Harry Wolfson spent sixty-six years at Harvard University, as undergraduate, graduate student, teacher, and professor emeritus. From 1925 until his retirement in 1958 he was Nathan Littauer Professor of Hebrew Literature and Philosophy at Harvard. He died in September 1974 at the age of 86.

STUDIES IN THE HISTORY OF
PHILOSOPHY AND RELIGION

STUDIES IN THE HISTORY OF PHILOSOPHY AND RELIGION

HARRY AUSTRYN WOLFSON

Volume Two

edited by Isadore Twersky and George H. Williams

Harvard University Press

Cambridge, Massachusetts

London, England

1977

Printed in the United States of America

Library of Congress Cataloging in Publication Data

Wolfson, Harry Austryn, 1887–1974
Studies in the history of philosophy and religion.

Includes bibliographical references.
Vol. 2 edited by I. Twersky and G. H. Williams
1. Philosophy—Collected works. 2. Religion—Collected works. I. Title.
B29.W646 100 72-86385
ISBN 0-674-84766-0 (v. 2)

EDITORS' FOREWORD

This volume of studies, although different in scope from its predecessor, *Studies in the History of Philosophy and Religion,* I, is a microcosm of the ramified scholarly oeuvre of Harry A. Wolfson, one of this century's most erudite, versatile, and creative scholars in the history of philosophy and religion. A cursory glance at the contents suggests that it is highly concentrated; the preponderant number of articles gathered here from widely dispersed journals and books deals with medieval Jewish philosophy—broadly defined, commodiously structured, and imaginatively interpreted. This collection thereby reflects the fact that the wide, almost universal range of his philosophical scholarship notwithstanding, its core, substantive and succulent, and foundation, firm and reassuring, remained Jewish religious philosophy. He frequently repeated and clearly emphasized that he was primarily a student of medieval Jewish philosophy. Indeed, this axial preoccupation is mirrored in the bibliographic parameters or contours of his illustrious career; his first book—growing out of his doctoral dissertation (1912–15) on parts of the *Or ha-Shem* of R. Hasdai Crescas[1]—is *Crescas' Critique of Aristotle: Problems of Aristotle's Physics in Jewish and Arabic Philosophy* (Harvard University Press, 1929), while *Kalam Repercussions in Jewish Philosophy* is still to be published posthumously. The beginning and the end, both scholarly tours de force—impressive literary monuments in every sense—are intertwined, underscoring the steady, smooth rhythmic movement from core to periphery and back.

Actually, however, core and periphery are almost blended. The core concentration in no way negates the universal exploration, for the requirements of genuine scholarly investigation and Wolfson's own conception of the history of philosophy converged to guarantee that the study of medieval Jewish philosophy would never be insular, would not be cut loose from its general cultural moorings. Obviously, the canons

[1] It may be interesting to note the original title of his thesis, recorded in a letter Wolfson wrote from Europe to Professor David Gordon Lyon: "The Philosophy of Chasdai Crescas Genetically and Critically Presented."

of scholarship necessitated that artificial or artful linguistic and cultural barriers be eliminated so that interlocking analyses of philosophic problems could be developed and comprehensive conceptualizations be elaborated. A scholar must strive to write in terms of what should be known rather than what he happens to know. He must learn to move across the frontiers of learning and become a naturalized citizen of the wide universe of knowledge. "The Aristotelian Predicables and Maimonides' Division of Attributes" (1938), for example, includes an A quintet—Ammonius, Augustine, Avicenna, Algazali, and Averroes—the triumvirate of Philo, Porphyry, and Plotinus, and the following pleiades of medieval Jewish authors: Saadia Gaon, Bahya ibn Pakuda, Joseph ibn Zaddik, Judah ha-Levi, Abraham ibn Daud, Joseph ibn Caspi, Moses Narboni, and M. Efodi (Duran). This holistic approach and integrative analysis—not merely erudition—is for Wolfson standard procedure.

Moreover, his basic conception of the history of philosophy, the catalyst and constitutive principle of all his writing, was determinative: since his new, anti-Hegelian periodization of the history of philosophy rested upon the special nature of Jewish philosophy from Philo to Spinoza—its paradigmatic value for that type of thought which produced a well-integrated interpretation of Scripture in terms of philosophy—the connections and repercussions, influences and parallels between Jewish, Christian, and Islamic thought had to be regularly ascertained and recorded. The process of identifying and exposing these connections often necessitated tireless sleuthing and imaginative philological probing—both microscopic textual explication and wide-ranging collation of topics, themes, and schemes from the large multi-lingual repertoire of philosophic writings. Hence, that characteristically Wolfsonian blend of erudition and intuition—graced by a literary virtuosity which made esoteric concepts or forbidding subjects attractive and intelligible—is discernible throughout this volume whether the topic is "Judah Hallevi on Causality and Miracles" or "Atomism in Saadia" or "Infinite and Privative Judgments in Aristotle, Averroes, and Kant" or "The Problem of the Origins of Matter in Mediaeval Jewish Philosophy and Its Analogy to the Modern Problem of the Origin of Life." In its own distinctive way, because of the relative homogeneity of topics included, this collection provides an unusually coherent and compact introduction to the substantive and methodological achievements of H. A. Wolfson, in which philosophical perceptivity, philological precision, and historical imagination constantly and constructively reenforce each other.[2]

The volume is also emblematic of Wolfson's scholarly career in a piquant chronological way: it contains his first and last published articles. The first, "Maimonides and Hallevi: A Study in Typical Jewish Attitudes towards Greek Philosophy in the Middle Ages," which he used to refer to fondly as an "undergraduate essay," appeared in the *Jewish Quarterly Review* (1912), while the last, "Answers to Criticism of My Discussion of the Ineffability of God," was published posthumously in the (belated) April 1974 issue of the *Harvard Theological Review*.[3] During his last years, he frequently reminisced, with pride and gratification, that he was probably the oldest living contributor to both these journals which, in their own ways, are twin foci of his long life and multi-faceted work.

Finally, the two Hebrew articles, "Emanation and Creation *Ex Nihilo* in Crescas" and "Testimony of Clement of Alexandria concerning an Unknown Custom in the Yom Kippur Service in the Temple," reveal Wolfson as the master of an idiomatic, expressive, finely honed Hebrew style and testify indisputably to one of his great but muted passions: Hebrew literature. For a long time, he thought of becoming a Hebrew writer; he wrote Hebrew poems and essays, and expounded original ideas about the proper development of modern Hebrew style. This belletristic aspiration was a casualty of his total immersion in historical scholarship.

The volume is thus a documentary of the growth and maturation of scholarly skills and sensitivities over a sixty-year period, marked by

[2] These articles would have become the basis of the frequently discussed volume on "Medieval Jewish Philosophy" with which he always hoped to cap his career. His files, which he left to Harvard, contain many fragments of unpublished works: a volume on Greek philosophy, planned as an introduction to the series on "The Structure and Growth of Philosophic Systems from Plato to Spinoza"; the second volume of the Philosophy of the Church Fathers; and a third volume on Spinoza which was intended to appear together with a revision of the original work.

[3] In an editorial postscript to that article, Isadore Twersky noted: "Regrettably, Professor Wolfson did not live to proofread this note, which was completed shortly before his death. Written while he was convalescing from surgery, his body racked with disease, it symbolizes his relentless commitment to scholarship while it illustrates the triumph of glorious mind over decaying matter."

unified interests and heterogeneous expressions. While some additions, corrections, and slight stylistic changes jotted down by the author on the margins of his copies were incorporated, no attempt was made to eliminate inconsistencies and repetitions. Changes and contradictions, varying nuances and divergent emphases, advances and refinements are to be expected in the course of a long, intense, unflaggingly creative career, in which the author worked assiduously day after day, year after year, and these signs of trial and triumph, modification or retraction are all preserved. Small Notes were also included; the scholarly intensity or methodological significance of some articles are not commensurate with their size.

The last note, "Answers to Criticisms of My Discussion of the Ineffability of God," leads us to call attention to two related features which deserve to be sharply delineated—fully appraised and praised. First of all, there is the dynamism of his research. He was constantly defining and refining the kind of textual analysis that was the methodological foundation for his work, a method which he successively described as hypothetico-deductive or the method of conjecture and verification. He repeatedly described and vindicated his method.[4] Concomitantly, he was scrutinizing the conclusions, interpretations, and conceptualizations, seeking a superior formulation, greater exactitude, a more resonant description of new problems or hitherto unperceived relationships in the history of philosophy. His great but disciplined powers of synthesis notwithstanding, he was constantly on guard against a pretentious, even partially unsubstantiated or conceptually flabby generalization and weighed each word and each phrase. Since, as he wrote, "scholarhip is the proper use of circumstantial evidence," it required relentlessly rigorous research and disciplined imagination. Proper use of circumstantial evidence was a corrective to a spiritless "bread and butter scholarship." As was noted in the Foreword to the posthumously published *The Philosophy of the Kalam*, Professor Wolfson would regularly re-read an entire work *in page proof*, checking for consistency in translation and transliteration as well as elegance of formulation and precision of conceptualization. Secondly, inasmuch as

[4] See, for example, *Crescas' Critique of Aristotle*, 24–27; *Philosophy of Spinoza*, 24–25; *The Philosophy of the Kalam*, viii; and Foreword to Volume I of these Studies, ix. See also "Studies in Crescas," reprinted in this volume.

Wolfson's conception of the history of philosophy and his method of analysis produced bold and iconoclastic propositions or positions, refreshing and challenging assertions or assumptions, he frequently found it necessary to confront critics, to defend his methodological procedures and conceptual conclusions. He did this with verve and vigor but with abundant grace and good taste. His polemical statements are soaked in wisdom, tinged with wit, but free of asperity or aspersion. He could be witty, trenchant, and satirical, but he was never demeaning, derisive, or pejorative. One is continually impressed with the delicacy and force of his polemical statements, their wry humor, and critical insight.

In fact, Professor Wolfson was careful to maximize the role of predecessors, always giving credit to previous, primary researches and citing the earliest scholarly literature on a given subject. Of special note is his skillful use of medieval commentaries and his adroit juxtaposition of their interpretations with those of modern scholars. There is not only gracefulness in his writing but graciousness in his presentations. *Coincidentia oppositorum*—rigor and grace, intellectual toughness with personal mildness and thoughtfulness. There was no disjunction between the shy person and the sovereign scholar.

CONTENTS

1 Hallevi and Maimonides on Design, Chance and Necessity
Proceedings of the American Academy for Jewish Research, 11 (1941): 105–163 1

2 Hallevi and Maimonides on Prophecy
The Jewish Quarterly Review, n.s. 32.4 (1942): 345–370, and 33.1 (1942): 49–82 60

3 Maimonides and Hallevi: A Study in Typical Jewish Attitudes towards Greek Philosophy in the Middle Ages
The Jewish Quarterly Review, n.s. 2.3 (1912): 297–337 120

4 The Aristotelian Predicables and Maimonides' Division of Attributes
Essays and Studies in Memory of Linda R. Miller (New York, Jewish Theological Seminary of America, 1938), pp. 201–234 161

5 Maimonides on Negative Attributes
Louis Ginzberg Jubilee Volume (New York: American Academy for Jewish Research, 1945), pp. 411–446 195

6 Maimonides and Gersonides on Divine Attributes as Ambiguous Terms
Mordecai M. Kaplan Jubilee Volume (New York: The Jewish Theological Seminary of America, 1953), pp. 515–530 231

7 Crescas on the Problem of Divine Attributes
The Jewish Quarterly Review, n.s. 7.1 (1916): 1–44, and 7.2 (1916): 175–221 247

8 The Kalam Problem of Nonexistence and Saadia's Second Theory of Creation
The Jewish Quarterly Review, n.s. 36.4 (1946): 371–391 338

9 Atomism in Saadia
The Jewish Quarterly Review, n.s. 37.2 (1946): 107–124 359

10 Arabic and Hebrew Terms for Matter and Element with Especial Reference to Saadia
The Jewish Quarterly Review, n.s. 38.1 (1947): 47–61 377

11 Saadia on the Trinity and Incarnation
Studies and Essays in Honor of Abraham A. Neuman (Philadelphia: Dropsie College, 1962), pp. 547–568 393

12 Judah Hallevi on Causality and Miracles
Meyer Waxman Jubilee Volume (Chicago: College of Jewish Studies Press, and Jerusalem: Mordecai Newman Press, 1966), pp. 137–153 415

13 Maimonides on the Unity and Incorporeality of God
The Jewish Quarterly Review, 56.2 (October 1965): 112–136 433

14 Studies in Crescas
Proceedings of the American Academy for Jewish Research, 5 (1934–1935): 155–175 458

15 Isaac Ibn Shem-Tob's Unknown Commentaries on the *Physics* and His Other Unknown Works
Studies in Jewish Bibliography and Related Subjects (New York: Alexander Kohut Memorial Foundation, 1929), pp. 279–290 479

16 The Problem of the Origin of Matter in Mediaeval Jewish Philosophy and Its Analogy to the Modern Problem of the Origin of Life
Proceedings of the International Congress of Philosophy (Philadelphia), 1926, pp. 602–608 491

17 St. Thomas on Divine Attributes
Mélanges offerts a Étienne Gilson (Toronto: Pontifical Institute of Medieval Studies, 1959), pp. 673–700 497

18 Answers to Criticisms of My Discussion of Patristic Philosophy
Harvard Theological Review, 57.2 (April 1964): 119–131 525

19 Answers to Criticisms of My Discussions of the Ineffability of God
Harvard Theological Review, 67 (1974), 186–190 538

20 Infinite and Privative Judgments in Aristotle, Averroes, and Kant
Philosophy and Phenomenological Research, 8.2 (December 1947): 173–187 542

21 Goichon's Three Books on Avicenna's Philosophy
The Moslem World, 31 (January 1941): 29–38 556

22 Synedrion in Greek Jewish Literature and Philo
The Jewish Quarterly Review, n.s. 36 (1946): 303–306 566

23 Two Comments Regarding the Plurality of Worlds in Jewish Sources
The Jewish Quarterly Review, 56.3 (January 1966): 245–247 570

24 Colcodea
The Jewish Quarterly Review, n.s. 36 (1945): 179–182 573

25 Some Guiding Principles in Determining Spinoza's Mediaeval Sources
The Jewish Quarterly Review, n.s. 27.4 (1937): 333–348 577

26 Spinoza's Mechanism, Attributes, and Panpsychism
The Philosophical Review, 46.3 (May 1937): 307–314 593

27 Towards an Accurate Understanding of Spinoza
The Journal of Philosophy, 23.10 (May 13, 1926): 268–273 601

28 Solomon Pappenheim on Time and Space and His Relation to Locke and Kant

Jewish Studies in Memory of Israel Abrahams (New York: Press of The Jewish Institute of Religion, 1927), pp. 426–440 606

Appendix

Emanation and Creation *Ex Nihilo* in Crescas (in Hebrew)

Sefer Assaf (Jerusalem: Magnes Press, 1953), pp. 230–236 623

Testimony of Clement of Alexandria Concerning an Unknown Custom in the Yom Kippur Service in the Temple (in Hebrew)

Horeb (New York: Yeshiva University), 3 (1936): 90–92 630

Index 633

STUDIES IN THE HISTORY OF
PHILOSOPHY AND RELIGION

I

HALLEVI AND MAIMONIDES ON DESIGN, CHANCE AND NECESSITY

1. Design, Chance and Necessity

The opposite of the view that God acts by free will with its corollary that the world came into being after it had not been is either the denial of God and causality altogether and the assertion that the world came into being by chance or the view that God acts by the necessity of his nature and that the world existed from eternity. In Halevi this distinction between chance and necessity as alternative opposites of free will is not formally made but it is implied throughout his work. The theory of chance is described by him in two ways, each of which goes back to a different Greek source. Sometimes he describes it as the view which held that "the world came into existence by chance"[1] or that "all things happen by chance"[2] and this view

[1] *Cuzari* V, 8: טענת אפיקורוס היוני אשר היה רואה כי העולם היה במקרה.

[2] *Ibid.* V, 20: דעת אפיקורוס היוני באמרו כי כל הדברים הם נופלים במקרה (באלאתּפאק).

The term מקרה used by Judah Ibn Tibbon (cf. also *Emunot we-De'ot* I, 3, 9th view, and *Ḥobot ha-Lebabot* I, 6) as well as by Samuel Ibn Tibbon as a translation of the Arabic اتّفاق in the sense of *chance* is the Greek τύχη. It is to be distinguished from מקרה used by the same translators for the Arabic عرض in the sense of *accident* which is the Greek συμβεβηκός. In the Hebrew translations of Averroes' commentaries on the *Physics* the term for τύχη, اتّفاق is הזדמן. Similarly in *Moreh Nebukim* II, 19, the expression כיף אתּפק is translated in Ibn Tibbon by כאשר הזדמן and in Ḥarizi by כפי מה שנזדמן. Cf. also the translation of אתּפאקיּה in *Moreh Nebukim* II, 48, by הזדמניות in *Moreh ha-Moreh*, ad loc. (quoted in Munk, *Guide* II, 48, p. 362, n. 3). But inasmuch as τύχη, according to Aristotle's own use of the term, does not refer to that which has no cause but rather to that of which the cause is *accidental*, the Arabic אתּפאק as well as the Hebrew הזדמן means also *accident*. Cf. below §4, text over nn. 6–7.

is attributed by him to Epicurus. But sometimes he describes it as a view which held that "things created themselves."[3] This evidently refers to the view of the Atomists of whom Aristotle says that "some (*τινες*)" ascribe "this heavenly sphere and all the worlds to spontaneity (*αὐτόματον*)"[4] or, as by implication he says later, to "chance (*τύχη*)."[5] Halevi's term here "created themselves" is thus to be taken to mean that it arose spontaneously.[6] Though modern scholarship has shown that the 'spontaneity' of Democritus is not the same as the 'chance' of Epicurus[7] and the former, unlike the latter, does not mean causelessness, mediaeval commentators made no such distinction and the 'spontaneity' of the one was taken to mean the same as the 'chance' of the other. As against this, however, the philosophers, by whom Halevi means Alfarabi and Avicenna, who to him as to all his contemporaries represented Aristotelianism, are not described by him as believing in chance. They are rather described by him as believing that God "is above all kinds of will and all kinds of design," that "the world is eternal,"[8] that it emanates from God by a series of intermediary causes and that "the causes and effects are connected by necessity."[9] In Maimonides, however, a formal distinction between chance and necessity is made. Like Halevi, he describes the theory of chance

[3] *Ibid.* II, 6: בראו הדברים את עצמם.

[4] *Phys.* II, 4, 196a, 24–26.

[5] *Ibid.*, 196a, 29.

[6] The expression בראו (תכלק) את עצמם here and similar expressions, such as עושים (כלקת) את עצמם (*Emunot we-De'ot* I, 2) and עושה (יצנע) את עצמו (*Ḥobot ha-Lebabot* I, 5), all reflect Aristotle's expression *ἀπὸ ταὐτομάτου γενέσθαι* (*Phys.* II, 4, 196a, 26). Maimonides' היה (כאן) מעצמו (quoted below in n. 11) is a literal translation of the Greek.

[7] Cf. Zeller, *Pre-Socratic Philosophy*, II, 237, n. 2; C. Bailey, *The Greek Atomists and Epicurus*, 142 and 325.

[8] *Cuzari* I, 1: נעלה מכל החפצים ומכל הכוונות . . . כי העולם קדמון.

[9] *Ibid.*: אבל הוא אצילות נאצלת ממנה סבה שנית ואחר כן שלישית ורביעית והתדבקו הסבות והמסובבות (ותלאזמת).

The term התדבקו (תלאזמת) here has the implication of necessity. In the *Moreh Nebukim* necessity is described by the term לזום which is translated by חיוב (II, 19 *et passim*).

in two ways and attributes them to two different Greek sources. In one place, he describes it as the view of "those who do not recognize the existence of God but believe that things are generated and destroyed by combination and separation according to chance" and attributes this view to Epicurus.[10] In another place, quoting the passage reproduced above from Aristotle, he describes it as the view of those who believe that "this world is the result of chance and that it came into existence spontaneously without any cause" and attributes it to "some of the earlier philosophers"[11] or to "others,"[12] the latter of which evidently represents the Arabic translation of Aristotle's ***τινες***.

Furthermore, Maimonides makes a distinction between what he considered the genuine view of Aristotle and the view of those whom he describes as "some recent philosophers." According to the genuine view of Aristotle, he says, while the world does not follow from God by that kind of necessity by which "a shadow follows from a body, or heat from fire, or light from the sun, as it is said by him who does not comprehend his words,"[13] still God is not its cause in the sense of an agent who acts by design and determination. God to Aristotle, he contends, can only be

[10] *Moreh Nebukim* II, 13 (3).

[11] *Ibid.* II, 20: מי שחשב מן הראשונים שזה העולם נפל במקרה ושהיה מעצמו בלא סבה.

[12] *Ibid.*: אנשים אחרים (קום אכ֗ר). So also in the Latin translation of the Arabic translation of the *Physics* included in Averroes Long Commentary on it (Liber Secundus, text. 44) the Greek *τινες* is translated by *quidam alii*.

[13] *Ibid.*: כהתחייב הצל מהגוף או התחייב החום מהאש או התחייב האור מהשמש כמו שיאמר עליו מי שלא יבין דבריו (כלזום אלט֗ל ען אלגסם או לזום אלחרארה̈ ען אלנאר או לזום אלצ֗ו ען אלשמס כמה יקול ענה מן לא יפהם קולה). The reference here is to Algazali who attributes to the philosophers the very same view which is rejected here by Maimonides. Cf. *Tahafut al-Falāsifah* III (ed. M. Bouyges), §3, p. 97, l. 2:

لزوم الظل من الشخص والنور من الشمس

Averroes similarly rejects Algazali's interpretation, exclaiming: "I say all this is false" (*Tahafut al-Tahafut* III (ed. M. Bouyges), §8, p. 150, l. 11). Avicenna's original view which is misinterpreted by Algazali reads as follows: "The procession of the universe from God is not by way of natural necessity so that it would imply that the existence of the universe proceeds from God without any knowledge (معرفة) and without any satisfaction (رضا) on the part of God" (*Najāt*, Cairo, 1331 A. H., p. 449, ll. 3–4).

called a conscious cause.[14] According to "some of the recent philosophers," however, he adds, while the world is still assumed to be an eternal emanation, God is said to act by will and design and determination. Maimonides expresses his doubt as to whether these recent philosophers meant their view to be an interpretation of the view of Aristotle or whether they meant it to be a modification of the view of Aristotle.[15] He dismisses this interpretation, however, on the ground that the terms will, design and determination, when applied to the eternal creation of the world, are meaningless terms, for in reality they mean nothing but necessity. "The conception of design and determination," says Maimonides, "applies only to a thing which does not yet exist but may either exist or not exist according to the design or determination of the agent."[16] Halevi refers to no such distinction between Aristotle and the "recent philosophers." Whether he was not cognizant at all of the existence of such a distinction, or whether, like Maimonides, he thought that the distinction between the new interpretation and the genuine view of Aristotle was only verbal, or else whether, unlike Maimonides, he agreed with those "recent philosophers" that on mere rational grounds the assumption of free will in God is compatible with the assumption of the eternity of the world, there is no direct way of telling. Such a statement by him as that when the philosophers use the term "creator" with reference to God they use it only in a metaphorical sense on the ground that they do not conceive of God as creating "by design" and that they believe that "the

[14] *Ibid.* The consciousness of God is expressed by Maimonides by his restatement of the emanationist formula that God is the cause of that which immediately emanates from Him as the intellect is the cause of the object conceived by it. אבל יאמין החיוב ההוא כחיוב המושכל מהשכל, כי השכל הוא פועל המושכל מצד היותו מושכל. Avicenna, as we have seen (above n. 13), directly states that the process of emanation is not without God's knowledge. Similarly Averroes in his criticism of Algazali says: "For the philosophers hold that God's action emanates from knowledge (علم)" (*Tahafut al-Tahafut* III, §9, 151, ll. 7–8).

[15] *Ibid.* end.

[16] *Ibid.* II, 21.

world is eternal"[17] is vague enough to lend itself to any of the three aforementioned possible interpretations of his view.

Logically and historically the arguments against the view that the world came into being after it had not been but that its coming into being was due to chance are different from the arguments against the view that the world is eternal but that it still has a cause and that its cause acts by necessity. Against chance the arguments are from the phenomena of order, regularity and harmony that are observed in the universe, on the assumption, rightly or wrongly, that no perfect order and regularity and harmony could result by mere chance. These are exactly the kinds of argument used by Aristotle in refutation of the Atomists to whom he attributes a theory of chance and in opposition to whom he sets up a theory of causality culminating in a God who acts as a prime cause by the necessity of his nature. Indeed Aristotle was aware of the existence of certain deviations from order, regularity and harmony both in the motions of the spheres and in the phenomena of the sublunar world but for all such deviations he found explanations in conformity with his theory of necessary causality, without having to resort to the assumption of free will in God. Against necessity, on the other hand, logically and historically, the arguments are from the evidence of certain deviations from order, regularity and harmony, coupled with an effort to show that such deviations could not be satisfactorily explained on any other ground except that of the free will of God. Historically, it may be said, all mediaeval arguments against chance are only a repetition or an elaboration of the arguments against chance used by Aristotle and similarly all the mediaeval arguments against necessity are refutations of Aristotle's attempt to explain the deviations from order, regularity and harmony observed in the universe.

This is a general observation in the light of which all mediaeval arguments for the establishment of free will in God, whether in Hebrew or in Arabic or in Latin authors, are to be studied and

[17] *Cuzari* I, 1: ואם יאמרו הפילוסופים שהוא בראך הם אומרים זה על דרך ההעברה . . . לא מפני שהוא בכונה מאתו . . . כי העולם קדמון.

examined and it is in the light of this observation that we shall examine the arguments for free will in God used by Halevi and Maimonides. With regard to each argument used by them we shall ask the following questions: Is this an argument from order or from deviation from order? Is it used by the author against chance or against necessity? Does the author mean to establish by it merely the existence of a cause or also the existence of a cause which acts by free will?

One more general observation is to be made, and this with regard to the relation of the arguments employed by Halevi and Maimonides for the free will of God to their proofs of the existence of God. These arguments obviously already assume the existence of God, but still they are in themselves no proofs for the existence of God. If they are from deviation from order and directed against the Aristotelian theory of necessity of God's action and eternity of the world, then it means that the existence of God has already been established by the proofs advanced by Aristotle himself. Now Maimonides reproduces these Aristotelian proofs and considers them as valid.[18] Halevi, however, does not reproduce these proofs and it cannot be ascertained whether he would consider them as valid or not. Again, if the arguments are from order and directed against the Epicurean theory of a world which has a beginning but whose beginning was due to chance, then, on the basis of this preassumed premise, the arguments against chance constitute at once a proof for both the existence and the free will of God. But inasmuch as the premise in these arguments is only preassumed but not proved, the arguments based on that premise cannot by themselves be considered as proofs for the existence of God. To raise these arguments to the status of proofs of the existence of God it will be necessary to establish by proof the preassumed premise of the beginningness of the world. Thus Saadia and Baḥya reproduce with approval the Kalam arguments for the creation of the world before they use the conclusion of those arguments as a premise for their proof of the existence of God.[19] Similarly Maimonides, though he does not accept the Kalam arguments for creation as

[18] *Moreh Nebukim* I, 1.

[19] *Emunot we-De'ot* I, 2; *Ḥobot ha-Lebabot* I, 5.

conclusive and hence does not use them as arguments leading toward a proof of the existence of God,[20] still he uses the arguments by which he disposes of necessity to dispose also of eternity and by disposing of eternity he establishes the greater probability of the belief in creation and once he establishes creation as a more probable hypothesis he uses it as a premise for a proof in the existence of God.[21] Halevi, however, though he makes the Rabbi at the urgings of the Cuzari reproduce the Kalam proof for the creation of the world, he lets the Rabbi express his own view of these arguments by his characterization of them as futile.[22] Consequently he has no proof of the existence of God after the manner of Saadia and Baḥya. But still, even without the Kalam arguments he believes in the beginningness of the world and with that as starting point he has rational arguments to show that it could not have come into being by chance. Consequently, whatever is found to be Halevi's basis for the belief in creation, and to him, it may be said, the Biblical account of creation is the ultimate basis, will also be his basis for the belief in the existence of God. Then, again, Halevi has arguments against necessity but, as we have seen, unlike Maimonides, he does not try to show that the disposal of necessity disposes also of eternity. Still, any argument against necessity constitutes an argument for the existence of God and consequently whatever will be found in the course of our subsequent discussion to Halevi's basis for the refutation of necessity will also be an additional basis for his belief in creation as well as the existence of God.

The arguments used by Halevi and Maimonides may be arranged under the following headings:

1. Arguments from the alleged process of emanation, which at the time of Halevi and Maimonides was attributed to Aristotle.

2. The Argument of Determination, including the (1) arguments from the motions of the celestial spheres and the (2) arguments from certain non-essential accidents in the structure of the world.

[20] *Moreh Nebukim* I, 74.

[21] *Ibid.* II, 2; III, 13; cf. below §5, n. 61.

[22] *Cuzari* V, 16: אין בזה תועלת.

3. Arguments from sublunar phenomena, namely, (1) the four elements, (2) minerals, and (3) plants and animals.

4. Arguments from miracles.

2. Emanation

The theory of emanation begins with the statement that inasmuch as the effect cannot contain more than its cause the first emanation from God must be one simple Intelligence. Then it proceeds to explain the rise of multiplicity by showing that within the first Intelligence, simple though it is, by the mere reason of its being the effect of a cause, there must emerge a multiplicity in the object of its knowledge, consisting as it inevitably must of (1) a knowledge of its cause and (2) a knowledge of itself, and also by showing how from this multiplicity in the object of its knowledge there emanate respectively two beings, (1) another Intelligence and (2) a sphere. Finally it concludes that, while this process repeats itself with reference to the second Intelligence and any of the other successive Intelligences, it does not go on infinitely but stops with the tenth Intelligence, known as the Active Intellect, and the ninth or lunar sphere.

In his strictures upon emanation Halevi does not specifically say that the arguments are directed against emanation primarily for its assumption that God as an emanative cause acts by necessity. But that this was the main object of his attack on the theory of emanation is to inferred not only from the nature of the arguments themselves but also from the manner in which they are used by Algazali who, as we shall see, is the source of these arguments employed by Halevi. In Maimonides there is a definite statement to the effect that his criticism of emanation is a criticism of the element of necessity involved in it.[1]

The arguments which Halevi raises against necessary emanation are three.

First, as a necessary process there is no reason why emanation should stop with the tenth Intelligence and the lunar sphere and

[1] *Moreh Nebukim* I, 22, where the criticism of emanation is concluded with the statement: הנה כבר התבאר לך שלא ימשכו אלו העניינים על צד החיוב.

why it should not go on to infinity. Halevi states this objection succinctly: "First, by what reason did this emanation cease: did the Prime Cause become impotent?"[2] The conclusion to be drawn from this is that even the philosophers will have to resort to the assumption of free will in God in order to explain why the process of emanation should come to an end at a given point.

Second, if the variety of objects of knowledge in any of the Intelligences is taken to constitute a variety of elements in its nature from which a corresponding variety of things can emanate, then in the third Intelligence, which, on the assumption of eight spheres,[3] will be the Intelligence which moves the seventh sphere or the sphere of Saturn, there will be four elements, and not two, for the objects of knowledge in it are four, namely, (1) its knowledge of its own self, (2) its knowledge of the second Intelligence, (3) its knowledge of the first Intelligence and (4) its knowledge of God. And just as the objects of knowledge in the third Intelligence are greater than those in the second and first Intelligences so the objects of knowledge in the succeeding Intelligences will continually increase in number and cor-

[2] *Cuzari* IV, 25 toward end: אחד מהם למה עמדה האצילות הזאת, הקצר יד מהראשון. Cf. V, 14: ואיך . . . עמדו השפעים אצל השׂכל הפוֹעל ולא יחוייב ממנו לא גלגל ולא מלאך.

[3] The restatement of the theory of emanation in IV, 25, assumes the existence of only eight spheres, as is evidenced by the fact that the sphere emanating from the first Intelligence is called the sphere of the fixed stars (גלגל הכוכבים הקיימים). Cf. *Ḳol Yehudah, ad loc.* In V, 14, the reference to emanation assumes the existence of nine spheres, as is evidenced by the expression "eleven stages (אחת עשרה מדרגות)" of emanation, the eleven being God and the ten Intelligences. So also Alfarabi refers to God and the ten Intelligences as eleven (cf. Dieterici, *Alfarabi's Abhandlung der Musterstaat*, Arabic: p. 19; German: pp. 29–30). There is no ground for *Ḳol Yehudah's* interpretation that it assumes ten spheres. Elsewhere throughout the *Cuzari* Hallevi assumes with Ptolemy the existence of a ninth sphere to which he refers as אלפלך אלאעלי: הגלגל העליון (II, 6; V, 2; V, 7), אלפלך אלאעטם: הגלגל הגדול (IV, 13). The unqulified גלגל in II, 54, IV, 1, and IV, 9 does not necessarily refer to the outermost sphere, as inaccurately, I think, stated by Cassel (*Das Buch Kuzari*, p. 94, n. 2). Nor does גלגל in V, 5, refer to the outermost sphere. In V, 3, the Hebrew הגלגל המקיף, on the basis of the Arabic text which has only אלמחיט, should read only המקיף and from the context, as the contrast of מרכז, it means only *periphery* and refers to the lunar sphere. In *Moreh Nebukim* II, 4, however, the term המקיף: אלמחיט definitely refers to the outermost sphere.

responding to this there will have to be a continuous increase in the number of emanations from each succeeding Intelligence. The brief and rather incomplete statement of this argument in Halevi reads as follows: "Secondly, it might be argued, why should not from the knowledge which [the Intelligence of the sphere of] Saturn has of what is immediately above it necessarily emanate one thing and from its knowledge of the first angel (*i. e.*, Intelligence) another thing, so that the emanations [from the Intelligence of the sphere] of Saturn will be four."[4] The conclusion to be drawn from this, too, is that the philosophers will have to resort to the assumption of free will in God in order to explain why only two and not four emanations should proceed from the third Intelligence.

Third, the entire theory of emanation is absurd, if we consider it as merely a necessary process. "Whence do we get the notion that if any being knows his own essence there will of necessity emanate from him a sphere and that if any being knows the Prime Cause there will of necessity emanate from him an angel? According to this notion, when Aristotle, for instance, pretends to have a knowledge of his own essence, one would of necessity have a right to expect that a sphere should emanate from him and, if he pretends to have a knowledge of the Prime Cause, one would similarly have a right to expect that an angel should emanate from him."[5] Here, too, the conclusion to be drawn is that the philosophers will have to resort to the assumption of free will in God in order to explain how knowledge can act and produce certain results, for, by the analogy of human beings, on the basis of Aristotle's own psychological theory, knowledge

[4] *Cuzari* IV, 25: ואחר כן נאמר למה לא התחייב מהשכלת שבתאי מה שלמעלה ממנו דבר אחר ומהשכלתו המלאך הראשון דבר אחר ותהיינה צורות אצילות (פתציר פיוץ̈) שבתאי ארבע.

The term צורות in the Hebrew should not be taken in the technical sense of "forms", for the emanations are not all forms, there being among them spheres. The expression צורות אצילות is merely a free way of translating the phrase פיוץ̈ and is the equivalent of אציליות.

[5] *Ibid.* IV, 25: ומאין לנו שמי שישכיל עצמו יתחייב ממנו גלגל ומי שהשכיל הראשון יתחייב ממנו מלאך ובעת אשר יטעון ארסטו שהוא משכיל את עצמו צריך שיהיה נתבע שיאצל ממנו גלגל ואם יטעון שהשכיל הראשון שיאצל ממנו מלאך. Cf. V, 14: ואיך התחייב מן המדע בראשון מלאך ומן המדע בעצמו גלגל.

becomes a motive force which acts and produces results only when combined with will.[6]

Now these three arguments are not original with Halevi. They are either suggested by, or based upon, or are merely paraphrases of, certain statements in Algazali's discussion of the theory of emanation, which contains a detailed restatement of the theory itself and five refutations thereof.[7]

Halevi's first argument, though not taken from any of Algazali's five refutations of emanation, seems to have been suggested by a statement which occurs in his exposition of the theory of emanation. That statement reads as follows: "It is not necessary that from each Intelligence there should infinitely proceed another, for these Intelligences are diverse in species and consequently that which is affirmed of any particular one of them does not necessarily have to apply to every one of them."[8] What he means to say is this. If all the Intelligences were alike in species but differed only by individual accidents, then, being of the same species, all the Intelligences, including the tenth Intelligence or Active Intellect, would have to emanate from themselves other Intelligences and consequently the process of emanation would have to go on to infinity. But inasmuch as they are each a

[6] Cf. *De Anima* III, 10, 433a, 9 ff.

[7] Hallevi himself may have hinted at his indebtedness to others for his criticism of emanation in his following introductory words: ומקשים עליה בכמה פנים: ויעתרץ בכם וגוה. This reflects Algazali's statement that his five refutations of emanation are וגוה מעדודה of אלאעתראץ̇ (*Tahafut al-Falasifah* III, §41, p. 117, ll. 1–2).

Kaufmann, in his discussion of the influence of Algazali on Hallevi, says with regards to the latter's criticism of emanation as follows: "Auch hier haben wir den Einfluss Gazzâlî's zu erblicken, der in der dritten Disputation gegen diese Lehre eine Reihe niederschlagender Widerlegungen vorführt, wenn auch die Einwände, die Jehuda Halewi äussert, von denselben verschieden sind und durchaus als seine eigenen gelten mussen" (*Attributenlehre*, p. 130). I do not think that his judgment is based upon a careful examination of the arguments in question.

[8] *Tahafut al-Falāsifah* III, § 38, p. 115, ll. 2–3: ولا يلزم ان يلزم من كل عقل عقل الى غير نهاية لان هذه العقول مختلفة الانواع فما ثبت لواحد لا يلزم للاخر.

different species, it is not illogical to assume that the Active Intellect, unlike the other Intelligences, is incapable of emanating from itself another Intelligence or sphere. What Halevi does in his first argument is to reproduce the tentative objection implied in Algazali's statement without reproducing his answer.

Halevi's second argument, wherein he contends that "the emanations [from the Intelligence] of Saturnus will be four," must have been suggested by Algazali's third refutation, wherein he similarly contends that in the first Intelligence there is a "quadruplicity"[9] with the implication that the emanations therefrom will similarly have to be four. That there must be a "quadruplicity" in the first Intelligence is demonstrated in Algazali's argument by certain subtle metaphysical speculations with regard to distinctions between essence and the knowledge of essence and between possibility and necessity. Evidently it was in order to simplify the argument for the general reader that Halevi transferred the argument from the first Intelligence to the third Intelligence, wherein he could show the existence of Algazali's "quadruplicity" in a more simple manner. Still, despite the new form given to the argument by Halevi, his dependence upon Algazali is evident in his selection of the third Intelligence as a case in point. Were it not for the fact that he wanted to retain Algazali's original contention of the existence of a "quadruplicity" in some of the Intelligences, he could have selected as a case in point the second Intelligence, in which by the same method of reasoning he could have found in it a triplicity of elements, namely, (1) its knowledge of itself, (2) its knowledge of the first Intelligence and (3) its knowledge of God, and this, for the purpose of his argument, would have served him just as well.

Halevi's third argument seems to be nothing but a paraphrase of Algazali's fifth refutation. The essential parts in Algazali's fifth refutation reads as follows: "How are you not ashamed of yourselves" to say that from the variety of the objects of knowledge in the first Intelligence there emanates a variety of beings! "What difference is there between what you say and some tall

[9] *Ibid.* III, § 53, p. 123, ll. 5–6: ويلزم فيه تربيع.

story told by some person about some mysterious man of his acquaintance whose existence is possible *per se* and who knows his own self and he knows also his Creator and from whose possibility of existence there emanates a sphere? . . . Such a story if told about a man would be laughed at; it deserves no more serious consideration when told about any other being."[10] There is nothing new in Halevi's version of this argument except the substitution of Aristotle for "some mysterious man."

The arguments which Maimonides raises against necessary emanation are two. These two arguments are not the same as the three arguments of Halevi, two of which, as we have seen, reflect respectively Algazali's *third* and *fifth* of his five refutations, but we shall try to show that they do reflect certain elements of Algazali's *second* and *fourth* refutations.[11]

In his first argument, after admitting that in the first Intelligence there is more than one object of knowledge, Maimonides still insists that this "first Intelligence is undoubtedly simple" and consequently he asks: "Whence then comes the composition which, according to Aristotle, exists by necessity in existent things?" or, "How could the Intelligences become the cause of the spheres emanating from them by necessity? What relation is there between material and immaterial beings?"[12] The crux of the argument, as will have been noticed, is the assumption that the first Intelligence, despite the two objects of knowledge that it comprehends, is still simple and consequently no composite material being, like a sphere, could emanate from it. But why

[10] *Ibid.* III, § 67, pp. 129, l. 8–130, l. 2: كيف لا تستحيون . . . وما الفصل بين هذا وبين قائل عرف وجود انسان غائب وانه ممكن الوجود وانه يعقل نفسه وصانعه فقال يلزم من كونه ممكن الوجود وجود فلك . . . وهذا اذا قيل فى انسان ضحك منه فكذى فى موجود آخر.

[11] A suggestion of Maimonides' dependence upon Algazali is to be found in Narboni's statement on *Moreh Nebukim* II, 22 (ed. Goldenthal, p. 34b; erroneously under פרק כ') that "The difficulty raised by Rabbi Moses is taken from Moslem philosophers" והיה הספק אשר ספקו רבינו משה לקוח מפילוסופי אלאסלם "The Moslem philosophers" are more correctly Algazali.

[12] *Moreh Nebukim* II, 22.

the Intelligence, despite the two objects of knowledge that it comprehends, should be assumed to be simple is not explained by Maimonides. The explanation, however, can be found in Algazali's second refutation of the process of emanation, where among other things he argues for the assumption that in the first Intelligence the thinking subject, the act of thinking and the object of thought should be identical. His statement reads in part as follows: "In the case of the [first Intelligence] caused [by God], the knowledge which it has of its essence is identical with its essence, for it is by its very substance that it knows and it is its own self that it knows and consequently with reference to it also that which knows and the act of knowing and the object known are one and the same. Now, since its knowledge of its own essence is identical with its own essence itself, it must have a knowledge of that essence as being something brought into effect by a cause. But, this being the case, then, inasmuch as in it that which knows coincides with that which is known, both of them revert to its essence and are one with it. Therefore, there is no multiplicity [in the first Intelligence]."[13] This first argument of Maimonides, therefore, though not exactly the same as any of Algazali's refutations, still reflects the latter's second refutation.

In his second argument Maimonides tries to show that on the assumption of necessity, according to which the effect must equal its cause, there are not enough elements in the Intelligences to account for the variety of elements which are to be found in the spheres which are supposed to emanate from the Intelligences. For in the spheres there are stars, which are assumed to be of a different matter than the spheres. Now, he argues, if all the stars are of the same matter, then in each sphere there will be at least four component parts, namely, the (1) matter and (2) form of the spheres and the (3) matter and (4) form of the stars.

[13] *Tahafut al-Falāsifah* III, § 45, p. 119, ll. 3–6: والمعلول عقله ذاته عين ذاته فانه عقل بجوهره فيعقل نفسه والعقل والعاقل والمعقول منه أيضا واحد ثم اذا كان عقله ذاته عين ذاته فليعقل ذاته معلولا لعلة فانه كذلك والعقل يطابق المعقول فيرجع الكل الى ذاته فلا كثرة.

And if the luminous stars are of a different matter than the non-luminous stars, then the component parts of each sphere will be still greater.[14] Thus, concludes Maimonides, there is not enough multiplicity in the Intelligences to account for all the elements of multiplicity in the spheres emanating from them. This argument, too, is based upon a part of Algazali's fourth refutation in which he contends that the three elements discernible in the second Intelligence will not account for the emanation of the second sphere, *i. e.*, the sphere of the fixed stars, "in which there are 1200 and more stars diverse in magnitude, in figure, in position, in color, in influence and in the power of bringing ill fortune and good fortune."[15]

3. Celestial Spheres

The argument from the motions of the spheres occur in Halevi in three places.

In one place it is stated in the form of what seems to be four questions hurled at "the Philosopher," *i. e.*, Aristotle.[1] "What thing is it," he asks, "which in thy opinion made (1) the Heavens[2] revolve continually and (2) the uppermost sphere, beyond which there is nothing,[3] carry all the other spheres,[4] without having

[14] *Moreh Nebukim* II, 22.

[15] *Tahafut al-Falāsifah* III, § 65, p. 128, ll. 4–6: وفيه ألف و نيف ومئتا كوكب وهى مختلفة العظم والشكل والوضع واللون والتأثير والنحوسة والسعادة.

[1] *Cuzari* II, 6: נאמר לו אתה הפילוסוף, מה הדבר (אלאמר) אשר שם אצלך השמים סובבים תמיד והגלגל העליון נושא הכל ואין מקום לו ואין נטייה בתנועתו וכדור הארץ מֻרְכָּז (מרכוזה) עומד באמצעיתו מבלי נטיה ולא סבה ושם סדר הכל על מה שהוא עליו מהכמות והאיכות והתמונות.

That the "philosopher" here is Aristotle, and not the philosophers generically, is evident from the many concrete references to Aristotle's writings contained in this passage.

[2] השמים. Cf. below n. 19.

[3] ואין מקום לו. Literally: "and it has no place". To be in place according to Aristotle, is to be enclosed within a body (*Phys.* IV, 5, 212a, 31–32). The outermost sphere, therefore, not being enclosed in any other body, is not in any place (*ibid.*, 212b, 8–9).

[4] נושא הכל: חאמל אלגְמיע. This expression is a literal translation of Aristotle's description of the sphere of the fixed stars which to him was the uppermost

any inclination[5] in its motion, and (3) the earth fixed as a centre stand still in the centre of the uppermost sphere,[6] without being rolled[7] and without having anything to rest upon,[8] and which also made (4) the order of the universe according to the quantity and quality and shapes which it happens to have?" All this, he says, refutes, besides the materialistic conception of God, also the view "that things created themselves," that is to say,

sphere: *τήν τε γὰρ τῶν ἀπλανῶν τὴν ἀπάσας φέρουσαν εἶναι* (*Met.* XII, 8, 10736, 25–26). "Carry" here means to cause all the other spheres to move, the equivalent of ויסבב עמו כל הגלגלים in V, 2.

[5] מיל: נטייה=ἔγκλισις (*De Gen. et Corr.* II, 10, 336b, 4).

[6] וכדור הארץ מָרכז (מרכוזה) עומד (ואקפה) באמצעיתו. Reflects Aristotle's statement that "the earth has its centre at the centre of the universe" (*De Caelo* II, 14, 296b, 17–18) which culminates his arguments that the earth is at rest and does not move. In the Latin translation of Averroes Long Commentary on *De Caelo* the Greek *τὸ μέσον ἔχει ἐν τῷ τοῦ παντὸς μέσῳ* is translated by *medium terrae est positum in medio totius* (Liber Secundus, text. 100) of which the Arabic must have been مركز الارض موضوع فى مركز الكل. Accordingly the term מרכוזה in this passage may mean not merely "fixed" but "fixed as a centre".

[7] מבלי נטייה: דון מיל. Though the same word מיל (נטייה) is used here as before with reference to the motion of the uppermost sphere, I have translated it by "being rolled" because this statement seems to refer to Aristotle's refutation of the theory, which he quotes from Plato's *Timaeus* (40 B) that the earth is rolled. Cf. *De Caelo* II, 13, 293b, 30–32: "Others, again, say that the earth, which lies at the centre, is rolled (ἴλλεσθαι), and thus in motion, about the axis of the whole heaven. So stands written in the *Timaeus*". Cf. also II, 14, 296a, 24 ff.

[8] ולא סבה: ולא סנד. The Arabic סנד means *support* whereas the Hebrew סבה means *reason, cause.* This does not necessarily mean that Judah Ibn Tibbon's text had the reading סבב for סנד. It is quite possible that he took the word סנד to mean here an intellectual support or reason. But the interesting thing about this passage is that both "support" and "reason" can be traced to Aristotle's discussion of the problem of the immovability of the earth. In that discussion Aristotle refers to some philosophers who seek "a reason (αἰτία) to explain why the earth remains at the centre" (*De Caelo* II, 13, 295a, 14–15). Thales, he says, explained it by saying that "the earth rests upon water" (*ibid.*, 294a, 28), i. e., water is its support. Aristotle's own opinion is that "it is absurd to look for a reason why the earth remains at the centre"; the only reason for it is that the centre is the natural place of the earth (*ibid.*, 295b, 25–29). Hence here it means both "without any reason" and "without any support."

that they arose spontaneously and by chance.[9] The conclusion which he wishes to establish by this argument is that all this is the result of that which is called "will or decree or whatever else you may wish to call it."[10] From the context of the entire discussion here it is evident that the term "will" used by him here is meant free will, that kind of will which, as he says, "the philosopher rejects."[11]

In another place the argument is from the outermost ninth sphere with only a vague reference to the internal spheres. The passage reads as follows: "The divine wise will ordained the revolution of the uppermost sphere, which completes one revolution in every twenty-four hours and causes the othere spheres to revolve along with it."[12] The argument implied in this passage is that the revolution of the outermost sphere once in twenty-four hours as well as the fact that it causes the internal spheres to revolve along with it is proof for the existence of "divine wise will," *i. e.*, of a will that is at once free and rational.

In a third place the argument is from the outermost ninth sphere and it is stated in the form of the following question: "And I should like to discuss with my opponent concerning the uppermost sphere itself. What is it that causes it to revolve? Is it the result of chance?"[13] The implication of this statement is that the motion of the outermost sphere cannot conceivably be regarded as the result of chance. It does not say, however, whether the argument implied in this statement is directed only against chance or also against necessity.

Now, it will have been noticed, that in the first and third of these three passages the target of the criticism is explicitly said to be "chance" and that in the first and second of these passages the conclusion sought to be established from the motion of the

[9] *Cuzari* II, 6: כי לא בראו הדברים עצמם. Cf. above §1, n. 6.

[10] *Ibid.*: לא תוכל להמלט מהודות בדבר (אלאמר) ההוא... קרא אותו אתה חפץ (ארארה֞) או דבר (אמרא) או כאשר תרצה.

[11] *Ibid.* II, 5: מה יצילך ממדת החפץ (אלארארה֞) שאתה מיחס אותה אל הבורא והפילוסוף מרחיק אותה ממנו.

[12] *Ibid.* V, 2: ואחר כן חייב חפץ האלהים וחכמתו (ארארה֞ אלחכמה֞ אלאלאהיה֞) סבוב הגלגל העליון אשר יסוב פעם בכל עשרים וארבע שעות ויסבב עמו כל הגלגלים.

[13] *Ibid.* V, 7: ואני אדבר עמו על הגלגל העליון עצמו, מה הוא שיגלגלהו, ההיה הדבר הזה במקרה.

spheres is explicitly said to be the free will of God. Furthermore, it will have been also noticed that the external phrasing of the argument from the motion of the spheres in all these three passages reads like an argument from the regularity and uniformity of that motion. But such an argument, as has already been pointed out, while it may be used as a refutation of chance, does not by itself establish free will in God. It may only establish the existence of a God who acts by the necessity of his nature. In fact, Aristotle uses the argument from the uniformity and regularity of the motions of the spheres as a refutation of chance,[14] and yet he does not believe that the Prime Cause of the motions of the spheres acts with free will. If therefore Halevi argues from the motion of the spheres in opposition to Aristotle and in favor of free will in God, then these arguments, despite their external phrasing, must have been meant by him to be arguments not from uniformity and regularity but rather from diversity and irregularity. The question, then, is: Do these arguments lend themselves to such an interpretation?

This question, with respect to the argument in the first passage, has been raised by Moscato in his commentary *Ḳol Yehudah* on the *Cuzari*.[15] His answer is that the passage in question cannot be interpreted as an argument from diversity and irregularity.[16] He therefore tries, rather hesitatingly and with some misgiving, to justify somehow Halevi's use of an argument from

[14] Cf. *Phys.* II, 4, 196b, 1–3; *De Caelo* II, 8, 289b, 21–27.

[15] *Ḳol Yehudah* on *Cuzari* II, 6: אולם אתה המעיין הבא נא ידך בחיקך ותחפש כל חדרי בטן על תשובת החבר בזה אם חומה היא לבנות עליה טירת כסף, כי הנה אויביה יהמיון בהבדילם בין חפץ לחפץ ובין רצון לרצון, כי יש חפץ ורצון שהוא הפך המקרה, והוא מה שיוכרח הפילוסוף להודות בו . . . ואפשר עוד להבין ממלת חפץ ורצון דבר יותר מזה, לא לבד על הפך המקרה, אבל ג״כ על כונה לדבר טרם היותו . . . וא״כ הפילוסוף ישים לו מקום אשר ינוס שמה לאמר לא ראי זה כראי זה, לא הרי החפץ אשר הכריחני העיון להודות בו, כהרי החפץ אשר בקשת ליחס לו ית׳ . . . והנה להיות שם חפץ ורצון מן השמות המשותפים אין לקפץ ולדלג בו מהוראה אחת אל זולתה.

[16] *Ibid.*: ואולם המאמר הזה שאני רוקד כנגדו למען לא יוכלו אויביו ליגע בו לרעה איני יכול ליגע בו מטוב טעם הרב המורה בשני פ׳ י״ט ומן זו והלאה כאשר בא אל בטול דעת הקדמות מצד ההתחלפות הנראה בגלגלים . . . כי הנה דברי החבר לא יסבלוהו להיות הטעם ההוא יסודתו על ההתחלפות, וטעמו של חבר מכותלי דבריו ניכר היותו מונח על הסדר, באמרו מה הדבר אשר שם אצלם השמים סובבים תמיד וכו׳ והם סדר הכל וכו׳. רק אם נאמר שכיון אל הסדור המסודר על בלי סדר, והרי זה לשון שאין רוח חכמים נוחה הימנו.

uniformity and regularity as a proof for free will in God.[17] But not fully satisfied with his own interpretation, he expresses a willingness to welcome some other kind of interpretation.[18]

Such another kind of interpretation we shall attempt to offer here — and one which will show that the argument from the motions of the spheres in the first passage as well as that in the other passages is an argument from diversity and irregularity.

To begin with, we suggest that in the first passage (II, 6) the fourth question should be separated from the preceding three questions. This fourth question, we shall show, constitutes a separate argument, with a different historical background. The repetition of the term "and made" before this question would also indicate that it is to be distinguished from the preceding questions. We are thus left only with the first three questions, one with regard to the "heavens" in general, by which term, we take it, Halevi meant to include also the eccentric spheres and epicycles,[19] another with regard to the uppermost sphere only and a third with regard to the earth. Of these three questions, the second and third, we further suggest, should be taken together as constituting one question, as is evidenced from the expression

[17] *Ibid.*: על כן אמרתי אעשה לו עזר כנגדו ויהיה טעמו ממולח טהור קדש על זה הדרך. הן הסדר הזה הנראה בדבר מורה על מסדר, והמסדר הוא מסדר לתכלית, כי זה הוא ענינו של סדר להיות החלקים מסודרים בו לתכלית מה, והמסדר לתכלית תאות לו הכונה אליו, ומה שהוא בכונת מכוין יתחייב היותו מחודש בחפץ פשוט, וכמו שכתב המורה בשני פרק כ׳, ועוד כתב בשלישי פ׳ י״ג . . . ועל זה אדני הרלב״ג הטבעו במופתיו המובאים על חדוש העולם בששי מספר מלחמותיו [חלק א׳] פ׳ ו׳ וז׳ כי בא הלום ברוב ענין וברוב דברים אשר לא נתנה ליכתב כאן לעוצם אריכותם . . . ועוד יבא מעין זה בחמישי סימן ג׳.

With regard to the reference in this passage to *Moreh Nebukim* III, 13, it will be shown later that the argument there against necessity is not from order but rather from deviation from order (cf. below §5, text above n. 62). Similarly in the chapters in the *Milḥamot Adonai* referred to no use is made of arguments from order against necessity. Cf. also our discussion of his reference to *Ḥobot ha-Lebabot* in *Ḳol Yehudah* on V, 3, below, §4, n. 2.

[18] *Ibid.*: הנה זאת חשבתי למשפט דברי החבר, ואם לא אפוא מי הוא הצד ציד ויבא לי כונתו הרצויה בהעביר קול טובו על פנינו נגילה ונשמחה בו ונברכהו גם ברוך יהיה. אך אם לא תגיע ידו די זה, ולקח הוא ושכנו את הקרוב אל בינתנו אשר למראה עינינו שפטנו, עד יחדש טובו אשר יאמר כי הוא זה ראה וקדש, ואז ישן מפני חדש נוציא.

[19] So also in Aristotle the term *οὐρανός* is sometimes used in a general sense to include what he considered all its component parts. Cf. Bonitz, *Index Aristotelicus*, sub *οὐρανός*, 2. i. q. caelum universe.

"in its centre"[20] where the pronoun *its* refers only to the uppermost sphere in the question immediately preceding it. We are thus left with two questions, one about all the spheres, including eccentric spheres and epicycles, and the other about the uppermost sphere. Now, we again suggest that these two questions should be also taken together as constituting one question and as intending to emphasize certain contrasts between the motion common to all the spheres and the motion which is particular to the uppermost sphere. What these contrasts are may be gathered from the characterizations by which Halevi describes the uppermost sphere. He says that the uppermost sphere has "no inclination in its motion," by which, we take it, he wishes to call attention to the fact that in the case of the other spheres there is an inclination in their motion.[21] Again, he says that the uppermost sphere moves round the earth as its centre, by which, we take it, he wishes to call attention to the fact that in the case of the other spheres there are motions which are not round the earth as a centre.[22] Thus interpreted, Halevi's argument is to be restated as follows: you say that all the spheres have circular motion by reason of the fact that they all consist of a common substance to which circular motion is natural. But if this were true, then all the spheres should move without inclination and round the earth as their centre. Why are there differences in these respects between the various spheres? The only explanation, Halevi concludes, is that all this is brought about by the free will of God. It will be noticed that no mention is made here by Halevi of the explanations that have been offered by Aristotle

[20] Cf. above quotation in n. 1.

[21] Hallevi elsewhere refers to such an inclination in the motion of some other spheres. Cf. *Cuzari* IV, 25: ורצינו בגלגל גלגל השמש הנוטה (פלך אלשמס אלמאיל).
The expression גלגל השמש הנוטה: פלך אלשמס אלמאיל reflects the Greek *ὁ ἥλιος καὶ ὁ λοξὸς κύκλος* (*Metaphys.* XII, 5, 1071a, 15–16).

[22] A similar contrast is referred to in the *Cuzari* IV, 13: כאשר הוא מבקש שיספר על הארץ על הדמיון שהוא במרכז הגלגל הגדול ואינה במרכז גלגל המזלות (פלך אלברוג). As for the meaning of גלגל המזלות in this passage, see commentaries *Ḳol Yehudah*, *Oẓar Neḥmad*, Satanow, Brecher, in Cassel (*ad loc.*). As far as the passage in II, 6, is concerned, we have shown that the term שמים may include also the epicycles whose centres are not the same as the centre of the uppermost sphere.

and others for these diversities in the motions of the spheres. Maimonides, as we shall see, does mention them and disposes of them.[23]

Similarly the argument from the motion of the spheres contained in Halevi's second passage (V, 2), is to be understood as implying a contrast between the motion of the outermost sphere and the motions of the other spheres. The nature of the contrast is again indicated in the characterization he uses of the outermost sphere. In this characterization he says that the uppermost sphere completes a revolution once "in every twenty-four hours" and that by its own revolution "it causes the other spheres to revolve along with it." The argument implied in this statement, we take it, is as follows: You say that all the spheres move by necessity according to a certain fixed law of causality. Now the outermost sphere completes a revolution once in every twenty-four hours, rising in the east and setting in the west. This means that the uppermost sphere moves along in a westward direction and with a certain definite velocity. We should therefore expect that all the other spheres should move in the same direction and with the same velocity. And yet we know that this is not the case.[24] The only explanation, Halevi concludes, is that these differences are brought about by the free will of God. Here, again, no reference is made to the attempted rational explanations of the diversity in direction and velocity in the motions of the spheres. But in so far as the attempted explanation was based upon the theory of Intelligences,[25] Halevi does refer to it elsewhere in his work and dismisses it rather summarily as something "which defies reason and is rejected by reason."[26]

[23] Cf. below nn. 43, 44, 46.

[24] In his comment on this passage *Ḳol Yehudah* seems to have felt the implication of some contrast between the motion of the uppermost sphere and the motions of the internal spheres. סבוב הגלגל העליון הסובב את כל ארץ כו"ש ממזרח למערב בכ"ד שעות, וכל יתר הגלגלים המתגלגלים בתנועת עצמם להפך ממערב למזרח, יסבו בלכתו אל עבר פניו מכח מרוצתו אשר העיר ממזרח בצדק יקראהו לרגלו.

[25] Cf. *Moreh Nebukim* II, 19, where reference is made to the use of the Intelligences as an explanation of the diversities in the motions of the spheres and Maimonides' refutation of it.

[26] *Cuzari* V, 14: ולהם בתחלה דעות מפסידות השכלים (אלעקל: השכל) יבזם השכל, כהעללתם בסבוב הגלגל שהוא יבקש שלמות יחסר לו כדי שיהיה נכחי לכל צד ולמה שלא

As for the argument in the third passage (V, 7), it contains only an allusion to the motion of the uppermost sphere, without any characterization, and it is used explicitly as a refutation of chance, without drawing any conclusion with regard to free will in God. Consequently, either it may refer to an argument from the uniformity of the motion of the uppermost sphere and is used only as a refutation of chance or it may refer to his previous arguments from the contrast between the motion of the outermost sphere and the motions of the inner spheres and is used not only as an argument against chance but also as a proof of free will in God.

A suggestion of this type of argument from the diversity of the motions of the spheres, though in phrasing unlike that used by Halevi, is to be found in Algazali, in a passage in which he tries to answer a certain objection raised by philosophers against the creation of the world and in the course of which he tries to force the philosophers to admit that the divine will of which they speak must be a free will. The philosophers' objection against creation quoted by Algazali is as follows: "Why was not the world created before the time in which it was created?"[27] In answer to this Algazali first maintains that "will is an attribute whose nature is to distinguish one thing from another thing which is like it"[28] and then on the basis of this he tries to show that inasmuch as some spheres move eastward while others move westward the philosophers themselves must assume that God by some act of deliberation, judgment and choice must have determined this diversity of directions in the motions of the spheres. To quote: "The second consequence concerns the direction of the motions of the spheres, some of which move from east to west while others move in the opposite direction, even though [with reference

יתכן זה תמיד לכל חלק יבקשהו על ההמרה והעקב. Cf. also IV, 26: מה הצורך אל אותיות
הו"י או אל מלאך וגלגל וזולת זה עם ההודאה בחפץ הבורא. V, 21: וקראו השכלים ההם
אלהים ומלאכים ועלות שניות וזולת זה מהשמות . . . וזה כלו דקדוק יקנה חדוד.

[27] *Tahafut al-Falāsifah* I, § 4, p. 23, l. 11: لِمَ لَمْ يحدث العالم قبل حدوثه. Cf. *Moreh Nebukim* II, 14 (6).

[28] *Ibid.* I, §30, p. 37, ll. 10–11: والارادة صفة من شانها تمييز الشيء عن مثله.

to the spheres] all directions are alike. What is the reason for that?"[29]

The logic of this argument from the diversities in the motions of the spheres is the same as that of the Kalam argument for the creation of the world known as the argument from Determination, which Halevi himself reproduces in the name of the Kalam.[30] The logic of the argument is this. If we find anything in the universe which cannot be considered as being essentially necessary to the nature of the universe so as to make the opposite thereof logically inadmissible, then we must consider that thing as being a selection out of two or more than two admissible alternatives and as such it must imply the existence of an agent who by the judgment of his free will has determined that selection. On the basis of this reasoning, those who employ the argument from the diversities in the motion of the spheres against the philosophers admit with the philosophers, at least for the sake of the argument, that the circularity of motion which is common to all the spheres may be something essentially necessary to the nature of the substance of the spheres, but they do not admit that the philosophers have succeeded in accounting for the diversities in the motions of the spheres as being essentially necessary to the nature of the substance of the spheres. These diversities, it is therefore maintained, are selections out of several alternative admissible possibilities and hence, it is argued, they must imply an agent who by his judgment and free will has determined these selections.

Now in the original Kalam argument from Determination, a great many things in the universe, which the philosophers consider as necessary, are assumed to be only of a possible nature.[31] These, of course, cannot be used as the basis of an argument against the philosophers. But there are certain things mentioned by the Kalam as being only of a possible nature which are ad-

[29] *Ibid.* I, §§37 ff. and §42, p. 45, ll. 3–4: الالزام الثانى تعيين جهة حركة الافلاك بعضها من المشرق الى المغرب وبعضها بالعكس مع تساوى الجهات ما سببها.

[30] *Cuzari* V, 18 (3).

[31] Cf. *Moreh Nebukim* I, 73 (10) and 74 (5).

mitted even by the philosophers as being of such a nature. Among such things of a merely possible nature are included the particular shape of things,[32] the particular magnitude of things,[33] the particular place of things[34] and in general all the other particular accidents of things.[35] These, of course, can be used as the basis of an argument against the philosophers. Accordingly, we find that Algazali, in addition to the argument from the diversity of the motion of the spheres, also argues from the fact that certain things in the world are white and others are black, that certain things are in motion and others at rest[36] and in general from the fact that "the world is determined by certain peculiar shapes (*hī'āt*), even though it was possible for it to be of other shapes."[37] The fact that there are in the world things which could have been otherwise proves, according to him, that there must be a determining cause which acts by free will.

It is this argument from certain particular unnecessary accidents that the world happens to have that is contained in the passage which we have suggested to detach from his argument from the motions of the spheres. The passage reads: "What thing is it which in your opinion . . . made the order of the universe have a certain particular quantity and quality and certain particular shapes?"[38] "Quantity," "quality" and "shape," as we have seen, are the terms which usually occur in the Kalam argument from Determination.

These two types of argument, one from the diversities in the motions of the spheres and the other from certain particular accidents in the structure of the universe, which are only alluded

[32] *Ibid.* I, 74 (5): Arabic: שכל, Hebrew: (1) תאר, (2) תכונה (Ibn Tibbon), (3) תבנית (Ḥarizi).

[33] *Ibid.*: שעור: מקדאר.

[34] *Ibid.*: מקום: מכאן.

[35] *Ibid.*: או במקרה (בערץ̇) מן המקרים.

[36] *Tahafut al-Falāsifah* I, § 28: بل فى البياض والسواد والحركة والسكون . . . وما الذى ميّز أحد الممكنين عن الآخر (p. 36, ll. 6–9).

[37] *Ibid.* I, § 29, p. 37, ll. 2–4: العالم مخصوص بهيئات مخصوصة كان يجوز أن يكون على هيئات اخرى.

[38] Cf. quotation above in n. 1.

to by Halevi, are stated by Maimonides with much greater clearness and with more considerable detail. From his introductory statement to these types of argument, where reference is made to the Kalam argument from Determination and where also a distinction is drawn between his own conception of determination and that of the Kalam,[39] as well as from his use of the term determination throughout his discussion of these arguments,[40] it is evident that Maimonides consciously considered these types of argument as a modification of the Kalam argument from Determination.

The diversities which Maimonides finds in the motions of the spheres are of three kinds. In the first place, there is a difference in the direction of the motions of the spheres. Some of them revolve from east to west, while others revolve from west to east.[41] Necessity, he argues, cannot explain that deviation from uniformity. In the second place, there is a difference in the velocity of the motion of the spheres. Some of the spheres revolve with less speed, while others revolve with greater speed.[42] Here, too, necessity cannot explain this deviation from uniformity. Indeed, says Maimonides, Aristotle has tried to explain this variety in the direction and velocity of the motions of the spheres by various devices.[43] But these explanations are critically examined by Maimonides and are rejected as unsatisfactory.[44] In the third place, there is also a difference in the courses of the motions of the planets.[45] Here, again, necessity cannot explain the deviation from one uniform course of motion. Indeed, an explanation for these differences has been offered either in the theory of epicycles or in the theory of eccentric spheres or in a theory which combines the two. But none of these theories, argues Maimonides, is quite fully satisfactory.[46] The conclusion to be drawn is that God acts by free will.

39 *Moreh Nebukim* II, 19.
40 *Ibid.*
41 *Ibid.*
42 *Ibid.*
43 *Ibid.*
44 *Ibid.*
45 *Ibid.*
46 *Ibid.* II, 19 and II, 24.

Interspersed among his arguments from the diversity in the motion of the sphere there is an argument from certain particular accidents in the structure of the universe, which, as we have seen, is also used by Algazali and Halevi. Three such kinds of accidents in the structure of the universe are mentioned by Maimonides. To begin with, while each of the seven planets has several spheres, the fixed stars, though large in number, are all in one sphere.[47] Then, the stars and spheres, though inseparably attached to each other, still differ from each other in that the former are at rest and opaque and the latter are in motion and transparent.[48] Finally, the stars in the eighth sphere are of various sizes and of unequal distances from each other.[49] Now none of these, argues Maimonides, are necessary by the nature of the heavenly bodies themselves; by their own nature it was possible for them to be otherwise. The fact that one of the several possible alternatives prevailed in preference to the others cannot be explained except by the assumption of a free will which determined the selection of one in preference to the others. All this, as will have been noticed, is only an elaboration of the argument which Algazali only describes by the terms "white" and "black" "motion" and "rest" and "shape" and which Halevi describes by the terms "quantity" "quality" and shapes."

4. Sublunar Phenomena

Strictly speaking, in Maimonides there are no arguments from sublunar phenomena for the existence of free will of God. His discussion of sublunar phenomena is intended only to show how in contrast to the translunar world, where Aristotle could not explain certain phenomena on the assumption of necessity, the phenomena in the sublunar world were explained by him quite adequately on such an assumption. In Halevi, however, the discussion of sublunar phenomena is presented in the form of an argument against something. Quite properly they are

47 *Ibid.* II, 19.
48 *Ibid.*
49 *Ibid.*

always presented as an argument against chance.[1] But inasmuch as the alternative of chance favored by him is not a God who acts by necessity but one who acts by free will, this particular view of his, for which the only arguments he has are those based on the diversity of the motions of the spheres and the non-essential accidents in the structure of the universe, is throughout his discussion from sublunar phenomena advanced as if it were the logical conclusion of his argument, thus giving the erroneous impression that the sublunar phenomena were used by him as a direct proof for free will in God.[2] Let us, then, try to trace logically the successive steps in his arguments from the sublunar phenomena.[3]

[1] *Cuzari* V, 3: ואני רואה אצלם מתחדשות במקרה (באלאתّפאק); V, 5: ומה הצריכנו לדחות טענת אפיקורוס היוני אשר היה רואה כי העולם לומר במקרה (באלאתّפאק); V, 8: היה במקרה.

[2] *Ḳol Yehudah* on V, 3, explicitly states that Hallevi arguments in refutation of chance are also valid as arguments in refutation of necessity: והראיה עצמה אשר תורה על בטול המקרה תבטל ג״כ טענת החיוב. His reference to *Ḥobot ha-Lebabot* I, 6, however, does not prove his point. Baḥya's argument from order is directed against the Epicurean theory which admits that the world has a beginning but denies that it has a cause. He does not argue against the Aristotelian assumption that the world is eternal and that it has a cause but that its cause acts by the necessity of its nature. Against this later view the arguments are to be not from order but from deviation from order. Cf. above §3, n. 17.

[3] Here is an analysis of the text of Cuzari V, 2–10, which contains the arguments from sublunar phenomena.

V, 2. Rabbi: the formation of elements, according to the philosophers, are due to their respective locations with reference to the spheres. [According to some philosophers, the formation of minerals are similarly due only to their mixtures (v, 10)].

V, 3. Cuzari: Does not this view imply that the formation of the elements is due to chance?

V, 4. Rabbi: Yes. But the philosophers themselves, realizing that chance could not account for the specific differences in the forms of (1) the four elements, (2) plants and (3) animals, have introduced to Active Intellect. [The specific form in plants and animals is called 'soul'. In plants it is called 'nature'. The various souls are also described as 'powers' (V, 10)].

V, 5. Cuzari: Don't you yourself believe that the specific forms of plants and animals are due to the direct act of the free will of God and not to the Active Intellect, which according to the philosophers is only an intermediate cause of a God acting by necessity? Why then should you not say outright

These arguments deal with the question of the rise of the elements out of matter, the rise of minerals out of the elements and the rise of life in plants and animals. Now with regard to the rise of the elements from matter, says Halevi, some interpreters of Aristotle maintain that matter becomes transformed into four elements as a result of the location in which it happens to be with reference to the celestial sphere within which it is enclosed, that part of the matter which is nearest the sphere thus becoming fire, that part which remotest from the sphere becoming earth and the intermediate parts becoming either air or water.[4] This view is characterized by Halevi as a view which makes the transformation of matter into the four elements dependent on chance.[5] By the term 'chance' here, we take it, Halevi does not mean 'chance' in the sense of causelessness which he

that by the analogy of plants and animals the specific forms of the elements are similarly due to the direct act of the free will of God?

V, 6. Rabbi: Yes, this is my belief. But this belief of mine is based only on the evidence of the historical miracles recorded in Scripture. To philosophers this kind of evidence is not convincing. Consequently, from their own point of view, were it not for the argument that specific differences in forms could not be explained by chance, they would say that even the specific forms of plants (and for that matter also of animals) were due only to chance. Cf. *Ḳol Yehudah ad loc.*

V, 7. Cuzari: It seems to me that besides this argument against chance (1) from specific forms, there is also an argument against it (2) from the motion of the uppermost sphere (cf. above §3) and (3) from the finite number of forms of plants and animals.

V, 8. Rabbi: Yes, and there is still another argument against chance (4) from the purposiveness and utility in the structure of animal organs.

[4] *Cuzari* V, 2: ותחלתם חמום האויר הקרוב מגלגל הירח בעבור קורבתו ממקום התנועה . . . ואחר כן כדור הארץ, אשר היא המרכז, בעבור רחקה ממקום התנועה.

Hallevi does not say here with reference to the elements, as he does say later with reference to minerals (V, 10), that only some philosophers hold this view (ולקצתם דעת במוצאים). From his subsequent statement אבל ההכרח יביאם להודות (V, 4) it would seem, quite the contrary, that in the case of the elements all the philosophers have found themselves compelled to introduce the intervention of the active Intellect. Historically, however, we know this not to be the case. Maimonides, as we shall see, follows a school of philosophers which does not assume the intervention of the Active Intellect in the case of the elements.

[5] *Ibid.* V, 3: ואני רואה אותם אצלם מתחדשות במקרה (באלאתּפאק) באמרם נקרה לאשר קרוב מהגלגל מאד שיהיה אש וכו' (אתּפק).

attributes to Epicurus, for the theory of the rise of the elements under discussion can hardly be described as 'chance' in this sense of the term, that is to say, in the sense of causelessness, for, even if it is the mere chance of the location of matter with reference to the lunar sphere that transforms matter into one of the four elements, the transformation itself is caused by the motion of the sphere. He uses the term 'chance' here, we take it, in its Aristotelian sense, that is, in the sense of 'accident.'[6] In this sense, 'chance' does not mean that which has no cause at all but rather that whose cause is accidental (*κατὰ συμβεβηκός*) and not essential (*καθ' αὑτό*).[7] In the case now under consideration, therefore, while the transformation of matter into the four elements is indeed caused by the motion of the spheres, the latter is not an essential cause but only an accidental cause, in view of the fact that the transformation of matter into a particular element does not take place except by the accidental location of that matter with reference to the spheres. The arguments which Halevi uses here in refutation of chance apply equally to both meanings of the term.

Similarly with regard to the rise of minerals, says Halevi, some philosophers believe that the powers and properties and substances of the various minerals arise only as a result of the various mixtures of these elements,[8] which mixtures are, of course, determined by the motions of the spheres.[9] This view is not characterized by Halevi as one of chance, though, following his own reasoning in the case of the elements, he could have used the same characterization also here in the case of minerals.

There are other philosophers, continues Halevi, who felt that the assumption that the elements arose out of matter by 'chance' or, as we have tried to interpret it, by 'accident,' would have to make the differences between the four elements only of an accidental nature, such as differences with reference to 'more and

[6] The Arabic *ittifāq* which Hallevi uses here means chance in the sense of causelessness as well as accident.

[7] *Phys.* II, 5, 196b, 24 ff.

[8] *Cuzari* V, 10: ולקצתם דעת במוצאים שכחותם (קואהא) וטבעיהם (=וטבאיעהא; וכואצה=וסגולותיהם) [ונואהרהא=ועצמיהם] מזגיים בלבד.

[9] Cf. below n. 21.

less' or to 'stronger and weaker,' but it would not account for the fact that each element differs from any of the other elements essentially by the "proper form" which peculiarly belongs to it.[10] Moreover, all the philosophers, even those who assume that elements arise by what Halevi describes as 'chance,' felt that this assumption was not sufficient to explain the rise of plants and animals, and this for the following two reasons: First, if plants and animals arose as a result only of the influence of the spherical constellations, there would have to have been an infinite variety of plants and animals, inasmuch as the spherical constellations are infinite in number. But this is contrary to observation.[11] Second, the evidence of wisdom and purposiveness in animals, such as has been described by Aristotle in his *De Partibus Animalium*[12] and by Galen in his *De Usu Partium Corporis Humani*,[13] is so striking that even according to Aristotle himself and other philosophers it precludes the possibility of their having arisen by mere chance.[14] Here he says definitely he uses chance in the Epicurean sense of the term.[15] But we know

[10] *Cuzari* V, 4: כי לא יפרד עצם האש מעצם האויר והאויר מן המים והמים מהארץ במעט וברב (באלאקל̈ ואלכת̇ר) ובחזק ובחלש (ואלאש̈ד ואלאצ̇עף) אבל בצורה מיוחדת לכל אחד (בצורה̈ כאצ̇ה̈).

The contrasting Arabic terms אקל̈ (מעט) and אכת̇ר (רב), אש̈ד (חזק) and אצ̇עף (חלש) are commonly used as translations of the contrasting Greek terms ἧττον and μᾶλλον, σφόδρα and ἠρέμα which occur in Aristotle as illustrations of variations of degree in accidental qualities (cf. *Categ.* ch. 8, 10b, 26; *Topics* III, 2, 117b, 23; cf. my paper "Amphibolous Terms in Aristotle, Arabic Philosophy and Maimonides," in *Harvard Theological Review*, 31 (1938), 157–158; in *Studies in the History of Philosophy*, I, 455–478.

[11] *Ibid.* V, 7: ואחר כן אדבר עמו בערכים ההם הגלגליים והם עד אין תכלית מרוב, ואנחנו רואים צורות הצמחים והחיים יש להם תכלית, עליהם אין להוסיף ומהם אין לגרוע, והיה ראוי שתתחדשנה עם חדוש הערכים צורות ותמחינה אחרות.

The reason why the number of species of plants and animals must be finite is stated by Gersonides as follows: "As for the species, they must of necessity be finite in number, for their essence must be comprehended by the Active Intellect and by God, but that which is not encompassed by number cannot be known" (*Milḥamot Adonai VI*, i, 8, p. 317). ואולם המינים יחוייב בהם שיהיו מוגבלי המספר, לפי שהוא מחוייב שיהיה מהותם מושכל לשכל הפועל ולשם יתברך, ומה שלא יקיף בו מספר לא יתכן שיהיה ידוע.

[12] בספר תועלת מיני החיים לאריסטו.

[13] בספר תועלת האברים לגלינוס.

[14] *Cuzari* V, 8.

[15] *Ibid.*: לדחות טענת אפיקורוס היוני אשר היה רואה כי העולם היה במקרה.

that Aristotle uses the same argument to eliminate even chance in his own sense of the term.

But in order to escape chance — we may now restate Halevi's thought, if not his words, — what do the philosophers do? They introduce the Active Intellect and make it the cause of the specific forms. Some of them, being consistent, introduce it at the very outset of the process in connection with the rise of the elements out of matter. Some of them, with an inexplicable inconsistency, introduce it only in connection with the rise of plants and animals. They all call that Active Intellect "something divine"[16] and speak of it as acting with "wisdom"[17] and hence believe to have found in it a sufficient explanation for the evidence of wisdom and purposiveness in animal life, such as is described by Aristotle and Galen. But what is really that Active Intellect? It is only one of the Intelligences, the tenth or the last Intelligence, to be exact, which according to the philosophers emanate by necessity from God and, like God himself from whom they emanate by necessity, act by necessity. Consequently what the philosophers have done is only to substitute necessity and eternity for chance and a temporal beginning of the world. Now against this explanation of the sublunar phenomena by the assumption that they are parts of an eternally established order dependent upon a cause which acts by necessity, Halevi advances no arguments. Evidently he agrees with the commonly accepted view that such a conception is logically tenable, for order and regularity and harmony, logically, require no free will on the part of God, except on the theory, independently established, that the world came into being after it had not been. But if one assumes that the world is eternal, then its order and regularity and harmony can be explained even on the assumption that God acts by the necessity of his nature.[18] To

[16] *Ibid.* V, 4: ענין אלהי (אמר אלאהי).

[17] *Ibid.*: אבל ההכרח יביאם להודות בחכמה (באלחכמה̈).

[18] In an essay published by the present writer many years ago ("Maimonides and Halevi", *Jewish Quarterly Review*, N. S., 2 (1912), 297–337), Hallevi's arguments from sublunar phenomena are restated as follows:

"Moreover, the argument from design is no proof for the existence of God. The order of the universe, if there is any, need not be a created order. Har-

prove that God acts by free will, without first proving on independent grounds that the world came into being after it had not been, one must resort to other arguments, such, for instance, as the diversity in the motions of the spheres or the existence of non-essential accidents in the structure of the universe, which, according to our interpretation, Halevi himself has made use of.

And now let us recast Maimonides' discussion of the sublunar phenomena into the same form in which we have put Halevi's agreement and see wherein he agrees with Halevi and wherein he differs from him.

In the case of the rise of the elements out of matter, Maimonides, like some of the philosophers to whom Halevi refers, represents Aristotle as believing that matter becomes transformed into four elements as a result of its location with reference to

mony, beauty and unity, the teleologic architectonic need no explanation. They are necessarily self-explaining, for they contain nothing problematic. If the possibility of change and the creation of *new* things in nature be not granted, then 'thy opponent and thou might agree that a vine e. g. grew in this place because a seed happens to have fallen here' (V, 7). If there were no changes in nature, if the world presented no difficult situations, man would never think of God. What raises questions in our mind, what needs explanations, is the discord and change in nature. These cannot be explained but by the presupposition of a Supreme Guide, for whom 'evidence is found in changes of nature' (V, 7), 'It is these that prove the existence of a creator of the world who can accomplish everything' (I, 67)." *Ibid.*, pp. 322–323. This paper is below, pp. 120–160.

I do by no means subscribe now to everything said in that undergraduate essay of mine, nor do I think that I had then a clear conception of the various implications of Hallevi's arguments from design. Essentially, however, the paragraph quoted happens to be correct, though in the light of my analysis of the question in the present paper I would rewrite certain statements in it to read differently. For example:

Moreover, the argument from design is no proof for the existence of God. This I would rewrite to read: Moreover, the argument from order and regularity is by itself no proof for the existence of God. It can become such a proof only if one proves at first the temporal beginning of the world. Indeed Hallevi argues from order and regularity against those who believed in chance which means also that he argues from order and regularity against those who denied the existence of a God, but this is only because his opponents assumed, even if they did not prove it, that the world had a beginning. (Cf. above §1).

The order of the universe, if there is any, need not be a created order. This I would rewrite to read: The order of the universe, if that order be fixed and

the celestial sphere within which it is enclosed.[19] Unlike Halevi, however, he does not characterize this conception of the rise of the elements as one which attributes their rise to chance or accident. On the contrary, he explicitly states that the rise of the elements out of matter by reason of the differences in the location of matter with reference to the sphere is the result of necessity, and not of chance or accident, and this because of the fact that these differences in location are eternally fixed by nature

unalterable, need not be an order created by the free will of God, for it might be an order existing from eternity by the necessary causality of God.

If the possibility of change and the creation of new things in nature be not granted, then 'thy opponent and thou might agree that a vine e. g. grew in this place because a seed happens to have fallen here' (V, 7). This I would rewrite to read: If the possibility of miraculous changes and the creation of new things in nature be not granted, then, without the arguments from specific forms (see above n. 3), "thy opponent might with equal force argue quite to the contrary (אסתוי מעך מנאטרך: ישתוה עמך הטוען עליך) that a vine e. g. grew in this place because a seed happens to have fallen here" (V, 6).

In a paper "Judah Halevi as Philosopher", in the *Jewish Quarterly Review*, N. S., 25 (1935), 201–225, Professor Isidore Epstein felt there was something wrong about my paragraph quoted above. But I am afraid he failed to see what was really the trouble with it. He objects to it on the ground that it assumes that (1) "Halevi in his distrust of human reason does not accept the argument of design" (*ibid.*, p. 202), contending that (2) such an assumption is based upon a misinterpretation of *Cuzari* V, 6 (*ibid.*) and (3) that the meaning of *Cuzari* V, 6, is that "once deny the possibility of change and the creation of *new* things by God, that is, once reduce the universe to fixed inexorable iron laws, shutting out all supernatural, there is no point in attacking the proposition that the world has no creator, as the question of the origin of things is of no value to religious beliefs in so far as it leads to the affirmation of an *Almighty* and *All-Powerful* Supreme Being, able to create *new* things and produce changes in the natural order" (*ibid.*, p. 208, n. 17).

In the light of my analysis of the question in the present paper, I imagine that Professor Epstein will want to revise his views with regard to the following:

(1) The real facts in the case and the meaning of Hallevi's use of the argument of design.

(2) The meaning of the argument contained in *Cuzari* V, 6, which according to the interpretation here presented has reference only to the question why the Rabbi has introduced the argument from specific forms as a refutation of chance (cf. above n. 3).

[19] *Moreh Nebukim* II, 19: ענה אריסטו על זה בשאמר חייב זה התחלף המקומות וכו'. Cf. I, 72.

and cannot therefore be considered as a mere chance or accident.[20] So also with regard to the formation of minerals out of the four elements Maimonides agrees with those philosophers referred to by Halevi that according to Aristotle they are due to the variety of mixtures of those elements as determined by the motions of the spheres.[21] No assistance of the Active Intellect is required, according to Maimonides, to account for the specific forms of the elements or for the specific forms of minerals. The Active Intellect to him is not the giver of all forms, but only of the specific forms of plants and animals which are called souls.[22] But like Halevi he believes that the Active Intellect, as conceived by the philosophers, acts by necessity[23] Again, like that which is only implied in Halevi's silence on the question, Maimonides states explicitly that the sublunar phenomena are satisfactorily explained on the assumption of necessity. "With regard to the things in the sublunary world which are various despite the fact that their matter is one, you can say, as we have shown, that the cause which determines their variation is to be found in the forces of the spheres and in the different positions of the matter with reference to the sphere, as has been taught by Aristotle."[24]

[20] *Ibid.* II, 19: והיה זה הכרחי כי מן השקר שיהיה החומר הזה לא במקום, או יהיה המקיף הוא המרכז והמרכז הוא המקיף, וזה חייב לו התייחדות בצורות מתחלפות, רוצה לומר ההכנה לקבל צורות, מתחלפות.

This statement is in direct oppositioh to the statement quoted above (n. 5) from Hallevi.

[21] *Ibid.*: וזה שהם יתערבו תחלה בתנועת הגלגל ואחר כן ימזגו ויתחדש ההתחלפות בהתערבות המורכבות מהם בשעורים מתחלפים.

[22] *Ibid.* I, 72: הנה כל תנועה שתמצא בעולם התחלתה הראשונה תנועת הגלגל וכל נפש שתמצא לבעל נפש בעולם התחלתה נפש הגלגל. ודע כי הכחות המגיעות מן הגלגלים לזה העולם כפי מה שהתבאר ארבע כחות: כח יחייב הערוב וההרכבה. ואין ספק שזה מספיק בהרכבת המחצבים. Cf. Shem Tob *ad loc.* and *Moreh ha-Moreh*, p. 45, and *Ḳol Yehudah* on *Cuzari* V, 10: ולקצתם דעת במוצאים.

[23] *Ibid.* II, 19, where, despite the Intelligences, the motions of the spheres are said by him to be moved by necessity according to Aristotle: אבל תראה מאמריו שהוא משתדל לסדר לנו מציאות הגלגלים כמו שסדר לנו מציאות מה שתחת גלגל הירח עד שיהיה הכל על צד החיוב הטבעי.

[24] *Ibid.*: כי כל מה שתחת הגלגל מן החלופים ואף על פי שהחמר שלהם אחד כמו שבארנו תוכל לשים מיחדם כחות גלגלים והנחות החמר מן הגלגל כמו שלמדנו אריסטו. And before that: כי כל מה שבאר לנו ממה שתחת גלגל הירח נסכם על סדר מסכים למציאות מבואר העלות ואפשר שיאמר בו שהוא על צד החיוב מתנועת הגלגל וכחותיו.

5. The Wisdom of Nature

In connection, directly or indirectly, with the evidence of sublunary phenomena, especially from the life of plants and animals, for free will in God, both Halevi and Maimonides discuss a certain view according to which 'nature' is said to be endowed with certain powers which are responsible for the wonders of structure and function which one observes in plants and animals. Now the attribution of such powers to nature is found both in Aristotle and the Stoics, as well as in later writers who followed either one or the other or both of them. There are, however, certain differences between Aristotle's use of the term nature and its use by the Stoics, two of which differences are pertinent to our discussion. Aristotle does not identify the term nature with God. Nature is formally defined by him as a principle or cause of motion which is inherent in that which is moved (ἐν ᾧ ὑπάρχει)[1] whereas God as the Prime Mover is separate from sensible things (κεχωρισμένη τῶν αἰσθητῶν)[2] of all of which he is the ultimate cause of motion. In other words, 'nature' as an inherent cause of motion, according to Aristotle, has itself God as a cause separate from it. To the Stoics, on the hand, God is a principle inherent in the universe, and not separate from it, and nature is one of the many terms which they apply to God.[3] Then, again, while Aristotle occasionally uses the term nature in its general sense of an inherent principle of motion to include also soul, he does not use it specifically in the sense of soul or in the sense of any particular faculty of the soul; on the contrary, quite often he uses it as the antithesis of soul. The Stoics, on the other hand, use the term nature specifically as designation of the vegetative soul.[4] In studying the passages in which Halevi and Maimonides deal with the wisdom of nature, whether they merely restate the view of others or whether they also comment upon it, we shall therefore have to determine in each instance the par-

[1] *Phys.* II, 192b, 22.

[2] *Metaphys.* XII, 7, 1073a, 4–5.

[3] Cf. Index to Arnim, *Stoicorum Veterum Fragmenta*, sub φύσις, p. 159, col. 1: θεὸς φ.

[4] Cf. *ibid.*: ἕξις: φ: ψυχή.

ticular conception of nature dealt by them, whether it is the Aristotelian or the Stoic or some combination of the two.

The discussion of "nature" is introduced by Halevi in the course of the Rabbi's endeavor to prove that the wisdom observed in animal life is due directly to the Will of God.[5] At this point the Cuzari interrupts him to say that according to "the philosophers" "this is attributed to the action of nature."[6] This term 'nature,' we are then informed by the Rabbi, is defined by "the Philosopher" as "the principle and the cause by which the thing in which it is inherent rests and is moved, essentially and not according to accident."[7] Now this is almost a literal translation of Aristotle's formal definition of motion.[8] Then we are further informed by the Cuzari that, following the philosophers, "we say that nature is wise and active."[9] This statement, too, reflects such statements of Aristotle as that the course of nature (*πέφυκε*) corresponds to the course of action (*πράττεται*)[10] and that the products of nature, like the products of art, are for the sake of an end[11] and that "nature, like a prudent (*φρόνιμος*) man, always apportions (*διανέμει*) to each the instrument it can use"[12] and that such creatures as spiders, ants and swallows work so skilfully for an end by nature (*φύσει*) that people wonder whether they do not work by intelligence (*νῷ*).[13] That Halevi has reference here to these statements of Aristotle becomes all the more obvious when in his opening statement about the wisdom which philosophers attribute to nature he mentions as an example "The wisdom apparent in the nature of an ant."[14]

[5] *Cuzari* I, 69.

[6] *Ibid.* I, 70–72.

[7] *Ibid.* I, 73: כי הוא ההתחלה והסבה אשר בה ינוח וינוע הדבר אשר הוא בו בעצם ולא במקרה.

[8] *Phys.* II, I, 192b, 20–23.

[9] *Cuzari* I, 76: באמרנו הטבע חכם (חכימ̈ה) פועל.

[10] *Phys.* II, 8, 199a, 9–10.

[11] *Ibid.* 199a, 17–18.

[12] *De Part. Anim.* IV, 10, 687a, 10–12. Hence (חכימ̈ה) חכם is *φρόνιμος*. But cf. below n. 64.

[13] *Phys.* II, 8, 199a, 20–30.

[14] *Cuzari* I, 69: זאת החכמה הנמצאת בבריאות (כ̇לק) הנמלה. The Arabic כ̇לק is to be taken here to read *ḫulk* or *ḫuluq*, and not *ḫalq*, whence its meaning here is not *creation* but rather *natural disposition* or *inborn quality*, reflecting the

But then Halevi proceeds to criticize the philosophers for their description of nature as "wise and active" on the ground that "they lead us astray by these words and cause us to give an associate to God . . . for, following out the meaning of their words, we might be led to say that nature is possessed of intelligence."[15] This cautious phrasing of his criticism makes it quite clear that he did not actually accuse Aristotle or his followers of attributing intelligence to nature, which shows an accurate understanding on Halevi's part of Aristotle's position, for in many places Aristotle explicitly uses the terms intelligence and nature as designating two distinct things.[16] Nor does he accuse Aristotle and his followers of making nature independent of God so as to place it on a par with God, for, quite the contrary, to Aristotle nature as the inherent principle of motion in the physical world depends upon God as its prime cause. The nearest that Aristotle comes in speaking of nature as a deity is such a statement as that "the divine encloses the whole nature,"[17] or as that "all things have by nature something divine in them,"[18] but all such statements are as far from pantheism as the many rabbinic statements about the omnipresence of God. All that Halevi does here is to warn his reader against misunderstanding the words of Aristotle.

Having thus warned the reader against drawing wrong inferences from the philosophers' description of nature as wise and active by attributing to it intelligence and by making it indepen-

Greek *φύσις* by which in the passage quoted ants are said to work. The same applies also to the statement: שחכמתו והנהגתו ביצירת (כֹלקה) הנמלה והדבורה later in III, 17. On the interpretation of this kind of *φύσις* in Arabic philosophy, see my "The Internal Senses in Latin, Arabic, and Hebrew Philosophic Texts," *Harvard Theological Review*, 28 (1935), 86–91, 109. On the Hebrew terms בריאה, יצירה in the sense of טבע, see Klatzkin, *Oẓar ha-Munaḥim ha-Pilosofiyyim*, s. v. "Internal Senses" is in *Studies*, I, 250.

[15] *Ibid.* I, 76: אם כן אני רואה שהתעינו בשמות האלה ושמינו משתפים עם הבורא (=כֹאלק; אללה=האלהים) באמרנו הטבע חכם פועל ואפשר שנבא לומר בורא (=כֹאלקה; עאקלה=משכיל) על טעם דבריהם.

[16] Cf., e. g., *Phys.* II, 8, 199a, 20–30, and II, 4, 196a, 30.

[17] *Metaphys.* XII, 8, 1074b, 3.

[18] *Eth. Nic.* VII, 13, 1153b, 32. Zeller (*Aristotle*, I, 421) finds a different connotation in this statement as well as in other similar statements of Aristotle.

dent of God, Halevi proceeds to show why such inferences would be wrong.

We have no objection, he says, to the use of the term nature as a description of the actions of the elements and the sun and the moon and the stars in their influence upon the generation of things in the sublunar world. It is to be admitted, he continues, that they all have a part in the processes of generation and that they all may be considered as causes. But the action ascribed to nature in this sense merely means a sort of "compulsory labor"[19] performed by the direction of some wise agent. It does not mean that nature has wisdom of its own. Thus in the generation of life, you may regard those physical agencies, such as the elements and the sun and the moon and the stars only as factors in the preparation of matter for the reception of life and hence only as contributory causes. You may describe their action, if you like, by the term nature. It is, however, not this nature, but rather a being above it, who is "wise, victorious and possessed of the power to decree things," that imparts life — that kind of life which manifests itself in such actions as "the shaping of the animal being, the determining of its size and the delivery of it."[20]

[19] *Cuzari* I, 77: מבלי שניחס להם חכמה רק עבודה (סכֿרה).

[20] *Ibid.*: אבל הציור (אלתצויר) והשיעור (אלתקדיר) וההזרעה (אלתבריז) וכל אשר יש בו חכמה לכונה לא יתיחס כי אם לחכם (לחכים) היכול (אלקאהר) המשער (אלקאדר).

אלתצויר: הציור, literally, the act of forming or shaping. Its use in connection with the faculty of reproduction is common (cf. S. Horovitz, *Die Psychologie der jüdischen Neuplatoniker*: *B. Josef Ibn Ṣaddik*, p. 181, n. 107). The Arabic التصوير is direct translation of the Greek *διάπλασις* and it refers to the action of the *δύναμις διαπλαστική* (Galen, *De Naturalibus Facultatibus* I, 6). Cf. *Cuzari* V, 21: כאשר אמר גאלינוס בכח המצייר (אלקוֿה אלמתצוֿרה). It is described as one of the activities of the process of generation (Galen, *op. cit.* I, 5). Cf. below n. 64.

אלתקדיר: השיעור, literally: the act of determining the measure or size or quantity of something. Hence it is used here with reference to the faculty of growth in the sense of determining the growth or increase of a living thing. In Aristotle the faculty of growth is described as "a limit (*πέρας*) or proportion (*λόγος*) which determines size (*μεγέθους*) and growth (*αὐξήσεως*)" (*De An.* II, 4, 416a, 17) and is said to refer to an animate thing in so far as it is quantitative (*ποσόν τι*) (*ibid.*, 416b, 12–13). Cf. also Galen's definition

In this passage, again, the term nature is still used in the general sense of motion which is imparted to the sublunar things by the heavenly bodies. Halevi's contention here that there must be a being above nature who compels nature to do its work is one which is maintained by Aristotle himself. There is, in fact, nothing in what Halevi says logically to lead to the conclusion maintained by him, in contradistinction to Aristotle, that the God beyond nature acts by free will.

So far, then, in his restatement of the philosophers' conception of nature, Halevi has used the term in its strictly Aristotelian sense, making it neither identical with God nor specifically identical with the vegetative soul, though he makes the vegetative soul, as soul in general, included under it. But to this general Aristotelian use of the term nature, in many places in the *Cuzari*, Halevi adds its Stoic use as a designation of the vegetative soul[21] — a usage which, it can be shown, has been introduced

of growth as a tridimensional increase (ἐπίδοσις) and expansion (διάστασις). *De Naturalibus Facultalibus* I, 5.

אלתבריז: ההזרעה. The Hebrew translation is evidently based on the reading אלתבזיר, i. e., the act of sprouting or of growing grain. The Hebrew הזרעה here is therefore to be taken not in the sense of *sowing* but rather in the sense of *yielding seed* after the expression מזריע זרע in Gen. 1, 11.

But it is not impossible that the reading אלתבריז is correct. The literal meaning of التبريز is the act of making come forth. It may thus be used in the general sense of the *expulsive faculty*, δύναμις ἀποκριτική, القوة الدافعة, הכח הדוחה. Now the expulsive faculty includes both *excretion* and *parturition* (cf. Galen, *De Naturalibus Facultalibus* III, 12), and the term تبريز is known to have the meaning of *excretion*. It is therefore not impossible that it is used here by Hallevi in the sense of *parturition*. Taken in this sense, the three terms here refer to three stages in the process of generation, namely, (1) the shaping of the body, (2) the growth of the body and (3) the delivery of the child.

It may be noted that in Persian both برز and بزر mean *seed* and that بزر means also *offspring*.

[21] *Cuzari* II, 14: וכמו שהטבע צופה למזג השוה באיכותיו שיחיל בו ויהיה צמח; IV, 25: והקדום חולק בין עולם הטבע ועולם החיים; V, 2: ואחר כן הטבע ואחר כן הנפש; V, 10: והיא הצמח . . . לחכמה הנפלאה התקועה בו הנקראת אצלם טבע. But here in addition to the Stoic "nature" he refers also to the Platonic "soul" and the Aristotelian "faculty" when he says of the vegetative soul or "nature": קרא אתה התכונה ההיא אם תחפוץ טבע או נפש או כח; V, 12: ומדרגת הטבע מהנפש.

into Arabic philosophy by way of (1) Neoplatonism and (2) Galen. In one of these places, describing the reproductive faculty of the vegetative soul, he says that the seed produced by a plant reproduces and preserves its kind "by some wonderful wisdom inherent in it, called by philosophers 'nature,' which is a power that takes care of the preservation of the species, inasmuch as the individual in itself, on account of its being composed of unstable parts, cannot have continuance of existence."[22] This is an exact restatement of a Stoic definition attributed to Zeno, according to which "Nature is a force moving of itself, producing (ἀποτελοῦσα) and preserving (συνέχουσα) in being its offspring in accordance with seminal principles within definite periods and effecting results homogeneous with their sources."[23] The combination, of the Aristotelian conception of nature as the general principle of motion in the universe and the Stoic conception thereof as a special principle of motion in plants and animals evidently was not uncommon in Arabic philosophy. A description of it is to be found in the following passage of Shahrastani: "Themistius states his view, as a tradition handed down from Aristotle, Plato, Theophrastus, Porphyry and Plutarch, to the effect that the whole world has one general nature and that each species of plants and animals possesses a peculiar nature of its own and they define the general nature as being the principle of motion in things as well as of rest therein according to the first thing of their essence, for it is the cause of motion in things which are moved and the cause of rest in things which are at rest."[24]

With this identification of the term nature specifically with the reproductive faculty of the vegetative soul, Halevi tries to show

[22] *Cuzari* V, 10: ויבקש הזרע ההוא כמו המעשה ההיא לחכמה הנפלאה התקועה בו הנקראת אצלם טבע והוא כח משתדל (תעני) בשמירת (בחפט̇) המין בעבור שלא היה אפשר להשאר האיש ההוא בעצמו שהוא מורכב מדברים משתנים (מסתחילה̈).

The Arabic תעני here reflects the Greek *προνοητική* used by Galen in his definition of nature as *εὐπαίδευτός τε καὶ δικαία καὶ τεχνικὴ καὶ προνοητικὴ τῶν ζώων* (*De usu partium corporis humani* V, 9, in *Opera*, ed. Kühn, III, 379). Hence משגיח would have been a better translation for תעני than משתדל. Elsewhere in the *Cuzari* ענאיה̈ is translated by השגחה (I, 4 *et passim*). Cf. below n. 64.

[23] Diogenes, *De Vitis* VII, 148 (The Loeb Classical Library).

[24] Shahrastani, 343, ll. 15–19 [II, 206].

how it is impossible for nature itself, without the assumption of a superior cause above it, to produce the phenomenon of life. Things generated by nature, he says, require such accuracy of measurements in the proportions of the elements of which they are composed that they are easily spoiled by a trifle.[25] If it were nature itself which did it, then it should be possible for us to produce, for instance, blood or milk from any kind of liquid, or bread from ingredients which have no nourishing powers; or it should be even possible for us to produce semen from any kind of liquid and thus be able to create living beings out of non-living matter.[26] There are indeed those, he says, who think that nature alone, without any cause above it, produces all these wonderful things in the world and consequently they try to imitate nature by various devices and to accomplish the same things, but they all fail in their efforts. Take, for example, the alchemists. Because they have seen that in living beings natural heat transforms food into blood, flesh, bone and other organs,[27] they think that by imitating nature they can transmute baser metals into gold. But they have so far failed in all their efforts. All they can boast of being able to do is to generate "bees out of the flesh of oxen and gnats out of wine." But this is not something which they themselves have figured out or which they themselves perform by their own skill; it is only an empirical fact of observation which they have happened to stumble upon and which they unduly claim credit for.[28] The conclusion which he stresses, therefore, is that only God can create life and that "the form by which one plant is distinguished from another and

[25] *Cuzari* III, 53: כאשר תראה ההויות הטבעיות משתערות ומתאזנות ונערכות בהמזגם מן הטבעים הארבעה . . . ובמעט דבר יפסד.

[26] *Ibid.* III, 23: ואלו היינו יכולים לשער אותם היינו יכולים לעשות דם וחלב דרך משל ושכבת זרע מלחיות שנשער מזגיהם עד שנוכל לברוא חיים שיחול הרוח בהם, או שנוכל לעשות מה שיעמוד במקום הלחם מדברים שאינם מן המזונות.

[27] *Ibid.* III, 53: הכמיים חשבו שישערו האש הטבעית במשקליהם עד שיהיה להם מה שירצו ותהפך להם העצמים כאשר תעשה אש החום הטבעי בחיים אשר יהפך המזון לדם ובשר ועצם ושאר האיברים וטורחים למצוא כאש הזאת. והתעו אותם נסיונות שמצאו אותם במקרה לא משעורם כאשר נמצא האדם נהיה מהנחת השכבת זרע ברחם.

[28] *Ibid* III, 23: וכבר ראינו חרפת כל מי שהשתדל בדבר מהדרכים האלה מבעלי הכימי"א . . . בעשות הדבורים מבשר הבקר והיתושין מהיין, כי זה איננו משעורם וחכמתם אבל הוא מנסיונות שמצאום (ומעשיהם = ועלמהם; ועמלהם =).

one animal from another is not the work of the four natural elements but the work of God"[29] and that similarly, "the calculation of proportions which give the human form belongs exclusively to the Creator."[30]

Here, again, Halevi's contention that it is not nature itself which produces life but rather a being above nature is a view maintained by Aristotle himself. A clear restatement of this Aristotelian view is found in a long passage in Themistius[31] which contains some of the characteristic terms and expressions used by Halevi. In that passage Themistius sets out to show how in the seed of every plant and animal there is a 'nature' in which is inherent a certain form or proportion which has the power to generate various species of animals, provided only the proper matter presents itself.[32] In the course of his discussion he states that it is 'nature' which explains such facts of our observation as that "a certain kind of wasp is generated from the bodies of horses, that bees are generated from the carcasses of oxen, that the frog is generated from slime and that gnats, which are a species of fly small in body, are generated from wine turned sour."[33] He also shows that it is 'nature' which explains why

[29] *Ibid.*: ואמרתי כי הצורה אשר בה יהיה עצם (=יתנַהֿר=יהיה נראה, יהיה נכר; יתטֿהר=יהיה נראה, יהיה נכר) צמח מבלתי צמח וחי מבלתי חי איננה מן הטבעים אך מעשה אלהי מאת האלהים יתברך. The reading יתנַהֿר is translated here by יהיה עצם, instead of יהיה נראה, probably under the influence of the statement תפריד את בעליה פרידה עצמית (מפארקה֗ גֿוהריה֗) in I, 39. Similarly in I, 41 the Hebrew has נפרדת בעצמה for the printed Arabic מפארקה֗ פי אלטֿאהר. Cf. S. Horovitz, MGWJ, 41 (1897), 267.

[30] *Ibid.*: ושעור הערכים שראויה להם הצורה האנושית איננה כי אם ליוצרה יתברך.

[31] *Themistius in Aristotelis Metaphysicorum Liber Lambda*, ed. S. Landauer, Hebrew: pp. 7, l. 8–8, l. 27; Latin: pp. 9, l. 3–10, l. 4. This passage is quoted with some verbal modifications by Averroes in his Long Commentary on *Metaphysics* XII, comm. 18.

[32] *Ibid.*, Hebrew: p. 8, ll. 5–7; Latin: p. 9, ll. 15–18: שהוא כבר הושם בטבע לפנים יחס מזומן מוכן לחדש איזה מין שיהיה אפשר ממיני החי עם מצאו חומר נאות להתחדש חי ממנו.

יחס, *proportio* = نسب = λόγος (?).

[33] *Ibid.*, Hebrew, pp. 7, l. 28–8, l. 1; Latin: p. 9, ll. 5–7: **כי אנחנו נראה סוג מן הצרעה יתילדו מן גופות הסוסים, ונראה כי הדבורים יתילדו מגופות השוורים המתים, ונראה הצפרדע תתילד מן העפוש, ונראה היתושים, והוא מין אחד מן הזבובים קטן הגוף, יתילדו מן היין כאשר יפסד.**

The general theory of spontaneous generation expressed here by Themistius

from certain plants and animals only certain plants and animals are generated so that "from the seed of man there can be generated no horse, nor from the seed of a horse a man, nor from the seed of any special kind of plant any other kind of plant."[34] He similarly shows how in the case of man, though begotten by man, it is not the father who imparts to his offspring that human form which is peculiar to him and than which no more suitable could be had by him, but rather that 'nature' which is inherent in the father.[35] Now all this emphasis upon nature would seem to be quite the opposite of Halevi's emphasis upon God above nature and one might therefore be

is based on Aristotle (*Historia Animalium* V, 19, 551a, 1 ff.). As for the four examples of spontaneous generation mentioned by him, the following brief observations may be made:

(1) The horse-born wasp is not of Aristotelian origin. For the origin and history of this belief, see C. C. Osten Sacken, *On the Oxen-born Bees of the Ancients* (*Bugonia*), 1894, pp. 15, n. 1, 22, and 53 ff.

(2) Similarly the ox-born bee is not of Aristotelian origin. See *idem*, *op. cit.*, pp. 8 and 26, and *Additional Notes in Explanation of the Bugonia-Lore of the Ancients*, 1895, pp. 6 ff.

(3) The account of the spontaneous generation of the frog (צפרדע, *rana*) is not Aristotelian. It corresponds to the account of the generation of frogs found in Pliny (*Naturalis Historia* IX, 51 (74), §159) and to the account of the generation of certain shell-fish found in both Aristotle (*op. cit.* V, 15, 547b, 13–15) and Pliny (*op. cit.*, §160). The term עפוש, *putredo aquae*, Averroes: *putrefactio aquae*, reflects the term *limus* in *Pliny* (*op. cit.*, §159) and the term *ἰλὺς τῶν φρεάτων* in Aristotle's description of the spontaneous generation of the *ἐμπὶς* (*op. cit.*, V, 19, 551b, 28). Cf. *ὕδατος ἰλύς* (*De Part. Anim.* II, 1, 647b, 2–3).

(4) The account of the spontaneous creation of gnats (יתושים, Averroes: *musciliones*) agrees exactly with Aristotle's description of the generation of the *κώνωψ* (*op. cit.*, V, 19, 552b, 4–5), the expression מן היין כאשר יפסד, *ex vino corrupto*, reflecting the Greek *ἐκ τῆς περὶ τὸ ὄξος ἰλύος*.

Cf. *Moreh Nebukim* I, 72: כמו מיני התולעים המתיילדים מן האשפות ומיני בעלי חיים המתילדים בפירות כשיתעפשו ומה שיתיילד מעיפוש הלחיות ותולעים מתיילדים במעיים וכיוצא בהם.

[34] *Ibid.*, Hebrew: p. 8, ll. 4–5; Latin: p. 9, ll. 11–14: שלא יהיה מזרע האדם סוס, ולא מזרע סוס אדם, ולא מזרע צמח מן הצמחים צמח זולתו.

[35] *Ibid.* Hebrew: p. 8, ll. 12–14; Latin: p. 9, ll. 25–28: כי האדם, ואם היה מתילד מאדם, הנה האב אין לו אומנות בהרכבתו זאת, אשר אי אפשר שתהיה בענין אחר הוא יותר טוב מענינו, ואמנם יהיה בזה הענין, בעבור שכבר הושם בטבע כל אחד מן העצמים מן היחס והצורות.

tempted to conclude that it is such a view as that maintained here by Themistius that must constitute the target of Halevi's attack. But as we read on in Themistius we find that, after he has shown that all this is not done by the external physical agent but rather by 'nature' that is inherent in that agent, he proceeds to state further that nature does not do all this by itself, that is it not conscious of what it is doing and that above it there are higher causes, at the top of which is God. "It is not surprising that nature, though it possesses no discerning intelligence, for nature does not actually perceive and understand that which it does, should lead that which it does to an intended end. This shows that the proportions are inspired by a cause which is more honorable and more noble and of a higher order than they, and that is the soul on earth[36] which according to Plato is generated by the secondary dieties[37] and according to Aristotle is generated by the sun and the oblique circle.[38] It is for this reason that nature does what it does; it is incited, as it were, by a desire for a certain intended end, without, however, understanding what that intended end is. It is analogous to the case of men who are inspired; they utter words, they predict the future, but they do not understand what they say."[39] There is not in this passage,

[36] I. e., the irrational soul, or what Plato in *Timaeus* 69c calls the mortal soul.

[37] *Timaeus* 41c; 69c ff.

[38] *De Gen. et Corr.* II, 10, 336b, 2 ff.

[39] Themistius *op. cit.*

Hebrew: p. 8, ll. 16–23: ואינו נפלא שיהיה הטבע, והוא לא יבין, מוליך מה שיעשהו אל הכונה המכוונת אליו, כי היה בלתי חושב ומשכיל בפועל מה שיעשה. וזה ממה שיורה אותך על שהם כבר התפעמו התפעמות אותם היחסים מסבת מי שהוא יותר נדיב מהם. ויותר נכבד, ומדרגתו יותר עליונה, והיא הנפש אשר

Latin: p. 9, ll. 31–40: neque mirandum naturam nescientem ea, quae *facit, ad fīnem, qui intenditur, adducere*; etenim ipsa nec quid agat intellegit, nec *actu* percipit. et hoc indicat proportiones illas *numine* honorabilioris nobiliorisque causae, quam ipsa sit, atque sublimiore gradu collocatae afflari, nempe anima, quae est in terra, quae secundum

Quotation in Averroes' Long Commentary on *Metaphysics* XII, com. 18: et non est mirum, quamvis natura non intelligat aliquid de huiusmodi, et tamen facit hoc inducendo aliquam intentionem. et hoc demonstrat quod aliquid rememo-tra ipsam de causis

to be sure, a direct statement that God is above nature. But this is the implication of the statement that above nature is the earthly soul which is generated by the 'oblique circle,' for the 'oblique circle,' which is one of the spheres, is moved by God who is the Prime Mover of all the spheres. The implication of this passage is brought out with unmistakable clearness in the paraphrase of it found in Shahrastani: "Themistius reports: Aristotle in Book Lambda [of the *Metaphysics*] says that nature does what it does with wisdom and in the right direction, even though it is not a living being; it is only inspired by a cause which is more noble than it is itself; and he indicates that the cause is God."[40]

And so there is nothing in this argument of Halevi but a restatement of the Aristotelian position as expounded by Themistius. But what is significant about this entire discussion of Halevi is the fact that it is used not as a warning against the possible error of investing nature with the powers of God but an argument against certain people who have actually committed that error. These people are called by him 'alchemists.' But from the nature of Halevi's criticism of these alchemists, it is quite evident that it is not their practice of alchemy that he objected to but rather the theory that lay behind their practice. This theory, as may be gathered from Halevi's criticism, is a sort of philosophy which attributed the origin of life, as well as

בארץ, אשר יראה אפלאטון שהיא נתחדשה מן האלהים השניים, ויראה אריסטוטליס שהיא נתחדשה מהשמש והגלגל הנוטה, ולכן היא עושה מה שעושה, והיא משתוקקת אל הכונה, והיא לא תבין הכונה, כמו שיראו האנשים אשר יתפעמו, שידברו הדבור, ינבאו על מה שיהיה, והם לא יבינו מה שיאמרו.

Platonem a diis secundis manat, secundum Aristotelem a sole provenit et a circulo obliquo. *et ideo facit illud, quod facit, desiderio intentionis, qua agitur, incensa, licet ipsa non intellegat intentionem*; quomodo afflantur homines, ut verba loquantur, cum futura vaticinantur, haud sane percipientes, quid ipsi dicant.

nobilioribus, ut anima, quae est in terra: de quo Plato dicit, quod sit ex Diis secundis, et Aristoteles ex Sole et orbe declivi. et ideo facit illud, quod facit, inducendo se paulatim ad intentionem, qua agitur, et ipsa non intelligit intentionem: sicut videmus homines loquentes futura, et nihil intelligunt de eo, quod dicunt.

[40] Shahrastani, 344, ll. 2–4 [II, 207].

of everything else in the world, to what it called 'nature' and which, furthermore, considered 'nature' as something material, as something inherent in the physical world itself and as something beyond which there was nothing superior and nothing immaterial. Now such a materialistic philosophy, while it may have been the philosophy of those particular alchemists whom Halevi criticizes, cannot be considered as the special kind of philosophy upon which alchemy as a practical science was based, for we know that Alfarabi, who was a good Aristotelian, and a Neoplatized Aristotelian at that, still believed in alchemy. It must have therefore been some kind of materialistic philosophy known to the Arabs at the time of Halevi which happened to have become the philosophy of those alchemists whom Halevi criticizes.

What that philosophy was and by what name it was known may perhaps be gathered from Halevi himself. It happens that in the two places where Halevi criticizes the alchemists, he couples them together with a class of people whom he describes as "Spiritualists."[41] One of the characteristic beliefs of these "Spiritualists," as described by Halevi, is their denial of the revealed nature of Scripture, declaring that "the prophets were only wise men of knowledge."[42] This exactly corresponds to a description we find in Shahrastani of a certain sect of the Sabians, who, on account of their admission of the existence of intelligible beings, are similarly called by him "Spiritualists"[43] and are similarly described by him as denying any divine revelation, at least after Seth and Enoch,[44] maintaining that "the prophets are our equals in species and our likenesses in form,"[45] or, as this idea is expressed by him elsewhere, "the founders of religions are men who possessed wisdom based on knowledge."[46] In con-

[41] *Cuzari* III, 23: בעלי הרוחניים (אהל אלרוחאניאת); III, 53: הרוחניים (אלרוחאניון).
[42] *Ibid.* III, 53: ושהנביאים אמנם היו חכמים מחוכמים (עלמא מתחכמין).
[43] Shahrastani, 203, l. 10 [II, 4]: اصحاب الروحانيات.
[44] *Ibid.*, 202, ll. 9–12 [II, 3].
[45] *Ibid.*, 204, ll. 6–7 [II, 6].
[46] *Ibid.*, 201, l. 13 [II, 2]: حكم علمية.

trast with these 'Spiritualists" Shahrastani mentions, among others, the "Naturalists,"[47] whom he describes as denying the existence of intelligible beings.[48] It is quite clear, then, that the materialistic philosophy of the alchemists, whom Halevi contrasts with "Spiritualists," is that philosophy which Shahrastani ascribes to the "Naturalists" whom he similarly contrasts with Spiritualists. Now, "Naturalists" is one of the terms which is used in Arabic philosophy as a description of the Stoics.[49] It follows therefore that in his criticism of the alchemists for their conception of nature Halevi is really criticizing the Stoics.

Halevi, as we have seen, carries on his discussion of the wisdom of nature in a rather militant fashion, arguing at first against a possible misunderstanding of that wisdom and then against some alchemists who did actually misunderstand it. Nowhere does he say explicitly that Aristotle has misused it. Nor does he ever use any new arguments to prove that Aristotle was wrong in his view that the God who is above nature acts by necessity. All that he does is to utilize Aristotle's own arguments from plant and animal life in proof that nature's wisdom belongs to a God above nature as arguments for his own particular view that the God who is above nature acts not only with wisdom but also by free will.

As distinguished from Halevi's treatment of the subject, Maimonides' treatment of it always seems to have the purpose of showing how Aristotle and all other philosophers have the right conception of the wisdom which they attribute to nature and how they all make nature dependent upon a God above it. Of course, he does express his dissent from the philosophic conception of that God above nature as a being who acts with wisdom but without free will. But he does not utilize the common philosophic arguments from plant and animal life as proof of his own particular conception of God. For this he relies upon his arguments from diversity and irregularity in the motions of the celestial bodies.

[47] *Ibid.*, 201, l. 6 [II, 1): الطبيعيون.

[48] *Ibid.*, 201, ll. 6–7 [II, 1]; 202, ll. 13–14 [II, 3].

[49] S. Horovitz, *Ueber den Einfluss der griechischen Philosophie auf die Entwicklung des Kalam*, p. 6.

We shall consider three passages where Maimonides deals with the wisdom of nature.

In one of these passages he describes in some detail the wonders of the structure of the eye and then raises the question: "Can any intelligent person imagine that all this is due to chance?" and answers this question himself: "Certainly not; but it must of necessity be by a design of nature as has been declared by every physician and every philosopher."[50] In this "every physician and every philosopher" we can readily recognize Galen and Aristotle and the Stoics from whose writing all descriptions of the wisdom of nature in both Halevi and Maimonides are derived. Halevi, it will be recalled, specifically mentions Aristotle and Galen in this connection.[51] But then Maimonides specifically mentions two views in explanation of this evidence of design in nature. One of these views, which he attributes to "the philosophers" in general, declares that "this artistic management emanates . . . from an intellectual principle . . . which causes it to issue forth from itself."[52] The other view, which he describes as "our own view," declares that "this artistic management . . . is the work of an intelligent being who has stamped these faculties upon everything that possesses a natural faculty . . . and brings it into existence."[53] In the contrast between these two views we can readily recognize the distinction which Maimonides always makes between the view held by Aristotle and his own view. Both of them agree that the order and the purposive action in the universe are due to some immaterial being beyond and above the universe. But to Aristotle that immaterial being is only an "intellectual principle" which acts indeed with consciousness and wisdom but still by necessity and without design and which only "causes it (*i. e.*, the artistic management in the world) to issue forth from itself;" to Maimonides that immaterial being is an "intelligent being" who acts by will and design and who

[50] *Moreh Nebukim* III, 19: האם יצייר משכיל שזה נפל במקרה. לא כן, אבל הוא בכונה מן הטבע בהכרח כמו שבאר כל רופא וכל פילוסוף.

[51] Cf. *Cuzari* V, 8.

[52] *Moreh Nebukim* III, 19: אבל זאת ההנהגה הדומה למלאכת מחשבת תבוא לפי דעת הפילוסופים מהתחלה שכלית (מבדא עקלי) . . . הגיע מאתו (חצלת ענה).

[53] *Ibid.*: והיא מפעולת בעל שכל (ד̇י עקל) לפי דעתנו, והוא אשר הטביע אלו הכחות בכל מה שימצא לו כח טבעי . . . המציא (אוג̇ד).

"brings it (*i. e.*, the artistic management in the world) into existence." But more than that: in the course of his discussion he states as a fact "upon which all the philosophers are in agreement" that by itself "nature has no intelligence and no power of management."[54] This statement reflects the indirect implications of certain statements of Aristotle to the effect that nature acts without inquiry (*ζήτησις*) and without deliberation (*βούλησις*) and that it is not the same as intelligence (*νοῦς*)[55] and it also reflects the more direct statement of Themistius, quoted above, that "nature does not actually perceive and understand what it does."[56] Elsewhere Maimonides similarly says that "nature has no thought and no reflection."[57] His sweeping statement that "all the philosophers are in agreement" upon this conception of nature may perhaps be somewhat exaggerated from the historical point of view. But to Maimonides, as to all his contemporaries in Arabic philosophy, the only true philosophers were the Peripatetics.

A similar clear statement of Aristotle's view as to the dependence of nature upon a God above it as well as a clear statement as to difference between his own conception of God and that of Aristotle occurs in another passage. In that passage he restates Aristotle's view to the effect that "every act of nature is necessarily for the sake of some end" and in support of this view he refers to Aristotle's own arguments from his observation that "plants are created for the sake of animals," that among other things also "some of them exist for the sake of others" and that such evidence of purpose is especially to be found "in the case of the organs of animals."[58] This, however, he says, does not lead Aristotle to attribute intelligence to nature itself. On the contrary, says Maimonides, "the existence of purpose of this kind in natural things has necessarily led philosophers to admit the existence of another principle apart from nature, which is called

[54] *Ibid.*: ואין הטבע בעל שכל והנהגה וזה מוסכם מן הפלוסופים כלם.

[55] *Phys.* II, 8, 199a, 20–30; cf. 199b, 27–28.

[56] Cf. above nn. 39, 40.

[57] *Moreh Nebukim* III, 43: כי הטבע אינו בעל מחשבה והשתכלות (דֹאת פכרהֹ ורויהֹ).

[58] *Ibid.* III, 13: וכבר באר ארסטו שהצמחים נבראו בעבור ב"ח וכן באר במקצת הנמצאות שזה מפני זה וכל שכן באברי בעלי חיים.

by Aristotle an intellectual or divine principle and it is this principle which makes one thing for the sake of another."[59] As elsewhere he makes sure to point out the difference between Aristotle and himself as to their conception of the relation of that intellectual or divine principle to nature above which it exists. According to Aristotle, the order of nature of which God is the cause is an order of "eternal and immutable necessity."[60] According to his own view, the order is a created order, and the proof that it is created, is the belief that God acts by free will, and the belief that God acts by free will is to be demonstrated by the fact "that every natural object serves a certain purpose and that one thing exists for the benefit of another."[61] This last statement does not mean, as would seem, that Maimonides utilizes Aristotle's own arguments from plants and animals as a proof against Aristotle's own theory of necessity and eternity, for, as we have already seen, Maimonides admits that sublunar phenomena can be explained satisfactorily even on the basis of Aristotle's theory of necessity. What this statement really means is this: Inasmuch as Aristotle himself admits that everything in nature serves some useful purpose, it must follow that, if something in nature is found to have no possible useful purpose and its existence cannot be adequately accounted for, the existence of that thing must inevitably be explained on the assumption of free will in God. Now it has already been shown by Maimonides elsewhere that certain phenomena in the motions of the spheres serve no useful purpose and that no adequate explanation for them can be discovered. Therefore, the inevitable conclusion is that God acts by the freedom of his will.[62]

[59] *Ibid.*: ודע שמציאות זאת התכלית בעניינים הטבעיים הביא הפילוסופים בהכרח להאמין התחלה אחרת זולת הטבע הוא אשר יקראה אריסטו התחלה שכלית (מבדאא עקלי״א) או אלהית (אלאה״יא) ואשר יעשה זה מפני זה.

[60] *Ibid.*: כי הכל אצלו על צד החיוב הנצחי אשר לא סר ולא יסור.

[61] *Ibid.*: ודע כי מן הגדולה שבראיות על חדוש העולם למי שמודה על האמת הוא מה שעמד עליו המופת בנמצאות הטבעיות כי לכל דבר מהם תכלית אחד ושזה מפני זה והיא ראיה על כוונת מכוין ולא יצויר כונה רק עם התחדשות מחדש.

[62] This would seem to be also the interpretation of this passage in Shem Tob *ad loc.*: ולמה שהאריך הרב בזה בחלק השני כי תנועות השמים והיותם שהם לתכלית הם וכל צבאם ואין בהם דבר לבטלה יורה על שהם נעשו בכוונה.

Cf. above §3, n. 17.

But in a third passage, reflecting the use of the term nature in the Stoic sense of the vegetative soul, to which Maimonides makes several references elsewhere in his works,[63] he applies it more specifically to the reproductive and nutritive faculties of the vegetative soul. The actions of the forces derived from the spheres, he says, are twofold, namely, "the preservation of the species perpetually and the preservation of the individual for a particular time, and this is the meaning of the term 'nature' of which it is said that it is wise, that it governs, that it takes care of the production of that which has life by workmanship like that of art and that it takes care of its preservation and perpetuation, producing formative powers which are the cause of its existence and nutritive powers which are the cause by which it endures and preserves itself for as long as it is possible."[64] But

[63] *Moreh Nebukim* II, 38: וזה הכח בכחות הנפשיות אצלי כדמות הכח הדוחה בכחות הטבעיות. III, 12: אבל הכחות כלם הטבעיות והנפשיות והחיוניות. *Shemonah Peraḳim*, ch. 1: עד ששם ראש הרופאים פתיחת ספרו שהנפשות שלש: טבעית וחיונית ונפשית. Cf. S. B. Scheyer, *Das Psychologische System des Maimonides*, p. 11, n. 3.

[64] *Ibid.* II, 10: שמירת מינו תמיד ושמירת אישיו זמן אחד, וזהו ענין הטבע אשר יאמר שהוא חכם (חכימה) מנהיג (מדבّרה) משגיח (מעתניה) בהמצאת (באיגאד) החי במלאכה כמחשבות (בצנאעה כאלמהניّה) משגיח בשמירתו (בחראסתה) והתמדתו בהמציא כחות נותנות צורה (קוי מצוّרה) הם סבת מציאותו וכחות זנות הם סבת עמידתו ושמירתו הזמן שאפשר. See Munk *ad loc.* (II, p. 89, n. 2) for emendation of the Hebrew text.

חכם, חכים. According to the sources quoted before, this term may reflect either (1) *φρόνιμος* (above n. 12), in which case it should be translated by *prudent* or (2) *εὐπαίδευτος* (above n. 22), in which case it should be translated by *skilful*, *clever*, *subtle*. Evidently in connection with 'nature' the latter meaning is more apt. In Themistius' commentary on Metaphysics XII (above n. 31) the term ערמה, *peritia* (Latin translation), *scientia* (quotation in Averroes' Long Commentary on Metaphysics XII, comm. 18), is applied to the artist with which nature is compared: שהוא פלא מן האומן, ערמתו בעשיית מה שיעשהו מן הטיט יותר מערמתו מה שיעשהו מן הזהב והשיש (Hebrew: p. 8, ll. 8–9: Latin: p. 9, ll. 19–21). Maimonides himself says that among the four meanings which the Hebrew term חכמה has one is that of ערמה, תלטّף, Ḥarizi: עצה *Moreh Nebukim* III, 54). Elsewhere he speaks of ערמת (תלטّף) השם וחכמתו בבריאת בעלי חיים (וחכמתה). Ḥarizi: חמלת האל (*ibid.* III, 32).

מנהיג, מדבّרה. This reflects the Greek *διανέμειν* in the passage quoted above (n. 13). It is this Greek term (*νόμος*, *νέμειν*) which underlies the term הנהגה, تدبير, in its combination with various other words.

משגיח, מעתניה. This reflects the Greek *προνοητική* which is applied to nature

in conformity with his expressed view elsewhere that according to both Aristotle and himself nature, which is here identified with the faculties of generation and nutrition, is itself dependent upon God above it, who is described by Aristotle as an "intellectual" or "divine principle" and by himself as an "intelligent being," Maimonides adds here in conclusion that "what is to be understood by the foregoing statement is that it (i. e., the object of the sphere's conception and desire) is that *al-amr al-ilhāhiyy* from which come the two aforementioned actions by means of the spheres."[65] One cannot determine from the context whether the

in the passage quoted above (n. 22). Cf. discussion of term משתדל in *Cuzari* above n. 22.

צנאעה̈ כאלמהניה̈, במלאכה כמחשבית, *Moreh ha-Moreh*: במלאכה כמו האומנות. This reflects the Greek τεχνική used as a description of nature in the passage quoted above (n. 22). Cf. Arnim, *Stoicorum Veterum Fragmenta* II, §§1132 ff.

איג̇אד, המצאה. This reflects the Greek ἀποτελεῖν in the passage quoted above (n. 23).

חראסה̈ (חפט̇ in *Cuzari* V, 10, above n. 22), שמירה. This reflects the Greek συνέχειν in the passage quoted above (n. 23). Cf. my paper "The Internal senses in Latin, Arabic, and Hebrew Philosophic Texts," *Harvard Theological Review*, 28 (1935), p. 102, n. 49, for other Greek terms underlying the Arabic حفظ when used in other connections. In *Studies*, I, 283.

קוה̈ מצורה̈: כח נותנת צורה (Ibn Tibbon); כח מצייר (Ḥarizi; *Moreh ha-Moreh*). This is the Greek δύναμις διαπλαστική. Cf. above, n. 20.

[65] *Ibid.* הכוונה הוא זה הענין האלהי המגיע ממנו (אלקצד הו ד̇לך אלאמר אלאלאהי אלואצל ענה) שתי הפעולות האלו.

This passage is rather difficult. From Maimonides' own statements here and elsewhere we know that שתי הפעולות האלו=הטבע but that God, called התחלה שכלית או אלהית by Aristotle (cf. above nn. 52, 59) and בעל שכל by Maimonides (cf. above n. 53), is above הטבע and hence above שתי הפעולות האלו. Accordingly, הוא: הו (which might be a corruption of היא: הי, the latter reading being given in *Moreh ha-Moreh*) cannot refer to הטבע: אלטביעה̈ mentioned previously, for that would make הענין האלהי=הטבע from which the שתי הפעולות האלו came. But this would be contrary to what we know to be the view of Aristotle as well as of Maimonides. I therefore take הוא: הו here to refer to the statement: ואי אפשר מבלתי נמצא אחד (מוג̇ד מא) והוא אשר צויר (תצור) והיה הכוסף (אלשיק) אליו כמו שבארנו which occurs earlier in the same chapter (II, 10). That statement refers to God, as may be seen from a parallel statement in an earlier chapter (II, 4): יתחייב גם כן מזה שיהיה לגלגל תשוקה (אשתיאק) למה שציירהו (למה תצורה) והוא הדבר האהוב (אלמעשוק) והוא האל יתעלה שמו.

The old Latin translation from Ḥarizi's Hebrew version (Paris, 1520) translates it (Lib. II, Cap. XI, fo. XLV, r. ll. 1–2): "Convenit autem quod

Arabic term is to be read *al-amr al-ilhāhiyy* and should be taken in the sense of "the divine thing," in which case it may be the equivalent of Aristotle's "intellectual" or "divine principle," or whether it is to be read *al-āmir al-ilhāhiyy* and should be taken in the sense of "the divine commander,"[66] in which case it would

sit mens spiritualis ex qua proveniunt illae duae res mediante caelo" and Buxtorf translates it from Ibn Tibbon's Hebrew version (Basel, 1629, p. 208): "Nihil enim aliud sibi vult, quam Divinum quid esse illud, a quo duae istae operationes ad nos mediantibus sphaeris coelestibus perveniunt." In both these translations it is not quite clear whether the "mens spiritualis" or the "Divinum quid" is meant to refer to the "natura" mentioned before or not. It is quite possible that Ḥarizi's statement was taken by the Latin translator to mean that in addition to "nature" mentioned previously there is also a "mens spiritualis" and similarly Ibn Tibbon's statement was taken by Buxtorf to mean that it is not "nature" previously mentioned but rather the "Divinum quid" from which the two actions proceed. In other words, these Latin translators may have taken the statement הכוונה הוא זה הענין האלהי המגיע ממנו to mean as if it read הכוונה זה הענין האלהי הוא המגיע ממנו. But it is quite evident that הוא in this passage refers to something previously mentioned. Munk, always exact in his translations, gives a rather evasive translation of this passage without any comment (Paris, 1861, II, p. 89): "en un mot, c'est là cette chose divine de laquelle viennent les deux actions en question, par l'intermédiare de la sphère céleste." Stern, in his German translation (Wien, 1864, p. 20a), follows Munk. Friedländer (London, 1885, II, p. 51) translates it: "It may be that by Nature the Divine Will is meant, which is the origin of these two kinds of faculties through the medium of the spheres" and adds the following explanation: "I. e., those who ascribe these results to Nature mean perhaps by this term the Divine Will." This would be a good translation as well as a good explanation; but Maimonides elsewhere, as we have seen, adopts the use of the term 'nature' in its original philosophic sense and merely changes the philosophic concept of God above nature by attributing to it free will. Weiss translates it (Leipzig 1924, II, p. 74): "und es ist möglich, dass das göttliche Ding, welches von Gott durch die Vermittelung der Sphäre zu uns gelangt, diese beiden Wirkungen bedeutet" and adds the following explanation: "Der Verf. will sagen, dass die Emanation in nichts anderem als in der Verleihung der zeugenden und erhaltenden Kräfte bestehe." The translation and the explanation are both wrong.

[66] In *Moreh Nebukim* II, 29, Maimonides definitely uses the expression אלאמר אלאלהאהי in the sense of divine decree or command. אלא כאשר חייב העניין האלהי (אלאמר אלאלאהי) בהכרח לכל מי שישיג שלמות שישפיעהו ועל זולתו כמו שנבאר בפרקים הבאים.

The term מגיע :ואצל used by Maimonides in this passage (see quotation above in n. 52) is not decisive, as it may refer to either emanation or creation or both (cf. above nn. 52, 53).

represent Maimonides' own view of God and would thus be the squivalent of Maimonides' "intelligent being." It is quite possible that Maimonides has purposely used here that ambiguous term in order to include both these views. In any case we have here again an assertion of the view stated by him elsewhere that above nature, it is generally admitted by all philosophers, there is God.

The fact that Maimonides constantly emphasizes that, according to Aristotle, the wisdom and purposiveness which are evidenced in the universe and which are attributed to nature is not the work of nature itself but of God who is above nature enables him to deduce from Aristotle's oft-repeated statement that nature does nothing in vain the conclusion that even according to Aristotle the actions of God contain nothing that is in vain.[67] This indirect method of proving that according to Aristotle God does nothing in vain occurs several times in Maimonides.[68] Nowhere does he ever attribute to Aristotle a direct statement that God does nothing in vain. Now in Aristotle, besides the many passages in which he speaks only of nature as doing nothing in vain,[69] there is one passage in which he says explicitly that both "God and nature do nothing in vain."[70] One should naturally like to know why that direct statement of Aristotle is not quoted by Maimonides. Perhaps the explanation for this is to be found in the possibility that in the Arabic translation of *De Caelo*, where alone the expression "God and nature" is used by Aristotle, the term God was omitted. As the original Arabic translation of *De Caelo* is not extant, one can prove this suggestion only indirectly through the Latin translation of that Arabic translation which is incorporated in Averroes' Long Commentary on *De Caelo*, where the term

[67] *Moreh Nebukim* II, 14 (7): ודרך אחר יאמרו פעולותיו יתעלה שלמות מאד אין בהם דבר מן החסרון ואין בהם דבר לבטלה ולא מוסיף וזהו העניין אשר ישבחו אריסטו תמיד ויאמר הטבע חכם ולא יעשה דבר לבטלה (עבת̇א).

[68] *Ibid.* III, 13: וארסטו אומר תמיד בפירוש שהטבע לא יעשה דבר לבטלה (עבת̇א) III, 25: וכן הוא גם כן דעת הפילוסופים שאין בעניינים הטבעיים כלם דבר על צד ההבל (אלעבת̇).

[69] See Bonitz, *Index Aristotelicus*, sub μάτην.

[70] *De Caelo* I, 4, 271a, 33.

"God" is omitted.[71] As far as I know, no passage has been quoted by scholars from Arabic literature, either Moslem or Jewish, in which Aristotle is quoted as having made the direct statement that God does nothing in vain.[72]

6. Argument from Miracles

We have seen, then, that throughout their discussion of sublunar phenomena neither Halevi nor Maimonides goes beyond the Aristotelian evidence of design in nature. And yet while Maimonides explicitly admits that this order in the sublunar world can be explained on the basis of eternity and necessity and always advances both the Aristotelian view and his own view as two alternative explanations of that order, Halevi, without arguing against the Aristotelian explanation and perhaps tacitly admitting its logical tenability, always presents his own particular view as the only explanation of that order in the sublunar world. There must have undoubtedly been something in his mind which he considered sufficiently valid to fill that logical gap between his arguments and the conclusion which he

[71] Averroes' Long Commentary on *De Caelo*, Liber II, text. 32: *Natura autem nihil facit ociosum.*

[72] Such a statement as that of Joseph Ibn Ẓaddiḳ in *'Olam Ḳaṭan* (ed. Horovitz, p. 38, l. 1a) שהבורא לא ברא שום דבר חסר (quoted by Kaufmann, *Attributenlehre*, p. 322, n. 138, and Diesendruck, "Die Teleologie bei Maimonides," *Hebrew Union College Annual* V (1928), p. 516, n. 274) does not reflect Aristotle's passage in *De Caelo* I, 4. It is a variation of another passage of Aristotle (cf. Diesendruck, *ibid.*, n. 375). Nor do such statements as החכם לא יפעל להבל וריק (*'Olam Ḳaṭan*, p. 62, l. 15) and והחכמה לא תתן דבר להבל וריק (עבתֿא) (*Cuzari* V, 12), both referred to by Diesendruck (*ibid.*, n. 274), reflect a reading of "God and nature" in *De Caelo* I; 4. The terms חכם and חכמה in both these passages refer not to 'God' but to 'nature' and they are substitutions of the commonly used expression הטבע חכם, the origin of which has been discussed above. Even Maimonides in II, 14 (7), when he was about to quote Aristotle verbally: הטבע לא יעשה דבר לבטלה, as he does in III, 13, could not refrain himself from changing הטבע into the conventional הטבע חכם (cf. above n. 67). Nor is Saadia's statement ושאיננו עושה השוא (אלעבת) (*Emunot we-De'ot* II, 13; cf. II, 5: שעשה אותם . . . לא על דרך השוא) a direct quotation of *De Caelo* I, 4.

seems unjustifiably to draw from those arguments. That missing link in his logical reasoning is to be found in the view expressed by him many a time throughout his work, outside of those passages in which he presents his rational arguments against chance and his inconsequent assertions of free will in God, and that is his view that even among sublunar phenomena there are certain deviations from order which cannot be explained on the assumption of the Aristotelian eternal necessity. These deviations from order are called by him by their traditional name of miracles — those historical miracles recorded in Scripture whereby things were changed into one another, as in Egypt, for instance, water was changed into blood,[1] and whereby also new things came into being, such, for instance, as the manna in the wilderness.[2] These, says Halevi, can be explained only by the assumption of a God who is omnipotent and who acts by wisdom, though a wisdom which we cannot always comprehend.[3] And so once, at least, in the midst of rational arguments from sublunar phenomena, when he happens to introduce the philosophic conception of an Active Intellect, which acts with wisdom but by necessity, as an explanation of the order in the sublunar phenomena, he makes the Cuzari interrupt him to say that this kind of order could be better explained by the assumption of free will in God. The Rabbi agrees with him that free will in God would indeed be a better and truer explanation, and in support of it he advances as proof the historical miracles recorded in Scripture. "This is the religious argument, and the evidence for it is to be found in the children of Israel, for whose sake changes of substances were wrought and new things created."[4] Miracles to Halevi constitute the chief argument for free will in God and if he happens to produce other arguments, such as the argument from order against chance or the arguments from the diversities in the motions of the spheres against necessity, they

[1] *Cuzari* I, 83.

[2] *Ibid.* I, 89; I, 91.

[3] *Ibid.* V, 5.

[4] *Ibid.* V, 6: וזאת היא הטענה התוריה ומופתה בני ישראל אשר הופך להם מן עיני העצמים מה שהופך ומה שנברא להם מן ההויות.

are merely arguments *ad hominem*, which have for their purpose only the confutation of the opponent, in pursuance of the rabbinic injunction "to learn what answer to give to a disbeliever."[5]

Unlike Halevi, however, Maimonides does not argue from the recorded miracles in Scripture for free will in God. Indeed, he believes in the possibility of miracles and certainly in the historicity of the miracles recorded in Scripture, still he does not think that they should be made use of in a rational discussion as evidence for the existence of free will and design in God. Accordingly, while he thought, like Halevi, that evidence for design can be found only in deviation from the ordinary, he sought such deviations, as we have seen, in the motion of the spheres and in the position of the stars and the spheres, but not in recorded miracles. A similar difference between them appears also with regard to the use of the miracles performed by Moses, in the historicity of which both Halevi and Maimonides believed, as evidence for the veracity of the teachings of Moses. Halevi makes use of them as evidence for that purpose;[6] Maimonides is openly against making such use of them.[7] To Maimonides the order of religious thought is to start with whatever rational arguments one can muster in defence of free will in God, by which one is enabled to establish the belief in creation, and once one has established this belief in creation, miracles as well as prophecy become possible. "Know," he says, "that with the acceptance of the creation of the world all the miracles become possible, so does also revelation become possible, and every objection that can be raised against either of these beliefs is removed."[8] To Halevi the starting point in religious thought is the acceptance of the scriptural accounts of the creation of the world, as well as of the miracles performed on various occasions, as historical facts. These establish directly the belief in the free will of God. One should not according to him, make use of

[5] *Ibid.* V, 16; M. Abot II, 14.

[6] *Ibid.* I, 9; I, 11; I, 41.

[7] *Mishneh Torah*: *Yesode ha-Torah*, VIII, 1; *Iggeret Teman*, *Ḳobeẓ*, p. 4vb.

[8] *Moreh Nebukim* II, 25: ודע כי עם האמנת חדוש העולם יהיו האותות כלם אפשריות ותהיה התורה אפשרית ותפול כל שאלה שתשאל בזה הענין.

rational arguments in support of these beliefs unless there is need for them for the purpose of quieting one's own doubts or of refuting heretics.[9]

7. Recapitulation

Let us now sum up the result of our annotations on Halevi's and Maimonides' discussions of design, chance and necessity. Both of them set out to disprove chance and necessity and to establish free will in God. In Maimonides there is a clear definition of the issue under consideration and throughout his discussion he directs his attack primarily against necessity, which in his time, owing to its revival by Alfarabi and Avicenna, was still a vital question. Chance is often mentioned by him, but that only for the purpose of rounding out the discussion; on the whole, it is treated by him as a theory already discredited in philosophy. Halevi, though primarily interested in establishing free will in God as against necessity, makes chance the open object of his attack more often than necessity, as if chance were still the main issue in the philosophic discussion of his time. In their arguments for the establishment of free will in God they make use, quite correctly, of arguments which logically disprove necessity. But whereas Maimonides makes it clear that these arguments are directed against necessity and he phrases them with unmistaken clearness as arguments directed primarily against necessity, Halevi introduces them as if they were arguments against chance and phrases them also if they were arguments against chance. The arguments which they both use for the establishment of free will in God are three: (1) from emanation, (2) from the diversities in the motions of the spheres, and (3) from certain non-essential accidents in the structure of the universe, the latter two types of argument being varieties of what is known as the argument of determination. None of these arguments is new; their immediate source in both Halevi and Maimonides is undoubtedly Algazali. But whereas Maimonides' restatement of these arguments is much clearer and fuller than

[9] *Cuzari* V, 1; V, 16.

in Algazali and are self-explanatory, Halevi's restatement of them is less clear and less full than in Algazali and are ambiguous to the point of being easily misunderstood. Both of them, in the course of their discussion, deal with the problem of the rise of elements and minerals in the sublunar world. But whereas Maimonides, whose expressed object of attack is necessity, uses it merely to point out the contrast between Aristotle's successful attempt to explain this phenomenon in the sublunar world on the assumption of necessity with his failure to explain certain phenomena in the translunar world on the basis of such an assumption, Halevi, who somehow treated chance as still a vital issue, uses it as a means of wresting from the philosophers the admission that chance is to be rejected. Both of them deal also with the conception of the wisdom of nature as evidenced in plant and animal life. But here, again, whereas Maimonides uses it only to show the reasonableness of philosophers of the Aristotelian school in their cautious use of this conception and in their scrupulous attempt to avoid any implication that nature is independent of God, Halevi argues, with argument borrowed from the philosophers themselves, against the possibility of a misunderstanding of this conception of nature and against those "alchemists" who did actually misunderstand it. Finally, while both Halevi and Maimonides believe in the historicity of the miracles recorded in Scripture, Maimonides does not use them as arguments for free will in God, confining himself only to arguments of reason, whereas Halevi does make use of these historical arguments.

Note. My conjecture above (pages 54–55) that the Arabic translation of *De Caelo* I, 4, 271a, 33, did not contain the word "God" has been corroborated with the publication of that translation in 1961, ed. A. Badawi.

2

HALLEVI AND MAIMONIDES ON PROPHECY

§1. Hallevi's and Maimonides' Approach to the Philosophic Conception of Prophecy

Hallevi and Maimonides approach the problem of prophecy with four presuppositions, on one of which they agree and on three of which they disagree. They both agree that God acts with free will and that in His action there is therefore an element of grace and election, opposing thereby the view which they both attributed to Aristotle and to the philosophers in general that God acts by the necessity of His nature.[1] They differ, however, as to the question whether that free will of God is exercised in the world directly or not.

Maimonides, who accepts the Neoplatonized Aristotelian conception of the physical universe that prevailed in his time, accepts the common view that the motions of the spheres, at least their regular motions, are produced by God by means of Intelligences and that also the souls of plants and animals as well as the intellect of man come from God by means of the last or tenth of the Intelligences known as the Active Intellect.[2] Hallevi, on the other hand, rejects the entire theory of Intelligences, including that of the Active Intellect.[3] Accordingly he attributes the

[1] *Cuzari*, II, 5; *Moreh Nebukim*, II, 19.

[2] *Moreh Nebukim*, II, 3; I, 72.

[3] *Cuzari*, V, 14: ולהם בתחלה דעות מפסידות השכל יבוז השכל, כהעללתם בסבוב הגלגל וכו'; IV, 26: מה הצורך אל אותיות הו"י או אל מלאך וגלגל וזולת זה עם ההודאה בחפץ הבורא; V, 21: וקראו השכלים ההם אלהים ומלאכים ועלות שניות וזולת זה מהשמות . . . וזה כלו דקדוק יקנה חדוד.

motion of the spheres as well as the forms and souls of plants and animals, including also the rational soul of man, to the direct action of God's will. The contrast between Hallevi and Maimonides on this point is brought out in two parallel passages in which they state their respective views as to the classification of intermediary causes. According to Hallevi, "the order and composition which are observed in animal and in plant and in the spheres" are caused by God directly,[4] and not through intermediary causes, and it is directly by the will of God, and not through intermediaries such as Intelligences, that the "heaven" is set in motion,[5] and consequently he finds that the causes of all the events that take place in the world are four: (1) divine, i. e., directly by God, (2) natural, (3) accidental and (4) volitional.[6] To Maimonides, however, all the events in the world are brought about by God through intermediary causes and consequently in his enumeration of causes he mentions only intermediate causes, namely: (1) essential or natural, (2) volitional and (3) accidental, leaving out that direct cause which Hallevi calls "divine."[7] In one place Maimonides definitely ex-

[4] Ibid., V, 20: ואומר כי כל הידיעות מיוחסות אל העלה הראשונה על שני דרכים, אם על הכונה הראשונה אם על דרך ההשתלשלות, ודמיון הדרך הראשון הסדור וההרכבה הנראים בחי ובצמח ובגלגלים.

[5] Ibid., I, 97: וכאשר אנחנו עושים בשמים ובכל דבר שאנו יודעים שתנועתו אמנם הוא בחפץ אלהים מבלי מקרה ולא רצון אדם ולא טבע. IV, 3: כן רומזים אל השמים, מפני שהוא כלי משמש בחפצו גרידא מבלי סבות אחרות אמצעיות ביניהם.

[6] Ibid., V, 20: המעשים יהיו אלהיים או טבעיים או מקריים או מבחריים.

[7] *Moreh Nebukim*, II, 48: דע כי הסבות הקרובות כלם אשר מהם יתחדש מה שיתחדש אין הפרש בין היות הסבות ההם עצמיות טבעיות או בבחירה או במקרה.
The omission of אלהיות here seems to have been taken by *Ḳol Yehudah* on *Cuzari*, V, 20, as being unintentional: היו הדברים האלה קרובים למה שכתב במורה בשני פרק מ"ח, אלא שלא הזכיר שם המעשים האלהיים בלא אמצעי. The omission of this term, however, is quite evidently intentional. Maimonides does not mention "divine" causes, because in the three examples of things mentioned by Hallevi as being directly caused by God (cf. above nn. 4 and 5) he believes there is the intermediary cause of Intelligences or of the Active Intellect.

plains the term "divine actions" as meaning "natural actions."[8] To him the order of nature is directed by God's will, to be sure, but by means of intermediary causes.

They differ also as to the relation of the observance of the Law to right belief and as to the relation of right belief to reason and philosophic speculation. To Hallevi, the observance of the Law is an end in itself[9] and right belief consists in the acceptance as a matter of implicit faith of certain well established doctrines; reason and speculation, while they may be necessary for the purpose of answering heretics or of quelling one's own doubts, are not essential to true religion.[10] To Maimonides, the observance of the Law has for its purpose the inculcation of right belief[11] and right belief, in its highest form, must be based on reason and philosophic speculation.[12]

With these their conceptions of the causality of God and of the position of the observance of the Law and of the meaning of right belief in religion, they begin their examination of what in their time was considered the philosophic conception of prophecy.

What the philosophers mean by prophecy is delineated by Hallevi and Maimonides themselves.[13] Above us is the astronomical heaven with its nine spheres. Corresponding to each sphere there is an immaterial being, called in philosophic language an Intelligence and in theological language an angel, which acts upon each sphere as a cause, or, to be more exact, a final cause, of its rotation. But below the lowest sphere, which is the sphere of the moon, there is a tenth Intelligence which has no corre-

[8] Ibid., III, 32: כשתתבונן בפעולות האלהיות רוצה לומר הפעולות הטבעיות.

[9] *Cuzari*, I, 79; I, 98; II, 49; III, 23.

[10] Ibid., V, 1; V, 16.

[11] *Moreh Nebukim*, III, 27 ff.

[12] Ibid., I, 50; III, 51; III, 54.

[13] *Cuzari*, I, 1; V, 12; *Moreh Nebukim*, II, 32 (2).

sponding sphere upon which it is to exercise its power as a cause of motion. This is called the Active Intellect[14] or the Universal Intellect[15] or the Divine Intellect[16] and metaphorically also a "light" of the "divine nature."[17] The sphere of operation of the Active Intellect is the sublunar world, the world of matter and of the four elements and of minerals, plants and animals. Though it is a subject of controversy whether the Active Intellect is responsible for the specific forms of the elements and minerals, it is generally admitted that it is responsible for the specific forms in plants, animals and men, which forms bear the special name of souls.[18] Then these souls, including the soul of man, like all the other forms, start on their career as something inseparable from the bodies to which they are attached. But in the case of man this soul is capable of growth and development and as it grows and develops it becomes gradually independent of the body. In the course of its development and its growing independence of the body, it may reach a stage wherein it becomes separated from the body, and reunites itself with the Active Intellect

[14] השכל הפועל: אלעקל אלפעאל, *Cuzari*, I, 1 et passim; *Moreh Nebukim*, I, 68 et passim.

[15] *Cuzari*, V, 12: ותוליד מהם תועלת התולדות בעזר השכל הכללי (אלעקל אלכלי) הסומך אותם . . . וכבר יצליח הכח הדברי בקצת האנשים מהתדבקו בשכל הכללי (אלעקלי אלכלי).

[16] *Moreh Nebukim*, I, 1: ונאמר באדם מפני זה הענין ר"ל מפני השכל האלהי (אלעקל אלאלאהי) המדובק בו שהוא בצלם האלהים ובדמותו. Cf. Munk, ad loc. *Cuzari*, V, 21: וקראו השכלים ההם אלהים (אללה). The designation of the intellect which is above the individual human intellect by the term "divine" or the application to it of the term "God" reflects such expressions as *νοῦς θεῖος* in Plato (*Philebus*, 22c), *νοῦς θειότερόν τι* in Aristotle (*De Anima*, I, 4, 408b, 29) and the use of the term *θεός* or *θεὸς δεύτερος* with reference to *νοῦς* by Plotinus (*Eunedas*, V, 5, 3). This term "divine" occurs throughout the history of philosophy as a designation of any intellect above the individual intellect whether called universal intellect or Active Intellect.

[17] *Cuzari*, I, 1: ידבק בו מן המין (נמט) האלהי אור שהוא נקרא השכל הפועל. Cf. below §3.

[18] *Cuzari*, V, 2, 4, 10; *Moreh Nebukim*, I, 72.

whence it had its origin. When that union occurs, man is said by the philosophers to reach the state of prophecy. Making use of religious terminology, the philosophers, and by these are meant especially the Moslem philosophers, call the Active Intellect by such names as the "Holy Spirit" and "Gabriel";[19] they say that, when that union with the Active Intellect occurs, man receives knowledge by means of "inspiration and revelation" and attains the distinction called "Holiness" and "Holy Spirit,"[20] and they apply to

[19] *Cuzari*, I, 87: שלא תהיה הנבואה כאשר חשבו הפילוסופים מנפש יזדככו מחשבותיה ותדבק בשכל הפועל (אלעקל אלפעאל) הנקרא רוח הקודש (רוח אלקדס) או בגבריאל. Cf. Alfarabi, *Kitāb fī Mabādi al-Maujūdāt*, Hyderabad, 1346 A. H., p. 3, 11. 18–19; Hebrew: *Sefer Hatḥalot ha-Nimza'ot* (Filipowsky's *Sefer he-Asif*, p. 2): והשכל הפועל הוא אשר ראוי שיאמן בו שהוא הרוח הנאמן ורוח הקודש. The terms "Faithful Spirit" and "Holy Spirit" both occur in the Koran (الروح الامين, Surah 26, 193; روح القدس, Surah 16, 104 et passim). Both these terms, according to Moslem authorities, refer to Gabriel. Corresponding to this Moslem identification of the Active Intellect with Gabriel is Maimonides' identification of it with מלאך or שרו של עולם (*Moreh Nebukim*, II, 6). So also ibid., II, 34, is the Active Intellect referred to by Maimonides simply as מלאך. Cf. D. Kaufmann, *Geschichte der Attributenlehre*, pp. 204–5, n. 181; S. Horovitz, *Die Psychologie bei den jüdischen Religionsphilosophen*, p. 265, n. 126.

[20] Ibid., V, 12: בלמוד (באלאלהאם) ונבואה (ואלוחי) ותקרא סגולתו זאת קדושה (קדיסא) ותקרא רוח הקדש (רוחא מקדסא). This statement, as well as the statement immediately preceding, is an exact quotation from Avicenna's treatise on psychology, ch. 8 end, ed. S. Landauer, *ZDMG*, XXIX (1876), 365.

The term الهام, literally *to cause to swallow* or *to gulp down*, means individual revelation as distinguished from وحى, נבואה, which means general revelation, the former referring to the revelation of a message for the instruction of the individual, while the latter to the revelation of a message to be communicated to mankind (cf. D. B. Macdonald, *Encyclopaedia of Islam*, sub *ilhām*). This distinction corresponds to the distinction made by Maimonides between the two kinds of prophets, one who feels himself compelled to communicate his prophecy to others and the other who receives a prophetic revelation only for the sake of self-instruction (*Moreh Nebukim*, II, 37, and cf. below §5). The Hebrew למוד in the *Cuzari*, or rather more fully למוד אלהי (ed. Hirschfeld, p. 315, 1. 23) is a translation not of the term *ilhām* itself but rather of its definition. The use of the term

that state of union the religious expression "pleasure of God."[21]

Now the characteristic features of this philosophic conception of prophecy are *five*. In the *first* place, it is a natural process, that is to say, the stage of prophecy follows by natural necessity from certain conditions, without any direct intervention of divine grace. In the *second* place, prophecy is effected by God not directly, but rather indirectly by means of an intermediary, the Active Intellect, which is conceived to be a real being, one of the many incorporeal beings known as Intelligences or angels. In the *third* place, the qualification of man for the attainment of prophecy is assumed by philosophers to be threefold: (1) the possession from birth of certain natural perfections with which the human race as a whole is endowed,[22] (2) the attainment by means of "training" of perfection in the "moral and practical virtues," and (3) the attainment by means of "instruction" of perfection in "the intellectual virtues,"[23] which intellectual virtues consist

instruction in connection with prophecy is found in the Christian Church Fathers in such expressions as "the mind of the prophetic and instructive (*διδασκαλικόν*) spirit" (Clement of Alexandria, *Stromata*, I, 9, PG, 8, 741B; ed. Otto Stählin, II, p. 30, ll. 3–4).

[21] Ibid., I, 1: וזה אשר יכונה ברצון אלהים (ברצֹא אללה) על דרך ההעברה או על דרך הקרוב. The reference here is to the Koranic expression رضى الله عنهم in Surah 5, 119 et passim. All these expressions are, of course, ultimately of Jewish origin. But in restating the philosophers' views Hallevi uses them as Moslem terms.

[22] Ibid., I, 1: ולכל איש מאישי העולם סבות שבהם יגמר ויש איש שנשלמו סבותיו ובא שלם. *Moreh Nebukim*, II, 32 (2): והוא שהנבואה שלמות אחד בטבע האדם.

[23] *Cuzari*, I, 1: והפילוסוף אשר לו נתכנו תכונות יקבל בהם המעלות (אלפצֹאיל) המדותיות (אלכֹלקיהֿ) והמדעיות (ואלעלמיהֿ) והמעשיות ולא חסר מאומה מן השלמות אבל השלמות הזה בכח צריך בהוצאתו לידי מעשה (אלפעל) אל למוד (אלתעלים) ומוסר (ואלתאדיב).

Moreh Nebukim, II, 32 (2): והשלמות ההוא לא יגיע לאיש מבני אדם אלא אחר למוד (ארתיאץֿ) יוציא מה שבכח המין לפעל (ללפעל) . . . והוא שהאיש המעולה השלם בשכליותיו (נטקיאתה) ובמדותיו (וכֹלקיאתה), כשיהיה כחו המדמה על מה שאפשר מן השלמות ויזמין עצמו ההזמנה ההיא אשר תשמענה, הוא יתנבא בהכרח, שזה

in the possession of a perfect knowledge of the arts and sciences whereby one may "become like the Active Intellect in distinguishing the truth, in describing everything by that which necessarily belongs to it and in believing it to

שהענין הטבעי שכל מי שראוי לפי בריאותו השלמות לנו בטבע. Ibid., II, 32 (3): (בחסב גֿבלתה) ויתלמד (וארתאץֿ) לפי גדולו (תרביתה) ולמודו (ותעלימה) שיתנבא.

On the basis of the corresponding passages in the *Nicomachean Ethics*, which are reflected in these quotations from the *Cuzari* and the *Moreh Nebukim*, the Greek equivalents of the Arabic and Hebrew terms contained in them can be definitely established as follows:

بحسب جبلته, IT: לפי בריאותו, Ḥ: לפי בריאותו ותולדתו, πεφυκώς (*Nic. Eth.*, II, 1, 1103a, 25).

فضيلة خلقية, מעלה מדותית, ἀρετὴ ἠθική (ibid., 1103a, 14–15).

فضيلة علمية, מעלה מדעית, ἀρετὴ ἐπιστημονική, *scientific virtue*, which is a subdivision of ἀρετὴ διανοητκή, *intellectual virtue* (ibid., VI, 1, 1139a, 12 and 15–17). The term فضيلة نطقية, IT: מעלה שכלית, Ḥ: מדה נפשית and מדה שכלית, in *Moreh Nebukim*, III, 54, is ἀρετὴ λογιστκή, *calculative virtue*, another subdivision of ἀρετὴ διανοητική (ibid., VI, 1, 1139a, 12 and 15–17), of which a literal Hebrew translation is מעלה דברית as in *Moreh Nebukim*, II, 32 (3) and in *Millot ha-Higgayon*, ch. 14, the term שכלית being a translation of διανοητκή, عقلية.

Ḥarizi's translation of פצילה כלקיה and פצילה עלמיה by מדה גופית and כח נפשי or כח שכלי is not literal.

فضيلة عملية, מעלה מעשית, ἀρετὴ πρακτική (ibid., X, 7, 1177b, 6–7).

تعليم, למוד, διδασκαλία (op. cit., II, 1, 1103a, 15), to be distinguished from تعلم, למוד (*Cuzari*, V, 12, Hebrew: p. 321, l. 26; Arabic: p. 322, l. 6), למידה (ibid., I, 1, p. 7, l. 12; p. 6, l. 13), which is μάθησις. Cf. also למוד, الهام, above n. 20.

تاديب, מוסר, ἔθος (op. cit., II, 1, 1103a, 17), ἐθίζεσθαι (1103b, 24).

ارتياض, IT: למוד; Ḥ: הרגיל עצמו; تربية, גדול, παιδεία (op. cit., II, 3, 1104b, 13). Cf. the various Hebrew translations of رياضة, παιδεία, in my paper "The Classification of Sciences in Mediaeval Jewish Philosophy," *Hebrew Union College Jubilee Volume* (1925), p. 268, and *Hebrew Union College Annual*, III (1926), 372. In *Studies*, I, 498, 547.

These passages quoted from the *Cuzari* and *Moreh Nebukim* reflect Aristotle's general statement in the *Nicomachean Ethics* that intellectual virtue owes its origin and development to teaching (διδασκαλία), whereas moral virtue comes from habit (ἔθος) (II, 1, 1103a, 14–18) and that we acquire habit by acting (ἐνεργήσαντες) (1103a, 31).

Hallevi's and Maimonides' attribution to the philosophers of the

be as it really is."[24] Then, in the *fourth* place, the moral and practical virtues are not considered by philosophers as an end in themselves; they are only important as auxiliary to the attainment of the intellectual virtues, so that in their exhortations to their followers they say: "Follow the most equitable of ways as regards moral virtues and practical virtues, because this will help thee to the conception of truth (i. e., the attainment of intellectual virtues), to the pursuit of learning and to the becoming similar to the Active Intellect."[25] *Fifth* and finally, there

view that prophecy is dependent on intellectual perfection represents Avicenna's view with regard to that type of prophecy which is called *ilhām* as distinguished from the other type which is called *waḥy* (cf. above n. 20). The *waḥy* type of prophecy, according to him, does not require intellectual perfection. On this distinction between these two types of prophecy, see A. M. Goichon, *La Distinction de l'Essence et de l'Existence d'après Ibn Sīnā*, 1937, pp. 327 ff. On Alfarabi's and Avicenna's theory of prophecy, cf. Leo Strauss, "Maimunis Lehre von der Prophetie und ihre Quellen," *Le Monde Oriental*, XXVIII (1934), pp. 114 ff.

[24] *Cuzari*, I, 1: בעבור ההדמות אל השכל הפועל בבחירת האמת וספור כל דבר במה שהוא ראוי לו (ודעתו) והאמנתו כאשר הוא.

[25] Ibid. והדבק בדרכי הצדיקים (אעדל אלטרק) במדות (אלאכלאק) ובמעשים (אלאעמאל) כי הם עזר בציור האמת ודבקות הלמידה (אלתעלם) וההדמות לשכל ההוא הפועל.

The various Arabic adjectives from the root عدل, which mean *just*, *righteous* or *equal*, are translated into Hebrew by צדיק (as in this quotation), ישר or שוה. Cf. *Cuzari*, II, 14 end: למזג השוה (אלמתאעדל); *Shemonah Peraḳim*, ch. 4: וישכון במדינות ביושר (באלעדל); המעשים השוים (אלמתעדלה̈); *Millot ha-Higgayon*, ch. 14, Ibn Tibbon: דרכי יושר; Aḥiṭub: עיקרים של צדק, of which the underlying Arabic must have been טרוק עדל in the case of Ibn Tibbon and ערוק עדל in the case of Aḥiṭub. So also Aristotle uses the term ἴσος, *equal*, in the sense of δίκαιος, *just* (*Nic. Eth.*, V, 1, 1129a, 34).

In Maimonides המעשים השוים: אלאפעאל אלמעתדלה̈ refers to actions which constitute "the mean between two extremes": אלמתוסטה̈ בין טרפין: הממוצעים בין שתי קצוות, (*Shemonah Peraḳim*, ch. 4), reflecting Aristotle's statement that "the equal (ἴσον) is a mean (μέσον τι) between excess and defect" (*Nic. Eth.*, II, 6, 1106a, 28–29). Hallevi, however, does not use the term דרכי הצדיקים: אעדל אלטרק (=הישרה בדרכים), which he attributes here to the philosophers, to imply that the philosophers to whom he refers follow the Aristotelian theory of the mean, for elsewhere he explicitly denies that these philosophers

is no special mode of conduct or of action which is recommended by philosophers as a means of attaining what they call prophecy. To them any of the existent revealed religions or any of the ethical systems which one may set up for himself or which has been set up by the philosophers may equally serve the purpose. They say: "Be not concerned about the manner of thy humility or thy belief or thy worship or about what formula or what language or what actions thou employest. Thou mayest invent a religion of thy own with a view to humility, worship, prayer and the management of thy own moral qualities, of thy household and of the people of thy country, if it is agreeable to them. Or take the rational laws set up by philosophers as thy religion and make the purity of thy soul thy aim and purpose."[26]

Let us now see how Hallevi and Maimonides, in their approach to the problem of prophecy from their respective conceptions of divine causality and religious perfection, deal with this problem.

§2. The Term *al-amr al-ilāhiyy* (*ha-'inyan ha-elohi*) in Hallevi

The five points in the philosophic conception of prophecy as presented by Hallevi himself in the *Cuzari* are all rejected by him. But before attempting to present his own partic-

have a theory of the mean in their ethics. Cf. *Cuzari*, IV, 18: עד שכל מי שנבדל (אעתדל) ונפרש (ותזהד) יאמר עליו ששב פילוסוף. The Arabic אעתדל of Hirschfeld's text in this passage has been corrected by Goldziher to read אעתזל, which is the Hebrew נבדל (*ZDMG*, XLI [1887], 703).

[26] Ibid.: אל תחוש על איזה תורה תהיה (=תשרעת; תכ̇שעת=כניעה תהיה) ובאי זה דת ובאי זה מעשה (=עמלת; עט̇מת=רוממות) ובאי זה דבור ובאי זה לשון [ובאי אעמל=ובאי זה מעשים] אתה. או בדה לעצמך דת לענין הכניעה ולרומם ולשבח ולהנהגת מדותיך וביתך ואנשי מדינתך אם הם סומכים עליה. או קח לך לדת הנימוסים השכליים אשר חברו הפילוסופים ושים מגמתך וכונתך זך נפשך. Cf. note by S. Horovitz on the text of this passage in *MGWJ*, XLI (1897), 266.

ular conception of prophecy, we must clarify the meaning of his Arabic term *al-amr al-ilāhiyy*, of which the Hebrew translation is *ha-'inyan ha-elohi*, and with it also a number of other terms which he uses in connection with prophecy.

It has been suggested — and this suggestion has gained acceptance — that the *amr ilāhiyy* in Hallevi's *Cuzari* designates a certain real being analogous to the Logos in the history of philosophy and in Christianity.[27] Support for such a suggestion would seem to come from the fact (1) that the term *al-amr al-ilāhiyy* occurs in the *Cuzari* in the speech of the Christian, where at first sight it would seem to stand for the Logos;[28] and also from the fact (2) that the term *amr rabbī*[29] or *amr allah*[30] and similar combinations of *amr* with the name of God occur in the Koran and in other Moslem literature, where it is sometimes said to refer to a hypostatic Logos.[31]

We shall therefore try to see whether there is any evidence for the use of *al-amr al-ilāhiyy* in the sense of a real, hypostatic being analogous to the hypostatic Logos, taking up first the use of that term in the speech of the Christian in the *Cuzari*.

That speech falls into two parts, the first dealing with

[27] I. Goldziher, "Mélange judéo-arabes: XXI. Le *amr ilāhī* (*ha-'inyan ha-elohi*) chez Juda Halévi," *REJ*, L (1905), 32–41. (The greater part of Goldziher's paper deals with the general historical background of this term as well as of other phases of Hallevi's philosophy, which, I think, could stand revision. The discussion in this paper, however, will touch only upon such statements of his which have a direct bearing upon Hallevi's use of the term under consideration.) H. Hirschfeld, *Judah Hallevi's Kitab al Khazari*, London, 1906, Introduction, p. 9.

[28] Hirschfeld, op. cit., n. 15 on pp. 297–98.

[29] Surah 17, 87.

[30] Surah 33, 37.

[31] H. Hirschfeld, loc. cit., referring to his *New Researches into the Composition and Exegesis of the Qoran*, London, 1902, pp. 15 ff., where reference is given to Grimme, *Muhammed*, II, 51. Goldziher, op. cit., p. 38, n. 3, referring to Grimme, *Die weltgeschichtliche Bedeutung Arabiens*, p. 60b.

the problem of Christology and the second with the problem of the Trinity. In the Christological part it states that "the Godhead (*al-lāhūtiyyah*) was incarnated and became an embryo in the womb of a virgin from the noblest ranks of Israelitish women. She gave birth to him, a being visibly human but invisibly divine, visibly a prophet sent forth but invisibly a god come down. He is the Messiah, who is called the Son of God."[32]

Then in the part dealing with the Trinity it states: "And God is the Father, the Son and the Holy Spirit. We believe that He is one in essence, even though Trinity appears in our speech. We believe in Him and in His having abided among the children of Israel as a mark of distinction to them, because the *amr ilāhiyy* had always been attached to them, until their masses rebelled against this Messiah and crucified him. Whereupon wrath became everlasting upon them and upon their masses and the good will was transferred to a few who followed the Messiah and then to those nations who followed these few."[33]

Now it will have been noticed that in the first part of the quotation that which has become incarnate is called

[32] *Cuzari*, I, 4: נגשמה האלהות (אללאהותיה̈) והיה עובר ברחם בתולה מנשיאות בני ישראל וילדה אותו אנושי הנראה אלהי הנסתר נביא שלוח בנראה אלוה שלוח בנסתר והוא המשיח הנקרא [ענדנא=אצלנו] בן אלהים.

[33] Ibid. והוא האב ו[הו=הוא] הבן והוא רוח הקודש, ואנחנו מיחדים אמתתו ואם נראה על לשוננו השילוש. נאמין בו ובשכנו בתוך בני ישראל לכבוד להם, כאשר היה הענין האלהי [אלאמר אלאלאהי] נדבק בהם, עד שמרו המוניהם במשיח הזה ותלוהו, ושב הקצף מתמיד עליהם ועל המונם והרצון ליחידים ההולכים אחרי המשיח ואחרי כן לאומות ההולכים אחרי היחידים.

The והוא in והוא האב cannot be parallel with והוא המשיח and refer to Jesus, as it is translated by both Cassel and Hirschfeld. I take it to refer to הבורא which occurs at the beginning of the Christian's address and is parallel with ושהוא ברא העולם which occurs subsequently in the address. Buxtorf translates it: *Hicque fuit Messias, dictus Filius Dei, qui est Pater, Filius, et Spiritus Sanctus*, where I presume *qui* correctly refers to *Dei* and not to *Hic*. The entire passage evidently deals with two distinct problems: (1) Christology and (2) Trinity, the latter problem beginning with והוא האב.

not *al-amr al-ilāhiyy* but rather *al-lāhūtiyyah,* whereas in the second part of the quotation that which had always been attached to the children of Israel is called *al-amr al-ilāhiyy.* The question before us therefore is whether these two terms mean the same thing, and also whether both of them refer to the Logos.

Let us take up first the first part of this passage. In this part of the passage it will have been noticed that (1) Jesus is described as being visibly human, a prophet, a Messiah, but that invisibly he retains that divine nature, designated by the term *al-lāhūtiyyah,* which became incarnate in him and that (2) it is that visible nature of Jesus, the man in him and not the God, which Mary gave birth to. All this indicates a certain definite position taken by the spokesman of Christianity in the *Cuzari* with regard to the controversial questions in the history of Christian theology as to whether the human and the divine in Jesus constituted one nature or two separate natures, and also as to whether Mary is to be called a God-bearer (*θεοτόκος*) or a man-bearer (*ἀνθρωποτόκος*). By its phrasing and terminology this passage seems to reflect the teachings of Theodore of Mopsuestia and Nestorius. The contrast which it draws between the visible humanity and the invisible deity in Jesus reflects Theodore's interpretation of Colossians 1.15, which is in opposition to the commonly accepted orthodox interpretation. The verse in question reads: "Who is the image (*εἰκὼν*) of the invisible God (*τοῦ θεοῦ τοῦ ἀοράτου*), the firstborn of every creature." According to the orthodox interpretation, the term image in this verse refers to the Logos and is therefore an invisible image, whereas according to Theodore the term "invisible God" refers to the Logos but the term image refers to the human Jesus and is therefore to be understood as meaning a visible image in whom the Logos is incarnate as an invisible God.[34] Then the statement that Mary gave birth to a man in so far as visible, but to a God in so far as invisible, reflects the view of both Theodore and Nestorius that the proper designation of Mary is ἀνθρωποτόκος, because it was a man whom she gave birth to, and if she is also to be called θεοτόκος, it is only because God was incarnate in the man whom she brought forth.[35]

Now it will have been noticed that in the passage quoted the Logos, which becomes incarnate in Jesus before his birth, is called *al-lāhūtiyyah* ("Godhead") and not *al-amr al-ilāhiyy*. That the term *al-lāhūtiyyah* for the Logos is used here with deliberate care as a technical term we may gather from a passage in Shahrastani, where in the course of his enumeration of the various Christological theories he restates what is evidently the Nestorian view of the incarnation of the Logos by saying that according to some Christians "the Godhead (*al-lāhūt*) was clothed with humanity as with a breastplate."[36] Here, in this restatement of the Nestorian view, the term "Godhead (*al-lāhūt*)" for Logos must have been used advisedly, for in the restatements of the other Christological views Shahrastani uses the term "Logos (*kalimah*)."[37] Similarly in the story

[34] Cf. H. B. Swete, *Theodori Episcopi Mopsuesteni in Epistolas B. Pauli Commentarii*, I, 261, l. 18, n. Cf. also ibid., p. 264, ll. 6–7, with reference to Romans 8.29: "to be conformed to the image of his son," *etenim illic non dixit conformes filii, sed imaginis filii, imaginem filii visibilem naturam evidenter dicens.*

[35] Theodore, *De Incarnatione*, XV, PG, 66, 991; F. Loofs, *Nestoriana*, Register C, p. 402, under "Maria."

[36] Shahrastani, p. 172, l. 7 [I, 260]: تدرّع اللاهوت بالناسوت.
The analogy of incarnation to being clothed reflects some such statement in Nestorius as the following: *propterea et omnium dominus indutus est nostram naturam, nunquam spoliabile videlicet deitatis vestimentum, inseparabile indumentum divinae substantiae* (F. Loofs, *Nestoriana*, p. 298). The breastplate part of the analogy reflects Isaiah 59.17.

[37] Ibid., p. 172, ll. 4–7 [I, 260], where five views are enumerated, of which the one quoted here is the fourth. Haarbrücker takes the term

of the Complaint of Animals against Man in the Encyclopedia of the Iḫwān al-Ṣafā, in the scene of a dialogue between representatives of various religions, including a Jew, before the king of the jinn, which undoubtedly had an influence upon the similar scene in the *Cuzari*, a Syrian Christian, evidently a Nestorian, presents his view as follows: "Praise be to God, who out of a spotless virgin chose for himself the body of humanity and joined to it the divine essence (*jauhar al-lāhūt*) and filled it with the Holy Spirit."[38] Here, again, the term "divine essence," which is the same as the term "Godhead" used in the *Cuzari* and Shahrastani, is used in the sense of the Logos. This deliberate choice of the use of the term Godhead for Logos in presenting the Nestorian Christology evidently reflects Theodore's interpretation of Colossians 1.15, quoted above, where the term "invisible God" is taken by him to refer to the Logos.[39] It is thus clear that so far in the Christian's speech in the *Cuzari* the Logos is not referred to as *al-amr al-ilāhiyy* but rather as *al-lāhūtiyyah.*

Let us now take up the second part of the Christian's speech and see whether the term *al-amr al-ilāhiyy* which occurs in it is the same as the term *allāhūtiyyah* which occurs in the first part. In this part of the speech, the Christian starts with a confession of faith in the Trinity. Now in the history of Christian doctrine, ever since the doctrine

"Jesus" (p. 171, l. 16) as the subject of all the verbs in ll. 4–7 on p. 172, including the verb in our quotation, and translates our quotation as follows: *er habe die Gottheit mit der Menschheit wie mit einem Panzer bekleidet.* But this is quite obviously wrong. The subject of all the verbs in ll. 4–7, exclusive of the verb in our quotation, is the term *kalimah* in l. 4.

[38] Fr. Dietrici, *Thier und Mensch vor dem König der Genien*, Arabic text, Leipzig, 1879, p. 63, ll. 18–19: والحمد لله الذى اتخذ من العذراء البتول جسد الناسوت وقرن به جوهر اللاهوت وايده بروح القدس.

[39] Cf. Swete, op. cit., I, 261. Cf. above, n. 34.

of the Trinity was formulated, the Holy Spirit has retained the original character of the term Holy Spirit in Judaism as a designation of the spirit of prophecy and as the principle of union between God and man. Furthermore, according to the Christian belief the Holy Spirit or the Spirit of Prophecy was removed from the Jews, with their rejection of Jesus, and was transferred to the followers of Christianity.[40] When therefore the Christian in the *Cuzari* says that he believes in God's "having abided among the children of Israel," prior to their rejection of Jesus, "because the *al-amr al-ilāhiyy* had always been attached to them," these words, translated into terms commonly used in Hebrew literature, mean that the Shekinah or the Divine Presence had always been among the children of Israel, because the Holy Spirit or the Spirit of Prophecy had always rested on a chosen few among them. Accordingly the term *al-amr al-ilāhiyy* in the speech of the Christian in the *Cuzari* is not the Logos but it rather refers to the Holy Spirit or the Spirit of Prophecy. Again, when he subsequently says that upon their rejection of Jesus, "the good will" was transferred from the Jews to the followers of Jesus, the term "good will" refers to the *amr ilāhiyy* or the Holy Spirit.[41]

With reference to the term *amr* in the Koran it is quite possible that, like the term *kalimah*,[42] it reflects the Logos in certain verses which deal with the birth of Jesus,[43] but this does not mean that whenever the term *amr* occurs in the Koran in connection with God, it must necessarily refer to the Logos. Such an expression as *amr rabbī*[44] or

[40] Cf. below §4, references to Justin Martyr and Clement of Alexandria.

[41] Cf. below n. 83.

[42] Surah 3, 40.

[43] Surah 19, 21.

[44] Surah 17, 87; cf. 18, 48; 51, 44.

amr allah[45] may indeed reflect the targumic *memra de-adonai* but this targumic *memra de-adonai* is not necessarily a hypostatic Logos; it is nothing more than the word of the Lord in the sense of the speech of the Lord or the command of the Lord.[46]

The difficulty of determining whether the term *amr* in a certain context means a hypostatic Logos or whether it means only "command" may be illustrated by the use of the term in the Iḫwān al-Ṣafā, Alfarabi and Shahrastani. The Iḫwān al-Ṣafā, referring to the Koranic verse (7.52): "Your Lord is God, who in six days created (*ḫalaqa*) the heavens and the earth . . . by His command (*bi-amrihi*); Is not all creation (*ḫalq*) and command (*amr*) His?", add the following comment: "Creation (*ḫalq*) refers here to corporeal things; command (*amr*) refers here to spiritual substances."[47] Shahrastani, in his discussion of the Batinites, represents them as saying that "God by His command (*amr*) brought into existence the first Intelligence."[48] Goldziher takes the *amr* in both these passages to refer to a hypostatic Logos.[49] Alfarabi, speaking of prophecy, says that the "spirit (*al-rūḥ*)" which is in man is derived "from the substance of the world of *amr*"[50] and that accordingly man consists "of the world of creation (*ḫalq*) and the world of *amr*, for thy spirit is of the *amr* of thy Lord and thy body of the creation (*ḫalq*) of thy Lord.[51] Horten

[45] Surah 33, 37.

[46] See Hirschfeld, *New Researches*, etc., loc. cit. (above n. 31), and cf. G. F. Moore, *Judaism*, I, 417 ff.

[47] *Rasā'il*, ed. Bombay, III, p. 42, ll. 9–10; Dieterici, *Die Abhandlungen der Ichwān es-Safā in Auswahl*, p. 217, l. 20.

[48] Shahrastani, p. 148, l. 1 [I, 22].

[49] Goldziher, op. cit., p. 38, n. 4; p. 37, n. 4.

[50] Alfarabi, *Fuṣuṣ al-Ḥikam*, §26. Horten, Arabic: *Zeitschrift für Assyriologie*, XVIII (1904), 272–94; German: *Das Buch der Ringsteine Farabis*, Münster, 1906. Dieterici, Arabic and German: *Alfarabi's philosophische Abhandlungen*, Leiden, 1890, pp. 66–83; 1892, pp. 108–38.

[51] Ibid., §27.

takes the *amr* in this passage to refer to a hypostatic Logos.[52] But all this I believe to be incorrect on general historical grounds into which I cannot enter here but which I discuss in great detail elsewhere. Here in connection with this I only wish to call attention to the general fact, that neither the Iḫwān al-Ṣafā nor the Batinites nor Alfarabi interposes a hypostatic Logos between God and what they call Intellect or the first Intelligence. In all these passages *amr* means the fiat of God, or perhaps also the *word* of God in the sense of the *fiat* of God, and they all reflect the verbal distinction in the above-quoted Koranic verse, according to which the intelligible world was brought forth by the command (*amr*) of God and the corporeal world was brought forth by the creation (*ḫalq*) of God.

Another illustration of the ease with which one may fall into the habit of seeing a hypostatic Logos in the expression *al-amr al-ilāhiyy* is another passage quoted by Goldziher. That passage reads as follows: "Before the coming of Alexander, the Greeks occupied themselves with the building of temples, which they named after the spiritual forces and the luminary celestial bodies, and took them each as an object of worship. Thus there was the temple of the Prime Cause (*al-'illah al-ūla*), who is to them the *amr ilāhiyy*, the temple of the Pure Intellect, the temple of the Absolute Dominion, the temple of the Soul and the Form."[53] Now Goldziher takes the *amr ilāhiyy* here to refer to a hypostatic Logos. But this, I believe, is quite obviously wrong. For the *amr ilāhiyy* in this passage is definitely identified with the Prime Cause, whereas the Logos, in whatever system of philosophy or theology it appears,

[52] Horten, op. cit., German: p. 20.

[53] Fakhr al-dīn al-Rāzi, *Mafātīḥ al-Ghaib*, ed. Cairo, I, p. 133 top, quoted by Goldziher, op. cit., p. 38, n. 5.

is never the Prime Cause but always a prime effect, for it is always conceived as something emanated or generated from God. As the Prime Cause inevitably refers here to God, the *amr ilāhiyy* must also refer here to God. Consequently the term *al-amr al-ilāhiyy* must mean here either (1) the "divine thing," in which sense it is the equivalent of such appellations of God as "divine essence," "divine substance" and "divine being," or (2) the "divine command," in which case the command of God is assumed here to be identical with the essence of God and hence used as the equivalent of the Prime Cause, or else (3) the Arabic term is to be read here *al-āmir al-ilāhiyy*, which means the "divine commander" and hence God or the Prime Cause.[54]

A clear use of the term *amr* in the sense of a divine fiat occurs in Saadia in his discussion of the Christian Trinity. For the Logos he uses the term *kalimah*.[55] Then in the course of his discussion of the scriptural verse: "By the word of the Lord were the heavens made,"[56] where, according to him, Christians took the Hebrew term word (*dabar*) to refer to the Logos (*kalimah*), he says that the term word in this verse, as well as in other similar verses, means only that the "Creator created the things by His edict (*qaul*), by His command (*amr*), by His wish (*murād*) or by His will (*mashī'ah*)."[57] Here, then, *amr*, in contradistinction to *kalimah*, does not refer to a hyperstatic Logos, but it rather means simply "command."

[54] This may also be the reading of the term in *Moreh Nebukim*, II, 10. Cf. the present writer's discussion on this point in "Hallevi and Maimonides on Design, Chance and Necessity," *Proceedings of the American Academy for Jewish Research*, XI (1941), 156–58. Above, pp. 52–54.

[55] *Emunot we-De'ot*, II, 5 (Arabic: p. 88, l. 2).

[56] Psalm 33.6.

[57] *Emunot we-De'ot*, II, 5 (p. 88, ll. 11–14): כי העושה עשה הדברים בצוויו (بقوله) או במאמרו (بامره) או בחפצו (بمراده) או ברצונו (بمشيئته).

External evidence, though of authors who lived after Hallevi, of the use of the term *al-amr al-ilāhiyy* in the general sense of a divine or theological or metaphysical matter, as contrasted with a human, mundane or physical matter, is to be found in Averroes and Maimonides. Averroes, speaking of miracles and of other religious beliefs which cannot be demonstrated by reason, says that all this is "something divine (*amr ilāhiyy*) which eludes the comprehensions of human intellects"[58] or that they are all "divine matters (*umūr ilāhiyyah*) which surpass human intellects but which one must accept despite a lack of knowledge of their reasons."[59] Similarly Maimonides speaks of "divine matters (*al-umūr al-ilāhiyyah*)" as those matters which, in contrast to matters for which there is a proof, contain certain things whose truth can be known and certain other things whose truth can only be approached.[60] Here "divine matters" refer to general theological and metaphysical concepts which cannot be perceived by the senses but which can be only indirectly, either fully or partially, demonstrated by reason. Similarly in another place, speaking of the "regulations and customs" established by "the sages of bygone nations,"[61] among whom he especially includes the Sabian sages,[62] he says:

[58] *Tahafut al-Tahafut* (ed. M. Bouyges), Phys. § 6, p. 514, l. 14: امر الهى معجز عن ادراك العقول الانسانية.

[59] Ibid., Phys. I (XVII), § 18, p. 527, l. 12: امور الهية تفوق العقول الانسانية.

[60] *Moreh Nebukim*, III, 51.

[61] *Millot ha-Higgayon*, ch. 14, Ibn Tibbon: וכן חכמי האומות השלמות יניחו הנהגות ודרכים; Aḥitub: וכמו כן חכמי האומות שכבר כלו מחברים הנהגות ועקרים. Cf. above n. 25 on the different Arabic terms underlying דרכים and עקרים.

[62] The evidence that the reference in *Millot ha-Higgayon*, ch. 14, includes the Sabians is as follows: (1) In *Moreh Nebukim*, II, 39, the Greeks and Sabians are described as אלמלל אלסאלפה̈, which expression must have been used in the original Arabic of *Millot ha-Higgayon*, ch. 14, as this is the only expression which can explain Aḥitub's translation האומות שכבר כלו as well as Ibn Tibbon's trans-

"We nowadays are not in need of all this, that is to say, of (1) the forms of worship and (2) the laws and (3) the man-made regimen in matters divine."[63] Here the term "matters divine" refers to the generality of religious beliefs and practices, for the three subjects mentioned here as those which "we nowadays are not in need of" correspond to the three topics mentioned by Maimonides elsewhere as being contained in what he refers to as Isaac the Sabian's "Great Book," namely, "the laws of the Sabians (=2),

lation האומות השלמות, the latter on the assumption that the term אלסאלפה was corrupted to אלסאלמה. (2) In *Moreh Nebukim*, III, 29, referring to certain pseudo-Aristotelian works and to Sabian works, Maimonides says: אלו כלם אשר זכרתי לך הם ספרי עבודה זרה אשר נעתקו ללשון ערבי ואין ספק שהם חלק קטן מאד ממה שלא נעתק ולא נמצא גם כן אך אבד ברוב השנים ואלה אשר הם נמצאים אצלנו היום יכללו רוב דעות הצאבה ומעשיהם. In *Millot ha-Higgayon*, ch. 14, he similarly says: ולפילוסופים בכל אלו הדברים ספרים רבים כבר יצאו אל לשון ערב, ואולי אשר לא יצאו יותר. Cf. my "Note on Maimonides' Classification of the Sciences," *JQR*, N. S., XXVI (1936), 375–76. In *Studies*, I, 557–558.

[63] *Millot ha-Higgayon*, ch. 14, Ibn Tibbon: והנה לא הוצרכנו באלו הזמנים אל כל זה, ר"ל הדתות והנמוסים והנהגת האנשים בענינים אלהיים. Aḥitub: וכבר הספיק באלו הזמנים מבלי כל זה, ר"ל בלי הנהגות והנמוסים והנהגת בני אדם בדברים האלהיים.

From the use of the terms ענינים and דברים in the Hebrew translations it is evident that the underlying Arabic term was אמור and not אואמר, the latter of which would have been translated by מצוות (cf. *Cuzari*, III, 23, quoted below n. 65; cf. n. 75).

In translating this passage here I have taken the expression הנהגת האדם to indicate a subjective genitive, thus reflecting by its contrast with הענינים האלהיים the contrast expressed in the following passage in *Moreh Nebukim*, II, 39 end: זאת התורה לבד היא אשר נקראת תורה אלהית, ואמנם זולתם מן ההנהגות המדיניות, כנמוסי היונים והזיות הצאבה וזולתם, כל זה מפעולות אנשים מנהיגים (אקואם מדברין) לא נביאים. It is not impossible, however, that the expression indicates an objective genitive, as in *Emunot we-De'ot*, X, 2 (Arabic: p. 283, l. 15): تدبر الانسان : הנהגת האדם, and accordingly its translation would be: the conduct of men, or the regimen governing men.

The reading והנהגת האנשים ה י א בענינים אלהיים, which occurs in the Basil edition and in many manuscripts and is adopted in ed. Ventura and ed. Efros of Ibn Tibbon's version, does not represent the original Arabic reading nor the original reading of Ibn Tibbon's version. By intrinsic evidence it can be shown that this reading is the result of a half-learned copyist's tampering with the text.

the details of their religion and festivals and sacrifices and prayers (=1) and other matters (*umūr*) of their religion (=3)."[64]

There is nothing then in the use of the term *amr* or *amr ilāhiyy* in Arabic works which would throw light upon the special use made of it by Hallevi. The meaning of the term *al-amr al-ilāhiyy* as used by Hallevi must therefore be determined on the basis of an examination of his own use of it in the *Cuzari* itself.

The fundamental meaning of the term *amr* in Arabic is like that of the term *dabar* in Hebrew and the term *milta* in Aramaic. It means (1) *order*, *edict*, whence also *power*, *dominion*. It means also that which has been ordered or has been made as a result of an order and hence (2) *thing*, *matter*, *business*, *case*, *affair*. There is no way of distinguishing the meaning of this term in its singular form except from the context in which it occurs. In the plural form of this term, however, if it is *awāmir*, and not *umūr*, it definitely means "commands" or "orders," and not "things." Then also, these three Arabic consonants, which we have transliterated by *amr*, may be also read *āmir* and, in that case, it means "commander." Now in many cases in the *Cuzari* it could not be determined from the context whether the expression means "the divine command" or "the divine thing" or "the divine commander," as any one of these three meanings would make good sense. Furthermore, even if the term is taken in the sense of "the divine thing," it may refer either to God himself or to the command or the decree of God or to some sacred object. Good illustrations of the possibility of construing the term *al-amr al-ilāhiyy* in the *Cuzari* in any of these

[64] *Moreh Nebukim*, III, 29: וספר יצחק הצאבי בטעון דת (מלה̈) הצאבה וספרו הגדול בנמוסי הצאבא ופרטי דתם (דינהם) וחגיהם וקרבניהם ותפלותיהם וזולתו (אמור דינהם) מעניני אמונתם.

senses are offered by Hallevi himself. In one place, he uses the term *awāmir allāh*, where from the context[65] as well as from the plural form *awāmir* it is clear that it means "the commands of God." Still in another place, he uses the term *al-umūr al-ilāhiyyah*, where from the plural form *umūr* it most likely means, though not necessarily so, "the divine things," but from its context it is quite clear that it refers to divine commands.[66] Then, again, in speaking of the union between God and His people, sometimes he speaks definitely of the attachment of "God" or the "Deity" to His people,[67] sometimes in the same passages he uses the terms Deity and *al-amr al-ilāhiyy* indiscriminately in connection with that attachment[68] and sometimes he speaks of the attachment of God's people to the *amr ilāhiyy*.[69] Moreover, in addition to this term *al-amr al-ilāhiyy*, which, as we have seen, includes the meanings of "divine thing" and "divine command," Hallevi uses terms which mean unmistakably either the "divine thing"[70] or the divine "word" or "decree."[71]

Nor can we get much light on the subject from the Hebrew translator. On the whole, he translates *amr* by

65 *Cuzari*, III, 23: שאין מתקרבים אל האלהים כי אם במצות האלהים (באואמר אללה) עצמם.

66 Ibid., III, 11: וכללו של דבר שישמור מהענינים האלהיים (אלאמור אלאלאהיה̈) מה שיוכל להיות נאמן באמרו לא עברתי ממצותיך.

67 Ibid., I, 27: מפני שהוציאנו ממצרים והתחברות כבודו (ואתצאלה=והתחברותו) אלינו. I, 43: הנביא . . . אשר נראה על ידו להמון התחברות הדבר האלהי (אלאלאהות=האלהות) בהם.

68 Ibid., I, 47: ולא התחבר בהם הענין האלהי (אמר אלאהי) . . . עד שהוליד יעקב שנים עשר שבטים כלם ראויים לענין האלהי (ללאמר אלאלאהי) ושבה האלהות (אלאלאהיה̈) בקהל רב.

69 Ibid., II, 34: אבל יש לנו התחברות בענין ההוא האלהי (בד̇לך אלאמר אלאלאהי).

70 Ibid., IV, 3: וכאשר יהיה הדבור עם דבר אלהי (לשי אלאהי) שרומזים אליו יאמר אדני באלף דלת נון יוד.

71 Ibid., I, 103: ורצה בספור ושמיעת הדבור האלהי (אלנטק אלאלאהי). IV, 25: הדבור (והקול) אבל הוא דבור אלהי (נטק אלאהי) קול דברי אלהים חיים. I, 87: ומה שנלוה אל הדבור האלהי (אלכלאם אלאלאהי) . . . כאשר שמעו אותם דבור אלהי (כ̇טאבא אלאהיא). II, 48: ואיך שמעו דבור האל (כ̇טאב אלרב).

'inyan, which indicates that he took the term in the sense of *affair*, *case*, *matter* and *thing*. But sometimes he translates it by *dabar*,[72] and while it is not always clear whether he uses this term in the sense of "thing" or "command," sometimes he definitely uses it in the sense of "command."[73] The plural form *awāmir* is translated by him by *mizwot*, *commands*, in contrast to the plural form *umūr* which is translated by him *inyanim*, *things*. Furthermore, in some places he uses the term *inyan elohi* or *dabar elohi* where the original Arabic has only the term "divine" or "Deity"[74] and it is not clear whether this is an indication that he considered the term *al-amr al-ilāhiyy* used in other places, or at least in some of the other places, to be the equivalent of "God" or "divine," or whether this is an indication that even in those few places where the term "God" or "divine" is used in the original Arabic he did not consider it to refer to God himself but rather to the *amr ilāhiyy*.

But despite the vagueness of the use of the term *al-amr al-ilāhiyy* in most of the passages, there are a few passages in which the context shows some various definite meanings in which the term is used. We shall try to enumerate these various meanings.

(1) In the sense of divine command.[75]

[72] Ibid., IV, 3: אבל אנחנו רואים אותם נעזבים אל הטבע והמקרה, טובתם ורעתם כפיהם, לא בענין (אמר) מתברר שהוא בדבר אלהי (באמר אלאהי). Cf. I, 98: כי אין האדם מגיע אל הענין האלהי (אלאמר אלאלאהי) אלא בדבר אלהי ([אלא באמר אלאהי]), רוצה לומר במעשים שיצום (יאמר) האלהים.

[73] Ibid., III, 73: שיציאת מצרים היתה בכונה (קצדא) מאת האלהים, לא במקרים ולא במצועים מתחבולות בני אדם וברוחניות כוכבים ומלאכים ושדים וכל אשר יעבור בלב מחשב אבל בדבר אלהים (באמרה תעאלי). Cf. also II, 6: קרא אותו אתה חפץ (אראדה̈) או דבר (אמרא) או כאשר תרצה.

[74] Ibid., I, 77: ואל יהיה רחוק בעיניך הראות רשמי ענינים אלהיים (אתֿאר אלאלאהיה̈) נכבדים בעולם הזה. I, 43: התחברות הדבר האלהי (אלאלאהות) בהם. In I, 103: נבדלים מבני אדם בענינים מיוחדים אלהיים (בכֿצוציה̈ אלאהיה̈), the expression ענינים מיוחדים is a translation of כֿצוציה̈ and it does not imply an underlying Arabic אמור.

[75] *Cuzari*, I, 87: ועשה להם משה במצות האלהים (באמר אללה) ארון. I, 97: וחטאתם היתה בציור אשר נאסר עליהם ושיחסו ענין אלהי (אמר אלאלאהיא) על מה

(2) In the sense of divine power, meaning thereby:

(a) the power of God which sustains the universe.[76]

(b) a divine or superrational faculty in man, whereby he can conceive things which cannot be comprehended by reason,[77] and hence also in the sense of prophetic faculty.[78]

(3) In the sense of God's control of everything and of His pre-ordination of everything.[79]

(4) In the sense of God's dominion over everything.[80]

שעשו בידם ורצונם מבלי מצות האלהים (אמר אללה). I, 98: כי אין אדם מגיע אל הענין האלהי (אלאמר אלאלאהי) אלא בדבר אלהי ([אלא באמר אלאהי]) רוצה לומר במעשים שיצום (יאמר) האלהים. II, 50: שתשמח במצוה (אלשריעה) עצמה מאהבתך המצוה בה (משרעהא) . . . ואם תעבור בך השמחה אל הנגון והרקוד היא עבודה ודבקה בענין האלהי (אלאמר אלאלאהי). III, 11: וכללו של דבר שישמור מהענינים האלהיים (אלאמור אלאלאהי̈ה) מה שיוכל להיות נאמן באמרו לא עברתי ממצותיך. III, 23: שאין מתקרבים אל האלהים כי אם במצות האלהים (באואמר אללה) עצמם.

In all these passages, with the exception of I, 98, where the Arabic text is missing, it will be noticed that when *amr* is followed by the noun *Allāh*, it means the "act of commanding," whereas when it is followed by the adjective *ilāhiyy*, it means "that which has been commanded" or something divine which is the result of God's command.

[76] Ibid., IV, 25: . . . רמז לענין האלהי (אלאמר אלאלאהי) המחבר בין ההפכים והעיר על הערך אשר בין אלה ובין הכח (אלקו̈ה) הסובל לכל שבו יתחברו ההפכים.

[77] Ibid., I, 95: והוא אשר קבל הנפש על תומה, והשכל על תכלית מה שביכולת האנושי, והכח האלהי (אלקו̈ה אלאלאהי̈ה) אחר השכל, רוצה לומר המעלה אשר בה ידבק באלהים וברוחניים וידע האמתות מבלי למוד אבל במחשבה קלה . . . והיה הענין האלהי (אלאמר אלאלאהי) דבק בהם מאבות אבותם אל בני בנים. V, 21: ניחסהו אל כח (קו̈ה) בלתי גשמי אבל (כח) אלהי (אלאהי̈ה) כאשר אמר גאלינוס בכח המצייר וישים לו יתרון על שאר הכחות ורואה שאיננו מחמת המזג אבל לענין אלהי (לאמר אלאהי).

[78] Ibid., I, 103: והאיך חל הענין האלהי [הנבואי] (אלאמר אלאלאהי אלנבוי) באיש שהיה לב האחים וסגלת האב.

[79] Ibid., I, 77: אבל הציור והשיעור וההזרעה וכל אשר יש בו חכמה לכונה לא יתיחס כי אם לחכם (חכים) היכול (אלקאהר) המשער (אלקאדר) . . . ואל יהיה רחוק בעיניך הראות רשמי ענינים אלהיים (אתֿאר אלאלאהי̈ה) נכבדים בעולם הזה.

In this passage the אתֿאר אלאלאהי̈ה which is the equivalent of אתֿאר אלאמור אלאלאהיה undoubtedly refers to the traces of the acts of God as a being who is חכים, קאהר and קאדר.

[80] Ibid., III, 17: וכי יתן אל לבו באהבת עולם, הדבק הענין האלהי (אלאמר אלאלאהי) בעדה המוכנת לקבולו כהדבק האור במראה הזכה ושהתורה (אלשריע̈ה) מאצלו התחלת החפץ (אראד̈ה) ממנו להראות מלכותו (מלכותהא) בארץ כהראותה

(5) In the sense of God's wisdom.[81]

(6) In the sense of God's will, wish and design.[82]

(7) In the sense of God's love and good will or pleasure.[83]

(8) In the sense of "divine thing" and hence as referring to God's covenant with Israel or the revealed Law.[84]

(9) Again in the sense of "divine thing" and hence as referring to the Divine Light,[85] of which we shall speak later.

בשמים . . . וכאשר יזך מהם יחיד או קהל יחול עליו האור האלהי . . . ויקרא זה ממנו אהבה ושמחה.

Here then הענין האלהי = (1) תורה, (2) חפץ, (3) מלכות, (4) האור האלהי and (5) אהבה ושמחה.

[81] Ibid., IV, 25: ואמר תלי בעולם כמלך על כסאו, גלגל בשנה כמלך במדינה, לב בנפש כמלך במלחמה . . . ורוצה לומר שהחכמה (אלחכמה̈) בשלשה אחת והענין האלהי (אלאמר אלאלאהי) אחד, והחלוף ביניהם איננו כי אם בהתחלפות היוליהם, ודמה הענין האלהי כשהוא מנהיג הרוחניים כמלך על כסאו . . . ודמהו כשהוא מנהיג הגלגלים כמלך במדינה . . . ודמהו כשהוא מנהיג החיים כמלך במלחמה. Cf. also I, 77, quoted above in n. 79.

[82] Ibid., V, 20: כי דבור הנביאים . . . מכוון מן הענין האלהי (אלאמר אלאלאהי), with which cf. IV, 3: הנביאים והחכמים והחסידים, כי הם ככלים הראשונים לחפץ האלהים (לאראדה̈ אללה). III, 73: שיציאת מצרים היתה בכונה (קצדא) מאת האלהים יתברך, לא במקרים ולא במצועים מתחבולות בני אדם וברוחניות כוכבים ומלאכים ושדים וכל אשר יעבור בלב מחשב אבל בדבר אלהים (באמרה תעאלי), with which cf. V, 20: המעשים יהיו אלהיים או טבעיים או מקריים או מבחריים, והאלהיים מהסבה הראשונה יוצאים על כל פנים אין להם סבה זולת רצון אלהים (משיה̈ אללה).

[83] Ibid., II, 50: וראה איך שב הענין האלהי (אלאמר אלאלאהי) הדבק באברהם ואחר כן בהמון סגולתו ובארץ הקדושה מביא הענין מדרגה אחר מדרגה . . . והניח אותם בטוב שבמקומות . . . באדמה הראויה לסגולה . . . מפני הראות אורו באלה כהראותו בשמים, אך במצוע עם ראוים לקבל האור ההוא, והוא מאציל אותו עליהם, ונקרא זה ממנו אהבה (אהבה). Cf. III, 17, quoted above in n. 80. III, 23: כי ההתחכמות [ואלתעקל = וההשתכלות] והסברא בתורה איננו מביא אל רצון אלהים (רצ̂א אללה) . . . וכבר אמרנו שאין מתקרבים אל האלהים (אללה) אלא במצות האלהים (באואמר אללה) עצמם . . . אשר בהשלמתם יהיה הרצון (אלרצ̂א) והדביקה בענין האלהי (בלאמר אלאלאהי).

[84] Ibid., IV, 3: . . . ויש שיקראו היחס שיש בין בני ישראל ובינו וההצטרף ה׳ רוצים שם ה׳ או ברית ה׳ או תורת ה׳, כי אין צרוף בינו ובין אומה מהאומות . . . אך אנחנו רואים אותם נעזבים אל הטבע והמקרה, טובתם ורעתם כפיהם ולא בענין (באמר) מתברר שהוא בדבר אלהי (באמר אלאהי) לבדו.

[85] Ibid., I, 103: ואיך חל הענין האלהי [הנבואי] (אלאמר אלאלאהי אלנבוי) באיש שהיה לב האחים וסגולת האב מקבל לאור (אלנור). III, 17: וכאשר ההוא יזך מהם יחיד או קהל יחול עליו האור האלהי (אלנור אלאלאהי) . . . ולא מצא הענין האלהי (אלאמר אלאלאהי) מקבל מסכית לדברו דבק בסדר אשר צוה בו אחר המאורות

These are some of the senses of *al-amr al-ilāhiyy* in the *Cuzari* which can be definitely determined by the context in which they occur. There is indeed in the *Cuzari* occasionally an attempt to personify the *amr ilāhiyy*,[86] but this attempt at personification should be taken only in a figurative sense. There is nowhere a definite assertion of real hypostatization. In all these meanings of the term there is that logical transition from its original meaning of ordering, with its implications of power, control, preordination, dominion, wisdom, will, wish, design, love, good will, to that which has been ordered by God or to that which has been created by His order, and hence he uses it with reference to the revealed Law and the Divine Light, both of which are real things and creations of God. "Divine Light," however, belongs to another group of terms, with special meanings of their own, which Hallevi uses in connection with prophecy. To this group of terms we shall now turn our attention.

והגלגלים אלא חסידי בני אדם היו יחידים מאדם ועד יעקב ואחר כן שבו קהל וחל עליהם הענין האלהי (אלאמר אלאלאהי) לאהבה להיות להם לאלהים. III, 20: מי שהוא מתפלל להדבק באור האלהי (אלנור אלאלאהי) בחייו . . . כי מי שדבקה נפשו בענין האלהי (אלאמר אלאלאהי) והיא טרודה במקרה הגוף.

[86] Hirschfeld (op. cit., p. 297, n. 15 on his Introduction) says: "In several places, e. g., iii, 17 (see quotation above in n. 85), it assumes quite a personal character." This is not quite correct. What we have in that passage, as well as in other similar passages, is only the usual attempt at personification.

§3. The Terms "Holy Spirit," "Divine Light" and Their Equivalents in Hallevi

The second group of terms used by Hallevi in connection with prophecy which, unlike the term *al-amr al-ilāhiyy* in its primary meaning, refers to something which has real existence as a creation of God, contains the following six terms: (1) Holy Spirit,[87] (2) Ray of Divine Light or Divine Light,[88] (3) Glory of God, (4) Kingdom of God, (5) Shekinah,[89] and (6) Messengership of God.[90] These terms, with the exception of the Light of God, are quoted by him within the Arabic text in their original Hebrew form, although in his presentation of the philosophic view on prophecy, as we have seen above, the term Holy

[87] רוח הקודש (II, 4).

[88] ניצוץ אור אלהי (II, 8); האור האלהי (III, 17).

[89] כבוד ה׳ ומלכות ה׳ ושכינת ה׳ (IV, 3). Hirschfeld's edition reads here ומלאכות ה׳ both in the Arabic (p. 244, l. 20) and in the Hebrew (p. 245, l. 26) text. But this is obviously a corruption, for the following reasons: (1) In the explanation which immediately follows there is the quotation ומלכותו בכל משלה (Ps. 103.19). (2) The same statement is repeated later in Arabic (p. 244, l. 23) and in Hebrew (p. 247, l. 1) and in both cases the reading is מלכות. (3) The early Hebrew editions read ומלכות.

The term מלכות is used by Hallevi as the equivalent of כבוד, after the expression כבוד מלכותך (Ps. 145.11), and it refers to the visible manifestation of God on earth. It is to be distinguished from the term מלכות אלסמא: מלכות שמים (III, 1) which he uses in the sense of the kingdom of God above.

[90] כבוד ה׳ ומלאכות ה׳ ושכינה (II, 7); ומלאכות ה׳ כנוי לשליחות (IV, 3). Cf. Haggai 1.13.

Spirit is quoted in its Arabic form[91] and although also the term Kingdom with reference to God and the term Shekinah occur also in Arabic.[92] The inference to be drawn from this is that in his discussion of the terms "Holy Spirit," "Glory of God," "Kingdom of God," "Shekinah" and "Messengership of God" he meant to interpret certain traditional Hebrew terms found in Scripture or in talmudic literature. As for "Divine Light," though allusions to it are to be found in Scripture and talmudic literature, at the time of Hallevi it was not yet crystallized into a technical Hebrew term.

Of these six terms, one term of which we have the clearest definition is Holy Spirit, with its equivalents, the terms Spirit of God[93] and Spirit.[94] It is defined by Hallevi as a "subtle spiritual substance" from which by the will of God are formed those "spiritual forms"[95] which "appear to the prophets"[96] during their prophetic experience. These "spiritual forms" arise by the divine will[97] out of this "subtle spiritual substance," called Holy Spirit, by means of a "ray of divine light" or a "divine light"[98] which acts upon the Holy Spirit, after the analogy of the action of the rays of sunlight upon the clouds which produce the colors of the rainbow.[99] As in the case of the sun and the ray of

[91] Cf. above, nn. 20, 21.

[92] ملكوت (Surah 23.90 et passim); سكينة (Surah 2.249).

[93] *Cuzari*, IV, 25: רוח אלהים והוא רוח הקודש.

[94] Ibid., IV, 15: ורוח כנוי לרוח הקודש.

[95] *Cuzari*, II, 4: וכן מצטייר מן הגשם הדק הרוחני (אלגִסם אללטיף אלרוחאני) הנקרא רוח הקדש הצורות הרוחניות הנקראות כבוד ה'. Hallevi's גשם :גִסם here is loosely used for גוֹהר: עצם, *οὐσία*; cf. below nn. 103 and 199.

[96] Ibid., II, 7: ונתגלגל לי ענין כבוד ה' ומלאכות ה' ושכינה ושהם נופלים על דברים נראים אצל הנביאים.

[97] Ibid., II, 6: והדבר ההוא שם האויר מצטייר בשמע בעשרת הדברים ושם המכתב מצטייר חרות בלוחות. קרא אותו אתה חפץ (אראדה̈) או דבר (אמרא) או כאשר תרצה.

[98] Ibid., II, 8: נצוץ אור אלהי; III, 17: אור אלהי.

[99] *Meteorologica*, III, 4, 273a, 32 ff.

sunlight and the many-colored rainbow, where the ray of sunlight is not identical with the sun and the rainbow is not identical with the ray of sunlight, so also in the case of God and the ray of divine light and spiritual forms, the ray of divine light is not identical with the essence of God; it is something created by God's will; nor are the "spiritual forms" identical with the "ray of the divine light"; they are something created out of the "Holy Spirit" by the action of the "ray of the divine light" upon it. The "Holy Spirit" or "the subtle spiritual substance" corresponds to the clouds in the phenomenon of the rainbow.[100]

[100] *Cuzari*, II, 7. Hallevi does not explicitly distinguish between Holy Spirit and Divine Light and, as we shall see (below, n. 121), no distinction is made between them by Saadia. But from the analogy he draws in II, 7, between Divine Light and sunlight and his reference in the case of the latter to the relation between sunlight and the bodies affected by it on a cloudy day *Ḳol Yehudah* infers that the relation between the Divine Light and the Holy Spirit is like that of an active principle to a passive principle. *Ḳol Yehudah's* interpretation is based upon Shem Tob's comment on Maimonides' reference to the rainbow in *Moreh Nebukim*, III, 7, which in its turn is based upon Narboni's comment on the same reference in Maimonides. This interpretation of *Ḳol Yehudah*, Shem Tob and Narboni, as I shall show in the subsequent paragraph, has a historical foundation.

Cf. *Ḳol Yehudah* on *Cuzari*, II, 7: הנה כה משפטו של הנצוץ אל מול פני הגשם הדק הרוחני הנ"ל הנקרא רוח הקדש, כי הגשם הזה נפעל בנכחו ויאור בו, ובכן יצטייר לכמה פנים, הוא מראה כבוד ה', לא שישתנה נצוצו ית' מצד עצמו. וכמאמר החבר ברביעי סימן ג' על כיוצא בזה: ורבו המדות והעצם אחד, בעבור התחלפות הדבר המקבל, כהתחלפות הניצוצות והגשם אחד וכ"ו . . . והמורה גם הוא לקח הרמז ממנו בשלישי פ' ז' על מראות אלהים המצטיירות בנפש הנביא המוכנת לנבואה מאור הניצוץ האלהי לדוגמת התחדשות הקשת בענן.

The passage in *Moreh Nebukim*, III, 7, referred to reads: אמר גם כן כמראה הקשת אשר יהיה בענן ביום הגשם כן מראה הנגה סביב הוא מראה דמות כבוד וגו'. חומר הקשת המתואר ואמתתו ידוע. וזה נפלא בדמיון ובהמשלה מאד, והוא בלא ספק בכח נבואה והבינהו.

Upon this passage Narboni makes the following comment (ed. Goldenthal, p. 48b): אמר גם כן במראה הקשת אשר יהיה בענן והוא המקבל, ר"ל כמו שיתרשמו המראים המתחלפים בענן המוכן ביום (הגשם) להראות ניצוץ השמש, כי השמש הוא הפועל ההכאה (ההכנה), כי הלחות נותן ההכאה (ההכנה) בענן לקבל הרושם ההוא כי יתהפך מעין אל עין נכחי ובו יראה הקשת בעל דרכים, כן מראה הנוגה סביב וכ"ו.

While the analogy of the rainbow definitely reflects the passage in

The "spiritual forms" are thus the result of the action of the ray of the divine light upon the Holy Spirit, the latter being related to the former as an active principle to a passive principle, or as form to matter.

Now this conception of Hallevi that there is a "subtle spiritual substance" which is acted upon by Divine Light as its form reflects a Neoplatonic view. Hallevi's "subtle spiritual substance" corresponds to that divine (θεία)[101] or intelligible (νοητή)[102] matter (ὕλη) or substance (οὐσία)[103] of which Plotinus speaks. Similarly Hallevi's Divine Light corresponds to that light (φῶς) which, according to Plotinus, proceeds from God and illuminates the intelligible matter, and which with reference to that matter is called reason (λόγος)[104] by which is meant form (εἶδος).[105] This Neoplatonic conception of an intelligible matter of which the form is spoken of as light was widespread in Arabic philosophy. Taking but one example of Arabic Jewish philosophy, we may mention Avicebron who similarly speaks of an "intelligible" or "spiritual matter"[106] as being acted upon by an "intelligible light" which emanates from the word or will of God and is described as form.[107]

Let us now see what becomes of the remaining terms,

Aristotle referred to above (n. 99), the argument that the sunlight is not identical with the sun and that the rainbow is not identical with the sunlight reflects Plato's argument, in his analogy of the sun with the idea of good, that just as "light and vision" are like the sun but not identical with it so also "knowledge and truth" are like the idea of good but not identical with it (*Rep.*, VI, 508E–509A).

Cf. also Shem Tob and Efodi ad loc.

101 *Enneads*, II, 4, 5 (ed. E. Bréhier, l. 15).

102 Ibid. (l. 24).

103 Ibid. (ll. 20–22).

104 Ibid. (ll. 7–8).

105 Ibid., II, 6, 2 (l. 15).

106 Cf. *Avicebrolis Fons Vitae*, ed. C. Baeumker, Index Rerum, p. 485, under *Materia intelligibilis*.

107 Ibid., V, 30, p. 313, ll. 9–20.

namely, Glory of God, Kingdom of God, Shekinah and Messengership of God.

These terms are said by Hallevi to be used as general designations of those "spiritual forms" which appear to prophets at the time of their receiving the prophetic communication. Not being physical forms, they are not perceived by all the people by means of the ordinary sense-perceptions, but they are in some miraculous way perceived by the prophets when they are possessed of the prophetic spirit and sometimes also by other privileged persons for whom the prophetic message was intended. These "spiritual forms" are such phenomena mentioned in Scripture as "a pillar of cloud" (Num. 12.5), "consuming fire" (Ex. 24.17), "a thick cloud" (Ex. 19.9), "the thick darkness" (Ex. 20.21), "fire" (Deut. 5.19), "brightness" (Ezek. 1.28),[108] "the cloud" (Ex. 16.10), "the image of God" (Gen. 1.27), "the similitude of the Lord" (Num. 12.8),[109] "the pillar of fire" (Ex. 13.22), and "a paved work of sapphire stone" (Ex. 24.10).[110]

But evidently Hallevi makes a distinction between the terms Glory of God, Kingdom of God and Shekinah on the one hand and the term Messengership of God on the other. The former terms are general descriptions of any of the phenomena which appear to the prophet at the time of his prophetic experience. The term Messengership of God, however, applies to that particular phenomenon which is called in Scripture "angel," who appears as the bearer of a

[108] *Cuzari*, II, 7: ונתגלגל לי הבנת ענין כבוד ה׳ ומלאכות ושכינה ושהם נופלים על דברים נראים אצל הנביאים כמו שאמר עמוד ענן ואש אוכלת ועב וערפל ואש ונוגה.

[109] Ibid., IV, 3: עד שהיו רואים אותו במצוע מה נקרא כבוד ושכינה ומלכות ואש וענן וצלם ותמונה ומראה הקשת וזולת זה.

By מראה הקשת I take it he means מראה הנגה or מראה דמות כבוד ה׳ which in Ezek. 1.28, is said to be כמראה הקשת and hence it is the same as נוגה in the passage quoted in the preceding note.

[110] Ibid. וכן רומזים אל עמוד האש. ועמוד הענן . . . וכן אל אש אוכלת . . . ואל הצורה הרוחנית אשר ראוה האצילים, ותחת רגליו כמעשה לבנת הספיר.

message of God. According to this view, then, the angels of Scripture are like all the other temporary perceptible phenomena by which the prophetic experience is attended, except, Hallevi seems to intimate, that unlike all those other temporary phenomena which, as he has said, are created from that "subtle spiritual substance," called "Holy Spirit," these temporary angels are created out of "the subtle elementary bodies," by which he presumably means the four simple elements.[111] Out of which of these elements the temporary angels are created he does not specify. But if his statement here has reference to the talmudic statement about ephemeral angels who are created out of the "fiery stream" mentioned in Daniel 7.10,[112] then they are created out of the element fire.[113] There is, however, continues Hallevi, another class of angels, who have a permanent existence, and of this class of angels he is willing to admit that they may be identical with what the philosophers call Intelligences, even though for himself he has dispensed with the Intelligences as intermediary causes of the motions of the spheres.[114] This class of angels who like the Intelligences of the philosophers are of permanent existence consist, according to Hallevi, not of "the subtle elementary bodies," i. e., the four elements, but rather of that "subtle spiritual body" which he calls Holy Spirit and which, as we have seen, corresponds to what Plotinus calls the "intelligible matter."[115]

Similarly with regard to the visions seen by Isaiah, Ezekiel and Daniel, such as the "throne," the "chariot,"

111 Ibid. והמלאך יש שיהיה נברא לעתו מן הגופים היסודיים הדקים (אלאגֿסאם אלענצריה̈ אללטיפה̈).

112 Ḥag. 14a. Cf. below, n. 198.

113 For parallels, see *Ḳol Yehudah* ad loc. and Kaufmann, *Attributenlehre*, p. 184, n. 194, and p. 505.

114 Cf. above, nn. 3 and 5.

115 *Cuzari*, IV, 3: ויש שיהיה מן המלאכים הנצחיים ושמא הם הרוחניים שאומרין הפילוסופים ואין עלינו לדחות דבריהם.

the "firmament," the "wheels" and the "wheelwork," Hallevi suggests that they may be either temporary phenomena created for the special occasion or permanent fixtures in the celestial world.[116] What substance they are made of in either of these two cases he does not say. But from the context as well as from his description of them as "spiritual" it may be gathered that he considered them as having been created out of that "subtle spiritual substance" which he calls Holy Spirit.

With regard to the term Glory of God, which on the whole he regards as a general term descriptive of the totality of the spiritual phenomena which appear at the time of the prophetic experience, Hallevi discerns in it also three other usages. (1) It is used as the equivalent of Holy Spirit and is accordingly defined by him as a "subtle substance,"[117] by which he evidently means, as he says of the Holy Spirit, a subtle spiritual body. (2) It is used as the equivalent of the "Ray of Divine Light," i. e., as the principle which acts as a form in its relation to the Holy Spirit, and accordingly he says that "the glory of God is a ray of the divine light."[118] (3) It is used as a general term designating the totality of those permanent celestial beings, such as angels, Throne, Chariot, Firmament and Wheels or the Wheelwork and others like them.[119]

These speculations about the meaning of the term "Glory of God" and its use by Hallevi as a designation of the totality of the immaterial beings created by God have

[116] Ibid. הספק במה שראה ישעיהו ויחזקאל ודניאל, אם הם מהנבראים לעת הצורך או מן הצורות הרוחניות הקיימות . . . אך על הדעת השנייה יהיה כבוד ה' כלל המלאכים והכלים הרוחניים כסא ומרכבה ורקיע ואופנים וגלגלים וזולת זה.

The term גלגלים in this passage stands for הגלגל in Ezek. 10.2, which is rendered as a plural in the Targum: גלגליא and is taken to refer to האופנים in 1.16. Cf. Rashi, ad loc., and below, n. 204.

[117] Ibid.: וכבוד ה' הוא הגוף הדק (אלגִסם אללטיף) . . . כפי הדעת הראשונה.

[118] Ibid., II, 8: הכבוד נצוץ אור אלהי.

[119] Ibid., IV, 3, quoted above in n. 116.

a long history. Already Philo uses the biblical term Glory of God as a designation of his Logos or the intelligible world, though he also suggests that it may mean men's glorification of God.[120] In Saadia the biblical term Glory of God which he identifies with the Shekinah and which according to *Sefer Yeẓirah* is also identified with the Spirit of God, i. e., the Holy Spirit, is said to refer to what he calls "the second and subtle air" or "light,"[121] which was created by God and out of which, as in Hallevi out of the subtle spiritual matter called Holy Spirit or Glory of God in one of its usages, are produced the various forms which appear to the prophet at the time of his prophetic experience. Among these forms he mentions, not only the visions seen by Jehoshaphat, Ezekiel and Daniel, such as the throne of God, heaven and the angels who carry the throne,[122] but also "pillar of cloud," "pillar of fire" and

[120] *Quaestiones in Exodum*, II, §45; *De Specialis Legibus*, I, 8, §§45–46.

[121] *Commentary on Sefer Yeẓirah*, IV, 1 (ed. M. Lambert), Arabic: p. 72; French: p. 94, and extract from Hebrew translation in J. Guttmann, *Die Religionsphilosophie des Saadia*, p. 119, n. 2: וכתבי הקדש קוראין האויר השני הדק (الهواء الثانى اللطيف) כבוד ... והאומה קוראה אותה שכינה. ... ובעל הספר הזה קראו רוח אלהים חיים. *Emunot we-De'ot*, II, 10; Arabic: p. 99, ll. 14–20: חדשו הבורא מאור (نور) אצל נביאו ... נקראת כבוד ה' ... ועליה אמרו החכמים שכינה.

For other literary parallels see Guttmann, loc. cit. Cf. also Kaufmann, *Attributenlehre*, p. 183, n. 146; Harkavy's additions to Rabinovitch's Hebrew translation of Graetz's *Gesch. d. Jud.*, V, pp. 16–18; my *Crescas' Critique of Aristotle*, pp. 460–62. A historical sketch of this metaphysical conception of light in the general history of philosophy is to be found in Clemens Baeumker, *Vitelo*, pp. 357 ff.

[122] *Emunot we-De'ot*, II, 10, Arabic: p. 99, l. 14: נענה כי זאת הצורה ברואה, וכן הכסא (الكرسى) והרקיע (والعرش) ונושאיו כלם מחודשים. References given by him are Ezek. 1.26; I Kings 22.19; Dan. 7.9.

The two Koranic terms كرسى (Surah 2.256) and عرش (Surah 69.17) used here by Saadia both mean the throne of God. But in the encyclopedia of the Iḫwān al-Ṣafā the term *kursiyy* is taken to refer to the sphere of the fixed stars and *'arsh* is taken to refer to the starless or ninth sphere (cf. *Rasā'il*, ed. Bombay, 1305 A. H. Vol. II, p. 17, ll. 21–22; Dieterici, *Die Abhandlungen der Ichwân es-Safâ in Auswahl*, p. 99, ll. 5–7; cf. also other references in Flügel, "Scha'rānī und sein

"bright light," the latter of which, he says, may be perceptible not only to the prophet but also to the people who are present with him.[123] As in Philo, so also in Hallevi, we find the suggestion that the term Glory of God, in addition to its meaning of the Holy Spirit or the Divine Light[124] or the totality of the permanent celestial beings,[125] may also mean men's glorification of God, for he says that the term Glory of God as well as Kingdom of God and Shekinah are sometimes metaphorically applied to the divine laws which govern nature and which evoke men's glorification of God.[126]

In all this, as suggested above, Hallevi meant to interpret certain old Hebrew technical theological terms. In the vague utterances about the "Holy Spirit" and the "Shekinah" in talmudic literature there is indeed sometimes the undoubted implication that they are real beings created by God. But there is never any definite statement that they are permanent beings, after the manner of the Logos and the Holy Spirit in Christianity, acting as intermediaries between God and men in the process of His communication with them. Hallevi, accordingly, interprets these terms as certain temporary visible manifestations

Werk über die muhammadanische Glaubenslehre," *ZDMG*, XX [1866], 28, n. 20). Consequently when the Hebrew translates here *'arsh* by רקיע it undoubtedly means thereby the sphere of the fixed stars, i. e., the eighth sphere, and when it translates *kursiyy* by כסא which is above the רקיע it undoubtedly means thereby the starless or ninth sphere (cf. below, nn. 207, 208, 210).

[123] Ibid., III, 5: והוא אם עמוד ענן או עמוד אש או אור בהיר מבלעדי האורים הרגילים וכאשר רואה הנביא זה יתברר לו בלי ספק כי הדבור מאת הבורא ואפשר שיראוהו גם כן העם.

[124] Cf. above, nn. 117, 118.

[125] Cf. above, n. 119.

[126] *Cuzari*, IV, 3: אך פעמים הושאלו גם כן למשפטים הטבעיים ואמרו מלא כל הארץ כבודו ומלכותו בכל משלה. To which the *Oẓar Neḥmad*, ad loc., adds: ופירש הרד"ק ז"ל: מלא כל הארץ כבודו, כי הוא ברא הכל ועל הכל יכבדוהו בעלי השכל, עכ"ל.

created by God during the process of His communication with men. The expression "the word of God" of Scripture and post-scriptural literature is not directly dealt with by Hallevi. In so far as it is implied in the term *al-amr al-ilāhiyy* it has all the variety of meaning of that term.

With the explanation of these terms which come into play in Hallevi's theory of prophecy, we may now sketch the outline of that theory itself.

§4. HALLEVI'S THEORY OF PROPHECY

Prophecy, according to Hallevi, comes to man by the *amr ilāhiyy*, that is to say, by God's wisdom, power, decree, dominion, command, love or will, but, he adds, that in the process of the prophetic experience, God shows to the prophet certain "spiritual forms" which are formed out of the Holy Spirit by the action of the Divine Light, these forms being known as Glory, Kingdom, Shekinah, and angels. It is in this sense that he says that "the speech of a prophet at the time when he is enwrapped by the Holy Spirit is in every part directed by the *amr ilāhiyy*,"[127] or that the term "spirit" used in Scripture in connection with prophecy refers "to the Holy Spirit which enwraps the prophet at the time of his uttering the prophecy,"[128] or that the servant of God who is exiled from the Holy Land "does not attach himself to the Divine Light so that he may become familiar with it as the prophets,"[129] or that philosophers had to have recourse to speculation "on account of the absence of prophecy and Divine Light among them."[130] In all these passages the *amr ilāhiyy*

[127] *Cuzari*, V, 20: כי דבור הנביאים בעת שלובשת אותם רוח הקדש בכל דבריהם מכוון מן הענין האלהי (אלאמר אלאלאהי).

[128] Ibid., IV, 15: ורוח כנוי על רוח הקודש הלובשת הנביא בעת הנבואה.

[129] Ibid., III, 1: והוא איננו דבק באור אלהי שימצא בו צות (יאנס אליה) כנביאים.

[130] Ibid., V, 14: ויש להם התנצלות למה שנצטרכו אל הקשיהם להעדר הנבואה והאור האלהי אצלם.

refers to the will or decree of God by which the gift of prophecy is granted to man, and the term Holy Spirit refers to that subtle spiritual substance which by the action of the Divine Light becomes spiritual forms which manifest themselves to the prophet.

The *amr ilāhiyy* of Hallevi, then, is nothing but the "divine will" and it is used by him merely for the purpose of denying that prophecy is a straight natural process of knowledge and of introducing into it an element of election by the Grace of God. In fact Hallevi himself sometimes uses the term "will" for *amr* and says that they both mean the same thing to him.[131] By his use of this term Hallevi has merely aligned himself with all religious thinkers in making prophecy a special gift of God. This then is his *first* point of departure from what he represented as the philosophic conception of prophecy.

Then he departs from the philosophic conception of prophecy on a *second* point. He eliminates the Active Intellect as an intermediary between God and man in the prophetic experience. Prophecy to him belongs to those acts which he describes as "divine," using the term "divine" in the sense that it is an act caused directly by the will of God without any intermediary causes, be they natural or volitional.[132] If angels sometimes appear as bearers of God's message to man, such angels are especially created by God for that purpose and they serve only as attending circumstances in the prophetic experience, such as the cloud, for instance, from the midst of which God may communicate His word to the people.[133] The knowledge

[131] *Cuzari*, II, 6: קרא אותו אתה חפץ (ארادה) או דבר (אמרא) או כאשר תרצה. Cf. above, n. 82, and below, n. 174.

[132] Ibid., V, 20: המעשים יהיו אלהיים או טבעיים או מקריים או מבחריים. והאלהיים מהסבה הראשונה יוצאים על כל פנים אין להם סבה זולת רצון האלהים (משיה אללה) . . . כי דבור הנביאים בעת שלובשת אותם רוח הקודש בכל דבריהם מכוון מן הענין האלהי (אלאמר אלאלאהי).

[133] Cf. above, n. 109.

imparted by God to the prophet is thus unique in its kind, dependent as it is entirely on the will of God, and accordingly he distinguishes prophecy as a special stage of knowledge, calling it "the divine and angelic stage,"[134] and similarly the faculty by which that stage of knowledge is attained he distinguishes as a special faculty, calling it "the divine faculty."[135]

Again, he differs with the philosophers on the *third*, *fourth* and *fifth* points in their theory of prophecy, namely, on the conditions set up by them as requirements for the gift of prophecy. To begin with, he eliminates that which the philosophers call intellectual perfection. Speculation and deduction and the knowledge of the arts and the sciences, he repeats in a variety of ways, do not prepare one for the divine gift of prophecy.[136] Then, as for what the philosophers call moral qualities, and right conduct, they are indeed necessary, but they are primary virtues and are not subordinate to intellectual virtues. Furthermore, the moral qualities and the right conduct which prepare one for the gift of prophecy are not those vague moral virtues for the attainment of which philosophers, in their unaccustomed humility, hesitate to prescribe a definite mode of action and tell you to choose your own religion or your own non-religion. They are, according to Hallevi, the way of life prescribed in the Law of Moses[137]

[134] Ibid., I, 42: אבל המעלה הזאת [היא] אלהית מלאכותית אם היא נמצאת, וזה מדין הענין האלהי (אלאמר אלאלאהי), לא מן השכלי (אלעקלי) ולא מן הנפשי (=אלנפסאני; אלאנסאני=האנושי) ולא [מן] הטבעי (אלטביעי). III, 22: זאת מדרגת התכלית אין אחריה כי אם מדרגת המלאכים והענין האלהי (אלאמר אלאלאהי) כמו צופה למי שראוי להדבק בו שיהיה לו לאלהים, כמו הנביאים והחסידים, כאשר השכל (אלעקל) צופה למי שנשלמו טבעיו ונשתוה נפשו ומדותיו שיחול בו על השלמות כפילוסופים, וכמו שהנפש (אלנפס) צופה למי שנשלמו כחותיו הטבעיים השלמה מזומנת למעלה יתרה ותחול בו כחיים, וכמו שהטבע (אלטביעה) צופה למזג השוה באיכותיו שיחול בו ויהיה צמח.

[135] Ibid., I, 95 and V, 21, quoted above in n. 77.

[136] Ibid., I, 79; I, 98; II, 49; III, 23.

[137] Ibid., III, 1; III, 5; III, 11; III, 23.

with all its mandatory and prohibitory laws. Finally, he adds two conditions, essential to prophecy, which are: First, prophecy is confined to the Jewish race only, who alone by a certain process of selection have inherited a predisposition for it from Adam who was created directly by God with a special predisposition for the gift of prophecy.[138] None of the other human races, though all of them are descendants of Adam, has inherited that particular predisposition for prophecy, and consequently, since this prophetic gift is a matter of heredity, it cannot be attained by one who is born of another race, even if he becomes converted to the Jewish religion.[139] Second, besides the racial condition of prophecy, there is also a geographical condition. Prophecy can flourish only in Palestine and, if we do find prophets who flourished outside of Palestine, it is because the burden of their prophecy was Palestine.[140]

There are several phases in Hallevi's theory of prophecy which reflect certain theological tendencies in the general history of the problem but which can be best and more fully treated in connection with other problems. But here we should like to comment upon his view that prophecy is confined to the Jewish race. This view, which Hallevi so vehemently upholds, was more current in Christianity than in Judaism. There is of course no such restriction in the Bible. In talmudic literature the view is expressed in a variety of ways that prophecy existed also among other

[138] Ibid., I, 95.

[139] Ibid., I, 115: ועם כל זה לא ישתוה הגר הנכנס בתורתנו עם האזרח כי האזרחים לבדם הם ראויים לנבואה, וזולתם תכלית ענינם שיקבלו מהם ושיהיו חכמים וחסידים אך לא נביאים. Cf. I, 27: וכל הנלוה אלינו מן האומות בפרט יגיעהו מן הטובה אשר ייטיב הבורא אלינו אך לא יהיה שוה עמנו.

[140] Ibid., II, 14. Cf. *Mekilta*, Bo, Proem, ed. Friedmann, p. 1a: "Ere Palestine was chosen, all the lands were fit for the revelation of the words of God; but as soon as Palestine was chosen, all the other lands were excluded from that destination." Cf. Ginzberg, *The Legends of the Jews*, V, 301, n. 215.

nations,[141] though statements are also to be found there which would seem to indicate that prophecy was restricted to Jews.[142] Philo emphasizes again and again that prophetic inspiration may come to all men who are qualified for it by moral perfection, though once in describing the prophetic revelations to Moses as evidences of divine graciousness and beneficence by which God "trains *all men* to noble conduct," he adds "and particularly the people dedicated to His service (*τὸ θεραπευτικὸν αὐτοῦ γένος*),"[143] by which expression, it may be taken, he refers to the Jewish people, for Israel, says Philo elsewhere is the best of races, since Israel means seeing God[144] or the contemplation of God, and the source of seeing God is the habit of service to God (*τὸ θεραπευτικῶς ἔχειν αὐτοῦ*).[145] Still while he considered the Jews as having been particularly favored to receive the gift of prophecy, he did not consider them as having been exclusively so favored. Among the Church Fathers, however, the view appeared that prophecy was confined to Jews, probably to enable them to transfer it, after the Jewish rejection of Jesus, exclusively to Christians. Thus Justin Martyr, addressing Trypho, says: "For prophetical gifts remain with us even to this time, from which you ought to understand that those which were formerly lodged with your

[141] The most characteristic of such statements is that in which seven non-Jewish prophets are enumerated. Cf. Baba Batra 15b.

[142] As, e. g., the statement that "when God causes His Shekinah to alight, He lets it alight only on families in Israel of traceable descent" (Ḳid. 70b), which is quoted in *Oẓar Neḥmad* on *Cuzari*, I, 115, as the source of Hallevi's view.

[143] *De vita Mosis*, II, 35, §189.

[144] *De congressu quaerendae eruditionis gratia*, 10, §51; *De posteritate Caini*, 26, §92.

[145] *De sacrificiis Abelis et Caini*, 36, §120. In *De vita contemplativa*, 2, §11, τὸ θεραπευτικὸν γένος refers to the Therapeutic sect and not to Israel as a whole.

nation are now transferred to us."[146] Clement of Alexandria, drawing upon Philo's method of allegorizing on scriptural characters, declares that from Adam three natures were begotten, the irrational in Cain, the rational in Abel and the spiritual, i. e., the prophetic, in Seth[147] and then goes on to say that "Israel is an allegory, the spiritual man who will see God"[148] and finally concludes that this spiritual or prophetic quality passed on to one part of the Church.[149] St. Augustine, however, approaching the original Jewish view, raises the question whether before Christian times there were prophets among other nations, and makes the statement that he does not think that the Jews themselves dare contend that there were no prophets among other nations, referring to Job as an example of a non-Jewish prophet. But evidently in order to safeguard the belief in the subsequent exclusiveness of prophecy to Christians, he speaks of all those non-Jewish prophets as belonging to that "heavenly fellowship," "the true Israelites," which had existed as the prototype of Christianity even before the advent of Christ.[150] Thus Hallevi's conception of prophecy as an exclusive gift of the Jews has its parallel, if not its origin, in non-Jewish literature. In view, however, of the fact that prophecy is considered in Judaism as being of various degrees, it is not impossible that, when Hallevi speaks of prophecy as being restricted to Jews, he has reference only to a special kind of prophecy. In fact, Hallevi himself says that a non-Jew may become a *waliyy*, which Arabic term, though translated into Hebrew *ḥasid*, *pious person*, is to be taken here to mean a *prophet* of a lower grade as contrasted with *nabiyy*, which

[146] *Dialogus cum Tryphone*, 82.
[147] *Excerpta ex Theodoto*, 54 (ed. R. P. Casey)
[148] Ibid., 56.
[149] Ibid., 58.
[150] *De Civ. Dei*, XVIII, 47.

means here a higher grade of prophet and hence a prophet in the true sense of the term.[151]

Similarly one of the most characteristic expressions used by Hallevi in describing the selection of Israel comes from a non-Jewish source, where it was used as a description of a non-Jewish people. The expression in question is Hallevi's description of the Jews as the heart, in the figurative sense of essence and purest part, of the nations.[152] This

[151] Cf. *Cuzari*, I, 115: יזולתם תכלית ענינם שיקבלו מהם ושיהיו חכמים וחסידים (אוליא) אך לא נביאים (אנביא). Elsewhere (V, 20, p. 342, ll. 23–24; p. 343, ll. 18–19), Hallevi attributes to *waliyy*, חסיד, as contrasted with *nabiyy*, נביא, "divine inspiration," *ilhāmāt*, למוד, evidently as contrasted with *waḥy*, נבואה, concerning which terms see above n. 20. It is not impossible that the *waliyy* of Hallevi corresponds to the lowest of the three degrees of prophecy enumerated by Abraham bar Ḥiyya in *Megillat ha-Megalleh*, II, p. 41, ll. 10 ff. (As to the origin of that threefold classification, see Guttmann's Introduction to that work, pp. XVIII–XIX). That Hallevi should designate the lowest degree of prophecy by a different term is quite understandable. So also Maimonides says that the prophet of his two lowest degrees of prophecy is not to be called *nabiyy*, נביא, in the true sense of the term (cf. below nn. 187, 188).

It may be observed that, whenever in the Hebrew translation of the *Cuzari*, the term *ḥasid* occurs as a description of a merely *pious* person the underlying Arabic term is not *waliyy* but rather *ḫayyir* (III, 1, 2 3, 4, 5, 11; V, 16) or *fāḍil* (III, 17, 21) or *taqiyy* (III, 31).

[152] Hallevi uses the following Arabic terms for "heart" with its derivative meanings of "essence," "best part," etc. All of these are translated into Hebrew by לב.

(1) لُباب, pure essence, pulp or marrow of fruit. *Cuzari*, I, 47: באיש שהיה לב (לבאב). I, 103: ואלה . . . היו לב (לבאב) האדם וסגולתו (וצפותה). II, 12: לעם שהם סגולה (אלצפוה̈) ולב (ואללבאב) האחים וסגולת (וצפוה̈) האב. IV, 3: ראיה על ענין הדברים ההם ולבותם (ולבאבהא). Here the Hebrew ולבותם is to be changed to the singular ולבתם in agreement with the Arabic.

(2) لُبابة, mind, intellect. I, 95: נתן לו תחתיו שת והיה דומה לאדם והיה סגולה (צפוה̈) ולב (ולבאבה̈). Hirschfeld (p. 44, l. 15) takes the final ה in these two Arabic words as pronominal suffixes and consequently takes the words themselves to be צפו and לבאב. This, however, does not seem to be correct, for the form צפוה̈ occurs throughout this section (p. 44, ll. 16, 23, 26, 27). Goldziher changes Hirschfeld's צפוה to צפותה (*ZDMG*, XLI [1887], 697). But this is not required by the

description occurs in that book on the Complaints of Animals against Man of the Iḫwān al-Ṣafā to which we have referred above, where it is put in the mouth of an Iraqian who speaks in praise of his people. He says: "We are the heart of men, men are the heart of animals, animals are the heart of plants, plants are the heart of minerals, minerals are the heart of the elements, and so we are the heart of hearts."[153] Evidently in using these Iraqian words Hallevi meant to reclaim for the Jews that distinctive position among the religions of the world which later other peoples have arrogated to themselves in their belief of being the rightful successors to the Jews. In fact, some of the phrases used by Hallevi in praise of Palestine and the Jews seem to be aimed directly at that Iraqian's speech in praise of his own country and his own people. When Hallevi speaks of Palestine as being the center of the inhabited

context and it certainly does not represent the reading underlying the Hebrew translation.

(3) لب, the principal part and middle, the purest and best, essence, marron, kernel, heart, mind, intellect. II, 14: והיה לב (לב) הסגולה ההיא אל המקום אשר בו תגמר השלמתו (אלצפוה̈).

(4) قلب. Cf. below, n. 159.

[153] Cf. Dieterici, *Thier und Mensch vor dem König der Genien*, p. 61, ll. 2-4: فنحن لب الناس والناس لب الحيوان والحيوان لب النبات والنبات لب المعادن والمعادن لب الاركان فنحن لب الالباب.

There are many striking similarities between this treatise of the Iḫwān al-Ṣafā and the *Cuzari*, some which indicate a literary dependence of the latter upon the former. One of these, because of its bearing upon the text of the treatise of the Iḫwān al-Ṣafā, I shall call attention to here. In *Cuzari*, I, 3, there is the following statement: אמר הפילוסוף אין בדת הפילוסופים הריגת אדם מפני שמגמתם השכל. This has its parallel in the following statement in the Hebrew version of the treatise of the Iḫwān al-Ṣafā, *Iggeret Ba'ale Ḥayyim*, V, 9 (ed. Mantua, 1557): אמר אמנם דע אדוננו המלך שאין בדת הפילוסופים הריגה. This statement, however, is not found in Dieterici's edition of the Arabic text (p. 126), which is based upon two Calcutta editions and two manuscripts. Nor is it found in the English translation of the same treatise from Hindustani (*Ikwánu-s Safá*; or, *Brothers of Purity*. Translated from the Hindustání, by John Dowson, London, 1869, p. 149). Cf. above, n. 38.

world,[154] reflecting therein a number of traditional Jewish statements to that effect,[155] he undoubtedly meant to counteract thereby the Iraqian's statement that Iraq is the center of all lands.[156] Similarly when Hallevi speaks of the Jews as having inherited the gift of prophecy from Adam, through Seth, Enos, Noab, Shem, Abraham, Isaac and Jacob,[157] he again undoubtedly means to counteract thereby the Iraqian's claim of the gift of prophecy for his people and his further claim that it is from the midst of his people that sprang such prophets as Noah, Idris (Enoch), Abraham, Moses, Jesus and Mohammed.[158] It must, however, be added that the extension of the analogy of Israel amidst the nations to the heart amidst the organs of the body to mean not only that it is the best and the most central part and the most healthy part of the body but also to mean that it is the most sensitive and the most easily affected part of the body has no parallel in the work of the Iḫwān al-Ṣafā.[159]

Since prophecy, according to Hallevi, requires no special intellectual perfection, it was logical for him to describe the revelation on Mount Sinai as a prophetic experience partaken by the entire people after they have been duly prepared for it morally and after they have performed certain

[154] *Cuzari*, II, 20: שארץ ישראל באמצע (באלוסט) לישוב.

[155] Tanhuma, Kedoshim, 10: ארץ ישראל נתונה באמצע העולם, שנאמר יושבי על טבור הארץ (יחזקאל ל"ח, י"ב), and parallels. Cf. Cassel, ad loc., p. 106, n. 1.

[156] Op. cit., p. 60, ll. 13–14: والحمد لله الذى خصنا باوسط البلاد.

[157] *Cuzari*, I, 47: אדם ושת ואנוש עד נח עד שם ועבר אל אברהם יצחק ויעקב עד משה. On the literary sources of this statement, see Guttmann's Introduction to Abraham bar Ḥiyya's *Megillat ha-Megalleh*, pp. XVI and XXI–XXII, referring to Ziemlich, "Abraham ben Chija und Jehuda Halewi," *MGWJ*, 29 (1880), 366–74. Cf. also passages referred to above, nn. 147, 148, 149.

[158] Op. cit., p. 6, ll. 18–20.

[159] *Cuzari*, II, 36: ישׂראל באומות כלב (במנזלה̈ אלקלב=במדרגת הלב) באיברים הוא רב חליים מכלם ורב בריאות מכלם.

religious acts.[160] "The people," he says, "heard with distinctness the words of the Ten Commandments which constitute the first principles and the roots of the Law . . . and these Ten Commandments were not received by the people through the intermediary of single individuals or a prophet but directly from God."[161] There is a striking resemblance between this statement of Hallevi and the statement with which Philo opens his discussion of the Ten Commandments. These Ten Commandments, says Philo, "God judged fit to deliver in His own person alone, without employing any other" and these laws "which He gave in His own person and by His own mouth alone include both laws in general and the heads of particular laws."[162] Elsewhere for "heads of particular laws" he uses the expression "the ten generic laws"[163] or "the generic heads, roots and principles of the vast multitude of particular laws, being the everlasting source of all the ordinances."[164] Moreover, as he goes on, Philo stresses the fact that the Ten Commandments were spoken by God with "clearness and distinctness" and that they reached the ears of the people in an "articulate voice."[165] The similarities are striking,

[160] *Cuzari*, I, 87.

[161] Ibid.: ושמע העם דבור צח (אלכטאב פציחא) בעשרת הדברים הם אמות (אמהאת) התורה ושרשיה (ואצולהא) . . . ואלה עשרת הדברים לא קבלם ההמון מאנשים יחידים ולא מנביא כי אם מאת אלהים.

[162] *De Decalogo*, 5, §§18–19.

[163] *Quis rerum divinarum heres sit*, 35, §167.

[164] *De congressu quaerendae eruditionis gratia*, 21, §120.

On the basis of these passages of Philo, the term امهات, אמות (above, n. 161), literally, *mothers*, but used in the sense of *origins*, *first principles*, *species*, reflects Philo's κεφάλαια (*Dec.*, §19), γενικὰ κεφάλαια, ἀρχαί and πηγαί (*De Cong.*, §120) and the term اصول, שרשים (above, n. 161) reflects Philo's ῥίζαι (*De Cong.*, §120). Cf. also description the Ten Commandments as اصل العلم, שרש החכמה in *Cuzari*, II, 28.

[165] *De Decalogo*, 9, §33.

Hence, Hallevi's خطاب فصيح, דבור צח, reflects Philo's σαφήνεια and τρανότης. Cf. تفصيل الكلام : הבדל הדברים in *Moreh Nebukim*, II, 33, below, n. 189.

though they are not exactly of such a nature that one could not assume that Hallevi has arrived at his view independently as a result of the scriptural text itself as well as the rabbinic traditions about it.[166] But as it is now well established that there existed a condensed Arabic version of Philo's *De Decalogo* before the time of Hallevi,[167] the possibility of a literary connection in this case is not to be excluded.

More striking still is the similarity between Philo and Hallevi in their treatment of the question of anthropomorphism that is involved in the story of the revelation on Mount Sinai, in the statement that the voice of God was heard by the people.

In his explanation of this anthropomorphism Philo says that it was not a physical voice with which God addressed the people, "for God is not like a man in need of a mouth and a tongue and a windpipe."[168] What really happened there is that God "wrought a miracle of a truly holy kind." He ordered "an invisible (i. e., an immaterial) sound to be created in the air," a sound which was "a rational soul full of clearness and distinctness," and this "invisible sound" or "rational soul" transformed the air into "a flaming fire" and sounded forth a loud "articulate

[166] Cf., for instance, the statement that the tablets of the Ten Commandments contained all the laws of the Torah (Song of Songs Rab., 5.14, 2). Cf. *Ḳol Yehudah* ad loc.

[167] Cf. the fragment of that condensed translation of *De Decalogo* in Hirschfeld, "The Arabic Portion of the Cairo Genizah of Cambridge," *JQR*, XVII (1905), 65–66.

Other verbal similarities between the *Cuzari* and the *De Decalogo*, besides those given above in nn. 164, 165, are the following:

Cuzari, I, 67: חדש מזמן ידוע: חאדת̇ מנד̇ מדה̈ מחצלה̈; *De Decalogo*, 12, §58: *ἀπό τινος χρόνου γενόμενον*.

Cuzari, V, 14: Arabic, p. 324, ll. 27–28: אד̇ תכ̇ילת ען הד̇א אלעאלם לם יכן; Hebrew: p. 325, l. 18: כשידומה מזה העולם שהוא לא היה; *De Decalogo*, loc. cit.: *καὶ ἦν ποτε χρόνος, ὅτε οὐκ ἦν*.

[168] *De Decalogo*, 9, §32.

voice"[169] that could be heard even by those who were stationed farthest away from the mountain, for this "newly created voice" was heard by the people with "another kind of hearing, far superior to the hearing of the ears."[170]

Similarly Hallevi declares emphatically that the voice in which God addressed the Ten Commandments was not a physical voice produced by organs of speech. Like Philo, he describes that voice as a miracle created by God for that particular occasion, a miracle like all the other miracles recorded in Scripture, the chief one among which is the creation of the world. Unlike Philo, however, he does not undertake to describe how that "articulate voice" which the people heard proceeded from that "invisible voice" which God created in the air. But he seems to have Philo in mind when he says: "We do not know how God's thought became corporealized so that it was transformed into speech which struck our ear, nor what new thing God created out of that which had no existence, nor again what existing thing did He employ [in creating this new thing]; for [all we know is that] God does not lack the power [to do any of these things]."[171] And consequently, "just as He created the heaven and the stars by His will alone . . . [and just as] the water stood at His command, and shaped itself at His will, so the air which touched the prophet's ear was shaped into sounds of letters, which conveyed the thoughts to be communicated by God to the prophet and the people."[172]

[169] Ibid., §33.

[170] Ibid., §35.

[171] *Cuzari*, I, 89: ונאמר שאין אנחנו יודעים איך נגשם הענין (אלמעני) עד ששב דבור (כלאמא) וקרע את אזנינו ולא מה שברא לו יתברך ממה שלא היה נמצא וכל מה שהעביד לו מן הנמצאים, כי לא יחסר לו יכולת.

[172] Ibid.: כאשר ברא את השמים והכוכבים במאמרו (במשיתה=בחפצו) בלבד . . . כי המים עמדו במאמרו (לאמרה) ונצטיירו בחפצו (במשיתה) וכן יצטייר האויר המגיע אל אוזן בצורות האותיות שהם מורות על הענינים שהוא חפץ להשמיעם אל הנביא או אל ההמון.

We may now present the essential features of Maimonides' view on prophecy both in its relation to what he calls the philosophic view and in its relation to the view of Hallevi.

§5. Maimonides' Theory of Prophecy

Of the *five* points in the philosophic conception of prophecy, the first point is explicitly rejected by Maimonides. Disagreeing with the philosophers on their *first* point, he does not believe that the state of prophecy must follow by necessity as a result of one's natural, moral and intellectual perfection. "For we believe," he says, "that, even he who is naturally fit for prophecy and has prepared himself for it may yet not actually prophesy, for the act of prophecy depends upon the divine will, and according to my opinion it is a miraculous act like all miracles and it occurs in the same manner."[173] The term used by him for "will" in this connection is the Arabic *mashi'ah*, used by Hallevi as the equivalent of *amr ilāhiyy*,[174] and once he even uses the term *amr ilāhiyy* as the eqivalent of *mashi'ah* in describing the cause of prophecy. This use of the term *amr ilāhiyy* occurs in a passage where he says that "*al-amr al-ilāhiyy* necessarily obliges everyone who has obtained some perfection to transmit it to others, as we shall explain it later in the chapters on prophecy."[175]

[173] *Moreh Nebukim*, II, 32(3): שאנחנו נאמין שהראוי לנבואה המכין עצמו לה אפשר שלא יתנבא וזה ברצון אלהים (במשיה̈ אלאהיה̈) וזה אצלי כדמות הנפלאות כלם ונמשך כמנהגם.

[174] *Cuzari*, V, 20: המעשים יהיו אלהיים או טבעיים או מקריים או מבחריים. והאלהיים מהסבה הראשונה יוצאים על כל פנים אין להם סבה זולת רצון האלהים (משיה̈ אללה) . . . כי דבור הנביאים בעת שלובשת אותם רוח הקודש בכל דבריהם מכוון מן הענין האלאלהי (אלאמר אלאלאהי).

[175] *Moreh Nebukim*, II, 29: אלא כאשר חייב הענין האלהי (אלאמר אלאלאהי) בהכרח לכל מי שישיג שלמות שישפיעהו ועל זולתו, כמו שנבאר בפרקים הבאים [בענין הנבואה].

The reference is to the distinction which he makes subsequently between two types of prophecy, of which one does not compel the prophet to communicate his message to others and another compels him to do so.[176] Now the compulsion which the prophet feels to communicate his message to others is said by Maimonides to come from the *amr ilāhiyy*, which term, judging from his definition of prophecy, can mean only the "will of God."[177]

But once he expresses his disagreement with the philosophers on this point, he agrees with them on the next three points. He agrees with them in their *second* point that prophecy, though dependent upon divine will, is not a direct act of God. With the philosophers he believes that God acts by the intermediary of the Active Intellect, so that in his formal definition of prophecy he says that "prophecy, in its truth and essence, is a free grace flowing from God through the medium of the Active Intellect to man's rational faculty first and then to his imagination faculty."[178] The only exception to this general theory of prophecy is Moses, who according to the generally accepted view based on Scripture, received his prophetic communications directly from God and not by any intermediary.[179] He also agrees with the philosophers on their

[176] Ibid., II, 39. Cf. above, n. 20.

[177] Ibid., II, 32(3). Cf. above, n. 173.

[178] Ibid., II, 36: כי אמתת הנבואה ומהותה הוא שפע שופע מאת השם יתעלה באמצעות השכל הפועל על הכח הדברי תחלה ואחר כן ישפע על הכח המדמה.

The term פיץ̇, שפע in this passage is usually translated by emanation (Munk, Friedländer, Stern, Weiss, Buxtorf: *influentia*). But the context as well as the historical background of the problem requires that the emphasis should be laid upon the element of liberality and generosity in the act of emanation. The old Latin translation (Paris, 1520) translates Ḥarīzī's כבוד here by *largitas*, which is what is required here.

[179] *Mishneh Torah*: *Yesode ha-Torah*, VII, 6; Introdcution to *Pereḳ Ḥeleḳ*, Article 7

third point that man must be qualified for this divine gift of prophecy by natural, intellectual and moral perfection, for it is a fundamental principle with us, he says, and one based on the authority of traditional statements, that "preparation and perfection in moral and rational virtues are necessary"[180] conditions for prophecy, and these two conditions are supplemented by him later by a third condition, namely, the possession of "an inborn highest possible perfection of the imaginative faculty," which perfection, he adds, "depends upon the most excellent mixture of the organ in which any bodily faculty resides, upon the best proportion of that mixture and upon the greatest purity of its matter."[181] With regard to intellectual perfection, he also agrees with them that it is attained by those "who have succeeded in finding a proof for everything for which there is a proof and who know in matters divine the truth of everything whose truth can be known or who comes near the truth of that whose truth can only be approached."[182] He also agrees with them on

[180] *Moreh Nebukim*, II, 32(3): אמנם היות יסודנו ההכנה והשלמות במדות (אלכֿלקיאת) ובדבריות (אלנטקיאת) על כל פנים.

[181] Ibid., II, 36: ... שלמות הכח המדמה בעקר היצירה בתכלית מה שאפשר נמשך לטוב שבמזגים שיהיה לאבר ההוא הנושא לכח ההוא ולטוב שבשעורים שיהיה לו ולזכה שבליחות.

[182] Ibid., III, 51: מי שהגיע לדעת מופת כל מה שנמצא עליו מופת וידע מן הענינים האלהיים (אלאמור אלאלאהיהֿ) אמתת כל מה שאפשר שתודע אמתתו, ויקרב לאמתת מה שאי אפשר בו רק להתקרב אל אמתתו.

Arabic philosophers, such, e. g., as Avicenna and Averroes, have relaxed in their requirements of intellectual perfection as an essential condition of prophecy, and this for the purpose of explaining the prophetic gift of Mohammed (cf. A. M. Goichon, loc. cit., and Leo Strauss, op. cit., p. 117, n. 4; cf. above, n. 23). Maimonides, however, was not hampered by such a consideration and hence he stressed intellectual perfection as an essential condition of prophecy for everybody, without any exception. As for Mohammed, he allusively places him within that class of people of whom he says that "the influence [of the Active Intellect] extends only to their imaginative faculty, their rational faculty remaining untouched by it, on account either of an innate deficiency in it or of a neglect in training," and among

their *fourth* point that moral virtues and practical virtues are subordinate to intellectual virtues.[183]

But as for the *fifth* point of the philosophers, namely, that there is no special virtue in any particular mode of conduct for the attainment of prophecy, Maimonides is not quite clear, for it is somewhat uncertain whether Maimonides insisted upon the particular practices prescribed by the Jewish religion as an essential condition leading to divine gift of prophecy. He does indeed take great pains to show that all the six hundred and thirteen commandments of the Law have for their purpose the development of intellectual, moral and practical virtues.[184] But it is not clear whether non-Jews, who are not bound by all these six hundred and thirteen commandments and who according to Maimonides attain the status of "pious gentiles" by the observance of the Noachian laws only,[185] would be excluded by him from the gift of prophecy. Equally vague is he in his direct discussion of the problem whether non-Jews, properly qualified by natural disposition and moral and intellectual qualities perfection, can attain the gift of prophecy. In his *Iggeret Teman* he argues against what he describes as the vulgar view that no non-Jew can become a prophet and refers to Job and Zophar and Bildad and Eliphaz and Elihu, all of whom were non-Jews, and still,

whom, he adds, some persons, "even while they are awake, perceive strange apparitions and dreams and astonishing images, and these are so much like a prophetic vision that they believe themselves to be prophets" (*Moreh Nebukim*, II, 37). Cf. Abrabanel, ad loc.: ואין ספק שרמז בזה אל נביא הישמעאלים.

[183] Ibid., III, 27: ודע ששתי הכוונות האלה האחת מהן בלא ספק קודמת במעלה, והוא תקון הנפש, רוצה לומר נתינת הדעות האמתיות.

[184] Ibid. כונת כלל התורה שני דברים, והם תקון הנפש ותקון הגוף. אמנם תקון הנפש הוא שינתנו להמון דעות אמתיות . . . ואמנם תקון הגוף . . . ישלם בשני דברים, האחד מהם להסיר החמס מביניהם . . . והשני ללמד כל איש מבני אדם מדות מועילות בהכרח.

[185] *Mishneh Torah*: *Melakim*, VIII, 11.

he says, they are all considered by us as prophets, concluding his statement with the remark that "we believe a prophet or we reject him only on the ground of the nature of his prophecy and not on the ground of his descent."[186] In his *Moreh Nebukim*, however, all the non-Jews mentioned in Scripture who might be taken as prophets, such as Job and his friends as well as Balaam, are placed by him in the second of the eleven degrees into which he divides prophecy, and concerning these first two degrees he definitely says that they are not degrees prophecy properly so called, but only "steps leading to prophecy,"[187] and any one belonging to either of these two degrees is not really a prophet and, if he happens to be called prophet, it is only in a loose use of the term, for the term prophet is applied to him only in the sense that "he is almost a prophet."[188] Now the question is whether Maimonides believed that no non-Jew could rise to a higher degree of prophecy than that of the second, or whether he believed that even a non-Jew could rise to a higher degree of prophecy; in the latter case, the fact that the non-Jewish prophets in Scripture belong to the second degree is not to be explained by their disqualification on racial grounds from attaining a higher degree of prophecy, but rather by their own personal shortcomings, even as David and Solomon and Daniel and other prophets of Jewish descent never rose above the second degree of prophecy, evidently by reason of their own personal shortcomings. If we should therefore assume, as suggested above, that Hallevi's

[186] *Iggeret Teman*, *Ḳobeẓ*, II, p. 4a: אבל שלא נאמין בנבואת זיד ועמר אין זה בשביל שאינם מישראל, כמו שחושבים ההמון, עד שנצטרך לדייק ממלת מקרבך מאחיך, שהרי איוב וצופר ובלדד ואליפז ואליהוא כלם אצלנו נביאים ואף על פי שאינם מישראל. וכן חנניה בן עזור נביא שקר ואף על פי שהוא מישראל, אבל נאמין בנביא או נכחישהו מצד נבואתו ולא מצד יחוסו.

[187] *Moreh Nebukim*, II, 45: אבל המדרגה הראשונה והשנית הם מעלות לנבואה.

[188] Ibid. ואם יקרא בקצת העתים נביא הוא לקצת כללות להיותו קרוב לנביאים מאד.

restriction of prophecy to Jews refers only to a special higher degree of prophecy, and if we should also assume that Maimonides excludes non-Jews from the higher degrees of prophecy, then there is really no difference between them on this point.

As a result of his view that prophecy requires intellectual perfection, Maimonides could not accept the view of both Philo and Hallevi that the revelation on Mount Sinai was a direct prophetic experience partaken of by the entire people. To him it was only Moses who heard "distinct words"; the people heard only a "sound," the meaning of which had to be explained to them by Moses.[189] Moreover, even that indistinct sound was heard by the people only in the case of the first two Commandments. In the case of the remaining eight Commandments, they heard not even the sound of the voice of God. These eight Commandments were communicated to the people through Moses.[190] He agrees, however, with both Philo and Hallevi in describing that indistinct sound of the first two Commandments as having been "created," i. e., as having been created as a miracle especially for that occasion. He thus refers to it as the "created sound from which the intelligible word was derived."[191] Elsewhere he similarly says that the term "to say" or "to speak," when it refers to some communication from God, implies that that communication was either by means of a "created sound" or by means of one of the several degrees of prophecy.[192]

[189] Ibid., II, 33: כי הדבור היה לו והם ישמעו הקול ההוא העצום לא הבדל הדברים (תפציל אלכלאם). Cf. above n. 165.

[190] Ibid.

[191] Ibid. הקול הנברא אשר ממנו הדבור.

[192] Ibid., I, 65: וכל אמירה ודבור שבאה מיוחסת לשם הם משני העניינים האחרונים, ר״ל שהם אם כנוי על הרצון והחפץ או כנוי על העניין המובן מאת השם, והוא אחד אם נודע בקול נברא או נודע בדרך מדרכי הנבואה אשר אבארם.

While the term *al-amr al-ilāhiyy* is used by Maimonides in connection with prophecy in exactly the same sense as it is used by Hallevi, his use of Hallevi's second group of terms, namely, Holy Spirit, Divine Light, Glory of God, Kingdom of God, Shekinah, and Messengership of God, shows some differences.

With regard to the term Holy Spirit, he seems to reject Hallevi's use of it in the sense of a "subtle spiritual substance" which, as we have seen, means the Neoplatonic "intelligible matter." To Maimonides the terms Holy Spirit and Spirit of God and Spirit are to be understood only as descriptions of the gift of prophecy in general[193] or more particularly as descriptions of the first and second of the eleven degrees of prophecy.[194]

Nor does he agree with Hallevi in his conception of the term Messengership of God, i. e., angels. The angels, whom he identifies with the separate Intelligences, are free of any matter.[195] Here we have the counterpart in Arabic, Jewish as well as Moslem, philosophy of a controversy which is to be found later in mediaeval Latin philosophy. Moreover, the angels to Maimonides are permanently existing beings.[196] Indeed he refers to the midrashic statement with regard to the existence of ephemeral angels and like Hallevi he concludes that some angels are permanent and some are transient.[197] But Maimonides' transient angels are unlike those of Hallevi's.

193 Ibid., I, 40: רוח . . . והוא גם כן השפע השכלי האלהי אשר ישפיע על הנביאים ויתנבאו בו . . . ואצלתי מן הרוח . . . רוח ה׳ דבר בי.

194 Ibid., II, 45 (1): וזאת תקרא רוח ה׳ . . . וכן נאמר בעמשא כאשר הגיעהו רוח הקודש לעזור את דוד ורוח לבשה את עמשא. II, 45 (2): וזהו אשר יאמר עליו שהוא מדבר ברוח הקודש . . . ועל כיוצא ברוח הקודש הזה אמר דוד רוח ה׳ דבר בי . . . ומזה הכת היו שבעים זקנים הנאמר עליהם ויהי כנוח עליהם הרוח ויתנבאו.

195 Ibid., I, 43; I, 49; II, 4; II, 6; II, 10.

196 Ibid., II, 6: וכן התבאר פעמים שהמלאכים חיים וקיימים.

197 Ibid. וכאשר הוקשה . . . יהיה המענה שמהם קיים ומהם אבד, כן הענין באמת.

They are in fact not real beings at all. They refer only to those physical and animal powers by which individuals are guided and guarded in their ordinary processes of life.[198]

Maimonides agrees, however, with Hallevi in the use of the terms Glory of God, Light of God and Shekinah. All these terms designate some physical phenomenon which manifests itself at the time of the prophetic experience. Such a phenomenon is described by him as being created by God out of some "substance" which is less material than the Aristotelian fifth substance out of which the celestial spheres consist but which is not of the same grade of immateriality as God.[199] Undoubtedly he would consider it also of a lower grade of immateriality than the Intelligences. This is close enough to Hallevi's "subtle spiritual body" or the Neoplatonic "intelligible matter." As an example of such a phenomenon he mentions the term "pillar of cloud,"[200] which occurs in Scripture as a manifestation of the Glory or Presence of God and which, as we have seen, is included by Hallevi in his long list of similar phenomena. It is not certain whether Maimonides would agree with Hallevi as to the meaning of all the other terms in that list. With regard to three of those terms, at least, he definitely disagrees with Hallevi. The term "image" in the verse "in the image of God created He him" (Gen. 1.27) is interpreted by him to refer to the specific form or intellect of man,[201] and the term

[198] Ibid. ומה שיחזק אצלך היות הכחות האישיות הטבעיות והנפשיות נקראות מלאכים אמרם במקומות רבים, ועקרו בבראשית רבה, כל יום הקב"ה בורא כת של מלאכים אומרים לפניו שירה והולכים להם.

[199] Ibid., I, 76 (2): וכמו שאין גשם הנצוצות אצלו הוא גשם כדור השמש כן יאמר שאין גשם האור הנברא, ר"ל השכינה, הוא גשם הגלגלים והככבים, ולא גשם השכינה או עמוד הענן הנברא הוא גשם האל יתעלה אצלו, אבל יאמר הגשם (אלג̇סם) ההוא העצם (אלד̇את) השלם הנכבד. Cf. above, n. 95, on the use of the term גשם in the general sense of substance.

[200] See quotation in preceding note.

[201] *Moreh Nebukim*, I, 1: ומפני ההשגה הזאת השכלית נאמר בו בצלם אלהים ברא אותו . . . אשר היא הצורה המינית.

"similitude" in the verse "and the similitude of the Lord doth he behold" (Num. 12.8) is interpreted by him to refer to the true essence of God.[202] The expression "a paved work of sapphire stone" (Ex. 24.10) is interpreted by him to refer to prime matter.[203]

Maimonides finally differs with Hallevi as to the meaning of the vision of Ezekiel and hence also as to the meaning of the visions of Isaiah and Daniel. In the vision of Ezekiel, he takes the "wheels" (1.16) and the "wheelwork" (10.2) to refer to the four sublunar elements,[204] the "four living creatures" (1.5), i. e., the "chariot,"[205] to refer to the sphere of the fixed stars, the spheres of the five planets, the sphere of the sun and the sphere of the moon,[206] the "firmament" (1.22) to refer to the concavity of the starless sphere,[207] and the "throne" (1.26) to refer to the convexity of the starless sphere.[208] Elsewhere in Scripture, according to him, the term "throne" refers either to the heaven in general[209] or to the ninth sphere[210] or to God's

[202] Ibid., I, 3: ותמונת ה' יביט עניינו ופירושו ואמתת השם ישיג.

[203] Ibid., II, 26: ותחת רגליו כמעשה לבנת הספיר שהם השיגו במראה הנבואה ההוא אמתת החומר הראשון והתחתון. Cf. I, 28.

[204] Ibid., III, 2: כבר גלה שהארבעה פנים אשר לאופן הם ארבעה אופנים. III, 3: שהאופנים הם הגלגלים, אמר לאו פנים להם קורא הגלגל באזני. Cf. above, n. 116.

[205] Ibid., I, 70: ארבע חיות קראוהו החכמים מרכבה. Cf. M. Ḥag. 2.1.

[206] Ibid., III, 2: זכר שראה ארבע חיות. Efodi, ad loc.: רוצה לומר ארבע כדורים, והם כדור הכוכבים הקיימים וכדור חמשה כוכבי הנבוכים וכדור חמה וכדור ירח. Cf. Maimonides' allusion to it, ibid., II, 9 end: וזה המספר הוא אצלי שרש גדול מאד לעניין עלה בדעתי.

[207] Ibid., ואמר שעל הארבע חיות רקיע. Shem Tob, ad loc. ואחרים פרשו שהרקיע הוא קבוב גלגל ערבות והוא הגלגל הט'. Cf. ibid., I, 70.

[208] Ibid. ועל הרקיע דמות כסא. Shem Tob, ad loc. ועל הרקיע כסא והוא גבנונית גלגל ערבות . . . וכן פי' החכם ר' שמואל אבן תבון. Cf. *Ma'amar Yiḳḳawu ha-Mayim*, Ch. 10, p. 47: דמות כסא שאמר עליו שהוא ממעל לרקיע . . . כאלו תאמר עליונו וגבנינותו. Cf. also Ch. 8, p. 28.

[209] Ibid., I, 9: ומפני זה הענין נקראו השמים כסא. Cf. also I, 28.

[210] Ibid., I, 70: ומכלם לא בחר כסא כבוד למלכותו אלא ערבות. Cf. above, n. 122.

attributes of greatness and power which are identical with His essence.[211]

Let us now summarize the result of our discussion. The problem of prophecy by the time of Hallevi and Maimonides was no longer a mere scriptural problem; it was already intricately enmeshed with the old philosophic discussions about divination and dreams and intuitive knowledge, and also with what the philosophers themselves called prophecy. Like any other scriptural problem which was collated with a corresponding philosophic problem, the problem of prophecy had a purely philosophic aspect and a purely religious aspect. The purely philosophic aspect concerned the question of the psychological basis of prophecy and of the part to be played in it by the various faculties of the soul. Maimonides dwells much on this aspect of the problem;[212] Hallevi hardly touches upon it. The religious aspect of it was the question whether prophecy is a purely natural process determined exclusively by the laws of necessary causality or whether there is an element of divine will in it. Both Hallevi and Maimonides agree that it is a process dependent upon the will of God. But in conformity with their respective views as to the operation of the divine will in nature, they differ also as to the operation of the divine will in prophecy. To Hallevi, it is a direct act of God's will; to Maimonides, it is an act of God's will through the intermediacy of the Active Intellect. In conformity also with their respective views as

[211] Ibid., II, 11: ולזה ירצה בכסא הנה ובכל מה שדומה לו גדולתו ועצמתו אשר אינם דבר יוצא מעצמו.

[212] For detailed studies of this aspect of the problem, see Z. Diesendruck, "Maimonides' Lehre von der Prophetie," *Jewish Studies in Memory of Israel Abrahams*, 1927, 74–134; Leo Strauss, "Maimunis Lehre von der Prophetie und ihre Quellen," *Le Monde Oriental*, XXVIII (1934), 99–139.

to what constitutes religious perfection in man, they differ also as to the prerequisite qualifications for prophecy. To Hallevi, right action as prescribed by the Law is sufficient; to Maimonides, intellectual perfection is an additional essential condition. As a result of this difference between them with regard to intellectual perfection as a condition of prophecy, they differ also with regard to the nature of the revelation on Mount Sinai. To Hallevi, it was a direct prophetic experience partaken of by the entire people; to Maimonides, the people were merely eyewitnesses of a prophetic experience which directly affected only Moses.

They both also believe that prophetic experience is attended by certain phenomena which are created by God, for that particular occasion, out of some "subtle spiritual substance," which is not exactly immaterial but at the same time it is not of such gross a nature as matter, even not as the fine matter out of which the heavens and the stars are made. Hallevi gives a rather long list of such phenomena, all derived from Scripture. One of these phenomena happens to be mentioned by Maimonides and is taken literally by him in the same sense as in Hallevi, while three other phenomena of Hallevi's list are fully discussed by him and are interpreted allegorically. A similar difference is to be discerned to exist between them with regard to the visions seen by Isaiah, Ezekiel and other prophets. To Hallevi, they are visions of certain real objects made of that "subtle spiritual substance" out of which all the phenomena attending prophecy are made, though he is not certain whether these objects were of enduring existence or only of temporary existence. To Maimonides, they are all to be interpreted allegorically. So also do they differ with regard to those bearers of divine communications which in Scripture are called angels. To Hallevi, they all refer to real beings, some of them of contemporary existence, created out of fire, and others of enduring existence, created out of that "subtle spiritual substance." To Maimonides, sometimes they refer to real beings, and in that case they are the Intelligences, who are immaterial and of enduring existence; but sometimes they do not refer to real beings, and in that case they are merely figurative terms descriptive of the physical and psychical powers through which God operates in the universe.

ADDITIONAL NOTES TO § 2.

At nn. 47–51 (preceding issue of this *Review*, pp. 360–61): That the Iḫwan al-Ṣafa (n. 47), the Bāṭinites quoted by Shahrastani (n. 48) and Alfarabi (n. 51) in their use of the terms *ḫalq* and *amr* were merely playing upon the verbal distinction of these two terms in Koran 7.52 may be supported by a similar passage in Abraham bar Ḥiyya's *Megillat ha-Megalleh*, III (ed. Poznanski and Guttmann), p. 51: "With regard to all created things that passed into actuality and became existent during the six days of creation, some of them passed into actuality by the word 'said' alone, as in the creations of the first and third days, but others passed into actuality by the words 'said' and 'created,' as in the creations of the fifth day, and still others passed into actuality and became existent by the words 'said' and 'made,' as in the creations of the second and fourth days and in the case of the cattle and beasts among the creations of the sixth day." שכל הנבראים היוצאים לידי מעשה וההוים בששת ימי בראשית יש מהם יוצאים למעשה אחר אמירה בלבד כגון בריות היום הראשון והיום השלישי. ויש מהם יוצאים לידי מעשה אחר אמירה ובריאה כגון בריות היום החמישי. ויש מהם יוצאים לידי מעשה והוים אחר אמירה ועשיה כגון בריות היום השני והיום הרביעי וגם בהמות וחיות מבריות היום הששי. Cf. *Hegyon ha-Nefesh*, I, p. 6a.

At nn. 53–54 (ibid., pp. 361–62): If, as suggested, the term *al-amr al-illāhiyy* in the passage quoted by Goldziher from Faḫr al-dīn al-Rāzi (n. 53) means "divine thing" in the sense of "divine essence," "divine substance," "divine being" and hence "the Deity," then it is merely a translation of the Greek term *τὸ θεῖον*, in which term the combination of adjective and article implies some noun, corresponding to *amr*. A definite connection between these Arabic and Greek terms is to be found in Hallevi's statement אין כילות אצל הענין האלהי: לא בכל ענד אלאמר אלאלאהי (*Cuzari*, V, 10, Arabic: p. 308, 1.14; Hebrew; p. 309, 11.12–13). Here the *amr illāhiyy* refers to God himself, for a little later Hallevi rephrases the same statement to read אין כילות לפניו ית': לא בכל ענד תע'

(p. 308, 1.28; p. 309, 1.27). Now this statement is undoubtedly based on Aristotle's statement οὔτε τὸ θεῖον φθονερὸν ἐνδέχεται εἶναι in *Metaphysics*, I, 2, 983a, 2 (cf. Plato, *Timaeus* 29E and *Phaedrus* 247A). Similarly in the popular Greek saying as quoted by Aristotle (op. cit., 982b, 32–983a, 1), against which his own statement is directed, the term used for God is τὸ θεῖον.

By the same token, the term *al-amr al-illāhiyy* in *Moreh Nebukim*, II, 10, referred to in n. 54, may mean the same as the term התחלה אלהית: מבדא אלאהי, which is attributed to Aristotle in *Moreh Nebukim*, III, 13, and in that case it again reflects the term τὸ θεῖον used by Aristotle in *Metaphysics*, XI, 7, 1064a, 37, in the sense of πρώτη ἀρχή.

3

MAIMONIDES AND HALEVI

A Study in Typical Jewish Attitudes towards Greek Philosophy in the Middle Ages

I

WHAT most characteristically distinguishes Jews and Greeks, is their respective views of life. That of the former was ethical, that of the latter was cosmological. Of course, neither was exclusive. In the process of the development of their respective ideas, Jews became interested in cosmology and Greeks in ethics. Rabbis of the Mishnic era assiduously cultivated cosmological studies (מעשה בראשית), and Greek philosophy ever since Socrates was for the most part ethical. Yet the emphasis has always been laid on the point of view with which they started. Jewish cosmology has always been ethical, while Greek ethics has always been cosmological.

The Jews beheld nature subjectively, and based their view of life on the inner experience, taken as produced by the response of their selves to the external world rather than on the flat observation of the external world itself. The flux of nature, sweeping over their spirit, stirred its chords to feelings pleasant or unpleasant, and out of these notes, registering the impact, they constructed their life-view. Thunder, lightning, and death were not for them merely physical events; nor was it the tremendous noise, the flashing light, and the sudden disappearance of life that they dwelt upon. Their concern was the shocking, dazzling, and terrifying effects of these phenomena upon their minds. All natural phenomena appeared to them as either physically good or bad, pleasing or painful. But things appeared to them not merely as physically good or bad but also as morally good or bad. Death, they recognized, is bad, and life is good; but why, they also asked, is murder more terrible than natural death, and why is the saving of another's life a pleasure to the saver? By putting this question, they realized the existence of moral good and evil, and began to judge things in these terms. So by means of introspection rather than inspection, from *their* version of the world rather than its own version of itself, the Jews developed their organized ethical view of life.[1]

The Greeks, on the other hand, beheld life objectively. They beheld things as they are, without their relation to man and his visions, fears and pleasures. True, the external world produces images in man's mind, stirs up his passions, rouses in him sadness and joy, but these are merely transitory moods and feelings, discovered only by introspection, by absorption in one's self, by digging into one's own nature—acts essentially alien to the spirit of Hellas. The Greek liked to observe the external world rather than to pour forth his soul. There was much in the nature of his country, in its skies and soil, to attract his attention to the world around him. What he saw in the world was a variety of forms with a common background. Life was a chain of interlacing links. Things were necessarily regenerations, producing other things, and events were leading,

[1] See D. Neumark, השקפת העולם והשקפת החיים, in השלח, XI.

according to law, to other events. This objective appreciation of orderly process gave rise to Hellenic cosmology.

The different points of view, from which Jews and Greeks beheld the world, involved a difference in their conception of reality. What is real, the stable or the changeful, the constant or the flux? The Jews who beheld life subjectively, as it had reflected itself in their own consciousness, saw in it only change and instability, for consciousness is a stream, and the pulse of life is never at rest. Furthermore, their feelings, moods, and states of mind, i. e. their inner reflection of the external world, are a chaotic disorder, capriciously changing without warning. Hence, reality, their consciousness of the world, was conceived by them as in flux. The Greeks, on the contrary, beholding the world objectively, saw the law and order existing in it, the principles governing natural phenomena, the perfect arrangement of the parts of the universe and their harmonic unity of interadaptation. Hence, reality was for them that observable unity, order, and stability of the world. These opposing conceptions of reality have been well summarized by Dr. H. M. Kallen in a recent paper on the subject. "For the Greeks, change is unreal and evil; for the Hebrews the essence of reality is change. The Greek view of reality is static and structural; the Hebrew view is dynamic and functional. The Hebrew saw the world as a history. For them the inwardness of reality lay in the movement of events. The Greeks saw the world as an immutable hierarchy of forms; for them the reality was the inert order of being."

A primary implication of these contrasting conceptions of reality, is the contrast in the conceived nature of divinity. When the Jews began to think of God, asking: "Would you suppose that the palace has no master?"[2] they inferred that "there must be an eye that sees and an ear that listens,"[3] and that the seeing eye and the hearing ear is God. This God moreover, is neither outside the world nor the world itself. God is the dynamic essence of the world, life, reality, *natura naturans.* God is reality, and as reality consists in the change of events, so God is changeful. And He is not changed by His own will but by the will and actions of men. "Said the God of Israel, I rule over men, who rules over Me?—The righteous; for I issue a decree, and the righteous man cancels it."[4] God's anger is kindled at the evil doings of men, but He regrets the evil He intended to bring upon them, as soon as they improve their ways. The relation between God and man is personal and mutual. "Return to Me and I will return to you."[5] God appears to man under different forms. He appeared "on the Red Sea as a warrior making war, at Sinai as a Scribe teaching the Law, in the days of Solomon as a young man, and in the days of Daniel as an old man full of mercy."[6] But above all God is the heavenly father. "Go and tell them: 'If you come to me, are you not coming to your heavenly father?' "[7]

The conception of God among the Greeks was of quite a different nature. With the exception of Socrates, whose

[2] תאמר שהבירה הזו בלא מנהיג, Gen. r., c. 39.

[3] יש עין רואה ואזן שומעת, Abot. 2, 1,

[4] אני מושל באדם מי מושל בי צדיק שאני גוזר גזרה והוא מבטלה, Moed ḳaṭan 16*b*.

[5] Mal. 3, 7.

[6] לפי שנראה להם הקב"ה בים כגבור עושה מלחמה ובסיני כסופר מלמד תורה ונראה להם בימי שלמה כבחור ובימי דניאל כזקן מלא רחמים וכו׳, Tanḥuma, יתרו.

[7] לך אמור להם, אִם אתם באים לא אצל אביכם שבשמים אתם באים, Pesiḳta derabbi Kahana, 25.

theology was independent of his philosophy, all Greek philosophers identify God with some logical or metaphysical term. To Plato God is identical with the Good, a mere term of discourse, without life and personality. If Plato did not explicitly deny the personality of God, as did Spinoza, it was because he never raised that question; he took it as a matter of fact.[8] The God of Aristotle again, does not come into contact with the sublunary world. "God is the *primum mobile* only in so far as he is the absolute end of the world, the governor, as it were, whose will all obey, but who never sets his own hand to the work."[9] In fact, the relation of Aristotle's God to the world constitutes for scholarship one of the problems of his metaphysics. It is, however, clear that the nature of Aristotle's deity consists of unceasing sleepless contemplation and absolutely perfect activity, an activity that cannot alter, since to a perfect being alteration would involve a loss of perfection.[10] "Evidently then, it thinks that which is most divine and precious, and it does not change; for change would be change for the worse, and this would be already a movement."[11] "Therefore it must be itself that thought thinks, and its thinking is a thinking on thinking."[12] Thus by confirming the function of the Divine Reason to a monotonous self-contemplation, not quickened into life by any change or development, Aristotle merges the notion of personality in a mere abstraction.[13]

The original diversity between the Hebraic and the Hellenic views of being becomes still more patent in their

[8] Zeller, Outline of the Hist. of Greek Phil., Eng. Tr., § 49.

[9] Zeller, Aristotle and the Earlier Peripatetics, Eng. Tr., I, 405.

[10] Zeller, *ibid.*, 397.

[11] Aristotle, Metaphys., XII, 9.

[12] Aristotle, *ibid.*

[13] Zeller, Aristotle and the Earlier Peripat., I, 402.

ideals of conduct and the end of life. The Jews who had a theory of creation as opposed to the Greek philosophical doctrine of the eternity of matter, the Highest Good was not that to which all things aim to reach but that for the sake of which all things had been created. Now, the purpose of creation has indisputably been declared to be the Torah (תורה). "But for the Torah, heaven and earth would not have existed."[14] Everything in the world was created according to the prescriptions of the Torah. "The Holy One looked in the Torah while creating the world."[15] Hence the Torah is the most adequate guide for human life, for it is the most relevant to human nature. Since "the Laws have been given for the purpose of refining men through them,[16] and since these laws can be realized only in a social organization, the perfect organization of society, based on the precepts of the Torah, is the Highest Good. The task of the individual is to adjust himself to such a social status, to obey the Torah, and thereby to contribute his share to the collectively integrated righteous society. But mere obedience, mere formality, mere practicing of virtue is not sufficient. The individual is not perfect unless the divine virtues, the formal code of ethics, become the acts of his inmost conscience, the spontaneous expression of his nature. "What God wants is the heart."[17] and "when a man performs his duties he shall perform them with a joyful heart."[18] The test of individual perfection is the perfect harmony or coincidence of his con-

[14] אלמלא תורה לא נתקימו שמים וארץ, Pesaḥim 65*b*.

[15] הקב"ה היה מביט בתורה ובורא העולם, Gen. r., c. 1.

[16] לא נתנו מצות אלא לצרף בהן את הבריות, Gen. r., c. 47; Tanḥuma, שמיני.

[17] הקב"ה לבא בעי, Sanhedrin 106*b*.

[18] כשיהא אדם עשה מצוה יהא עושה בלב שמח, Levit. r., c. 34.

science with his deeds and the residing joy therein. "Whenever a man is satisfied with his own right conduct, it is a good omen for him; whenever a man is not satisfied with his own conduct, it is a bad omen for him."[19] The perfect man is the *"Beautiful Soul,"* beautiful because his instinct and righteousness coincide.

To the Greeks, on the other hand, the Highest Good resides in the individual, in the perfection of all his mental and physical qualities and in the attainment of the supreme good of rationality. The state is, of course, necessary, for the faculties essential to the excellence of the individual have in the state their only opportunity of development. But the state as such is not an end but an instrument. "It is perhaps better for the wise man in his speculation to have fellow-workers; but nevertheless he is in the highest degree self-sufficient."[20] And virtues are also merely means of conducing to happiness, in themselves neither good nor bad. "Thus, in place of a series of hard and fast rules, a rigid and uncompromising distinction of acts and affections into good and bad, the former to be absolutely chosen and the latter absolutely eschewed, Aristotle presents us with the general type of a subtle and shifting problem, the solution of which must be worked out afresh by each individual in each particular case."[21] The highest individual perfection is speculative wisdom, the excellence of that purely intellectual part called reason.[22]

[19] כל שרוח עצמו נוחה בשלו סימן יפה לו; אין רוח עצמו נוחה בשלו סימן רע לו, Tosefta Berakot 3, 4.

[20] Aristotle, Ethics, X, 7.

[21] Dickinson, Greek View of Life, 136.

[22] Comp. Aristotle, Ethics, I, 6.

"The speculative is the only activity which is loved for its own sake as it has no result except speculation."[23]

These, then, present the most obvious distinctions between the Jewish and the Greek insight. In the first place there was the distinction in their idea of God, who, according to the Jews, was the living One, personally related to man, and who, according to the Greek philosophers, was the Prime Mover, existing outside the world. Then, there was the distinction in their ethical system. To the Jew the aim of life was to live happily as a member of the total polity. To the Greek the essence of man is to be rational. Virtues are good in so far as they conduce to the highest good; and society likewise is merely a means to facilitate man's reaching the Highest Good.

The struggle between these two views of life, which began with the Jews' coming in contact with Greek civilization and resulted on the one hand in Philo's Neo-Platonism and on the other hand in Pauline Christianity, was renewed in the tenth century among the Jews of the Mohammedan countries. The intrusion of Greek philosophical ideas into Jewish thought, chiefly through Arabic channels, gave rise to the need of a new reconciliation between Judaism and Hellenism. The attempt to satisfy that need resulted in the creation of a religious philosophy which, though different from Philo's in content, was very much like it in spirit and general outlook. Like Philo, the philosophers of the Middle Ages aimed at reconciling Jewish religion with Greek philosophy, by recasting the substance of the former in the form of the latter. The principles upon which they worked were (1) that the practical religious organization of Jewish life must be pre-

[23] *Ibid.*, X, 7.

served, but (2) that they must be justified and defended in accordance with the principles of Greek philosophy. Thus Hellenic theory was to bolster Hebraic dogma, and Greek speculation became the basis for Jewish conduct. The carrying out of this programme, therefore, unlike that of Pauline Christianity, involved neither change in the practice of the religion, nor abrogation of the Law. There was simply a shifting of emphasis from the practical to the speculative element of religion. Philo and the mediæval philosophers continued to worship God in the Jewish fashion, but their conception of God became de-Judaized. They continued to commend the observation of the Law, but this observation lost caste and became less worthy than the "theoretic life." Practice and theory fell apart logically; instead there arose an artificial parallelism of theoretic with practical obligations.

As against this tendency to subordinate Judaism to Hellenic speculation, there arose a counter-movement in mediæval Jewish philosophy which aimed to find in Judaism itself satisfaction for the theoretical as well as the practical interest. This movement developed a school which, though appreciative of the virtues of Aristotelianism, still saw their difference in temper and attitude toward life and considered any attempt at reconciliation as a mere dallying with meanings distorted by abstraction from their contexts. As this school aimed to justify Judaism by its own principles, it sought to indicate its characteristic features, and to assert its right to autonomous intellectual existence, the peer of Hellenism, because of its very diversity therefrom. Consequently, the work of this school has a double character. It had, on the one hand, to criticise Greek philosophy and undermine the common belief of its contemporaries in its absolute truth, and, on the other hand, it had to differentiate and define the Jewish position.

Of the Hellenizers in Judaism, the most typical representative is Moses Maimonides (1135-1204); of the Hebraizers, Judah Halevi (1085?-1140?). These two men represent the opposite poles of Jewish thought in the Middle Ages. Maimonides is a true convert to Aristotelian philosophy. To him the thorough understanding of Aristotle is the highest achievement to which man can attain. Halevi, on the contrary, is full of doubts about the truth of Aristotle's theories, "which can be established by arguments which are partially satisfactory, and still much less capable of being proved."[24] Maimonides is ruled by reason, nothing is true which is not rational, his interest is mainly logical. Halevi is ruled by feeling and sentiment, full of scepticism as to the validity of reason, and he is chiefly interested in ethics. Maimonides' chief philosophic work, "Moreh Nebukim (מורה נבוכים)"[25] is a formal, impersonal treatment of his philosophy. Halevi's "Kuzari" (כוזרי) [26] is written in dialogue and its problems are attacked not *more scholastico* but in the more spontaneous literary and intense fashion of Job. Maimonides' chief contribution besides his "Moreh" was the codification of the talmudic Law; Halevi's chief work besides the "Kuzari," was the composition of synagogal hymns of highly lyrical quality.

In point of time, Halevi preceded Maimonides. Yet in comparing them we must treat Halevi as the critic of the tendency which Maimonides represented, the tendency

[24] Kuzari I, 13.

[25] Guide of the Perplexed, Eng. Tr. by Friedländer.

[26] Translated into English by Hirschfeld under title of "Kitab al Khazari."

which began long before Halevi and reached its climax in Maimonides. Maimonides may be considered as swimming with the stream, he was the expression of his age; Halevi was swimming against the stream, he was the insurgent, the utterer of paradoxes. Halevi does not criticise any specific system of philosophy. The system portrayed in the opening of the "Kuzari," is a medley of distorted views of Aristotle and Neo-Platonism. But the "Kuzari" is a criticism of philosophy in general, of the philosophic method and temper of Halevi's time, and especially of the universal attempt to identify it with theology and religion.

II

In the introduction to the "Moreh Nebukim" Maimonides describes the book's aim. He intends it "to afford a guide for the perplexed, to thinkers whose studies have brought them into collision with religion, who have studied philosophy and have acquired sound knowledge, and who, while firm in religious matters, are perplexed and bewildered on account of the ambiguous and figurative expressions employed in the holy writings." He does not, however, examine the views of the philosophers with the object of supporting the Jewish traditional interpretation of religious principles. His aim is solely to show that Scriptures and Talmud, correctly interpreted, strictly harmonize with the philosophical writings of Aristotle.

Starting with Aristotle's metaphysics, Maimonides attempts to demonstrate that the scriptural "God" does not differ from the "Prime Cause" of the philosophers. But here he encounters a great difficulty. It had been held by the conservative theologians of Maimonides' time, that the conception of God as Cause necessitates the belief in the eternity of matter, for if we were to say that God is the Cause, the co-existence of the Cause with that which was produced by that Cause would necessarily be implied; this again involves the belief that the universe is eternal, and that it is inseparable from God."[27] On the other hand, when we say that God is *agens,* the co-existence of the *agens* with its product is not implied, for the *agens* may exist anterior to its product. Maimonides who rejected Aristotle's doctrine of the eternity of matter on purely dialectical grounds, wishing, however, to identify "God" with the "Cause," had to show that the latter view does not necessarily imply the former. His argument is this. If you take terms "cause" and *"agens"* in the sense of reality, then both terms must necessarily imply the co-existence of the world with God, for God would be called neither *"agens"* nor "cause" in reality before the actual making of the world began. On the other hand, if you take terms "cause" and *"agens"* in the sense of a mere potentiality, then in both cases God preceded the world, for God was potentially both the Cause and the *agens* of the world even before it came into being. Therefore the term "cause" and *"agens"* are identical. The reason why Aristotle calls God "the Cause," says Maimonides, is to be sought not in his belief that the universe is eternal, but in another motive; it is "in order to express that God unites in Himself three of the four causes, viz., that He is the *agens,* the form, and the final cause of the universe."[28]

Maimonides adds to his adaptation of Aristotle's conception of God, also an adaptation of Aristotelian cosmological and logical proofs of God's existence. The unso-

[27] *Moreh Neb.* I, 69.

[28] *Moreh Neb.,* I, 69, and comp. translator's note about the application of the material cause to God.

phisticated Jews, to whom God was the power and the behavior of the universe, felt no need of proof that He exists. To them His existence was self-evident, for His power manifested itself in all the works of nature. "God said to Moses: Do you want to know My name?—I am designated by My actions."[29] But when Maimonides conceived God as a metaphysical, transcendent entity, proofs of His existence became necessary. Divine actions, according to Maimonides, are merely names used to symbolize God's nature, the only instruments of description that are available. They do not signify His existence in *propria persona;* that must be proved logically and cosmologically. The arguments, moreover, must demonstrate not only that God exists, but also that it is impossible that He should not exist.

God's existence is demonstrated in the proof of the necessity for a Prime Mover. But another difficulty comes. The Bible contains many anthropomorphisms which describe the mode of action of the Divine Being. The question arises whether they are applied to the Deity and to other things in one and the same sense, or equivocally. Maimonides accepts the latter view and seeks carefully to define the meaning of each term taken as an attribute of God, and to give it a transcendental, or metaphysical significance. Maimonides is very strict in this respect. He does not admit the propriety of assigning attributes to God. God is absolute, His existence, His life, and His knowledge are absolute, and there can never be new elements in Him. Consequently, God exists, lives, and knows without possessing the attributes of existence, life, and knowledge. The only way of defining Him is by negative attributes.

[29] שמי אתה חפץ לידע לפי מעשי אני נקרא, Exod. r., c. 3.

You can tell what He is not, but you cannot tell what He is. All we can discover about God is that He is. "In the contemplation of His Essence, our comprehension and knowledge prove insufficient; in the examination of His works, how they necessarily result from His will, our knowledge proves to be ignorance, and in the endeavor to extol Him in words, all our efforts in speech are mere weakness and failure."[40]

With this, however, Maimonides' idea of God comes to a vanishing point. The highest that a man can obtain of the true essence of God is to know that He is unknowable. And the more conscious one becomes of his ignorance of God, the nearer to God he draws, "for just as each additional attribute renders objects more concrete, and brings them nearer the true apprehension of the observer, so each additional negative attribute advances you to the knowledge of God. By its means you are nearer this knowledge than he who does not negate in reference to God, those qualities, which you are convincecd by proofs must be negated."[31] God cannot be the object of human apprehension, none but Himself comprehends what He is; hence men should not indulge in excessive prayer to God. "It is more becoming to be silent, and to be content with intellectual reflection, as has been recommended by men of highest culture, in the words, "Commune with your own heart upon your bed, and be still (Ps. 4, 4),"[32] "We cannot approve of those foolish persons who are extravagant in praise, fluent and prolix in the prayers they compose and in the hymns they make in their desire to approach the Creator."[33]

[30] *Moreh Neb.*, I, 69.

[31] *Ibid.*

[32] *Ibid.*

[33] *Moreh Neb.*, I, 69.

An Aristotelian, though with limitations, in metaphysics, Maimonides is also an Aristotelian in ethics. Though Maimonides accepts the theory of creation *ex nihilo,* he nevertheless agrees with Aristotle that there is no occasion to inquire into the purpose of the existence of the universe.[34] He considers the question of cosmic purpose as futile. No adequate answer, he argues, can be adduced. Even if we admit that the universe exists for man's sake and man exists for the purpose of serving God, the question remains, What is the end of serving God? God does not become more perfect; and if the service of God is intended for our own perfection, then the question might be repeated, What is the object of being perfect? The question must, therefore, be left unanswered, for "we must in continuing the inquiry as to the purpose of the creation at last arrive at the answer, It was the will of God, or His wisdom decreed it."[34]

But within the limits of the universe as it exists now, the immediate purpose of all things is man, for we notice that in the "course of genesis and destruction" every individual thing strives to reach "its greatest possible perfection," and since "it is clear that man is the most perfect being formed of matter," "in this respect it can hardly be said that all earthly things exist for man."[35]

We may, however, still ask: What is the end of man? Whereto Maimonides replies, with Aristotle, that the end of man is the perfection of his specific form. But there are four varieties of perfection.[36] The earliest in the order of excellence, is perfection in respect of worldly possess-

[34] *Moreh Neb.,* III, 13.
[35] *Moreh Neb.,* III, 13.
[36] *Moreh Neb.,* III, 64.

ions; the next is perfection in respect of physical beauty and well-being. The third is moral perfection, the highest degree of excellence in character. None of these is the ultimate perfection of man, for ultimate perfection is complete self-sufficiency. How clearly Maimonides here follows the Hellenic tradition is obvious. He takes the individual as unit of supreme excellence, self-sufficient both with regard to other values and with regard to other men. None of these three orders of moral adequacy are self-sufficient with regard to both relations. The first and second perfections are self-sufficient with regard to other persons, for they would exist even if the universe contained only one man, but they are insufficient as regards other values, for when a man has wealth and health, they become merely means conducing to other values. Even moral perfection, virtue, is not self-sufficient, for all principles of conduct concern the relation of man to his neighbor. "Imagine a person being alone, and having no connection whatever with any other person, all his good moral principles are at rest, they are not required, and contribute to man no perfection whatever."[37] They are, therefore, only necessary and useful when man comes into relation with others. Hence self-sufficiency is external to all these, for it must involve no external conditions; it must depend upon nothing but itself. It is to be found in the perfection of the intellect, the development of the loftiest intellectual faculties, the possession of such notions which lead to true metaphysical opinions about God. "With this perception (the right view of God) man has obtained his final object; it gives him true human perception; it remains

[37] *Moreh Neb.*, III, 60.

to him alone; it gives him immortality; and on its account he is called man."[38]

Thus the highest perfection of man consists in his becoming an "actually intelligent being." The acts conducing to that are the virtues. Acts are, therefore, in themselves neither good nor bad; their moral value is determined by their furthering or preventing the Highest Perfection. Hence there is no virtue in doing righteousness for its own sake. "The multitude who observe the divine commandments, but are ignorant, never enter the royal palace."[39] Not only are virtues for their own sake unimportant, but they are not even the best means of reaching the Highest Perfection. Speculation and knowledge will lead to it sooner than practice and right conduct. "Of these two ways—knowledge and conduct—the one, the communication of correct opinions, comes undoubtedly first in rank."[40] "For the Highest Perfection certainly does not include any action or good conduct, but only knowledge, which is arrived at by speculation, or established by research."[41]

"But one cannot procure all this; it is impossible for a single man to obtain this comfort; it is only possible in society, since man, as it is well known, is by nature social."[42] Hence the object of society is to provide the conditions favorable to the production of "actually intelligent men." All mankind live only for the few who can reach the Highest Perfection, just as all earthly beings exist for men. "Common men exist for two reasons; first.

[38] *Ibid.*

[39] *Moreh Neb.*, III, 51.

[40] *Moreh Neb.*, III, 27.

[41] *Ibid.*

[42] *Ibid.*

to do the work that is needed in the state in order that the actually intelligent man should be provided with all his wants and be able to pursue his studies; second, to accompany the wise lest they feel lonely, since the number of wise men is small."[43]

It is on the basis of this ethical system that Maimonides evaluates the Jewish Law. In its speculative part the Law contains Aristotle's metaphysics couched in language suitable for the intelligence of the common people. In its practical part, it is a scheme of a social organization planned to produce "actually intelligent beings." That the practice of the Law will not alone conduce to the Highest Perfection, we have already seen. That must be reached by reason. But Maimonides argues that such practice is meant to prepare the environment favorable to the attainment of the perfection of self-sufficiency. Hence religion and tradition are not superior to reason, for God who endowed man with reason, so that he might reach the Highest Perfection, would not demand of him deeds contrary to this God-given reason. No man, hence, must believe in anything contrary to reason, even though he may see miracles, "for reason that denies the testimony is more reliable than his eye that witnesses the miracles."[43]

Such a view, it is clear, could hardly be more Hellenic and still save even a semblance of Judaism. Maimonides was not a rabbi employing Greek logic and categories of thought in order to interpret Jewish religion; he was rather a true mediæval Aristotelian, using Jewish religion as an illustration of the Stagirite's metaphysical supremacy. Maimonides adheres staunchly to the Law, or course, but

[43] Introduction to סדר זרעים; see also אחד העם, שלטון השכל in השלח, XV.

his adherence is not the logical consequence of his system. It has its basis in his heredity and practical interests; it is not the logical implication of his philosophy. Judaism designated the established social order of life, in which Maimonides lived and moved and had his being; and it was logically as remote from his intellectual interests as he was historically remote from Aristotle. That, naturally, he was unaware of the dualism must be clear. Indeed, he thought he had made a synthesis, and had given scientific demonstrations of poetic conceptions. Therein he was like the Italian priest and astronomer Angelo Secchi, who, while performing his religious services, dropped Copernican astronomy, and, while in the observatory, dropped his church doctrines. Maimonides really saw no incompatibility between his Judaism and his philosophy; he was a Jew in letter and philosopher in spirit throughout his life. As a rationalist he could not but consider that religion and philosophy, both of which seemed reasonable to him, were identical. No doubt it was Moses ben Maimon whom Joseph ben Shem Tob had in mind when he wrote that in spite of the identification by Jewish philosophers, of the contemplative life with the obedience of the Law, that obedience was still assigned as the road to salvation of the common people, while contemplation was reserved for the select theorizers.[44]

[44] אמר יוסף ומפני שראו חכמי עמנו אשר עינו בפילוסופיא כי ההצלחה האחרונה היא בהשלמת האדם במעלות המדות ובמעלות השכליות וראו מופת אריסטו שהמדות בעבור השכליות כמו שהתבאר וחשבו שהשגת ההשארות הוא בהצלחה וההצלחה התבארה בפילוסופיא ושהתורה תיעד יעוד רוחני כמו שהתפרש מענייננה וקבלו שהמביא אל ההצלהה אי אפשר בדרכים מתחלפים במין ובמהות ושחשבו שדרכי התורה ודרכי הפילוסופיה אחדות במין ויתחלפו בענין הלמוד כי התורה להיותה לרבים והם עמי הארץ אשר לא ידעו משפט המושכלות ולא נתפרדו מהמוח היה מחויב שתהיה למודה למוד כולל כל עדת האנשים והסתרים רמוזים בה

III

Diametrically opposed to Maimonides, in insight, in conception of life and destiny, is Judah Halevi. In his discussion of God, His existence, His nature and His relation to the world, Halevi displays, for his time, a remarkable freshness and originality of view. In a period when Hellenic thought dominated Jewish and Arabic intellect, he was, though as familiar with it as the closest student of the Greeks, remarkably free of its influence. He sees clearly, in contradistinction to most Jewish thinkers of his time, the essential differences between the Jewish and the Greek ideas of God, of conduct and of human destiny. From Philo to Maimonides, Jewish dialecticians were intent upon thinning the concrete formalism of the biblical God to the abstract and tenuous formalism of the Aristotelian Prime Mover. They reduced differences, so far as they could, to expression and terminology, and sought to eliminate whatever more fundamental diversity there remained by explaining it away. They failed to note the tremendous scope of the diversity, how it reached down into the very nature and temperaments of people and spread to the unbounded cosmos itself. Halevi alone among the philosophizing rabbis recognized the ineradicable reality of the difference, and pointed out with unmistakable clearness the essential distinctions between the Prime Mover of the Greeks and God of the Jews.

The Kuzari, a dialogue between the King of the Chazars and a rabbi, in which these views of Halevi's are developed, is not a systematic philosophical work. Its order is conversational rather than structural, and it is less allied

.והפלוסופיא למוד מסוגל למורגלים בהשגת הדברים הבלתי מבוארים בתחלת הדעת

Joseph b. Shemṭob. כבוד אלהים, Ferrara 1555.

to Plato than to Job. The ideas suggest more than they express; they carry the conviction of insight rather the force of demonstration. Halevi is less explicit than Maimonides, less careful about making manifest implication of his system. He needs more interpretation than the other. He and those who think like him are genuinely Hebraic. They repudiate the Hellenizing tendency which, to them, vitiates Jewish thought, and they do so often with a critical acumen that anticipates the controversy between the eternalists and the temporalists of our times.

For the Jews, Halevi argues, God is an efficient cause; for the Greeks He is a final cause. Hellenism accepts God as the inert and excellent form of reality; Judaism demands an efficacious relation between man and the personal ground of the Universe. "The philosopher only seeks Him that he may be able to describe Him accurately in detail, as he would describe the earth, explaining that it is in the center of the great sphere, but not in that of the zodiac."[45] The religionist seeks God "not only for the sake of knowing Him, but also for the great benefits which they derive therefrom,"[45] for to them God is a personal, spiritual *guide* in the world. To the philosopher, "ignorance of God would be more injurious than would ignorance concerning the earth be injurious to those who consider it flat;"[45] God has no pragmatic significance for them; He makes no difference in their life and action. To the religionist, ignorance of God implies a difference in one's life. To the philosopher God is merely a logical necessity, a final link, arbitrarily chosen to terminate the otherwise endless chain of potentiality and actuality. "We cannot blame philosophers for missing the mark, since they only arrived at this

[45] Kuzari IV, 13.

knowledge by way of speculation, and the result could not have been different."[45] To the religionist, God is the satisfying object, an inner need, without whom man cannot dwell upon the earth. When the religionist begins to doubt the existence of God, there is a sudden disruption of all of life's values, and there ensues a state of suspense in which any positive action is impossible. The God of religion is not arrived at by dialectic procedures and the operations of logic. Knowledge of Him is empirical and uncriticised personal and human experience. Judah Halevi further expounds the distinction by the different uses of the two divine names, אלהים and יהוה. So early as in the talmudic times, rabbis had distinguished between the meanings of these two names. אלהים, they held, expresses the quality of justice (דין), the unchangeable laws of nature, while יהוה expresses God's quality of mercy (רחמים), the God who stands in personal relations with man.[46] Halevi, probably drawing on this ancient commentary, elaborates its intent, by using אלהים to designate the philosophical idea of God, and by יהוה the religious. "The meaning of אלהים can be grasped by way of speculation, because a Guide and a Manager of the world is a postulate of reason. The meaning of יהוה, however, cannot be grasped by speculation, but only by that intuition and prophetic vision which separates man from his kind and brings him into contact with angelic beings, imbuing him with a new spirit."[47]

The philosophic God, being merely *a postulate of reason,* is not as inspiring to, as influential in, human action as is the God of a living religion. Truly, the philosopher after

[46] בכל מקום שנאמר ה' מדת הרחמים בכ"מ שנאמר אלהים מדת הדין, Gen. r., c. 33.

[47] Kuzari IV, 14.

ascertaining by speculation the existence of an absolute remote God, acquires a veneration for that absolute Being of his. Rigid dialectic may be merely the starting point, but having once left that starting point, the philosopher may be as full of veneration for his God as the religionist for his. In the opening of the Kuzari, the philosopher speaks about his "veneration of the Prime Cause."[48] Yet, there exists a wide difference between philosophical and religious veneration. The philosopher's veneration is merely an attitude, having no real object for its content. It is merely a psychological phenomenon, akin to the love of the artist toward his handiwork. The veneration of the religionist is directed toward a specific object; it has its source in something external to man; it is the love of the creature to its creator.[49] "Now, I understand how far the God of Abraham is different from that of Aristotle."[50] "Man yearns for the Jewish God as a matter of taste and conviction," hence the religious attitude is native and inherent in man, whilst attachment to אלהים is the result of speculation,"[50] and the attitudinal quality is merelf acquired. The religionist's veneration for his God, being innate is of lifelong duration, it is a part of his constitution, he lives for his God. To the philosopher, feeling for the divine is a temporal interest which lives besides other interests, but is not in spite of them; it disappears as soon as it becomes discordant with other interests. "A feeling of the former kind (i. e. the constitutional) invites its votaries to give their life for His sake, and to prefer death to His absence. Speculation, however, makes veneration only a necessity as

[48] I, 1.

[49] אבל זאת האהבה היא אהבת העשוי לעושהו, Joseph b. Shemṭob, כבוד ה׳.

[50] Kuzari IV, 16.

long as it entails no harm, but bears no pain for its sake.[51] There is also a difference in the vital function of these diverse apprehensions of divinity. Since the religious attitude arises from inner vision, it is active, it determines man's life, it shapes his deeds, it moulds his destiny. The veneration of theory, on the contrary, is passive, it is led and shaped by the residual man, it has no efficacy, and is attached to no efficacious object. Indeed, it is, perhaps, ignorant of virtue and is certainly no justification for it. "I would excuse Aristotle," Halevi makes the rabbi say, "for thinking lightly about the observation of the Law, since he doubts whether God has any cognizance thereof."[51]

Such then are the differences between God of philosophy and God of positive religion, and the attitudes they evoke. But practice may be based on illusion, and inactivity may yet be truth. Which, then, of these opposed conceptions has the greater stronghold in truth? For which, asks Halevi, is there more evidence? His answer is empirical and pragmatic. The truer is that which is warranted by the experience of the many and which serves human purposes most adequately. The conception of a transcendent Deity is intelligible only to a few, to select ones, to those who are trained in the art of metaphysical speculation. The mass of the people do not understand such a God, they do not understand Him in spite of all the eloquence, all the ratiocination of philosophers. If the latter reply, "What of that? Truth has its own justification, regardless of its intelligibility or unintelligibility to the common masses," they must recall that one of the proofs they themselves offer of God's existence is its universal acknowledgment by men. They claim that the existence of God is deduced from

[51] Kuzari IV, 16.

reflection upon self-revealing traces of the divine nature in the presentiments of the soul, in the conscience of the human mind.[52] But these presentiments are against the philosophers. The presentiments of the soul are not of the existence of a Prime Mover, of a God who, having once started the motion of the world, has left it to its own fate. They are indications of the existence of a God who is guiding the world, who is taking active part in its machinery. Men call Him "God of the land, because he possesses a special power in its air, soil and climate, which in connexion with the tilling of the ground, assists in improving the species."[53] This is what all mankind have a presentiment of, and for this reason they are so obedient to religious teachers. "The soul finds satisfaction in their teachings in spite of the simplicity of their speech and ruggedness of their similes,"[53] while philosophers have never been able to attract the attention of the people. "With their eloquence and fine teachings, however great the impressiveness of their arguments, the masses of the people do not follow them, because the human soul has a presentiment of the truth, as it is said: 'The words of truth will be recognized.' "[53]

As dialectic is a perversion of inner experience coming immediately and empirically, so the argument from design is a perversion of empirical fact. The world has beauty and its parts are harmoniously connected. This points, according to the philosophers, to a Being placed far above the world, from whom alone its simple movement and admirable coördination proceed.[54] Halevi denies the total allegation. The philosophers are mistaken in their descrip-

[52] See Zeller, Aristotle and the Earlier Perip., I, 300, and notes.

[53] Kuzari IV, 17.

[54] See Zeller, Aristotle and the Earlier Peripatetics, I, 391, and note 2.

tion of the world. The world is not one and harmonious, and its parts do not hang together according to fixed and eternal laws. The world is a chaos, whose sole and miraculous unifying principle is a supreme Will, which is itself unstable and capriciously changing. The world is full of "miracles and the changing of ordinary, things newly arising, or changing one into another."[55] The philosophers fail to observe the irreversible flux and change which permeates nature, because they project their own mental traits therein, and unify the natural diversity through the instrumentality of their intellects. "And this abstract speculation which made for eternity prevailed, and he found no need to inquire into the chronology or derivation of those who lived before him."[56] Thus the unified nature which philosophers speak of is merely an artifact, the result of conceiving it in analogy with the soul. And this speculative nature has been substituted by philosophers for nature as she is.

Moreover, the argument from design is no proof for the existence of God. The order of the universe, if there is any, need not be a created order. Harmony, beauty and unity, the teleologic architectonic need no explanation. They are necessarily self-explaining, for they contain nothing problematic. If the possibility of change and the creation of *new* things in nature be not granted, then "thy opponent and thou might agree that a vine e. g. grew in this place because a seed happens to have fallen here."[57] If there were no changes in nature, if the world presented no difficult situations, man would never think of God. What rouses questions in our mind, what needs explana-

[55] Kuzari I, 67.

[56] *Ibid.*, 65.

[57] Kuzari V, 7.

tions, is the discord and change in nature. These cannot be explained but by the presupposition of a Supreme Guide, for whom "evidence is found in changes of nature."[57] "It is these that prove the existence of a creator of the world who can accomplish everything."[58]

In addition to the evidence of novelty, i. e. spontaneity in nature, Judah Halevi presents another proof for the existence of God; this is the history of human experience. Like Socrates, Halevi considers that real science is not physics but ethics. He regards personality and the relation of persons to one another as the essence of reality. But he goes further than Socrates; he takes as the basis of his science not the conduct of individuals but the conduct of humanity in history. He accuses the Greeks of lacking historic sense, of considering the history of each man as beginning with himself.[59] Therein he is quite the antithesis of the Greek philosophers. The latter reflected upon the purposiveness of nature but saw no teleology in the flux of history; Halevi, on the other hand, denies the purposiveness of nature, but asserts the onward march of history to a clearly-defined end. "Generations come and generations go," and yet history seems to have a purpose; human destiny seems to be guided by some pre-defined plan. God is not the God of the universe only; He is the God of human destiny. This view is stated quaintly, chiefly by use of illustrations drawn from the Bible. "Moses said to Pharaoh: 'The God of Abraham, Isaac and Jacob,' but he did not say: 'The God of heaven and earth,' nor 'My creator

[58] Kuzari I, 67.

[59] Comp. Kuzari I, 63.

and thine sent me.' "[60] "In the same way God commenced His speech to the assembled people of Israel: 'I am the God whom you worship, who led you out of the land of Egypt,' but He did not say: 'I am the creator of the world and your creator.' "[60] A review of the experiences of the human race reveals enough empirical evidence to prove the existence of a Supreme Being guiding human actions.

The experience of the race would be sufficient, but private experience, Halevi thinks, also reveals the existence of God. The use of private religious experience as proof was, of course, in vogue among the Arabic philosophers of Halevi's time. Arisen among the mystic sect of the Sufis, it had been rendered by the powerful arguments of Ghazali the accepted proof of Moslem theology. Halevi makes use of the term personal experience in a sense somewhat different and wider than that given it by Moslem divines. He does not mean the personal experience of the individual generated by certain conditions of mind and body. He means personal experience as revelation or intuition. It is objectively perceptive and contains nothing "mystical." Thus the revelation on Mount Sinai was nothing more or less than the personal experience of the entire Jewish congregation. Not all other religions, hence, are in true sense revealed religions, because the revelation was not to the whole people, severally and collectively. The other religions depend chiefly on the veracity and authority of a single individual whose experience has been conceded as true and regulative. Judaism, on the contrary, is based on the personal experience of each and all of the people. Hence, "the revelation on Sinai, this grand and

[60] Kuzari I, 25.

lofty spectacle, cannot be denied."[61] "Every one who was present at that time became convinced that the matter proceeded from God direct."[62] And the witnesses transmitted their experience to succeeding generations by an unbroken chain of tradition. "Thus all Israel know these things, first, from personal experience, and afterwards through uninterrupted tradition which is equal to the former."[63] "The first man would never have known God, if he had not addressed, rewarded, and punished him."[64] "Cain and Abel were made acquainted with the nature of His being by communication of their father as well as by prophetic intuition."[64]

The empiricism is extraordinarily bold, even for our time. For Halevi's position is tantamount to asserting that unless men perceived God, meeting Him face to face, they cannot know Him at all. Thus the knowledge of God is *natural* knowledge. He appears to individuals and to masses, He speaks, He rewards, He punishes. He is known as other beings are known, by prophetic intuition, and by derived evidence, i. e. by tradition.

Now prophetic intuition and tradition, were lacking to the Greek philosophers. "These things, which cannot be approached by speculation, have been rejected by Greek philosophers because speculation denies everything the like of which it has not seen."[65] "Had the Greek philosophers seen them (the prophets) when they prophesied and performed miracles, they would have acknowledged them, and sought by speculative means to discover how to achieve such things."[65] The implication is that observation or intuition is

[61] Kuzari I, 88.
[62] *Ibid.*, I, 91.
[63] *Ibid.*, I, 25.
[64] *Ibid.*, IV, 3.
[65] Kuzari IV, 3.

prior to reason, that reason elaborates but does not discover, that the true is what is *perceived,* not what is reasoned. Indeed, on this not very clear notion, Haelvi develops a complete theory of race psychology, in which the *dominant* instruments of explanation are notions concerning *preceived environment*—the soil, the climate, etc. Reason is merely the tool which manipulates these perceived objects and it is they that are potent in the psychology of race.

The best application of this doctrine is perhaps to be seen in Halevi's discussion of the efficacy of prayer and the use of anthropomorphic terminology. His explanation of the latter is psychological. Using as his text the talmudic saying "The Torah spoke in the language of man,"[66] he points out that man cannot grasp metaphysical problems by means of abstract intellect alone, without the assistance of anything that can be conceived or seen, such as words, writing, or any visible or imaginary form.[67] Man shows fear whenever he meets with anything terrible, but not at the mere report of such a thing; he is likewise attracted by a beautiful form which strikes his eye, but not so much by one that is only spoken of. That the prophets should picture God by visible images is, then, inevitable.[68] How very different is this from the Maimonidean identification of anthropomorphisms with metaphysical terms![69]

Prayer, again, is likewise a psychological necessity. Prayer is not a means of approaching God, to rouse His mercy and assuage His anger, but it is the spontaneous expression of the individual at moments of strong emotions. Jewish metaphysicians have mistaken the prime object of

[66] דברה תורה כלשון בני אדם, Berakot 31*b*.

[67] Kuzari IV, 5.

[68] *Ibid.*

[69] Comp. Friedländer's analysis of the "Guide of the Perplexed," p. XIV.

prayer and had therefore split hair over such questions as: How is it possible to change God's mind by prayer? Can we praise God sufficiently? The result was Maimonides' condemnation of excessive prayer. According to Halevi, prayer can never be excessive. So long as man feels the need of praying, of pouring forth his accumulated passions and feeling, he cannot be restrained by external barriers. Prayer is the art of self-expression just as are music, dance, and song which often accompany it. It occupies in the Jewish life the same position that music and athletic games used to hold in Greek life. It is a catharsis of the pent-up energies. It is primarily not a petition to God but a voluntary exercise of the soul. The perception or thought of God merely excites prayer, just as the sight of beauty calls forth the practice of other arts. "Prayer is for the soul what nourishment is for the body. During prayer a man purges his soul from all that passed over it, and prepares for the future."[70]

To an empiric and intuitionist like Halevi, the residual problems of the metaphysicians had to seem empty. Denying the absoluteness of design, the adequacy of reason, the unity of the world, insisting on acts, facts, observation, his treatment of the typical problems of Jewish metaphysicians was rather superior and high-handed. There was, for example, the problem of the eternity of matter. We have seen how Maimonides has treated it. No Jewish theologian save RaLBaG[71] ventured to agree with Aristotle in the doctrine of the eternity of matter. Halevi, however, dismisses the whole problem as futile. If the doctrine merely asserts the existence of an eternal matter, it may be accepted or

[70] Kuzari III, 5.

[71] Rabbi Levi ben Gershon (d. about 1344).

rejected without making any difference in one's view of life. It is primarily a question of observation not of logic or religion, and it must be solved by experimental evidence. And if anybody has proved to his own satisfaction that an eternal non-divine element does exist, what of it? Does it alter his conduct or view of life? What is really of practical importance is whether the historic movement of the world is real or not. The world exists for us in so far as we know it, and do we know it *sub specie aeternitatis* or *sub specie generationis?* Assuredly our earliest records of the past date from a certain period, and everything before that period is wrapt in a mist. We may infer what had happened before that time, but that is merely "abstract speculations which *make* eternity." It is not actual proof. As far as our knowledge goes, we must assume that the world was created in time, though by abstract speculations we may infer that the world is eternal. Hence, "if, after all, a believer of the Law finds himself compelled to admit an eternal matter and the existence of many worlds prior to this one, this would not impair his belief that this world was created at a certain epoch, and that Adam and Noah were the first human beings."[72]

But the philosophers trust that their inferences are as true as the records of events. They say that science is not merely hypothesis, but a true description of things. Halevi proceeds to criticise contemporary science. His criticism, which was undoubtedly inspired by Ghazali's "The Destruction of Philosophy," is mainly a criticism of the scientific method of his time not for the purpose of substituting a new, improved method, but to discredit science. His criticism, therefore, was not like that of

[72] Kuzari I, 67.

Bacon's, but rather like that of modern religionists who try to prove the truth of religion by the limitation of science.

The science of the philosophers, he argues, is based on logic rather than on experience. The laws of nature do not really describe the nature of things, but are merely rules of action. Take for example the theory of the four elements which is entirely hypothetical, for we have never seen elementary fire, earth, air, or water.[73] Their real existence can be verified neither by a synthetic nor by an analytic process. "Where have we ever witnessed an igneous or atmospheric substance entering into the substance of the plant or animal, and asserted that it was composed of all four elements?"[73] "Or when did we ever see things dissolve into the four real elements?"[73] Science, it is true, forces us to accept the theory that cold, moisture and dryness are primary qualities, the influence of which nobody can escape; this is, however, only conception and nomenclature; it does not mean that they can emerge from mere theory into reality, and produce, by combination, all existing things.[73]

Had the philosophers merely recorded facts and not undertaken to explain their cause and origin, there would be no objection against them. The philosophers, however, go further than that; they conceive the classified facts as metaphysical abstractions which produce these very facts. They call these abstractions or powers by the name of Nature, and ascribe all the phenomena of the universe to the actions of nature. But "what is Nature?"[74] The common people think it is a certain power which is known only to the philosophers.[75] But "the philosophers know as

[73] Kuzari V, 14.

[74] Kuzari I, 71.

[75] *Ibid.*, I, 72.

much as we do. Aristotle defined it as the beginning and primary cause through which a thing moves or rests, not by accidents, but on account of its innate essence."[76] Though these words "astonish those who hear them, nothing else springs from the knowledge of nature."[77] All we notice in the world is things in motion and in rest, which we call by the general name Nature, but the philosophers "mislead us by names, and cause us to place another being on par with God, if we say that nature is wise and active.[78] To be sure, the elements, sun, moon, and stars, have power such as warming, cooling, moistening, and drying, "but these are merely functions." "There is no harm in calling the power which arranges matter by means of heat and cooling, 'Nature,' but all intelligence must be denied to them."[79]

Science being disposed of, the right conception of God and the universe defined, we may turn to Halevi's ethical doctrines. Here, too, he begins with polemic. The real difficulty with science lies in the fact that philosophers' interest in the world is theoretical rather than practical. They consider the knowledge of handling things inferior to the knowledge of "describing things in a fitting manner."[80] And they extend this preference of speculation to action even in the fields of ethics. The highest good, according to the philosopher, is the "Pleasure of God,"[80] which is obtained when one "becomes like the active intellect in finding the truth, in describing everything in a fitting manner, and in rightly recognizing its basis."[80] The way of reaching

[76] *Ibid.*, I, 73; comp. also Arist., Phys., II, 1.

[77] Kuzari, I, 75.

[78] *Ibid.*, I, 76.

[79] Kuzari I, 77.

[80] *Ibid.*, I, 1.

it is not by action nor is it prescribed. The philosophers say, "Fashion thy religion according to the laws of reason set up by philosophers, and be not concerned about the word or language or actions thou employest."[81]

In criticising this ethical system Halevi and his followers try to prove that reason is unreliable both as a guide in life and as a means of knowing things, that virtues are inefficient if they possess no intrinsic values, that man can never become like the "Active Intellect," and that the "Active Intellect" cannot be the highest happiness.

To begin with, intellect can not be a guide of life. If all men were to follow their own intellects they would be led to different points, never coming to an agreement. "Why do Christian and Moslem who divide the inhabited world between them fight with one another?"[82] They do not fight over matters of practice, for in their ethics and worship of God they differ very little, "both serve God with pure intention, living either as monks or hermits, fasting and praying."[82] They fight only over speculative creeds and doctrines. It is that speculative element in religion that breeds all kinds of differences of opinion. that causes schisms and dissensions. If men did not rely on their intellect and admitted the fallibility of reason, difference of opinion would be recognized as inevitable, and no man would attempt to force his views upon others. In fact, it is better for the progress of humanity that there exists diversity of opinion.[83] In short, intellects must differ, and therefore should not determine action.

But not only does reason fail to be a guide of life, it is also fallible as a way of getting a true understanding of

[81] Kuzari I, 1.

[82] *Ibid.*, I, 2.

[83] Comp. Kuzari I, 102, 103.

things. There are things in heaven and things in earth that one cannot get by mere reasoning. The unsophisticated person, who does not set the universe in a logical frame-work, who beholds man and nature acting freely in their undelineable boundaries, sees all their irregularities, all their defiance of system and law, in spite of their occasionally apparent regularity. There are miracles in nature and mysteries in human nature, which cannot be grasped and explained by bare reason. Man must possess another faculty to understand them, and he must have recourse to another language to communicate them. There is prophecy, divine influence, and inner vision which are quite different from reason and independent of it. Persons who have not been devoted to study and to the development of their intellect have often been endowed with supernatural powers by which they have been enabled to discover truth which philosophers with their superior intellect have in vain striven after.[84] "This proves that the divine influence as well as the souls have a secret which is not identical with the intellect."[84]

You will say that philosophers, too, recognize the value of moral virtue, and "recommend good and dissuade from evil in the most admirable manner."[85] But what is the moral force that will cause one to do good and desist from doing evil? The philosophers "have contrived laws or rather regulations without binding force, which may be overridden in times of need."[85] Reason alone cannot be a binding force; one's knowledge that by doing evil to others he does evil to himself is not strong enough to overcome his momentary impulses to do evil. These can be over-

[84] Kuzari I, 4.

[85] *Ibid.*, IV, 19.

come but by an inhibiting impulse, by a consciousness of responsibility, by a sentiment that certain actions are wrong in themselves. You may say that the fear of punishment will inhibit a man from doing evil, but how can the fear of a remote uncertain pain inhibit man from immediate pleasure? The inhibition of evil conduct must be present in the action just as is the desire to do it. Man would not desist from doing evil unless together with the desire of evil there comes an opposed desire not to do it. What can this opposed desire be if not the same that certain actions are wrong in themselves, that they are prohibited by Authority, and are, "like the work of nature, entirely determined by God, but beyond the power of man?"[87] The doing of good likewise must be inspired by a social sentiment, by a feeling that "the relation of the individual to society is as the relation of the single limb to the body"[87] and that "it is the duty of the individual to bear hardships, or even death, for the sake of the welfare of the commonwealth."[87] Philosophy does not offer such binding forces. Philosophers "love solitude to refine their thoughts"[88] and do not consider their relation to society as that of the single limb to the body. They have no sense of social obligation. "They only desire the society of disciples who stimulate their research and retentiveness, just as he who is bent upon making money would only surround himself with persons with whom he could do lucrative business."[89]

But inasmuch as the philosophers recommend moral virtues, the difference reduces itself to this: Do moral virtues exist for intellectual virtues, or intellectual virtues for

[86] Kuzari III, 53.
[87] *Ibid.*, III, 19.
[88] *Ibid.*, III, 1.
[89] Kuzari III, 1.

moral? Joseph ben Shemṭob (1400-1460), attempts to answer the question.[90] Regarding religion as identical with life he concludes that speculation (עיון) arises for the sake of action, (מעשה). Though in some sense religious practices are themselves a means to a particular sort of speculation, to the pure or mystical knowledge, i. e. possession of God, most men cannot attain this stage of happiness. Only a few saints, like Simon bar Joḥai and his son (ר' שמעון בר יוחאי ובנו), achieved the heights on which they could be absolved from the practice of the Law. In this case their mere existence *was* the source and existence of law. But the great majority of men cannot be merged in God in this way, and must subordinate speculation to life.

Thus it is evident that intellectual excellence, the pleasure derived from "finding the truth, from describing everything in a fitting manner, and rightly recognizing its basis,"[91] can be attained only after man had completely adapted himself to nature. Play does not begin till after all work is done. But can man completely adapt himself to nature? This would be possible if man were the only being, living on a planet made for his special purposes, and meeting all his needs. But man is placed in a world not altogether fit for his purposes; he must make terms with it; his chief concern is to adjust himself to the universe in order that he may survive in it. And the process of adjustment is an eternal endless process, for each adjustment is only between one small part of man and one small part of the universe, and after the adjustment between any such two parts is completed, there comes forth

[90] Comp. Joseph b. Shemṭob, כבוד אלהים.

[91] Kuzari I, 1.

the need of a new adjustment between other parts. Contemplation, therefore, cannot be an end in itself, since man can never adapt himself completely to the universe. Of course, individual persons, instead of adapting themselves to the world, may renounce it, withdraw in caves and deserts and spend their lives in contemplation. But mankind as a whole live in the world and do not retire from it. It is, therefore, not sufficient for man to comprehend things objectively and "describe them in a fitting manner." What he needs is to understand everything in its relation to his purposes. Knowledge must be an instrument for action. "Reason must rather obey, just as a sick person must obey the physician in applying his medicine and advice."[92]

Finally, the philosophers place speculation above action because they consider speculation as the greatest, the only self-sufficient happiness. But speculation can afford man no happiness unless it has its basis in action, unless it has been called forth by some practical motive. In order to derive intellectual pleasure from seeing things as they are, there must first be a problem, a difficulty in seeing those things. Intellectual pleasure consists in the transition from a state of perplexity to that of certainty, in the unraveling of a problem, in the suspense and repose we experience after a state of confusion. "The pleasures of our life consist in the getting of things we desire; and the desire for a thing consists in our being potentially in the possession of that thing but actually deprived of it."[93] We can have no intellectual pleasure unless we are conscious of its com-

[92] Kuzari III, 8.

[93] הערבות אשר נמצא בחיינו הוא להשגת הדבר הנכסף כי למה שהאדם כחיי אל השגת המושכלות והוא הכוסף אליהם, והיה הכוסף איננו זולת המרצת הרצון להשיג הדבר הנכסף. Kreskas, אור ה׳, ed. Vienna, 55*b*.

ing. We all take pleasure in our senses, and yet it is not those permanent sensations impressed upon us by external forces that give us the greatest pleasure, but those sensations which we ourselves bring upon us by intention and desire. The mathematician may take pleasure in solving problems, but certainly not in the self-evident truth of the multiplication table. "We see this in the fact that we do not take pleasure in the comprehension of self-evident truths. The reason is because there was no transition from potentiality to actuality, and hence there was no desire to comprehend them."[94] Intellectual pleasure, then, cannot result but from a problem; but how can you have any problem if you have no practical interest in the world, if you already had conquered it, and are going to live in it on mere contemplation?

With this Halevi's criticism of philosophy is completed His general point of view, it will be gathered, is Hebraic. His implicit standards of criticism involve the empirical method, the voluntaristic assumptions, the historic sense, and the high *morality* which are embodied in the Jewish Scriptures. But we have not here to deal with his constructive doctrine compounded of religion, tradition, and criticism. Our task has been to separate and exhibit the bearing of two opposed tendencies toward Greek philosophy in the thought of the Jews of the Middle Ages, as these tendencies are expressed in their most representative protagonists, especially Moses ben Maimon and Judah Halevi. Maimonides is Hellenist, Halevi a Hebraist; Maimonides is a rationalist, Halevi an empiricist. Maimon-

[94] והנה ממה שיודה על זה אשר אמרנו מה שנמצא בהשגותינו המושכלות הראשונות שלא נרגיש בהן ערבות כלל, וזה אמנם למה שלא היה להם העתק מורגש מן הכח אל הפעל ולא היה בהשגותם כוסף קודם שהושגו, Kreskas, *ibid.*

ides subordinates everything to reason, which, for him, is alone the master of man. Halevi, too, serves only one master, but he recognizes and regards the other. He thinks will fundamental but offers reason its proper place. Though he criticises the works of reason, and is skeptical about the validity of theory, he accepts it within limitations. and seeks to conform theory to practice. We cannot know the world as it is, but we can know it so as to live in it. In form, the philosophy of both men, Maimonides and Halevi, is antiquated, yet the substance of their differences is still operative. Maimonides, however, is more truly mediæval; his thought is closely allied to that of the Schoolmen; while Halevi's is old wine that is even now bursting new bottles. Contemporary thought, the whole pragmatic movement, may find its visions foreshadowed in Halevi's discussions. Maimonides intended his book to be the "Guide of the Perplexed," and it can now be taken but for a scholastic apology of religion; Halevi called his work: "Book of Argument and Demonstration in the Aid of the Despised Faith," and it must now be considered the most logical of mediæval expositions of the practical spirit as contrasted with the speculative.

4

THE ARISTOTELIAN PREDICABLES AND MAIMONIDES' DIVISION OF ATTRIBUTES

THE problem of attributes was not invented by Maimonides. Back of it at the time of Maimonides was a history of over four centuries of speculation on the attributes of God in Arabic philosophy, and back of these speculations in Arabic philosophy were, according to Maimonides himself,[1] similar speculations in the writings of the Christian Church Fathers, and back of these, it may be added, was the problem of attributes in the works of Philo. Maimonides draws upon these sources, and directly so upon Arabic sources, for his own discussion of the problem. There is hardly a phase of the problem dealt with by Maimonides which has not its parallel in the works of his predecessors. But this old problem receives at his hands a fresh treatment, more thorough, more comprehensive and more systematic than in any of his sources. Particularly new is his treatment of attributes as a problem of logical judgment. To his predecessors the problem was primarily metaphysical; he stresses the logical aspect of it. To his predecessors the problem was solved once one has arrived at the conclusion that the

[1] *Moreh Nebukim* I, 71.

terms predicated of God are not to be taken literally, that they are His essence, or that they are according to His essence, or however else the denial of the existence of attributes in God was expressed. To Maimonides, however, this did not mark the end of the problem. For, arriving at the conclusion that terms predicated of God are His essence, he asks himself: What is the logical meaning and significance of these terms when predicated of God? And so throughout his discussion, even when operating with terms and ideas borrowed from others, he gives to these terms and ideas a new turn, a new twist, and makes them fit into the framework of the problem as he has formulated it.

The present paper, however, will confine itself to the single topic of Maimonides' familiar division of attributes into five classes and will endeavor to show how by drawing upon older sources, and especially upon Aristotle's various classifications of predicables, Maimonides arrived at a new type of classification.

The statement with which Maimonides opens his general discussion of the problem of attributes in Ch. 50 (of *Moreh Nebukim* I) may be also considered as the logical starting point of his classification of attributes which comes subsequently in Chs. 51–52. For, in this statement, as we shall see, he lays down the principle, which is essential to his entire treatment of the problem, that terms predicated of God must conform to all the rules which govern the use of predicables in logical judgments. He says: "Belief does not refer to something uttered with the lips but rather to something conceived by the soul when that conception of the soul is attended by the belief that it is in reality as it is conceived."[2] The sentiment expressed in this statement is an old one, and parallels to it have been cited[3] and more parallels can still be cited. But in the new phrasing and setting given to it by Maimonides it assumes a new meaning. This passage, as will be noticed, contains two statements. First, a contrast between that which is only "uttered with the lips" and that which is not a mere utterance of the lips but a conception of the soul. Second, the association of belief with a conception of the soul which corresponds to external reality. Now, the contrast between a mere verbal utterance and that which is not a mere verbal utterance reminds one of Aristotle's contrast between a verbal sentence (λόγος) and a logical proposition (λόγος ἀποφαντικός).[4] It is thus quite evident that by a conception of the soul which is not a mere verbal utterance Maimonides means that which Aristotle calls a logical proposition. Not so evident, however, at first sight, is the Aristotelian origin of Maimonides' statement that belief is to be associated with a conception of the soul which corresponds to reality. But when we recall that a logical proposition is defined by Aristotle

[2] *Ibid.* I, 50.
[3] Kaufmann, *Attributenlehre*, p. 369, n. 9.
[4] *De Interpretatione*, Ch. 1, 16a, 2, and Ch. 4, 17a, 2–3.

as a combination of terms in which there is "either truth or falsity"[5] and that truth is to be tested by the correspondence of the ideas in our mind to the objects outside our mind[6] and that such truth can be established mainly by syllogism[7] but partly also by induction[8] and, finally, that every belief is founded upon the evidence of either syllogism or induction,[9] we can easily see how on the basis of these statements of Aristotle one could arrive at a definition of belief such as given here by Maimonides. What Maimonides therefore means to say is that belief is that which can be expressed by a logical proposition. Since this is what is meant by belief, then every statement made about God which is to express any of our beliefs about His nature must of necessity constitute a logical proposition the truth of which is to be tested by its correspondence to the reality of the nature of God. Irresponsible terms, such as religious people are in the habit of applying to God in their prayer, however laudatory they may sound, do not constitute a true expression of religious belief, and, according to Maimonides, their use is to be discouraged.[10] "A prayer," says Aristotle, "is a verbal sentence" and not a logical proposition, inasmuch as it is "neither true nor false."[11]

[5] *Ibid.*, Ch. 4, 17a, 2–3.
[6] *Metaphysics* IV, 7, 1011b, 27.
[7] *Analytica Posteriora* I, 2, 71b, 17–18.
[8] *Ibid.* II, 5, 91b, 34–35.
[9] *Analytica Priora* II, 23, 68b, 13.
[10] *Moreh Nebukim* I, 59.
[11] *De Interpretatione*, Ch. 4, 17a, 4–5.

Similarly Maimonides would say that exaltations and glorifications of God are not proper expressions of true religious belief, inasmuch as they do not constitute logical propositions.

Having laid down in Ch. 50 the principle that predications about God must constitute logical propositions, Maimonides proceeds to give in Ch. 51 a general classification of such propositions. There are two kinds of logical propositions, he says, one in which the predicate signifies something superadded to the essence of the subject and the other in which the predicate signifies that which is the essence of the subject. In the first type of logical propositions, he says in effect, the predicate is to be called accident, irrespective of the fact whether it has only a transient existence in the subject of which it is predicated or whether it is co-eternal with that subject.[12] In the second kind of logical propositions, he continues, the predicate may be a term having the same meaning as that of the subject, as, e. g., in the proposition "man is man" or it may be the "explanation of a term" (*perush shem*), as, e. g., in the proposition "man is a rational animal." Propositions like 'man is man,' however, are not regarded by him as logical propositions and are dismissed by him as mere tautologies. Propositions like

[12] Based upon the following statement in *Moreh Nebukim* I, 51: ולא בשלילת שם המקרה ישולל ענינו, כי כל ענין מוסף על העצם הוא משיג אותו בלתי משלים אמתתו, וזהו ענין המקרה, מחובר אל מה שיתחייב מהיות דברים רבים קדומים. That accidents may be eternal is stated by Aristotle in *Metaphysics* V, 30, 1025a, 30–34. This kind of accidents is what Aristotle otherwise calls 'property' (cf. Ross's commentary on the *Metaphysics*, *ad loc.*).

'man is a rational animal,' on the other hand, are taken by him as exemplifications of logical propositions of the type in which the predicates signify the essence of the subject.

The expression "explanation of a term" seemingly reflects Aristotle's expression "a phrase of what a term signifies" (*λόγος τοῦ τί σημαίνει τὸ ὄνομα*),[13] which is rendered in Averroes' Middle Commentary on *Posterior Analytics* by "a phrase explaining a term,"[14] as contrasted with the expression "a phrase of what a thing is" (*λόγος τοῦ τί ἐστι*),[15] which is rendered in Averroes' work as referring to a phrase "which shows the essence of a being."[16] In Aristotle the former expression is used as a description of what is generally called a nominal definition, whereas the latter expression is used as a description of what by way of contrast is called a real definition, or, as Aristotle describes it in that particular passage in *Posterior Analytics* II, 10, a definition which indicates the cause of the definitum.[17] Similarly Avicenna, in a passage which is evidently based upon the passages in the *Posterior Analytics* just

[13] *Analytica Posteriora* II, 10, 93b, 30.

[14] *Averrois Expositio Media in Librum Demonstrationis Aristotelis*, Tractatus II (*Aristotelis . . . opera*, Venice 1574, Volume I, Part III, p. 29 E): "Oratio declarans nomen." Hebrew: המאמר המפרש לשם (Averroes Middle Commentary on the *Organon*, MS. Jewish Theological Seminary, fol. 216a).

[15] *Analytica Posteriora* II, 10, 93b, 29.

[16] "Quod doceat substanitiam entis." (*loc. cit.*). Hebrew: מודיע לעצם הנמצא (*loc. cit.*).

[17] *Analytica Posteriora* II, 10, 93b, 39. Averroes calls this kind of definition "definitio in veritate" (*loc. cit.*). Hebrew: הגדר באמת (*loc. cit.*).

referred to, makes use of the expression "explaining the meaning of a term"[18] with reference to a nominal definition. Taken in this sense, the expression "explanation of a term" used here by Maimonides with reference to the definition "man is a rational animal" would seem to imply that Maimonides considered a definition of this type to be only a nominal definition. But this can hardly be the case, for several reasons. In the first place, both Aristotle and Avicenna, whose logical views Maimonides is following here, consider a definition of the type of 'man is a rational animal' as an example of a real definition. In the second place, from the context of the passage in which Maimonides uses the expression 'explanation of a term' it is quite evident that unlike its corresponding Aristotelian and Avicennian expression it is used by him with reference to a real definition, for while indeed he speaks of the phrase "rational animal" as being only the "explanation of a term", he also speaks of it as expressing "the true essence of man"[19] which reflects the expression "a phrase of what a thing is" quoted above from Aristotle as a description of a real definition. Moreover, the expression 'explanation of a term' applied by Maimonides to the predicate 'rational animal' is explained by himself subsequently to mean that "the thing referred to by the term 'man' is that thing which is

[18] *Najat* I: Logic, ed. Rome 1593, p. 20, 11.51 sqq.; ed. Cairo 1913, pp. 130–131.

[19] *Moreh Nebukim* I, 51: כי החי המדבר הוא עצם האדם ואמתתו.

composed of animality and rationality."[20] This explanation certainly cannot refer to a nominal definition. Finally, later when Maimonides takes up the question whether a definition is predicable of God or not, he rejects it on the ground that the elements of a definition constitute the causes of the definitum.[21] This corresponds exactly to the description of a real definition used by Aristotle and his followers,[22] and Maimonides would not have made use of this description unless he considered a definition of the type 'man is a rational animal' to be a real definition. There can be no doubt, therefore, that, unlike Aristotle and Avicenna, Maimonides uses the expression 'explanation of a term' with reference to a real definition . What justification he had in making use of that old expression in a new sense will now be explained.

The locus classicus of Aristotle's discussion of the predicables is in Topics I, 4–9. There Aristotle begins with a general division of predicables into those which signify the essence of the subject and those which do not signify the essence of the subject, calling the former definition and the latter, rather loosely, as he says, property.[23] This, as will be noticed, corresponds exactly to Maimonides' general classification of attributes into those which signify the essence of the subject and those

[20] *Ibid.*: שהדבר אשר שמו אדם הוא הדבר המורכב מן החיים והדבור.

[21] *Ibid.*, I, 52: וזה המין מן התאר מרוחק מן האל יתברך אצל כל אדם שהוא יתעלה אין לו סבות קודמות שהם סבת מציאותו.

[22] Cf. above n. 17.

[23] *Topics* I, 4, 101b, 19–23.

which signify something superadded to the subject. Then, taking up those predicates which signify the essence of the subject, i. e., real definitions, he distinguishes between what is to be properly called 'definition' (ὅρος) and what is to be called only 'definitory' (ὁρικόν). A definition, he says, is always 'a certain phrase' (λόγος τίς), that is to say, "a phrase signifying a thing's essence" (λόγος ὁ τὸ τί ἦν εἶναι σημαίνων),[24] though the subject of the definition, that is, the definitum, may be either a term or a phrase, for a definition, says Aristotle, may be "either a phrase in lieu of a term or a phrase in lieu of another phrase".[25] In Averroes' Middle Commentary on the *Topics* this Aristotelian expression "a phrase in lieu of a term" is rendered by the statement "it explains that which a simple term signifies" and is illustrated by the proposition "man is a rational, mortal animal."[26] In contradistinction to a definition, which is always "a certain phrase", a "definitory", says Aristotle, is that which explains one term by some other synonymous term, as, for example, the explanation of the term 'seemly' (πρέπον) by 'beautiful' (καλόν).

From the foregoing analysis of passages we may

[24] *Ibid.*, 101a, 39.

[25] *Ibid.*, I, 5, 102a, 1.

[26] *Averrois Expositio Media in octo libros Topicorum*, Liber I, Cap. 4: "Explicat quid simplex nomen significet, prout dicimus, an homo sit animal rationale [mortale]" (op. cit., p. 8 G). Hebrew: מודיע למה שיורה עליו שם נפרד כאמרנו האדם חי מדבר מת (op. cit., fol. 231b). The occasional addition of the term 'mortal' in the definition of man is referred to by Maimonides himself in *Millot ha-Higgayon*, Ch. 10.

gather that the expression 'explanation of a term' was used in Arabic versions of Aristotle's logic in two distinct senses. First, it was used, as in the passages quoted from Avicenna and from Averroes' Middle Commentary on the *Posterior Analytics,* in the sense of a nominal definition in contrast to a real definition, being thus the equivalent of Aristotle's expression λόγος τοῦ τί σημαίνει τὸ ὄνομα ("a phrase of what a term signifies") in *Posterior Analytics* II, 10, 93b, 30, as contrasted with the expression λόγος τοῦ τί ἐστι ("a phrase of what a thing is"). Second, it was used, as in the passage quoted from Averroes' Middle Commentary on the *Topics,* in the sense of a real definition (ὅρος) in contrast to that which is only "definitory" (ὁρικόν), being thus the equivalent of Aristotle's expression λόγος ἀντ' ὀνόματος ("a phrase in lieu of a term") in *Topics* I, 5, 102a, 1, as contrasted with the explanation of one term by another synonymous term. Or, to put it more simply: according to the first sense of the expression "explanation of a term", the word 'term' (Arabic: *ism,* Hebrew: *shem,* ὄνομα) is used as the opposite of the word 'essence' (Arabic: *ḏāt* or *māhiyyah,* Hebrew: *'eẓem* (*'aẓmut*) or *mahut,* τὸ τί ἐστι; τὸ τί ἦν εἶναι). According to the second sense of the same expression, the word 'term' is used as the opposite of 'explanation' (Arabic: *sharḥ,* Hebrew: *perush*) in which case 'explanation' is the equivalent of the word 'phrase' (Arabic: *ḳaul,* Hebrew: *ma'amar,* λόγος). Now the passage of Maimonides under consideration, as will have been noticed, corresponds to the passage of Aristotle in the *Topics*. In both of them the contrast is between a predicate which signifies the essence of the subject by a single term, such as "the seemly is beautiful" in Aristotle and "man is man" in Maimonides, and a predicate which signifies the essence of the subject by a phrase, such as "man is a rational animal", in both Aristotle and Maimonides—in the former according to the paraphrase of Averroes. Consequently, Maimonides' use of the expression 'explanation of a term' with reference to 'rational animal' reflects Aristotle's expression "a phrase in lieu of a term" in *Topics* I, S, 102a, 1, the word 'explanation' (*sharḥ, perush*) thus having here the meaning of the word 'phrase' (λόγος, *ḳaul, ma'mar*), and does not therefore imply that he considered 'rational animal' as only a nominal definition of 'man'.

In the light of what has been said, the passage in Chapter 51 in which Maimonides uses the expression 'explanation of a term' is to be rendered as follows: "If that attribute signified the essence of the subject, then [either it would be a single term synonymous with that of the subject, in which case] it would be a mere tautology, as if, for example, one would say 'man is man', [26a] or it would be a phrase explaining a term, as

[26a] Though in Maimonides' illustration (אלאנסאן הו אלאנסאן, האדם הוא האדם) the term used for the predicate is the same as that used for the subject, his statement that the proposition is tautological would be true even if the predicate were a term synonymous with the subject. Cf. Moses ha-Lavi, *Ma'mar Elohi*, MS. Bodleian 1324.5, fol. 120b: ואמנם כשהיה נשואה ונושאה דבר

if, for example, one would say 'man is a rational animal', [in which case the attribute would be neither a tautology nor an additional element to the essence of the subject], for the phrase 'rational animal' signifies the true essence of man, emphasizing as it does, [first], that no third element besides 'rational' and 'animal' enters into the essence of man, and, [second], that it is man alone that can be described by the terms animality and rationality. This attribute is thus only a phrase explaining a term without the implication of any element superadded to the essence designated by that term, being only an assertion, as it were, that the thing which is referred to by the term 'man' is that thing which is composed of animality and rationality." Similarly in Chapter 52, when he says with reference to a definition of the type 'man is a rational animal' that it is "the explanation of a term and nothing else,"[27] he does not mean that it is the explanation of a term only and not the explanation of the essence, but rather that it is the explanation of a term denoting the essence and not the explanation of something added to the essence.

Corroborative evidence that the expression "explanation of a term" is used here by Maimonides with reference to a real definition may be found in another passage of Avicenna which would seem to be the under-

אחד בעינו, הנה אין שם נושא ונשוא באמת, אבל יהיה מובן המאמר אשר בזה לא יגיע ממנו תועלת, בין שהולץ באותו הענין בשם אחד, כאמרנו שהאדם אדם, או בשני שמות נרדפים, כאמרנו שהחמור עיר, כי זה [המאמר שוה] לאמרנו שהחמור חמור.

[27] פירוש שם לא דבר אחר.

lying source of Maimonides' passage here under consideration. In that passage Avicenna tries to show how the simplicity of God is to be understood to exclude three kinds of divisibility. It reads: "We also say that the essence of the Necessary Being cannot have (1) principles out of the aggregate of which that Necessary Being would be constituted, nor (2) parts of quantity, nor (3) parts of a definition (*ḥadd* = ὅρος) or a phrase (*ḳaul* = λόγος). [As for principles], it makes no difference whether they are principles like matter and form or principles of some other kind. But [in the case of parts], if they are parts of a *phrase explaining the meaning of the term* 'God', then each one of the parts must signify something which in existence is essentially different from any other part. The reason why God cannot have parts of a definition is this. If anything is described by parts of the kind mentioned, then the essence of any part of it will not be the same as the essence of any other part nor will it be the same as the essence of the whole, so that even though it is possible for each of its parts to have a separate existence for itself, the whole could not possibly have an existence without those parts and could not therefore be said to have necessary existence".[28]

[28] *Najat* III: *Metaphysics*, ed. Rome, p. 63, 11.1 sqq.; ed. Cairo, p. 371; Latin: *Avicennae Metaphysices Compendium*, by K. Carame, Rome 1926, pp. 72–73. The bracketed additions in my translation are necessary for the purpose of making the meaning of the text intelligible and are based upon Avicenna's own subsequent analysis of this passage on p. 63, ll. 10–12 (ed. Rome), p. 372, ll. 3–6 (ed. Cairo), p. 74, ll. 1–7 (Latin).

From the context of the passage it is quite clear that the definition or phrase referred to is a real definition. Still Avicenna speaks of it as the explanation of the meaning of a term — the very same words used by him in the passage quoted previously with reference to a nominal definition.

The general twofold classification of attributes given by Maimonides in Chapter 51 is increased by him to a fivefold classification in Chapter 52. These five classes of attributes are given by him the names of 'definition', 'part of definition', 'quality', 'relation' and 'action'. To this may be added a sixth one, namely, 'negation', which Maimonides discusses later but omits from his formal classification, for the reason that in this chapter, as explicitly stated in the opening sentence, he confines himself to positive attributes. No literary precedent, as far as I know, is to be found for this fivefold classification of attributes. The nearest analogy to it is the fivefold classification of attributes by Algazali[29] and the fourfold classification by Abraham ibn Daud[30] which is evidently based upon that of Algazali. Thus corresponding to Maimonides' 'definition' and 'part of definition' are Algazali's and Abraham ibn Daud's first class of attributes which they call 'essential attributes', under which Algazali mentions 'genus' and 'difference' and Abraham ibn

[29] *Maḳaṣid al-Falasifah* II: *Metaphysics* III, ed. Cairo (without date), p. 150; Latin: *Algazel's Metaphysics*, ed. J. T. Muckle, pp. 62–63.
[30] *Emunah Ramah* II, iii, p. 54.

Daud mentions 'genus'. Similarly corresponding to Maimonides' 'quality' are their 'accidental attributes', which in Algazali are subdivided into two classes,[31] and corresponding to Maimonides' 'relation' is the attribute of relation in both of them. Finally, corresponding to Maimonides' 'negation', which, as we have observed, is placed by him outside his formal classification, is the last class in both Algazali's and Abraham ibn Daud's lists, where it is likewise called 'negation'. But while Maimonides' classification has undoubtedly been influenced by that of Algazali and Abraham ibn Daud, still it contains certain differences of both arrangement and terminology which would seem to indicate that there were some other sources and some other considerations which had led Maimonides to adopt his own particular classification. What these sources and considerations were will now be explained.

In those chapters in the *Topics*, which we have shown to be the underlying sources of Maimonides' preliminary twofold classification of attributes in Chapter 51, Aristotle, after having made his general twofold division of predicables into those which signify the essence of the subject and those which do not signify its essence, subdivides them further into two classes each. Those which signify the essence of the subject are subdivided by him into definition and genus. Those which do not signify the essence of the subject are subdivided by

[31] Cf. my *Crescas' Critique of Aristotle*, p. 686, n. 4.

him into property and accident.[32] Property and accident, though both of them are considered by Aristotle as predicates which do not signify the essence of the subject, differ from each other according to him in that the former "is present (ὑπάρχει) to a certain thing alone"[33] whereas the latter is "something which may be present or may not be present with any one and the self-same thing".[34] Elsewhere, however, he designates both accident and property as accident.[35]

But, then, after arriving at his fourfold classification of 'predicables' (κατηγορήματα), Aristotle seems to have reminded himself of his tenfold classification of the 'predicaments' (κατηγορίαι), or categories, as they are usually called, and makes the suggestion that the four predicables may be combined with the ten categories, for, as he says, "the accident and genus and property and definition will always be in one of these categories".[36] The obvious implication of this statement is that the categories, which are a classification of being, can also be treated as predicables, which are a classification of logical relations, so that instead of speaking of four predicables one could speak of ten predicables or of any other number into which Aristotle occasionally divides his categories.

In the history of Aristotelian philosophy, however,

[32] *Topics* I, 4, 101b, 17–25.
[33] *Ibid.* I, 5, 102a, 18–19.
[34] *Ibid.*, 102b, 6–7.
[35] Cf. above, n. 12.
[36] *Topics* I, 9, 103b, 23–25.

this suggested combination was not taken up. Categories and predicables, as a rule, were kept apart,[37] and while philosophers did not exactly speak of four predicables as they spoke of ten categories they did speak of five predicables, the five being Porphyry's modification or Aristotle's list, in which the latter's 'definition', 'genus', 'property' and 'accident' became 'genus', 'species', 'difference', 'property' and 'accident'.[38]

On the basis of these facts, then, Maimonides had before him three possible enumerations of predicables or, as he calls them, attributes. (1) He could have followed Aristotle's formal statement in the *Topics* and enumerated four attributes. (2) He could have followed Porphyry and enumerated five attributes. (3) He could have followed Aristotle's later suggestion in the *Topics* and enumerated ten attributes, corresponding to the ten categories. Now, in his formal treatise on logical terms, Maimonides follows Porphyry's enumeration, which by his time had already become standardized in philosophic literature, and he concludes his reproduction of Porphyry's five predicables with the following characteristic statement: "These are the five universal notions as they have been enumerated by the ancients."[39] Here,[40] however,

[37] An indirect suggestion as to the use of the ten categories as predicables may be found in Saadia's *Emunot we-De'ot* II, 8–12. A similar suggestion as to the use of the ten categories as predicables is to be found also in St. Augustine's *De Trinitate* V, 8 (VII).

[38] *Porphyrii Isagoge et in Aristotelis Categorias Commentarium*, ed. Busse, pp. 1 sqq.

[39] *Millot ha-Higgayon*, Cf. 10.

[40] *Moreh Nebukim* I, 52.

in his discussion of divine attributes, he combines all the three possible types of classifications we have mentioned. From Porphyry he borrows the number 'five' and in conformity with it he divides his attributes into five classes, as was done also by Algazali, evidently for the same reason. But having paid tribute to custom and retained the Porphyrian term five, he returns to the original fourfold classification of Aristotle and he follows it faithfully in the first and second parts of his enumeration. His first class of attributes is called by him definition, exactly as it is in Aristotle, and his second class of attributes, illustrated by the terms 'animality' and 'rationality', that is to say, genus and difference, is called by him 'part of definition', which is only another way of expressing what Aristotle calls 'genus', for the term 'genus' is used by Aristotle to include also 'difference', for, as he says, "difference, being attached to genus, is to be ranked alongside with genus".[41] Furthermore, in the passage quoted above from Avicenna, the terms 'genus' and 'difference' are referred to as 'parts of definition'.[42] Then evidently acting upon Aristotle's suggestion in the *Topics* as to the possibility of combining the predicables with the categories, he substitutes for the general terms 'property' and 'accident' a complete enumeration of the nine accidental categories, for 'property', as we have seen, is to Aristotle only a special kind of 'accident'.

[41] Topics I, 4, 101b, 18–19.
[42] Cf. above p. 213 and n. 28.

But inasmuch as Aristotle himself sometimes has a threefold classification of categories in which the nine non-substantial categories are grouped together under the headings of *τὰ πάθη*, modifications, i. e., qualities, and *τὰ πρός τι*, relations,[43] and furthermore inasmuch as for his own particular problem of divine attributes the categories which may be grouped together under the heading of relation presented a different problem than those under the heading of quality, Maimonides mentions only the categories of 'quality' and 'relation'. Under these two categories, however, we shall try to show, Maimonides explicitly mentions, or indirectly refers to, all the nine categories.

'Quality' is divided by Maimonides, after Aristotle,[44] into four main classes and is used by him as a general term under which he includes also the categories of possession, action, passion and quantity. Thus in the first class of quality, which Aristotle as well as Maimonides calls 'habit' and 'disposition',[45] the term 'habit' (ἕξις, Arabic: *milkah,* Hebrew: *ḳinyan*) suggests the category of *habere* (ἔχειν,[46] Arabic: *al-milk,* Hebrew: *ha-ḳinyan*), i. e., 'possession'. Furthermore, Maimonides in his restatement of this kind of 'quality' includes under 'habit' not only what Aristotle calls habits of 'knowledge' (ἐπιστῆμαι Arabic: *'ilm,* Hebrew: *ḥakmah*)

[43] *Metaphysics* XIV, 2, 1089b, 23–24. The term *πάθη* in this passage is generally understood to be used by Aristotle in the sense of *ποιά*.

[44] *Categories*, Ch. 8.

[45] *Ibid.*, Ch. 8, 8b, 27.

[46] Cf. *ibid.*, Ch. 15, 15b, 18.

and of 'virtue' (ἀρετη, Arabic: *ḫulḳ*, Hebrew: *middah*)[47] but also what he himself calls habits of 'art' (Arabic: *ṣinā'ah,* Hebrew: *melakah,* τέχνη) which he illustrates by the term 'carpenter', and thus the term habit suggests also the category of 'action'. In the second kind of 'quality', which is described by both Aristotle and Maimonides as including all those terms which refer to "natural power or lack of power", the expression "natural power or lack of power" is explained by Aristotle, though left unexplained here by Maimonides, as a natural power or lack of power "of doing something easily",[48] the term 'doing' (ποιῆσαι) thus reflecting the category of 'action' (ποιεῖν). The category of 'passion' (πάσχειν) is reflected in the third class of quality which is described by both Aristotle and Maimonides as that of "passive (παθητικαί) qualities and passions (πάθη)".[49] Finally, the fourth kind of quality is that of "figure and shape", which Maimonides, after Alfarabi, explicitly describes as "quality resulting from quantity as such",[50] thus reflecting the category of quantity. And so under quality Maimonides really includes, besides the category of quality, also the categories of possession, action, passion and quantity.

Similarly 'relation' is used by Maimonides as a general term under which he includes three categories or, as he says, three kinds of relations: (1) the relation

[47] *Ibid.*, Ch. 8, 8b, 29.
[48] *Ibid.*, 9a, 18–19.
[49] *Ibid.*, 9a, 28–29.
[50] Cf. Munk, *Guide* I, p. 196, n. 5.

of a thing to place, (2) the relation of a thing to time, and (3) the relation of one thing to another thing. The last of these three kinds of relation corresponds to Aristotle's general definition of relation as that which explains one thing with reference to another thing, Maimonides' expressions לזולתו and לאיש אחר thus reflecting Aristotle's expression πρὸς ἕτερον.[51] Though Aristotle himself does not put the categories of place and time under relation, Maimonides' combination of these three categories is not without precedent, for we find that Plotinus argues for the inclusion of time and place under relation.[52] Avicenna, too, takes relation to include the categories of time and place, though he goes even further and includes under it all the other categories,[53] as does also Maimonides' contemporary Averroes.[54] The term relation, furthermore, may also have been used by Maimonides to include the category of position, though no specific mention is made of it by him here, for we know that Aristotle's category of relation sometimes includes also the category of position.[55]

These three kinds of relation are illustrated by Maimonides by four examples, namely, (1) A is the

[51] *Categories*, Ch. 7, 6a, 37.

[52] *Enneades* VI, i, 14.

[53] *Shifā'*, fol. 27a, 18–22, quoted in I. Madkour, *L'Organon d'Aristote dans le monde arabe*, p. 93, n. 8.

[54] *Epitome in Metaphysicorum libros*, Lib. I (*Aristotelis opera* . . . Venetiis apud Iutnas, 1574, Vol. V, p. 359 B-C); Arabic: ed. Quiros, § 29, p. 17; German: M. Horten, *Die Metaphysik des Averroes*, p. 16, S. van den Bergh, *Die Epitome der Metaphysik des Averroes*, p. 12.

[55] *Categories*, Ch. 9, 11b, 8–10; cf. Ch. 7, 6b, 3.

father of B, (2) A is the partner of B, (3) A is the resident of a certain place, (4) A is he who lived at a certain time. Of these four examples the third and fourth are quite obviously meant to illustrate respectively the relations of place and time, whereas the first and second are presumably meant to illustrate what Maimonides calls the relation of one thing to another. Thus while only one example each is given for the relations of place and time, two examples are given for the relation of one thing to another. Furthermore, later, in the course of his discussion, Maimonides subdivides the relation of one thing to another into what he vaguely calls (a) correlation and (b) some relation.[56] What he exactly means by these two subdivisions he does not explain. But from his arguments against their applicability to God it may be gathered that by 'correlation' he means the mutual relation between two things which are dependent upon each other as cause and effect and that by 'some relation' he means the numerical relation between two things which share something in common but in different proportions, for against the admissibility of the former as a divine attribute he argues that God as cause is independent of His effects, and against the admissibility of the latter he argues that there can be no relation of more and less or equality between God and other beings.[57] The question naturally arises in

[56] (a) הצטרפות, (b) קצת יחס.

[57] Cf. Shem-tob on *Moreh Nebukim, ad loc.*

our mind whether the two examples Maimonides mentions as illustrations of the relation of one thing to another correspond to his two subsequent subdivisions of that kind of relation. I shall show, by a study of the history and meaning of these two subdivisions, that this is exactly the purpose which the two examples were intended for by Maimonides.

In his *Metaphysics*[58] Aristotle divides relation into three kinds, two of which, necessary for our purpose here, are mentioned by him also in his *Physics*.[59]

The first kind of relation is called by Aristotle the relation of "the active to the passive"[60] or the relation of "agent and patient"[61] and he illustrates it by the example of a father who "is called father of his son" because "the one has acted, and the other has been acted on in a certain way".[62] The second kind of relation is called by Aristotle "numerical relation"[63] or the relation of "that which exceeds to that which is exceeded"[64] or the relation between "excess and defect"[65] and he illustrates it by the examples of "double", "triple", and "greater".[66] Under this kind of relation he includes also the relation of "sameness", "likeness" and "equality".[67] The main characteristic

[58] *Metaphysics* V, 15, 1020b, 26 sqq.
[59] *Physics* III, 1, 200b, 28–30.
[60] 1020b, 30.
[61] 200b, 30.
[62] 1021a, 23–25.
[63] 1020b, 32–33.
[64] 1020b, 28.
[65] 200b, 29.
[66] 1020b, 26–23; cf. *Categories*, Ch. 7, 6a, 39, 6b, 18–19, 31.
[67] 1021b, 8–10.

of this numerical relation is that the things so related must have something in common with reference to which they can be compared, for, as Aristotle says, "those things are the same whose substance is one; those are like whose quality is one; those are equal whose quantity is one".[68]

In the light of these statements of Aristotle it is quite clear that Maimonides' distinction between 'correlation' and 'some relation' corresponds to Aristotle's distinction between relation of 'agent and patient' and 'numerical relation' and also that, as in Aristotle, his example of father-son relation was meant by him to serve as an illustration of agent-patient relation or of what he himself subsequently calls 'correlation'. In view of this it is not unreasonable to assume that his example of partnership was likewise meant by him to serve as an illustration of numerical relation or what he himself subsequently calls 'some relation'. The aptness of the example of partnership as an illustration of numerical relation will be more readily understood when it is recalled that by numerical relation Aristotle means a relation existing between two things which share the same substance or quality or quantity in either unequal or equal proportions.[69] In using the example of 'A is partner of B' Maimonides means therefore to say that 'numerical relation' is a sort of 'partnership' between two things which share the same

[68] 1021b, 10–12.

[69] Cf. above nn. 66, 67.

substance or quantity or quality in either unequal or equal proportions. Still more clear does the aptness of this illustration become when taken in connection with his subsequent refutation of the existence of a numerical relation between God and creatures, on the ground that all terms applied to God must be understood in an equivocal sense, even as "the term 'existence' is applied to Him and to other beings, according to our opinion, only in an equivocal sense".[70] When we recall that in Arabic the term for 'equivocalness' (*ishtirāk*) is based upon a word meaning 'to be a partner' (*sharik*), we may see the pointedness of this contention of Maimonides in arguing that there can be no 'numerical relation', i. e., partnership, between terms predicated of God and terms predicated of other beings on account of the fact that they are predicated of them "in an equivocal sense". In its original literal meaning Maimonides' argument is this: There is no 'partnership' between God and other beings except in so far as they share in the same sound of certain words which are applied to them in absolutely unrelated meanings.

The first four kinds of Maimonides' classification thus have their origin in Aristotle, based as they are upon a combination of his fourfold classification of predicables and his tenfold and threefold classification of categories. In view of this, it is quite natural for

[70] *Moreh Nebukim* I, 52 (4) ואיך יצוייר יחס בין מי שאין בינו ובין מה שזולתו עניין שיכללם בשום פנים, כי המציאה אמנם תאמר אצלנו עליו יתעלה ועל זולתו בשתוף גמור.

us to inquire whether his fifth attribute, which he calls action, has a similar origin, or whether it is something of his own device, dictated by the exigency of the problem of divine attributes, in which action had to be separated from all the other attributes, inasmuch as it is the only attribute which according to him can be predicated of God affirmatively. This question seems to have occurred to Joseph Caspi, for he makes the following comment: "I do not remember to have come across this [fifth] class of attributes in any of the books on logic or physics, that is to say, that it should be treated as a special class of attributes, and I am inclined to think that it is a distinction made by Maimonides out of his own head".[71] He furthermore states that Maimonides' attribute of action is "a subdivision of relation",[72] which he subsequently qualifies by saying that it is "the lowest of the subdivisions of relation".[73]

By the last statement Caspi undoubtedly means to say that Maimonides' action is to be identified with that kind of relation which, as we have seen, Aristotle describes as the relation of "agent and patient" or "the active to the passive". In this Caspi is quite obviously wrong, for it can be shown that in that part

[71] *Maskiyyot Kesef, ad loc.* in *'Ammude Kesef u-Maskiyyot Kesef*, ed. Werbluner, p. 58: והחלק החמישי מתארי החיוב וג', זאת החלוקה לא אזכור שהיא בספרי ההגיון והטבע, רצוני שיעשה מזה חלוקה מיוחדת, אבל מדעתי הוא דיוק מהמורה.

[72] *Ibid.*: והכוונה בזה שזה ממיני המצטרף.

[73] *Ibid.*, p. 59: אם כן מבואר שזה החלק החמישי הוא הסעיף השפל שבסעיף (read שבסעיפי) ההצטרפות.

of his discussion of relation, in which Maimonides tries to show that relations such as that of father to son cannot be predicated of God, h s discussion is a direct criticism of all his predecessors, Jewish, Moslem and Christian, ever since Philo, who invariably admitted such a kind of relation, i. e., the relation of agent and patient, as an attribute of God, which kind of relation, according to a comment by Narboni on Algazali, is also to be called action.[74] Furthermore, it can also be shown that even such philosophers as Baḥya ibn Paḳuda,[75] Joseph ibn Ẓaddiḳ[76] and Judah ha-Levi,[77] who explicitly speak of an attribute of action, mean by action the relation of agent and patient which is rejected here by Maimonides. What Maimonides really means by action that is not a relation is not the subject of the present paper. For the present we shall confine ourselves to the problem raised by Caspi in the first part of his statement and shall try to show that in Aristotle's discussion of predicables there is to be found a passage which will account for Maimonides' treatment of action as an attribute to be distinguished from the other four attributes.

[74] Narboni on *Kawwanot ha-Pilosofim* II: Metaphysics III, MS. Bibliotheque Nationale, Paris, Cod. Heb. 901, fol. 73b: Algazali: הרביעי הטוב והוא ישוב אל צרוף העצמות אל פועל סודר ממנו. Narboni: הרביעי תארי הפעולות והוא צרוף העצמות אל פועל סודר ממנו.

[75] *Hobot ha-Lebabot* I, 10.

[76] *'Olam Ḳaṭan* III, ed. Horovitz, p. 48.

[77] *Cuzari* II, 2. Judah ha-Levi's relative attributes (אצֿאפיה״, טפליות), which he distinguishes from actional attributes (תאת׳יריה״, מעשיות), are of a different nature and have a different origin, as I hope to show elsewhere.

In Aristotle, besides the fourfold and tenfold classifications of predicables which he discusses in *Topics*, I, 4–9, there is also another type of classification to which he makes reference in *De Interpretatione*, Chs. 5 and 10. Sometimes the predicate of a proposition, he seems to say, is connected with its subject by the copula 'is' (τὸ ἔστι), which is described by him as being "additionally predicated as a third element" (τρίτον προσκατηγορῆται),[78] and sometimes the predicate and the copula are combined into one word which he refers to as "a verb" (ῥῆμα).[79] This distinction, which in Aristotle is only slightly suggested, has been fully developed by Ammonius who also invented the terms by which it has been known to subsequent logicians. Propositions in which the copula is distinct from the predicate are described by him as propositions of the third adjacent (προτάσεις ἐκ τρίτου κατηγορουμένου, *propositiones tertii adjacentis*),[80] whereas propositions in which the copula is merged with the predicate are described by him as propositions of the second adjacent (ἐκ δύο . . . ἀποτελοῦνται, *propositiones secundi adjacentis*).[81]

This distinction between a predicate which Aristotle describes as a 'verb' and a predicate which in the lan-

[78] *De Interpretatione*, Ch. 10, 19b, 19–20.

[79] *Ibid.*, Ch. 5, 17a, 10.

[80] *Ammonius in Aristotelis De Interpretatione Commentarius*, ed. Busse, p. 14, 1.23; cf. also p. 8, 11.5–6. Cf. Wm. Hamilton, *Lectures on Logic*, Vol. I, pp. 228, 230.

[81] Ammonius, *op. cit.*, p. 7, 11.30–31.

guage of Aristotle is connected with the subject by the copula 'is' "additionally predicated as a third element" is also made use of by Maimonides in his treatise on logical terms.[82] Furthermore, like Ammonius he describes a proposition in which the predicate is only a 'verb' as a "two-termed proposition",[83] and it is called a two-termed proposition even when other terms are contained in it as direct objects of the verb. The illustrations used by him for two-termed propositions are "A stood", "A killed B".[84] Similarly a proposition in which the predicate is a noun or an adjective or a participle connected with its subject by some form of the copula 'to be', which in Arabic as well as in Hebrew is either expressed or only understood, is described by him as a "three-termed proposition".[85] The illustrations used by him for this kind of proposition are: "A is standing", "A was standing", "A will be standing".[86] Now in Greek and Latin and all other European languages, in which there is a present tense as well as a past and future tense, propositions of the second adjacent can be expressed by a verb in the present tense as well as by one in the past or future tense. But in Arabic and in Hebrew there is no present tense. The present tense is always expressed by a participle

[82] *Millot ha-Higgayon*, Ch. 3, and cf. ed. Leon Roth, p. 13, n. 3, and ed. M. Ventura, p. 36, n. 5.

[83] *Ibid.*: משפט שניי.

[84] *Ibid.*: ראובן עמד; ראובן הרג את שמעון.

[85] *Ibid.*: משפט שלישיי.

[86] *Ibid.*: ראובן הוא עתה עומד או היה עומד או ימצא עומד.

which has an adjectival meaning as well as the meaning of a *nomen agentis*. It is impossible, therefore, to have in these languages a proposition of the second adjacent expressed in the present tense. The sentence "God creates" could be rendered into Arabic and Hebrew only by a sentence which would literally mean "God is a creator" or "God is creating". The only way of forming a proposition of the second adjacent in Arabic and Hebrew is to use the perfect or imperfect tense of the verb 'to create'.

This is exactly the meaning of Maimonides' attribute of action as distinguished from the other four attributes. The four attributes of definition, part of definition, quality and relation are all used as predicates in propositions of the third adjacent; they are all to be connected with the subject by a copula which is either to be expressed or to be understood. The attribute of action, on the other hand, is always to be used in a proposition of the second adjacent, in which the predicate and copula are combined in what Aristotle as well as Maimonides calls a 'verb'.[87] And when we scrutinize the passage in which Maimonides himself draws a distinction between action in the sense of quality and action in the sense in which he uses it we shall find that it is mainly based upon the distinction between propositions of the third adjacent and propositions of the second adjacent. Action as a quality, he says in effect, is always expressed in a proposition of

[87] Cf. below n. 89.

the third adjacent, as, e. g., "A is a carpenter", "A is a smith". Action in the sense in which he uses it, on the other hand, is always to be expressed in a proposition of the second adjacent, as, e. g., "A made this door", "A built this house", "A wove this garment",[88] and if in Scripture it happens to be expressed in a proposition of the third adjacent it must be interpreted to stand for a proposition of the second adjacent. The reason for this is quite understandable. In a proposition of the third adjacent the predicate will always be a participle which, having the meaning of an adjective or *nomen agentis*, may imply the existence of a habit or disposition or natural power in the subject to which the action is attributed. In a proposition of the second adjacent, however, where the predicate is a verb, the action attributed to the subject is to be taken as pure action without any implication of habit or disposition or natural power. Accordingly, this fifth kind of attribute may be referred to as 'verb' as well as 'action', and the Arabic term *fi'l* (Hebrew: *pe'ulah*) which Maimonides uses here in connection with his fifth kind of attribute may have the meaning of the term *fi'l* (Hebrew: *po'el*) in his *Millot ha-Higgayon* where it is used in the sense of 'verb' as distinguished from participle, which he calls 'noun' (Arabic: *ism*; Hebrew: *shem*),[89] thus reflecting the Greek term ῥῆμα which is

[88] *Moreh Nebukim* I, 52 (5).

[89] *Millot ha-Higgayon*, Chs. 1 and 13, and cf. n. 1 on p. 87 in ed. Leon Roth. It is to be noted that the Greek ῥῆμα in *De Interpretatione*, Ch. 10, 19b, 22 is rendered in Isḥāḳ ibn Ḥonian's Arabic translation of that book

used by Aristotle in his description of propositions of the second adjacent.

In the light of the foregoing discussion of the various parts of Maimonides' fivefold classification of attributes, we may arrive at the conclusion that his classification is the result of a combination of four types of classification. First, Aristotle's classification of predicables into those which he calls 'verbs' and those which are connected with their subject by the copula 'is'. Second, Aristotle's classification of predicables according to his various classifications of the categories. Third, Aristotle's formal fourfold classification of predicables. Fourth, Porphyry's augmentation of Aristotle's four predicables to five. It is also possible for us to retrace the steps by which Maimonides arrived at his classification. He must have started with the general division of attributes into 'verbs', which combine in themselves the copula, and nouns or adjectives or phrases, which require a distinct copula to connect them with the subject. Under the former he placed all the terms which belong to the category of action — action considered as a distinct category and not as included under the categories of quality and relation.[90]

(*Die Hermeneutik des Aristoteles*, ed. Isidor Pollak, 1913) by the term *kalimah* (Hebrew: *dibbur*)—the very same term which in *Millot ha-Higgayon*, Chs. 3 and 13, Maimonides uses in the same sense as the term *fi'l* (Hebrew: *po'el*).

[90] Aristotle himself, according to Simplicius, uses action as a distinct category in a sense different from action as a relation. Cf. Trendelenburg,

Under the latter he placed all the attributes belonging to the other eight categories, including among them also action used in the sense of relation. Then taking the attributes of this latter type, he divided them according to the most general division of the categories to which they belong, namely, substance and accident. But following Aristotle's division of the category of substance into the predicables of 'definition' and 'genus', the latter used in the sense of both 'genus' and 'difference', he designated the predicates belonging to the category of substance as the attributes of 'definition' and 'part of definition', the expression 'part of definition' having been borrowed by him from Avicenna. Then, again, following Aristotle's occasional classification of the accidental categories into 'quality' and 'relation', he placed all the accidental categories, minus the distinct category of 'action', under the categories of 'quality' and 'relation' and designated them as the attributes of 'quality' and 'relation', substituting them for the two predicables which Aristotle calls 'property' and 'accident'. Finally, taking the resulting new classification of predicables or attributes, he coordinated them and referred to them as the five attributes, corresponding to the conventional reference to the five predicables of Porphyrian origin.

Geschichte der Kategorienlehre, p. 132. It is to be understood, of course, that in its application to God action is not taken by Maimonides as an accident. Cf. Efodi on *Moreh Nebukim* I, 52 (5).

This classification of attributes by Maimonides, quite apart from its specific theological application, may be considered, in its bearing upon the general problem of the nature of logical judgment, as a new and independent revision of Aristotle's list of predicables—one on a par with the revision introduced by Porphyry, and perhaps even of greater importance than the Porphyrian revision. Consequently, histories of philosophy or of logic, which hitherto have assumed that nothing new had happened in the classification of predicables from the time of Porphyry to that of Kant, may now report that a new list of predicables was introduced in the 12th century by Maimonides, and by the side of Porphyry's five predicables of 'genus', 'species', 'difference', 'property' and 'accident' they may now place Maimonides' five predicables of 'definition', 'part of definition', 'quality', 'relation' and 'verb'.

5

MAIMONIDES ON NEGATIVE ATTRIBUTES

In his discussion of the problem of divine attributes Maimonides has introduced a new element — the treatment of all terms affirmed of God as predicates in logical propositions. To his predecessors the problem was only whether attributes, conceived as real incorporeal beings distinct from God's essence, existed in God or not. Their interpretation of predicates affirmed of God as actions or negations was used by them only as a means of expressing their belief that none of the terms predicated of God in Scripture or Koran, in liturgy or in the common speech of men, is to be taken to signify the existence of real attributes in God. To Maimonides, however, the denial of the existence of real attributes is only the groundwork of the problem. The main problem to him makes its appearance only as a logical consequence of such a denial. For logically, with the denial of real attributes, all the terms affirmed of God become predicates which are identical with the subject. They are all tantamount to saying that God is God. But propositions about God, according to him, must have the form and meaning of logical propositions, and logical propositions, by the generally accepted view, must express some kind of relation between subject and predicate other than a relation of identity. This is the main burden of his inquiry, and it is to justify the logical nature of the tautological propositions about God that he uses the old-time device of interpreting all divine predicates as actions or negations.

In a previous paper[1] we have dealt with Maimonides' division of the various kinds of relations that must be assumed to exist between subject and predicate in logical propositions, and we

[1] "The Aristotelian Predicables and Maimonides' Division of Attributes," *Essays and Studies in Memory of Linda R. Miller*, 1938, pp. 201–234. Above, pp. 161–194.

have also touched upon the meaning of his interpretation of predicates as actions. By his interpretation of predicates as actions, we have tried to show, he means that propositions about God are not to be taken as propositions of the third adjacent, i. e., propositions consisting of a subject and predicate connected by the copula *is*, but rather as propositions of the second adjacent, i. e., propositions consisting of a subject and finite verb. In propositions of the third adjacent there must be some relation, other than identity, between subject and predicate; in propositions of the second adjacent, wherein the copula and predicate are combined to form what Maimonides calls "verb" as well as "action," the predicate and subject may be logically identical without making the proposition tautological. This solution of the problem is first stated by Maimonides in a general way;[2] then he shows how all propositions in which "life", "power", "knowledge", and "will" are predicated of God are to be taken as propositions of the second adjacent rather than propositions of the third adjacent.[3] Thus interpreted, this solution of Maimonides of the problem of divine attributes may have its historical background in the solution of the problem of the one and the many as reproduced by Aristotle from some anonymous philosophers. The problem dealt with by Aristotle is like that dealt with here by Maimonides. It was argued that no proposition in which the subject and predicate were different was logically admissible, for any such proposition would make the subject, which is one, to be many. The answer as reported by Aristotle reads that some philosophers were led "to change the mode of expression and say 'the man has been whitened' instead of 'is white', and 'walks' instead of 'is walking', for fear that if they added the word 'is' they should be making the one to be many."[4] In other words, they have changed every proposition of the third adjacent into a proposition of the second adjacent.

In the present paper we shall deal with Maimonides' interpretation of attributes as negations, which is offered by him as

[2] *Moreh Nebukim* I, 52 (5).

[3] *Ibid.*, 53.

[4] *Phys.* I, 2, 185 b, 28–31.

an alternative to his previous interpretation of them as actions. According to this alternative interpretation, all propositions in which any term is predicated of God are to be taken as propositions of the third adjacent, and the relation between subject and predicate in all such propositions is therefore one of identity. But in order to justify such seemingly tautological propositions he advances the negative interpretation.

His discussion of the subject falls into two parts. First, he tries to show how in affirmative propositions about God the predicate is to be understood as being an equivocal term. Second, he further tries to show how such affirmative propositions with equivocal predicates are also to be understood as having a negative meaning. The former phase of the discussion is to be found in Ch. 57, which begins with the statement: "Of attributes, remarks more recondite than the preceding." The latter phase of the discussion is to be found in Ch. 58, which begins with the statement: "This chapter is even more recondite than the preceding." As the subject of his discussion of the negative interpretation of predicates he takes the terms "existence," "unity," and "firstness," the last of which is the scriptural term for "eternity" in the specific sense of eternity *a parte ante*. The initial selection of these three terms as examples of predicates which are to be explained negatively is due to historical precedents. Before him Baḥya, for instance, who similarly explained predicates as either actions or negations, selected as the subject of the latter kind of explanation the same predicates of "existence," "unity," and "firstness."[5] But in order to show that these are not the only predicates which can be explained as negations, Maimonides, in the midst of his discussion of this list of these three predicates, slips into it three of the other four predicates, namely, "life," "power," and "knowledge,"[6] which previously have been explained by him as actions.

In his discussion of the significance of the affirmative form of the predications of God, confining himself directly to the three

[5] *Ḥobot ha-Lebabot* I, 10.

[6] *Moreh Nebukim* I, 57: ואם כן הוא נמצא ולא במציאות, וכן חי לא בחיים, ויודע לא במדע, ויכול לא ביכלת, וחכם לא בחכמה.

terms "existence," "unity" and "firstness," Maimonides says that in their application to created beings, or, if creation is not admitted, in their application to possible beings, i. e., beings whose existence depends upon a cause, are all accidents superadded to the essence of the subject to which they apply. This view, in so far as it relates to "existence" and "unity," represents the view of Alfarabi and Avicenna which during the lifetime of Maimonides was called into question by his contemporary Averroes.[7] Maimonides, however, was unacquainted with the objections raised against it by Averroes[8] and he states it here as the generally accepted view among philosophers. Now according to this prevalent view, in all things whose existence depends upon a cause, that is to say, whose existence by its own nature is only possible, existence is only an accident, just as the fact of their being white or black, great or small, is only an accident. Similarly, in all things, and this includes all things below God, in which there are such distinctions as genus and species, matter and form, substance and accident, unity is only an accident, for they are one only because they happen to be united by some external union; internally, they are more than one, even though the internal plurality which they possess is one that may be discerned only by our mind. That the term "first" or eternal *a parte ante*, is an accident is more obvious, for to be first means to be first in time, and as time is an accident of motion, which in its turn, is an accident of body, "firstness" is of necessity only an accident of things.

All this, he continues, is true only when the terms "existence," "unity" and "firstness" are applied to beings outside of God. When applied to God, however, these terms are to be understood as having an entirely different sense. They are to be understood as equivocal terms which in meaning are absolutely unrelated to similarly sounding terms which are applied to other beings. As equivocal terms they are in their application to God no longer

[7] Cf. *Moreh ha-Moreh*, Narboni and Munk *ad loc.*

[8] Cf. discussion of the question as to Maimonides' acquaintance with the works of Averroes in *Crescas' Critique of Aristotle*, p. 323. Shem-Ṭob Falaquera, *Moreh ha-Moreh*, Introduction, p. 8, however, assumes that Maimonides had a knowledge of Averroes.

universal terms, they are rather individual terms which can be predicated only of God. They do not, therefore, as do the similarly sounding universal accidents of "existence," "unity" and "firstness," signify the inherence of any accidents in the essence of God, but rather like the name Jahveh, which is the proper name of God,[9] they signify the very essence of God. And having given this explanation of the terms "existence," "unity" and "firstness," Maimonides suggests that the four terms of "life," "power," "knowledge" [and "will"] can similarly be explained as terms signifying the very essence of God, even though previously he has tried to show how they could be converted into actions. All these terms predicated of God thus affirm that they are the same as God. They form together with the term God, of which they are predicated, propositions of the third adjacent wherein the relation between subject and predicate is that of identity.

To express this view as to the significance of the affirmative form in which terms are predicated of God, Maimonides uses two formulae. The first formula, stated by him in the course of his discussion of negative attributes, reads as follows: "God is existent, but not according to existence; and similarly He is knowing, but not according to knowledge; and He is powerful, but not according to power."[10] The second formula is stated by him in the course of his discussion of divine knowledge, and it reads: "God has not any attribute external to His essence, but His essence is His knowledge and His knowledge is His essence."[11] Combining these two formulae into one, it would read: God is knowing, but not according to knowledge, for His knowledge is His essence and His essence is His knowledge. Now this combined formula is a reproduction, with but one slight change in wording, of a formula attributed to Naẓẓām, which reads: "God is incessantly knowing, living, powerful, hearing, eternal according to His essence (*binafsihi*), not according to knowledge, power,

[9] *Moreh Nebukim* I, 61.

[10] *Ibid.*, I, 57. Cf. quotation in n. 6 above.

[11] *Ibid.*, III, 20: שהם בארו במופת שעצמו יתעלה אין רבוי בו ולא תאר לו חוץ לעצמו אבל עצמו מדעו ומדעו עצמו.

life, hearing, seeing, and eternity."[12] In using this formula Naẓẓām meant to express by it his denial of the existence not only of attributes but also of modes.[13] This exactly corresponds to the view of Maimonides, for not only does he repudiate the view of the Ash'arites, to which he refers in his statement concerning those who believe that "God is one, but that He possesses many attributes, and that He with His attributes are one"[14] but he also repudiates Abū Ḥāshim's theory of modes, to which he refers in his statement concerning "some thinkers" who say the "attributes are neither His essence nor anything extraneous to His essence."[15] Agreeing with Naẓẓām in his denial of both attributes and modes, Maimonides quite naturally adopted Naẓẓām's formula to express his view.

But, as we have remarked above, in his reproduction of Naẓẓām's formula, Maimonides has made one change in the wording. He has substituted the expression "God's knowledge is His essence" for Naẓẓām's expression "God is knowing according to His essence." This substitution, we shall try to show, was done by Maimonides quite deliberately, and for the following reason. In Arabic philosophy the expression "according to His essence" was used as signifying two opposite theories of attributes, represented respectively by Jubbāi and Abū Ḥāshim. Concerning Jubbāi it is reported: "Jubbāi says that the Creator is knowing according to His essence (*li-dhātihi*), powerful, living according to His essence, and his use of the expression 'according to His essence' shows that he does not take the statement that God is knowing to imply an attribute, which constitutes the knowledge itself, or a mode, which makes God to be knowing."[16] Concerning Abū Ḥāshim it is reported: "Abū Ḥāshim, however,

[12] *Al-Ash'ari*, ed. H. Ritter, p. 486, ll. 11–12. The same formula is reproduced by Shahrastani, ed. Cureton, p. 34, l. 17, without giving the name of its author.

[13] Shahrastani, p. 34, l. 18.

[14] *Moreh Nebukim* I, 50; (Hebrew, p. 70b, l. 1; Arabic, p. 57a, ll. 8–9): הוא אחד אבל הוא בעל תארים רבים, והוא ותאריו אחד.

[15] *Ibid.*, I, 51; (Hebrew, p. 71b, l. 6; Arabic, p. 58a, ll. 20–21): וכבר הגיע המאמר באנשים מבעלי העיון, באמרם כי תאריו יתעלה אינם עצמו ולא דבר יוצא מעצמו.

[16] Shahrastani, p. 55, l. 19–p. 56, l. 1.

takes the statement 'He is knowing according to His essence' to mean that He is endowed with a mode (*ḥālah*)."[17] Now, Maimonides, as we have seen, is opposed not only to the attributes of the Ash'arites but also to the modes of Abū Ḥāshim. Furthermore, Abū Ḥāshim's view is reproduced by him in its original formula by the use of the expression "according to His essence," for it its undoubtedly Abū Ḥāshim whom he refers to in his repudiation of "the statement of one of them that God is powerful according to His essence (*li-dhātihi*), knowing according to His essence, living according to His own essence, willing according to His essence."[18] It is quite evident therefore that it is because the expression "according to His essence" was used by Abū Ḥāshim as signifying the existence of modes that Maimonides, in his reproduction of Naẓẓām's formula, has substituted for it, the expression "is His essence."

Besides its association with Abū Ḥāshim's theory of modes, another reason why Maimonides should have objected to the expression "according to His essence" is to be found in his own particular classification of predicables and his use of it as a classification of divine predicates. The expression "according to His essence", of which the Arabic is *li-dhātihi* or *bi-dhātihi* or *bi-nafsihi* or *li-'ainhi*, reflects the Greek *καθ' αὑτό*. Thus Aristotle's statement that "the activity of God according to its essence (*καθ' αὑτὴν*) is life most good and most eternal"[19] is paraphrased in Arabic by the statement "God is living according to His essence (*bi-dhātihi*) and is eternally enduring according to His essence".[20] Technically the Greek phrase *καθ' αὑτό* in Aristotle is used as a designation of what he calls property (*ἴδιον*).[21] Now, on some other occasion, we shall show that before Maimonides, those who denied the existence of real attributes, took the predicates of God to be properties of God, and this either together with the actional and negative interpretation

[17] *Ibid.*, p. 56, ll. 1–2.

[18] *Moreh Nebukim* I, 53: כמאמר קצתם, יכול לעצמו (לראתה), חכם לעצמו, חי לעצמו, רוצה לעצמו.

[19] *Metaph.* XII, 7, 1072b, 27–28.

[20] Shahrastani, p. 315, ll. 13–14.

[21] *Metaph.* V, 18, 1022a, 35–36, and *Top.*, I, 5, 102a, 18–19.

or without it. Maimonides, however, as we have already shown in our discussion of his classification of attributes, considered properties as accidents.[22] To him nothing short of complete identity of the predicate with the subject is permissible in propositions about God. It is for this reason that the expression "according to His essence" was disapproved of by him, and he substituted for it the expression "is His essence".

The expression "is His essence" in itself, however, is adopted by Maimonides from 'Allāf, who uses it as part of a formula which expresses a view to which Maimonides is openly opposed. The formula as reported in the name of 'Allāf reads as follows: "God is knowing according to knowledge and the knowledge is His essence, powerful according to power and the power is His essence, living according to life and the life is His essence."[23] 'Allāf's formula is said to differ from Naẓẓām's formula, and its difference from the latter formula is that, unlike the latter, it implies some kind of existence of attributes, analogous to what Abū Ḥāshim later called modes.[24] What Maimonides, therefore, did in his two formulae is this. In his first formula, he took from Naẓẓām the expression "knowing, not according to knowledge," but left out the expression "according to His essence," on account of its use by Abū Ḥāshim in expressing his theory of modes. In his second formula, he took from 'Allāf the expression "His knowledge is His essence," but left out the expression "according to knowledge," again on account of its use by 'Allaf as expressing a view which is like Abū Ḥāshim's theory of modes.

The rigidity with which Maimonides uses these various formulae may be contrasted with the looseness with which earlier Jewish philosophers have used them. Al-Muḳammaṣ, who denied the existence of real attributes, uses the formula "God is living without life, but He is living according to His essence,"[25] thus, unlike Maimonides, he has no objection to the expression "according to life"; but, then, like Maimonides, he uses also

[22] *Op. cit.* (above n. 1), pp. 215–216, 218
[23] Shahrastani, p. 34, ll. 13–14.
[24] *Ibid.*, p. 34, ll. 17–20.
[25] *Halikot Ḳedem*, p. 75, l. 9: שהוא חי בלא חיים, אבל הוא חי בנפשו.

the formula "His life is His essence" and explains that it means the same as the formula "He is living without life."[26] Saadia, who also denies the existence of real attributes, again, unlike Maimonides, has no objection to the use of the formula "He is living according to His essence (*li-'ainihi*) and He is knowing according to His essence."[27]

Thus, even though Maimonides has rejected Naẓẓām's expression "according to His essence," on account, as we have tried to show, of its having been used by Abū Ḥāshim as signifying the existence of modes, still in the phrasing of his own formulae he tries to stress the significance of the positive form of the various propositions about God. In his first formula, the

[26] *Ibid.*, ll. 2–4: ואם יאמר כי החיים שלו הוא הוא, היה אומר כי השם הוא חי בלא חיים, אבל חילוף הלשון ולא נתחלף הענין.

Judah Ha-Levi (*Cuzari* V, 18, 10), in his restatement of the doctrines of the Kalam, uses the following formula: "He is living according to the life of His essence . . . powerful according to His own power, and willing according to His own will" חי בחיות עצמותו (בחיאה̈ דאתה) . . . יכול ביכלתו וחפץ בחפצו. He then adds a statement which occurs in two versions: (1) In the original Arabic it reads: "One cannot say 'He is powerful without power', (קאדר בלא קדרה̈), without the addition of some qualifying statement". (2) In the Hebrew translation it reads: "One cannot say concerning Him 'He is powerful according to power' (יכול ביכולת), without the addition of some qualifying statement". If the Arabic reading is adopted, then the formula reproduced by Ha-Levi is the same as that used by Al-Muḳammaṣ, the expression "living according to the life of His essence" in Ha-Levi being the equivalent of the expressions "living according to His essence" and "His life is His essence" in Al-Muḳammaṣ. Al-Muḳammaṣ's formula in itself is a combination of both Naẓẓām's and Allāf's formulas. If the Hebrew reading is adopted, then the formula reproduced by Ha-Levi may be either that of Naẓẓām or that of Allāf, in the former case the expression "living according to the life of His essence" being the equivalent of Naẓẓām's "living according to His essence", whereas in the latter case the same expression being the equivalent of Allāf's "and the life is His essence".

[27] *Emunot we-De'ot*, II, 5, p. 92, l. 22; Arabic, p. 87, ll. 9–10: התחייב בלא ספק שיהיה חי לעצמו (لعينه) וחכם לעצמו. Kaufmann (*Attributenlehre*, pp. 33 f.) is not right in identifying this formula with that of 'Allāf. It has neither of the two characteristic expressions which mark 'Allāf's formula, namely, (1) living according to life; knowing according to knowledge, and (2) His life is His essence; His knowledge is His essence (cf. above n. 23). The formula used here by Saadia is that of Naẓẓām.

assertion "God is existent, living, knowing, and powerful" is just as important for him as the qualification "but not according to existence, not according to life, not according to knowledge, and not according to power." In his second formula, the second part thereof, namely, "God's essence is His knowledge and His knowledge is His essence," is used by him as an explanation of its first part, namely, "God has not any attribute external to His essence". The affirmative form of the predication is thus as important for him as its negative implication. The question therefore arises as to what logical justification there is for propositions which merely assert that the predicate is identical with the subject. If all the predicates affirmed of God are identical with God, then the propositions in which they stand are tautological, tantamount to saying God is God.

It is in answer to this question that Maimonides takes up the old device of the negative interpretation. In all such propositions, he seems to say, the affirmation of the identity of subject and predicate is used for the purpose of emphasizing the negation of the opposite of that predicate which is affirmed of the subject. The identity affirmed is indeed by means of equivocal terms, which convey to us no positive meaning. Still it is not altogether tautological or useless, for it serves the useful purpose of the negation of something which otherwise might be considered as admissible of God. A tautology ceases to be a tautology, Maimonides seems to say, when its affirmation is in answer to a challenge and implies a negation of the opposite. Even such proposition as "A is A" may have a logical significance if, for some reason, such, for instance, as the answer to the challenge that "A is B", it is necessary to affirm that "A is A" in order to emphasize that "A is not B". In propositions about God, according to Maimonides, it is always necessary to affirm that such predicates as "living", knowing", powerful" and "willing" are identical with God's essence, because on the one hand there are some who consider them as being real attributes distinct from God's essence, while on the other hand there are others who deny them of God altogether. To affirm of God predicates in an equivocal sense serves the purpose of showing that we understand by God a being most perfect, "to whose perfect essence nothing can be superadded and whose perfection means the negation of imperfections".[28] The use of the negative interpretation of affirmatively expressed propositions is first introduced by Maimonides indirectly in Ch. 57, in connection with the discussion of the term "first";[29] but it is then directly discussed in Ch. 58, in connection with attributes in general.[30]

In his direct discussion of negative attributes Maimonides illustrates his explanation by a list of propositions, all of the third adjacent, in which the affirmative predication of certain terms is shown to be an emphasis of the negation of respectively corresponding opposite terms. The list contains eight terms, the seven already mentioned by him before, with the addition of one new term. These eight terms, in the order in which they are presented by Maimonides are as follows: (1) existence, (2) life, (3) incorporeality, (4) firstness, (5) power, (6) knowledge, (7) will, (8) unity. In his treatment of the subject, he constructs out of seven of these eight terms affirmative propositions with God as the subject and shows how in meaning these propositions are negative. "He is existent" or, as it literally reads in Arabic and Hebrew, "He is found", means "He is not missed"; "He is living" means "He is not dead"; "He is first" means "He is not caused"; "He is powerful" means "He is not weak"; "He is knowing" means "He is not foolish"; "He is willing" means "He is not rash or neglectful"; "He is one" means "He is not many."[31] Only in the case of the negative proposition "He is not corporeal"[32] does he fail to give a corresponding affirmative proposition. Such an affirmative proposition would be "He is pure form." The reason why he does not give it is probably to be found in the fact that such a proposition is not in common usage.

[28] *Moreh Nebukim* I, 58: ולא ישנהו ענין מוסף על עצמו השלם, אשר ענין שלמותו שלילת החסרונות ממנו.

[29] *Ibid.*, I, 57.

[30] *Ibid.*, I, 58.

[31] *Ibid.* . . . ואמרנו בו שהוא נמצא (מוֹגֹד), הענין כי מן השקר העדרו (עדמה) . . . חי (חי) אינו מת (ליס במאית) . . . קדמון (קדים) . . . אין לו סבה (ליס לה סבב) המציאתו . . . יכול (קאדר) וחכם (ועאלם) ורוצה (ומריד) . . . שאינו לואה (ליס בעאגֹז) ולא סכל (ולא גֹאהל) ולא נבהל או עוזב (ולא דֹאהל ולא מהמל) . . . אחד (ואחד) . . . הרחקת הרבוי (נפי אלכתֹרה).

[32] *Ibid.*: שהוא אינו גוף (אנה ליס בגֹסם).

Maimonides' treatment of these eight terms follows a certain definite plan. He arranges them in such a way as to show how, when taken as the negation of their opposites, they constitute a complete description, logically and orderly arranged, of the dissimilarity between God and all other beings. He naturally begins with the term "existence" which is common to all beings. But in order to negate any similarity between God who is said to exist and all other beings who are likewise said to exist, one must interpret the direct affirmative attribution of "existence" to God to mean an indirect negation of the "privation" which is inevitably implied in the existence of all other beings by the reason of the fact that in all other beings existence is only accidental and hence only possible if not also transient. Now existent beings are generally divided into three classes: the sublunar elements, the celestial spheres and the intelligences. The sublunar elements are inanimate or dead bodies; the celestial spheres are living beings but they are still corporeal; the intelligences are incorporeal but they are still the effects of a cause. Consequently, immediately after the term "existence" Maimonides takes up the terms "life" and "firstness" and inserts between them the hitherto unmentioned term "corporeality", in order to show how by their predication of God they negate any similarity between God and these three classes of beings. The affirmative predication of "life" indirectly negates the likeness of God to the sublunar elements which are "dead"; the direct negation of "corporeality" shows the unlikeness of God to the celestial bodies which are "corporeal"; and again the affirmative predication of "firstness", which means "not being caused", indirectly negates the likeness of God to the Intelligences who are "caused." Then Maimonides takes up the three terms of "power," "knowledge" and "will," and shows how by their predication of God they indirectly negate any similarity between the causality of God's essence and the causality of any of the other beings. The affirmative predication of "power" indirectly negates the likeness of God to other beings, who are "weak," that is to say, incapable to produce certain things. The affirmative predication of "knowledge" indirectly negates the likeness of God to certain other beings, who are "foolish," that is to say, they are blind forces acting by necessity and unconscious of the results produced by them. The affirmative predication of "will" indirectly negates the likeness of God to some other beings, who are "rash" and "neglectful," that is to say, they act without any purpose. Finally, he takes up the remaining term "unity," which in its sense of "uniqueness" sums up all the other negations, and shows how its affirmative predication of God negates indirectly that there is anything like God.[33]

In his statement how the affirmative predication of certain terms of God is to be taken as meaning the negation of certain corresponding opposite terms of Him, Maimonides does not say, as we should expect him to say, that such affirmations mean the "negation of their opposite." Instead he says that they mean the "negation of their privation."[34] The use of the term "privation" here instead of the term "opposite" refers to the special type of opposite which in Aristotle is called "privation." The term opposite, according to Aristotle, is used in four senses: (1) as correlatives to one another, such as, double and half; (2) as contraries to one another, such as, bad and good; (3) as privation and habit, such as, blindness and sight; (4) as affirmation and negation, such as, he sits and he does not sit.[35] This classification of the four types of opposite is reproduced by Maimonides in his *Millot ha-Higgayon*.[36] What Maimonides means to say here, therefore, is simply that the opposites which are negated of God in all the affirmative propositions which he has mentioned are all of the type known as the opposites of "habit" and "privation," and not of the type known as the opposities of "contraries." The reason why he insists upon their being "privations" and not "contraries" is this. He wants to say that every affirmation of one term in propositions about God implies the negation of its opposite. Now if the opposites are "habit" and "privation," then this statement is universally

[33] *Ibid.*

[34] *Ibid.*: הנה כבר התבאר לך כי כל תאר שנתארהו בו, הוא אם תאר פעולה, או יהיה ענינו שלילת העדרו (כלב עדמהא), אם היתה הכונה בו השגת עצמו לא פעולתו.

[35] *Categ.*, Ch. 10, 11b, 15 ff.

[36] *Millot ha-Higgayon*, Ch. 11.

true, for by the law of the excluded middle every proposition "A is B" implies the proposition "A is not not-B." But if the opposites are "contraries," then Maimonides' statement would not be universally true, for, according to Aristotle, between certain contraries there are intermediates, and in such cases it would not be true to say that every affirmation of one contrary implies the negation of its opposite contrary. Thus, for instance, it does not necessarily follow that the proposition "A is good" means "A is not bad" or the proposition "A is white" means "A is not black," for the "A" in the proposition may be something which is intermediate between good and bad or between black and white and thus it may be at the same time both good and bad or both black and white.[37] Thus all the seven pairs of opposition enumerated by him are each considered by him as an opposition of "habit" and "privation": existent — being missed; living — dead; first — caused; powerful — weak; knowing or wise — foolish; willing — rash or neglectful; one — many. I have purposely translated the opposites of "existent," "powerful" and "knowing" by "being missed," "weak" and "foolish," rather than by "non-existent," "powerless" and "ignorant," because in Arabic as well as in Hebrew these terms are positive in form. They are "privations" only in meaning, after the manner of the term "blindness," which Aristotle, as we have seen, calls privation and the opposite of the term "sight." Of terms which are negative in form, such, for instance, as "unseeing" or "sightless", we shall speak later.[38]

But here a question must have arisen in the mind of Maimonides. The very same law of excluded middle which makes every proposition "A is B" imply "A is not not-B" also makes every proposition "A is not not-B" imply that "A is B." Consequently, if we object to the affirmation of a "habit" of God, we cannot justify such an affirmation by saying that it means the negation of its opposite privation, for the negation of the privation reciprocally means the affirmation of its opposite habit. In other words, if we cannot say "God is living," then we cannot justify our saying it by maintaining that it means

[37] *Categ.*, Ch. 10, 12a, 13–20. [38] Cf. below nn. 55–58.

"God is not dead," for the latter proposition, logically, means "God is living."

Maimonides does not raise this question directly but he anticipates it in certain passages which are full of allusions to various statements in Aristotle and in the commentary of Alexander on Aristotle. We shall present this historical background first.

On several occasions Aristotle speaks of a distinction between privation (στέρησις), and negation (ἀπόφασις), or between privative negation (στερητικὴ ἀπόφασις) and negation,[39] that is to say, between an affirmative proposition in which the predicate is a privation and a negative proposition in which the predicate is a habit. In the case of a proposition in which a privation is affirmed of a subject, he says that "it is a universal rule" that the privation of a habit "is predicated of that in which the 'habit' in question can naturally exist."[40] He explains it by the illustration that we can say of a man that he is blind, not simply because he has no sight, but because he has no sight at a time when by nature he should have it.[41] As contrasted with this is the case of a proposition in which a "habit" is negated of a subject, for in any such proposition, he says, as, e. g., the proposition "A is not one", the negation of unity means just "the absence (ἀπουσία) thereof",[42] without the implication that the subject "A" can naturally be one. Alexander in his commentary on Aristotle's *Metaphysics* explains the difference between "negation" and "privation" by the two propositions "A is not seeing" and "A is blind", "for," he says, "the expression 'is not seeing' may indeed be appropriately said both of a blind man and of a wall, the latter of which is absolutely incapable of having sight . . . not so, however, is the case of blindness."[43] In other words, you can say "the wall is not seeing" but you cannot say "the wall is blind."

39 *Metaph.* IV, 2, 1004a, 14–16; IV, 6, 1011b, 18 ff.; X, 5, 1056a, 17.

40 *Categ.*, Ch. 10, 12a, 27–29.

41 *Ibid.*, 31–34.

42 *Metaph.* IV, 2, 1004a, 14–15.

43 *Alexander in Metaphysica*, ed. M. Hayduck, p. 327, ll. 18–20, on *Metaph.* IV, 6, 1011b, 15 ff. τὸ γὰρ οὐχ ὁρᾷ καὶ ἐπὶ τοῦ τυφλοῦ ἀληθὲς καὶ ἐπὶ τοῦ τοίχου, ὅς οὐδὲ ὅλως ὄψεως δεκτικός . . . οὐχ οὕτω καὶ ἡ τυφλότης.

Thus, according to Aristotle, a predicate can be negated of a subject, in a proposition which is negative in form, or, as it is usually called, negative in quality, irrespective of the fact whether the subject by its very nature can have that predicate which is negated of it or it cannot have it. The meaning of the negation, however, will differ in accordance with the difference in the nature of the subject as to whether it can have the predicate negated of it or it cannot have it. In negating of a subject something which that subject may naturally have, as, e. g., in the proposition "the man is not seeing," the negation merely means the assertion that of a class of beings which ordinarily are seeing a certain individual for some reason does not happen to be seeing. In negating of a subject something which that subject cannot naturally have, as, e. g., in the proposition "the wall is not seeing," the negation means the assertion that the subject in question belongs to a class of beings which by their very nature cannot see. In other words, negation in the latter case means a denial that the predicate in question can be appropriately affirmed of the subject. Narboni, referring vaguely to works on logic, without specifying them, expresses this view by distinguishing within what Aristotle and Alexander call "negation" between "particular negation" and "absolute negation," illustrating the former by the proposition "Balaam is not seeing" and the latter by the proposition "the wall is not seeing."[44] This illustration of Balaam is very apt. When one recalls that Balaam of Biblical fame is depicted in Jewish tradition as having been blind of one eye[45] and, according to the Biblical narrative itself, he was blind to the presence of the angel until "the Lord opened his eyes,"[46] one can see how Narboni came to use the example of the proposition "Balaam is not seeing" as a substitution for Aristotle's own implied example of the proposition "the blind man is not seeing."

[44] Narboni on *Moreh Nebukim* I, 58: כבר ידעת ממה שקראת ממלאכת ההגיון כי השלילה שני מינים: האחת השלילה המיוחדת, כמו שנאמר בלעם אינו רואה, והיא השלילה האמתית; והשני השלילה המשולחת, והוא שישלול מן הנושא מה שאין דרכו שימצא בו, כמו הכותל אינו רואה, והיא השלילה הכוללת.

[45] *Sanhedrin* 105a; *Niddah* 31a.

[46] Num. 22.31.

In these passages of Aristotle and Alexander, it will be noticed, three statements are made. (1) We cannot say the wall is seeing", nor (2) can we say "the wall is blind", but (3) we can say (3) "the wall is not seeing." Nothing is said by them with regard to the proposition "the wall is not blind. "But we may reasonably assume that they would admit that on purely logical grounds we can say "the wall is not blind," even though, according to them, we cannot say "the wall is blind." In other words, the proposition "the wall is not blind" does not mean an indirect assertion that "the wall is seeing"; it only means that the term "blind" is inapplicable to the term wall, because "blindness" is foreign to its nature, just as the negative proposition "the wall is not seeing" only means that the term "seeing" is inapplicable to the term wall, because "sight" is foreign to its nature.

This distinction between "privation" and "negation," together with Alexander's illustration of a wall, is reproduced by Maimonides. With regard to "privation," he says: "Nothing can have a term of 'privation' as its predicate except that in which the 'habit' opposite to that 'privation' can naturally exist, for we do not say of a wall that it is foolish or blind or dumb."[47] With regard to "negation," he says: "Sometimes one negates of a thing that which cannot naturally exist in it, as, for instance, we say concerning a wall that it is not seeing."[48] In other words, as in Alexander's explanation of Aristotle, we cannot say "the wall is blind" but we can say "the wall is not seeing." Now since every affirmative proposition about God, such, for instance, as "God is powerful" is to be understood as meaning not a "privation" but rather a "negation," namely, "God is not weak," it follows that the negation of weakness in such a proposition does not necessarily imply that its opposite power, in its ordinary sense as the opposite of weakness, is indirectly predicated of God. He thus says that "even with respect to these negations you

[47] *Millot ha-Higgayon*, Ch. 11: ולא יתואר בשם ההעדר כי אם מי שטבעו שימצא לו הקנין ההוא הנכוחי להעדר ההוא, כי אנחנו לא נאמר בכותל שהוא סכל ולא עור ולא אלם.

[48] *Moreh Nebukim* I, 58: ולא תעשה גם כן אלו השלילות ולא תתירם עליו יתעלה אלא בפנים אשר כבר ידעת, שפעמים ישולל מהדבר מה שאין דרכו שימצא לו, כמו שנאמר בכותל לא רואה (לא בציר).

cannot make use of them and apply them to God except in the way which you know, namely, that sometimes one negates of a thing that which cannot naturally exist in it, as, for instance, we say concerning a wall that it is not seeing."[49] In other words, just as in the proposition "the wall is not seeing" the negation means that the term "seeing" is inapplicable to the wall, so in any proposition like "God is not weak" the negation only means that the term "weak" is inapplicable to God; it does not mean that the term "powerful" in its ordinary sense as the mere opposite of the term "weak" is applicable to God. Indeed one does say "God is powerful," but in such a proposition, Maimonides maintains, the term "powerful" is an equivocal term and affirms of God His own power which is identical with His essence. When, therefore, Maimonides maintains that by saying "God is powerful" we mean "God is not weak," the negation of the term "weak" means at the same time also the negation of the term "powerful" in its ordinary sense, for the term "powerful" in its ordinary sense is only weakness when compared with God's own power. This view, that by affirming of God any such term as "powerful" in an equivocal sense we thereby negate of Him not only the term "weak" but also the term "powerful" in its ordinary sense, is brought out by Maimonides in his statement that God, on account of His not being subject to the accident of time, "cannot be truly described either as 'first' (*qadim*) or as 'created', just as 'sweetness' cannot be described as 'crooked' or 'straight' and just as 'voice' cannot be described as 'salty' or 'vapid'."[50] Now elsewhere, as we have seen, Maimonides

[49] *Ibid.* Cf. quotation in preceding note.

[50] *Moreh Nebukim* I, 57: לא יאמר עליו באמת לא קדמון (קדים) ולא חדש (חאדת׳), כמו שלא יאמר במתיקות לא מעוותת ולא ישרה, ולא יאמר בקול לא מליח ולא תפל (תפה). In this passage I have purposely translated the Arabic تفه, תפל, by "vapid." The translation of this term by *insulsa* (Justinianus; Buxtorf), *geschmacklos* (Fürstenthal; Weiss), *insipide* (Munk), and *insipid* (Friedländer) is literally correct but logically, in this particular passage, wrong; and for the following reason. The Arabic as well as the Hebrew term here is not negative but rather privative. Using here a term which is privative, Maimonides could very well state that we cannct say "the voice is vapid," for in the same way, according to Aristotle, we cannot say "the wall is blind" (cf. above n. 43). But if we translate it by "insipid" or "tasteless" or any other term which is negative,

explicitly states quite on the contrary that we can say "God is first (*qadim*)", provided we use the term 'first' in an equivocal sense, as something identical with the essence of God, meaning thereby that "God is not caused",[51] i. e., that He is not created. What he therefore means here by his statement that "God cannot be truly described either as first or as created" is merely to explain that when we say "God is first" and use the term first in an equivocal sense, we mean thereby not ony that "God is not created" but also that "God is not first" in the ordinary sense of the term first.

But we shall now try to show that besides expressing negative attributes by means of the "negation of privation" Maimonides also uses another method of expressing negative attributes, and that is by means of the "affirmation of privation", provided that the privation is a negative term, that is, a term with a negative prefix or affix.

Maimonides does not deal directly with negative attributes expressed by the "affirmation of privation", that is, by affirmative propositions in which the predicate is a negative term. All the eight propositions of which he says that they are negations of privations are negative propositions in which the predicates, as we have seen, are only privations in meaning but not negative in form.[52] They are all expressed by him in the technical form in which negative propositions are usually expressed in Arabic.[53] Still there is in Maimonides an indirect reference to affirmative propositions with predicates which are negative terms, and from this indirect reference we may infer that such propositions were regarded by him, in connection with the problem of divine attributes, as being the equivalent of negative propositions. The indirect reference in question is to be found in the passage quoted

Maimonides could not state that we cannot say "the voice is insipid or tasteless", for, as we shall see, according to Aristotle, we can say "the voice is invisible" (cf. below n. 55).

[51] *Ibid.*, I, 58.

[52] Cf. above n. 31.

[53] The technical form of negative propositions, as given by Maimonides himself in *Millot ha-Higgayon*, Ch. 2, is אין ראובן חכם : ליס זיד עאלם; cf. also below n. 65 and above n. 31.

above, wherein Maimonides says that "sometimes one negates of a thing that which cannot naturally exist in it, as, for instance, we say concerning a wall that it is not seeing".[54] The Arabic in this passage for what we have provisionally translated by "not seeing" is *lā baṣīr*. The negative *lā*, I take it, is used here in the same sense as the negative *gair*, corresponding to our negative prefix *un*. The terms *lā baṣir* in this passage should therefore be translated not by "not seeing" but rather by "unseeing". The logical principle involved here is that, according to Maimonides, there is a distinction between a privation which is expressed by a positive term, such, e. g., as "blind", and a privation which is expressed by a negative term, such e. g., as "unseeing". In the former case, it can be affirmed only of a subject in which the opposite habit "seeing" would naturally exist, and therefore one cannot say "the wall is blind"; in the latter case, it can be affirmed even of a subject in which the opposite habit "seeing" would not naturally exist, and therefore we can say "the wall is unseeing". By the same token, according to Maimonides, we can describe God not only in negative propositions, such as "God is not mortal" and "God is not corruptible", but also in affirmative propositions with negative predicates, such as "God is immortal" and "God is incorruptible".

This distinction which we have found in Maimonides between a privation which is expressed by a positive term and a privation which is a negative term is not discussed by Aristotle. But, I think, it is implied in several passages. In three passages, Aristotle intimates that a "voice" can be said to be "invisible" (ἀόρατος), even though visibility cannot naturally exist in a voice.[55] From this it may be inferred that, according to him, while one cannot say "the wall is blind", one can say "the wall is unseeing". In another passage, he states that one can say "a plant is deprived of eyes (ὀμμάτων ἐστερῆσθαι)", even though it cannot naturally have eyes.[56] From his subsequent remark that "there are as many kinds of privations as there are of words

[54] *Moreh Nebukim* I, 58; cf. above n. 48.

[55] *Phys.* III, 5, 204a, 13–14; V, 2, 226b, 10–11; *Metaph.* XI, 10, 1066a, 36.

[56] *Metaph.* V, 22, 1022b, 23–24.

with negative prefixes or affixes"[57] we may gather that, according to him, one can express his previous statement "a plant is deprived of eyes" by the statement "a plant is eyeless (ἀνόμματον)". From this again it may be inferred that, according to Arsitotle, one can say "the wall is unseeing" or "the wall is sightless" even though one cannot say "the wall is blind".[58]

That an affirmative proposition in which the predicate is a term with a negative prefix or affix is to be regarded as a negative proposition can be shown to have been also the view of Avicenna and Averroes. In Arabic there are no negative prefixes or affixes, but such prefixes and affixes can be expressed by the negative particle *gair* or *lā*. Now, with regard to the use of these negative particles, there is a statement by Avicenna that the Arabic proposition *Zaid lā baṣīr* may sometimes mean the same as the negative proposition *inna Zaidan laisa huwa bi-baṣīrin*, which logically means that "Zaid is not seeing".[59] This, as we shall explain later, refers to the case when *lā baṣīr* is taken in the sense of "unseeing".[60] A similar use of *lā baṣīr* in the sense of "unseeing" and of the proposition "Zaid is unseeing" as the equivalent of a negative proposition is to be discerned also, as we shall show, in Averroes.[61] So does also Averroes use the proposition "God is *lā mā'it* and *lā fāsid*"[62] as an illustration of that kind of privation of which Aristotle says that it can be applied even to a subject in which the opposite habit does not ordinarily exist, such as the privation of eyes in a plant. In this illustration of Averroes it is quite evident that the terms *lā mā'it* and *lā fāsid* are used by him in the sense of "immortal" and "incorruptible" respectively, corresponding to the Greek ἀθάνατος and ἄφθαρτος.

We have thus far shown that, according to Aristotle and

[57] *Ibid.*, 32–33.

[58] Students of Aristotle, as far as I know, have failed to notice this distinction in Aristotle's treatment of privative and negative propositions. The Stoics, however, do not make this distinction, for they treat a proposition like "this man is inhuman (ἀφιλάνθρωπος)" as a privative proposition (Diogenes Laertius, VII, 70).

[59] *Najāt*, Cairo, 1331 A. H., p. 23, ll. 12–13.

[60] Cf. below n. 73.

[61] Cf. below n. 80.

[62] *Epitome of the Metaphysics* (ed. C. Quiros), I, 47, p. 27, l. 7.

Arabic philosophers and Maimonides, there are three ways by which a certain "habit", say "sight", can be negated of a subject. First, by a proposition like "A is blind". This proposition is affirmative in quality with a predicate which is privative in meaning but positive in form. Such a proposition is described by Aristotle as a "privation" or a "privative negation" and the predicate "blind" in it can be applied to the subject "A" only when "A" is something which naturally would be "seeing", say a "man". If "A" is a "wall", the term "blind" cannot be predicated of it. Second, by a proposition like "A is not seeing". This proposition is negative in quality, the negative particle "not" belonging to the copula "is", and the term "seeing" can be negated of the subject "A", even if "A" is a "wall". Third, by a proposition like "A is unseeing". This proposition is affirmative in quality, but with a predicate which is both privative in meaning and negative in form. Such a proposition has the force of a negative proposition, and the term "unseeing" can be predicated of the subject "A", even if "A" is a "wall".

Besides propositions which are negative in quality, such as "A is not seeing" and propositions which are affirmative in quality, but with predicates which are negative terms, such as "A is unseeing", Aristotle discusses another kind of proposition, again affirmative in quality, but with a predicate which he calls an "indefinite term" (*ὄνομα ἀόριστον*),[63] such as "A is not-seeing". Aristotle himself illustrates this last kind of proposition by "man is not-just"[64] which he contrasts with the negative proposition "man is not just".[65] By many examples Aristotle tries to show how an affirmative proposition with an indefinite predicate differs from a negative proposition.[66] For the purpose

[63] *De Interpretatione*, Ch. 2, 16a, 32. Arabic (Isḥaq ibn Ḥunain's translation, ed. I. Pollak): غير محصل; Hebrew: בלתי מגיע (Averroes' *Kol Meleket Higgayon: Meliẓah*, Riva di Trento, 1559, p. 10a), בלתי נשלם (*ibid.;* also *Middle Commentary on the Organon*, Israel Levi MS., Jewish Theological Seminary, p. 34b).

[64] *Ibid.*, Ch. 10, 19b, 28: *ἔστιν οὐ δίκαιος ἄνθρωπος*, يوجد انسان لا عدلا, אדם ימצא לא צדיק.

[65] *Ibid.*, 27–28: *οὐκ ἔστι δίκαιος ἄνθρωπος*, ليس يوجد انسان عدلا, אדם לא ימצא צדיק.

[66] *Anal Priora* I, 46, 51a, 3–52b, 34.

of our present discussion, however, it is more appropriate to quote the difference between these two types of proposition as stated by Avicenna, Algazali and Averroes, which undoubtedly reflects a view commonly held in Arabic philosophy.

In Avicenna, a proposition in which either the subject or the predicate is an "indefinite term" is described by the expression *qaḍiyyah ma'dūlah*.[67] The term *ma'dūlah* in this expression is translated into Latin, directly from the Arabic, by *privativa*[67a] and, indirectly through the Hebrew, by *remotiva*;[67b] two modern scholars translate it by *infinita*[68] and *équivalente*.[69] None of these terms, as can be readily seen, are exact translations of the original Arabic term. In mediaeval Hebrew translations from the Arabic, however, the expression *qaḍiyyah ma'dūlah* is translated by *mishpaṭ musar* or *gezarah noṭah*.[70] From this it is quite evident that the term *ma'dūlah* in this expression is taken by those Hebrew translators to mean "deviated" or "turned aside" — a meaning to which the Arabic term etymologically lends itself. If, then, with these Hebrew translators we take the expression *qaḍiyyah ma'dūlah* to mean a "deviated proposition", i. e., a proposition deviated from its logically affirmative form to what appears to be a negation, we can reasonably conclude that this expression has its origin in the Greek expression **πρότασις ἐκ μεταθέσεως**," proposition by transposition", which

[67] *Najāt*, p. 22, l. 6.

[67a] Cf. below n. 70.

[67b] Cf. below n. 70.

[68] M. Horten, *Die spekulative und positive Theologie des Islam*, 1912, p. 203.

[69] A.-M. Goichon, *Lexique de la Langue philosophique d'Ibn Sina*, 1938, § 411.

[70] Cf. Algazali, *Maqāṣid al-Falāsifah*, Cairo, no date, p. 22. l. 17: قضية معدولة; Hebrew: משפט מוסר (Judah Nathan's translation, MS. Jewish Theological Seminary, Adler 1015, p. 23a); גזירה נוטה (Albalag's translation, MS. *ibid.*, Adler 131, p. 9b); Latin: *propositio privativa* (quoted in Prantl, *Geschichte der Logik*, II, 2nd ed., 1885, p. 373, n. 260). In the Latin translation, from the Hebrew, of Averroes' *Epitome of De Interpretatione*, Cap. 4, the term מוסרים (see quotation below n. 82) is translated by *remotivae* (*Aristotelis opera*, Venice, 1574, I, ii, fol. 41 I).

It is to be noted that the term נוטה in this expression has not the same meaning as the term נוטה in the expression שם נוטה, "inflected noun", in *Millot ha-Higgayon*, Ch. 13. In the latter case, the underlying Arabic term probably was منصرف.

Greek expression, as reported by Ammonius, was used by Theophrastus as a description of any proposition in which the predicate is an indefinite term.[71] An accurate English translation of the Arabic *qaḍiyyah ma'dūlah* would therefore be "transposed proposition". Now with regard to such "transposed propositions", Avicenna makes two statements, (1) that they differ from negative propositions[72] and (2) that they can be used even when the subject does not by nature possess the predicates in question.[73] On some other occasion, I hope to show that in Arabic philosophy, owing to the impossibility of reproducing the distinction between such terms as "not-seeing" and "unseeing", there arose a confusion between an affirmative proposition in which the predicate is an indefinite term, such as "A is not-seeing", and an affirmative proposition in which the predicate is a term with a privative prefix, such as "A is unseeing", also that both these types of proposition came to be known as *qaḍiyyah ma'dūlah*, and finally that the two statements of Avicenna refer to these two types of proposition respectively.

Similarly Algazali explicitly says that a proposition with an indefinite predicate has the force of a privation and not of a negation. Taking the proposition "Zaid is not-seeing (*gair baṣīr*)" as the subject of his discussion, he describes it, like Avicenna, as a 'transposed proposition" (*qaḍiyyah ma'dūlah*) and explains that the indefinite "not-seeing" has the same meaning as the privation "blind" (*a'ma*).[74]

Of Averroes' discussions of the difference between a negative proposition and a proposition with an indefinite predicate we shall quote two passages. These passages of Averroes, which undoubtedly reflect a traditional interpretation of Aristotle, will make it quite clear that in Arabic philosophy an indefinite predicate, such as "not-seeing", has the same logical status in a proposition as a privation, such as "blind".

In one passage, the difference is stated by him as follows:

[71] *Ammonius de Interpretatione*, ed. A. Busse, p. 161, ll. 10 and 128.
[72] *Najāt*, p. 23, ll. 2–6.
[73] *Ibid.*, ll. 6–10; *'Ishārāt*, ed. J. Forget, Leiden, 1892, p. 28, ll. 10–12.
[74] *Maqāṣid*, p. 22, l. 14–p. 23, l. 4.

"Our saying 'the man is not just' may apply to a wicked man or to a man who is neither wicked nor just, that is, a man who does not naturally possess the habit [of wickedness and justice]; but when we say 'the man is not-just', the statement applies only to a man who is wicked, for our predicate 'not-just' signifies a privation, and privation is the remotion of a habit from a subject in which it would naturally exist at a time when it would naturally exist in it".[75]

In another passage, discussing various types of proposition, he says: "Some of them are by transposition, and these are those propositions of which the predicate is an indefinite noun or verb, as when we say, for instance, 'Reuben is not-healthy' or 'Simon is not-seeing.' It happens[76] that this kind of proposition is not used in the Arabic language. Some of them are privative propositions, and they are those of which the predicate is a privative noun or verb. It is a universal rule that privation is predicated of a subject with reference to that which would naturally exist in it at a time it would naturally exist in it,[77] as when we say, for instance, 'Reuben is blind' or 'Simon is sick.' The force of indefinite terms in those languages in which they are used is like the force of privative terms, for our saying 'not-seeing' is of the same order of our saying 'blind'[78] and our saying 'not-healthy' is of the same order as 'sick.' Inasmuch as indefinite terms are not used in the Arabic language, the negative particle is regarded by Arabic logicians as one of the ambiguous particles, for sometimes they use it generally and mean thereby merely privation[79] and sometimes they mean thereby absolute

[75] *Middle Commentary on De Interpretatione*, p. 47b: כי אמרנו האדם לא ימצא צדיק יצדק על האדם הרשע ועל האדם שאינו רשע ולא צדיק, והוא בלתי בעל הקנין. ואמרנו האדם ימצא לא צדיק אמנם יצדק על הרשע לבד, כי אמרנו לא צדיק יורה על ההעדר. וההעדר הוא העלות הדבר ממה שדרכו שימצא בו בעת שדרכו שימצא בו.

[76] אפשר. I take this Hebrew term here to be a translation of the Arabic ربما.

[77] *Categ.*, Ch. 10, 12a, 27–29; cf. above n. 40.

[78] Cf. above n. 43.

[79] As in the application of the terms לא רואה [لا بصير] to Reuben [Zaid] in this passage, where they are used in the sense of "not-seeing" and are therefore the equivalent of "blind".

negation.[80] It is this consideration that has compelled men of this art [i. e., logic] to speak of 'indefinite terms',[81] for if we are not careful about these 'indefinite terms' and pay no heed to their being technically equivalent to privations, we might be led into error and take that which is indefinite to mean negation, and vice versa."[82]

From all this we may gather that while propositions of the type "A is unseeing" is the equivalent of the negation "A is not seeing," propositions of the type "A is not-seeing" is the equivalent of the privation "A is blind." By the same token, propositions of the type "A is not-blind" are to be treated in the same way as propositions of the type "A is not-seeing," and therefore one cannot affirm the indefinite term "not-blind" of "A" unless one can affirm of "A" also the term "blind". In other words, one cannot say "the wall is not-blind".

A direct discussion of propositions with indefinite predicates is found in Maimonides. "As for the term which we call indefinite," he says, "it is a term composed of the negative 'not' and a 'habit,' as, for instance, 'not-seeing,' 'not-wise,' 'not-

[80] As in the application of the terms لا مائت and لا فاسد to God by Averroes himself (cf. above n. 62), where they are used in the sense of "immortal" and "incorruptible", and also in the application of the terms لا بصير, לא רואה to a wall by Maimonides (cf. above n. 54), where they are used in the sense of "unseeing". So also would be the use of the terms لا مائت in opposition to a preceding affirmative proposition, as, e. g., "God is living, not mortal (*lā mā'it*)"; cf. Caspari-Wright, *A Grammar of the Arabic Language*, II, 184, a.

[81] Literally, "transposed terms."

[82] Averroes, *Kol Meleket Higgayon*: *Meliẓah*, p. 10a, ll. 4–19: ומהם מוסרים, והם אשר נשואם שם או פעל בלתי מגיע, כמו אמרנו ראובן לא בריא ושמעון לא רואה. וזה הנה אפשר שלא יורגל בלשון הערב. ומהם העדרים, והם אשר נשואם שם העדרי או פעל העדרי. וההעדר בכלל הוא שיקשור הנושא במה שדרכו שימצא בו בעת שדרכו שימצא בו, כמו אמרנו ראובן עור ושמעון חולה. וכח השמות בלתי מגיעים בלשונות אשר ישתמשו בהם כח השמות ההעדריים, שאמרנו לא רואה במדרגת אמרנו עור ואמרנו לא בריא במדרגת חולה. ובעבור שלא היו אלה השמות בלשון הערב היתה מלת השלילה אצלם מהמלות המסופקות, לפי שהם יחליטום וירצו בו ענין ההעדר ופעם ירצו בו השלילה המוחלטת. וזהו אשר הכריח אנשי זאת המלאכה לדבר בשמות המוסרים, לפי שכאשר לא נשמור בהם ונניח בהם זאת ההנחה אפשר שנטעה ונקח מה שהוא בלתי מגיע על מה שהוא שלילה ובהפך.

rational.' "[83] Nothing is said by Maimonides as to whether such propositions are privations or negations. We may assume, however, that as in the interpretation of Averroes they are privations after the manner of "A is blind", and one cannot therefore say "A is not-seeing" unless one can also say that "A is seeing." In other words, propositions of the type "A is not-seeing" can be used only when "A" could naturally be "seeing", and similarly propositions of the type "A is not-blind" can be used only when "A", who could naturally be "seeing", could naturally also be "blind". Consequently we may infer that Maimonides would not admit propositions about God such as "God is not-mortal" or "God is not-weak," inasmuch as God could not naturally be "mortal" or "weak".

There are thus according to Maimonides three ways in which propositions of the third adjacent can be framed with God as the subject.

1. Affirmative propositions. One can say, for instance, "God is living," in which the predicate "living" is used as an equivocal term. Such a proposition, though affirmative in form, is negative in meaning. The affirmation of "life" in an equivocal sense, which is the essence of God, negates "life" in its ordinary sense, which is not the essence of God. Since "life" in its ordinary sense, as compared with the "life" of God, is really "death" or "mortality," the affirmative proposition "God is living" really means "God is not dead" or "God is not mortal."

2. Negative propositions. One can say "God is not mortal," even though God by His nature cannot be mortal, for in the same way one can say "the wall is not seeing," even though the wall by its nature cannot be seeing.

3. Affirmative propositions with predicates which are negative

[83] *Millot ha-Higgayon*, Ch. 13. The term בלתי מגיע in Ibn Tibbon's translation, as well as the variants בלתי נשלם and בלתי מושלם recorded in ed. Efros, and also the term בלתי נלקח in Aḥitub's translation are all literal translations of the Arabic *gair muḥaṣṣal* (cf. above n. 63). The change to בלתי מסוים suggested in ed. Roth is uncalled for.

terms. One can say "God is immortal." Such a proposition has the same force as the negative proposition "God is not mortal," and one can therefore say "God is immortal," even though God by His nature cannot be its opposite "mortal."

But Maimonides would not admit, with reference to God, affirmative propositions with predicates which are indefinite terms. Thus, according to him, one could not say "God is not-mortal," for such a proposition is not what Aristotle calls a "negation" but rather what he calls a "privation." It is not like the proposition "A is not seeing"; it is like the proposition "A is blind." And just as the term "blind" cannot be applied to the term "wall," because "wall" by its nature cannot be its opposite "seeing," so also the term "not-mortal" cannot be applied to God, because God by His nature cannot be its opposite "mortal." In other words, unlike Kant, who takes a proposition with an indefinite predicate, such as "the soul is not-mortal", to mean the exclusion of the soul from the sphere of mortality, Maimonides would take such a proposition to mean that the soul, which may be mortal, happens to be immortal.[84]

[84] In my paper, "Crescas on the Problem of Divine Attributes," *Jewish Quarterly Review*, N. S., 7 (1916), pp. 20–22, impressed by Maimonides' statement that his "negation of the privation" does not imply the affirmation of its corresponding "habit," I tried to show that by negative attributes Maimonides does not really mean negative propositions, such as "God is not many," but rather affirmative propositions, with indefinite predicates, such as "God is not-many." I compared it to what Kant calls "infinite judgment," which he illustrates by the proposition "the soul is not-mortal." This is a kind of interpretation that would naturally suggest itself to any student of philosophy. I have since convinced myself, however, that this interpretation is wrong, and for the following reasons: (1) As I have shown here, the expression "negation of privation" means a negative proposition in which the predicate is a "privation" instead of a "habit," and not an affirmative proposition in which the predicate is an "indefinite term." (2) Negative propositions, according to Aristotle, do exactly what Maimonides says he means by his negative attributes, namely, they negate something of a subject without necessarily implying that the subject in question can by its nature have the opposite of the predicate negated. (3) Again, as I have shown here, in Arabic philosophy affirmative propositions with indefinite predicates, such as Kant's proposition "the soul is not-mortal", have the force of what Aristotle calls "privation" and not of what he calls "negation", and consequently a proposi-

Finally, Maimonides makes three important qualifications with regard to the use of negative and affirmative attributes.

The first qualification is with regard to affirming of God "privations" in an equivocal sense. Though, according to Maimonides, "habits," such as power and knowledge, can be affirmed of God equivocally even though they cannot be affirmed of Him in their ordinary sense, it does not follow that in the same manner "privations", such as powerlessness and ignorance, which cannot be affirmed of God in their ordinary sense, could be appropriately affirmed of Him in an equivocal sense. Maimonides will always insist that privations, and everything that denotes a deficiency and an imperfection in ordinary speech, cannot be affirmed of God even when understood as equivocal terms. God cannot be said to be ignorant or powerless or blind even if these terms were to be used in an equivocal sense and one absolutely unrelated to what we ordinarily mean by them. Not only is this to be inferred from the chapters in which Maimonides deals directly with negative attributes, but there is also an explicit statement to this effect in his earlier discussion of the anthropomorphisms of the Bible. "We have already stated several times," he says "that anything which is considered by ordinary men as an imperfection or which cannot be conceived as compatible with God has not been ascribed to God in the prophetic books even metaphorically, although such terms may not otherwise be different from those which were employed as

tion about God such as "God is not-mortal" would not be considered admissible by Maimonides. This paper is below, p. 247.

The interpretation of Maimonides' negative attributes as infinite judgments after the analogy of Kant had been vaguely intimated, prior to the publication of my paper, in Hermann Cohen's use of the Kantian term "infinite judgment" for Maimonides' expression "negation of privation" (cf. "Charakteristik der Ethik Maimunis", *Moses ben Maimon*, ed. Jacob Guttmann, 1908, I, p. 102; more fully later in his *Die Religion der Vernunft*, 1919, pp. 71–72). Z. Diesendruck in "Maimonides' Theory of the Negation of Privation", *Proceedings of the American Academy for Jewish Research*, 6 (1934–5), pp. 139–151, referring to Hermann Cohen, operates with the same assumption that Maimonides' negative attributes constitute propositions in wuich the predicates are indefinite terms.

metaphors in relation to God."[85] When therefore Gersonides,[86] in his criticism of Maimonides' equivocal interpretation of attributes, raises the question why God should not be described as corporeal in an equivocal sense, Maimonides would answer that it is because the term corporeality, by its mere sound and irrespective of its meaning, carries with it the implication of an imperfection in God.

The second qualification is with regard to the excessive use of affirmative predicates, even when one takes them in an equivocal sense and as having a negative meaning. Though such predicates are philosophically and logically defensible, still one should not use them more than has been sanctioned by Scripture and liturgy. Besides proofs for this which he cites from Scripture and the rabbis,[87] he proceeds to support it also by reason. It is not all certain, he argues, that the understanding of affirmative predicates as negations will safeguard one against the misconception that such predicates signify the existence of real attributes in God, for one may take such predicates to mean negations and still believe that they express real attributes in God. Take, for instance, "those who believe in attributes,"[88] that is to say, the Ash'arites. According to their belief, the attributes are all eternal like God himself.[89] From this Maimonides infers that, according to the Ash'arites, too, every perfection predicated of

[85] *Moreh Nebukim* I, 47.

[86] *Milhamot Adonai* III, 3, p. 134: וזה כי לאומר שיאמר, דרך משל, שהשם יתברך הוא גשם ולא ירצה בזה הגשם דבר בעל כמה, אבל דבר משותף שתוף גמור עם מה שנקראהו גשם. Cf. *'Olam Ḳatan* III (ed. Horovitz), p. 46, l. 11: ולמה לא תאמר גוף ולא כשאר הגופים.

[87] *Moreh Nebukim* I, 59.

[88] *Ibid.*, I, 60. The argument of this chapter is not clear. Munk encloses the reference to the attributists within brackets. By doing so, he makes the argument to be an explanation on the part of Maimonides that his own theory of attributes does not imply the existence of an infinite number of unknown attributes. But such an explanation is entirely superfluous, inasmuch as he has already stated his denial of the existence of attributes in any sense whatsoever. The argument, as analyzed by us here, is an exposition by Maimonides of the view of the attributists for the purpose of cautioning his reader against the excessive use of affirmative predicates even when understood as equivocal terms and negations.

[89] *Shahrastani*, p. 67, l. 10.

God affirmatively "is not of the same kind of perfection as that imagined by us, but is used only as an equivocal term,"[90] just as Maimonides himself has said about his own conception of predicates, and hence, again, as in Maimonides' own conception of predicates, each affirmative predicate, in the Ash'arite theory, "does necessarily amount to a negation."[91] Consequently, when the Ash'arites say that "God is knowing according to knowledge,"[92] inasmuch as the knowledge which they predicate of God is an eternal attribute and hence unlike our own knowledge, they really mean, says Maimonides, that "God is knowing not according to a knowledge that is like our own."[93] Thus, if you are an Ash'arite, "you necessarily arrive at negations, and, while you do not obtain a true knowledge of an essential attribute, you are led to the establishment of a plurality in God and to the belief that He is one essence which has unknown attributes."[94] The point which Maimonides wishes to establish by this argument is that the use of affirmative predicates, even when understood as negations, might lead one to a belief in the existence of real attributes like those maintained by the Ash'arites, and consequently he warns his reader that "in the description of God by affirmative predicates there is a great danger."[95]

The third qualification is with regard to negating of God "habits" in their ordinary sense. Though, according to Maimonides, "habits," such as power and knowledge, can never be predicated of God in their ordinary sense, still it does not follow that they can be negated of God in their ordinary sense. Maimonides will always insist that habits, and everything that denotes excellency and a perfection in ordinary speech, even though it cannot be affirmed of God in its ordinary sense, cannot

[90] *Moreh Nebukim* I, 60: כי כבר התבאר שכל מה שנחשבהו שלמות, אפילו אם היה השלמות ההוא נמצא לו, לדעת האומרים בתארים, שאינו ממין השלמות אשר נחשבהו, אבל בהשתתף השם יאמר לבד כפי מה שבארנו.

[91] *Ibid.*: הנה בהכרח תצא לענין השלילה.

[92] *Shahrastani*, p. 67, l. 8.

[93] *Moreh Nebukim*, I, 60: הנה כבר גלית שהוא יודע לא במדע כמדענו.

[94] *Ibid.*: הנה כבר באת בשוללות בהכרח, ולא עמדת על אמתת תאר עצמי, אבל עמדת על הרבוי, והיותך מאמין שהוא עצם אחד יש לו תארים נסכלים.

[95] *Ibid.*: אמנם תארו יתעלה במחייבות יש בו סכנה גדולה.

also be negated of Him. It must always be affirmed of Him in an equivocal sense. In this he differs from Aristotle. When Aristotle says, that a god has "no vice (κακία) or virtue (ἀρετή)," because his state is "higher than virtue",[96] he would undoubtedly have no more objection to the negative proposition "God is not virtuous" (οὐκ ἔστι καλὸς θεός) than to the negative proposition "God is not vicious" (οὐκ ἔστι κακὸς θεός). Maimonides, however, would be opposed to this. He would say that even though virtue in its ordinary sense cannot be affirmed of God, still it cannot be directly negated of Him. It must be affirmed of God as an equivocal term, identical with His essence, and such an affirmation must be justified on the ground that it implies the negation of its opposite "vice" as well as "virtue" in the ordinary sense of the term. That this represents the exact view of Maimonides can be inferred, again, not only from the general tenor of his discussion in the chapters which deal directly with negative attributes,[97] but also from a statement toward the end of his discussion of the attribute of action, before he has yet introduced the negative interpretation of attributes. The passage, which contains two statements, reads as follows: (a) "This is what one must believe concerning the predicates occurring in the books of the prophets; (b) or else one may believe concerning some of them that they are predicates to be taken as indicating a perfection by way of comparison with what we consider as perfections in us, as we shall explain."[98] Now the first part of the statement quite obviously refers to his explanation of predicates as actions. But what does the second part of the statement refer to? It cannot refer to the chapter immediately following it (Ch. 54), for in that chapter he continues to show how the so-called thirteen predicates of Exodus XXIV.6--7 are all reducible to actions. Nor can it refer to the subsequent two chapters (Chs. 55–56), for these chapters continue his arguments against the existence of essential

[96] *Eth. Nic.* VII, 1145a, 25–27.

[97] *Moreh Nebukim* I, 58; III, 20.

[98] *Ibid.* I, 53: זה הוא אשר צריך שיאמן בהם בתארים הנזכרים בספרי הנביאים, או שיאמן בקצתם שהם תארים יורו בהם על השלמות על צד הדמיון בשלימותנו המובנות אצלינו כמו שנבאר. Shem-Ṭob (*ad. loc.*) gives another interpretation of these words.

attributes. It must therefore refer to Chs. 57–58, where he shows how the non-actional predicates are to be taken as negations. It is thus clear from this reference to negative predicates that the affirmative form in which these predicates are expressed have a certain definite purpose which, in his own words, is to indicate "a perfection by way of comparison with what we consider as perfections in us."

And so according to Maimonides, even when terms affirmatively predicated of God are to be understood as negations of their opposites, the affirmative form of the predication is not altogether useless. It has for its purpose the affirmation that nothing which is ordinarily regarded by us as a perfection is alien to God's nature. While in us, indeed, such perfections may be only accidents added to our essence, or universals of which our essence is composed, in God they are His essence. The proposition "God is knowing" means logically, to be sure, "God is not foolish," but it is not sufficient to say that "God is not foolish"; it must also be said that "God is knowing," not indeed in the sense that knowledge is either an attribute or a mode of God, but in the sense, as Maimonides explains it elsewhere, that "God's essence is His knowledge and His knowledge is His essence."

The significance of the affirmative form of the propositions which Maimonides interprets as negations was first discussed by me in a paper "Crescas on the Problem of Divine Attributes," *Jewish Quarterly Review*, N. S., 7 (1916), pp. 1–44, 175–221. Julius Guttmann, in his *Die Philosophie des Judentums*, 1933, pp. 389–390, n. 438, agrees with the general point of view that Maimonides' negative interpretation does not completely deprive God of the perfections connoted by the various predicates, but he disagrees with my contention that Maimonides attaches significance to the affirmative form in which propositions about God are framed. He especially objects to the following two statements in my paper: (1) "In the following statement of Maimonides, 'God is existent without existence, living without life,' etc., we clearly see that 'God is existent' does not merely mean 'God is not absent,' but what it means is that God is existent with an existence of His own, identical with His own essence." (p. 20). (2) "God, by virtue of His absolute perfection in every sense, has an infinite number of aspects in His essence; and had we only the means of doing so, we should be able to express them all in human language. But on account of the unknowability of the divine essence, we can express none of its infinite aspects in positive terms; we can only indirectly hint at them by negating of Him our own knowable perfections" (p. 23). Such an interpretation, according to Guttmann, would make Maimonides' view the same as the view ascribed by Maimonides himself to those who say, i. e., the Ash'arites, that "God is one but that he possesses many attributes, and that He with His attributes are one" (*Moreh Nebukim* I, 50; Arabic, p. 57a, ll. 8–9; Hebrew, p. 70b, l. 1). He also finds my second statement explicitly rejected by Maimonides in his statement that his theory of attributes would reject the belief that "God is one essence having unknowable attributes" (*ibid.*, I, 60; Arabic, p. 76, ll. 16–17; Hebrew, p. 90, l. 3). A similar criticism is made by Jacob Teicher, in "Observations critiques sur l'Interprétation tradionelle de la Doctrine des Attributs negâtifs chez Maimonide," *Revue des Etudes Juives*, 99 (1935), pp. 64–65.

I hope that my present discussion has removed these objections. I have shown here how by a deliberate change of formula Maimonides himself distinguishes between his own view and the views of the attributists and the modists. All the three of them, the attributists and the modists and Maimonides, indeed be ieve that it is necessary to predicate of God perfections in propositions which are to be expressed affirmatively. But they differ as to what these predicated perfections signify. To the Ash'arites, they signify real attributes, distinct from the essence of God, though not actually separable from it. These attributes, according to Maimonides, may be even conceived by the Ash'arites as equivocal terms and as having a negative meaning; still, though unknowable, they signify real attributes.[99] To Abū Ḥāshim, these perfections signify modes, which are characterized by Maimonides as being "neither the essence of God nor extraneous

[99] Cf. above (nn. 88–95) our analysis and interpretation of this argument.

to the essence of God."[100] To Maimonides, these perfections, as he himself says, are identical with God.[101] They are, of course, unknowable, but we can still express them in equivocal terms, which do nothing but affirm that they are the essence of God. Such an affirmation of the identity of subject and predicate, of course, makes the proposition in question tautological, but still it is not altogether useless, for it emphasizes a negation. In my earlier paper, in order to distinguish these predicated perfections as they are conceived by Maimonides from the predicated perfections as they are conceived by the attributists and modists, I referred to them as the "infinite aspects" of the "divine essence."[102]

Let us now summarize the result of our discussion of Maimonides' theory of attributes.

Metaphysically, we have said, there is for him no problem of attributes, for, with his conception of God as a purely immaterial and absolutely simple being, he can without any difficulty deny the existence of real attributes in Him. The terms that are usually predicated of God are taken by him to be identical with God's essence and hence, like the essence of God, are unknowable in their meaning, and are used only in an equivocal sense.

The problem to him is primarily logical, arising from his view that any statement about God must have the validity of a logical proposition. The question, as seen by him, is merely whether identity is a logical relation.

In his answer to this question, he first tries to examine the nature of the various logical relations that must exist between subject and predicate in logical propositions. His discussions on this point, as we have seen, resulted in a new list of predicables, which should be placed by the side of the known lists of Aristotle and Porphyry.

[100] Cf. above n. 15. [101] Cf. above n. 11.

[102] In that paper, in order to avoid confusion, I was careful not to describe the perfections, as they are conceived by Maimonides, by the term attributes. In one place, however, I find that inadvertently I called them "qualities" (p. 22, ll. 19–20), which is not a good term. It should be changed to "perfections."

Then, having arrived at the conclusion that identity is not a logical relation, he tries to find some explanation by which he could justify the affirmation of predicates of God. Two such explanations are found by him; first, they are actions; second, they are negations. Neither of these explanations is original with him, but they are both used by him in an original way.

As for actions, before Maimonides, actions meant relations, and relations were assumed to be predicable of God. Maimonides, however, uses the term actions only to indicate that propositions about God, whatever their external logical form, are to be understood as propositions of the second adjacent.

As for negations, before Maimonides, the negative interpretation of divine predicates was used only to indicate that terms predicated of God are to be understood as a denial of their opposite; in their affirmative form they are to have no meaning at all. Maimonides, however, uses the negative interpretation of divine predicates only as a means of justifying the affirmative form in which certain terms must be predicated of God.

Because of this special logical sense of the negative interpretation of divine predicates, the use of negations are, according to him, to be governed by certain rules. *A*. Terms which with reference to us are perfections must be predicated of God in (1) affirmative propositions, such as "God is living", though logically they are to be taken to emphasize the negation of the opposite, such as "God is not mortal". *B*. Terms which with reference to us are imperfections must be predicated of God either in (2) negative propositions, such as "God is not mortal", or in (3) affirmative propositions with predicates which are negative in form, such as "God is immortal". But we have reason to assume that he would not allow, in the case of terms which with reference to us are imperfections, to predicate them of God in (4) affirmative propositions with predicates which are indefinite in form, such as "God is not-mortal".

6

MAIMONIDES AND GERSONIDES ON DIVINE ATTRIBUTES AS AMBIGUOUS TERMS

One of the distinguishing characteristics of Maimonides' conception of our knowledge of God is his view that divine attributes are equivocal terms. No other philosopher before him, whether writing in Greek or Latin or Arabic or Hebrew, has explicitly interpreted divine attributes as equivocal terms. Whether any of them, without explicitly describing attributes as equivocal terms, meant them to be equivocal,[1] is a point which perhaps may be debated. But Maimonides it was who explicitly argued that attributes can neither be univocal terms (متواطية, מוסכמים, συνώνυμα) nor ambiguous terms (مشككة, מסופקים, ἀμφίβολα), concluding therefore that they must be equivocal terms (مشتركة, משותפים, ὁμώνυμα).[2]

Now there are several types of ambiguous or amphibolous terms.[3] One of these is described as a term applied to two things according to prior and posterior, that is to say, to one of these things it is applied primarily and to the other it is applied only secondarily through its dependence upon the first thing, and this dependence, as says Alfarabi, is either (a) the dependence of an effect upon a cause[4] or (b) the dependence of a copy upon its exemplar.[5] Though in his discussion of ambiguous terms in his *Millot ha-Higgayon*, 13, and *Moreh Nebukim*, I, 56, Maimonides makes no mention of the phrase "according to prior and posterior," still it is this type of ambiguity that Maimonides had in mind, as may be inferred from the explanation given by him of the meaning of this term in both these passages.

In *Moreh Nebukim*, I, 56, Maimonides explains ambiguous terms as terms "which are predicated of two things, between which there is

[1] Cf. my paper "Negative Attributes in the Church Fathers and Basilides" in the George La Piana issue of *Ricerche Religiose*, 22 (1953), and the formula "God is living without life" in my paper "Maimonides on Negative Attributes," *Ginzberg Jubilee Volume*, 1945, pp. 418 ff., and in Joseph Ibn Ẓaddiḳ below at n. 39. See *Studies*, I, 131–142, and above, pp. 195–230.

[2] Cf. *Moreh Nebukim*, I, 56.

[3] Cf. my paper "The Amphibolous Terms in Aristotle, Arabic Philosophy and Maimonides." *Harvard Theological Review*, 31 (1938), 151–173. In *Studies*, I, 455–477.

[4] Cf. below n. 18.

[5] Cf. below n. 19.

a similarity in respect to something, and that something is an accident in them and does not constitute the essence of either one of them."[6] By this statement Maimonides undoubtedly had in mind the term "existent," which to him is an accident,[7] in its application as a predicate of a "substance" and of another "accident,"[8] for this is one of the common examples of ambiguous terms. But the term "existent" is said by Aristotle as well as by his followers in Arabic philosophy to be applied to "substance" priorily and to "accident" posteriorly.[9]

In *Millot ha-Higgayon*, 13, he explains an ambiguous term as "a term which is predicated of two or more substances because of something which they have in common but which something does not constitute the essence of either one of them" and illustrates it by the example of the term "man," in the sense of the human figure and shape, when predicated of a real human being, of the corpse of a man, and of the statue or painting of a man. Now the explanation of an ambiguous term here differs somewhat from that in *Moreh Nebukim*, I, 56, for "man-shaped," according to Maimonides, would not be an "accident" but rather a "property," as may be judged from his description of "broad-chested," "standing erect" and "straight-nailed" as "properties" rather than as "accidents."[10] But still "property" is also described by Aristotle as "accident" in the general sense of the term and though, unlike "accident," it is described as that "which belongs to each thing in virtue of itself (καθ' αὑτό)," still, like "accident," it is described as that which "is not in the

[6] *Moreh*, I, 56: כי השמות אשר יאמרו בהסתפק הם אשר יאמרו על שני דברים שביניהם דמיון בעניין אחד והעניין ההוא מקרה בהם ואינו מעמיד עצם כל אחד מהם.

[7] Cf. *Moreh*, I, 57.

[8] Efodi on *Moreh Nebukim*, *ad loc.*: והענין ההוא מקרה בהם, ר"ל וזה במציאות לעצם ולמקרה.

[9] Cf. "Amphibolous Terms," *op. cit.*, pp. 153, 154, 157.

[10] *Millot ha-Higgayon*, 10: וכן רוחב החזה, והיותו נצב הקומה, ורוחב הצפרנים, כל אחד מאלו נקראהו סגולה לאדם, based on Aristotle, *Historia Animalium*, II, I, 497b, 33–34; III, 9, 517a, 33–517b, 2; *De Partibus Animalium*, II, 10, 656a, 12–13.

The underlying Arabic for רוחב הצפרנים must have been عريض الاظفار (cf. Avicenna, *Kitāb al-'Ishārāt wal-Tanbīāt*, ed. J. Forget, 1892, p. 19, l. 3), which literally means "broad-nailed." But the underlying Greek term εὐθυώνυχος (*Hist. Anim.* 517a, 33) means "straight-nailed."

While in *Millot ha-Higgayon* 13 the term "man" in its application to a real man and to the statue or painting of a man is described by Maimonides as an "ambiguous" term, in *Moreh Nebukim* I, 1, he says that "the term 'form' is either an 'equivocal' or an 'ambiguous' term, being applicable both to a specific form and to an artificial form" (צלם שם משתתף או מסופק, יאמר על הצורה המינית ועל הצורה המלאכית). The explanation of the difference between these two statements is to be

essence (ἐν τῇ οὐσίᾳ) of a thing."[11] But, however different may be the example given in the *Millot ha-Higgayon* from that hinted at in the *Moreh Nebukim*, the application of the predicate "man-shaped" to a real living man and to the corpse of a man or to the statue or painting of a man is quite evidently according to prior and posterior, for it is primarily applied to a real living man and then only secondarily to a corpse and a statue or painting, and this because of their similarity to the real living man as their exemplar.

The reason for his rejection of amphiboly or ambiguity as an interpretation of divine attributes is, as he plainly says, that ambiguous terms imply a similarity between the things of which they are predicated. For, Maimonides would seem to argue, whether the ambiguous terms are accidents or properties they imply, in the former case, that the things of which they are predicated belong to the same species and, in the latter case, that the things of which they are predicated belong either to the same genus or to the same species; but, since God is not similar to anything and has no genus or species, the terms predicated of Him cannot be taken as ambiguous terms. They must be taken as equivocal terms.

This rejection of the ambiguous interpretation of divine attributes is in direct opposition to all the major Arabic philosophers, such as Alfarabi, Avicenna, Algazali's restatement of the views of those whom he calls "the philosophers," and also to Maimonides' own contemporary Averroes.[12] For all these philosophers, though denying that there is any similarity between God and other beings and though also denying that God belongs to a genus or species and though maintaining that all terms predicated of God are properties of God which are unique to Him, still believe that all these terms predicated of God should be taken in an ambiguous sense according to prior and posterior.

found in the fact that the Greek term *homōnyma*, which is used by Aristotle as a description of the term "animal" in its application both to "man" and to "the picture of a man" (*Categ.* 1, 1a, 1–3), is translated into Arabic by terms which may mean either "equivocal" or "ambiguous" (cf. ("Amphibolous Terms", *op. cit.*, pp. 168–171). In *Moreh Nebukim* I, 3, the term "form" (תמונה) is rightly said by Maimonides to be used ambiguously (בספוק) in its application to (1) a sensible form, (2) an imaginary form, and (3) an intelligible form, inasmuch as the term in question is predicable of these three kinds of form in accordance to prior and posterior.

[11] *Metaphysics*, V, 30, 1025a, 31–32; cf. also *Millot ha-Higgayon*, 10: . . . הסגולה אלא שאינו מעמיד [לאמתת האדם].

[12] What follows about these Arabic philosophers is more fully treated in my paper "Avicenna, Algazali, and Averroes on Divine Attributes" to be published in the Jubilee volume in honor of Professor José M. Millás Vallicrosa. In *Studies*, I, 143.

We shall illustrate this assertion by quoting key passages from each of these four Arabic philosophers.

Alfarabi, who defines ambiguous terms as terms applied to two things according to prior and posterior,[13] says that the common terms which are predicated of both God and of other beings are predicated of God "firstly" (*awwalan*)[14] or "in a prior manner" (*bi-aqdam al-anḥā'*)[15] and of other beings "secondly" (*thāniyan*)[16] or "in a posterior manner" (*bi-anḥā' muta'aḫḫirah*).[17] This statement is explained by him to mean that terms which are predicated both of God and of other beings are predicated of other beings only in either of the following two senses: (a) in the sense that "they derive their substantiality (متجوهرة, מתעצמים) from the First and acquire their portion (مقتبسة, נחלקים) from Him and gain their benefit (مستفادة, נקנים) from Him"[18] and (b) in the sense of" what one may imagine to see in them with regard to a similarity to the existence of the First, be it a great similarity or a small similarity."[19]

In Avicenna there is the statement that the term "one" is predicated of God and of other beings "in an ambiguous sense (*bil-tashkīk*)."[20]

In Algazali there is the following statement: "If one says: Is not the term existent predicated of both the Necessary Being and other beings besides Him? and is not existence therefore a general term, thus resulting that the Necessary Being and other beings are ranged under a genus? But this is impossible, for these other beings must inevitably be distinguished from the Necessary Being by some differentia, and it would thus follow that the Necessary Being had a definition. To him the answer is as follows: No, the Necessary Being would leave no definition, inasmuch as existence is applied to him and to other beings by way of priority (*al-taqaddum*) and posteriority (*al-ta'aḫḫur*), for thus also with reference to substances and accidents, as we have shown, the term existence applies to them in a similar

[13] *Risālat fi Jawābi Masā'il 'anhā*, § 12, ed. F. Dieterici, *Alfārābī's philosophische Abhandlungen*: Arabic (1890), p. 88; German (1892), pp. 145–146.

[14] *Kitāb al-Siyāsāt*, p. 20, l. 11 (Hyderabad, 1346 A. H.); Hebrew: *Sefer ha-Hatḥalot*, p. 16, l. 18 (in Z. Filipowski, *Sefer ha-Asif*, Leipzig, 1849).

[15] *Ibid.*, p. 20, l. 17 (p. 16, l. 26).

[16] *Ibid.*, p. 20, l. 11 (p. 16, l. 18).

[17] *Ibid.*, p. 20, l. 18 (p. 16, l. 27).

[18] *Ibid.*, p. 20, ll. 13–14 (p. 16, ll. 21–23).

[19] *Ibid.*, ll. 16–17 (ll. 24–26).

[20] *Tafsīr al-Ṣamadiyyah*, 20, l. I (quoted in Goichon, *Lexique de la langue philosophique d'Ibn Sīnā*, p. 162, § 328).

manner. Consequently, the term existence is not predicated by way of univocality (*al-tawāṭu'*), and whatever is not predicated by way of univocality is not a genus."[21]

Averroes expresses his agreement with Avicenna that terms predicated of God and of other beings, such as "existent" (*al-maujūd*), "thing" (*al-shai*), "being" (*al-huwiyyah*),[22] and "substance" (*al-dhāt*), are not to be taken as being predicated of them "univocally" (*bi-tawāṭu*)[23] but rather ambiguously (*bi-tashrīk*), that is to say, according to priority (*bi-taqdīm*) and posteriority (*wa-ta'ḫīr*)."[24] Similarly in another place he says that the terms "mover" and "form," like the terms "one" and "existent," are predicated of God and of other beings not "univocally" but only ambiguously and "according to the prior and the posterior."[25]

The issue between Maimonides and the generality of Arabic philosophers is thus sharply drawn. To Maimonides, divine attributes are equivocal terms; to the generality of Arabic philosophers they are ambiguous terms.

It is the uniqueness of Maimonides' position among all those who discussed the problem of divine attributes that has caused philosophers after the time of Maimonides, both Jewish and Christian, to come out against his interpretation of divine attributes as equivocal terms. Rejecting this Maimonidean interpretation, they all follow the Arabic philosophers in interpreting divine attributes as ambiguous terms of the prior and posterior type.

The leaders of the assault upon Maimonides are, in Latin philosophy, Thomas Aquinas and, in Hebrew philosophy, Gersonides. We shall deal here with Gersonides.

Gersonides' criticism of Maimonides' view with regard to equivocality of divine predicates is included in his wider discussion of Maimonides' theory of the knowledge of God.[26] Out of this discussion of the general problem of God's knowledge we shall select those arguments which have a direct bearing upon the more specific problem of the equivocality or ambiguity of divine predicates.

[21] *Maqāṣid al-Falāsifah*, II, 2, p. 145, ll. 1–7 (ed. Cairo, n. d.) Latin: *Algazel's Metaphysics*, p. 58, ll. 3–11 (ed. J. T. Mückle, 1933).

[22] *Tahāfut al Tahāfut*, VII, 4, p. 369, l. 8 (ed. Bouyges); Latin: in *Aristotelis opera*, Venice, 1573, Vol. IX, p. 93 H.

[23] *Ibid.*, l. 4.

[24] *Ibid.*, ll. 6–7.

[25] *Kol Meleket Higgayon*, p. 42b, l. 20 (*Riva di Trento*, 1559); Latin: in *Aristotelis opera*, Venice, 1574, Vol. I, Pars. II, p. 58 D.

[26] *Milḥamot Adonai*, III, 3, pp. 132–137 (ed. Leipzig, 1866).

First, argues Gersonides, "it would seem that God's knowledge is associated with our knowledge by a relation of priority and posteriority, that is to say, the term knowledge is predicated of God priorily and of any other being posteriorily, inasmuch as the knowledge possessed by God comes to Him from His own essence, whereas the knowledge possessed by any other being follows as an effect from the knowledge possessed by God, and consequently, as in any case of that kind, the term knowledge is predicated of God priorily, whereas of other beings of whom it is predicated it is predicated posteriorily."[27]

In this passage, Gersonides tries to show that Maimonides himself, on the basis of certain premises admitted by himself, is bound to admit that the term "knowing" predicated of God is to be taken as an ambiguous term. Maimonides himself admits, he seems to say, "that everything produced must have an immediate cause which produced it and that that cause must have again a cause, and so on until one reach the First Cause, namely, the free will of God."[28] Now, according to Maimonides, the knowledge of God is identical with His will and both of them are identical with His essence.[29] Consequently we may say that God's knowledge is the cause of human knowledge and hence that knowledge is applied to God priorily and to man posteriorily. But, when a term is applied to two things according to prior and posterior, it is an ambiguous term. Hence, the divine attribute of knowledge is an ambiguous term.

Second, argues Gersonides, the term knowledge cannot be predicated of God in an equivocal sense. Maimonides himself admits that we attribute knowledge to God by reason of the fact that we possess knowledge, and furthermore that the possession of knowledge by us is a perfection, and still further that God cannot be devoid of anything which in us is a perfection, for thus he says: "It is undoubtedly a primary notion that to God must belong all the perfections and that all deficiencies must be negated of Him. It is also almost a primary notion that ignorance in anything whatsoever is a deficiency, and that God, therefore, cannot be ignorant of anything."[30] Putting this argument in logical form, we have then the following syllogism:

[27] *Ibid.*, p. 132, ll. 21–25: שכבר ידומה שתהיה ידיעתו ית' משותפת עם ידיעתנו בקודם ואיחור, ר"ל ששם הידיעה נאמר בשם יתברך בקודם ובזולתו באיחור. וזה כי ידיעתו לו מעצמותו, וידיעת זולתו היא עלולה מידיעתו, ומה שזה דרכו, הנה השם נאמר בו בקודם, ובשאר הענינים אשר יאמר עליהם באחור.

[28] *Moreh Nebukim*, II, 48: מבואר הוא מאד שכל דבר מחודש אי אפשר לו מבלתי סבה קרובה חדשה אותו, ולסבה ההיא סבה, וכן עד שיגיע זה לסבה הראשונה לכל דבר, ר"ל רצון השם ובחירתו.

[29] *Ibid.*, I, 53.

[30] *Ibid.*, III, 19: מושכל ראשון הוא בלא ספק שהשם יתעלה צריך שימצאו לו כל השלמיות

If knowledge is a perfection in man, God has knowledge.
But knowledge is a perfection in man.
Therefore, God has knowledge.

Now, in this syllogism, the term "knowledge" in the antecedent of the major premise as well as in the consequent of the major premise and hence also in the conclusion must be the same kind of knowledge, for otherwise they would be equivocal terms and the syllogism would commit what Aristotle calls the fallacy of "equivocation" (ὁμωνυμία).[31] Thus, on the basis of his own statement as to the proof that God possesses knowledge, Maimonides cannot maintain that the knowledge predicated of God is an equivocal term.

The argument as phrased by Gersonides himself reads as follows: "It is evident that we arrive at a knowledge concerning matters which we affirm of God from matters which we observe in ourselves, as, for instance, we affirm concerning God that He possesses knowledge by reason of the fact that knowledge is possessed by us. To continue with this illustration: It is because we have conceived from the knowledge that is possessed by our intellect that knowledge is a perfection in it, without which it cannot do, if it is to be at all an actual intellect, that we assert that God has knowledge, seeing that it has already been demonstrated to our satisfaction, beyond any doubt, that God is an actual intellect. Now it is self-evident that if any predicate is affirmed of a certain thing by reason of its belonging to another thing, that predicate cannot be affirmed of both these things as an absolute equivocal term, for between things which are related to each other by absolute equivocation there can be no analogy. To illustrate: Just as it cannot be logically inferred that man is rational from the premise that body is continuous, so could not that inference be drawn, even if in both the premise and the conclusion one single term were used in an absolute equivocal sense to mean, in one case, 'rational' and, in the other, 'continuous.' This is self-evident."[32]

וירוחקו מעליו כל החסרונות, וכמעט שהוא מושכל ראשון שהסכלות באי זה דבר שיהיה הוא חסרון, ושהוא יתעלה לא יסכל דבר.

[31] *De Soph. Elench.*, 4, 165b, 26.

[32] *Milḥamot Adonai*, III, 3, p. 133, ll. 6–17: וזה כי הוא מבואר שאנחנו דורכים בענינים אשר נחייבם בשם יתברך מהענינים אשר אצלנו, כאלו תאמר שאנחנו חייבנו בשם יתברך שהוא יודע מפני מה שנמצא בנו מהידיעה. והמשל שאנחנו, מפני מה שהשגנו מהידיעה הנמצאת בשכלנו שהיא שלמות לשכל אי אפשר לו מזולתה, ובמה שהוא שכל בפועל, נאמר שהוא יתברך יודע, מצד מה שהתבאר לנו ממה שהוא שכל בפועל בלי ספק. ומן המבואר בנפשו שנשוא אחד, כשחוייב לדבר מה מפני מציאותו לדבר אחר, הוא בלתי נאמר בשני הדברים בשתוף השם גמור, כי הדברים המשותפים שתוף גמור לא יפול ביניהם הקש. והמשל שכמו שלא יתכן שיאמר שהאדם הוא משכיל מפני שהגשם הוא מתדבק, כן לא יתכן זה, אם הנחנו שם אחד לשכל ולמתדבק יהיה נאמר עליהם כשתוף גמור, וזה מבואר בנפשו.

Exactly the same argument against Maimonides' equivocal interpretation of divine attributes is to be found in Thomas Aquinas. He says: "When one thing is predicated of several by pure equivocation, we cannot be led from the one to the knowledge of the other, for the knowledge of things depends not on words but on the meaning of names. Now we come to a knowledge of things divine from our observation of other things . . . Therefore attributes of this kind are not pure equivocations when said of God and other things."[33] Again: "Now since our intellect knows God from creatures, it knows Him as far as creatures represent Him . . . Hence every creature represents Him, and is like Him, so far as it possesses some perfection: yet not so far as to represent Him as something of the same species or genus."[34]

Third, the same argument, Gersonides continues to say, follows also from Aristotle's views, to which Maimonides subscribes, with regard to contradictory propositions. To begin with, according to Aristotle, of contradictory propositions, one must be true and one false.[35] Then, also, according to Aristotle, contradictory propositions are those "which have the same predicate and subject, without equivocation of terms."[36] Accordingly, since Maimonides believes that of the two propositions "God is knowing" and "God is not knowing" only the first is true, whereas the second is false, he must of necessity admit that these two propositions are contradictory propositions. But since he must admit that they are contradictory propositions, he must also admit that the term "knowing" used as a predicate in the affirmative proposition must mean the same as the term "knowing" used as a predicate in the negative proposition. But in the negative proposition the term "knowing" is not used in an equivocal sense. Consequently in the affirmative proposition also the term "knowing" is not used in an equivocal sense.

The argument as phrased by Gersonides himself reads as follows: "This conclusion, namely, that God's knowledge does not differ from our knowledge after the manner of the difference mentioned by Maimonides, may also be arrived at logically in another way, as follows. When we investigate with regard to certain predicates whether they should be affirmed of God or negated of Him, these predicates, it is quite clear, are to be understood by us in our investiga-

[33] *Contra Gentiles*, I, 33 (3).

[34] *Sum Theol.*, I, 13, 2 C.

[35] *De Interpr.*, 7, 17b, 26–29.

[36] *Ibid.*, 6, 17a, 34–35.

tion to mean the same thing both in the affirmation and in the negation. To illustrate: If we investigate whether God is a body or whether He is not a body, the term body, it is quite clear, must be taken by us to have the same meaning in some respect in both these alternative propositions, for if the term body in the negative proposition were predicated by us of God in absolute equivocation as compared with the same term predicated of Him in the affirmative proposition, then the two alternative propositions would not have been conceived by us as contradictory to each other. This is self-evident . . . Since this is so and since also it is evident that the predicates which we negate of God are not applied to Him and to ourselves in an equivocal sense, it must be evident that the predicates which we affirm of God are not to be applied to Him and to ourselves in an equivocal sense."[37]

Fourth, says Gersonides, "in general, if the things which we affirm of God are affirmed of Him and of ourselves according to an absolute equivocation, then there would be no term, among the many terms used with reference to ourselves, which would be more fitting to be used as a negation with reference to God than as an affirmation, or as an affirmation than as a negation. Thus, for instance, one might say that God is a body, insisting that he does not mean by the term body something which has quantity but rather something which has no analogy with that which we call body except by the absolute equivocation of the term applied to both of them. By the same token, he might say that God is not knowing, insisting that the term knowing does not mean with him in this proposition what it usually means when we describe a thing as knowing."[38]

The same argument occurs in Joseph Ibn Ẓaddik, aimed not at the explicit use of the equivocal interpretation of divine attributes, for

[37] *Milḥamot Adonai*, III, 3, p. 133, l. 28–p. 134, l. 2 and ll. 15–17: וכבר יתבאר זה מצד העיון באופן אחר, ר"ל שידיעת השם יתברך בלתי מתחלפת לידיעתנו זה האופן מהחלוף אשר זכרו הרב המורה זכרונו לברכה. וזה שהענינים אשר נחקור עליהם אם הם נמצאים לשם יתברך או הם נשללים ממנו, הוא מבואר שאנחנו נשפט על הנשואים ההם בכונה אחת בעינה בחיוב ובשלילה. והמשל שנחקור אם השם יתברך גשם או איננו גשם, הוא מבואר ששם הגשם הוא מורה אצלנו הוראה אחת באופן מה בשתי החלוקות האלו. וזה שאם היה שם הגשם נאמר אצלנו בחלק השולל מאלו החלקים בשתוף גמור עם מה שיאמר עליו בחלק המחייב, לא היו אלו החלוקות חלקי הסותר אצל מחשבתנו. וזה מבואר בנפשו . . . ובהיות הענין כן, והיה מבואר שהנשואים אשר נשלל מהשם יתברך אינן נאמרים בו יתברך ובנו בשתוף גמור, הוא מבואר שהנשואים אשר נחייבם לו יתברך אינם נאמרים בו יתברך ובנו בשתוף גמור.

[38] *Ibid.*, p. 134, ll. 20–26: ובכלל אם היו הדברים אשר נחייבם לו יתברך נאמרים בו יתברך ובנו בשתוף גמור, לא יהיה כאן שם משמות הדברים אשר אצלנו שיהיה יותר ראוי בשוללות השם יתברך מבחיוב, ובחיוב מבשוללות. וזה כי לאומר שיאמר, דרך משל, שהשם יתברך הוא גשם ולא ירצה בזה הגשם דבר בעל כמה, אבל דבר הוא משותף שתוף גמור עם מה שנקראהו גשם. וכן יאמר כי השם יתברך בלתי יודע, לפי ששם הידיעה לא יורה אצלו בזה המאמר כל מה שיורה עליו במה שנקראהו ידיעה.

the term equivocal does not occur in the text, but at the figurative interpretation of attributes in general, as expressed in the Mutazilite formula "He is living without life." If one can attribute to God the term "life," without meaning thereby what is generally meant by life, he argues, "why then should you not predicate of God the term body with the implication that the body predicated is unlike other bodies."[39]

A similar argument, though with a different point, is used also by Thomas Aquinas. After quoting Maimonides' interpretation of attributes as negations, he tries to refute it on the ground that if, as maintained by Maimonides, "when we say that God lives, we mean that God is not like an inanimate thing," then so also may we say that He is a body, with the explanation that we mean thereby "that He is not a mere potentiality as is primary matter."[40]

Gersonides, however, was aware that Maimonides himself, in anticipation of this objection insists that no term which denotes a deficiency or an imperfection in ordinary speech can be predicated of God even in an equivocal sense. "We have already stated several times," he says, "that anything which is considered by ordinary men as a deficiency or as that which cannot be conceived as compatible with God has not been ascribed to God in the prophetic books even metaphorically, although such terms may not otherwise be different from those which were employed as metaphors in relation to God."[41] It is evidently with this passage of Maimonides in mind that Gersonides says: "One may not answer this objection by saying that we negate corporeality of God only because it is a deficiency with reference to us, but we affirm knowledge of Him because with reference to us it is a perfection, for this answer may be rebutted as follows: It is not the term corporeality that is a deficiency, nor is it the mere term that we negate of God, but rather that which is meant by the term. Evidence for this is the fact that if we used the term corporeality to designate that which is designated now by the term knowledge or conversely the term knowledge for that which is designated now by the term corporeality, then corporeality would be a perfection with reference to us and knowledge a deficiency. Then also, we do not affirm anything

[39] *'Olam Ḳaṭan*, III, p. 46, l. 11 (ed. Horovitz): ולמה לא תאמרו גוף ולא כשאר הגופים Cf. Kaufmann, *Attributenlehre*, p. 269, n. 47.

[40] *Sum. Theol.*, I, 13, 2 c.

[41] *Moreh Nebukim*, I, 47: כבר זכרנו פעמים כי כל מה שידמהו ההמון חסרון או אי אפשר לציירו בחק השם יתעלה לא השאילוהו ספרי הנבואה לו יתעלה, ואף על פי שמשפטו משפט הדברים אשר הושאלו לו. Cf. Dionysius, *De Myst. Theol.* IV (PG 3, 1040 D).

of God or negate anything of Him unless we first investigate whether that thing is fitting to be affirmed of Him or whether it is unfitting. But we do affirm or negate something of God without any investigation on our part whether that something is a perfection with reference to us or whether it is an imperfection with reference to us."[42]

But here a question must have come up in the mind of Gersonides. If any term predicated of God is not an equivocal term, then, by the statement quoted above from Aristotle,[43] it must have the same meaning as when it is predicated of some other being, as, for instance, the term "animal" when predicated of "man" and "horse" or as the term "man" when predicated of Socrates and Plato. In other words, it must be either a "genus" or a "species." In either case, any term predicated of God would be what Maimonides calls "part of a definition" and, as such, as Maimonides rightly contends, it would imply that God's essence is "compound,"[44] that is to say, it would imply a "plurality" in God's essence.[45] Moreover, if any term predicated of God is a species, then, according to Maimonides, there would be a "similarity" and hence also a "relation" between God and other beings of whom the same term is predicated, for, as it is argued by Maimonides, "similarity is a certain relation between two things"[46] and "whenever two things are under the same species . . . they are necessarily similar to each other"[47] and also "relation is necessarily always to be found only between things which are under the same proximate species."[48]

In answer to this question in its two phases, Gersonides will try to show that by his denying that divine attributes are equivocal terms it does not necessarily follow, first, that they are each a genus and hence imply a "plurality" in God's essence and, second, that they are each a species and hence imply a "relation" between God and other beings.

[42] *Milḥamot Adonai*, III, 3, p. 134, ll. 26–34. ואין לאומר שיאמר כי אנחנו אמנם נשלול ממנו הגשמות להיות חסרון לנו, ונחייב הידיעה להיותה שלמות, וזה כי אין שם הגשמות חסרון, והוא אשר נשללהו ממנו, אבל ענינו. והראיה שאם היינו מורים בשם הגשמות על מה שיורה עליו שם הידיעה, ובשם הידיעה על מה שיורה עליו שם הגשמות, היה הגשמות שלמות לנו והידיעה חסרון. ועוד שאנחנו לא נחייב לשם יתברך דבר ולא נשללהו ממנו, אלא כשנחקור תחלה אם מציאות הדבר ההוא ראוי לו יתברך או בלתי ראוי, לא נשים חקירתנו בזה אם היא שלמות לנו אי בלתי שלמות לנו.

[43] Cf. above quotation referred to in n. 36.

[44] *Moreh Nebukim*, I, 51: תהיה מהותו מורכבת.

[45] *Milḥamot Adonai*, III, 3, p. 135, l. 20: להיות כל תואר מחייב רבוי.

[46] *Moreh Nebukim*, I, 56: ההדמות היא יחס אחד בין שני דברים.

[47] *Ibid.*, כל שני דברים שהם תחת מין אחד . . . הנה שניהם מתדמים בהכרח.

[48] *Ibid.*, I, 52: היחס אמנם ימצא לעולם בין שני דברים שתחת מין אחד קרוב בהכרח.

His answer to the first phase of the question reads as follows: "After due reflection it becomes apparent that there are attributes which are predicated of God and of other beings according to priority and posteriority, without implying any plurality in Him. For not every statement that is predicated of a thing in any manner whatsoever does necessarily imply plurality in that thing. It implies plurality in it only when the thing of which the statement is predicated is related to the predicate as a subject of existence. But if it is not related to it as a subject of existence, even though it is a subject of discourse, there is no implication of plurality in the subject. For instance, if we state about a certain particular redness that it is a color [which is] red, it does not imply that the redness in question is composed of color and redness, for color is not something existent as a subject of redness; it is a subject only in discourse."[49]

This passage, I take it, reflects the discussions found in Alfarabi, Avicenna, Algazali, and Averroes with regard to terms which are predicated of two things ambiguously according to prior and posterior.[50] Any such term, says Algazali, is not a genus for "whatever is not predicated by way of univocality is not a genus."[51] Not being a genus, any such ambiguous universal term combined with a differentia does not form a "definition" in the technical sense of the term; it forms a "description" (*rasm*). This view is constantly repeated by Alfarabi, Avicenna, Algazali, and Averroes. Now while the term "description" goes back to the Stoics, it corresponds to what Aristotle would call a nominal definition, described by him as "a statement declaring what a name signifies,"[52] in contradistinction to what he would call a real definition, described by him as "a statement declaring why a thing exists."[53] As an illustration of a nominal definition Aristotle says, "as, for instance, what signifies that which is called

[49] *Milḥamot Adonai*, III, 3, p. 135, l.28–p. 136, l. 15: ונאמר שכבר יראה עם התבוננות הטוב שבכאן תארים נאמרים בשם יתברך ובזולתו בקודם ובאחור, ואינם מחייבים לו רבוי. וזה שאין כל מאמר אשר יאמר על הדבר מדרך מה הוא מחייב לו רבוי, אבל אמנם יחייב לו רבוי אם היה החלק האחד במדרגת הנושא במציאות לחלק השני, ואם לא היה לו נושא במציאות, אף על פי שהוא נושא במאמר, הנה אינו מחייב לו רבוי. והמשל כאשר נאמר באדמימות הרמוז אליו שהוא מראה אדום, הנה לא יחוייב מפני זה שיהיה האדמימות מורכב מהמראה והאודם, כי אין המראה דבר נמצא נושא לאודם, אבל הוא נושא במאמר לבד.

[50] What follows is more fully discussed in my paper "Avicenna, Algazali, and Averroes on Divine Attributes" mentioned above (n. 12).

[51] *Maqāṣid al-Falāsifah*, II, 2, p. 145, ll. 6–7.

[52] *Anal. Post.*, II, 10, 93b, 30.

[53] *Ibid.*, 39.

triangle,"[54] which is interpreted by Averroes,[55] as well as by Philoponus,[56] as referring to the definition of a triangle as a "figure contained by three sides."[57] Various similar examples are quoted by these Arabic philosophers. On the basis of this denial that an ambiguous term is a genus and on the basis also of this conception that a statement containing an ambiguous term is a nominal definition or description, all these Arabic philosophers maintain that terms predicated of God, by reason of their being ambiguous terms, are not genera and hence do not form real definitions; they form only nominal definitions or descriptions.

All these considerations, we take it, lie behind the passage we have quoted from Gersonides. A proposition which contains a "genus" and constitutes a real definition is described by him as having a "subject of existence." The expression "subject of existence" thus reflects Aristotle's description of a real definition as a "statement declaring why a thing exists." A proposition which contains an ambiguous term and constitutes only a nominal definition is described by him as having a "subject of discourse." The expression "subject of discourse" thus reflects Aristotle's description of a nominal definition as a "statement declaring what a name signifies." His illustration of what he calls a "subject of discourse" by the statement that redness is "a color which is red" reflects the illustration of a "nominal definition" by the statement, quoted above from Averroes, that a triangle is "a figure contained by three sides." From this, like his predecessors among the Arabic philosophers, Gersonides concludes that the terms predicated of God, by reason of their being ambiguous terms, are not genera and do not form parts of real definitions and consequently they do not imply plurality in God's essence.

Gersonides' answer to the second phase of the question reads as follows: "It can be demonstrated that even though we admit that there is a relation between God and His creatures, the attributes predicated of Him may still be applied to Him and to other beings according to priority and posteriority, for among terms which are applied according to priority and posteriority we do find some that

54 *Ibid.*, 31–32.

55 Long Commentary on *Analytica Posteriora* II, Comm. 44, p. 470 D, in *Aristotelis opera*, Venice, 1574, Vol. I, Pars II.

56 *Joannes Philoponus in Analytica Posteriora cum Anonymo* (ed. M. Wallies), p. 372, ll. 18–19.

57 So phrased in Averroes. Cf. Euclid, *Elements*, I, Def. 19.

are predicable of things between which there is no relation. For instance, the term 'existent' is predicable of both 'substance' and 'accident' according to priority and posteriority, as has been shown in the *Metaphysics*, and yet it is evident that there is no relation between substance and accidents."[58]

Behind this argument there are three statements of Aristotle. First, there is his statement that "existent" (ὄν) is not to be taken as the "genus" of the ten categories ranged under it,[59] the ten categories being "substance" and nine "accidents." Second, there is his statement that each category, that is, substance and each of the nine accidents, constitutes a genus.[60] Third, there is his statement that the term "existent" as applied to "substance" and the nine "accidents" is used neither "equivocally" nor "in the same sense," that is, "univocally," from which Alexander Aphrodisiensis as well as the Arabic philosophers infer that it is used "ambiguously."[61] With these three statements in mind, Gersonides argues against Maimonides as follows. You say that an ambiguous term must imply "similarity" by which you undoubtedly mean that terms can be applied ambiguously only to things which belong to the same species, for, according to your own statement, similarity is to be found only between things which are of the same species. But this is not true. The term "existent," according to Aristotle himself, is applied ambiguously to "substance" and "accident," and still substance and accident do not belong to the same species; they do not even belong to the same genus; they each constitute a genus. The conclusion to be drawn therefore is that ambiguous terms do not imply similarity and hence terms predicated of God should be allowed to be taken as ambiguous terms.

These arguments against the equivocal use of divine predicates are directly aimed, as we have said, at Maimonides' view of divine knowledge. But in the course of his discussion Gersonides extends their application also to all the other attributes. Toward the end of his first argument, which deals specifically with the attribute of knowledge, he says: "The same view must hold true also with reference to the terms 'existent', 'one', 'substance', and other terms of the

[58] *Milḥamot Adonai*, III, 3, p. 136, ll. 18–23: וכבר יתאמת שהתארים הנאמרים בשם יתברך נאמרים בו בקודם ובשאר הנמצאים באחור, עם הודאתינו שאין יחס בין השם יתברך ובין נבראיו. וזה כי כבר ימצא מהשמות הנאמרים בקודם ובאחור מה שמנהגם זה המנהג. והמשל ששם הנמצא נאמר על העצם בקודם ועל המקרים באחור, כמו שהתבאר במה שאחר הטבע, והיא מבואר שאין יחס בין העצם והמקרים.

[59] *Metaph.*, III, 3, 998b, 22; VIII, 6, 1045b, 5–6.

[60] *Ibid.*, V, 28, 1024b, 9–10 and 12–15; *Phys.*, V, 4, 227b, 4–5.

[61] Cf. "Amphibolous Terms," *op. cit.*, pp. 153–154.

same order, namely, that they are applied to God priorily and to other beings posteriorily."[62] The same view with regard to "existent," "one," and "substance" is repeated by him at the end[63] of the last passage we have quoted from him, to which he then adds the terms "intellect," "living," "comprehending," "beneficient," "powerful," and "willing."[64] In both these places he refers to his direct discussion of attributes later in his work,[65] where other terms are mentioned, all of which are evidently taken by him as ambiguous terms.

In this paper, confining ourselves to the problem whether divine attributes are to be taken as equivocal or as ambiguous terms, we have tried to show that Maimonides' interpretation of divine attributes as equivocal terms is unique in the history of philosophy, that Moslem philosophers took them to be ambiguous terms, and that Gersonides has adopted this view of the Moslem philosophers and presented it in opposition to that of Maimonides. We have also tried to explain Gersonides' arguments against Maimonides.

One general observation may now be added. The interpretation of divine attributes as ambiguous terms does not mean the assertion of the existence of the so-called "essential attributes" in God after the manner of the orthodox Moslem believers in essential attributes who are criticized by Maimonides.[66] It only means that, granted that God has no essential attributes, the terms predicated of God are to be interpreted as ambiguous terms. This is exactly the view of Alfarabi, Avicenna, Algazali, and Averroes, as well as of Gersonides. Then, also, the ambiguous interpretation of terms predicated of God does not necessarily mean the rejection of the interpretation of such terms as having an actional or negational meaning, for, again, granted that some terms predicated of God are to be taken as actions, these actional predicates may still be interpreted as ambiguous terms; similarly, granted that some terms predicated of God are to be taken as negations, this does not necessarily mean that some other terms usually predicated of God cannot be taken as ambiguous terms. While indeed Gersonides does not explicitly deal with the actional and negational interpretation of divine attributes by the side of his treatment of ambiguous interpretation, his Arabic predecessors do deal with the interpretation of some attributes as actions and some

[62] *Milḥamot Adonai*, III, 3, p. 132b ll. 15–17: וכן ראוי שימשך הענין בשם הנמצא והאחד והעצם ושאר השמות הנוהגים מנהגם, שהם נאמרים בשם יתברך בקודם, ובזולתו באיחור.

[63] *Ibid.*, p. 136, l. 23–p. 137, l. 6.

[64] *Ibid.*, p. 137, ll. 6 ff.

[65] *Ibid.*, V, 12, pp. 278 ff.

[66] *Moreh Nebukim*, I, 53.

of them as negation by the side of their discussion of the interpretation of attributes as ambiguous terms. When therefore Abraham Shalom in his *Neveh Shalom* states that "those who, like Gersonides and his followers, understand that things are predicated of God and of ourselves according to priority and posteriority and not according to an absolute equivocation, maintain that God has essential and positive attributes,"[67] his statement is not true as a generalization of all those who interpret divine predicates as ambiguous terms, and certainly it is not true of Gersonides, though it is partly true of Crescas.[68]

[67] Cf. *Neveh Shalom*, XII, I, 2, p. 199a (ed. Venice, 1575): אמנם מי שיבין שהדברים נאמרים בו ית' ובנו בקדימה ואיחור לא בשתוף גמור כהר"לבג והאוחזים דרכו יאמרו שיש לו תארים עצמיים וחיוביים.

[68] Cf. my paper "Crescas on the Problem of Divine Attributes," *Jewish Quarterly Review*, N. S., 7 (1916), 198 ff. Below, 314 ff.

7

CRESCAS ON THE PROBLEM OF DIVINE ATTRIBUTES

PREFATORY NOTE.

IT has been well said that in Arabic, and for that matter also in Jewish philosophy, the problem of Universals had never acquired, as it did later on in Scholasticism, the importance of an independent subject of inquiry. Still, the problem was not altogether unknown. Always latent, it occasionally cropped out in various philosophical discussions. We need only slightly penetrate below the surface of some controversies of the time in Metaphysics and Psychology to discover the lurking presence of the problem of Universals. For the true problem of Universals began with the rejection of Platonic Realism. Admitting with the Aristotelians that genera and species are mere products of the mind, the question was then raised as to what was the nature of those intellectual conceptions and their relation to the individual beings. It was this field of inquiry that proved a fertile ground for the crop of the many subtle and hardly distinguishable mediaeval theories of Universals. Now the same problem must inevitably appear whenever the mind perceives a distinction of a purely intellectual character in an object, and the solution of that problem will of necessity prove more difficult when, in addition to defining the nature of that intellectual distinction, we must at the same time safeguard the unity of the object. Thus, for instance, in the case of the soul, one and homogeneous, we may ask what is the relation between the essence and its faculties. And in the case of God, too, the absolutely simple, how are His attributes related to His essence?

It is as a problem of Universals in disguise that the problem of Attributes will be herein presented. I shall therefore forego the discussion of the lexicographical and exegetical aspect of the problem, namely, the enumeration of all the Attributes found in the Bible, and their explanation by Jewish philosophers, the object of this paper being to discuss the general principles underlying the problem and its solution. As part of a larger work upon the philosophy of Crescas, it deals more fully with that author. The two chapters devoted to him are intended both to present a constructive view of his theory and to serve as a commentary on his text. They are preceded by a chapter devoted to a general treatment of certain representative authors advisedly selected for their value as an introduction to the study of Crescas.

CHAPTER I

AN ANALYSIS OF THE PROBLEM AND SOME REPRESENTATIVE SOLUTIONS.

I.

THERE are four initial assumptions underlying the problem of divine attributes in mediaeval philosophy. The starting-point of the problem is the rationalistic attempt to invest the Scriptural predications of God with the validity of logical judgements. Then, a logical judgement is defined, after Aristotle, as having a double content, synthesizing as it does two distinct terms, of which one must be a universal, by bringing them together by one of the several relations obtaining between subject and predicate. In addition to these two assumptions, while Platonic Realism is not an essential prerequisite, the problem of attributes involves an anti-nominalistic conception of Universals. Finally, it follows Avicenna in identifying God with the metaphysical conception of necessary existence, whose simplicity by definition precludes from its being not only actual composition, but likewise any suggestion of noetic plurality and relativity. The question is then raised, How can we form a logical judgement about God without at the same time creating the anomaly of having the unrelatable Necessarily Existent brought into some logical relation with some predicate distinct from Himself? It is this apparent incompatibility of the formal interpretation of Biblical phraseology, the synthetic conception of a logical judgement, the anti-nominalistic view of universals, and the Avicennean definition of necessary existence that lies at the basis of the problem of attributes.

In Maimonides' treatment of Attributes we find a clear if not a formal statement of the problem. He sets out with a rationalistic definition of faith. Faith is not the correlative of reason, but rather the consummation of the reasoning process. Nor is it a mere attitude of mind, an inane state of consciousness; it is the comprehension of some objective reality. Furthermore, faith is not immediate comprehension or intuitive knowledge, the claim of mysticism, but it is resultant knowledge, the positive intellectual certainty arrived at after a process of ratiocinative reasoning. Faith thus being knowledge, derivative and logically demonstrable, the profession of faith must, therefore, have the force of logical judgements. They cannot be mere verbal utterance, mere irresponsible exclamations indicative but inexpressive of an attitudinal belief; they must be the embodiment of the conclusions of logical syllogisms, in which the premisses, though not stated, are assumed. Consequently the articles of faith, containing asseverations about the nature and being of God, based upon corresponding affirmations taken from the Scriptures, are perforce logical propositions conforming to all the regimens regulating such propositions.[1]

But a logical proposition must contain a synthesis of two distinct terms. Identity, contends Maimonides, is not a relation. A proposition in which the subject and predicate indicate one and the same thing is logically meaningless, for to assert that *A* is *A* is a mere tautology.[2] In this as well as in his subsequent elaborate statement of what he considers as real, logical relations, though at first sight he does not appear to do so, Maimonides is really following in the footprints of his Stagirite master. In order to show

[1] Cf. *Moreh*, I, 50. [2] Cf. *Moreh*, I, 51.

this congruity, let us first give a genetic analysis of Aristotle's predicables.

It is from his classification of the Categories that Aristotle derives his predicables, for whatever other purpose that classification might have originally served in Aristotle's system, its function as expressing logical relations between subject and predicate is unquestionable.[3] When Aristotle, however, uses the categories in their restrictive application of predicables, instead of their common tenfold classification, he adopts their less current division into two, Substance and Accident.[4] Thus the predicate of a proposition may be either a Substance or an Accident. Neither of these, however, can be a particular. Two individual substances, denoting one and the same thing, cannot be related as subject and predicate. Likewise a definite accident cannot be predicated of a subject. 'John is John' and 'The table is *this definite red*' are not logical propositions. Conse-

[3] Whether the Categories were originally intended by Aristotle as logical or ontological divisions is a moot point (cf. Zeller, *Aristotle*, vol. I, p. 274, note 3; p. 275, note 1; Grote, *Aristotle*, vol. I, ch. iii). No question on this point, however, existed for the Arabic and Jewish philosophers. To them it was clear that the Categories were both logical and metaphysical, and are treated as such in the works of Alfarabi, Avicenna, and Algazali. Likewise in the Scholastic philosophy, the Categories had logical as well as metaphysical significance (cf. De Wulf, *Scholasticism Old and New*, p. 141).

[4] Averroes, in his paraphrase of Aristotle's Categories (ספר המאמרות לבן רש״ד), has the following classification: (1) Universal Substance (העצם הכולל), which is predicable of a subject but does not exist in it (ינשא על נושא ואיננו בנושא). (2) Particular accident (מקרה נרמז הוא בנושא ולא ינשא על נושא), which exists in a subject but is not predicable of it (הוא בנושא ולא ינשא על נושא). (3) Universal accident (המקרה הכולל), which both exists in a subject and is predicable of it (ינשא על נושא והוא ג״כ בנושא). (4) Particular Substance (איש העצם), which neither exists in a subject nor is predicable thereof (לא ינשא על נושא ואיננו בנושא). Cf. Organon, *The Categories*, ch. ii.

quently, whether substance or accident, the predicables must be universals. Now, a universal substance may denote either the genus or the species of a thing, and a universal accident may be differentiated, with respect to its applicability, as more or less essential to the subject. In this way Aristotle derives his four predicables: genus, species, property, and accident, which, raised to five in Porphyry's 'Introduction' by the addition of 'specific difference', were referred to by mediaeval logicians as the five predicables.[5]

Herein, if I am not mistaken, we may find the origin of Maimonides' fivefold division of the possible relations between subject and attribute. Their difference in nomenclature is more apparent than real, and the process of their derivation from the Categories will be shown to tally with that followed by Aristotle. As already mentioned, Maimonides rejects identity as a logical relation, that is, the attributes cannot be taken as individual, first substances. What is now left is the alternative, that they must be either universal substances or universal accidents. In the words of Maimonides: 'It will now be clear that the attributes must be one of two things; either the essence of the object described—in that case it is a mere explanation of a name, &c.—or the attribute is something different from the object described' (*Moreh*, I, 51). This general twofold classification is now subdivided by Maimonides into five classes. Taking universal substance, from which the Aristotelians get genus, species, and specific difference, Maimonides

[5] Cf. *Intentions*, Logic. Algazali enumerates these five universals (הכוללים הנפרדים; הנפרדים החמישה) which may be predicated of a subject, namely, סוג, מין, הבדל, סגולה, מקרה. Sharastani likewise names the same five predicables: الفصل, الخاصّة, العرض العام, الجنس, النوع (ed. Cureton, p. 350).

divides it with respect to its function rather than with respect to its content, thus obtaining two classes, Definition and Part of Definition, for the combination of genus with species or with specific difference forms a definition, whence any one of these three may be properly called Part of Definition. Then again, taking universal accident, which by Aristotle is roughly subdivided into property and (general) accident, bearing upon the tenfold division of Categories, Maimonides divides it more minutely into three classes. The Categories of quantity and quality yield the relation of *Property*; those of Relation, Space, Time, Situation, and Possession are placed under the heading of *External Relations,* whereas the Categories of Action and Passion are designated by him as *Dynamic Relations.* Applying this theory of logical relations to the interpretation of divine attributes, Maimonides arrives at the following conclusion. The divine attributes cannot be identical with their subject, and, while they must be distinct, their relation to it must be equivalent to that of a Definition, Part of Definition, Property, External Relation or Action.[6]

If in the Biblical predications of God, as it has been shown, the attribute must be distinct from but related to the subject, the question then arises, By which of the five enumerated relations are they conjoined? To answer this question it must first be determined what is the nature of the subject of those attributes, or God, in so far as it is known by the proof for His Existence. Now, so much is known about the nature of God, that He is necessary existence, a term used by Avicenna, and corresponding to the Aristotelian Prime Mover. For just as Aristotle, taking motion as the starting-point of his physical inquiries, ulti-

[6] Cf. *Moreh*, I, 52.

mately arrived at the inevitable existence of a Prime Immovable Mover, so Avicenna, reflecting upon the nature of necessity and contingency, eventually concluded that there must be something that is Necessary Existence.[7] Whether Aristotle's Prime Mover should be identified with Avicenna's Necessary Existence is a controversial point which does not concern us now, and will be taken up elsewhere.[8] It is, however, clear that in his discussion of divine attributes Maimonides starts out with the Avicennean conception of Necessary Existence, the proof for which is incorporated by Maimonides within his various proofs for the existence of God.[9] Now, in the Avicennean application of the term, necessary or absolute existence means the negation of any cause whatsoever, the final as well as the efficient, the formal as well as the material. Thus the term Necessary Existence, negative in its original meaning with respect to causation, has ultimately acquired by the negation of all causes whatsoever the additional meaning of absolute simplicity and all which that connotes. The Necessarily Existent must, therefore, be absolutely simple, that is, its essence must exclude not only actual plurality, but metaphysical and epistemological plurality as well, being in no less degree impervious to the distinction between matter and form, genus and species, than to actual, physical disintegration and composition. Absolute simplicity, according to Avicenna, excludes the five possible kinds of plurality: (1)

[7] This will be fully discussed in a chapter on 'The Proofs for the Existence of God'. Cf. *Moreh*, II, 1, Third Argument.

[8] Cf. *ibid.*

[9] Cf. *Moreh*, II, 1, Third Philosophical Argument. This Avicennean argument is introduced by Maimonides as follows: 'This is taken from the words of Aristotle, though he gives it in a different form' (cf. Hebrew commentaries).

Actual plurality as that of physical objects; (2) noetic plurality as that of matter and form; (3) of subject and attribute; (4) of genus and species; and (5) of essence and existence.[10]

Absolute simplicity is thus the main fact known about necessary existence. And so, says Maimonides, when the necessarily existent is placed as the subject of a proposition, it cannot be related to its predicate by any of the first four of the five classes of relations enumerated. The reasons for that are variously stated by Maimonides, but it seems to me that they can all be classified under two headings: first, the implication of plurality; and second, the implication of similarity.[11]

[10] Cf. *Destruction of the Philosophers*, Disputation V.

[11] The classification of Maimonides' arguments into these two divisions is based upon the following facts: In chapters 50 and 51, Maimonides explicitly states that his ground for the rejection of attributes is to be found in the simplicity of the divine substance. In chapter 52, in his enumeration of the five classes of attributes, the first three are rejected for the following reasons: Definition because God has no previous causes (שהוא ית׳ אין לו סבות קודמות); Part of Definition because it would imply that in God essences were compound, and so it could have a definition which has been excluded on account of the implication of previous causation (cf. Afodi's commentary); Property because God is not a magnitude, He is not affected by external influences, He is not subject to physical conditions, and He is not an animate being. Now, all these reasons are in fact nothing but modifications of the chief reason, namely, the implication of the composition of the divine essence. They are thus summed up by Maimonides himself: 'Consequently, these three classes of attributes, describing the essence of a thing, or part of the essence, or a quality of it, are clearly inadmissible in reference to God, for they imply composition.' והנה אלו שלשה חלקים מן התארים, והם מה שיורה על מהות, או על איכות אחת נמצאת במהות, כבר התבאר המנעה בחקו יתעלה מפני שהם כלם מורים על הרכבה. The fourth class of attributes, that of external relation, are rejected by Maimonides not because they imply composition in the divine essence, but because a real external relation must not be assumed to exist between God and created beings. Why that must not be assumed, however, is explained

As for the first of these reasons, Maimonides restates Avicenna's conception of absolute simplicity. 'There cannot be any belief in the unity of God except by admitting that He is one simple substance, without any composition or plurality of elements; one from whatever side you view it, and by whatever test you examine it; not divisible into two parts in any way and by any cause, nor capable of any form or plurality either objectively or subjectively' (*Moreh*,

by him later on in chapter 56 on the ground that every relation implies similarity, the latter of which is inadmissible on independent grounds. Thus all the arguments against attributes may be reduced to the two classes I have named. In chapter 55 Maimonides advances the following four arguments against attributes: They imply (1) corporeality, (2) passiveness (הפעלות), (3) non-existence or potentiality (העדר, בכח), (4) similarity (דמוי). Here, too, the first three reasons are all reducible to the single reason that they imply composition. Likewise Crescas, in his restatement of Maimonides' arguments against positive attributes, classifies those arguments in the two parts I have mentioned. He says: 'If his contention were true that attributes must be negated on account of the inadmissibility of *composition* and of *relation or similarity* between God and others.' ומהם שאם היה החיוב שחייבו משללת התארים אמתי, להמנעות ההרכבה ולהמנעות שום יחס ודמיון בינו ובין זולתו (מ"א, כ"ג, פ"א (p. 25a. Abrabanel, however, reduces Maimonides' arguments to the following threefold classification: (1) on account of God's incorporeality, (2) on account of His eternity, and (3) on account of His unity (cf. commentary on the *Moreh*, I, 51): ועיין שעשה הרב כאן באמונת התארים ג' בטולים, הא' מצד היות הש"י מסולק מן הגשמות, הב' מצד היותו קדמון, והג' מצד היותו אחד. Kaufmann approves of Abrabanel's classification (cf. *Attributenlehre*, p. 377, note 22).

Abraham Shalom has the following classification: (1) On account of the implication of plurality in God, (2) on account of the limitation of human understanding, and (3) on account of the implication of similarity or relation between God and His creatures (cf. *Neveh Shalom*, XII, i, iii). ... האחת להיותו ית' מחוייב המציאות אינו מורכב מחלקים ... השנית היא מצדנו שהב"ת לא יוכל לתאר הבב"ת באמת, השלישית ... ואין לו ית' שום יחס ודמיון עם בריותיו. As will be noticed, the second of these three arguments is not found among the formal arguments of Maimonides.

Albo's classification of arguments against positive attributes (cf. *infra*, Chap. III, note 125) is not based upon Maimonides' text.

I, 51). Consequently, predicates taken in the sense of definition, part of definition, and accretion are inadmissible with respect to God. They all imply plurality in some sense or other. That accretive qualities are inadmissible goes without saying, since they imply that the subject is composed of external attributes inherent in or adherent to its substance. The inadmissibility of a definition or its parts is not so obvious. To affirm of God attributes which, like the parts of a definition, are merely descriptive of the substantial essence without implying the composition of the substance with anything unessential, would at first sight seem to be quite appropriate. That too, however, is inadmissible, for while the parts of a definition do not imply the composition of the defined substance with something external thereto, there is still the implication that the substance itself is composed, as it were, of two essences, the particular and the universal. It is here that Maimonides' theory of universals comes into play. For nominalism, it may be inferred, Maimonides had the same abhorrence as for logical verbalism.[12] There is the ring of a genuine

[12] It is generally stated that Arabic as well as Jewish philosophers were all nominalists (cf. Munk's *Mélanges*, p. 327), 'Les Péripatéticiens arabes, comme on le pense bien, devaient tous professer le nominalisme d'une manière absolue, et plusieurs d'entre eux se prononcent à cet égard dans les termes les plus explicites'. Among the last referred to he includes, in note 1, also Maimonides, who in *Moreh*, III, 18 states that 'species have no existence except in our own minds' (שאין חוץ לשכל שום נמצא, אבל המין נשאר הכלליות דברים שכליים). Cf. also Kaufmann's *Attributenlehre*, p. 379, note 29, 'Was aber Maimûni's Stellung in dem Streite über die Universalien angeht, so bekennt er sich als Aristoteliker zum strengen Nominalismus und läugnet entschieden deren Realität'. Of course, to say that one is a nominalist does not mean anything unless it is definitely explained how the term nominalism is employed. With regard to Maimonides it must be positively stated that his nominalism did not go further than the rejection of Platonic realism. His statement to the effect that the universals are in

feeling of contempt, characteristic of his rationalistic temper of mind, in his sneers at a *flatus vocis*, at 'things that are only said, existing only in words, not in thought, much less in reality' (*Moreh*, I, 51). Platonic realism, claiming the reality of ideas apart from the world of sense, had been discredited with the advent of Aristotelianism long before the age of Maimonides.[13] In various works on Logic and Metaphysics the absurdity of such a conception is pointed out without even recording a dissenting opinion. Conceptualism, to be sure, had found adherents among Arabic philosophers, but Maimonides, no less than Avicenna, evidently rejected that view. To him the assertion of ideal without real existence could have no meaning. Subjective reality, if it means anything, could merely mean that the reality affirmed has only a verbal significance. It is undoubtedly with reference to Conceptualism that Maimonides points out the meaninglessness of ideal existence and the incongruity in 'the assertion of some thinkers, that the ideas, i.e. the universals, are neither existent nor non-existent'[14] (*Moreh*, I, 51). What Maimonides, as a follower of Avicenna and in common with all his contemporaries, conceived of universals is that they have both ideal and real existence. Universals, to be sure, exist in the mind, but the human mind does not *invent* them out of nothing.

mind does not commit him to anything definite. That very same statement had been used by Averroes in quite a different sense. The question is, as we shall see, how much in mind they are, and this can only be determined by analysis of such problems where the existence of universals is involved. From our analysis of Maimonides' theory of Attributes it will be gathered that it can hardly be said of him that he was a nominalist 'd'une manière absolue' or that he declared his adherence 'zum strengen Nominalismus'.

[13] Cf. Munk's *Mélanges*, p. 327.

[14] Cf. Munk's and Friedländer's notes on this passage; Munk's *Mélanges* pp. 327 and 328, n. 1; Kaufmann, *Attributenlehre*, p. 379, n. 29.

What the mind does is only to *discover* them in the multifarious individuals. For prior to the rise of individual beings the universals exist in the mind of God as independent entities, and they remain as such even when they enter upon plurality in material form, though their presence in the individuals is indiscernible except by mental activity.[15] Consequently even in essential attributes, as those which form a definition, there must necessarily be the implication of plurality in the subject. For the definition is not merely a verbal description of the essence, the latter being in itself one and uniform, but, as said Avicenna, the parts of the definition are the predicates of the thing defined. And so, since genus and specific difference are real in a certain sense, and not mere words, the thing defined by its genus and specific difference must be composite in so far as that genus and specific difference are real. That composition, to be sure, would only be mentally discernible, but still it would be inconsistent with the conception of absolute simplicity.

Let us now assume that the universals predicated of God are neither essential nor accidental qualities, but rather external relations between God and His creatures. This interpretation of attributes though sanctioned by the traditional philosophy of his time[16] is rejected by Maimonides

[15] Cf. Avicenna's *Eš-šefah*, translated by M. Horten under the title of *Die Metaphysik Avicenna's*, Part V, ch. 1; De Boer's *Philosophy in Islam* (Eng. tr.), p. 135; Prantl's *Geschichte der Logik*, vol. II, in his exposition of Alfarabi, pp. 305–6, and in that of Avicenna, pp. 347 and 384, especially note 181; Carra de Vaux, *Avicenne*, pp. 224–5.

[16] In his *Intentions of the Philosophers* (*Metaphysics*, Part III, On the Attributes), Algazali restates Avicenna's interpretation of divine attributes as (1) negations (שלילה) and (2) relations (צרוף). Under relations he includes both what Maimonides calls 'external relations' and what he calls 'actions'. The same view is repeated by him in his *Destruction of the Philosophers*, Disputation V. Among Jewish philosophers, Abraham Ibn

as inadequate. In their ultimate analysis he says all such relations may be shown either to have no meaning at all, or, if they do have any meaning, to imply similarity between God and other beings. Relations are fourfold: temporal, spatial, reciprocative, and comparative. God, being incorporeal, cannot have any temporal or spatial relations. Again, His self-sufficiency and absolute independence precludes the relation of reciprocity, for His creativeness, His knowledge, and His beneficence are absolutely independent of the created, known and beneficiary objects. Finally, a relation of comparison exists only when things compared involved a specific identity, and differ only in individual diversity. White and green on that account are incomparable terms, even though they are identical as to their genus colour. Nor are they related terms; they are rather correlative and antithetical, their diversity being specific. God cannot, therefore, be compared with and related to other beings with respect to any predicate affirmed of Him, since all His predicates are indicative of attributes which are identical with essence, and hence absolute and immutable.[17] Nor can we claim that the attributes are some kind of subjective external relations, for every relation must imply a similarity.[18] If two things are related they are in so far

Daud, in his *Emunah Ramah* (Book II, Principle III), permits the use of relational attributes. In fact Maimonides was the first to distinguish between external relations and actions, and while permitting the latter to proscribe the former. Cf. *infra*, Chap. II.

[17] Cf. *Moreh*, I, 52.

[18] Cf. *ibid.* 'Besides, if any relation existed between them, God would be subject to the accident of relation, and although that would not be an accident to the essence of God, it would still be, to some extent, a kind of accident.' To which Shem-tob adds the following explanation: 'If any relation was affirmed of Him, even though an unreal relation, God would be subject to the accident of relation, that is to say, God would have to

similar, and so if a subjective relation means anything there must also be some meaning to subjective similarity. But there can be no similarity between God and other beings; hence, there cannot be any relation between them. For the preclusion of similarity Maimonides advances no arguments.[19] He refers to it as a well-accepted principle which seems to be exclusively based upon Scriptural inferences.

Of the five logical relations originally postulated by Maimonides there is now only one left, the dynamic, which has not been disqualified as a possible explanation of divine attributes. This is retained by Maimonides. The divine attributes are dynamic relations, that is to say, they are descriptive of the operating process of the activity rather than of the qualification therefor.[20] That the assertion of

resemble some other creature, even though that relation would not be an accident added to His essence.' ואם יתיחס לו שום יחס אפילו שיהיה בלתי אמתי ישיגהו מקרה היחס, והוא שיהיה דומה לשום נברא אעפ״י שאינו מקרה נוסף עליו. Shem-tob's explanation is probably based upon chapter 56, wherein Maimonides elaborately explains the interdependence of relativism and similarity.

[19] For the negation of similarity Maimonides advances no argument except that of authority. 'Another thing likewise to be denied in reference to God is similarity to any existing being. This has been generally accepted [even by the Mutakallemim, cf. Shem-tob's commentary], and is also mentioned in the books of the Prophets; e. g. "To whom, then, will you liken me?" [Isa. 40. 25].' ומה שראוי בהכרח שירוחק ממנו ג״כ הדמוי לשום דבר מן הנמצאות, וזה דבר כבר הרגיש בו כל אדם [ואפילו המדברים, שם טוב] וכבר גלה בספרי הנביאים בהרחקת הדמוי ואמר, ואל מי תדמיון אל. Though later on he adds, 'It is necessary to demonstrate by proof that nothing can be predicated of God that implies similarity' (ראוי בהכרח להרחיקו ממנו במופת . . . מה שיביא לדמיון), he does not, however, state the proof for this, except that by inference he maintains that similarity must imply a real and not only an external relation. Cf. Ḥobot ha-Lebabot, I, 7 והששי.

[20] Cf. *Moreh*, I, 52. 'I do not mean by *its actions* the inherent capacity for a certain work, as is expressed in *carpenter*, *painter*, or *smith*, for these

activities implies no plurality in the subject is apparent, for activities denote some external relation of the subject to its environment. In point of fact, most of the Arabic as well as Jewish philosophers do not treat activities as a special logical relation; but, including them together with space and time under the heading of External Relation, admit them all as divine attributes.[21] The separation of activities as a distinct class of logical relations is effected here by Maimonides because of his rejection of non-dynamic external relations on account of their implication of similarity. It might be questioned, indeed, Why should not activities, too, be excluded on account of similarity? As we shall see later on, this difficulty has not been allowed to pass unchallenged by Crescas.[22] For our present purpose, it suffices to state that dynamic relations, according to Maimonides, imply no plurality in the subject, and consequently the divine attributes must be interpreted as designations of activities.

There are, however, two points with regard to dynamic attributes which need some further explanation. First, while it is true that the assertion of any action in itself does not necessarily imply the existence of an accidental quality in the subject, the assertion of many diverse actions, it would seem, must of necessity be accounted for by some kind of diversity in its source, the subject. Second, while some of the Scriptural attributes, as knowledge, can be easily turned into actions, there are others, as life, which do not appear to have any active implication whatsoever. As to

belong to the class of qualities which have been mentioned above; but I mean the action the latter has performed. We speak, e. g. of Zaid, who made this door, built that wall, wove that garment.'

[21] Cf. *supra*, note 16. [22] Cf. *infra*, Chap. II.

the first, Maimonides maintains that the various activities affirmed of God are in reality emanating as a single act from the divine essence, its manifold ramification being only apparent.[23] As a single ray of light emanating from a luminous object, by striking through a lens breaks into many rays, so the single act of God becomes diversified by striking the lower strata of reality. One in essence, its manifoldness is due merely to the various aspects in which the divine action appears to the human eyes. As for the second point, Maimonides shows inductively how all the Biblical predications have active implications.[24] To do that, however, there was no need for him to go through the entire list of attributes found in the Bible. Most of them had been admitted by the Attributists themselves to be actions;[25] some of them were a matter of controversy. There were only four, which, unable to interpret as actions, the Attributists considered as essential attributes. These four—life, knowledge, will, power—are shown by Maimonides, in their ultimate analysis, to be actions, and one single action withal.

While the controversial attributes of life, knowledge, will, and power are interpreted by Maimonides as dynamic relations, the attributes of existence, unity, and eternity are admitted by him to be nothing but static.[26] And yet they are not attributes; they are absolutely identical with the divine essence. In created beings, to be sure, Maimonides, following Avicenna and the early Arabic philosophers, declares existence and unity to be adjoined to the essence;

23 Cf. *Moreh*, I, 53.

24 Cf. *ibid.*

25 Cf. Abrabanel's quotation from Averroes in his commentary on the *Moreh*, I, 53.

26 Cf. *Moreh*, I, 57.

in the case of God, however, they are the essence itself.[27] But if you argue that since identity is not a relation, the proposition that 'God is existent' or that 'God is one' would be tautological, the answer is that the predicates in this case, though positive in form, are negative in meaning; that logically 'God is existent' is equivalent to 'God is not absent', and 'God is one' to 'God is not many'. And having once stated this new solution of the problem of attributes, reverting now to those predicates he has previously interpreted as actions, Maimonides declares that even those may be taken as static and interpreted as negations.[28]

The admissibility of negative attributes, which is at first stated by Maimonides as an incontestable fact, is afterwards subjected to a searching examination.[29] In an elaborate discussion, illustrated by concrete examples, he clearly points out the distinction between the knowledge of a determinate and of an indeterminate object. Negative attributes as well as positive ones define and limit the object of knowledge, but they do so in different ways. Positive attributes limit the number of all the possible conjectures about an unknown object by singling out a few which constitute its essence; negative attributes eliminate all those conjectures by showing that neither one nor all of them constitute its essence. The former, therefore, is a characterization of the object; the latter is only a circumscription and individualization thereof. As the divine

[27] Cf. *Moreh*, I, 57, and *infra*, Chap. II.

[28] This may be deduced from the following passage: 'Consequently God exists without existence. Similarly He lives without life, knows without knowledge, is omnipotent without omnipotence, and is wise without wisdom' (*ibid.*).

[29] Cf. *Moreh*, I, 58.

essence is without determinations and is unknowable, negative attributes are permissible, whereas positive ones are proscribed.

In this statement of Maimonides' negative interpretation of attributes I have followed the traditional view. Maimonides, according to this, attaches no significance whatsoever to the positive form of those attributes which are interpreted by him negatively.[30] 'God is existent' means 'God is not absent', the positive form of the former proposition being absolutely meaningless. This interpretation of Maimonides, though prevalent and widespread, does not, however, seem to me quite correct. I think he attributes some logical significance to the positive form of judgements about God as well as to their negative contents. Let us just briefly restate the problem which Maimonides was called upon to solve. His main problem was not whether God possesses any essential attributes. That assumption was ruled out of court by the absolute simplicity of God on the one hand, and by the Avicennean theory of universals on the other; his main problem concerned the meaning of the logical predicate affirmed of God. These predicates, not being universals, and of necessity identical with the divine essence, must consequently form tautological propositions. It is this avoidance of a tautology, I think, that Maimonides aims at in his negative interpretation of attributes. The divine predicates, he says, though expressing a relation of identity with the subject, are not tautological, for the affirmation of identity has an emphatic meaning, implying as it does the negation of diversity. 'God is existent' is, to be sure, equivalent to

[30] Cf. Gersonides' criticism of Maimonides in *Milḥamot*, III, 3, which is quoted below in note 54.

the affirmation that 'God is God', but still even the latter proposition may be logically justified if it means to emphasize that 'God is not Man'. Similarly 'God is existent' emphasizes the negation of absentness. The justification of identity as a logical relation by means of its emphatic use, is found in the Logic of Alfarabi.[31] Thus, the positive forms of predicates are not altogether useless according to Maimonides. And this is exactly what he means by saying that the divine predicates are homonymous terms. Not being universal, and expressing a relation of identity, divine predicates are absolutely unrelated with similarly sounding predicates describing other beings. In the following statements of Maimonides, 'God exists without existence, lives without life', &c., we clearly see that 'God is existent' does not merely mean that 'God is not absent', but what it means is that God is existent with an existence of His own, identical with His own essence. To affirm this is to emphasize the negation of existence used as a universal term.

If, as we have just said, by negative attributes Maimonides means that the divine predicates affirm a relation of identity, emphasizing the negation of a non-identical relation, it follows that the term *negative* must have been used by Maimonides in some special sense. By negative attributes he does not mean that the proposition in which a predicate is affirmed of God is negative in quality. He means that although the proposition itself is positive in quality, the predicate is to be understood to have a negative prefix.

[31] 'In a proposition like the following, the predicate and subject can both be individual: "The one who is sitting is Reuben"' (Alfarabi, *Book on Syllogism*). הנשוא יכל להיות ג"כ אישי עם הנושא אישי במשפט הזה: זה היושב הוא ראובן. (אלפרבי בספר ההקש Brit. Mus. Harley 5523, p. 71)

Thus, 'God is one' is not to be convertible into 'God is not many', but the term 'one' must be taken to mean 'not-many', the quality of the proposition as a whole remaining unaltered. In order fully to appreciate this distinction, let us briefly restate what Aristotle had said about the quality of propositions. There is, he points out, a distinction between a proposition wherein the negative particle modifies the copula, and that wherein it modifies the subject or the predicate. The former is a negative proposition, the latter is an affirmative proposition with an indefinite subject or predicate, as the case may be.[32] A negative proposition expresses the privation of the subject of one of two alternative qualities, thus always implying its possession of the other; an affirmative proposition with an indefinite predicate expresses the exclusion of the subject of a certain class of qualities which are irrelevant to its nature. The latter kind of proposition is said to express what Kant would call an infinite or limiting judgement, as is to be distinguished from a negative judgement, as the proposition 'The soul is not-mortal' is to be distinguished in meaning from that of 'The soul is not mortal'.[33] It is in the sense of the Aristotelian indefinite predicate that Maimonides uses the expression 'negative attribute', the negative particle being hyphenated with the predicate, thus excluding the subject not only from the stated predicate, but also from implication of its antithesis. This seems to me to constitute the significance of the following passage: 'Even the negative attributes must not be found and applied to God, except in the way in which, as you know, sometimes an attribute is negatived with reference to a thing, although that attribute

[32] Cf. *Organon*, On Interpretation, ch. x, and *Metaphysics*, IV, 22.

[33] Cf. Sigwart's *Logic*, vol. I, ch. iv.

can naturally never be applied to it in the same sense; as, e.g. we say, "The wall is not seeing"' (*Moreh*, I, 58). It is quite evident that we never say 'the wall is not seeing', except in the sense of 'the wall is not-seeing'.[34]

The rejection of positive essential attributes and the admission only of negatives, which is tantamount to a confession of our ignorance of the divine essence, gives rise to the question whether thereby it would be possible at all to mark any gradation in human knowledge of the divine being. But that one's comprehension of God is commensurable with one's intellectual and moral virtues is a postulate of both reason and tradition.[35] In answer to this difficulty, Maimonides maintains that knowledge arrived at by negation is as capable of increase as knowledge attained by determination. The negative interpretation of attributes, since it has been explained to express the affirmation of the relation of identity emphasizing the negation of irrelevant qualities, has a double meaning. While excluding God from knowable universal qualities, the attributes affirm of Him some unknowable qualities, peculiar to Himself, and identical with His essence. When we exclude God from

[34] That this is what has been meant by Maimonides is quite clear from his statement in his *Milot ha-Higayon*, which asserts that it cannot be said that 'The wall is blind'. ולא יתואר בשם ההעדר כי אם אשר מטבעו שימצא לו הקנין ההוא הנוכחי להעדר ההוא, כי אנחנו לא נאמר בכתל שהוא סכל ולא עור ולא אלם. (מלות ההגיון, שער י"א) Narboni in his commentary on the *Moreh* calls this kind of negation, referred to here by Maimonides, 'general' or 'absolute' (המשלחת), a term which has been adopted by the modern commentators, as Munk, Kaufmann, and Friedländer, in explaining the text. כבר ידעת ממה שקראת ממלאכת ההגיון, כי השלילה שני מינים: האחת השלילה המיוחדת [כמו בלעם אינו רואה] .... והשני השלילה המשלחת ... [כמו הכתל אינו רואה] Cf. *Metaphysics*, IV, 22.

[35] Cf. *Moreh*, I, 59.

the attribute of ordinary existence, for example, at the same time we affirm that He exists with an existence of His own. God, by virtue of His absolute perfection in every sense, has an infinite number of aspects in His essence ; and had we only the means of doing so, we should be able to express them all in human language. But on account of the unknowability of the divine essence, we can express none of its infinite aspects in positive terms ; we can only indirectly hint at them by negating of Him our own knowable perfections. Not only must our affirmations of divine infinite perfections be indirect, they must also be limited in number, since the knowable human perfections that are negated of Him are finite in number. This limitation on our part involves a serious difficulty. For in the conditional reality of the world we know there is always a line of demarcation between what is always already actually known and what is actually unknown but is knowable. In so far as we are cognizant of conditional reality we are able to distinguish God from the world, the absolute from the conditional. By negations, we exclude Him from the known quantity of perfections and indirectly affirm of Him a corresponding number of unknowable divine perfections. Beyond that boundary line, which marks off that which is known from that which is unknown in the knowable world, God and the world appear to us to merge together, and though we do not say so, since we are unable to negate it, we assume as it were that God possesses all the knowable qualities of the undiscovered part of reality. But this limitation which springs from our disability varies with each individual. The boundary line between the known and the unknown in the knowable world shifts backward and forward in accordance with one's own intellectual attainments. To the more informed the known part of reality is greater than to the less informed. The former hence can directly deny more knowable human perfections of God, and indirectly affirm more unknowable divine perfections than the latter. Thus, while neither possesses positive knowledge of the divine essence, their indirect knowledge of God varies widely. Furthermore, the realm of the knowable has not yet been completely laid bare, and, consequently, as our knowledge of conditional existence has before it ample opportunity of growth and expansion, so our knowledge of absolute existence of God might gradually draw nearer to perfection. Thus by means of the quantitative distinction in the knowledge of conditional reality between different individuals, and by means of the multiplicability of that knowledge in each individual, Maimonides conceives the possibility of a rising scale in men's knowledge of the divine essence.[36]

Maimonides' theory of attributes is typical rather than original. None before him, to be sure, had analysed the problem so minutely and comprehensively as he, but his constructive view does not differ from those of his predecessors. Negative and dynamic interpretations of divine attributes had been the common stock-in-trade of Arabic and Jewish philosophers ever since Philo.[37] As thus far noticed, Maimonides departs from the commonly accepted view solely by differentiating between actions and external relations and his disqualification of the latter. Again, with the exception of the naïve theologians, referred to by

[36] Cf. *ibid.* While I have given here a rather free interpretation of the chapter, I hope I have remained true to its spirit.

[37] Cf. Munk, *Guide*, I, ch. 58, p. 238, note 1, and Kaufmann's *Attributenlehre*, p. 481.

Maimonides himself, none of the rational thinkers admitted the propriety of accretive attributes. The discussion was focused mainly on the so-called essential attributes, that is, the universal predicates which enter into the formation of definitions. Thus the problem of attributes runs parallel to that of universals and to that of the nature of logical propositions. We have seen how all these problems converge in the theory of Maimonides. Taking universals to be present as something distinct within individuals, and finding the predication of such universals to be inconsistent with the absolute simplicity of God; believing that a logical proposition must affirm a real relation unless that affirmation is emphatic, he was forced to declare all divine predicates to be relations of identity emphasizing a negation. In his own language, the divine predicates are homonymous terms, having nothing in common with terms of the same sound. Following the same analysis of the problem, we shall now expound several other representative theories of attributes. Algazali's criticism of Avicenna will be taken as our starting-point, after which we shall discuss Averroes and two of his Jewish followers, Gersonides and Moses Halavi, and finally we shall give a rather full account of an entirely new view proposed by Crescas on this subject of divine attributes.

II

Algazali's approach to the solution of the problem is unique in its kind. He dares what nobody else before him had ever thought of doing, to impugn the Avicennean definition of necessary existence. Does necessary existence preclude noetic plurality? that is the main burden of his inquiry. His answer is in the negative. The primary meaning of necessary existence, he contends, is the absence of efficient causation.[38] The Avicennean proof for the conception itself, indeed, merely establishes the fact of an ultimate terminus to the interlacing chain of cause and effect. That terminus is necessary in the sense that its springing into being had not been effected by the operation of a pre-existent agent. The phrase *necessary existence*, therefore, means nothing but primary existence, the term *necessary* signifying in this phrase a description of the spatial and temporal relation of a certain being in a series of causally interrelated entities rather than a qualitative determination of the nature of that being. If we are now asked, Can the necessarily existent be composite? the answer would depend upon the circumstance whether the composition in question would be subversive to the uncon-

[38] Cf. *Destruction of the Philosophers*, Disputation VII. 'The source of error and blunder in all this discussion is to be found in the expression "necessary existence". But to us the expression seems to be irrelevant, for we do not admit that the proof for necessary existence establishes anything except the existence of something eternal which had not been preceded by an efficient agent. If that is its meaning, the expression "necessary existence" must be dropped out of discussion. You must state your contention plainly, that it is impossible that there should be plurality and distinction in an eternal existence which had not been preceded by an efficient agent. But this you will be unable to prove.' ומקור השבוש וההמעדה בכל זה הוא מליצת מחוייב המציאות, ולכן לא תזכר ולא תפקד, כי אנחנו לא נודה שהראיה תורה על מחוייב המציאות אלא א״כ יהיה הנרצה בו קדמון שאין לו פועל, ואם היה זה הנרצה, תעזב נא מליצת מחוייב המציאות, ויאמר בפירוש שהוא מן השקר שימצא רבוי והבדל בנמצא קדמון שאין לו פועל, ודה אין לכם ראיה עליו (הפלת הפילוסופים, שאלה ז׳).

The same argument recurs in Disputations V, VI, VIII, IX, and X.

This seems to me to be the central argument made by Algazali. Curiously enough, De Boer, in his *Der Widerspruch der Philosophie nach al-Gazali*, does not even mention it. Neither is it mentioned in Carra de Vaux's *Gazali*, ch. II, where he discusses the latter's theory of attributes.

ditional existence of the being, unconditional in the sense that it is not grounded in an efficient cause. If the compositeness be not subversive to such unconditional being, then the necessarily existent may be composite. By means of the conception of necessary existence so stated, Algazali proceeds to show that the necessarily existent, according to Avicenna's own definition, might be composed of matter and form,[39] of substance and attribute;[40] it might also be defined in terms of genus and difference;[41] and, finally, that it might also have existence superadded to its essence.[42] Indeed, Algazali goes even farther. The original conception of necessary existence does not, he holds, preclude the duality of absolutely existent beings.[43] Unity, simplicity, and incorporeality are all unwarranted by necessary existence. It is only by vitiating the primary meaning of the term, by extending the proof for the absence of any efficient cause whatsoever, that necessary existence had come to be used by philosophers in the sense of absolute simplicity; and, again, it is by a kind of vicious intellectualism which reasons from the conception of absolute simplicity rather than from the conception of necessary existence, that the philosophers had erroneously inferred the necessity of the first unconditionally existent being as one, simple, undefinable, and unrelatable.

[39] Cf. Disputation IX: בלאותם מהעמיד ראיה על שהראשון אינו גשם.

[40] Cf. Disputation VI: בהסכימם על שקרות קיום המדע, והיכלת, והרצון, להתחלה ראשונה.

[41] Cf. Disputation VII: בבטול אמרם שמציאות הראשון אי״א שישתתף עם זולתו בסוג ויובדל ממנו בהבדל.

[42] Cf. Disputation VIII: בבטול אמרם שמציאות הראשון פשוט, כלומר, הוא מציאות גמור ואין מהות ולא אמתות יצורף המציאות עליהם.

[43] Cf. Disputation V: בבאור לאותם מהעמיד ראיה על שהאל אחד ושאי״א להניח שני מחויבי המציאות כל אחד אין עלה לו.

Algazali's argument against Avicenna's conception of necessary existence is based upon the latter's use of the term 'possibility'. Possibility, according to mediaeval Jewish and Arabic logicians, has two meanings. In the first place, it applies to a thing which without any cause whatsoever may by its own nature come or not come into being. This is the real and primary meaning of possibility. In the second place, the term applies to a thing which cannot come into existence save through an external cause, in the sense that in so far as the thing is dependent upon a cause, with respect to itself it is only possible, since its existence is determined by the presence or absence of that cause. This is the unreal and derivative meaning of possibility.[44] Real possibility is thus the antithesis of impossibi-

[44] Moses Halavi, in his Treatise 'On the First Mover', discussing Avicenna's proof for necessary existence, makes the following comment: 'The term possibility is not used here in the sense in which it is used in the Logic, namely, that which may or may not exist. But we must understand that the expression of having by itself only possible existence is another way of saying that it owes its existence to something else. Necessity and impossibility are not, therefore, its antitheses. For the existence which accrues to some external cause may sometimes be necessary and sometimes not. In both cases, however, we call it possible by itself, by which we mean that of whatever nature the existence in reality is, it is due to some external cause.' To this the Hebrew translator adds the following note: 'In general, he [i.e. Avicenna] does not mean by possibility that whose antithesis is necessity, but that whose antithesis is self-sufficiency.' "וזה שהוא לא נשא מלת האפשר בכאן על הבנתה במלאכת ההגיון, והוא אשר יתחייב לו אפשר שלא ימצא, אלא ידענו שאמרנו בכאן אפשר המציאות לעצמותו הוא מליצה מק[נין] המציאות מהזולת, וההכרח פה והעדרו בלתי נוכחיים, כי לפעמים יהיה המציאות הנקנה מהזולת הכרחי, ולפעמים לא יהיה כן. ונאמר בשני ענינים שהוא אפשר המציאות לעצמותו, רצוני, שמציאותו איזה דרך היה מדרכי המציאות נקנה מזולתו" המעתיק העברי הוסיף בכאן על הגליון: "ובכלל אין כוונתו כאן במלת אפשרי אשר מקבילו ההכרח, אלא אשר מקבילו ההסתפקות בעצמו".

lity and necessity; unreal possibility is the antithesis of self-sufficiency. Now, in his proof of the existence of God, Avicenna uses the term possibility in its unreal meaning.[45] From the observation that all existences, sublunary as well as translunary, are with respect to themselves only possible, on account of the presence of an external cause, he concludes that there must be a prime cause which is necessary even with respect to itself. In what sense, according to Avicenna, must that prime cause be necessary with respect to itself? Certainly in the same sense as that in which the other existences are possible, namely, with respect to external causation. Consequently his proof for the presence of a necessarily existent being merely establishes the self-sufficiency of that being; that is, its independence with respect to external causation, without, however, disproving its dependence upon internal causation. Hence, Algazali's criticism against Avicenna's identification of necessary existence with absolute simplicity.

That Algazali's criticism is incontrovertible is generally admitted. In his *Destruction of the Destruction* Averroes refutes Algazali's contentions not by justifying Avicenna, but by showing that Avicenna is misrepresenting the philo-

[45] Cf. Averroes' *Destruction of the Destruction*, Disputation X. 'It was Avicenna's intention to have his distinction between possibility and necessity correspond to the philosophers' view of existences, for according to all the philosophers the celestial spheres are said to be necessary with respect to their cause. But still we may ask whether that which is necessary with respect to its cause has really any possibility by itself.' ואמנם רצה בן סיני שיסכים בזאת החלוקה [בגליון: ממחוייב ואפשר למה שיש לו עלה ולמה שאין לו עלה] אל דעת הפילוסופים בנמצאות; וזה שהגרם השמימיי אצל כל הפילוסופים הוא הכרחי בזולתו. ואמנם האם הוא הכרחי בזולתו יש בו אפשרות בצרוף אל עצמו, בו עיון. ולזה היתה זאת הדרך מעוקשת כשילכו בה זה המהלך. Likewise in *Moreh ha-Moreh*, II, Prop. 12.

sophers in the use of the terms possibility and necessity.[46] Possibility, to Averroes, has only one meaning, and that is the real and primary one. Nothing whose existence is dependent upon external causes can, he holds, be called possible in any sense whatsoever. Avicenna's designation of sublunar and celestial elements as possible is, therefore, untenable; and his consequent proof for a self-existent cause is likewise invalid. The indivisibility of the divine essence as well as the unity of God does not follow indirectly from the proof of His necessary existence, but from the arguments, of which there are several, which directly prove His simplicity and unity.[47] And so, while disagreeing with Avicenna as to the proof, Averroes agrees with him that the divine attributes must be interpreted (1) as negatives, and (2) as external relations, the latter of which include

[46] Cf. *Destruction of the Destruction*, Disputation X. 'It has already been made clear from our arguments that if by necessary existence is understood that which has no cause, and by possible existence that which has a cause [i. e. the Avicennean view], the division of being into these two classes [i. e. necessary and possible] could not be asserted, for the opponent might deny this alleged division, maintaining that every existent being is without a cause. But if by absolute existence is meant necessary existence, and by possible is understood real possibility [i. e. the Averroean view], the series must undoubtedly terminate at an existence which has no cause.' כבר קדם ממאמרנו שכאשר יובן מחוייב המציאות מה שאין עלה לו, ויובן מאפשר המציאות מה שיש עלה לו, לא תהיה חלוקת הנמצא בשני אלה הפרקים ידוע בה, כאשר לבעל דין לחלוק שאינו כמו שזכר, אבל כל נמצא אין עלה לו; אכן כאשר יובן ממחוייב המציאות הנמצא ההכרחי ומן האפשר, האפשר האמתי יכלה הענין בלא ספק אל נמצא אין עלה לו.

[47] Cf. Averroes' *Destruction of the Destruction*, Disputation VI. 'I say that this is a refutation of him who, like Avicenna, argues for the rejection of attributes from the premise of necessary existence by itself. But the best method to be followed in this inquiry is to argue from unity.' אמרתי זה כלו סתירה למי שהלך בהרחקת התארים דרך בן סיני, בהעמיד מחוייב המציאות בעצמותו; ואמנם הדרך היותר טובה בזה בחייוב ההתאחדות.

both the category of relation and that of action.[48] But these are not the only explanation of attributes. By a new theory of universals, which will presently be set forth, Averroes maintains that some attributes may be positive and essential.

Avicenna, as we have seen, holds the universals to have reality *in re* and *post rem* because of their reality *ante rem* in the mind of God. The pre-existent universals, according to him, are present in the multitudinous individuals. What then does Avicenna mean by his assertion that universals exist only in mind? He means by that that the presence of those universals in the individuals and our abstraction of them cannot be *discovered* except by the mind, though their presence in the individuals is independent of the mind. Averroes differs with him on that point. He thinks the very presence of the universals in the individuals a mere mental invention. The phrase that universals are in the mind he interprets to mean that the very presence of the universals in the individuals and their distinction therefrom is *invented* by the mind. The difference between Avicenna and Averroes is similar to the difference between the objective and subjective interpretations of Spinoza's definition of attribute in modern philosophy. Consequently in any definition the distinction between the individual substance which is defined and the universal substance by which it is defined has no reality whatsoever. The individual substance only appears to the mind in universal aspects. It is exactly this mentally invented distinction, says Averroes, that Aristotle conceives to exist between the faculties of the soul and its essence, and that also the Christian theologians conceive to exist between the three

[48] Cf. *Destruction of the Destruction*, Disputation V.

Personalities and the Godhead, though both the soul-essence and the Godhead are in reality one and absolutely indivisible.[49]

By this Averroes could have solved the entire problem of attributes. He could have said that the predicates attributed to God all designate certain aspects in which the divine essence appears to the human mind. He does not,

[49] Cf. *ibid.* 'It is in the nature of essential attributes that they do not actually diversify their subject; they diversify it only in the same sense as the parts of a definition are said to diversify the object defined, that is, what is called by the philosophers a mental plurality in contradistinction to an actual plurality. Take, for instance, the definition of man as a rational animal, in which case neither of these attributes nor both of them are actually added to the individual human essence, though man is diversified by the attributes describing appearance and form. Hence, it will follow that he who admits that the existence of the soul is absolutely independent of matter, will also have to admit that among immaterial existences there are such that are one in actuality though many in definition [that is to say, the soul is one in essence but many in faculties]. This is also the Christian doctrine of the Trinity, that is, they do not believe in attributes adjoined to the essence, for the attributes to them are only in definition, the manifoldness of which are not in actuality but in potentiality. Hence, they claim that these [personalities] are three and yet one, i. e. one in actuality but three in potentiality.' מדרך התארים העצמיים שלא יתרבה בם הנושא הסובל להם, אבל אמנם יתרבה בצד אשר יתרבה המוגדר בחלקי הגדר, וזה שהוא רבוי שכלי אצלם, לא רבוי בפועל, ר״ל, ודמיון זה, שהאדם אדם חי מדבר, ואין הדבור והחיות כל אחד מהם וכו׳ מחברו בו, ר״ל, בפועל. והמראה והתמונה מתרבה בו, ר״ל, ולזה יתחייב למי שיודה שהנפש אין מתנאי מציאותה החומר שיודה שכבר ימצא בנמצאות הנבדלות מה שהוא אחד בפועל, ר״ל, הרבה בגדר. וזהו דעת הנוצרים בשלוש, וזה, שהם לא יראים תארים נוספים על העצם, ואמנם הם אצלם מתרבים בגדר, והם רבים בכח ולא בפועל, ולזה יאמרו שהם שלשה ואחד, כלומר, אחד בפועל שלשה בכח.

This passage is paraphrased by Narboni in his commentary on the *Moreh* (I, 58), but he disagrees with Averroes as to the latter's interpretation of the Trinity. The Trinity according to the Christian belief, he says, are not potential but actual. והנראה לי כי התארים הג׳ בפועל אצל הנוצרים והעצם אחד, לא שיהיה בכח כמו שיאמר ב״ר.

however, say so. He admits with Avicenna that all the attributes, which with regard to created beings are accidental, with regard to God must be interpreted either as negations or as dynamic and external relations.[50] There is one attribute, however, which he insists must be taken positively, and that is the attribute of Intelligence. Intelligence, says Averroes, is the essence of God. He maintains this to be the view of the Peripatetics in opposition to that of Plato.[51] Intelligence is therefore merely another word for God. In the proposition, 'God is intelligent', the relation affirmed between subject and predicate is not real but formal. And likewise the universality of that term, which is implied in its application to God and to human beings, is only nominal and formal.

Still, the nominalist interpretation of a universal term disposes only of the assumption of an underlying identity running through various individuals. But it has to assume the existence of some kind of relation and resemblance between different things. Without such an assumption the mind could not form universal terms at all. What is then the relation that must be assumed to exist between God and other creatures in order to justify the common application of the term Intelligence? The relation, according to Averroes, is that of cause and effect. God is a thinking being in whom the subject, object, and process of thinking are all one and the same thing. But His thinking is creative, and all the Intelligences as well as the human intelligence are offshoots of the divine intelligence. The application, therefore, of the term intelligence to God and to human beings does not mean that both share alike in

[50] Cf. *Destruction of the Destruction*, Disputation V.

[51] Cf. *ibid.*

a common property; it means than man derives his intelligence from God, in whom it is not a property but the very essence.

The universalization of an individual term by means of its application to the effects of that individual with which the term has originated is distinguished by Averroes as a class by itself. He designates such terms as ambiguous with respect to priority and posteriority of application. To get at the meaning of this phrase, we need enumerate all the other kinds of applicability of universal terms with which this new one is contrasted. Thus: single terms may be universally applied to different individuals in three ways—equivocally, univocally, and ambiguously.[52] A term is used equivocally when it is applied to two or more things which share nothing in common, either in essential or in non-essential properties. Such a term is a perfect homonym, and its several applications in reality are perfectly unrelated, as, to use an old example, the word *grammatica*, meaning the art of grammar and a woman. A univocal term is one which is applied to two things that share in an essential quality, as, for instance, the term 'man' applied to individual human beings. A term is ambiguous when it is applied to different individuals which share only in non-essential properties, e.g. '*white* snow' and '*white* paper'. We may recall that in Maimonides' theory the divine attributes are used neither univocally nor ambiguously, God sharing with other beings neither in essential nor in non-essential qualities. In that theory the attributes must be taken in

[52] Equivocal = משותפים or משתתפים; univocal = מוסכמים or מסכימים; ambiguous = מסופקים. Cf. Algazali's *Intentions*, I, *Logic*, I, 5 (כונות, הגיון, אופן א', חלוקה ה'), and Maimonides' מלות ההגיון. Cf. Aristotle's Ὁμώνυμα, Συνώνυμα, Παρώνυμα, *Categories*, I.

an equivocal or homonymous sense. Divine intelligence, therefore, is absolutely unrelated with human intelligence, and is applied to God negatively. Now, Averroes proposes a new usage of a universal term in the case of its application to two things which share in a common quality only, in so far as one of them derives its quality from the other, to which it is essential. God, therefore, does not participate with man in intelligence, but God being intelligence, man derives his intelligence from Him. That special sense, in which a term may be applied to different things, was according to Averroes' testimony unknown to Avicenna.[53]

[53] Cf. Averroes' *Destruction of the Destruction*, Disputation VII. 'Ait Averroes: Si intellexisti id, quod diximus antea eo, quod sunt hic aliquae, quae includuntur uno nomine, non inclusione rerum univocarum, nec inclusione rerum aequivocarum, sed inclusione rerum relatarum ad aliud, quae dicuntur secundum prius, et posterius, et qualis proprietas harum rerum ut deveniant ad primum in illo genere, quod est causa prima omnibus, quibus imponitur hoc nomen, ut est nomen calidi, quod dicitur de igne, et aliis rebus calidis, et sicut est nomen entis, quod dicitur de substantia, et aliis accidentibus, et sicut nomen motus, quod dicitur de locali, et aliis motibus, non deficies scire inane, quod ingreditur in hoc sermone, nam nomen intellectus dicitur de intellectibus separatis apud philosophos secundum prius et posterius, quorum est intellectus primus, qui est causa aliorum, et sic est in substantia. Et ratio, quae demonstrat quod non habent naturam communem, est quoniam aliquis eorum est causa alterius, et id, quod est causa rei, est prius causati, et impossibile est ut sit natura causae, et causati uno genere, nisi in causis individualibus, et haec quidem species communicationis est contradicens communicationi genericae vero, quoniam communia genere, non est in eis primum, quod est causa aliorum, sed omnia sunt in gradu, et non reperitur in eis aliquid simplex, sed communia in re, quae dicuntur secundum prius, et posterius, necesse est ut sit in eis primum, et simplex, et hoc primum impossibile est ut imaginetur ei secundatio. Nam quotienscunque ponatur ei secundum, necesse est ut sit in gradu eius, quo ad esse, et naturam: et erit ibi natura communis eis, qua communicat communicatione generis veri; et necesse est ut differant differentiis additis generi: ergo erit unumquodque; eorum compositum ex genere, et differentia, et omne quod huiusmodi est innovatum. Demum id, quod est in ultimitate perfectionis in esse, necesse est ut sit unum. Nam, nisi esset unum, im-

The new distinction in the universalization of terms which had been advanced by Averroes was adopted by Gersonides in his theory of divine attributes. Gersonides' constructive view may be gathered from his refutation of Maimonides. He commences by pointing out an inherent fallacy in the homonymous interpretation of positive attributes. Since all positive attributes that are not actions must be taken as homonyms, that is to say, affirming, according to the interpretation given above, a relation of perfect identity which emphasizes the negation of non-identity; and since consequently any predicate could thus be interpreted homonymously, what would account for the fact that some attributes are found in positive form whereas others occur only in negative form? Why should not the latter as well as the former be expressed in positive language? Take, for instance, the attributes of existence and incorporeality. If the former is perfectly homonymous, why should we not likewise affirm of God corporeality in an homonymous sense? To say that the sound of the word corporeality in itself, irrespective of its special meaning, is derogatory to the divine being, does not explain the matter. In dealing with the problem of attributes, we

possibile est ut sit ei ultimitas esse, id enim, quod est ultimitate non communicat ei aliud, nam, sicut linea una non habet ex uno latere duos fines, sic res, quae succedunt in esse, diversae quidem in additione, et diminutione, non habent duos fines ex uno latere. Avicenna autem nescivit in esse hanc naturam mediam inter naturam, quam significat nomen univocum et naturas, quae non communicant nisi nominibus tantum, aut accidenti remoto, et evenit ei haec dubitatio.' (Latin translation from the Hebrew of Averroes' *Hapalath ha-Hapalah*, in the tenth volume of Aristotle's collected works, p. 232 a–b, Venice, 1560.)

It should be observed that this special kind of generic terms, which, according to Averroes, was unknown to Avicenna, is mentioned by Algazali in his *Intentions*, I; Logic, I, 5: נאותים . . . והוא קיים בקדימה ואיחור, וכבר יקרא זה מסופק לחזרתו (כונות, הגיון, אופן א׳, חלוקה ה׳).

are chiefly concerned with the meaning of the terms as they are employed, and not with their associative connotations. Furthermore, the admissibility of attributes is decided upon the ground of their logical consonance with the conception of necessary existence, and not upon the consideration whether in human analogies they are regarded as perfections or imperfections. If the distinction of affirmative and negative prevails in the form of attributes, it follows that for quite different reasons the term existence, even when taken in a sense not entirely unrelated with its ordinary usage, may be affirmed of God, whereas the term corporeality under the same circumstances must not be affirmed of Him.[54]

[54] Cf. Gersonides' *Milḥamot*, III, 3. 'In general, if the things which we predicate of Him were applied to God and to ourselves in perfect homonymy, none of the terms which we use in designating ordinary things would be more appropriately used in reference to God as negation rather than affirmations or as affirmations rather than negations. Thus, for instance, one would be able to state that God is corporeal, provided he did not mean by that corporeality anything possessing quantity, but something which is perfectly homonymous with what we usually call corporeality. Likewise, one would be able to state that God is unknowing, if the term knowing in that proposition was not used to designate the same thing as that which we ordinarily call knowledge. Nor can it be maintained that we negate of God corporeality because with respect to ourselves it is an imperfection, but we affirm of Him knowledge because it is a perfection. For it is not the term corporeality, which is alone negated of God, that is an imperfection; the imperfection is rather contained in its meaning. That this is so can be proved by the fact that were we to designate by the term corporeality what is now designated by the term knowledge, and by the term knowledge what is now designated by the term corporeality, then corporeality would have been in respect to ourselves, perfection and knowledge would have been an imperfection. Furthermore, we do not affirm nor negate anything of God unless we had first ascertained as to whether the existence of that thing is appropriate of God or not, but it is not imperative upon us to inquire as to whether that thing is a perfection or an imperfection with respect to ourselves.'

Thus divine attributes are to be taken, according to Gersonides, as universal terms. But now the two objections raised by Maimonides recur. First, the attributes being universals, according to the accepted theory of universals, exist as parts in the objective individuals; this, however, is impossible in the case of God. Secondly, by attributing universals, you imply some kind of relation between God and created beings, and *ipso facto* you imply a similarity between them, and such a similarity is impossible.

Gersonides' answer to these two possible objections, as we have said, betrays the unmistakable influence of Averroes. He distinguishes between a real, or rather existential, universal and a nominal, the latter being found in the case where an individual quality of a cause, which is identical with the essence of that cause, is in common language applied to the effects of that cause. That term, with respect to the object with whose essence it is identical, is only an invented universal. When joined in a proposition, the relation between the subject and predicate is, therefore, not real but verbal. A subject of that kind, says Gersonides, may be called a 'subject of discourse', for in reality the subject and predicate are identical. It is only when the predicate is an accident that its relation with the subject is real, the latter being called a 'subject of existence', that is to say, the subject of inhesion of the accidental predicate. Now, in God all the attributes are identical with His essence, or, in other words, they have no separate existence whatsoever. In any proposition, therefore, in which we predicate some attributes of God we really state a relation of identity. Still, such statements are not tautological. For logical propositions do not merely express *real* relations, but *formal* relations also. God is the 'subject of discourse' of the attributes predicated of Him, and in discourse there is no tautology, for in discourse all the attributes predicated of God are universal terms. 'Knowledge', 'power', 'will', and all the other attributes, are affirmed of God and other beings in a related sense, the relation being that of cause and effect. 'But there is the following radical distinction between divine and human attributes. In God attributes are identical with His essence; in man they are accidental to it. In the technical language of the time this notion may be expressed as follows: The divine predicates are to be understood in a sense neither 'equivocal' nor 'univocal'; they are used in an 'ambiguous' sense with reference to the distinction of 'priority and posteriority'. To quote now Gersonides' own words:

'We say that after due reflection it appears that there are attributes that are applicable primarily to God and subsequently to other things besides Him without, however, implying plurality in God. For not every proposition in which something is affirmed of something implies plurality of that thing. There is implication of plurality only when one part of the proposition is the subject with respect to *existence* of the other part. But if it is not its subject with respect to existence, though it is its subject in the proposition, it does not follow that the subject is composite. For instance, if we state about a definite redness that it is a red colour, it does not follow that the redness is composed of colour and red, for colour is not the existent subject of red, but its subject of *discourse* only.'[55]

But would not a nominal universal which is derived from two individuals correlated as cause and effect, imply the existence of some real relation and similarity between the two individuals? Gersonides endeavours to show that it would not. If any relation is to be implied it will be

[55] Cf. *Milḥamot*, III, 3.

nominal, just as the universal itself is nominal. He cites an analogous case from the meaning of existence. Existence, according to Averroes, whose view is followed by Gersonides, is identical with the essence of the subject of which it is affirmed. Now, accidents exist through substances, the latter thus being the causes of the former. The term existence, therefore, is with respect to substances and accidents, a nominal universal implied to individuals which are causatively related. And yet there is no implication of the existence of any real relation between substance and accident. To quote Gersonides again:

'It can be shown, even though we admit that there can be no relation between God and His creatures, that the attributes predicated of God may be applied to Him primarily and to other beings subsequently. For there are some terms which, though they are applied to some things primarily and to others subsequently, do not imply a relation between those things. For instance, the term existence is applied to substance primarily and to accident subsequently as stated in the Metaphysics. Still it is clear that there is no relation between substance and accidents.' [56]

We turn now to the theory of divine attributes formulated by Moses Halavi.[57] Unlike Gersonides, Moses Halavi works out his theory independently of Maimonides, to whom he does not make the slightest allusion. His theory may be summarized as follows: Attributes are either positive or negative. Of the negative, some are so both in form (בשם) and in content (בענין), as, for instance, 'incorporeality'. Others are negative only in content and positive in form, as, for instance, 'eternity', the real meaning of which is 'without beginning or end'. Both of these kinds of attri-

[56] Cf. *ibid.* [57] Cf. Steinschneider, *Uebersetzungen*, § 239.

butes are admissible. Thus far he is in perfect agreement with Maimonides.

Positive attributes are next divided by the author into three classes. First, attributes which are identical with the essence of the subject, as, for instance, animality in the predication of man. Second, attributes adjoined to the essence, as, for instance, whiteness, &c. Third, attributes which are merely descriptive of some external relation of the subject, as, for instance, actions and the relations of time and space. Of these three classes, the first and the last are admissible, but the second is inadmissible, for, adds the author, not only is any composition within the divine essence unthinkable, but likewise the composition of His essence with something outside itself.[58]

The points of difference between this theory and that of Maimonides are worth attention. First, according to Maimonides, actions and external relations are two different classes of attributes, the one admissible, the other inadmis-

[58] ואמנם התארים החיוביים, שם וענין, מהם תארים הם מהות המתואר, בתארנו אדם כשהוא חי: ומהם תארים אינם הם חלק מהות אלא יוצאים ממנו, ואבל הם יורו על תכונה במתואר מחוברת למהותו, בתארנו גד׳ שהוא לבן; ומהם תוארים אינם מהות המתואר ולא הם תכונה מחוברת למהות, ואבל הם הלצות למתואר בצרוף אל דבר יוצא ממנו, בתארנו גד בשהוא לימין דן, ואלה יקראו התוארים הצרופיים. אמנם התארים אשר הם חלק המהות אינם מיוחסים לו ית׳, אחר שכבר התבאר שעצמותו ית׳ בלתי מתחלקת. ואמנם התארים אשר הם במהות המתואר, הנה מן הידוע שתאר אותו ית׳ בהם אפשרי, אחר שלא יורו על ענין נוסף על המהות כלל . . . ומפני שתארי ית׳ באלו התארים הצרופיים נכון, אנחנו מתארים אותו בסביית, ובהתחליית . . . כי אלה כלם תארים צרופיים . . . הנה התבאר שהוא ית׳ נכון לתארו בתארים השוללים, וזה אם במלות וענין, ואם בענין בלתי מלות, ושתארי החיובים אשר בעצמותו ואשר הם על דרך הצרוף עובר.

sible; according to Moses Halavi both fall under the heading of external relations and both are admissible.[59] Halavi, again, in contradistinction to Maimonides, calls essential universal attributes identical with the individual essence, and admits the usage in divine predications. This unmistakably proves that to him universals are merely mental inventions.

Reverting, then, to his first class of positive attributes, to those designating a universal essential quality, which he holds to be identical with the essence of the individual subject, like Gersonides, Moses Halavi endeavours to obviate the possible objection based on the proposition that identity cannot be a relation in a logical proposition. 'In answer to such an objection', he says, 'we maintain that the predicate of a proposition, as, for example, "He is knowing", with respect to its general meaning of the comprehension of external objects, is not identical with the subject. Nay, they are radically different terms, for the term "knowing" does not imply the specific subject of the proposition. It is with respect to this general meaning that the predicate bears a real and unidentical relation to the subject. Sometimes, however, it may be warranted by the context of the proposition, that the apprehension implied in the predicate with regard to the subject should be taken in a specific sense which is identical with the subject, as, for example, in the proposition, "God is knowing". It is in accordance with this distinction between the two aspects of the predicate that we are enabled to attribute to God essential qualities which are distinct from Him as subject

[59] ומפני שתארי ית׳ באלו התארים הצרופיים נכון, אנחנו מתארים אותו בסביית, ובהתחליית, ובבריאה, ובעשייה, וזולת זה מה שדומה לו, כי אלה כלם תארים צרופיים, כי ענינם שמציאות זולתו נשפעת ממציאותו.

and predicate, but do not imply plurality in His essence.' [60]

The implication of this passage is clear. Essential attributes are universalized by the mind. They are mere aspects of the individual objects in which they have neither objective nor subjective existence. But it is that mentally invented universal aspect of the individual subject that is affirmed in a logical proposition. The relation between subject and predicate is, therefore, merely formal, and God, though identical with His attributes, can still be their formal subject in a proposition.

In these five theories of divine attributes, which we have analysed, the points of agreement and disagreement are clear. They all agree that Biblical predications of God should be taken as logical judgements. All but Algazali accept the Avicennean definition of the absolute simplicity of the divine essence, though they do so for different reasons. The controversy turns merely on the reality of the universal predicates and their distinction from the

[60] וכבר יקשה המקשה, הנה תאמר שכל גזרה יחוייב שנשואה ונושאה יהיו משתנים עם היות אחד מהם נושא לאחר. ואמנם כשהיה נשואה ונושאה דבר אחד בעינו, הנה אין שם נושא ונשוא באמת, אבל יהיה מובן המאמר אשר בזה לא יגיע ממנו תועלת בין שהולץ מאותן הענין בשם אחד כמו שאמרנו שהאדם אדם, או בשני שמות נרדפים, באמרנו שהחמור עיר, כי זה [דומה] לאמרנו שהחמור חמור... והתשובה על זאת הקושיא, שנשוא זאת הגזרה, והוא אמרנו יודע בבחינה הוראתה על ענין הידיעה משולח אינו נרדף לנושאה, אבל הם שני שמות נבדלים, כי אמרנו יודע לו מובן בלתי מובן נושא הגזרה, ומזה הצד לוקח אחד מהם נשוא והאחר נושא. אכן קרה לידיעה בצרוף אל זה חעצמות המתואר בה שהיו דבר אחד בעינו במציאות, וזה דבר יוצא ממובן הגזרה, והוא אמרנו שהאל יודע, הנה על דרך הזה יתאמת שיתואר ית' בתארים אשר הם עצמותו, ויתחייב מזה הנושא והנשוא, מבלתי שיתחייב הרכבה בעצמות.

subject. And on this point, too, they all further agree that in God the universal cannot in any way be distinct from His individuality. The inquiry is, therefore, reduced to the following two questions: First, are the universal essential attributes in beings other than God distinct from their individual essence or not? Second, in what sense are these universals applied to God as predicates? The answer to the latter questions is dependent upon that given to the former. Maimonides, believing that in other beings the universals are distinct from the individual essences, is forced to interpret the divine predicates as homonymous, that is to say, as absolutely individual terms, entirely unrelated with other terms of the same sound. Averroes, however, believing that all essential universals are mere names, interprets the predicate of intelligence in its application to God as a universal term used ambiguously *secundum prius et posterius*. Gersonides and Halavi follow Averroes, but extend his interpretation of the predicate Intelligence to all other predicates. With this, we are ready for our discussion of Crescas.

CHAPTER II

CRESCAS'S CRITICISM OF MAIMONIDES.

POSITIVE attributes, contends Crescas, cannot be inadmissible, for that would reduce the accomplished metaphysician in his knowledge of the divine being to the same level with the novice. But that the knowledge of the divine is commensurate with one's moral and intellectual perfections is generally admitted.[61] True, Maimonides had forestalled that objection by declaring that though there can be no rising scale in the positive knowledge of God there can still be one in the discovery of additional negations. His explanation, however, is inadequate, for the augmentation of negative attributes cannot mark an increase in knowledge. True knowledge must be scientific and demonstrative, a principle which had been advanced by Aristotle[62] and upheld by Maimonides.[63] It is not the acquisition of new facts, but rather the invention of new proofs that knowledge grows by. Now, that positive attributes are to be rejected is demonstrable by a simple argument based upon the proposition of divine absolute existence—an argument which can be easily mastered even

[61] Cf. *Moreh*, I. 59.

[62] Cf. *Physics*, I, 1.

[63] Cf. *Moreh*, I, 55.

by those uninitiated in philosophy. And once one has mastered demonstration of the divine absolute existence one can prove the inadmissibility of any positive attribute that may come up. Any additional negation merely involves a new application of the identical argument, and thus adds nothing to the content of knowledge. Hence Crescas asks with added emphasis: Since the divine essence is unknowable, and if you also deny the existence of essential attributes, how can there be a rising scale in the knowledge of the divine being?[64]

Again, the inadmissibility of divine attributes is irreconcilable with tradition. If the divine qualities are all identical with the divine essence, then in the prayer of Moses, to be shown God's glory,[65] what the prophet had asked for was to attain the knowledge of God's essence. But it is highly improbable that Moses should have been ignorant of the fact that the divine essence was unknowable. Furthermore, tradition has differentiated the Ineffable Name from other divine names in that the former refers to the divine nature itself, whereas the latter are derivative of His actions. Now, since the divine essence is unknowable the Ineffable Name could not have been a designation thereof. And if you also say that no essential attributes are existent, then it could not as well designate any divine attribute. What part of the divine nature could it then have referred to? You could not say that it designated God's absolute existence or some of His negative attributes, for if that were the case, the meaning of the Ineffable Name would not have been kept in secrecy. Hence, positive attributes are not inadmissible.[66]

[64] Cf. *Or Adonai*, I, III, 3, p. 23 a.

[65] Cf. Exodus 33. 18.

[66] Cf. *Or Adonai*, I, III, 3, p. 23 b.

Nor are relative attributes inadmissible. If you say that predications expressing temporal, spatial, or some other external relations of God, though not implying a plurality in His essence, are inadmissible because all such relations, if real, imply similarity, why then is the affirmation of actions admissible? Actions, to be sure, when conceived as emanative from the divine essence, co-existing *with* Him always in energy and never *within* Him as a mere capacity, do not by themselves imply the inherence of external, imperfect qualities. On that account, Maimonides is perfectly consistent in rejecting positive attributes and admitting actions. But still actions are external relations. However they are taken, actions express some relation between God and the external, created reality, a relation which, like transient qualities, is changeable and transitional, even though unlike the latter it does not imply changeability and transitionality in the essences of the related objects. For even though we may explain the apparent changeability in the divine actions as due to the material objects operated upon rather than to the operative agent, those actions, when not viewed as dynamic forces, but as external static relations between the agent and its object, must of necessity like all external relations, and especially like the relation between transient agents and their objects, be changeable and transitional. That actions present a phase of external relativity is an indisputable assumption. In fact, as we have already pointed out, Maimonides stands alone in differentiating between actions and external relations and separating them into two distinct classes of predicables. Most of the philosophers had included actions in the class of external relations, permitting the use of the latter as well as that of the former. And so, since Maimonides prohibits external relations on account of similarity, why should he not for the same reason prohibit actions? [67]

In his discussion of external relations, Maimonides especially mentions the two classes enumerated by Aristotle; [68] first, the relation of reciprocity, and, second, the rotation of degree of comparison. The former is designated by him by the term הצטרפות, Arabic اضافة, and the latter by the term יחס, Arabic نسبة. Both of these kinds are inadmissible. In rejecting the former kind, he states its reason that it is characteristic of such correlatives to be reciprocally convertible. The contention of this phrase has been variously interpreted by the commentators, and, as usual,

[67] Cf. *Or Adonai*, I, III, 3, p. 23 a. 'Since attributes by which a thing is described in its relation to something else, which implies non-existence, are inadmissible with respect to God, as e. g. the transition of an object from a state of potentiality to that of actuality [*Moreh*, II, 55], how then does he allow the use of attributes which only describe the actions of an object, as e. g. doing, acting, creating; since these, too, imply non-existence; for before the deed, act or creation, the agent was potential and afterwards became actual.'

The meaning of this argument had been misunderstood by Abraham Shalom and Isaac Abrabanel. They interpreted the argument as follows: Since essential attributes are to be rejected on account of the implication of transition from potentiality to actuality, why should not actions be rejected for the same reason. And so both of them point out Crescas's error in overlooking the distinction drawn by Maimonides himself between essential attributes and actions. (Cf. נוה שלום, מ' י"ב, דרוש א', פ"ר.)

הנה התבאר ממה שאמר הרב שאין תוארי הפעולות לומר פעל ועשה יורה שהיה בכח ושב בפועל, כמו שאמר זה החכם. ויש להפליא ממנו איך אמר זה אחרי ראותו לשון הרב פ' י"ח הנזכר.

Cf. also Abrabanel's commentary on the *Moreh*, I, 55. The rendering of this argument by Dr. Julius Wolfsohn (*Der Einfluss Gazali's auf Chisdai Crescas*, p. 38, note 2) is uncritical. Cf. also Kaufmann, *Attributenlehre*, p. 416, note 85.

[68] Cf. *Organon*, *Categories*, ch. 7.

the ancients like Profiat Duran, Asher Crescas, Shem-tob, and Abrabanel had come nearer the truth than the moderns, like Solomon Maimon, Munk, and Friedländer. From the *Organon* [69] we may gather the meaning of the statement to be as follows. Correlations are reciprocal not because of a reciprocal relation existing between two objects in reality, but because terms by which the related objects are designated are mutually implicative. Thus, 'slave' and 'master' are reciprocally correlative, but 'John' and 'master' are not so, though in reality John may be the slave of the master. Likewise, 'wing' and 'winged creature' are reciprocally correlative, but 'wing' and 'bird' are not, though the bird is a winged creature. Suppose now that the term 'slave' were used homonymously, in a sense absolutely divorced from its original meaning, would it still be correlative with 'master'? In other words, must a reciprocal correlation be so in reality as well as in name? Maimonides seems to think that the two conditions are necessary. Reciprocally correlative terms must be mutually implicative in name and mutually interdependent in reality. Consequently he maintains that by whatever term you designate God, that term taken as it must be in an absolute sense is perforce a homonym, and therefore no reciprocal relation can exist between God and other beings. Thus, even if God is called the First Cause or Principle, unlike all other causes and principles, it is absolutely independent of its effect and consequence. 'For', says Maimonides, 'it is characteristic of two correlatives by reciprocation to be mutually convertible, and God being necessary existence and everything besides being possible existence, there can be no such correlation between them.' But, argues Crescas,

[69] Cf. *ibid.*

while it is true that the divine existence, viewed as mere existence, is absolute and independent of anything else, when however it is viewed as causative existence it is because that in its causative nature it is even in reality dependent upon the existence of effects emanating from its essence. His existence is necessary because it is not anteceded by any prior cause, but it is causative because it is creative. The fact that His causativity is dependent upon the existence of its effects does not detract from the necessity of His own existence. For necessary existence means nothing but the absence of efficient causation. And thus while the divine existence is absolute, the divine causation is not.[70]

Furthermore, if time be eternal, God would share with it in the common property of eternity. To understand the full significance of this criticism we must first cite Aristotle's

[70] Cf. *Or Adonai*, I, III, 3, p. 23 b. 'It is difficult to comprehend the statement made by Maimonides, namely, that there can be no perfect relation between God and His creatures on account of the condition that objects which are correlative must be reciprocally convertible. For, as a matter of fact, God must inevitably be conceived as Cause and Principle. Since a cause is so with respect to its effects and a principle likewise with respect to what follows from it, it is therefore evident that in this respect there exists some relation between them.'

I take this argument of Crescas to be an application of Algazali's contention that necessary existence only implies the negation of prior causes. Algazali's contention, as will be seen, reappears again in Crescas's exposition of his own theory of Attributes (cf. *infra*, ch. III, note 110). In this argument, therefore, Crescas is reasoning from his own premise. It is, truly speaking, not an argument against Maimonides. Of the same nature, as will be pointed out, is Crescas's next argument from time.

This underlying postulate of Crescas's argument seems to have been overlooked by Abraham Shalom (cf. נוה שלום, מ׳ י״ב, ד״א, פ״ג) and Abrabanel (cf. פירוש המורה ח״א פ׳ נ״ב), cf. also Kaufmann, *Attributenlehre*, p. 389, note 47, and Julius Wolfsohn, *Der Einfluss Gazali's auf Chisdai Crescas*, p. 38, note 1.

definition of the phrase 'being in time'. To be in time may mean two things, one, to co-exist *with* time, and, the other, to exist *in* time and be measured by it.[71] The second meaning, however, is rejected by Aristotle as being untrue. When, therefore, Maimonides queries whether there be any relation between God and time, he simply means whether it could be affirmed that God has existence *in* time, to which his answer is in the negative, for since time is consequent to motion, and motion to magnitude,[72] an inextended being cannot be said to have temporal existence in that sense. But the question is now raised by Crescas: Why cannot temporal relation be affirmed of God in the sense of co-existence *with* time, or to be when time is? The relation would then not be, as in the first case, of the dependence of God upon time, but rather of the commonality of eternal co-existence of two independent entities, God and time. The hypothesis of eternal time, to be sure, is rejected by Maimonides, but that is on quite other grounds, and not because time, were it eternal, could not share with God the property of eternity.[73]

Maimonides' rejection of temporal relation in the case of God is still less justifiable 'in view of what has been said in the second part in refutation of the premise that time is an accident consequent to motion'.[74] Herein Crescas is pitting his own definition of time with all its corollaries against that of Maimonides, rather than criticizing the latter

[71] Cf. *Physics*, IV, 12, § 8.

[72] Cf. *ibid.*, IV, 12, § 6.

[73] Cf. *Or Adonai*, I, III, 3, p. 23 b. 'Likewise with regard to his statement that there is no relation between God and time, even if we admit that time is one of the conditions of motion, the latter of which is a condition of corporeal objects, there can still be a relation and similarity between God and time with respect to eternity, especially if we assume that time is eternal.'

[74] Cf. *ibid.*

from his own premises. Following Aristotle, Maimonides defines time as an accident adjoined to motion, and to be in time is circumscribed by two conditions. In the first place, the temporal object must have motion,[75] and in the second place, it must be comprehended by the time,[76] thus not co-existing with the whole of the time, but only with a part thereof. Therefore, the eternal translunary spheres, according to Aristotle, which are endowed with rotary motion, thus satisfying only one of the conditions, are said to be in time only by accident. The eternal immovable Intelligences, however, satisfying neither of the conditions, are not in time at all. And so God has no temporal relation. Though God is said to have existed prior to the world, the priority referred to is causal rather than temporal, since prior to the emergence of matter there had been no time. But Crescas defines time as an accident of both motion and rest, meaning by the latter some positive entity and not a mere absence of motion.[77] Time, therefore, being independent of motion, is likewise independent of matter, and had existed even before the creation of the universe. And so, the immovable eternal beings as well as God may be said to have existence in time.

Finally,[78] the divine negative attributes cannot form a privative judgement; they must of necessity form a negative judgement, thus involving an indirect affirmation. Privative judgements are possible only in the case where the subject belongs to a different universe of discourse from that which the predicate belongs to. When we say that 'a mathematical point is not red', the judgement must truly be

[75] Cf. *Physics*, IV, 12, § 11. [76] Cf. *ibid.*, IV, 12, § 10.

[77] *Or Adonai*, I, I, XVI, p. 11 a, and I, II, XI, p. 19 a.

[78] *Ibid.*, I, III, III, p. 25 a.

privative, denying red as well as all its correlatives, 'not red' thus meaning colourless, because in the universe of mathematical points there is no colour. But in the proposition 'God is not ignorant', while we negate not only human ignorance but also human knowledge, still, according to Maimonides, we affirm of God some knowledge which is identical with the divine essence, and which has no known relation with human knowledge. Thus the negation of knowledge in the case of God cannot be an absolute privation of knowledge; it must only be a negation of human knowledge which indirectly implies the affirmation of divine knowledge. Since divine knowledge is thus affirmed by the negation of human knowledge, the two must have some kind of relation, however vague and inarticulate. Divine knowledge, says Crescas, must accordingly be 'some kind of apprehension'. Now, let us designate that 'some kind of apprehension' by the letter *X*, and see whereabouts it would lead us.[79]

[79] Cf. *Or Adonai*, I, III, 3, p. 25 a. 'It is quite evident that when we attribute to God knowledge and power in a particular sense, meaning by knowledge the negation of its counterpart, namely, *human knowledge* [literally, ignorance], and by power, the negation of *human power* [literally, impotence], either of these two terms ascribed to Him must of necessity imply something positive. For even though His knowledge is as different from our knowledge as His essence differs from our essence, still that which is implied in the negation of *human knowledge* [literally, ignorance] must be some kind of comprehension or perception. That the negation of *human knowledge* [literally, ignorance] must imply [the affirmation of] something positive and cognoscible, is beyond dispute, since [being] the counterpart of that [negated] *human knowledge* [literally, ignorance], [it] must indicate a certain [positive] thing, namely, some kind of perception.'

I have translated the term סותר by 'counterpart' rather than by 'contrary', throughout these passages. I have likewise taken the terms סכלות and לאות to mean respectively human knowledge and human ignorance in general, which in contrast with divine knowledge and power,

First, what would be the relation of that *X* to the divine essence? It cannot be accidental nor essential to it, since both are debarred by Maimonides. It must, therefore, be identical with the essence. But *X*, as we have said, is not entirely unknowable; for so much is known of it that it is 'some kind of apprehension'. The question is now, Is it co-extensive with the essence or not? In the former case, the essence would have to be knowable; and in the latter, the essence would have to be composed of a knowable and unknowable part.[80]

Furthermore, as *X* stands for the divine correlative of human knowledge, so would *Y* stand for the divine correlative of human power. Now, since human knowledge and power are different, *X* and *Y* will have to be different.

are nothing but ignorance and impotence at their best. For I think that Crescas understood the term 'negative attributes', used by Maimonides, in the same sense as I interpreted it in ch. I. According to my rendering and interpretation of this argument as well as of those that follow, the objections raised against them by Abraham Shalom in his *Neveh Shalom* are ill-founded. (Cf. *Neveh Shalom*, XII, I, IV; Jöel, *Don Chasdai Crescas*, p. 31; cf. also *Ez Ḥayyim* by Aaron ben Elijah the Karaite, ch. 71.)

80 Cf. *Or Adonai*, I, III, 3, p. 25 a. 'Therefore I say that if this comprehension and whatever it implies were not something positive and essential to the Blessed One, it would have to be His essence itself, inasmuch as it could not be an accidental attribute, since God can bear no relation whatsoever to accidents. Now, if it were His essence itself, it would give rise to either of these two absurdities. First, were His essence to include nothing but what we understand by the term comprehension, His essence would then have to be knowable. Second, were His essence to include something besides what we understand by the term comprehension, it would then have to be composed of two parts, namely, that which we understand by the term comprehension and that of which we have no knowledge at all. Either of these two consequences is absolutely absurd. That the divine essence cannot be an object of our knowledge, is well known to every novice in Metaphysics; and that His essence cannot likewise be composed of two parts is due to the fact that God would in that case have one possible existence.' (Cf. *Neveh Shalom*, *ibid.*)

Hence, if these attributes were identical with God's essence, His essence would be composite.

Finally, suppose, however, that X is absolutely unrelated with human knowledge, and that is not even 'some kind of apprehension'. The proposition 'God is knowing', which according to Maimonides means that 'God is not ignorant', would, therefore, be the exclusion of human knowledge and the lack thereof without at the same time affirming divine knowledge.[81] But the judgement could not be privative, for though the divine knowledge is absolutely unrelated to the human knowledge, and cannot therefore be indirectly affirmed by the negation of the latter, there is, however, an absolutely unique divine knowledge which cannot be denied in the same way as we can deny mathematical colour. And so, negative attributes form negative judgements. But according to Maimonides negative attributes mean that God neither possesses those attributes as they are stated, nor their opposites. This, however, is contrary to the law of excluded middle.[82]

[81] Cf. *ibid.* 'Again, it has been shown, that the terms knowledge and power, when applied to God, must mean something positive and cognoscible, since in the case of negating [of God] either *human knowledge* [literally, ignorance] or *human power* [literally, impotence] we must understand [indirectly to affirm of Him] something [positive], namely, either the [divine] counterpart of *human knowledge* [literally, ignorance] or the [divine] counterpart of *human power* [literally, impotence]. But it is clear that whatever is meant by the [divine] counterpart of *human knowledge* [literally, ignorance] is not identical with whatever is meant by the [divine] counterpart of *human power* [literally, impotence]. Consequently the meaning of the one must differ from that of the other. Hence it follows that neither of them can be taken as identical with the divine essence, for in that case His essence would be composed of different parts.' (Cf. *Neveh Shalom*, *ibid.*)

[82] Cf. *ibid.* 'Again, if his conclusion with regard to the denial of essential attributes were true . . . . . it would be impossible to affirm of God any positive implication of those attributes, inasmuch as the denial thereof is not because we are ignorant of any of His essential attributes but because

From his arguments against Maimonides' theory of attributes, Crescas passes over to a discussion of the relation between essence and existence. In its origin, among the Arabs and Jews, the problem of essence and existence was much simpler than in its later development among the Schoolmen. To the latter the problem presented itself in the following form. Assuming the presence of a distinction between essence and existence within actual beings they ask, What does that distinction consist in?[83] The various answers given to the question ran parallel to the solutions offered to the problem of universals, real, conceptual, or nominal. This evolved form of the problem, however, bears only a remote resemblance to what seems to have been its nucleus, namely, the controversy of Avicenna and Averroes. To these Arabic thinkers the problem of essence and existence presented itself in the form whether existence is an accidental or an essential universal, and it originated in the following manner:

That which is divided into the ten Categories is designated by Aristotle by the word *τὸ ὄν*. The corresponding Arabic term is الموجود, a passive participle from a root meaning 'to find' (وجد). In the Arabic language that

He does not possess any. Thus, God will have to be deprived of whatever we understand by comprehension or power. Neither of these can, therefore, be ascribed to Him either as parts of His essence or as essential attributes. But as it is evident that any kind of ignorance or impotence [i. e. human knowledge and power] must be negated of Him, it follows that He is negated both contraries or opposites, namely, knowledge [i. e. divine] and ignorance [i. e. human knowledge], power [i. e. divine], and impotence [i. e. human power].' But that is most absurd and inane (cf. *Neveh Shalom, ibid.*; Joël, *Don Chasdai Crescas*, p. 31; Kaufmann, *Attributenlehre*, p. 478, note 162; Julius Wolfsohn, *Einfluss Algazalis*, p. 40).

[83] Cf. R. P. Kleutgen, *La Philosophie scholastique*, vol. III, chap. II; M. De Wulf, *Scholasticism Old and New*, pp. 108-9.

passive participle joined to a noun *A* in the nominative case forms a proposition meaning '*A* is existent'. Now, in this proposition, it is clear, that the existence affirmed of *A* must be accidental to it, for were it identical with the essence of *A*, argues Avicenna, '*A* is existent' would mean '*A* is *A*'. Existence is thus an accident. 'Being', τὸ ὄν, or الموجود, which is divided into the ten categories, is therefore resolvable into 'that which is', having itself existence superadded to its essence, and so is existence accidental to the essence of all the ten categories. And, like all accidents, existence is applied to different subjects in unequal sense. Meaning independent reality outside the mind, existence is primarily applied to substances which are self-existent, and through these to the accidents of quality and quantity, and through qualitatively or quantitatively modified substances, it is also applied to the residual accidents.[84] As the com-

[84] According to Isaac Albalag (commentary on Algazali's *Intentions*) the problem of essence and existence and unity had its origin in two apparently contradictory statements which he alleges to be found in the works of Aristotle. In the Metaphysics (IV, 2) Aristotle identifies being (τὸ ὄν) and unity (τὸ ἕν) with the essence of the subject of which they are predicated. In *De Anima*, however, says Albalag, being and unity are stated to be accidental to essence.

ואבוחמד טעה בזה, לפי שלקח המצוי הנאמר על ענין הראשון, והוא אשר אליו כיון אריסטו בספר הנפש תחת המצוי הנאמר על ענין השני, והוא אשר כיון במה שאחר הטבע (יצחק אלבלג, פירוש על הכונות, אלהיות, מ״א).

I was, however, unable to identify Albalag's reference in *De Anima*. In *De Anima*, II, 1, 7, the only place in that book where being and unity are discussed, there is no indication that Aristotle had considered them as accidents.

Cf. also Shemtob's commentary on the *Moreh*, I, 57.

In my exposition of the reason that had led Avicenna to consider existence as an accident, I have followed Averroes. (Cf. *Destruction of the Destruction*, Disputation VII; *Epitome of the Metaphysics*, I. The latter passage is quoted by Munk, *Guide*, vol. I, ch. 57, p. 231. Paraphrases of

position of essence and existence, which is now assumed in every being, must necessarily be occasioned by a preceding cause, that cause itself, in order to avoid an infinite

this passage of Averroes is found in almost every commentary on the *Moreh*; cf. also *infra*, note 86).

The following observation on the meaning of the Hebrew words מהות, מציאות, ישות, may be of some interest. In early Hebrew translations from the Arabic the terms ישות (being) and מציאות (existence), were synonymous, both contrasted with מהות (quiddity), cf. Hebrew translation of Algazali's *Intentions*, Part II, Metaphysics.

וזה יראה מה שזכרנוהו קודם מפני הישות אשר הוא מליצה מהמציאות בלתי המהות.

In the Hebrew translation of Aegidius de Colonna's *De Esse et Essentia*, however, the term מציאות is used as synonymous with מהות, both of which are contrasted with ישות.

א"כ מבואר הוא שהישות הוא דבר אחר מהמציאות או המהות לבד (p. 96).

The following explanation seems to me to be quite plausible.

The Arabs, and after them the Jews, rendered the Greek *οὐσία* and *τὸ ὄν*, both from a root meaning 'to be', by وجود (מציאות) and موجود (נמצא), which, derived from the root 'to find', usually mean 'existence' and 'existent', respectively. In addition to 'existence', they coined the term ماهيّة (מהות, that is, 'quiddity'. 'Existence' was to them the accident of 'quiddity'. And so even when *οὐσία* and *τὸ ὄν* are translated literally by كون (היות or ישות) and كاين (הוה), from 'to be', the latter are considered as synonymous with 'existence' and therefore accidents of 'quiddity'. According to Averroes, as we shall see, the distinction of 'existence' and 'quiddity' originally sprang from that inaccurate Arabic translation of the term *οὐσία*.

Now, the Scholastics used the term *essentia* among other terms for the Greek *οὐσία*. Adopting from the Arabs the *quidditas* they used it synonymously with *essentia*. Again, the Arabic وجود (מציאות) became *esse* which, as is well known, is used by the Schoolmen in the sense of *existentia*. Likewise, the Arabic موجود (נמצא) became *ens*. And just as the Arabs and Jews used to speak of the distinction between 'existence' and 'quiddity' so they speak of the distinction between *esse* and *essentia seu quidditas* or *ens* and *essentia seu quidditas*.

Thus while the Hebrew מציאות and the Latin *essentia* are both originally translations from the Greek *οὐσία*, in the historical development of ideas

chain of cause and effect, we must assume to be free from that composition. Thus Avicenna concludes that in God there is no distinction of essence and existence.[85]

they have drifted away far apart from each other. *Essentia* is identical with **מהות**, which is quite the opposite of **מציאות**, and **מציאות** is identical with *esse*, which is the antithesis of *essentia*.

Some of the Hebrew translators from the Latin saw that point clearly. Thus the translator of Thomas Aquinas renders the title of the latter's *De ente et essentia* by **מאמר בנמצא ובמהות** (quoted by Steinschneider, *Uebersetzungen*, § 295, 5). He likewise translates literally *essentia* by **היות** and *ens* by **הוה**, giving, however, for the latter its traditional Hebrew equivalent **נמצא**.

שאלה א׳, אם שם ההיות, ובלשונם אישינסיא, הוא לקוח משם ההוה, ר״ל, הנמצא, ובלשונם אינש, במהות ובמציאות מטומש (quoted *ibid.*).

The translator of Aegidius, however, renders the title *De esse et essentia* by **מאמר הנמצא והמציאות**. This, as we have seen, is inaccurate. For *ens* is **נמצא**, and *esse* is **מציאות**. Again, while both *essentia* and **מציאות** are translations from the Greek *οὐσία*, their meanings are quite different. He likewise renders the phrase *essentia seu quidditas* by **המציאות או המהות**, the first part of which is wrong again for the same reason. It should be observed that the phrase *seu quidditas*, which the translator had in his Latin text, is not found in the Venice edition of 1503 of Aegidius's *De esse et essentia*.

85 There is a very important question which I wish to raise at this point. In the literature dealing with the problem of essence and existence we find two different formulas which are invariably used in affirming the absence of any distinction between essence and existence in the divine being.

The first formula employed by Maimonides and some of his commentators states that in God *essence and existence are identical*. The following quotations will illustrate it:

תהיה מציאותו עצמו ואמתתו, ועצמו מציאותו (מורה, ח״א, פ׳, נ״ז)

אחר שהש״י הוא מחויב המציאות, ומציאותו ומהותו דבר אחד (שם טוב, פרוש על המורה שם).

לפי שמציאותו ומהותו אחד . . . אבל מציאותו הוא מהותו (אפודי, שם, פ׳ נ״ח).

הנה הם מסכימים על הנמצא הנאמר על האלוה ית׳ שאינו דבר יוצא מעצמו (אור ה׳, מ״א, כ״ג, פ״א).

In opposition to this view, Averroes maintains that existence is identical with essence. The two are indistinguishable even in thought. Anything thought of is thought

The second formula used by Avicenna and Algazali states that God is *existence without essence added to it.* To illustrate:

ולכן היתה העלה הראשונה מציאות בלי מהות נוספת (אלגזלי, כונות, אלהיות, מ"א).

בבטול אמרם שהראשון הוא נמצא פשוט בלי מהות (הנ"ל, הפלת הפילוסופים, שאלה ח').

The question may now be raised whether these two different formulas are advisedly used, implying two distinct theories, or not. For several reasons it would seem that the two formulas do not imply two different theories. First, as far as we know, there is no record of any controversy between Maimonides and Avicenna and Algazali as to whether in God essence and existence are identical or He is existence without essence. Maimonides is generally believed to follow Avicenna and Algazali on that point, even though they use different formulas. Second, from the following quotations it may be conclusively deduced that the two formulas are used indiscriminately.

והש"י אמרו בו שהוא מציאות ולא מהות, לפי שהישות והמהות הוא אחד בו (קרשקש, פירוש על המורה ח"א, פ', נ"ז).

ואינו מחוייב מזה שנשיג ישותו המיוחדת אשר הוא מהותו, שהוא מציאות בלי מהות נוסף, וכמו שאמר אבוחמ"ד אין מציאות בלי מהות כי אם לאל (הנ"ל, שם, פ' נ"ח).

But the following passage from Isaac Albalag's commentary on Algazali's *Intentions of the Philosophers*, would on the other hand indicate quite clearly that Albalag had taken the latter's formula that God is *existence without essence* quite literally.

לפיכך אמר שהעילה הראשונה מציאות בלא מהות, וזה תימה גדול, איך שלל לעילה הראשונה המהות שאינו דבר נוסף על העצם וחייב לו המציאות שהוא מקרה (אלבלג, כונות, אלהיות, מ"א).

Again, from the following passage in Averroes' *Destruction of the Destruction*, Disputation VIII, it would also seem that this was a point at issue between Algazali and Averroes as to the interpretation of Avicenna's theory, the former maintaining that it meant that God is *existence without essence*, the latter that in God *essence and existence are identical.*

אמר ב"ר . . . זה הפרק כלו מטעה, כי האנשים לא יניחו לראשון

of as existent. This essential existence, to be sure, cannot be affirmed as the predicate of a subject in a logical proposition without involving tautology. But conceptual existences may have counterparts in reality, or may not have them. The idea of God and angels, for instance, has something in reality to correspond with it. The idea of centaurs on the other hand, though likewise involving existence, has nothing outside the mind to correspond with it. The former idea is, therefore, a true one (ἀληθής—صادق—צודק), the latter idea is a false one (ψευδής—كاذب—כוזב). For truth is the correspondence of what is conceived with what is perceived. To express this distinction between a true and a false idea we either affirm or deny of a thing its existence outside the mind. The test of such existence is knowledge, direct or indirect. Of a true idea we, therefore, affirm that it is directly perceived or otherwise known to agree with reality. Now, in the Arabic language, says

מציאות בלא מהות ולא מהות בלא מציאות; ואמום האמינו שהמציאות במורכב תואר נוסף על עצמותו, ושזה התאר אמנם קנאו מהפועל, והאמינו במה שהוא פשוט שזה התאר לו אינו נוסף על המהות, ושהוא אין לו מהות מתחלף למציאות, לא שהוא אין לו מהות כלל כמו שבנה הוא כלל דבורו בסתירתם (הפלת ההפלה, שאלה ח׳).

That these two formulas represent two distinct theories, would also seem to follow from this passage of Thomas Aquinas's *De ente et essentia*. 'Aliquid enim est, sicut Deus, cuius essentia est ipsum suum esse; et ideo inveniuntur *aliqui philosophi* dicentes quod Deus non habet essentiam, quia essentia eius non est aliud quam esse eius.' As to who the *aliqui philosophi* were, Cajetan identifies them with the Platonists, a term, as has been observed, used by him loosely to indicate some gnostic sect (cf. *De ente et essentia*, ed. Émile Bruneteau, Paris, 1914, p. 114, note 1). It is more probable that Thomas refers there to Algazali. Professor Maurice De Wulf, however, was kind enough to advise me that in his opinion the phrase *aliqui philosophi* refers to some contemporary teachers in the University of Paris and not necessarily to some well-known philosophers.

Averroes, the same root وجد 'to find', which signifies the essential existence, means also to find out the presence of something by means of the senses or of the intellect. Thus 'God is existent' means that God is perceived or known to have objective reality corresponding to our subjective idea of Him. In the proposition 'centaurs are not existent' we likewise mean to deny the perception of centaurs to agree with our conception thereof. In either case, however, ideal existence is identical with essence.[86]

The same difference of opinion between Avicenna and Averroes recurs with regard to the attribute of unity.

[86] Cf. Narboni's Commentary on Algazali's *Intentions*, Metaphysics, Part I.

וכתב אבן רשד, זה לשונו: טעות אבן סינא, שהוא בעבור שראה שם הנמצא מורה על הצודק בדבור הערבי והיה אשר מורה על הצודק מורה על מקרה בלי ספק, אבל גם באמתות על מושכל מן המושכלות השניות, רצוני לומר, הדבריות, חשב שכאשר עשאוהו המעתיקים אמנם יורה על זה הענין, ואין הענין כן. אבל אמנם כונו בו המעתיקים שיורו בו על אשר יורה עליו שם העצמות והדבר. וכבר באר זה אבונצר בספר האותיות, וידע שאחת מסבות הטעות הנופלות בזה הוא ששם הנמצא הוא בתנועת נגזר, והנגזר יורה על מקרה, אבל הוא בשרש הלשון נגזר, אלא שהמעתיקים אחר שלא מצאו בלשון הערב תיבה מורה על זה הענין, אשר היו הקודמים חולקים אותו אל העצם והמקרה, ואל הכח והפעל, רצוני לומר, תיבה היא המשל ראשון, הורו עליו קצתם בשם הנמצא, לא על שיובן ממנו ענין הגזרה, ויורה על מקרה, אבל ענין אשר יורה עליו שם העצמות, והוא כל דבר הוה, והוא שם מלאכותיי, לא לשוניי ע"כ.

But Aristotle himself, as is well known, distinguishes four different usages of the term *τὸ ὄν*, two of which correspond to those mentioned by Averroes, namely, (1) in the sense of truth and falsehood (*Τὸ ὂν λέγεται τὸ μὲν κατὰ συμβεβηκός*), (2) that which is divided into the categories (*Ἔτι τὸ εἶναι σημαίνει καὶ τὸ ἔστιν ὅτι ἀληθές, τὸ δὲ μὴ εἶναι ὅτι οὐκ ἀληθὲς ἀλλὰ ψεῦδος*) (cf. Metaphysics, IV, 7, V, 2; Grote, *Aristotle*, vol. I, chap. III). Thus it is not altogether the translator's fault that Avicenna confused the two meanings of the term (see the interpretation of Averroes' criticism given by Munk, *Guide*, vol. I, p. 231).

Here, again, for similar reasons Avicenna maintains that, like existence, unity is only accidental to essence. Averroes, on the contrary, maintains that unity is identical with essence, but distinguishing between absolute and numerical unity, he admits the latter to be accidental, and it is this accidental kind of unity that is always referred to in propositions affirming unity.

Among Jewish philosophers, Maimonides and his immediate disciples[87] followed Avicenna. All later Jewish thinkers accepted the view of Averroes.[88] Having a new theory of his own, Crescas undertakes to expose the untenability of both the old systems.

Whatever the meaning of existence with respect to creatures may be, contends Crescas, with respect to God it is generally admitted, by both the Avicennean and the Averroesean groups, that existence is identical with the divine essence. Hence it must be inferred that they all interpret the attribute of existence homonymously, for as there is no relation between the divine and the created essence, so there cannot be any relation between their

[87] Cf. *Drei Abhandlungen von Josef b. Jehuda* (מאמר ר׳ יוסף ב״ר יהודה תלמיד הרמב״ם), edited by Moritz Löwy, Berlin, 1879, Hebrew text, p. 15.

[88] Cf. commentaries on the *Moreh*, as well as the commentaries of Narboni and Albalag on Algazali's *Intentions*. Cf. also Albo's *Ikkarim*, II, ch. I. Narboni, in his commentary on the *Intentions*, after quoting at length Averroes' arguments against Avicenna, adds the following remark: 'I have dwelt rather too long on this subject, because I have noticed that the savant, our Master Moses [i. e. Maimonides], following Algazali and Avicenna, had begun one of his chapters by saying that "existence is an accident superadded to the existent being". Would that that statement had not existed.'

והארכתי בבאור זה; למה שראיתי החכם רבינו משה נמשך בספריו אחר דעת אבו חמד ואבן סינא בזה, עד שהתחיל בפרק מפרקיו, המציאות מקרה קרה לנמצא, ומי יתן ולא נמצא.

existences. Consequently, queries Crescas, 'Would that I could conceive what is the significance of the term existence when applied to God, for our affirmation that God is existent, in which the latter term is not different from the former, is tantamount to our saying that God is God'.[89] Two inaccuracies of this argument of Crescas must not be passed over unnoticed. In the first place the inference that the homonymous interpretation of the term existence must follow its identification with the divine essence, is erroneous. Gersonides, for instance, follows Averroes in the identification of essence and existence, and still interprets the latter ambiguously, according to the distinction of priority and posteriority.[90] In the second place, in interpreting existence homonymously Maimonides circumvents the objection of tautology by taking it as an emphasis of the negation of non-existence.[91]

But the objection may be urged even with regard to created existences if we accept the view of Averroes and his followers, who consider existence to be nothing but the essence. For, according to this view, the proposition 'man is existent' or 'white is existent' would be equivalent to saying 'man is man' or 'white is white'.[92] This criticism is neither original nor irrefutable. In fact, it is the very same argument that had been advanced by Algazali in support of the Avicennean theory of the distinction between existence and essence.[93] Again, Averroes's refutation

[89] *Or Adonai*, I, III, 1, p. 21 b–22 a.

[90] Cf. *Milhamot*, V, III, 12, p. 46 b, and III, 3, p. 23 a.

[91] Cf. *Moreh*, I, 58.

[92] *Or Adonai*, I, III, 1, p. 22 a.

[93] Cf. Algazali's *Intentions*, Metaphysics: In refutation of the view that existence and essence are identical, he says: 'This is refutable on two grounds: first, when we say the substance is existent it is evidently a proposition conjoined of two terms. Now if the existence of the substance

thereof, based upon a distinction in the use of the term existence, was well known and had been quoted by all the commentators on the *Moreh*.[94]

The view held by Avicenna that existence is only accidental to the essence, says Crescas, is still less tenable. The term accident had been used by Avicenna in two senses, a general and a specific.[95] In its general sense the term is applied to everything which requires a subject of inhesion. In its specific sense, however, it is applied only to those that require a subject of inhesion, and of which the subject of inhesion is independent, as, for instance, *white* and *cloth*. Form, therefore, though an accident in the general meaning, having no existence apart from matter, is not an accident in the specific meaning of the term, since Matter in its turn has no subsistence without Form. And so Form is included among the four Substances. It is with reference to these two meanings of the term accident, if I am not mistaken, that Crescas urges the next two arguments against Avicenna's accidental interpretation of

were the essence of it, our statement would assert that substance is substance.'

. . . וזה נפסד משני פנים, אחד מהם, שאמרנו העצם נמצא דבור מחובר מובן, ולו היה מציאות העצם עין העצם, היה כאמרנו העצם עצם.

[94] Cf. *supra*, notes 84 and 86.

[95] Cf. Algazali's *Intentions*, Metaphysics, I. He divides there existence (מציאות) into two classes; one, which needs an abode (משכן) as accidents (מקרים), and another, which has no need for an abode. Those which need an abode are again divided into two classes: one, where the abode is independent of the accident, and, another, where the abode is dependent upon the accident. In the former case the accident bears the name accident (מקרה), whereas the abode is called the subject (נושא). In the latter case the accident is called *Form* (צורה) whereas the abode is called ὕλη (היולי). In fact the inclusion of the Form among the Substances is opposed by the Mutakallemim, who consider it as a mere accident dependent upon its abode (cf. *Moreh*, I, 73, proposition 8).

existence. Assuming at first that by interpreting existence as an accident Avicenna uses the term accident in its specific sense, Crescas attempts to reduce that view to an absurdity.[96] If anything, said to be existent, has its existence added to its essence, that existence, which we may designate as primary, being merely an accident, cannot be self-subsistent. In compliance with the definition of accident it must have existence in something else. Thus accidental primary existence will have accidental secondary existence. By analogous reasoning the secondary existence will need to have tertiary, and so the process may go on *ad infinitum*.[97]

96 *Or Adonai*, I, III, 1, p. 22 a. 'No less a difficulty may be pointed out in the view of him who states that existence in all other beings is outside the essence to which the former is superadded as an accident. For if existence is an accident it must have a subject of inhesion, and thus existence will have existence. If the other existence is also an accident, that, too, will require a subject of inhesion and thus will have a still other existence, and so on to infinity.'

97 This argument had been anticipated by many authors. Joseph Ben Judah, Ibn Aknin, a disciple of Maimonides, both raises and answers this objection (cf. *Drei Abhandlungen von Josef b. Jehuda*, von Moritz Löwy, Berlin, 1879, Hebrew text, p. 15:

ואם נאמר כאשר היה המציאות תאר לנמצא הנה הוא תאר נמצא, הנה הוא נמצא במציאות וכן יהיה זה המציאות נמצא במציאות, וילך הענין אל בלתי תכלית).

It is also found in Albalag's commentary on the *Intentions*, Metaphysics:

אם תאמר שהוא [כלומר, תאר המציאות] נוסף, יתחייב שיהיה למציאות מציאות, ולמציאות מציאות, וכן עד בלתי תכלית.

The argument is also found in Aegidius's *De esse et essentia*, which had been translated into Hebrew at about the middle of the fourteenth century (Jews' College, London, 268):

א"כ צריך שכל דבר שישותו הוא דבר מטבעו, יהיה לו הישות מדבר אחר, ובעבור שהישות, שהוא כולל דבר אחר, יובא אל אותו הישות שהוא בעצמו, כמו שיובא העלול לסבה הראשונה, צריך שיהיה דבר אחר

If you say, as had been really suggested by Algazali, that existence, like Form, is an accident only in the general acceptation of the term, on account of its dependence upon essence, but again like Form it is a substance, and thus capable of self-subsistence, the question is, Why should existence be called accident any more than Form, since both, though accidents in the general sense of the term, are not accidents in its specific sense?[98] Thus, existence can be neither identical with the essence nor accidental to it.

Nor can unity be identical with or accidental to the essence. The arguments employed here by Crescas are merely a repetition of those employed by him in the case of existence. There is, however, one novel argument. Quoting the commonly accepted definition of unity as the negation of diversity, he continues: 'and if we say that unity, signifying the absence of plurality, is identical with

שיהיה סבת הישות לכל הנמצאים, בעבור שהוא ישות לבד, ועל תכונה אחרת היתה ההליכה בסבות לבלתי תכלית.

Likewise Gersonides urges the same argument against the accidentality of unity, which he says may also be applied to the accidentality of existence; cf. *Milḥamot*, V, 12.

ועוד שאם היה כל דבר אחד מצד מקרה מה נמצא בו, הנה יחוייב בזה המקרה כשהודינו עליו בשם בלתי נגזר, שיהיה מתואר בשהוא אחד מצד מקרה אחר נמצאנו בו, וילך אל לא תכלית . . . . . ולזאת הסבה ג"כ נאמר שעצם כל דבר נמצא, ר"ל, שלא יורה הנמצא עליו מצד מקרה נוסף על המהות.

98 'Furthermore, existence is like Form in its relation to Matter, since, according to their contention, without that accident [i. e. existence] the subject would have been nonexistent. And so, since that accident bestows existence and permanency upon the substance, it deserves to be called Substance prior to the subject, just as Form is called Substance prior to Matter, as it has been stated in the *Physics*, Book I. But existence is called by them accident, which is an incorrigible contradiction.'

the essence of the object predicated by one, it would follow that all objects described by one are one in essence'.[99] This argument may be easily identified as the application of the well-known mediaeval argument against the identity theory of universals as well as against monopsychism.[100]

CHAPTER III

CRESCAS'S THEORY OF ATTRIBUTES.

IT would be comparatively easy and not altogether unjustifiable to dismiss Crescas's theory of attributes as a conglomeration of incongruous statements. Such, indeed, was the verdict passed upon it by an early critic.[101] The difficulties which one encounters in the attempt to give a constructive presentation of his view are many. Besides the lack of coherence and definiteness in his exposition, Crescas seems radically to contradict himself. Starting out to prove that divine attributes are positive, upon getting embroiled in the inevitable difficulties consequent to such a thesis, without much ado Crescas quite unostentatiously concludes that after all some of the attributes are negative

99 *Or Adonai*, I, III, 3, p. 22 b.

100 Cf. Gersonides, *Milḥamot*, V, 12. 'For if unity were a genus it could not be predicated of the *differentiae* by which the species which are included under it are classified, for the genus cannot be predicated of the *differentiae* by which its subordinate species are classified. For example, animality is not predicable of rationality and volatility.'

שאם היה האחד סוג, היה בלתי אפשר שינשא האחד על ההבדלים אשר יחלקו בהם המינים אשר יקיף בהם, והמשל כי החי לא ינשא על הדבור והעופפות.

101 Cf. Abraham Shalom's *Neveh Shalom*, XII, I, 3. 'It is surprising how that author changes his view in an instant.'

ומהפלא מזה החכם ומסברתו ההפוכה כמו רגע.

in meaning. If negativity is to be the ultimate solution of some of the attributes, it had been asked, why should it not be equally applied to all the attributes, and what is then the meaning of all his contentions against Maimonides?[102] This inconsistency, however, is too apparent to be real, and the absence of any explanation on the part of the author of what appears to be an abrupt reversal of his own position, leads us at least to suspect whether his final statement does really reverse his original thesis. While we do not hold a brief for the author, defending him against his critics as to the adequacy of his justification of positive essential attributes, we shall, however, endeavour to give a constructive and consistent view of his attempt to do so.

If the problem of attributes, as I have attempted to show in the first chapter, is in its final analysis a question as to the relation of the universal essence to the individual; in order to understand Crescas's position on attributes we must first construct his theory of universals. Suggestions available for the construction of his theory of universals are abundant. He differs with both Avicenna and Averroes, and with the latter more than with the former. Admitting with Avicenna that the universal substance is distinct from the individual, he differs with him as to the relation between these two. According to Avicenna,

[102] Cf. *ibid.*, XII, I, 4. 'This author has just stated that existence means not nonexistence, and that unity means the absence of plurality. How then could he have said, just an instant before, that existence and unity are essential attributes?'

והנה החכם הזה הוא האומר שהמציאות יורה על היותו בלתי נעדר, והאחדות על היותו בזולת רבוי, ואיך היה דעתו לשמה כרגע לומר שהנמצא והאחד תארים עצמיים.

while the universal does not exist apart from the individual, nor the individual apart from the universal, they can both at least be thought of as separate existences. But Crescas insists upon their mutual interdependence in thought. Differentiated in thought though they are, still in thought they are inseparable. Not only cannot rationality or animality be conceivable without the individual human essence, but likewise the individual human essence cannot be conceived without the universal conceptions of rationality and animality. Such 'essential universals', he says, are 'conditions' of the individual essences, not mere mental abstractions or inventions, but real entities, so united as not to be distinguishable except by thought; but they are also so mutually implicative as not to be thought of one without the other.

What essential universals, which form the definition, are to the individual essence of the defined object, all the attributes are to the divine essence, and they are positive. But before proceeding any further let us explain the special sense in which Crescas uses the term positive attribute. Positive attribute may mean two things. In the first place it means the existence of qualities distinct from the essence. In the second place, it means that any predicate affirmed of God is used in a sense not entirely unrelated to its original, ordinary meaning. In Hebrew the same word (תאר) is used in these two senses. In English, however, we may call the one 'attribute' and the other 'predicate'. Now, in the different theories of attributes which we have analysed in a previous chapter, the main controversy was not about the 'attributes', but rather about the 'predicates'. Both Maimonides and Gersonides admit that God does not possess any attributes distinct from His essence. Their reasons, however, vary. The former maintains that in this respect God is absolutely different from other beings, whereas the latter believes that even in created beings essential universals are not distinguishable from the individual essence except in name. And so, while both deny the distinction of essence and 'attribute' within the divine substance, Maimonides interprets the 'predicates' as negatives, that is to say, as homonymous terms, but Gersonides interprets them as positives, that is to say, as ambiguous terms applied to God and to other beings in a related sense, *secundum prius et posterius*. Now, Crescas, as we shall see, endeavours to prove that attributes are positive both in the sense that the divine substance is composed of essence and attribute, and in the sense that the predicate affirmed of God is a related term. This, however, does not mean to say that every single attribute is positive in both these senses. If it can be shown that a certain attribute, even in its application to other beings, has no positive meaning, it can still be called positive predicate, because of its being applied to God and to other beings in a related sense. In the proposition A is X, for instance, let us say that X means $-Y$. If we then affirm that 'God is X', using here X in the same sense as in the proposition 'A is X', we may then say that X in its application to God is a positive predicate, even though its meaning is negative. 'Positive' in this sense would not refer at all to the *positive content* of the term employed as the predicate of the proposition ; it would rather refer to the *positive relation* of the content of the term in its application to God, to the content of the same term in its application to other beings, the content itself being either positive or negative.

Of all the attributes, existence and unity stand out as

a class by themselves. They are to every individual essence what its essential universals by which it is defined are to it. Man, for instance, besides his two essential universals, animality and rationality, and his many adventitious qualities, has also the two attributes existence and unity, which like the former are inseparable from his essence. For existence and unity are conditions of thought, without which nothing is conceivable. 'Every essence must unconditionally have objective reality outside the mind',[103] which is the meaning of existence; and every such actually existent substance must be one and limited.[104]

The relation that commonly obtains between the attributes of existence and unity and every individual essence, likewise holds true between both these attributes and the divine essence. As to the meaning of existence, however, there are two phases, a general and a specific. The general meaning is negative and invariable, but the specific meaning is positive and subject to variations. The general meaning of existence is non-subjectivity; that of unity is non-plurality. In that sense, each of these attributes is invariably applied, without any shade of difference, to accidents, substances, and God. The specific meaning of existence, however, is objectivity, and the specific meaning of unity is simplicity. In this positive phase each of these attributes is applied in different degrees to accidents, substances, and God. Substances are more objective than

[103] *Or Adonai*, I, III, 1, p. 22 a.

וזה שמתנאי המהות היותו נמצא חוץ לשכל.

and cf. quotation in note 105.

[104] *Ibid.*, I, III, 3, p. 22 b.

ולזה הוא מבואר שאין היחוד . . . אלא דבר עצמי לכל הנמצא בפועל ומוגבל.

and cf. quotation in note 105.

accidents, since the latter have no reality except as part of the former. Likewise, substances are more simple than accidents, since the latter, again, are divisible not only by their own potentiality, but also by that of their subject of inhesion. And than both God is more real and more simple in a superlative degree.[105]

All other attributes, however, that with respect to created beings are only accidental, differ in their application to God not only in degree but also in the manner of their relation to His essence, for all the divine attributes are inseparable and essential. Crescas especially mentions the attributes of Priority, Knowledge, and Power. Priority implies time, and time is an accident related to motion in all created being, and is subject to the variation of more or less. With respect to God, however, it is essential and

[105] *Ibid.*, I, III, 1, p. 22 a. 'It has thus been shown by an irrefutable argument that existence cannot be accidental to the essence. It must therefore be either identical with the essence itself or essential to it. Since it cannot be the essence itself, as it has been shown in the first argument, it must be essential to it, that is to say, that it is one of the conditions of the essence to exist outside the mind. Just as animality and rationality are said to be the human essence, so it is one of the conditions of the essence to have extra-mental existence. And so the term existence is applied univocally to all beings that are not prior to one another, that is, excluding accidents. Of substances and accidents, therefore, the term is applied ambiguously, since extramental existence is primarily applied to substance and through it subsequently to accidents. The general meaning, however, is that whatever is predicated by existence is not absent. It is in this sense of non-absence that the term is applied to God and to other substances, except that to God it is applied primarily and to other beings subsequently. It is thus clear that the term existence in its application to God and to other beings is not a perfect homonym, but it is a certain kind of ambiguity' [i. e. *secundum prius et posterius*]. Cf. also *ibid.*, I, III, 1, p. 22 b. 'It is thus clear that unity is not the essence itself . . . . . . nor anything added to the essence. It is something essential to everything that is actually existent and limited, and is a mental distinction with respect to the absence of plurality.' Cf. Ḥobot ha-Lebabot, I, 8.

inseparable as if it were His definition. Furthermore, it is used in a superlative sense; thus acquiring the meaning of first, eternal, or rather that of uncreated. The same holds also true of Knowledge and Power. In created beings they are acquired and accidental; in God they are inseparably essential. Again, in created beings they are each in a limited degree, in God they are in the highest degree possible. Thus all the divine attributes are ambiguous, but not homonymous terms. While they differ from their ordinary usage in degree, or in both degree and relation to essence, they all share in common their primary meaning. Existence, unity, priority, knowledge, and power, in their application to God, are in their primary meaning related to the corresponding terms in their application to created beings.[106]

But would not that relation imply similarity? Crescas tries to answer this question as follows: Related terms are similar, when the relation has some numerical value; that is to say, when the related terms are both finite. When one of the terms, however, is infinite, its relation to a finite term has no numerical value, and hence they are dissimilar. The divine attributes, as has been stated, are used in a superlative degree. His knowledge is infinite, and so are all his other attributes. Thus, while they are related in meaning to created attributes, their relation has no numerical value, whence it does not imply similarity.[107]

[106] Cf. *supra* quotations in note 105.

[107] *Ibid.*, I, III, 3, pp. 23 b–24 a. 'We say, there is no doubt that any similarity between God and His creatures must be dismissed as impossible. Still, though the perfection [attributed to God and to His creatures] belong to the same genus, there is no similarity between them, since they are so widely distinguished whether with respect to necessity and possibility of existence or with respect to finitude and infinity. This is the meaning

There is another difficulty which Crescas endeavours to obviate. 'It is now imperative upon us', he says, 'to explain why the negation of essential attributes does not necessarily follow our acceptance of the proposition that everything that is composed of two elements cannot be necessary existence.' This difficulty presents itself in two ways. First, since there are many attributes, each of which is distinct from all others, it would follow that the attribute part of God, which is not unidentical with but is inseparable from His essence, would have to be composite. Second, the aggregate of those attributes taken as a whole, being distinct from the divine essence, would together with that essence imply a plurality in the divine substance. With regard to the first, Crescas maintains that all the attributes are mental modifications of the single attribute of Goodness. Though not identical with goodness, all the other attributes cannot be separated from it even in thought. The relation, therefore, of the individual attributes to the general goodness is similar to that of the attribute as a whole to the essence.[108] It is this mental inseparability which makes

of the verse "To whom then will ye liken God? or what likeness will ye compare unto Him?" [Isa. 40. 18]. The prophet thereby explains that only that kind of similarity is forbidden to attribute to God which implies a certain comparison. But as the alleged similarity between God and His creatures is incomparable, for there can be no relation and also comparison between the infinite and the finite, there is no implication of real similarity in the affirmation of attributes.'

108 That the relation of the individual attributes to Goodness is, according to Crescas, similar to the relation of Goodness, or the totality of attributes, to the essence, may be inferred from the following passage: 'Just as essence cannot be conceived without existence nor existence without essence, so the attribute cannot be conceived without its subject nor the subject without its attribute. And all the attributes are likewise comprehended in absolute goodness, which is the sum total of all perfections'. *Or Adonai*, I, III, 3, p. 25 b.

them all one. In this, indeed, he follows Maimonides' explanation of the plurality of divine activities, with only the following two exceptions. Maimonides takes intelligence as the unifying principle, whereas Crescas takes goodness; and, again, Maimonides considers all other activities as different aspects of intelligence which are in reality identical with it, whereas Crescas considers the other attributes to be distinct from goodness. Upon the fundamental difference between intelligence and goodness more will be said later on.[109] With regard to the second, Crescas maintains that the mental distinction between essence and attribute is not contradictory to the conception of necessary existence, since they are inseparable in thought. Necessary existence excludes composition only in so far as that composition would necessitate an external agent by which that existence would have been rendered conditional. Such would be the case if the divine substance were conceived to consist of parts which could in any way be separately conceived of. But in the divine substance the attributes and the essence cannot be thought of one without the other, just as the essence and the radiative quality of a luminous object cannot be thought of separately. It is the possibility of being separately conceived and not the mere fact of a mental distinction that militates against necessary existence.[110] This answer, however, concludes Crescas, must be resorted to only in the case of attributes whose primary meaning is positive, as, for instance, Power and Knowledge. There are some attri-

[109] In the chapters on Crescas's theory of Divine Omniscience and the Purpose of the Universe which are not included in this thesis.

[110] This line of reasoning sounds like a modified and moderated restatement of Algazali's definition of absolute simplicity (cf. *supra*, chap. I, note 38 and chap. II, note 70).

butes whose positive meaning in the final analysis is nothing but a negation. The positive meaning of Existence, for instance, is nothing but a mental antithesis of absence; that of unity is a mental antithesis of plurality; that of priority when applied in a superlative sense of infinite priority comes to mean not-having-been-created, which is eternity, and in its final analysis, the absence of temporal relation. Though these attributes, too, are applied to God in the same positive sense as to created beings, their positive sense, however, in both cases is only a negation.[111]

[111] *Or Adonai*, I, III, 3, p. 24 b. 'It is now left for us to explain that the negation of essential attributes must not necessarily follow the accepted proposition which states that whatever is composite cannot have necessary existence. The explanation of this is not difficult, and it may be stated in two ways. First, though with respect to ourselves the attributes are separate, with respect to God they are unified. The infinite goodness which is essential to God comprehends all the attributes rendering them one. Second, that proposition is true only under a certain condition, namely, when the joined and composite object is such that it requires an agent to perform its composition as, for instance, when each part of the composition is part of its essence, in which case we must say that the composition brought about by the composing agent is the cause of the composite object. But the Blessed One has no divided substance, for His substance is simple in an absolute sense, and goodness in general follows from him essentially. Why, then, is it impossible that God should be necessary existence by His essence even though goodness in general or infinite knowledge, power, and the other perfections in particular, follow from Him essentially, just as light could have eradiated from a luminous object, even if that object were assumed to be necessary existence by its essence? Would the assumption of necessary existence render the radiation of the light impossible? No! For the light is not something essentially different from the substance of the luminous object, and thus does not require an external agent to bring about its composition with the latter; it is rather something essential to the luminous object and appropriately predicable thereof. That is exactly the meaning of divine attrributes. So much the more the attribute *priority* which is a mental distinction of His not having been created, *existence* which is an indication of His

This would seem entirely to dispose of the negative interpretation of Attributes. The burden of authority, however, weighed heavily, and while Crescas dared disagree with Maimonides, for which there had been many precedents, he could not completely ignore the views of Ibn Gabirol, Judah Halevi, Baḥya Ibn Pekudah, and others, all of whom had incorporated the negative interpretation in their respective solutions of the problem of attributes. To avoid this predicament, Crescas interprets the texts of those authors so as to harmonize with his own view. His interpretation is based upon the distinction we have already pointed out between the two usages of the Hebrew word תאר, one meaning 'attribute', the other 'predicate'. The existence of essential attributes in the divine being, says Crescas, had never been denied by the ancients. They had only maintained that some 'predicates' must be interpreted negatively, and those, too, only in the case when the predicates denote the essence itself. God, however, possesses essential attributes, and terms connoting those attributes are not to be taken as negatives. In the words of the author: 'We must, therefore, say that whenever some of the savants exclude the positive meaning of attributes, interpreting them all as negations, they must be understood to refer only to such predicates as describe the essence itself. These alone cannot be taken in a positive sense. And note this distinction.' [112]

Thus the divine being consists of an essence and essential attributes, the unity of the former being preserved by the

not being absent, and *unity* which indicates that there is no plurality in His essence and that in no way does He contain any duality.'

[112] *Or Adonai*, I, III, 4, p. 26 a:

ולזה צריך שנאמר שאם היו קצת החכמים . . .

mental inseparability of its parts. This view, says Crescas, is in conformity with the following statement which is found in the mystic writing called the Book of Creation. 'The manner in which the flame is united with the coal is an illustration of the irruptible unity.'[113] The implication of this statement, continues he, is as follows: 'Just as essence cannot be conceived without existence nor existence without essence, so the attribute cannot be conceived without its subject nor the subject without its attribute; and all the attributes are comprehended in absolute goodness, which is the sum total of all perfections.'[114] It is due to their failure to distinguish inseparable essential attributes from separable attributes that the philosophers, and especially Maimonides, were compelled to reject the existence of divine attributes altogether. To them only two alternatives presented themselves, either attributes are identical with the essence or they are different from it, in the latter case implying plurality. That attributes may be unidentical with the essence and still both together be one, they failed to perceive. A similar error was made by them in their theory of knowledge. Finding it impossible to conceive the subject, object, and process of knowing as different things, they were forced to declare them all identical—

[113] *Ibid.*, I, III, 3, p. 25b. The text of the *Sefer Yezira* is paraphrased by Crescas. Originally the passage reads as follows: 'Their end [i. e. of the Ten Sefirot] is inserted in their beginning, and their beginning in their end, even as the flame is joined to the coal. Know, think, and imagine, that the Lord is one and the Creator is one, and there is no second to that oneness, and before one what number can you name?'

נעוץ סופן בתחלתן, ותחלתן בסופן, כשלהבת קשורה בגחלת, דע וחשוב וצור שאדון יחיד והיוצר אחד, ואין שני לו, ולפני אחד מה אתה סופר?

(cf. *Sefer Yezira*, Goldschmidt's edition, p. 51).

[114] *Ibid.*

a view which is untenable for many reasons. But there, too, 'the philosophers tripped and fell because they did not distinguish the essential from the identical'.[115] The *ens intelligens* is not identical with the *intellectus*, but is essential to and inseparable from it. Attributes are, therefore, positive, and have their real counterpart in the divine being. With this the knowability of God is no longer impossible. His essence, to be sure, can never be known; His essential attributes, however, can be comprehended.

While to Crescas the compatibility of essential attributes with absolute existence and unity seemed clear and indisputable, his position has not escaped cavilling criticism. It has indeed been charged to be open to the same objection that in his *Refutation of the Christian Principles*[116] Crescas himself had pointed out in the Christian doctrine of the Trinity. The type of trinitarian doctrine which Crescas deals with in his polemic is, generally speaking, that of the Western Church, though as to its identification with any specific creed I am not in a position to express an opinion.[117] He outlines it as follows. The divine substance or Godhead consists of one essence and three

[115] *Or Adonai*, IV, 11, p. 91 a.

[116] Cf. בטול עקרי הנוצרים, originally written in Spanish, and translated into Hebrew by Joseph b. Shemtob.

[117] Professor George Foot Moore was kind enough to make the following observation. 'The peculiar definition of the Christian theory of the Trinity which you find in Crescas is also to be found in Ramban's Disputation with the controvertite Pablo before King James of Aragon, in 1263, the text of which was printed by Wagenseil in a volume under the title *Tela Ignea Satanae*, 1681. The passage is near the end of the Disputation. Ramban gives for the three persons of the Trinity, החכמה והחפץ והיכולת. I take that Crescas's רצון, and Ramban's חפץ are equivalent, not to *voluntas*, but *benignitas*, or *caritas*, i. e. not "will" but "good-will". In this form, Power, Wisdom, Good-Will, we have the theory of the Trinity set forth by Abelard (died 1142), which was condemned by a synod at Soissons, in 1121.'

distinct persons, Father, Son, and Holy Ghost, corresponding respectively to the attributes of Power, Wisdom, and Will. The Persons are not identical with the essence. The Persons, furthermore, are distinct from each other, and are interrelated as cause and effect, the Father being the cause of the Son, and these two of the Holy Ghost. Again, the Persons are the causes of their respectively corresponding three attributes. Finally, the three Persons are co-equal, all of them being Gods.[118] In his criticism, Crescas chiefly assails that part of the doctrine which maintains the distinctness of the Persons from the essence, showing that conception to be at variance with divine unity.[119] But according to the testimony of the translator, Isaac ben Shemtob, the same arguments that Crescas had urged against the distinctness of the Persons were urged by others against his own theory of divine attributes. 'I have noticed', he says, 'that some scholars had raised the same difficulties with respect to our author's theory of divine attributes.'[120] The translator, however, comes to

118 הפ׳ הג׳ בשלוש. האמונה הנוצרית מנחת שהעצם האלהי יכלל על ג׳ תארים, פירשונאש [persones] בלשונם, ומהות אחד: אב, בן, ורוח הקודש יכולת, חכמה, ורצון. האב מוליד הבן, ומאהבת שניהם הרוה״ק הוא נאצל. מהאב הוא היכולת, מהבן הוא החכמה, מהרוח הרצון. והג׳ במהות אלה אל אחד, הם נבדלים אבל בתארים. וכל אחד מהם הוא אלוה. זאת היא אמונתם בזה העקר (*Ibid.*)

119 והעקר הג׳ הוא השלוש . . . . . ההקדמות המתחלפות ג׳: א׳, שהנוצרי אומר שיש בעל ית׳ ג׳ תוארים נבדלים, בלשונם פריסונאש, והיהודי כופר בזה. ב׳, שהנוצרי מאמין שיש באל ית׳ תאר נקרא בן נולד מאב, והיהודי כופר בזה. ג׳, שהנוצרי מאמין שיש באל ית׳ תאר נאצל מהאב והבן נקרא רוח, והיהודי כופר בכל (*Ibid.*)

120 והוצרכתי להעירך עליו, יען כי ראיתי קצת משכילים ישבו על סברת זה החכם, בהאמינו התארים העצמיים, קצת מאלה הבטולים (*Ibid.*)

Crescas's defence by pointing out a radical distinction between personalities and attributes, namely, that the former being causatively interrelated are necessarily many, whereas the latter are absolutely unified by absolute goodness.[121]

The abstruseness of Crescas's reconciliation of essential attributes with absolute unity has also been pointed out by Abraham Shalom in his *Dwelling of Peace*.[122] 'We may ask the author [i. e. Crescas] as follows: Are there essential attributes identical with the essence or added to it? for these are the only two possible alternatives. If he says that they are identical, he has gained nothing by interpreting Moses' prayer to refer to essential attributes. . . . If he says that these attributes, though distinct with respect to ourselves, are one with respect to God, then it must mean that they are identical. . . . If the author retorts that the essential Attributes are indistinguishable from the essence except in thought, we may ask him again: Are they conceived in

121 אמר יוסף, דרוש התארים עמוק מאד . . . . והרב הזה החזיק בתארים העצמיים . . . אבל ראוי שתדע שהמקיים התארים העצמיים איננו תחת זה הסוג, ואנחנו לא מצאנו מלה אחרת יותר נאותה בהעתקה למלת פריסונה זולת התאר. אבל אין מובנם אחד. וזה מבואר. שהם אמרו שהאב המוליד הבן. ומי שמניח שבו ית' יכולת וחכמה לא יחשוב חלילה שהיכולת יפעל לחכמה, ולא שהיכולת אלוה, והחכמה אלוה (*Ibid.*)

122 Cf. *Neveh Shalom*, XII, I, 3:

נשאל לחכם ונאמר, אם אלה התארים העצמיים הם עצמותו, אם הם נוסף על עצמותו, שזה חלוקה הכרחית. אם יאמר שהם עצמותו, א"כ לא הרויח דבר בהניחו בקשת משה רבינו ע"ה התארים העצמיים . . . . אם יאמר שהתארים האלה, עם היותם נבדלים בחקנו, הם מתאחדים בחקו, אם כן גם עצמותו . . . . ואם יענה זה החכם שהשגת תאריו העצמיים הם בחינות שכליות, נשאלהו מאותם הבחינות, האם יובחנו בכח השכל היותם עצם או מקרה, וישוב הספק הא' למקומו, ואין לדבר סוף.

thought to be essential or accidental? and thus we land again on the horns of our previous dilemma, and so we may go on asking and answering like that *ad infinitum*.' The main point of this criticism, as it may be gathered, is that if things are one they must be identical, and if they are not identical they cannot be one. To take an object which is physically one, and call it two, because it is so conceived in thought, and then call it one again, because its parts are inseparable in thought, is past comprehension.

Another derogatory reference to Crescas's theory of attributes is found in Abrabanel's commentary on the *Moreh*. In his discussion of Attributes, Maimonides cites the view of a certain class of thinkers who had held that besides those attributes, which must be either identical with the essence or accidental to it, there are some which 'are neither His essence nor anything extraneous to his essence'. Dismissing this view as an utter absurdity, Maimonides remarks that 'it exists only in words, not in thought, much less in reality'; and that 'if a man were to examine for himself his own belief on the subject, he would see nothing but confusion and stupidity in an endeavour to prove the existence of things that do not exist, or to find a means between two opposites that have no means'. Commenting upon this passage, Abrabanel makes the statement that this view, which had been spurned by Maimonides, was afterwards taken up by Crescas.[123]

The influence of Crescas's theory of divine attributes

123 Cf. Abrabanel's commentary on the *Moreh*, I, 51:
אחרי שבטל הרב היות התארים עצמו . . . . ולא שיהיו יוצאים מעצמו . . . . זכר דעת ג׳, שהיה אצל קצת המדברים, שאמרו שהתארים המתוארים בו ית׳ אינם עצמו ואינם מקרה יוצא מעצמו, אבל הם דברים עצמיים בו, וזהו דעת הר׳ חסדאי במ״א מספרו.

may be traced in the *Principles*[124] of his pupil Joseph Albo. Albo's theory of attributes is eclectic rather than systematic, and Crescas's view is partly adapted by him as a prerequisite of his conception of necessary existence. Necessary existence, according to Albo, implies four conditions: unity, incorporeality, timelessness, and indeficiency;[125] a classification which, it must be observed, overlaps and could not stand the test of a logical analysis. The first of these conditions excludes separable attributes, both accidental and essential; the second excludes bodily emotions; the third, by inference, negates relation and similarity; the fourth rejects any implication of deficiency. Accordingly divine attributes are interpreted by Albo in the following ways: First, they are merely explanatory terms of necessary existence,[126] or what Maimonides calls 'names'.[127] Second, they are negations.[128] Third, they are actions.[129] Fourth, they are external relations, these being admissible.[130] But by arguments not unlike those employed by Crescas he is compelled by force of the fourth condition of necessary existence, namely, indeficiency, to omit the existence of essential positive attributes.[131] The compatibility of such attributes with unity is explained by him in a way which is again reminiscent of that of Crescas's explanation. Attributes, he says, have two aspects, in one of which they appear as perfections, and in the other as imperfections. Imperfections they are when they are acquired and in any way separable from the essence. They are pure perfections when they are innate in the

[124] *Ikkarim.* [125] Cf. II, 7. [126] Cf. II, 6 and 21.
[127] Cf. *Moreh*, I, 61. [128] Cf. *Ikkarim*, II, 10, 23, and 24.
[129] Cf. *ibid.*, II, 8. [130] Cf. *ibid.*
[131] Cf. *ibid.*, II, 21.

essence and inseparable from it. In God they are inseparable parts of His essence, and, therefore, they are pure perfections and likewise not subversive of His unity. That these pure perfections were not considered by him as identical with the essence, but rather essential to it, is quite clear from the context of his discussion, and that he was here consciously following Crescas may be inferred from his following conclusion: 'Note this well', he says, 'for it is a correct and true interpretation, and one which had been adopted by conservative theologians both ancient and modern.'[132] By ancient he undoubtedly refers to Saadia, and by modern he could not have meant anybody but Crescas, for Gersonides' reputation was not that of a conservative.

Joseph Albo, however, is inconsistent. Having accepted Crescas's explanation that inseparable attributes are not incompatible with divine unity, he rejects the same in the case of existence and unity. In a passage which has been entirely misunderstood by the Hebrew commentators he makes the following statement: 'The meaning of existence in its application to all created beings is by some philosophers taken to be accidental, while by others it is taken as something essential.' Now, the Hebrew commentators have understood this passage to refer to the Avicennean and the Averroesean controversy, 'something essential' thus meaning 'something identical with the essence'.[133] This is, however, manifestly wrong. By 'something essen-

[132] Cf. *ibid.*

[133] Cf. *ibid.*, II, I, and the commentary שרשים *ad loc.* The difficulties of this interpretation have been pointed out in a note (הגה"ה) which appears in the latest undated Wilna edition. The author of that note, too, has failed to see that Albo's reference is to the controversy between Crescas and the Avicennean group rather than that between the latter and Averroes.

tial' he could not have referred to anything but Crescas's theory, which reference alone can be construed with the rest of the text. After thus stating Avicenna's and Crescas's views with regard to the meaning of existence in its ordinary application, Albo proceeds as follows: 'But the term existence in its application to God cannot be accidental, for God is not subject to accidents, as will be demonstrated in the ninth chapter of this part, nor can it be something essential and superadded to its essence, for in this case the divine being would consist of two elements, which is impossible, as will be brought out in the fifth chapter of this part. Consequently existence in the case of God cannot be anything but identical with His essence.' The implication of this passage is clear. Crescas's interpretation of existence as an essential and inseparable condition of essence is discarded by Albo on the ground of its conflict with unity. Albo thus reverses his own position on the other attributes.

In our analysis of Moses Halavi's theory of divine attributes in a previous chapter, we have shown that the attributes to him are mere inventions of the mind, and thus while he interprets divine predicates positively, he does not admit the existence of divine attributes. Yet Crescas endeavours to show that Halavi, too, had believed in the existence of essential attributes. He proves his point indirectly, as an inference of Halavi's theory as to the emanation of plurality from unity. In order to be able fully to understand and appraise the force of Crescas's reasoning, let us give a brief analysis of the nature of the problem of emanation.

Assuming as an axiomatic truth that God is absolute simplicity, and that a simple cause can generate only a simple effect,[134] the question arises as to the origin of the plurality of elements that we observe in the universe. The answer to this question is based upon a combination of Plotinus's theory of emanation and Aristotle's theory of the spheres. There is God, the Absolute One, the Necessarily Existent, or by whatever other name He may be designated, whose knowledge of Himself, being a generative principle, produces the first intelligence. This Intelligence, says Alfarabi, consists of two generative elements, one due to its knowledge of God, and the other due to its knowledge of itself, the former producing the Second Intelligence, and the latter producing the outermost sphere.[135] Alfarabi's statement of the solution is correct in principle, but it is too general to account for the different elements of which the celestial spheres are supposed to be composed. For, according to the early Arabic philosophers, and Avicenna in particular, each sphere is composed, like the sublunar elements, of Matter and Form, and is endowed with a Soul, which is the efficient cause of its motion, and is presided over by an Intelligence, which is the final cause of the same. In Avicenna's statement of the solution, therefore, the self-knowledge of the First Intelligence is declared to contain as many elements as are necessary to explain all the component parts of the spheres. Avicenna's statement is variously reproduced in subsequent works. According to Sharastani, the reflection of the First Intelligence of his own spiritual essence produces the Form as well as the Soul of the First Sphere, the latter being

[134] As for the origin of this proposition, see Munk, *Mélanges*, p. 361; *Guide*, II, 22, p. 172, note 1; Steinschneider, *Al-Farabi*, p. 9, note 20; Kaufmann, *Attributenlehre*, p. 371, note 11.

[135] Cf. Alfarabi's ספר ההתחלות הנמצאות,
השניים . . . ישכיל הראשון וישכיל עצמותו.

nothing but the consummation of the former, whereas the existence of that Intelligence being mere possibility, produces the matter of the sphere.[136] Algazali's restatement of the case in his *Destruction of the Philosophers* is similar to that of Sharastani's, but, unlike the latter, he maintains that the self-knowledge of the First Intelligence would only account for the Soul of the Sphere, and consequently criticizes Avicenna for his failure to account for the origin of its Form.[137] In all these restatements, the origin of the Second Intelligence is said to be due, as is said by Alfarabi, to the reflection of the First Intelligence of God. In his *Intentions of the Philosophers*, however, Algazali gives a somewhat different and rather inadequate version of the case. The First Intelligence, he says, has two aspects. It is necessary existence in so far as it must come into being through its cause, but it is only possible existence when it is considered with respect to itself. Its necessary aspect, therefore, produces the Second Intelligence, whereas its possible aspect produces the First Sphere.[138] Abraham Ibn Daud, in his *Sublime Faith*, finds three elements in the First Intelligence, from which proceed the Second Intelligence, the First Sphere and its soul.[139] But curiously enough he does not state what these three elements are. Maimonides is probably following Alfarabi, naming only two elements in the First Intelligence, its knowledge of itself which produces the sphere and its knowledge of God which produces the Second Intelligence, and, like Algazali, he argues that this explanation does not account for the

[136] Cf. *Sharastani*, pp. 380-81 (Cureton's edition).

[137] Cf. Algazali's *Destruction of the Philosophers*, Disputation III.

[138] Cf. Algazali's *Intentions*, Metaphysics, V.

[139] Cf. *Emunah Ramah*, II, IV, 3.

component parts of the spheres.[140] Joseph Ibn Aknin, in his special treatise on the subject,[141] finds in the First Intelligence three elements: knowledge of God, knowledge of self, and knowledge of its being mere possible existence. The restatement of the case in later Hebrew works are unimportant, as they all follow secondary Hebrew authorities.

It is significant that in all the statements cited the knowledge of God on the part of the First Intelligence is referred to as one of the component parts, the most important one, producing the Second Intelligence. None of these authors, however, specifies what is meant by that knowledge of God, though we may infer that what they meant by it is the knowledge that God is the cause of its existence, since the divine essence itself must be unknowable. Again, the least important element, that which produces the Matter of the Sphere, is designated by them *the mere possibility of existence*.[142] Now, in Moses Halavi's enumeration of the threefold division in the First Intelligence, the first element is, as usual, called the *knowledge of God*,[143] but the third is described as *the knowledge of its being brought into being by the Necessarily Existent*,[144] which, of course, is another way of saying the *knowledge of its mere possible existence*. But in Crescas's paraphrase that expression is changed into *the knowledge of God as its cause and of itself as His effect*.[145] And so Crescas asks, what could Halavi have meant by

140 Cf. *Moreh*, II, 22.

141 Edited and translated into English by J. L. Magnes (Berlin, 1904).

142 אפשרות המציאות.

143 ישכיל מחוייב המציאות.

144 וישכיל עצמותו שהוא עלול למחוייב המציאות.

145 ואם מה שישיג היות עצמותו ית׳ עלה לו והוא עלול ממנו (Crescas's paraphrase, *Or Adonai*, I, III, 3, p. 25 b .

describing the first element as *knowledge of God*? The divine essence itself is unknowable. The comprehension of God as cause is in Crescas's paraphrase of Halavi exactly the phrase by which the third element is described. And to say that it refers to a negative knowledge of God is likewise impossible, since the negative knowledge of God is in its ultimate analysis the knowledge of His causality. Hence it must refer to the knowledge of God's essential attributes, which, concludes Crescas, goes to show that Moses Halavi admitted the existence of essential attributes. And in the same manner it can also be shown that Alfarabi, Avicenna, and Averroes admitted the existence of the same. Averroes, to be sure, rejects the theory of intermediary emanations, believing that all the Intelligences and Spheres emanate directly from the divine essence. Still, contends Crescas, while denying the causal interrelation of the Intelligences, Averroes believes in the presence of some qualitative differentiation between them. That qualitative differentiation must, of course, be due to a corresponding gradation in the simplicity of their comprehension of God. But that comprehension cannot be of the divine essence itself; it must be of the divine attributes, which, therefore, have existence. But, as we have seen, while Averroes admits that the term Intelligence in its application to God is a positive predicate, he is far from believing that it is an essential attribute of God in the same sense as it is understood by Crescas.

Let us now summarize the results we have arrived at in our inquiry. The origin of the problem of attributes, we have stated, lies in the incompatibility of four initial assumptions: the logical interpretation of Scriptural phraseology, the reality of logical relations, the anti-nominalistic view of universals, and the Avicennean definition of absolute simplicity. We have seen how the various attempts to solve the problem tended either to reject one or more of these assumptions, or to find some explanation in accordance with them. The naïve theologians, referred to by Maimonides, rejected the first assumption that the Scriptural predications are logical propositions. Maimonides retains all the four assumptions, and denying the existence of essential attributes in the divine being, interprets the Scriptural predications of God as privative judgements. Averroes, Gersonides, and Halavi, too, deny the existence of essential attributes in the divine being, but accepting of a nominalistic view of universals, and therewithal the non-reality of logical relations, interpret the Scriptural predications of God as positive judgements in which subject and predicate are only verbally related. Algazali's criticism of Avicenna aims to disqualify the latter's definition of absolute simplicity, and thereby affirms the existence of essential attributes. Finally, by advancing a new theory of universals, Crescas attempts to show the compatibility of essential attributes and absolute simplicity.

8

THE KALAM PROBLEM OF NONEXISTENCE AND SAADIA'S SECOND THEORY OF CREATION

THE second theory of creation reproduced by Saadia in his *Emunot ve-De'ot* presents intrinsically no difficulty. It has been fully explained, annotated and equipped with all the necessary and relevant references to sources. The main question, however, still remains unsolved and that is the origin of that theory in the form in which it is reproduced by him. While some students of Saadia are content with identifying it with a single theory in Greek philosophy, either atomism[1] or the Platonic theory of ideas,[2] others do not fail to see its composite nature. Jacob Guttmann sees in it a combination of the Platonic theory of an antemundate eternal matter and the theory of atomism,[3] while Neumark sees in it a combination of the Platonic theory of ideas and the theory of atomism.[4]

An examination of the text, however, leaves no doubt that this theory of creation contains all the three elements

[1] J. Fürst, *Glaubenslehre und Philosophie*, 1845, p. 69; A. Schmiedl, *Studien über jüdische, insonders jüdisch-arabische philosophie*, 1869, p. 281; M. Lambert, *Commentaire sur le Sefer Yesira*, 1891, French, p. 17, n. 3.

[2] W. Bacher, *Die Bibelexegese der jüdischen Religionsphilosophen*, 1892, p. 15, n. 2; M. Schreiner, *Der Kalâm in der jüdischen Literatur*, 1895, p. 9, n. 5.

[3] Jacob Guttmann, *Die Religionsphilosophie des Saadia*, 1882, p. 45; M. Ventura, *La Philosophie de Saadia Gaon*, 1934, p. 117.

[4] D. Neumark, *Geschichte der jüdischen Philosophie des Mittelalters*, I, 1907, pp. 448–449; *Toledot ha-Pilosofiah be-Yisrael*, II, 1929, pp. 120–121; *Toledot ha-'Ikkarim be-Yisra'el*, II, 1919, pp. 100–102; H. Malter, *Saadia Gaon*, 1921, p. 203.

which have been brought into play in the discusssion of its origin. That it contains the theory of atomism is indicated by the fact that that from which the world is created is described as "indivisible particles."[5] That it contains also the theory of an antemundane matter is indicated by the fact that its entire description of the process of creation,[6] with but a few slight variations, follows the description in the *Timaeus*.[7] That, finally, it contains the theory of ideas is indicated by the fact that Saadia finds supporters of this view among those who believed in the theory of ideas.[8] But how these three theories came to be combined, either by Saadia himself or by someone preceding him, is the question which needs an answer.

In our present paper we shall try to find such an answer. We shall first try to show how two of the elements which make up this composite second theory of creation reproduced by Saadia have already been combined in another problem discussed in the Kalam. Then we shall try to show how the third element happened to become combined with the other two.

The Kalam problem in which we shall try to find evidence of the first part of that combination is the problem of "privation" and "nonexistence." In its logical form this problem turns on the question as to what kind of opposites are "privation" as contrasted with "habit," and "nonexistence" as contrasted with "existence." Opposites (*ἀντικείμενα*, *mutaqabilāt*), according to Aristotle, may be either the opposites of contraries, (*ἐναντία*, *muḍādah*) or the opposites of privation (*στέρησις*, *'adam*) and habit

[5] *Emunot ve-De'ot* II, 3, Second Theory, Hebrew, p. 63, ll. 23–24; p. 64, l. 14; Arabic, p. 41, l. 15; p. 42, l. 12.

[6] *Ibid.*, Hebrew, pp. 63–64; Arabic, p. 41, l. 16–p. 42, l. 3.

[7] Cf. Guttmann, *op. cit.*, p. 46, nn. 2 and 3, and p. 47, n. 1.

[8] Hebrew, p. 65; Arabic, p. 43, l. 17 ff.; cf. Guttmann, *op. cit.*, pp. 47–48; Neumark, *loc. cit.*

(ἕξις, *malakah*). An illustration of the former is the opposites "goodness" and "badness;" an illustration of the latter is the opposites "sight" and "blindness."[9] Now in the case of the opposites of contraries, quite clearly each of the opposites is something, for "goodness" and "badness," for instance, are each something. But in the case of the opposition of "habit" and "privation," one of the opposites, like the habit "sight," for instance, is quite clearly something, but as for its opposite privation, like "blindness," for instance, the question may be raised whether it is something or nothing. A similar question may also be raised with regard to the term "nonexistent" (μὴ ὄν) as the opposite of the term "existent" (ὄν), which two terms are translated into Arabic by *ma'dūm* and *maujūd*. The question here is whether the terms "existent" and "nonexistent" are opposites of "contraries" or opposites of "habit" and "privation." If the former, then "nonexistent" is "something;" if the latter, then the question may be raised whether "nonexistent" is "something" or "nothing." There are thus two phases to the problem, one with regard to any "privation" as the opposite of some "habit," and the other with regard to the privation of "nonexistence" as the opposite of the habit "existence."

Let us now quote a few representative passages in which these two phases of the problem are stated.

The "privation" phase of the problem is restated by Maimonides in his exposition of the views of the Kalam. As defined by him, the Kalam held that "the nature of 'habits' is the same as the nature of their 'privation,' both being really existent accidents,"[10] which, as explained by

[9] Categ., c. 10, 11b, 13; cf. *Millot ha-Higgayon*, Ch. 11.
[10] *Moreh Nebukim* I, 73, Prop. 7.

him later, means that "the 'privations' of 'habits' are real things which exist in a body and superadded to its substance."[11] The meaning of this proposition, as may be gathered from Maimonides' own illustrations, is that "blindness," for instance, which Aristotle considers as the "privation" of "sight" and not as its "contrary," is considered by them as the "contrary" of sight and not as its "privation." According to them, therefore, every privation, such as "blindness," "rest," "death," is "something," in the same way as every member of two contraries, like "hot" and "cold," "white" and "green," good" and "bad," is something, according to Aristotle.[12]

The "nonexistent" phase of the problem is well stated in a lengthy passage in Baghdadi, of which I shall give here a brief but comprehensive analysis. (1) Al-Ṣāliḥī, agreeing on this point with the orthodox, held that the nonexistent (*al-ma'dūm*) is neither an object of knowledge (*ma'lūm*) nor an object of memory (*madhkūr*), nor a thing (*shai*), nor an essence (*dhāt*) or substance (*jauhar*), nor an accident (*'araḍ*). (2) Al-Ka'bī held that the nonexistent is a thing and an object of knowledge and an object of memory, but that it is not a substance nor an accident. (3) Al-Jubbā'ī and his son Abū Ḥāshim held that the nonexistent is a substance and an accident, but cannot be called a body (*jism*). (4) Al-Khaiyāt held that the nonexistent can also be called body but cannot be described as being in motion.[13] In the restatement of this last view by Shahrastani, al-Khaiyāt is said to have held that the "nonexistent" is an object of knowledge and an object of discourse (*mā yu'lamu wa-yukhbaru 'anihi*) and, while it cannot be described by the term existence (*wujūd*) or by

[11] *Ibid.*; discussion of Prop. 7.

[12] *Ibid.*

[13] Baghdadi, Cairo, 1910, p. 163, l. 17–p. 164, l. 14.

any of the terms which imply existence and creation (*ḥudūth*), it can be described by the term perseverance (*thubūt*).[14]

Historically, it is our opinion, the problem originally started with its "nonexistent" phase and that its subsequent extension to include the "privation" phase was due to the fact that in Arabic the same word *'adam* is the translation both of the Greek term for "nonexistence" and the Greek term for "privation." In our present paper, for the purpose of the inquiry at hand, we shall deal only with the "nonexistent" phase of the problem.

How the Kalam happened to raise the question whether the "nonexistent" is "something" or "nothing" has been explained in a variety of ways. Five possible origins of this problem have been suggested.

First, the Vaiśeṣika philosophy. In this philosophy, it is said, just as among some of the masters of the Kalam, the nonexistent is regarded as something real.[15] Now, it happens that the discussion of the problem of the nonexistence in the Kalam is couched in terms borrowed directly from Greek philosophy and consequently, whatever influence the Vaiśeṣika philosophy may have had on the Mutakallimūn, the problem itself was consciously associated by them with certain problems in Greek philosophy, and it is this association with problems in Greek philosophy for which we are to look.

Second, Democritus and Leucippus.[16] Both of these philosophers, according to Aristotle, affirmed the existence

[14] Shahrastani, ed. Cureton, p. 53, ll. 11–15.

[15] M. Horten, *Die philosophischen Systeme der spekulativen Theologen im Islam*, 1912, p. 4; cf. S. Pines, *Beiträge zur islamischen Atomenlehre*, 1936, p. 116, n. 2.

[16] M. Schreiner, *Der Kalâm in der jüdischen Literatur*, 1895, n. 5 on pp. 8–9; cf M. Horten, *Die philosophischen Probleme der Spekulativen Theologie im Islam*, 1910, p. 72, n. 1.

of a void in addition to that of a plenum, calling the former nonexistent (τὸ μὴ ὄν) and the latter existent (τὸ ὄν); as a result they were led to say that "the existent is in no respect more existent than the nonexistent,"[17] or, as it is reported directly in the name of Democritus, that "something (τὸ δέν) is in no respect more existent than nothing (τὸ μηδέν)."[18] Now, there can be no doubt that the Kalam in its discussion of the problem of the nonexistent has drawn upon the vocabulary used by Democritus and Leucippus, but the problem of the nonexistent discussed by the Kalam, as may be judged from the various contexts in which it occurs, has nothing to do with the question whether a vacuum does or does not exist.

Third, the Stoics.[19] In Stoicism, it is said, nonexistent things, such as centaurs and giants and other fictitious mythical beings, are described as an indefinite something (τί).[20] Here again, while the Stoic phraseology may have been used by those in the Kalam who discussed the problem of the nonexistent, this Kalam problem as to whether the nonexistent, prior to its coming into existence, is to be regarded as something, is logically quite different from the Stoic view that fictitious concepts which never come into existence are to be regarded as something.

Fourth, Plato's theory of ideas. Plato, it is argued, believes that existence is only an accident supervenient to a thing, and consequently that things in their ideal existence, even before their acquisition of the accident of existence, are still things.[21] Now, that there is an element

[17] *Metaph.* I, 4, 985b, 4–8.

[18] H. Diels, *Die Fragmente der Vorsokratiker*, 413, 11, quoting Plutarch, *Adv. Colot.* 4, p. 1108F.

[19] Pines, *op. cit.*, p. 117.

[20] Seneca, *Epistola* LVIII.

[21] S. Horovitz, *Ueber den Einfluss der griechischen Philosophie auf die Entwicklung des Kalam*, 1909, pp. 71–72.

of the Platonic theory of ideas in the Kalam problem of the nonexistent is, as we shall see, quite correct. But to say that what the Kalam calls nonexistent refers to Platonic ideas, and that these ideas are called nonexistent because they have not yet acquired the accidental or temporal existence characteristic of sensible things, is an assumption which cannot be sustained. Plato himself never describes the ideas as nonexistent. On the contrary, the ideas in their totality are described by him as "true substance" (*ἀληθινὴ οὐσία*),[22] as "existing in reality" (*ὄντως ὄν*),[23] as "existing absolutely" (*παντελῶς ὄν*),[24] and as "existing eternally" (*ἀεὶ ὄν*).[25] How then could these Platonic ideas come to be described as "nonexistent"?

Fifth, Plotinus. Plotinus in the Arabic version of his work, it is said, compares the ideas to a seed which is described by him as first hidden ((*ḫafiyyah*) in the earth and then appearing (*bān*) in the open and walking the road of existence (*kaun*) and actuality (*fi'l*).[26] On the basis of this comparison it is argued that though, according to Plotinus, the ideas while "hidden" in the intelligible world are to be regarded as "nonexistent," still even in their nonexistence they are to be regarded as "something."[27] But here, again, as in the preceding interpretation, despite this comparison to a seed, Protinus never describes the ideas as "nonexistent." On the contrary, like Plato, he describes them as "existent things" (*ὄντα*) and as "substances" (*οὐσίαι*).[28]

On the whole, the entire approach to the problem must

[22] *Sophist* 246B.

[23] *Phaedrus* 247E.

[24] *Sophist* 248E.

[25] *Timaeus* 27D.

[26] *Die sogenanute Theologie des Aristoteles*, ed. Fr. Dieterici, Arabic, p. 78, ll. 6–12.

[27] H. S. Nyberg, *Kleinere Schriften des Ibn al-Arabī*, 1919, pp. 51–52.

[28] *Enneads* V, 8, 5.

be different. We must not treat the Kalam discussion of whether the "nonexistent" is "something" or "nothing" as a mere collocation of terms, the origin of which is to be explained by some similar collocation of terms. We must assume that this discussion started with some real problem of vital importance to those who participated in it. In our study of this discussion, we must therefore first find the real and vital problem concealed behind it and then look for some reason why that problem was expressed in the form of a question as to whether the "nonexistent" is "something" or "nothing."

The real and vital problem, which to our mind is behind the discussion as to whether the "nonexistent" is "nothing" or "something," is the problem whether the world was created out of nothing or out of an antemundane matter. Islam, like Judaism and Christianity, started with a belief that this world of ours once had not existed and then came into existence. On this point the Koran is quite explicit. Restating the words of the Hebrew Scripture, it says: "We created the heavens and the earth and all that is between them in six days."[29] But as to the manner of creation, whether it was out of nothing or out of something, the Koran is no more explicit than the Hebrew Scripture. In fact quite a number of statements, such for instance, as that in which the Koran says, "Then He applied himself to the creation of heaven which then was but smoke,"[30] indicate that the creation of the world was out of something.[31] Now the philosophic religious tradition, known to Isalm undoubtedly from Christian speculations on the subject, formulated the belief of creation as a belief in the creation of the world out of the "nonexistent." Thus, the

[29] Sura 50:7; cf. also 11:9; 16:3;

[30] Sura 41:10.

[31] Cf. *Philosophie und Theologie von Averroes*, ed. M. J. Müller, Arabic, p. 13.

Second Book of Maccabees says that God made the heaven and earth "from things not existent (ἐξ οὐκ ὄντων).[32] Philo speaks of God as bringing forth "things that were nonexistent (τὰ μὴ ὄντα),"[33] and in Christianity the belief of creation is spoken of as a belief in the creation of all things "from the nonexistent" (ἐκ τοῦ μὴ ὄντος).[34] But all such formulations of the belief of creation were in themselves indecisive with regard to the nature of creation, for in philosophic vocabulary the term "nonexistent" (μὴ ὄν) had two distinct meanings. On the one hand, it meant "nothing." Thus Aristotle says that "the nonexistent (τὸ μὴ ὄν) is nothing (μηδέν)" and not a "something (τὶ)."[35] But on the other hand, the "nonexistent" meant "matter." Thus, again, Aristotle says that the Platonists who refer to matter as "the great and small" identify it with the nonexsitent (τὸ μὴ ὄν).[36] In the light of this common formulation of the belief of creation in terms of "nonexistent" and in the light also of these two meanings of the term "nonexistent," the problem whether the world was created out of nothing or out of an antemundane matter thus took the form of a question whether the term "nonexistent" in the common formulation of the belief of creation was "nothing" or "something." Those who believed the world was created out of nothing maintained that the term "nonexistent" meant "nothing;" those who believed in creation out of an antemundane matter maintained that the "nonexistent" meant "something." Thus the seemingly verbal problem whether the nonexistent is something or nothing started with what was then one of the most vital problems, namely, whether the world was created out of an antemundane matter or out of nothing.

[32] 2 Macc. 7.28.

[33] *De Opificio Mundi* 26, 81; *De Mutatione Nominum* 5, 46.

[34] *Shepherd of Hermas*, Book II, Command. 1.

[35] *De Gen. et Corr.* I, 3, 318a, 15.

[36] *Physics* I, 9, 192a, 6–7.

But it will be noticed that those in the Kalam who believed in an antemundane matter are not satisfied with the mere description of the term "nonexistent" in the common formula of creation as "something." They all maintain that it is to be described not only as "something" but also as being (1) an object of knowledge, (2) an object of memory, and (3) an object of discourse.[37] Now these three descriptions of the "nonexistent" are reminiscent of the descriptions of the Platonic ideas, for the Platonic ideas are said to have the following characteristics: (1) they are the object of knowledge (*γνῶσις*,[38] *ἐπιστήμη*[39]); (2) they are "an object for thought (*τὸ νοεῖν*)," i. e., an object of memory, for they are remembered, even when the practical things of which they are the ideas have perished;[40] (3) they enable us to carry on a discussion (*διαλέγεσθαι*.),[41] i. e., they are an object of discourse. Furthermore, the controversy as to whether the nonexistent can be described as substance and accident[42] seems to reflect Aristotle's argument against the Platonic theory of ideas on the ground that on the one hand there must be ideas both of substances and accidents and on the other there can be no ideas of accidents.[43] So also when it is said that the nonexistent cannot be described as body and as being in motion,[44] it corresponds to Plato's description of the ideas as incorporeal (*ἀσώματα*)[45] and as remaining for ever immovably (*ἀκινήτως*) in the same state.[46] Finally, the statement that the nonexistent cannot be described

[37] Cf. above, at nn. 13 and 14.
[38] *Cratylus* 440B.
[39] *Metaph.* I, 9, 990b, 11–12.
[40] *Ibid.*, 14–15.
[41] *Parmenides* 135C.
[42] Cf. above, at n. 13.
[43] *Metaph.* I, 9, 990b, 22–991a, 8.
[44] Cf. above, at n. 13.
[45] *Sophist* 246B.
[46] *Timaeus* 38A.

by terms suggestive of existence dependent upon creation but can be described by the term perseverance,[47] undoubtedly means that it cannot be described by any of the terms suggestive of temporal existence, but can be described by terms meaning non-temporal existence. This undoubtedly reflects such statements in Plato in which he says that before creation there was no time and that in the world of ideas there is only unchanging eternity but no time, the latter being only a moving likeness of eternity.[48]

From all this it is quite evident that those in the Kalam who adopted the Platonic theory of an antemundane matter, calling it "nonexistent" and describing it as "something," conceived of it also after the manner of the Platonic ideas and described it by all the characteristic terms of the Platonic ideas. In other words the Platonic antemundane matter becomes with those Mutakallamūn one of the Platonic ideas, with the result that when they said the world was created out of an antemundane matter they meant that the world was created out of an ideal matter. Now such a view could not have arisen directly from Plato, for in Plato the antemundane matter is definitely something apart from the ideas, and is not included within the ideas, nor does it arise from them. Still, we shall try to show, this transformation of the nature of the antemundane matter was not done by them arbitrarily; it was due to the influence of Plotinus, whose philosophy is not only based upon a special interpretation of Plato but was also taken in Arabic philosophy to represent true Platonism.

In Plotinus, as understood by his Arabic interpreters, matter is not something apart from the ideas; it is something which emanates from the ideas. Within the totality of the ideas, which he calls Intelligence or the intelligible

[47] Cf. above, at n. 14.

[48] *Timaeus* 37C–38B.

world, there is according to him an intelligible matter (ὕλη νοητή) out of which the matter of the sensible world comes into existence by a process of emanation. Since, however, Plotinus, unlike Plato, does not consider the world as having been created in time, his intelligible matter out of which the world emanated did not precede the world. His intelligible matter, therefore, cannot be described as an antemundane matter; it can be described only as a supramundane matter. Now those Mutakallimūn who maintain that the nonexistent is something, while following Plotinus in his conception of an intelligible matter, agree with Plato in his belief in the creation of the world. The Plotinian supramundane matter thus becomes with them also a Platonic antemundane matter. With them, therefore, the old formula that the world was created out of the nonexistent came to mean, on the one hand, as in Plato, out of an antemundane matter, but on the other hand, as in Plotinus, out of a supramundane matter, which supramundane matter is not only something but is also to be described by all those predicates characteristic of the ideas. If those Mutakallimūn were to quote proof-texts in justification of their view, they could have quoted those passages in Plotinus in which he says that "matter" (ὕλη) or "nonexistence" (τὸ μὴ ὄν) or privation (στέρησις), in the sense of the opposite of "things that exist in reason" (τὰ ἐν λόγῳ ὄντα) or of "habit" (ἕξις), is a "something" (τι)[49] and that intelligible matter is still further to be described as "existent" (ὄν)[50] and as "substance" (οὐσία).[51]

That the problem of whether the "nonexistent" is "nothing" or "something" is, as we have tried to show,

[49] *Enneads* II, 4, 16.
[50] *Ibid.*
[51] *Ibid.* II, 4, 5.

primarily a circuitous way of stating the problem whether the world was created out of nothing or out of an antemundane eternal matter, may be corroborated by a statement in Baghdadi. In the passage reproduced above, after enumerating the various views among those who maintained that the nonexistent is something, he says that Al-Jubbaā'ī has condemned Al-Khaiyāt's view on the ground that it leads to the belief in "the eternity of bodies,"[52] and he himself condemns Al-Jubbā'ī also on the ground that his view similarly leads to the belief in the "eternity of substances and accidents."[53] In other words, the various views as to the meaning of the doctrine that the nonexistent is something, all mean that the world was created out of an eternal antemundane matter, and consequently they all imply that the world, though created, is somehow eternal.

We have thus shown how two of the three elements in Saadia's second theory of creation, namely, the antemundane matter and the ideas of Plato, have already been combined in the view of those Mutakallimūn who maintained that the "nonexistent" is "something." We shall now try to show the reasoning by which either Saadia himself, or somebody before him, has added to these two elements also the element of atomism.

The Mutakallimūn were atomists. To them the world is composed of atoms. On this point there was no difference between those who maintained that the world was created out of nothing and those who maintained that it was created out of an antemundane matter. There was, however, a difference between them. To the former group, consistent with their belief in creation out of nothing, the atoms out of which the world is composed were them-

[52] Baghdadi, p. 165, ll. 3–5.
[53] *Ibid.*, p. 165, ll. 5–9.

selves created by God out of nothing. To the latter group, consistent with their belief in an antemundane matter, the atoms out of which the world is composed were themselves eternal and constituted that antemundane matter out of which the world was created. Accordingly, those in the Kalam who interpreted the term "nonexistent" in the traditional formula of creation as being "something," i. e., the Platonic antemundane matter, and as being an object of knowledge and of memory and of discourse or also as a substance and accident, i. e., the Plotinian intelligible matter, considered it also as being a conglomeration of atoms, and these atoms naturally had to be intelligible or ideal atoms. On some other occasion, in a special study of Plato, we shall try to explain what justification there was for this superimposition of the atomic theory upon his antemundane matter.

These three elements are combined in Saadia's second theory of creation as stated by him in his *Emunot ve-De'ot*. The opening statement is rather vague. It reads: "The second theory is that of him who says that [composite] bodies have a Creator, with whom from eternity there had been spiritual things, out of which He created these composite bodies."[54] In this statement, it will be noticed, all that Saadia says of that out of which the "composite bodies" were created is that it is to be called "spiritual things." Now the terms "spiritual things" by themselves mean neither atoms nor antemundane matter, nor does the term "spiritual" by itself mean "ideal," for the term "spiritual" (*ruḥāniyy*), reflecting as it does the Greek term πνευματικός, does not necessarily mean "intelligible" or

[54] *Emunot ve-De'ot* I, Hebrew, p. 63; Arabic, p. 41, ll. 10–12. The reading of the Hebrew text is to be corrected on the basis of the Arabic to read as follows: והדעת השנית דעת מי שאמר שיש בורא לגשמים ועמו דברים רוחניים קדמונים ומהם ברא אלה הגשמים המורכבים. Cf. Bacher, *loc. cit.*

"ideal" (νοητικός). But in the course of his discussion, as we have pointed out above, Saadia makes it quite clear that this theory has reference to the Platonic antemundane matter. He makes it also quite clear that it has reference to atoms. While indeed he does not make it explicitly clear that the term spiritual is used by him in the sense of ideal, from his statement that some Jews identified these "spiritual things" with the Platonic ideas, it is quite evident that at least according to some upholders of this view these antemundane atoms were ideal atoms. In his statement that the world was created out of "spiritual things," the term "things" undoubtedly has reference to the view that the "nonexistent" out of which the world was created was a "thing." We thus find that there is both a reason and a history to the combination of the three doctrines in Saadia's second theory of creation.

Unlike the second theory of creation in the *Emunot ve-De'ot*, which is a combination of three elements, is the second theory of creation in the Commentary on *Sefer Yeṣirah*.[55] Of the three elements combined in the theory of the former work, namely, atoms, antemundane matter, and ideas, the theory of the latter work contains only two, namely, atoms and antemundane matter. In its bare outline, this theory is represented here as maintaining that the visible and composite things in the world have their origin in a simple thing" (*shai basīt*), described also as the root" (*aṣl*) of "these [composite] things" (*hadhihi al-ashyā'*).[55a] That the second theory in the Commentary on *Sefer Yeṣirah* reflects the atomistic view is clearly brought out in his description of that "simple thing" or "root," i. e., the matter, from which the world was created as consisting

[55] *Tafsīr Kitāb al-Mabadī*, ed. M. Lambert, p. 4, l. 5 ff.

[55a] *Ibid.*, p. 4, ll. 5–7. I take the words *hadhihi al-ashyā'* to mean 'these [composite] things" rather than "these [simple] things."

of "indivisible parts" (*ajzā' lā tatajazza'*)[56] which is a direct translation of the Greek ἄτομα. That it also reflects the Platonic antemundane matter may be discerned in Saadia's description of that "simple root" as mother (*umm*), clay (*ṭīnah*) and hyle (*hayūla*),[57] terms which either Plato himself or Aristotle had used in describing the antemundane matter.[58] Further evidence for the combination of atomism and the Platonic antemundane matter in the presentation of this view is to be discerned in Saadia's statement that the upholders of this theory are divided into three groups (1) "Those who maintain that that eternal element was completely combined and composed by the Creation, so that nothing remained of it in its original state; (2) those who maintain that the Creator did not combine it completely, that this world has used up only part of it, and that the remainder is still unused, subsisting in its state of simplicity and tenuity; (3) those who maintain that while all of it has been used up in composition, not all of it has been used up by this world, for there proceeded from it an innumerable number of worlds, of which this world of ours is only one."[59] Now of these three groups, the first reproduces what Plato himself says of the four elements out of which the world was created, namely, that "the making of the universe took up the whole bulk of each of these four elements" so that "nothing was left over whereof another world should be formed."[60] The second and third

[56] *Ibid.*, p. 4, l. 7. [57] *Ibid.*, p. 4, l. 11.

[58] The term "mother" (*umm*) as a description of matter occurs in *Timaeus* 51A. The term "hyle" (*hayūla*) for matter is Aristotelian. The term "clay" (*ṭinah*), I think, is here a translation of the Greek ἐκμαγεῖον, "that on which an impression is made," such as a lump of wax or clay or any other similar stuff, which is used by Plato in *Timaeus* 50C as a description of matter. This is probably also the origin of the use of the Hebrew term חומר as a translation of the Greek *hyle.*

[59] *Tafsīr*, p. 5, ll. 4–9; French, pp. 18–19.

[60] *Timaeus* 32C–33A.

groups represent two phases of the atomistic theory, first, that not all the atoms were used up at one time, so that in the infinite space atoms are still floating aimlessly, from which, worlds are from time to time being formed,[61] and, second, that our world is one of an innumerable number of worlds.[62] But, it will be noticed, throughout his entire discussion of this second theory in his commentary on *Sefer Yeṣirah*, Saadia makes no allusion at all to the theory of ideas.

Saadia himself, however, out of all the theories of creation enumerated by him in his *Emunot ve-De'ot* and his commentary on *Sefer Yeṣirah*, has selected the theory of creation from absolute nothing as representing what he considered as the true scriptural belief of creation. By his denial of the Platonic theory of an antemundane matter, which, as we have seen, is based upon the interpretation of the term "nonexistent" as meaning a "thing," Saadia thus aligns himself with those who maintain, in the language of the time, that the nonexistent is not a thing (*al-ma'dūm laisa shai*).[63] Consequently in his statement of what he believes to be the true scriptural belief of creation he describes it as a belief that creation is "not from something" (*lā min shai*),[64] intimating thereby that the term "nonexistent" in the traditional formula of creation does not mean that it is "something." So also with regard to the "privation" phase of the problem, he similarly aligns himself with those who deny that "privation" is "something." In one place, arguing against Manichaeism, he maintains that darkness is not the contrary (*muḍādah*) of lights but a privation (*'adam*) thereof, and in the course of

[61] Diogenes, X, 89.
[62] *Idem*, X, 45 and 73.
[63] Ibn Ḥazm, V, Cairo, 1317–21, A. H. p. 42, l. 11.
[64] *Emunot ve-De'ot* I, Hebrew, p. 54: לא מדבר; Arabic, p. 30, l. 18; *Tafsir Kitāb al-Mabādī*, p. 5, 1.3.

his discussion he makes it clear that "privation" to him is not something.[65] In another place he says that "bodies" have no contrariety (*ḍidd*) to them, with the result that if God does not create them "there will not exist anything except God,"[66] the implication being that the opposite of body is not a "contrary" but rather a "privation," and that "privation" is "not something."

That by his use of the expression "not from something" in the formulation of what he considered the true belief of creation Saadia had reference to the problem whether the "nonexistent" is "something" or "nothing," is clearly brought out by him in his commentary on *Sefer Yeṣirah.* Explaining the meaning of his formula, he says: "We say 'He created something not from something,' but we do not say 'He created something from nothing.' In the same way we have translated the verse [in Job 26.7] to read 'He hangeth the earth not upon something' and we have not translated it to read 'He hangeth earth upon nothing.'[67] We hint thereby to the opinion that 'nothing' is 'something,' for the principle of belief laid down here is that the Creator created air not from something."[68] The passage would seem to be a mere quibble in words. But this what Saadia means to say. The Arabic *lā shai* which we have translated tentatively by the negative term "nothing" may in Arabic be translated also by the term "no-thing." The latter is what Aristotle, and after him Arabic logicians, call an indefinite or infinite term (*ὄνομα ἀόριστον, ism ghair*

[65] *Emmunot ve-De'ot* I, Fifth theory, Hebrew, p. 70, Arabic, p. 53, ll. 7 ff.

[66] *Ibid.* I, 4, Hebrew, p. 82; Arabic, p. 72, ll. 14–15; cf. also IV, 3, Hebrew, p. 128; Arabic, p. 151, ll. 14–15. Cf. Guttmann, *op. cit.*, pp. 82–83.

[67] Cf. *Version arabe du livre de Job de R. Saadia*, ed. W. Bacher, 1899, p. 80.

[68] Cf. *Tafsīr Kitāb al-Mabādī* IV, 5, p. 84, ll. 3–6; French, p. 106.

muḥaṣṣal).[69] Now, in Aristotle, as interpreted in Arabic philosophy, the indefinite judgment "A is not-just," as distinguished from the negative judgment "A is not just," does *not* mean that the subject "A" is *not* by its very nature "just."[69a] By the same token, whenever any subject "A" is said to be "no-thing," it does *not* mean that that subject is *not* by its very nature a "thing." Accordingly, as the Arabic phrase *min la shai* may mean "from no-thing," the term "no-thing" may thus be an indefinite term, with all the implications of such a term, whereas the Arabic phrase *la min shai*, meaning "not from something," cannot be taken as an indefinite term. The same distinction is also to be made between the two Arabic phrases which may be translated respectively by "upon no-thing" and "not upon something." Now, says Saadia, in view of the fact that some Mutakallimūn maintain that the "nonexistent" in the traditional formula of creation means "something" and that the world therefore was created out of an antemundane matter, if we use the formula *min lā shai*, it may be taken to mean "from no-thing," and that "no-thing," being not a negative term but rather an indefinite term, may be taken to mean "something." Such a formula of creation could thus be taken to mean that the world was created out of "something." In the formula of creation we must therefore use the phrase *lā min shai*,[70] which means "not from something," thus removing any misapprehension.

[69] *De Interpr.*, c. 12, 16a, 32a.

[69a] Concerning this interpretation of Aristotle, see my papers "Infinite and Privative Judgments in Aristotle, Arabic Philosophy, and Kant," to be published in *Philosophy and Phenomenological Research*, and "Maimonides on Negative Attributes," *Ginzberg Jubilee Volume*, pp. 432–437. Above, p. 195.

[70] So also Alfarabi uses the expression *lā 'an shai* (*Alfārābī's philosophische abhandlungen*, Arabic text, ed. Fr. Dieterici, 1899, p. 23 ll. 15–16). In Judah bar Barzilai's *Perush Sefer Yeṣirah*, p. 76, l. 20, however, the formula for creation reads: וברא הכל מלא כלום ומלא דבר ומאין ומאפס.

In the light of this interpretation of the statement of Saadia, we can understand why Maimonides, in his phrasing of his belief in creation, uses the expression "not from something" (*lā min shai*) and "after nonexistence" (*ba'd 'adam*),[71] instead of the expressions "from nothing" (*min lā shai*) and "from nonexistence" (*min 'adam*). The reason why he does not approve of the latter two expressions is that they might be taken to mean, as Saadia said, that the world was created from "no-thing" or "nonexistent" which may be "something" or "matter." The mediaeval Latin translation of Maimonides renders the two expressions here by *non est de aliquo* and *post privationem*.[72] St. Thomas, evidently having understood the significance of the phrasing used by Maimonides, maintains that the true meaning of the phrase *ex nihilo* in the common expression *creatio ex nihilo* is either (1) *post nihil*, i. e., Maimonides' *post privationem*, or (2) *non fit ex aliquando*, i. e., Maimonides' *non est de aliquo*.[73] All this ultimately goes back to Saadia's attempt to express his opposition to the view that the "nonexistent" is "something."

We have thus seen how for various reasons in the Kalam, the antemundane matter of Plato was combined with the intelligible matter of Plotinus, whereby it became an ideal matter, and also how these two were combined with atoms, whereby the atoms became ideal atoms. Various combinations of these doctrines have been examined by us here.

[71] *Moreh Nebukim* II, 13, Second View, end: שאנחנו נאמין היות השמים לא מדבר אלא אחר ההעדר. Earlier in the same view there occurs the expression *min lā shai*. But from the Hebrew translation of this phrase by לא מדבר, rather than מן לא דבר, both in Ibn Tibbon and in Ḥarizi, it may be inferred that the original reading in the Arabic was *lā min shai*. For the use of the expression *ba'd 'adam*, see also *Moreh Nebukim* II, 2.

[72] *Rabi Mosei Aegyptij Dux seu Director dubitantium aut perplexorum* Lib. II, cap. XIV, Paris, 1520, fol. 47a, l. 18.

[73] *Sum. Theol.* I, 45, 1, ad 3.

First, in the doctrine of some of the Mutakallimūn that "nonexistence" is "something" we have found a combination, through the influence of Plotinus, of Plato's antemundane matter with his ideas. Second, in Saadia's second theory of creation in his commentary on *Sefer Yeṣirah*, we have found that the combination is only of Plato's antemundane matter with atomism. Third, in Saadia's second theory of creation in his *Emunot ve-De'ot*, there is a combination of all the three elements. Then we have also seen how Saadia's formulation of his belief of creation as a creation "not from something" is directly aimed at the belief of an antemundane matter which is implied in the doctrine that "the nonexistent is something." This formulation of the belief of creation is adopted by Maimonides and through him also by St. Thomas.

9

ATOMISM IN SAADIA

IN OUR paper on "The Kalam Problem of Nonexistence and Saadia's Second Theory of Creation,"[1] we have tried to show that the second theory of creation in the *Emunot ve-De'ot* consists of a combination of three elements, namely, atomism, antemundane matter, and ideas. The first two elements in the combination are explicitly described as such by Saadia himself; the third element is only indirectly indicated by him in his testimony that the "spiritual things" were identified by some Jews with the preexistent Wisdom in Proverbs, ch. 8. So interpreted, the second theory of creation maintains that the world was created directly out of an ideal atomic matter. While there is no historical antecedent of a theory stating that the world was created directly out of an ideal atomic matter, there is a historical antecedent of a theory that the world was created indirectly out of an ideal atomic matter, for those Kalam atomists who maintained that the "nonexistent" is "something" meant thereby, as we have tried to show, that the atomic matter out of which the world was created was in its turn created out of an ideal atomic matter. We have also tried to show that the second theory of creation in Saadia's Commentary on *Sefer Yeṣirah* is a combination of only two elements, atoms and antemundane matter, with the result that according to this theory the world was created out of an atomic matter not necessarily ideal. For this latter combination, we may add, there is a definite source, and

[1] *JQR*, 36 (1946), 371–391. Above, pp. 338–358.

that is Muḥammad b. Zakkariyyā al-Rāzī (d. 923/24 C.E.), according to whom the world was created out of atoms, which atoms he calls "absolute matter" (*al-hayūla al-mutlaqah*) — terms reflecting the Greek χωριστὴ ὕλη (*De Caelo* II, 1, 329b, 13 and 15), by which Aristotle describes the Platonic antemundane matter.[2] Al-Rāzī's theory is thus a combination of atomism and antemundane matter.

In both these versions of the second theory of creation, then, except for the difference that in one version the immediate antemundane atomic matter is ideal, whereas in the other it is not ideal, the world was created out of atoms. It is our purpose now to find out which of the particular conceptions of atoms current at his time Saadia had in mind. For already at the time of Saadia there existed a difference of opinion in Arabic philosophy with regard to the question whether atoms have magnitude or have no magnitude.[3] Now Saadia, in his description of the atoms, in his second theory in the *Emunot ve-De'ot*, happens to describe atoms as "points." The question naturally arises whether by his use of the term "points" as the equivalent of the term "atoms" he meant to indicate that the atoms spoken of by him are like mathematical points without magnitude.

In attempting to answer the question, we shall try to examine the various implications of the identification of the term atom with the term point, or the comparison between these two terms, found in certain texts relevant to our inquiry.

The earliest Arabic text in which the terms "atom" and "point" are known to have been identified is found in Isaac Israeli's *Sefer ha-Yesodot*. In one place in that work,

[2] Cf. S. Pines, *Beiträge zur islamischen Atomenlehre*, 1936, pp. 40–45.

[3] *Kitābu 'l-masā'il fi'l-ḫilaf bejn al-Baṣrijjīn wa'l-Baġdādijjīn*, ed. A. Biram, 1902, Text, p. 38; Introd., p. 46.

referring to the Mu'tazilites, he reproduces their view in the form of a statement that "bodies are composed of atoms,"[4] but in another place, previous to the statement just quoted, referring again to the Mu'tazilites in general, and to Naẓẓām in particular,[5] he says that "what may be understood from their words is that body is composed of atoms, that is to say, points."[6] From this identification of the atoms of the Mu'tazilites with points one would be tempted to infer that the atomists in this statement conceived of the atoms as having no magnitude. But the validity of such an inference is somewhat shaken when one studies closely Israeli's refutation of this Mu'tazilite type of atomism. In his refutation he argues that the atoms must inevitably either have magnitude or have no magnitude,[7] both of which alternatives he shows to be untenable. Now this suggestion of two alternative possibilities with regard to the nature of atoms may be nothing but a purely logical division of the problem. Still, inasmuch as we know that at the time of Israeli there was a controversy over this very question, we may be justified in assuming that his logical division of the problem is an allusion to two views which existed among his contemporaries. Accordingly, the designation of atoms as points may mean here merely a general comparison between these two terms with regard to indivisibility which is characteristic of both of them, without any commitment on the question whether the atoms have magnitude or have no magnitude.

[4] *Sefer ha-Yesodot*, ed. S. Fried, p. 49: הגופים מורכבים מחלקים שאינם מתחלקים.

[5] On the question whether Naẓẓām's view is misrepresented by Israeli or not, see Jacob Guttmann, *Die philosophischen Lehren des Isaak ben Salomon Israeli*, 1911, p. 17, n. 1; Pines, *op. cit.*, p. 95, n. 2.

[6] *Ibid.*, p. 43: הגוף מורכב מחלקים שאינם נחלקים, שר"ל הנקודות.

[7] *Ibid.*, pp. 49–50: מפני שהחלקים שאינם מתחלקים לא יסורו מלהיות אם בעלי מרחק או לא בעלי מרחק.

Similarly, referring to Democritus, Israeli attributes to him the statement that "a body is composed of planes and planes are composed of lines and lines are composed of points."[8] Here, too, it would seem that his conception of the atom of Democritus is that of something analogous to a point which has no magnitude. Still in his discussion of this statement of Democritus he seems to be in doubt whether by atom called point is meant something which has magnitude or something which has no magnitude, even though he is certain that it is indivisible. Inasmuch, however, as we know that the genuine view of Democritus concerning the atoms is that they have magnitude and that they are indivisible only physically but not mathematically,[9] we may ask ourselves whether this was not exactly what Israeli took Democritus' view to be and, if he does call the atoms points, perhaps he calls them points, again, only by way of a general comparison with regard to their indivisibility.[10]

The uncertainty as to what Israeli meant by his identification of the term "point" with the term "atom" does not exist in another such identification which is to be found in Shahrastani. In a chapter devoted to an exposition of the atomism of the Kalam, after stating that a point is

[8] *Ibid.*, p. 43: כי החכם דימאקראטוס היה אומר הגוף מורכב משטחים והשטחים מורכבים מקוים והקוים מורכבים מנקודות.

[9] Cf. Zeller, *Die Philosophie der Griechen* II, 1[5], p. 857, n. 3. (English, II, p. 225, n. 2); Burnet, *Early Greek Philosophy*[3], p. 336; E. Frank, *Plato und die sogenanten Pythagoreer*, p. 52 ff.

[10] Isaac Israeli is assumed to have misunderstood Democritus (cf. Jacob Guttmann, *op. cit.*, pp. 13 and 62. But as we shall see (n. 20), the designation of Democritus' atoms as points is found in Aristotle. Moreover, shortly before the passage in which Aristotle designates Democritus' atoms or points (*De Anima* I, 4, 409a, 11–12), there occurs the statement "that a line by its motion generates a surface and that a point by its motion generates a line" (4–5). Israeli's restatement of the view of Democritus is undoubtedly based upon these two statements in Aristotle.

"something indivisible," he adds "and this is the atom according to the Mutakallimun."[11] Immediately after that, however, he explicitly states that the atom of the Mutakallimun, unlike a point, is "a magnitude (*hajm*) which has body (*juththah*) and measurement (*misāḥah*)."[12] From the context of the discussion it is quite evident that the analogy of the point is introduced only as an illustration of the indivisibility of the atom, without any implication that the atom has no magnitude. In other words, despite this analogy of the point, the atom is still conceived as having magnitude, its indivisibility being only physical and not mathematical. In the light of this, is it not possible that Israeli's description of Democritus' atoms as points means nothing more than that?

A third instance of the identification of the terms "atom" and "point" is found in Ibn Gabirol's *Fons Vitae*. In the course of the dialogue between the Master and the Disciple, the latter happens to remark: "I do not say that a body is composed of parts which are indivisible (*ex partibus quae non dividuntur*) in actuality, that is to say, points."[13] As the Latin expression *partes quae non dividuntur* is a literal translation of the Arabic *al-ajzā' allatī lā tatajazzā'*, the latter of which is the Arabic technical expression for "atoms," the Disciple has thus identified atoms with points. Thereupon the Master rebukes him, saying that the "ambiguity of terms" has led him to think that "the term point and the term atom are to be taken to have the same meaning."[14]

[11] *Kitāb Nihāyat al-Iqdām fī 'ilm al-Kalām*, ed. A. Guillaume, 1934, p. 507. 11.14–15.

[12] *Ibid.*, 1. 19.

Pines (*op. cit.*, p. 96, n.) mentions also Faḫr al-Dīn as one who identifies atoms with points. The identification of atoms with points occurs also in Shem-Ṭob on *Moreh Nebukim* I, 73, Prop. 1, and Eṣ Ḥayyim, Ch. 4, p. 14.

[13] *Fons Vitae* II, 16, p. 52, ll. 16–17 (ed. C. Baeumker).

[14] *Ibid.*, ll. 22–24.

From the Master's subsequent remark it becomes clear that the reason for this confusion on the part of the Disciple is due to the fact that both atom and point are described as being "the smallest part (*minimam partem*) of a quantity."[15] There is no indication, however, as to whether the atom, on the basis of its analogy with the point, was also conceived as having no magnitude.

These identifications of the term atom with the term point, we shall now try to show, go back to certain analogies made by Aristotle between the atom and the point, and in Aristotle, as we shall see, these analogies between the atom and the point are made even though the atom spoken of by him is that of Democritus, concerning which he explicitly says that it has magnitude. Two such analogies are found in Aristotle.

The first analogy occurs in a passage in which, speaking of the Platonists, he says that from one standpoint they treat unity, which is their first principle, as a mathematical point and, when they do so, then like the atomists "they put things together out of that which is the smallest part."[16] Here it is quite clear that the point spoken of is a mathematical one and is without magnitude and the atom spoken of is one which has magnitude. Still an analogy is drawn between them. But, when we examine the nature of the analogy, we find that it is only for a special limited purpose, namely, to show that the unit of the Platonists is to be regarded as the matter out of which numbers are composed, just as the atom of the atomists is regarded as the matter out of which existing things are composed. But it will be noticed that in this passage the term "smallest part" (ἐλάχιστον) is applied by Aristotle to the "atom" and the Platonists are accused by him of treating their points

[15] *Ibid.*, l. 25.

[16] *Metaph.* XIII, 8, 1084b, 25–28.

as if they were atoms and smallest parts. This is undoubtedly the source of Ibn Gabirol's statement that the Disciple's confusion of the terms "atom" and "point" was due to the fact that both of these seemed to him to have been described by the term "the smallest part (*minima pars*)."

The second analogy occurs in a passage which I shall analyze here according to the Arabic version of that passage and also according to Averroes' interpretation of it, as both of these are found in Averroes' Long Commentary on *De Anima*. In that passage, Aristotle argues against Xenocrates who maintains that the soul is a self-moving number, that is to say, a number consisting of units having position, i.e., points, each of which is self-moving.[17] At first, Aristotle tries to show that such units, because they have only position and no magnitude, could not be self-moving.[18] Then, conceding that Xenocrates might be using the term point not in its strictly mathematical sense but in the sense of a small extended body or the atom of Democritus, he tries to show that even then Xenocrates' definition of soul would be open to objections.[19] The passage in which the term point is said to be used in the sense of a small extended body or the atom of Democritus reads, according to the Arabic version of Aristotle, as follows: "One might say that there is no difference between the units spoken of under this assumption and the small bodies, for the little round atoms of Democritus become points."[20] On the last part of this quotation Averroes comments as follows: "What Aristotle means thereby, as it seems to

[17] *De Anima* I, 4, 408b, 32 ff.

[18] *Ibid.*, 409a, 1–3.

[19] *Ibid.*, 10–18.

[20] *De Anima*, Liber I, Text. 69 (*Aristotlis opera omnia*, Venice, 1574, Vol. VI, fol. 35F): *Et potest homo dicere quod nulla est differentia inter unitates et corpora parva, fiunt enim ex sphaeris Democriti parvis puncta*. Cf. *De Anima*, 409a, 10–12.

me, is this: And similarly he who assumes that it is possible for a point to be self-moving will admit that as a consequence of his assumption it must follow that the point is a body. Accordingly we may well say that the self-moving round atoms of Democritus, in so far as they are small, may be called points, for a point, according to this assumption, is nothing but a body."[21]

From all these passages we may gather that in any analogy between atom and point, or in any identification of the terms atom and point, the terms atom and point may have been used in three possible ways. First, both terms may have been used in the sense of having no magnitude. Second, the term atom may have been used in the sense of having magnitude, whereas the term point may have been used in the sense of having no magnitude. Third, both terms may have been used in the sense of having magnitude.

Coming now to Saadia, we shall try to show, on the basis of his own statements, that in his identification of the terms atoms and points both terms are used by him in the sense of bodies having magnitude.

The statement in which Saadia describes the atom in what would seem to be mathematical terms reads as follows: "We picture to ourselves that the Creator had collected out of those spiritual things small points, and these are the parts which are indivisible, . . . and out of these small points he made a line."[22] Now in this passage the expression "parts which are indivisible"[23] is the technical

[21] *Ibid.*, Comm. 69 (fol. 36A): *Intendit, ut mihi videtur, et similiter qui ponit quod possibile est ut punctus moveatur concedit quod contingit ei quod punctus sit corpus, et ideo bene possumus dicere quod sphaerae Democriti, quae moventur ex se, adeo sunt parvae, quod dicuntur puncta, punctus enim secundum hanc positionem non est nisi corpus.*

[22] *Emunot ve-De'ot* I, Hebrew, p. 63, Arabic, p. 41, ll. 14–16: נדמה לנו שהוא קבץ מהם נקודות קטנות, והם החלקים אשר לא יחלקו . . . ועשה מהם קו ישר.

[23] החלקים אשר לא יחלקו: אלאג̇זאء אלתי לא תתג̇זאء.

Arabic expression for atoms. So let us refer to them as atoms. Following Aristotle, he calls them also "points;" but evidently knowing that by calling the atoms "points" Aristotle does not mean mathematical points but rather "small bodies" (σωμάτια μικρά)[24] or "small round atoms" (σφαιρία),[25] Saadia takes care to add the adjective "small" to the term "points." The expression "small points,"[26] Saadia must have felt quite certain, could not be mistaken for mathematical points, for mathematical points are neither small nor great. Saadia has thus made it quite clear that the atoms which he calls small points are bodies which have magnitude. Since the atoms spoken of by Saadia are assumed by him to have magnitude, they are also described by him as "thinner than anything thin and smaller than anything small,"[27] which description reflects the Greek term **ἐλάχιστον**, "the smallest part," by which, as we have seen, the extended atom of Democritus is described by Aristotle.[28] And we have reason to believe that just as the term "point" is explicitly said by Saadia not to be taken in the sense of a mathematical point, so also the term "line" in the same passage is not meant by him to be taken in a mathematical sense. The Arabic term *haṭṭ* as well as the Hebrew term *ḳav* underlying here the term "line," should thus be taken in the sense of "band" or "piece of fabric" or "strip," something long and narrow and thin but not altogether without width and thickness. This would make the statement of Saadia correspond exactly to Plato's statement in the *Timaeus* which it reflects.[29]

[24] *De Anima* I, 4, 409a, 11.

[25] *Ibid.*, 12.

[26] נקודות קטנות: נקט צנאר.

[27] *Tafsir*, p. 4, 11, 7 8: אדק מן כל דקיק ואצנאר מן כל צניר; *Emunot ve-De'ot*, Hebrew, p. 64; Arabic, p. 42, ll. 11–12: דק מכל דק: אדק מן כל דקיק.

[28] *Metaph.* XIII, 8, 1084b, 27.

[29] *Timaeus* 36 B ff.

In Greek philosophy, even though the atoms are assumed to have magnitude, they are not assumed to have qualities.[30] In the Kalam, however, there were those who like the Greek atomists assumed the atoms to have magnitude[31] and not to have qualities,[32] but there were others who, while denying that the atoms have magnitude,[33] affirmed that they have the qualities of "color, taste, smell, heat, cold, moisture, and dryness."[34] Now, in Greek philosophy the absence of qualities in atoms was the most vulnerable spot in atomism, and one which has laid it open to a stock criticism repeated by Plutarch, Galen, and Simplicius.[35] The gist of this criticism is as follows. On the assumption that the atoms have no distinguishing qualities there is no explanation for the existence of such distinguishing qualities in bodies composed of those atoms. As stated by Plutarch, it argues that atomists have failed to show "how bodies (i. e., atoms) which have not any quality can bring all sorts of qualities to others only by their meetings and joining together, as, for instance — to take that which comes next to hand — whence does that which we call heat proceed, and how is it engendered in the atoms, if they neither had heat when they came, nor are become hot after their being joined together?"[36]

This controversy in the Kalam with regard to the existence of qualities and magnitude in atoms and also this stock argument in Greek philosophy against atomism are drawn upon by Saadia in his second and third refutations of the second theory. In these two refutations, it will be

[30] Cf. above, n. 9.
[31] Cf. *Masā'il*, p. 38, 1.15 (Abū Hāshim).
[32] *Ibid.*, p. 43, ll. 6–7 (ditto).
[33] *Ibid.*, p. 38, ll. 16–17 (Abū al-Qasim).
[34] *Ibid.*, p. 43, ll. 20–21 (ditto).
[35] Cf. Usener, *Epicurea*, § 288; Bailey, *Greek Atomists*, p. 292.
[36] *Adversus Coloten* 8.

noticed, Saadia introduces his arguments by such expressions as "I think," "I furthermore think," and "I consider as far-fetched and even as false" — expressions the like of which he does not use in his first and fourth refutations. In the second and third refutations, we take it, therefore, Saadia is not arguing merely against the particular conception of atoms reproduced by him in his second theory nor is he arguing against it from its own premises; he is arguing against the various conceptions of atoms found in the Kalam, both attacking their premises and driving toward a different conclusion.

In the second refutation, Saadia comes out against both those who endow atoms with qualities and deprive them of magnitude and those who endow them with magnitude and deprive them of qualities, contending that, if atoms are assumed to exist, they can have neither magnitude nor qualities and concluding that the existence of something which has no magnitude and qualities is inconceivable. To begin with, he says, in his judgment atoms cannot have the four primary qualities of "heat" and "cold" and "moisture" and "dryness," for these primary qualities, on the assumption of the existence of atoms, are created out of the atoms.[37] Then, again, in his judgment, they cannot have the secondary qualities of "color" and "taste" and "smell," for these qualities are attributes of bodies which are supposed by the atomists to be created out of the atoms, and for this very same reason, also in his judgment, they cannot have "limit" and "measure," i. e., magnitude, and cannot be "in place" and "in time."[38] But the existence of that which has no magnitude and qualities is something excessively

[37] והשנית, אני רואה כי אלה הדברים אשר טענו לא יתכן שיהיו חמים ולא קרים ולא לחים ולא יבשים, מפני שהם אומרים שאלה הד׳ טבעים מהם נבראו.

[38] ואני רואה עוד שלא יתכן להיות להם מראה ולא טעם ולא ריח ולא גבול ולא שיעור, ולא רוב ולא מיעוט, ולא במקום ולא בזמן, מפני שאלה הדברים הם תארי הגשמים, והדברים ההם הם אצלם קודם הגשמים.

inconceivable and, on purely rational grounds, it is even more inconceivable than creation out of nothing.[39]

In his third refutation, he takes up the stock argument against atomism. Having stated that in his judgment atoms, if assumed to exist, can have neither qualities nor magnitude, he now argues from this judgment of his that such atoms could not be transformed into the four elements with their distinctive primary four qualities nor could they be transformed into magnitudes possessing length and breadth and depth nor could they acquire any of the secondary qualities.[40] If the proponents of the second theory, he concludes, could assume a Creator capable of effecting such a transformation, one could assume also a Creator capable of effecting creation out of nothing.[41] The "Creator" who according to Saadia is assumed by the proponents of the second theory to effect such a transformation is, of course, the Demiurge of Plato's *Timaeus*.

The same conception of atoms as extended bodies is also implied in Saadia's presentation of the ninth theory of Creation, that of Epicurus. This theory is not presented by him as a theory of the creation of the world out of atoms, but rather as a theory of the creation of the world by chance, that is to say, it is presented by him not as a theory of what the world was created from, but as a theory of how the world was created. In his presentation of this theory he merely refers to it as the "theory of chance" and describes its upholders as those "who imagined that

39 וזה תוספת למה שלא יושכל, וברחו מהיות דבר לא מדבר ונכנסו במה שהוא יותר רחוק ועמוק ממנו.

40 והשלישית, שאני מרחיק ואחשוב לשקר התהפכות דבר לא מצוייר בצורה עד שיצוייר בצורת האש והמים והאויר והעפר והצטיירות מה שאינו ארוך ולא רחב ולא עמוק עד שהיה ממנו הארוך הרחב העמוק, וכן השתנות מה שאין לו ענין עד שיהיו לו כל הענינים הנראים עתה.

41 ואם אצלם שנתקנו לו כל ההפוכים והשנוים מפני שהבורא חכם יכל להפכם ולשנותם, חכמתו אם כן ויכלתו לברא דבר לא מדבר.

their reason convinced them that the heavens and the earth came into existence by chance without the design of him who designs and without the action of an agent, whether endowed with the power of choice or lifeless."[42] Similarly, in his refutation of this theory, his main arguments are directed against creation by chance and only in his supplementary arguments does he touch upon the impossibility of creation out of atoms.[43] This is due to the fact that neither in Greek philosophy nor in Arabic philosophy was Epicurus considered as the founder of atomism. In Greek philosophy, in connection with a statement by Epicurus that "he supposes the same principles with Democritus," Plutarch ironically remarks that what he really did was "to steal from Democritus."[44] In Arabic philosophy, whenever any direct reference to the Greek origin of Kalam atomism is made it is always the name of Democritus that is mentioned. It is thus Democritus that is mentioned by Isaac Israeli,[45] Faḫr al-Dīn, Jurjānī, and Shīrāzī.[46] Similarly Maimonides attributes atomism to "the ancient philosophers,"[47] by whom he means Leucippus and Democritus from among the pre-Socratic philosophers.[48] Epicurus is only referred to as the one who has introduced into the atomic theory the view that the world was created by chance.[49]

[42] *Ibid.*, Hebrew, p. 75; Arabic, p. 61, ll. 12–14: והדעת התשיעית דעת המקרה. אלה האנשים חשבו כי שכלם הורה אותם שהשמים והארץ הוא במקרה בלא כוונת מכוין ובלא [פועל] פועל, לא בוחר ולא דומם.

[43] Beginning with וכאשר בארתי טעותם במאמרם במקרה כן אבארהו בשאר מה שסברו וחשבו.

[44] *Adversus Coloten* 8.

[45] Cf. above, n. 8.

[46] Pines, *op. cit.*, pp. 96–97.

[47] *Moreh Nebukim* I,71: הפילוסופים הראשונים: אלפלאספה̈ אלמתקדמין. But Epicurus as one of the exponents of atomism is mentioned in I, 73, Prop. 1.

[48] Cf. my *Crescas' Critique of Aristotle*, p. 321.

[49] *Moreh Nebukim* II, 13; *Eṣ Ḥayyim*, Ch. 4, p. 15.

Still Arabic philosophers, including Saadia, did know that the world which was created by chance, as maintained by Epicurus, was created also out of atoms, and consequently from Saadia's description of this Epicurean theory we may gather some information as to how he conceived of the nature of the Epicurean atoms. Now, with reference to the question whether the Epicurean atoms had magnitude or not he makes it quite clear that in this respect they were like the atoms in his second theory, for he refers to them as bodies.[50] But with reference to the question whether the atoms of the Epicureans have qualities, he merely says that "what they are is unknown"[51] and challenges the Epicureans to tell us "what the atoms were before they were brought together, whether they were the same as the bodies now composed of them or whether they were something different, and, if their state [of quality] was different from that of the bodies now composed of them, how do they conceive of that quality."[52] Evidently in the transmission of the Epicurean atomism there was some vagueness as to the nature of the atoms with regard to qualities, which vagueness caused Saadia to hesitate to make any definite statement about what the Epicureans thought about the qualities of the atoms. In the original Greek sources, however, it is definitely stated that the Epicurean atoms "possess none of the qualities belonging to things which come under observation, except shape, weight, and size."[53]

The care taken by Saadia to qualify the term "points"

[50] *Emunot ve-De'ot*, Hebrew, p. 75; Arabic, p. 61, 1.15: גשמים: אג̇סאם; cf. below, n. 58.

[51] *Ibid.*: לא יודע מה הם: לא יערף מא הי.

[52] *Ibid.*, Hebrew, p. 76, Arabic, p. 62, ll. 14–16: יאמרו איך היו מקודם זה הקבוץ, העל מה שהם או על זולתו. ואם היה ענינם (חאלהא) בהפך מה שהם עליו, איך חושבים האיכות (אלכיפיה̈) ההיא.

[53] *Diogenes*, X, 54.

when used by him as a description of "atoms" is an indication of the faithfulness with which philosophic formulae and terms as a rule were reproduced in Arabic philosophy. Despite the variety of interpretations of the views of ancient Greek philosophy found among Arabic philosophers — interpretations often erroneous — there were system and order in these interpretations, and this system and order can be traced in the use of terms and formulae. In connection with the term "point" under consideration, this term has been used in the history of philosophy as a link between the atoms of Democritus and the numbers of Pythagoras. Both the atoms and the numbers have in the course of their history been called points. With regard to the atom, though the names by which Aristotle calls it are the full (πλῆρες),[54] the solid (στερεόν),[55] the indivisible magnitude (μέγεθος ἄτομος),[56] the smallest part (ἐλάχιστον),[57] and "body" (σῶμα),[58] he also calls it, as we have seen, point (στιγμή),[59] using the term point in the sense of a point which has magnitude. So also with regard to the Pythagoreans, though their view is usually given by Aristotle as stating that number is the substance of all things,[60] or that all things consist of numbers,[61] he reproduces it also as stating that "the limits of body, i.e., surface, line, point and unit, are substances."[62] Here, too, Aristotle evidently uses the term point in the sense of a point which has magnitude, for he explicitly says that the numbers of

54 *Mataph.* I, 4, 985b, 7.

55 *Ibid.*

56 *Ibid.* VII, 13, 1039a, 10; also "primary magnitudes" (πρῶτα μεγέθη) *De Caelo* III, 4, 303a, 5.

57 *Ibid.* XIII, 8, 1084b, 27.

58 *De Caelo* III, 4, 303a, 11.

59 Cf. above, n. 20.

60 *Metaph.* I, 5, 987a, 19.

61 *Ibid.* XIII, 6, 1080b, 18–19; XIII, 8, 1083b, 11–12.

62 *Ibid.* VII, 2, 1028b, 15–17.

the Pythagoreans are "not numbers consisting of abstract units" but of units which they suppose "to have magnitude,"[63] and hence that the numbers themselves have magnitude.[64] On the basis of this conception of Pythagorean numbers in the Aristotelian passages quoted, there would seem to be, with reference to the question of magnitude, no difference between the numbers of Pythagoras and the atoms of Democritus, and, in fact, this is exactly what Aristotle explicitly says in certain passages. In one passage, he compares numbers to atoms, and applies a statement of Democritus with regard to atoms to the numbers of Pythagoras;[65] in another passage he identifies numbers with atoms, saying that Democritus' view that all things are generated by the combination and involution of atoms "in a sense makes things out to be numbers or composed of numbers."[66] Similarly among the followers of the Pythagoreans there was Ecphantus who is reported to have taken the Pythagorean units, which are the constituents of number, as the "indivisible bodies" of Democritus[67] and hence to have said that the world is composed of atoms.[68]

In the light of the facts unfolded here, we can well imagine how some student of philosophy at the time of the Kalam could have reproduced in the name of some unspecified Greek philosopher a statement to the effect that the world was generated out of points. Had that been done, it would have been legitimate for some scholar today to raise the question whether the term points in question referred to atoms or numbers, inasmuch as we have seen that both of

63 *Ibid.* XIII, 6, 1080 b, 18–20.

64 *Ibid.*, 30–33.

65 *Ibid.* VII, 13, 1039a, 9–14.

66 *De Caelo* III, 4, 303a, 8–9.

67 Stobaeus, *Eclogae* I, p. 127, ll. 16–17 (ed. Wachsmuth).

68 *Ibid.*, I, p. 186, ll. 2–3. Cf. Zeller, *Die philosophie der Griechen*, I, 1[6], p. 605, n. 2. (English, I, p. 528, n. 2).

these are described as points by Aristotle. Similarly we can also well imagine how some ill-trained or half-learned student of philosophy at the time of the Kalam could have confused the term atom with the term number and used the one when he really meant the other. But there is no evidence of such ignorance or confusion among students of philosophy of that time — at least not among those who allowed themselves to commit their thoughts to writing or among those whose writings have come down to us. Whatever conception philosophers of that time had of the numbers of Pythagoras and of the atoms of Democritus, their use of the Arabic translation of the term number is a clear indication that the reference is to the view of Pythagoras and so also their use of the Arabic translation of the term atom is a clear indication that the reference is to the view of Democritus. This careful use of terminology is especially noticeable in Saadia. When in his second theory of creation, both in his *Emunot ve-De'ot* and in his Commentary on *Sefer Yeṣirah*, he wanted to describe atomism, he used the Arabic technical translation of the term atom, and with it also the expression "thinner than anything thin and smaller than anything small."[69] When, again, following Aristotle, he wanted to describe the atoms by the term "points," he took care to indicate by the use of the qualifying adjective "small"[70] that he did not mean thereby mathematical points. Even the term "spiritual" by which he describes the atoms in his second theory in *Emunot ve-De'ot* may by itself merely mean "invisible" or "imperceptible"[71] and thus reflect both the terms invisible (ἀόρ-

[69] Cf. above, n. 27.

[70] Cf. above, n. 26.

[71] See discussion on the use of the term "spiritual" in the sense of something "invisible," though it may become visible to a prophet during his prophetic experience, in my paper "Hallevi and Maimonides on Prophecy," *JQR*, 33 (1942), 50–58. Above, pp. 87–95.

ατον) and imperceptible (*ἀναίσθητον*) which are applied to the ideas[72] and the expression perceptible only by reason (*λόγῳ θεωρητά*) which is applied to the atoms.[73] But when in his Commentary on *Sefer Yeṣirah* he wished to refer to the Pythagorean theory, he quite accurately uses the term "numbers."[74] His brief description of these "numbers," reflecting as it does the Neopythagoreanism current in Arabic philosophy of the time, shows that they were different both from the "atoms" as described by himself and from the Pythagorean "numbers" as described by Aristotle in the passages in which he compares them with atoms.

The upshot of our discussion is that, in Saadia's second theory, the atoms are represented as having magnitude. If Saadia calls these atoms points, he indicates by the qualifying adjective "small" that he does not use the term points in a mathematical sense. In this he follows a statement in Aristotle, especially in its Arabic version, which statement was also drawn upon by other Arabic philosophers in their identification of the terms atom and point. In his refutation of this second theory, he makes allusions to the controversy not only over the question whether atoms have magnitude but also over the question whether atoms have qualities. He himself, however, maintains that, if atoms are assumed to exist, they must be assumed to have neither magnitude nor qualities. Similarly in his ninth theory, the Epicurean atoms alluded to are represented as having magnitude. But with regard to qualities, there is an expression of uncertainty as to what was the exact Epicurean view on the subject.

72 *Timaeus*, 52A.

73 Aetius, I, 3, 18 (Diels, *Doxography Graeci*, p. 285). Cf. *Eṣ Ḥayyim*, ch. 4, p. 14: כי אין אנחנו רואים אותה . . . שלא אמתו מציאות הדק . . . בהרגש, אלא נתחייב מציאותו מהכרח דעת, והנה השכל אמת מציאותו.

74 *Tafsīr*, Seventh Theory, p. 9, l. 23; French, p. 25.

10

ARABIC AND HEBREW TERMS FOR MATTER AND ELEMENT WITH ESPECIAL REFERENCE TO SAADIA

In the paper on "The Kalam Problem of Nonexistence and Saadia's Second Theory of Creation," I remarked that the use of the Hebrew term *ḥomer* as a translation of the Greek *hyle* has its origin in the Arabic *ṭīnah* which in turn is a translation of Plato's *ekmageion*.[1] On the appearance of that paper Professor Erich Frank handed me a few references to Aristotle, where as an illustration of matter (ὕλη) in contrast to form he uses the example of the "bricks" and "clay" (πηλός) and "wood" out of which a house is built (*De Part. Animal.* I, 5, 645a, 34) or of the "clay" out of which a clay statue is made (*Metaph. VII*, 10, 1035a, 32). I shall take this occasion to amplify my brief remark in the previous paper and to give a full-length discussion of the Hebrew term *ḥomer* as well as of other related terms in Hebrew and in Arabic.

In Arabic, four terms are used specifically in the sense of matter. They are *hayūla*, *māddah*, *ṭīnah*, and *ḫamīrah*.[2]

The term *hayūla* is, of course, a transliteration of the Greek ὕλη. That the Arabs who used the term *hayūla* for matter knew that its original meaning was wood may

[1] *JQR*, N.S., 36 (1946), p. 386, n. 58. Above, p. 353.

[2] The first three terms are enumerated in Avicenna, *Shifā'* I, 6 (quoted in A. -M. Goichon, *Lexique de la Langue Philosophique d'Ibn Sīnā*, §404); the first, third and fourth terms are enumerated in Ibn Ḥazm, *Kitāb al-Fiṣal*, V, p. 70, 1.4 (quoted in S. Pines, *Beiträge zur islamischen atomenlehre*, p. 39, n. 2).

be gathered from the fact that Avicenna illustrates its meaning by the example of "wood" (*ḫashab*) in its relation to the "bed" into which it is changed or in its relation to the "ashes" to which it is reduced.[3]

The term *māddah* would seem to be of original Arabic usage. How that term came to be used for matter may be conjecturally explained by what we know of the prevailing view in Arabic philosophy as to the meaning of the term *hyle* as used by Aristotle.[4] The Aristotelian term *hyle*, as may be gathered from the Iḫwān al-Ṣafā, was divided into two kinds, the "first *hyle*" (*al-hayūla al-ūlā*)[5] and the "second *hyle*" (*al-hayūla al-thaniyyah*).[6] The "first *hyle*" was conceived as being inseparably joined to a "corporal form," (*ṣūrah jismiyyah*) and the combination of these two, forming the "second *hyle*," was the common underlying matter of the four elements.[7] Now the "corporeal form" was generally described as that which endows the "first *hyle*" with three distances (*ab'ad*)[8] or extensions (*imtidādāt*),[9] that is to say, dimensions, terms which are

[3] Cf. *Shifā'* I, 6 (quoted in Goichon, *Lexique*, §736, p. 414); *Ḥudūd* in *Tisu' Rasā'il fī al-Ḥikmah wal-Tabī'īyat*, Cairo, 1326/1908, p. 76, 1.9 (French: *Introduction a Avicenne*, by A. -M. Goichon).

[4] What follows is based upon my discussion of the subject in *Crescas' Critique of Aristotle*, pp. 579–590.

[5] Iḫwan al-Ṣafā, *Rasā'il* (ed. Dieterici), p. 13, 1.9; p. 25, 1. 15.

[6] *Ibid.*, p. 13, 11. 11–12.

[7] These "first" and "second" *hyle* in Arabic philosophy are not the same as the prime (πρώτη) and ultimate (τελευταία) *hyle* of Aristotle in *Metaph.* V, 6, 1017a, 5. The latter two terms refer respectively to an immediate matter which is nearest to its form and to a remote matter which is furthest from it (cf. *ibid.*, V, 7, 1016a, 20). Aristotle's "prime matter" in this sense is therefore explained by Averroes to mean *materia propinqua* (=Arabic *qarībah*). See his Long Commentary in *Aristotle's opera*, Venice, 1574, Vol. 8, fol. 108 E, on *Metaph.* V, 4, 1015a, 7. Cf. also Maimonides, *Millot ha-Higgayon*, Ch. 9: חומר קרוב and חומר רחוק. On *qarib*, קרוב for πρῶτον, see also *Crescas' Critique of Aristotle*, p. 700, n. 8.

[8] *Najāt* III, p. 327, 11, 12–16.

[9] *Ibid.*, p. 332, 1. 14.

translations of the Greek διάστημα.[10] The "second *hyle*," as distinguished from the "first *hyle*," is thus a matter which has extension. In view of all this, it was quite natural for Arabic philosophers to take up the Arabic term *māddah*, which literally means "extending," or "that which is extended," and use it as designation of the "extended" or "second *hayūla*."

It would seem, however, that this original distinction between the "first *hayūla*" and the "second *hayūla*" as well as this original use of the term *māddah* in the specific sense of the "second *hayūla*" soon disappeared. The reason for this was undoubtedly the commonly accepted view that the "first *hayūla*," that is, the *hayūla* underlying the "corporeal form," never existed without its "corporeal form," which was tantamount to saying that there was no *hayūla* which existed without extension, or, in other words, there was no *hayūla* which was not a *māddah*. As a result of this, naturally, the term *hayūla* became interchangeable with the term *māddah* and what was formerly called "first *hayūla*" came to be called also "first *māddah*." Moreover, owing also to the view that there was no *hayūla* without a corporeal form, which logically meant that every *hayūla* was a *māddah*, or something extended, the original use of the term "first" as distinguishing the inextended *hayūla*, underlying the corporeal form, from the extended *hayūla*, underlying the four elements, similarly disappeared, and the term "first" came to be applied to the *hayūla* or *māddah* which was underlying the simple four elements, to distinguish it from the *hayūla* or *māddah* which was underlying objects composed of the four elements.

Both these changes are reflected in the writings of Alfarabi, Avicenna, Averroes, and their followers or contemporaries. With regard to the matter underlying the

[10] Cf. *Crescas' Critique of Aristotle*, p. 591.

corporeal form, which the Iḫwān al-Ṣafā describe as "first *hayūla*," Avincenna describes it indiscriminately either as simply *hayūla*[11] or as "absolute (*mutlaqah*) *hayūla*"[12] or as "first (*ūlā*) *hayūla*"[13] or as "first *māddah*,"[14] and similarly Averroes, in his restatement of Avicenna, describes it either as "first *hayūla*"[15] or as "first *māddah*."[16] With regard to the matter underlying the four elements, which the Iḫwān al-Ṣafā describes as "second *hayūla*," Alfarabi describes it as the "first *māddah*,"[17] and Averroes as the "first *hayūla*."[18] The term *māddah* with the qualifying adjective "first" and the term *hayūla* without any qualifying adjective are used for the matter of the four elements by Bahya,[19] Halevi,[20] and Maimonides.[21] In view of this ultimate identification of these two terms, the terms *hayūla* and *māddah* are both to be translated simply by the term "matter."[22]

Thus *hayūla* and *māddah* are both of Aristotelian origin, the former having been introduced by Aristotle himself into philosophic vocabulary, the latter having been made

[11] *Najāt* III, p. 328, ll. 14–15.
[12] *Ḥudūd*, p. 83, l. 17.
[13] *Najāt* III, p. 349, l. 4.
[14] *Ibid.*, p. 362, l. 12.
[15] *Epitome of the Metaphysics*, (ed. Quiros), §73, p. 76, l. 15.
[16] *Ibid.*, l. 18.
[17] *Al-Siyāsāt al-Madaniyyah*, Hyderabad, 1346 A.H., p. 28, ll. 1–2.
[18] *Op. cit.*, I, §60, p. 33, l. 19.
[19] *Ḥobot ha-Lebabot* I, 6 (ed. A. S. Yahuda), p. 47, ll. 14–15.
[20] *Cuzari* IV, 25 (ed. Hirschfeld), p. 278, l. 10; V, 2, p. 294, l. 19.
[21] *Moreh Nebukim* I, 28; *Millot ha-Higgayon*, ch. 9.
[22] Goichon, both in *Lexique*, *loc. cit.*, and in *Introduction*, pp. 75 and 80, translates *hayūla* by "first matter" and *māddah* by "second matter," using the term "second matter" as a designation of the matter underlying things composed of the four elements (cf. *Introduction*, p. 17, n. 10). This, I think, is not an apt translation of the terms. As we have seen, in Arabic, the term *hayūla* is sometimes qualified by the adjective "second" (cf. above, n. 6) and the term *māddah* is sometimes qualified by the adjective "first" (cf. above, nn. 16 and 17). Also Avicenna, who is the special subject of Goichon's studies, qualifies both *hayūla* and *māddah* by the term "first" (cf. above, nn. 13 and 14).

use of in Arabic as a result of a special interpretation of Aristotle's *hyle*. The term *ṭīnah*, however, is not of Aristotelian but rather of Platonic origin. While Aristotle, in the passages cited above, does indeed use the term "clay" among his illustrations of the meaning of the term *hyle*, he never uses it as a technical term in the sense of matter. This term, we take it, reflects the term ἐκμαγεῖον, which is used by Plato in his *Timaeus* as a description of matter.[23] Now Plato himself uses this term both in a general and in a specific sense. In the *Timaeus*, as a description of matter, he uses it in the general sense of anything plastic which is capable of receiving various impressions. In the *Theaetetus*, in connection with the soul, he uses it more specifically in the sense of a "lump of wax" (κήρινον ἐκμαγεῖον) upon which impressions are made by seal rings.[24] However, we know that wax was not the only material used for impressions by seal rings; Lemnian earth or clay was also so used. In fact, Philo, in comparing Plato's ideas to seals, says of the latter, with evident reference to the term *ekmageion* in the *Timaeus*, that "when brought into contact with wax or some similar material, they stamp upon it any number of impressions."[25] Thus Plato's *ekmageion* in the *Timaeus* refers not only to wax but also to clay or any other material used with seal rings. Now the Arabic *ṭīnah*, just as its equivalent the Hebrew *ḥomer*,[26] is not only clay used for building purposes or clay molded by the proverbial potter's hand, but is also the particular kind of clay used for sealing.[27] In fact, Abraham Ibn Daud quotes the scriptural reference to sealing clay as an illustration of the philosophic concept of matter. He says: "Among the re-

[23] *Timaeus* 50 C.
[24] *Theaetetus* 191 C–D.
[25] *De Spec. Leg.* I, 8, §47.
[26] Cf. Ibn Janah, *Sefer ha-Shorashim*, s.v.
[27] Cf. Saadia's version of Job 38.14.

markable allusions in Scripture to the fact that all existent things contain matter (חומר) after the analogy of clay (חומר=Arabic *ṭīnah*) in which forms may succeed one after another in a circular manner, as if they were impressions on clay, is the word of God to Job: it is turned as seal-clay (Job 58.14)."[28] Thus the Arabic *ṭīnah* is really a fair translation of the Greek *ekmageion* in the *Timaeus*. I may add, however, the following statement of Plotinus with regard to matter (ὕλη): "We say that it is the matter of some and the form of others, just as clay (πηλὸν) is matter in respect to the potter, without being matter absolutely" (*Enneads* II, 4, 8).

By the same token, we may assume that the Arabic term *ḥamīrah* is another attempt to translate the term *ekmageion* of the *Timaeus*, for this Arabic term, which originally means "leaven" or "leavened bread," has also the meaning of "plastic material."

The first three of these four Arabic terms for matter are used by Saadia in his *Emunot ve-De'ot*.

In one passage, referring to the Platonic theory of creation, by which he means, as we have shown, an ideal atomic matter, he describes its followers as "those who believe in an eternal matter," using here for "matter" the term *ṭīnah*, "clay," which, as we have seen, is of Platonic origin. But then immediately after the words "those who believe in an eternal clay" he adds the words "propose to take it in the sense of *hayūla*, something in which there is no heat and no cold and no moisture and no dryness."[29] What

[28] *Emunah Ramah* I, 2, p. 12: האל ומן הדברים הנפלאים שבאו בכתובים מן הרמז אל ש[ל]הנמצאות חומר כמו הטיט, יחזור עליו הַלִילָה צורות כמו פתוחים אל הטיט, מאמר יתʹ לאיוב: תתהפך כחמר חותם. The expression יחזור עליו חלילה צורות in this passage as well as the expression (according to the reading corrected by Munk) ענינים ההווים בה חלילה in *Moreh Nebukim* I, 11, reflects the Greek *ἀνακυκλεῖν καὶ ἀνακάμπτειν* in *De Generatione et Corruptione* II, 11, 338a, 4–5.

[29] *Emunot ve-De'ot* I, Hebrew (ed. Yosefov), p. 55; Arabic, p. 31, 11. 16–17: ובעלי החומר (אלטינה) הקדמון הם מכוונים לקיימו היולי, דבר שאין בו חום ולא קור ולא לחות ולא יובש.

Saadia means to say here is that the Platonic antemundane eternal matter, called *ṭīnah*, is described by Plato's followers in terms of Aristotle's *hyle*. This identification of Plato's *ekmageion* (*ṭīnah*) with *hyle*, it may be remarked, is already found in Aristotle himself.[30]

In other passages, however, where the term *māddah* occurs, Saadia uses it in two senses, which correspond exactly to two senses in which the term matter is used by Aristotle. First, using the term *māddah* in the Aristotelian sense of matter as that "out of which" (*ἐξ οὗ*) things came to be,[31] that is to say, as the source of things, he speaks of "the materials (*mawadd*) of truth,"[32] that is, the sources of truth, and also of the Torah as the "matter (*māddah*) of our religion,"[33] that is, the source of our religion. Secondly using the term *māddah* in the Aristotelian sense of matter as "the substratum" (*ὑποκείμενον*) or as that which underlies all the processes of change that occur,[34] he says that "a thing which occurs by chance has no continuance of existence because it has no substratum (*aṣl*) in which the thing may occur permanently nor a matter (*māddah*) which may give to it duration."[35]

In Judah Ibn Tibbon's Hebrew translation of the *Emunot ve-De'ot*, these three Arabic terms for matter are each translated with etymological accuracy. The Arabic *ṭīnah* is translated by the Hebrew *ḥomer*, "clay"; the Greek *hyle*, transliterated into Arabic by *hayūla*, is similarly transliterated into Hebrew; the Arabic *māddah* is translated

[30] *Metaph.* I, 6, 988a, 1 and 10.

[31] Cf. *Ibid.*, VII, 7, 1032a, 17.

[32] *Emunot ve-De'ot, Haḳdamah*, Hebrew, p. 43; Arabic, p. 12, 1. 18: משכי (מואד̈) האמת.

[33] *Ibid.*, III, 10, Hebrew, p. 122; Arabic, p. 140, 1. 17: המשך לתורתנו (מאד̈תנא פי דיננא).

[34] *Metaph.* VIII, 1, 1042a, 32–34.

[35] *Emunot ve-De'ot* I, Ninth Theory, Hebrew, p. 75; Arabic, p. 62, 11. 6–8: שהדבר הנופל במקרה אין לו קיימא, מפני שאין לו שורש (אצל) הולך עליו ולא משך (מאד̈ה) שמכלכל אותו ההתמדה. On *aṣl*, see below, n. 46.

by the Hebrew משך, a term already used by Solomon Ibn Gabirol as well as by Saadia himself as the Hebrew for the Arabic *māddah*.[36] In his translations of *Ḥobot ha-Lebabot* and *Cuzari*, however, he invariably uses the Hebrew *ḥomer* as a translation of the Arabic *māddah*. The reason for this was probably his feeling that while משך is etymologically a more accurate rendering of *māddah*, the term חומר would be more intelligible to the Hebrew reader. The term חומר was also selected by both Samuel Ibn Tibbon and Ḥarizi[37] as a translation of the term *māddah* in *Moreh Nebukim*, and from that time on it was used as the most common Hebrew term for matter and as synonymous with the term היולי. In the case of Samuel Ibn Tibbon, we have his own explanation why he translated the Arabic *māddah* by the Hebrew *ḥomer*. "Know," he says, "the term which we have translated by *ḥomer* is a term which in Arabic refers to a certain thing which is capable of receiving various forms differing either specifically or individually."[38] The Arabic term referred to here is *māddah*, for that is the term which he translates by *ḥomer*. Then he says: "Such also is the case of clay (*ḥomer*) in the hand of the potter, who shapes it into vessels of innumerable forms which are devised by him in accordance with his power to perform skilful work. It is for this reason that we have used this term figuratively as a designation for anything capable of

[36] *Keter Malkut* (ed. Davidson) 1. 97, and ומשך החכמה אתה in *ha-Baḳḳashah ha-Ri'shonah* of Saadia; cf. Kaufmann, *Attributenlehere*, p. 1, n. 2. The Arabic translation of the *Baḳḳashah* uses *yambū'* and *ma'din* for משך. Cf. Siddur, ed. Davidson, Assaf, and Joel, p. 47.

[37] The translation of the Arabic *māddah* by the Hebrew טבע in the printed edition of Ḥarizi (p. 16, col. 2, last line) is either a misprint or a scribal error, for in the Latin translation from Ḥarizi (Paris 1520) the term in the corresponding passage is *materia* (folio 4, 1. 16).

[38] *Perush me-ha-Millot Zorot*, under היולי: דע, המלה שהעתקנוה במלת חומר היא מלה מורה בערבי על דבר אחד שמקבל צורות חלוקות במין או באישים.

receiving various forms."[39] By all this he evidently tries to explain why he did not translate the term *māddah* literally by some such term as *meshek*. Of the "first *ḥomer*," that is, the "first *māddah*," he quite rightly says that it is the matter underlying the four elements.[40] The term *hayūla*, according to him, primarily applies to what he calls "first matter," that is, the matter underlying the four elements, but, by the extension of meaning, it also applies to "second matter," that is, the matter underlying things composed of the four elements.[41]

A list of various Hebrew translations of various Arabic terms for matter occurs in two Hebrew versions of Saadia's commentary on the *Sefer Yeṣirah*, one anonymous quoted by Judah bar Barzillai[42] and the other by Moses ben Joseph of Lucena.[43]

In the original passage in Arabic, Saadia says that the antemundane atomic matter in his second theory of creation is called (1) *al-aṣl al-basīt*, (2) *al-'unṣur*, (3) *al-umm*, (4) *al-ṭīnah*, and (5) *al-hayūla*.[44] In this passage, it will be noticed, the first two terms refer to "elements," whereas the last three terms refer to "matter," for the atoms, which are usually conceived as "elements,"[45] are taken by Saadia in

[39] *Ibid.*: וכן הוא ענין ההומר ביד היוצר שעושה ממנו כלים חלוף הצורות אין מספר בכל אשר יחדשו בכח מלאכת מחשבת. על כן שאלנו שם הומר לכל דבר מוכן לקבל צורות חלוקות.

[40] *Ibid.*: ואולם ענין החומר הראשון הוא הדבר הנחשב או המדומה שקבל צורות ארבע היסודות.

[41] *Ibid.*

[42] *Perush Sefer Yeṣirah*, pp. 268–278.

[43] Excerpts quoted from manuscript in Steinschneider, *Hebr. Uebers.*, p. 447; cf. also Jacob Guttmann, *Die Religions-philosophie der Saadia*, p. 46, n. 1.

On these two versions, see Malter, *Life and Works of Saadia Gaon*, pp. 356 ff.

[44] *Commentaire sur le Sefer Yesira par le Gaon Saadya de Foyyoum*, Ed. M. Lambert, p. 4, 1. 11.

[45] Cf. Diels, *Die Fragmente der Vorsokratiker*, 345, 3.

For the application of the term *hyle* to the atoms, see Averroes, *Epitome of the Metaphysics* I (ed. Quiros), §60, p. 33, 11. 5–7.

this theory to constitute Plato's antemundane matter.

Before taking up the Hebrew translations of these terms, let us comment upon the first two of these Arabic terms for "elements."

The term *aṣl* is a literal translation of the Greek **ῥίζωμα**, which, literally meaning "root," is also used by Empedocles in the philosophical sense of "element."[46]

The term *'unṣur*, which comes from the verb *in'iṣar*, "be pressed out," like juice or fluid, was probably used originally as a translation of the Greek **χυμός**, which from its original meaning of "juice" or "fluid" came to be used in the medical sense of "humor." The Arabic *'unsur*, therefore, must have originally meant "humor." How it came to mean "element" may be accounted for by the following statement in Galen: "What in the world is an element (στοιχεῖον) is in animals a humor (χυμός)."[47] The medical origin of the term *'unsur* is also indirectly attested by Maimonides, in his statement concerning "matter" that "many of the philosophers and physicians call it *al-'unṣur*."[48]

[46] Cf. Diels, *op. cit.*, 175, 8; cf. also ῥίζα in Philo, *De Plantatione*, 120. Or, the term *aṣl*, יסוד, may reflect the Greek τεμέλιος, "foundation," which is similarly used in the sense of "element" (cf. Aristotle, *Metaph.* V, 1, 1013a, 5 and 20; Philo, *Quis Rerum Divinarum Heres*, 134).

[47] Galen, *De Humoribus* (*op.*, ed. Kühn, vol. 19, p. 485). See passages in Klatzkin, *Oṣar ha-Munaḥim*, under לחה, in which the four humors and the four elements are compared or identified. All these passages reflect the passage of Galen.

[48] *Millot ha-Higgayon*, Ch. 9: וכן רבים מהפילוסופים והרופאים יקראוהו אלעֻנצר. The substance of the argument for 'unṣur from χυμός is as follows:

1. χυμός when used in the sense of flavor is al-kīmūs (deAn. II, 6, 418a, 13; II, 10, 422a, 10 et alia). In Pseudo-Plutarch, Placita IV, 18 p. 407, 1.14: διακρίνεσθαι τοὺς χυμοὺς = alladhī yudhāg (= taste).
2. for χυμοί in the sense of the (ones) humors is always akhlāt = mixtures, of which the Hebrew ליחות is *not* a translation.
3. 'unṣur is that which is prior to, and underlying, the 4 akhlaṭ (*Milal*, p. 294, l. 12ff.) and hence represents the term χυμός in the sense of "humor."

In the anonymous version, the passage in question with its five terms is translated as follows:

והם קוראים לזה הדבר (1) שורש הנמתח (מתוח), (2) התעלה, (3) היסוד, (4) זה חומר, (5) ואל כולי.

Correcting the obviously corrupted זה חומר to והחומר and ואל כולי to ואלהיולי,[49] the fourth and fifth terms are self-explanatory. In the third term, יסוד is a good translation for *umm* in its sense of "element," a sense which in turn is derived from its original sense of "mother."[50] In the first term, the use of נמתח or מתוח for *basīt* may be explained on the ground that the term *basīt* in Arabic means both "extensive" and "simple" and consequently the Hebrew translator here has used the term נמתח or מתוח, which literally means "extensive," also in the sense of "simple," analogous to the Hebrew term פשוט. As for the term התעלה, it is difficult. In this passage it undoubtedly stands for the Arabic *al-'unṣur*, as it also does quite obviously in two other passages.[51] But how did the term תעלה, which literally means "ditch," "channel," come to be used as a translation of the Arabic *'unṣur?* If one tried one could undoubtedly find some fanciful explanation for it. But we shall not even try it. Since the word תעלה here is impossible, we may assume that it is a corruption of some other word; after such an assumption, we may further assume that it is a corruption of the Arabic word *'unṣur* which the anonymous Hebrew translator has reproduced here in Hebrew transliteration as ענצר. Such an adoption of an Arabic term into Hebrew was a common practice among Hebrew translators from the Arabic.[52] In the case of the term in

[49] Steinschneider (*loc. cit.*) takes it to be the Arabic אלכלי.

[50] Cf. below, nn. 64 and 70.

[51] Hebrew, p. 268, l. 29 = Arabic, p. 1, l. 7. Hebrew, p. 270, ll. 13–14 = Arabic, p. 5, l. 5.

[52] Cf. Samuel Ibn Tibbon in his Preface to his *Perush me-ha-Millot Zorot.*

question, even after the term יסוד had become established as a translation of the Arabic *'unṣur*, the latter term was still reproduced in its original Arabic form in the Hebrew translations of the *Millot ha-Higgayon*, Ch. 9. How the four letters ענצר were corrupted into the four letters תעלה by a copyist who did not know the meaning of the transliterated Arabic and perhaps could not even decipher it is quite understandable.

But it seems that after having reproduced in Hebrew letters the Arabic word *'unṣur*, the anonymous translator himself attempted to render it into Hebrew either by עיקר[53] or by יסוד[54] or by יסוד ועיקר[55] or by עיקר ושורש.[56] In one place, where the word *'unṣur* was left untranslated, probably the same copyist, or some other copyist, tried to substitute עיקר for ענצר, but as he must have failed to cross out this latter word, the resulted reading, which occurs in the printed edition, is עיקר תעלת המים.[57] In the corresponding passage in the original Arabic, for the Hebrew עיקר תעלת there is only *'unṣur*.[58]

In Moses of Lucena's version, the same passage with its five terms is translated as follows:

והם קוראים ענין זה (1) יסוד הפשוט, (2) והמעין, (3) והממש, (4) והאבן הקדומה, (5) ויסוד.

Of these five terms only יסוד הפשוט can with certainty be said to stand for the Arabic *al-aṣl al-basīt*. As for the other four terms, they do not seem to reflect the same text as that of the printed edition. From other passages in the same translation, to be quoted later, we may gather that

53 Hebrew, p. 271, 11. 19–20 = Arabic, p. 7, 1. 18.
54 Hebrew, p. 271, 1. 22 = Arabic, p. 8, 1. 1.
55 Hebrew, p. 271, 1. 26 = Arabic, p. 8, 1. 6.
56 Hebrew, p. 221, 1. 27 = Arabic, p. 8. 1. 6.
57 Hebrew, p. 271, 1. 18.
58 Arabic, p. 7, 1. 15.

aṣl is translated by שורש;[59] ממש stands for *'unṣur*[60] and its equivalent *istaqis*;[61] יסוד stands for *'unṣur*;[62] and עיקר stands for *hayūla*.[63] In this passage, therefore, disregarding the order of the terms, we may assume that ממש stands for *'unṣur*; מעין may stand again as a literal translation of *'unṣur*; [64] and יסוד, like עיקר in the other passage, may stand for *hayūla*. But what does האבן הקדומה stand for? Is it *ṭīnah*? But why should such a common word as *ṭīnah*, for which there is such a good Hebrew translation as חומר, be translated here by the unusual expression האבן הקדומה?

The suggestion we wish to make is that האבן הקדומה stands here for the Arabic *al-jauhar al-qadīm*, which must have been the reading in the underlying Arabic text. The term *jauhar*, which, in its technical sense of substance, is usually translated into Hebrew by עצם, literally means "precious stone" and also "any stone from which is extracted, or elicited, anything by which one may profit.[65] Consequently we may assume that the term אבן here is an attempt to give a literal translation of the Arabic word for substance. The expression האבן הקדומה, therefore, means "the eternal substance," in the sense of the eternal atom, which in the theory under consideration is identical with the Platonic antemundane eternal matter. As will be recalled, the Arabic *jauhar* is also used in the sense of atom.

59 Cf. below n. 70.

60 בממש הראשון אשר יצאו ממנו כלל הממשים; cf. Arabic, p. 1, ll. 7–8.

61 Cf. below, n. 70 and cf. n. 68. In the anonymous paraphrase of the *Emunot ve-De'ot*, the term הממשים quoted by Klatzkin, s.v., stands for the Arabic (p. 2, l. 4) *al-ashyā'*, "things," Ibn Tibbon: הדברים.

62 Cf. below, n. 70.

63 Cf. below, n. 70.

64 For *umm* taken in its derivative sense of "origin" or "source" see below, n. 70.

65 Cf. Lane, *s.v.* Cf. Averroes' Epitome of *Metaphysics* I, 26, p. 16, ll. 9–13: *jauhar* is applied to the term substance because, just as the pearl is the most precious of stones, so is substance the most precious of the categories.

And since the atom is also called ממש, "element," the expression ממש קדמונית is used in the same translation as the equivalent of האבן הקדומה.[66]

Two other passages in the commentary on the *Sefer Yeṣirah* contain terms used in the sense of matter.

In one of these passages, commenting on the term אמות in *Sefer Yeṣirah* I, 1, Saadia interprets it to mean *uṣūl* and refers to his previous statement, quoted above, to the effect that (1) *'anāṣir* is also called (2) *usūl*, (3) *ummahāt*, (4) *hayūla*, and (5) *istiqisāt*.[67] This statement is not exactly a reproduction of the previous statement referred to by him. For one thing, the term *ṭīnah* is omitted. For another, it contains the new term *istiqisāt*, which is the plural form of the Arabic transliteration of the Greek στοιχεῖον and is used, on the whole, as the equivalent of the Arabic *'unṣur*.[68] Of the two Hebrew versions of this passage, the anonymous version used by Judah bar Barzillai is hopelessly corrupted,[69] but the one of Moses of Lucena is an accurate translation in which we can easily correlate the five Hebrew terms to the five original Arabic terms. It reads as follows:

ופרשתי אמות שרשים כאשר הקדמתי כי (1) היסודות יאמר לו (2) שרשים (3) ואמהות (4) ועיקרים (5) וממשים.

In the other passage, commenting on the term אבות in *Sefer Yeṣirah* I, 4, Saadia says: "I have translated (1) *abot* by (2) *ummahāt* for as I have said before the terms (1) *ābā'* (2) *ummahāt*, (3) *uṣūl*, (4) *hayūla*, (5) *'anāṣir*, and (6) *is-*

[66] Quoted by Steinschneider, *loc. cit.*: אבן הקדומה הנקראת ממש קדמונית. Cf. also *Perush Sefer Yeṣirah* by Jacob ben Nissim in Dukes, *Konteros ha-Masorah*, p. 80: שהתחלתו לאבן קדומה, כלומר לממש הקדמוני.

[67] Arabic, p. 14, 11. 6–7.

[68] Cf. *Cuzari* V, 2 (ed. Herschfeld), p. 294, 1. 20: אלאסטקסאת and p. 296, 1. 25: ענאצר.

[69] p. 274, ll. 25–26: ומדרש אמות שורש כמו שאמרנו בתחלת הספר שורש ויסוד ותעלה מדרש אמות והוא אם הדבר ואמות הדרך.

tiqisāt all have the same meaning."[70] There is no translation of this passage in Judah bar Barzillai. But the translation of Moses of Lucena is almost literal, and each Hebrew term in it may be identified with its corresponding term in Arabic. It reads as follows:

פירשתי (1) אבות (2) אמהות כפי מה שהקדמתי כי היסודות נקראות (2) אמות (1) ואבות (3) ושרשים (4) ועיקרים (5) יסודות (6) וממשים שכל אלה אחד.

As a result of our discussion, then, the Hebrew *ḥomer* is not a translation of either the Greek *hyle* or of the Arabic *māddah*; it is a translation, through the Arabic *ṭīnah*, of the Platonic *ekmageion*, but, starting with Judah Ibn Tibbon, it has been conventionally used as the equivalent of *māddah* and sometimes also of *hyle*.

The Arabic *māddah* is not a translation of the Greek *hyle*; it is an original Arabic term first used as a designation of the matter of the four elements to indicate that it had extension, but it soon came to be used as a designation of matter in general. The Hebrew for it, literally, is משך.

Nor is the Hebrew האבן הקדומה a translation of the Greek *hyle*; it is a translation of the Arabic *al-jauhar al-qadīm*, and hence the equivalent of the Hebrew העצם הקדום.

The Hebrew ממש is not in itself used in the sense of "matter" nor of "eternal matter" nor of "body."[71] Technically it is used in the sense of "element," the equivalent of יסוד, and hence, with the qualifying adjective קדמון, in the sense of "eternal element."[72] Nontechnically, it is

[70] Arabic, p. 31, 11. 9–10.

[71] Cf. Ben Yehuda, *Millon*, s. v.: ובלשון המחקר, כנוי להחומר הקדמון, Klatzkin, *Osar*, s. v.: בהוראת חומר או גוף, וביחוד: החומר הקדמון והיסודות.

[72] Cf. above, n. 66. In this sense it is quite evidently used also in Berechiah ha-Nakdan, *Sefer Maṣref*, ed. Gollancz, §33: החכמים קוראים את אחד הממשים חום. Or, perhaps more accurately, it is used here in the sense of one of the four elementary properties (cf. *De Gen. et Corr.* II, 2, 330b, 3 ff.).

used in the sense of "thing" or "something," as the equivalent of דבר.[73]

The term תעלה in the sense of "matter" is a corruption of ענצר, the Hebrew transliteration of the Arabic *'unṣur*. As for the Arabic *'unṣur*, it was originally used as a translation of the Greek χυμός "humor," whence it became "element" and then also "matter."

[73] Cf. above, n. 61.

II

SAADIA ON THE TRINITY AND INCARNATION

IN HIS DISCUSSION of the Trinity, Saadia refers to two conceptions of it current among Christians. He describes them as the view "of the common people (عوامّ, עמי הארץ) among them" who "confess a Trinity which is conceived of only in corporeal terms" and "the elite (חכמים خواصّ) among them." [1] The expression "common people" as a description of one of the two contrasting views referred to by him does not give us an accurate idea of the view he had in mind. The exact meaning of the view which he had in mind here may be gathered from the work of his contemprary Yaḥyā ibn ʿAdī, a Christian apologist writing in Arabic. In that work, Yaḥyā tries to answer a certain Muslim critic of Christianity who argued that the Trinitarian formula "one substance (جوهر), three hypostases (اقانيم)," supplemented by the Christian belief that each hypostasis is God, must logically mean a belief in three substances and hence threee Gods. [2] In answer, Yaḥyā draws a distinction between "what the ignorant (جهّال) among Christians imagine concerning the hypostases" and "what the most learned (علماء) among Christians and those versed in their doctrine say," ascribing

[1] *Emunot ve-Deʿot* II, 5, p. 86, ll. 5-7. Chapter references are to the Yozefov edition; page and line references are to the Arabic text edited by S. Landauer; English quotations are from Samuel Rosenblatt's translation, except where the discussion of the subject required a more literal translation of the text.

[2] Cf. *Petits Traités Apologétiques de Yaḥyā ben ʿAdī.* Texte arabe . . . et traduit en français par Augustin Périer, Paris, 1920, p. 44, l. 5-p. 45, l. 2.

to the former the view that "the hypostases are essences of three subjects each of which differs from the other in virtue of its own self" and characterizing this view as being "only error and impiety, and one from which indeed it would have to follow that its exponents believed that the Creator is three substances and three Gods." [1] Now it can be shown, I believe, that by "the ignorant among Christians" Yaḥyā does not refer simply to mere uninformed people. He refers to that Christian sect known as the Tritheites, whose chief representatives were John Askusnages and John Philoponus, for the description of "the ignorant among Christians" as given by Yaḥyā corresponds exactly to the description of the Tritheites in Photius, which reads as follows: "Some of the more shameless, having taken nature (φύσιν) and hypostasis (ὑπόστασιν) and substance (οὐσίαν) to mean the same, did not shrink from affirming also that in the Holy Trinity there are three substances (οὐσίας), whence they teach, if not in word, yet at least in thought, that there are three Gods and three Divinities." [2] Like Yaḥyā's "ignorant among Christians," therefore, Saadia's "common people among them" is to be taken to refer to the Tritheites as represented by John Askusnages and John Philoponus. Accordingly, as we shall see, he couples these Christian Tritheites with the Dualists and criticizes both of them from a common principle. The Dualists he had in mind are the various followers of Zoroastrian Dualism, such as Manichaeans, Mazdakites, Bardaisanites, and Marcionites, who were known to the Muslims of the time of Saadia, and even after his time, and were to them still a subject of vital discussion. [3]

The common principle from which he criticizes the ditheism of the various forms of Zoroastrianism and the tritheism of

[1] *Ibid.*, p. 45, ll. 2-8.

[2] Photius, *Bibliotheca* 230 (PG 103, 1080 BC).

[3] *Cf.* A. S. Halkin's note in his translation of Baghdādī's *Al-Farḳ bain al-Firāḳ*, p. 179, n. 2; *cf.* also *Ibn Ḥazm, al-Fiṣal, fi'l-Milal* (Cairo, 1317-27), I, pp. 34 ff.

the Christian sect is the belief in the unity of God in the sense of numerical unity, as a denial of any form of polytheism. This principle he establishes first by quoting, as he says, "from the books of the prophets,"[1] various verses which affirm that God is one and there is no other God with Him[2] and then supporting it by various arguments which he describes as being "by the way of speculation."[3] With this as an established belief, he proceeds to discuss the view of the Dualists, to whom he explicitly refers as the believers in "two principles" (שני שרשים اصلين),[4] first refuting the arguments by which they support their view[5] and then refuting their view itself.[6] But then he conjures up a straw-man who raises two questions.

In one of the questions, he asks: "But in that case, what is the meaning of these two names, Lord (*Adonay*) and God (*Elohim*) that are constantly employed in the Bible with reference to God?"[7] This is quite evidently an attempt to show that a sort of Dualism is implied in the Bible itself. It reflects a passage in which the rabbis of old suggest that the Dualists might find an excuse for their belief in "two powers" (שתי רשויות) in the names "Lord" and "God" which are used in the Bible.[8]

In the second question he asks: "But what is the meaning of the statement in Scripture, 'And now the Lord God hath sent me and His spirit'" (Isa 48: 16).[9] This is not a question raised from the point of view of Dualism; it is a question raised from the point of view of the Trinity, for the very

[1] *Emunot ve-De'ot* II, 1, p. 80, ll. 6-7.

[2] *Ibid.*, p. 79, l. 15-p. 80, l. 6.

[3] *Ibid.*, p. 80, l. 7-p. 81, l. 2. So also in his Commentary on his Arabic translation of Proverbs (9: 13-18; 24: 21-22; ed. Derenbourg, pp. 53, 138), Saadia couples the Dualists and the Trinitarians in his discussion.

[4] *Ibid.*, p. 81, l. 6.

[5] *Ibid.*, p. 81, l. 3-p. 82, l. 5.

[6] *Ibid.*, p. 82, ll. 5-14.

[7] *Ibid.* II, 3, p. 83, ll. 3-4.

[8] *Mekilta Baḥodesh* 5 (ed. Lauterbach, II, p. 231).

[9] *Emunot ve-De'ot* II, 3, p. 84, ll. 6-7.

same verse is quoted in an Arabic work by the Christian Abucara as referring to the Chiristian Trinity.[1] It is to be noted, however, that there is a difference between the Trinity taken by Abucara to be referred to in the verse quoted by him and the Trinity taken by Saadia's questioner to be referred to in the same verse quoted by him. Abucara's Trinity is not that of the Tritheites but rather that which he ascribes to "the most learned among Christians," for Abucara explicitly rejects Tritheism, of which, he says, "certain unwise people" have accused the Christians.[2] The Trinity of Saadia's hypothetical questioner is, as we have seen, the Trinity of the Tritheites, inasmuch as his question is coupled by Saadia with the Dualistic question and is answered by the same principle of numerical unity. Quite evidently Saadia has allowed himself to take the verse quoted by Abucara as proof-text for his non-Tritheistic conception of the Trinity and put it in the mouth of his fictitious questioner and make him use it as proof-text for his Tritheistic conception of the Trinity.

Having disposed of the Trinitarian view of the "common people" among the Christians, that is to say, the common people who in their simple-mindedness, and perhaps unbeknown to themselves, have a conception of the Trinity like that of the professed Tritheites, Saadia takes up the Trinitarian view of "the elite" among them, who maintain that their belief in the Trinity is based upon rational speculation and subtle reasoning."[3] Not all those who were opposed to Tritheism are taken up by Saadia. No mention is made by him of such extreme opponents of Tritheism as the Sabellians and Arians. The "elite" whom he speaks of are those who represent the orthodox conception of the Trinity as approved of by the Oecumenical Church Councils. The corresponding "most learned among Christians" of Yaḥyā ibn ʿAdī are

[1] Georg Graf, *Die arabischen Schriften des Theodor Abū Qurra* III, 10 (1910), p. 153; VII, 15, pp. 193-194.

[2] *Ibid.*, III, 17, p. 149.

[3] *Emunot ve-Deʿot* II, 5, p. 96, ll. 7-8.

more precisely described as "the learned Imams (الائمّة العلماء), such as Dionysius [the Areopagite], Gregory [of Nazianzus or of Nyssa], Basil the Great, John Chrysostomos,"[1] on whose Trinitarian view "all the three sects of Christians agree,"[2] by which three sects he means the Malkites, the Nestorians, and the Jacobites. It is this orthodox conception of the Trinity that Saadia undertakes to discuss. Now this orthodox conception of the Trinity insisted upon the belief in the unity of God. But it maintained that the unity of God does not mean absolute unity but only relative unity, a unity which may be conceived as consisting after a certain manner of inseparable parts. In his discussion of this orthodox conception of the Trinity, Saadia, therefore, tries to establish first the principle that the unity of God means absolute unity, that is, absolute simplicity, and then, from that principle, he proceeds to discuss the Trinity.

Preliminary to taking up Saadia's discussion of the subject, I should like to make three general observations.

First, the unity of God in the sense of absolute unity or absolute simplicity, with all its implications, was unknown in Greek philosophy. In Greek philosophy, the unity and simplicity of God went only so far as to deny of Him the composition of matter and form. Nor could the conception of unity in the sense of absolute simplicity be derived directly from the biblical insistence upon the unity of God. The unity of God insisted upon in Scripture means only numerical unity. The conception of the unity of God in the sense of absolute simplicity, with all its implications, was first introduced into philosophy and religion by Philo. He arrived at that view by the rigid application of philosophic reasoning to the biblical principle of the unlikeness of God to anything else in the world. This I have explained in the chapter on "The Unknowability of God and Divine Attributes" in *Philo*, Vol. II, pp. 94-164.

[1] *Petits* (above p. 1, n. 2), p. 53, ll. 4-6.
[2] *Ibid.*, p. 54, l. 8-p. 55, l. 1.

Second, the Trinitarian controversies in Christianity turned on the question whether the unity of God should be conceived of as interpreted by Philo in the sense of absolute simplicity or whether it should be conceived of in one of the various forms of relative unity enumerated by Aristotle. This I have explained in the chapters on "The Mystery of the Trinity" and "Heresies" in *The Philosophy of the Church Fathers*, Vol. I, pp. 305-365 and pp. 575-608.

Third, the controversies of divine attributes in Islam, which had arisen shortly after the Muslim conquest of Syria in the course of religious debates between Christians and Muslims, similarly turned on the question whether the unity of God should be conceived as interpreted by Christian orthodoxy in the sense of relative unity or whether it should be conceived of as interpreted by the heretical Sabellians and Arians in the sense of absolute simplicity. In these debates, we have reason to believe, the Christians represented the first person of the Trinity, the Father, as meaning "essence" or "existence" or "goodness," the second person, the Word or the Son, as meaning "life" or "knowledge," and the third person, the Holy Spirit, as meaning "knowledge" or "life" or "power". We may also assume that the Christian debaters tried to convince the Muslims that the second and third persons of the Trinity are nothing but the terms "knowing" and "powerful" or "knowing" and "living" or "living" and "knowing" or "living" and "powerful," by which God is described in the Koran and that there is nothing in the Koran against the Christian belief that the predication of God of either pair of these terms reflects the existence in God of real beings, or rather persons or hypostases, as they were called. The Muslims could find no flaw in the reasoning and no objection to the conclusion. They therefore accepted the view that in God there were real beings to correspond to certain terms predicated of God in the Koran. But then, when the Christian debaters continued to argue that these two persons of the Trinity, the second and the third, are

Gods like the first person, the Muslim balked and quoted against them the Koranic verses, "say not three... God is only one God" (4: 169) and "they surely are infidels who say, God is the third of three, for there is no God but one God" (5: 77). Thus there had arisen in Islam the belief, which became the orthodox belief, that certain terms predicated of God in the Koran have, corresponding to them, real beings in God, called attributes, which are coeternal with God, but eternally inseparable from Him, and because they were eternally inseparable from God and also because they were not called Gods, the unity of God, so vehemently insisted upon in the Koran, is preserved. The unity, however, like the unity in Christian orthodoxy, was only a relative unity.

The establishment of this belief in the existence of real attributes evoked opposition. This opposition was like the Sabellian opposition in Christianity to the reality of the second and third persons of the Trinity. It saw in the assumption of real attributes, even though not called Gods, a violation of the true unity of God, which, as laid down by Philo and followed by Sabellianism, they regarded as absolute simplicity. Like Sabellianism in Christianity, therefore, which declared the second and third persons of the Trinity to be mere names of God designating His actions, this opposition declared the terms predicated of God in the Koran to be only names of God, designating His actions. In their interpretation of terms predicated of God, these Muslim Antiattributists thus arrived at a position first formulated by Philo. And just as in Christianity, counterbalancing the Sabellian opponents to the orthodox conception of the Trinity there were opponents whose conception of the Trinity degenerated into Tritheism, so in Islam, counterbalancing these Antiattributistic opponents to the orthodox conception of Attributes, there were opponents with whom the belief in attributes degenerated into a crude anthropomorphism. The name given to them was "the Likeners" (المشبّهة), because they likened God to other beings.

That this is how the problem of attributes had originated in Islam can be shown by arguments evidential, terminological, and contextual. To begin with, in Islam itself, the opponents of the reality of attributes argued that the orthodox conception of attributes is analogous to the Christian doctrine of the Trinity. Then, two Arabic terms used for what we call "attributes," namely, *ṣifāt* and *maʿāniyy*, are translations of two Greek terms, χαρακτηριστικά and πράγματα, which were part of the technical vocabulary of the Trinity. Finally, the terms upon which the earliest controversies over attributes centered correspond exactly to the terms by which the second and third persons of the Trinity were known to the Muslims. Thus in the reports of the earliest discussions of the problem of attributes, the controversies turn always either on the attributes "knowledge and power" or on the attributes "life and knowledge" or on a combination of these two pairs of attributes, namely, "knowledge, power, and life." All this I have explained in my papers on "The Muslim Attributes and the Christian Trinity," *Harvard Theological Review*, vol. 49 (1956), 1-18, and "Philosophical Implications of Divine Attributes in the Kalam," *Journal of the American Oriental Society*, vol. 70 (1950), 73-80.

This is what Saadia knew about the question as to whether the unity of God means only relative unity or absolute unity, when he was about to take up this problem preparatory to his criticism of the orthodox Christian doctrine of the Trinity. In Islam, he knew, it was involved in the problem as to the meaning of the terms "knowing" and "powerful" or "living" and "knowing" or all these three terms, "knowing, powerful, and living," when predicated of God. He naturally knew that among the Muslims there were three views on the problem and that the view which maintained that these three terms mean the existence of three real attributes in God was charged by its opponents to be analogous to the orthodox Christian doctrine that the second and third persons of the Trinity are real beings really distinct from each other. Finally, he knew that of the three persons of the Trinity the Father was described by the term "essence" or "existence" or "goodness," the Son by the term "life" or "knowledge", and the Holy Spirit by the term "knowledge" or "life" or "power."

With all this in the back of his mind, when, as a basis for his criticism of the Trinity, he wanted to establish the view that the unity of God is absolute unity, instead of attacking the problem directly, as did, for instance, his contemporary al-Muḳammaṣ, [1] he attacked it indirectly by discussing the meaning of the terms "living, powerful, and knowing," which are predicated of God in Scripture. [2] In the course of his discussion, he alludes to the three views current in Islam on the meaning of these three terms, without actually naming the sects sponsoring them. Having in mind, "the Likeners," to whom he refers as those who "compare God to His creatures" or as those who take every term predicated of God in Scripture "in its corporeal rather than in its metaphorical sense," [3] he establishes the unlikeness between God and any of His creatures as a scriptural principle. [4] Then, having in mind the Muslim Attributists' view that terms predicated of God reflect the existence in him of real beings called *ṣifāt*, "attributes," or *ma'āniyy*, "things" (πράγματα), he says: "Let no one imagine that in God there are different things (עניינים معان)." [5] Having so briefly dismissed the view of the Attributists, he aligns himself with the Antiattributists and at great length he tries to show how the terms "living, powerful, knowing," when predicated of God, are "expalanations (פרושי شروح) of the term Creator." [6] These three terms, as we have seen, were the terms upon which the early controversies about attributes were centered.

Thus Saadia has established, indirectly, by rational argu-

1 See *Perush Sefer Yeṣirah* by Judah ben Barzilai, p. 78. ll. 1-3.
2 *Emunot ve-De'ot* II, l. p. 79, l. 19-p. 80, l. 4; II, 4, p. 54, ll. 14 ff.
3 *Ibid.*, II, l. p. 80, ll. 10-11.
4 *Ibid.*, p. 79, ll. 13-14; p. 80, ll. 5-6.
5 *Ibid.* II, 4, p. 85, ll. 6-7.
6 *Ibid.*, ll. 17-18.

ments, that the unity of God does not mean only relative or numerical unity: it means also absolute or internal unity, that is, absolute simplicity. Having thus arrived by rational arguments that unity means absolute unity he tries to find scriptural proof-texts for it. He cites three verses, [1] of which the first and the third are as follows: (1) "There is none else beside Him" (Deut 4: 35); (3) "the Lord shall be one and His name one" (Zech 14: 9). Of these two verses, the first has been previously quoted by him as a scriptural proof-text for numerical unity. [2] On what ground he quotes it now again as scriptural proof-text for internal unity is not clear. Perhaps on the basis of his own Arabic translation of the Pentateuch, where this verse is translated by him to read, "There is no other than He and there is none except Him", the verse was taken by him to contain two kinds of denial: (1) a denial of any other God; (2) a denial of anything else, eternal like Him, within Him. [3] More certain it is that his third verse has been taken by him to contain in its two parts affirmations of two kinds of unity: the expression "the Lord shall be one" was taken to mean numerical unity, and the expression "and His name one" was taken to mean that "His name," that is, name "Creator," is "one," because the terms "living," "powerful," and "knowing" are only, as he himself has said, explanations of it.

As for the second of the three proof-texts, it is a quotation in the Arabic text of his work of the original Hebrew of a part of a verse in Job, here italicized, which in the Authorized Version reads as follows: "Lo, these are parts of His ways: *but how a little portion is heard of Him?*" (Job 26: 14). What

[1] *Ibid.* II, 4, p. 85, l. 21-p. 86, l. 2.

[2] *Ibid.* II, 2, p. 82, ll. 15-16.

[3] The Hebrew of Deut. 4: 39, אין עוד מבלעדו, is translated by Saadia into Arabic: לא גירה ולא סואה, as if the Hebrew had read אין עוד ואין מבלעדו, "there is no other than He and there is none (or nothing) except Him". Elsewhere similar Hebrew expression ואין עוד מבלעדי (Isa. 45: 21) is translated by Saadia simply by ולא אלאה גירי. In Deut. 4: 39 there occurs only the expression אין עוד which Saadia translates by לא סואה.

relevance this quoted part of the verse has here to his attempt to show that the unity of God means internal unity is not clear. Fortunately in this case, Saadia's Arabic version of the Book of Job clears up the matter quite satisfactorily. His Arabic version of this verse reads as follows: "Lo, these are some of His descriptions (אוצאפה), but what thing thereof (שי מן אלאמור) is heard of Him?" Now the term *shay*, "thing," is used in the Kalam as synonymous with the term *ma'na*, which I have shown to be a translation of the Greek πρᾶγμα, as another word for *ṣifah*, "attribute." Thus al-Ash'arī is quoted by Ibn Ḥazm as calling the attributes *ashyā'*, [1] whereas Shahrastānī quotes the Ash'arites as calling them *ma'āniyy* [2] The use of the term *shay* as the equivalent of *ma'na* and *ṣifah* is also implied in al-Ash'arī's statement that "'Abdallah ibn Kullāb used to call the *ma'āniyy* which subsists in bodies accidents and he used to call them *ashyā'* and he used to call them *ṣifāt*." [3] Saadia himself [4] and so also Ibn Ḥazm [5] speak of the second and third persons of the Trinity, which are regarded as analogous to the orthodox Muslim attributes, as *shay'ani*, "two things," and Ibn Ḥazm speaks of all the three persons of the Trinity as "three things (*ashyā'*). [6] Accordingly, in quoting the verse of Job as proof-text for the internal unity of God, Saadia takes that verse to mean that none of "His descriptions," that is, none of the terms which are predicated of God, is a "thing," that is, a real attribute existing in God as something other than He.

Once he has established the absolute or internal unity, that is, the absolute simplicity, of God, Saadia proceeds to deal with the Trinity. "Hereupon," he begins, "I wish to say that, with regard to this doctrine of the unity of God, the Christians went astray and came to believe that there is in

[1] *Al-Fiṣal fī al-Milal* IV, p. 207, l. 13.
[2] *Nihāyat al-Ikdām* (ed. Guillaume, 1934), 181, l. 4.
[3] *Makālāt al-Islāmīyīn* (ed. Ritter, 1929), p. 370, ll. 11-12.
[4] *Emunot ve-De'ot* II, 5, pp. 86, l. 10.
[5] Ibn Ḥazm, *Fiṣal* IV, p. 207, l. 22.
[6] *Ibid.* I, p. 49, l. 1.

God an otherness (غيريه [ת]ולתות), which led them to make Him three, thus deviating from the true belief in the unity of God." [1] He therefore undertakes to refute them by rational arguments, and, as he says, with the help of "Him who is one in the true sense of the term unity." [2] And he is not going to deal, he says, with the Tritheites, to whom he refers as the "common people" among the Christians and whose use of a scriptural proof-text for their view, as we have seen, he has already refuted; nor, without telling us, is he dealing with the heretical Sabellians, whom he does not even mention; he is going to deal, he tells us, only with the view of the authoritative representatives of orthodoxy. Reflecting the opinion common among the Antiattributists that the view of the orthodox Attributists is analogous to the orthodox Christian Trinity, he speaks loosely of the three "hypostases" as "attributes" and reproduces the reasoning by which they claim to have arrived at "their belief in [the hypostases of] the Trinity" as follows: "They arrived at these three attributes (صفات, מדות) and adhered to them by asserting that only a thing that is living and knowing can create and, because they believed that the life and knowledge of that thing which is the Creator are two things (شيئين, שני דברים) other than His essence, these became for them three." [3] The three hypostases of the Trinity are thus represented by him to be "essence" (ذات, עצם), "life" حيوة, חיות), and "knowledge" (علم, חכמה). The description of the first person as "essence" and the description of the second and third persons as "life" and "knowledge," are to be found, as we have seen, in the various trinitarian formulae reproduced in Arabic works.

The arguments raised by Saadia against this orthodox conception of the Trinity are two.

First, he argues in effect that the belief in the Trinity involves a violation of the Law of Contradiction, for, on the

1 *Emunot ve-De'ot* II, 5, p. 86, ll. 2-3.
2 *Ibid.*, ll. 3-4.
3 *Ibid.*, II, 5, p. 86, ll. 8-10.

one hand, the Christians insist that in God there is a numerical distinction between three persons and, on the other, they profess that God is immaterial. Having in mind the Aristotelian statement that 'all things that are many in number have matter,"[1] he phrases his argument as follows: "If [as they openly profess] they do not believe that God is a body, then their allegation that there exists in Him an otherness (غيرية, שנוי = זולתיות) to the extent that one attribute [*i.e.*, hypostasis] of His is not identical with any other attribute of His is equivalent to an allegation on their part that He is really corporeal, to which they only give expression by another term, for anything in which there is otherness is inevitably a body."[2]

It is to be noted here that this type of argument, phrased in various terms, has been discussed in Christian literature ever since the rise of the problem among the Church Fathers and it was a subject of disputation between Christians and Muslims during the time of Saadia. An analysis of the problem and of its solutions is to be found in my discussion of the mystery of the Trinity referred to above.

Second, he argues again in effect that, if the Christians believe that the existence of the second and third persons in the sense of the attributes of life and knowledge is compatible with the unity of God, why did they limit the persons to these two and did not add other persons to correspond to the attributes of power and hearing and seeing and the like.[3] A similar criticism of the doctrine of the Trinity is reported by ibn Ḥazm in the name of the Ash'arites, who, as he was told by one of them, found fault with the Christians "because

[1] *Metaph.* XII, 8, 1074a, 33-34.

[2] *Emunot ve-De'ot* II, 5, p. 86, ll. 13-16.

For the term שנוי in this passage the context requires **זולתיות**. The underlying Arabic term غيرية, as a translation of the Greek ἑτερότης means both "otherness" and "alteration". Judah ibn Tibbon took it here wrongly in the sense of "alteration". *See* Neumark, *op. cit.* (below p. 15, n. 6), p. 210. 4.

[3] *Ibid.* II, 5, p. p. 87, ll. 11-19.

they assume that there coexist with God only two things (شيئين) and do not assume that there coexist with Him a greater number of things,"[1] of which he mentions the number "fifteen."[2]

Following this refutation, Saadia undertakes to refute Christian interpretation of certain verses in the Hebrew Bible as refering to the Trinity.[3] The number of such verses quoted by him is six. Of these six verses, the four middle ones, namely, Job 33: 4, Ps. 33/32: 6, Prov 8: 22, Gen 1: 26, are, again, to be found so interpreted in Abucara's work.[4] As for the other two verses, the sixth, "And the Lord appeared unto him... and, lo, three men" (Gen 18: 1-2), it is taken by some Church Fathers to refer to the persons of the Trinity;[5] but I could not find any work where the first verse, "The spirit of the Lord spoke by me and His word was upon my tongue" (2 Sam 23: 2), was similarly used as a proof-text for the Trinity. It is to be noted how careful Saadia is in his choice of words. The four verses which he himself must have seen used by Abucara as proof-texts for the Trinity he introduces by such expressions as "I find some of them cite as proof[6].... Also they say";[7] "I also found one of them who interpreted";[8] "I have seen others who rely on... and say."[9] The sixth verse, which he has not found in Abucara

[1] Ibn Ḥazm, *Fiṣal* IV, p. 207, ll. 22-23. *Cf.* answer to this kind of objection by Elias of Nisibis in David Kaufmann, *Gesammelte Schriften*, III (1915), p. 65.

[2] *Ibid.*, l. 21.

[3] *Ibid.*, II, 5-6, p. 88, l. 2-p. 90, l. 16.

[4] *Op. cit.*, above p. 4, n. 1. The verses occur in Abucara as follows:
(2) Job 23: 4 in III, 10, p. 143;
(3) Ps. 33/32: 6 in VII, 16, p. 196;
(4) Prov. 8: 22 in III, 20, p. 153; VII, 14, p. 193;
(5) Gen. 1: 26 in III, 20, p. 153, VII, 16, pp. 195-196.

[5] *Cf.*, e.g., Justin Martyr, *Dialogus cum Tryphone Judaeo* 56 and 126; Irenaeus, *Adversus Haereses* IV, 10, l; Eusebius, *Historia Ecclesiastica* I, 2, 7.

[6] *Emunot ve-De'ot* II, 5, p. 88, l. 9.

[7] *Ibid.*, l. 11.

[8] *Ibid.* III, 6, p. 89, ll. 9-10.

[9] *Ibid.*, ll. 16-17.

but must have heard that it had been used by the Church Fathers, is introduced, by the words "Others conjecture... and say," [1] whereas the first, for which he evidently had no source at all, is introduced by the words "If they derive their proof from Scripture, as, for example, someone of them might assert." [2] In other words, he himself supplied the Christians with a proof-text only to refute it.

While Saadia's treatment of the Trinity, with the exception of an allusion to the Tritheites, does not contain a classification of the various sects in Christianity, such as may be found in Arabic works dealing with Christianity, [3] his treatment of Christology does contain a classification of views of the various sects. [4] He enumerates four sects, three of whom he describes as older and one as that which appeared only recently. [5] It would be futile to identify these four sects with any of the sects known to us from modern works on the history of Christian doctrine; attempts made by students of Saadia to identify these sects by that method have proved only confusing. [6] We must go to descriptions of Christian sects in Arabic sources for the identification of these four

[1] *Ibid.* II, 6. p. 90, l. 1.2.

[2] *Ibid.* II, 5, p. 87, l. 20-p. 88, l. 1.

[3] *Cf.* Ibn Ḥazm, *Fiṣal* I, pp. 48 ff.; Shahrastānī, *Al-Milal wa'l-Niḥal* (ed. Cureton), pp. 171 ff.

[4] *Emunot ve-De'ot* II, 7, p. 90, l. 17-p. 91, l. 16.

[5] *Ibid.*, p. 90, ll. 17-18.

[6] Here are attempts to identify these four sects by the following authors: (1) Kaufmann, *Attributenlehre* (1877), pp. 50-51; Jacob Guttmann, *Die Religionsphilosophie des Saadia* (1882), pp. 108-113; Neumark, *Geschichte der jüdischen Philosophie des Mittelalters*, Zweiter Band 2 (1928), pp. 191-192; Ventura, *La Philosophie de Saadia Gaon* (1934), p. 184.

Kaufmann: (1) No identification; (2) Apollinaris; (3) Theodore of Mopsuestia; (4) Ebionites and Monarchians.

Guttmann: (1) Monarchianism and Sabellius; (2) Arianism; (3) Paul of Semosata; (4) [Spanish] Adoptionism.

Neumark: (1) Monophysites; (2) Dyophysites; (3) and (4) No identification.

Ventura: (1) Docetism of various Gnostic sects; (2) Chalcedonian Creed; (3) Roman Adoptionism; (4) Spanish Adoptionism.

sects enumerated by Saadia. Though the sources which we shall quote come from a time after Saadia, they undoubtedly reproduce Christological views as understood by Muslim writes at the time of Saadia.

The first sect is described by Saadia as that which believes that "both the body and the spirit of their Messiah are from the Creator." [1] Before we try to identify this sect, let us comment on the terms "body" and "spirit" which are used by Saadia in his description of the various views of these sects on Christology. These two terms, we take it, stand for what in Christological controversies is known as the contrast between the "humanity" (الناسوت, ἀνθρωπότης) and "divinity" (اللاهوت, θεότης) in Jesus, for it is the question of the "humanity" and "divinity" in Jesus, and in the case of Apollinaris also the question of "soul" or of "rational soul" in Jesus, and not that of the "body" and "spirit" in him, that was the main point at issue in the Christological controversies. A similar use of the term "spirit," in the sense of "divinity," in contrast to "body," in the sense of "humanity," is implied in a passage in Shahrastānī, where, comparing two ways in which Christians explain the union of the Word with the body in Jesus, he reports that they either say that "it appears in it like the appearance of the spiritual in the corporeal" or they say that "the divinity puts on the humanity as a breastplate." [2] Taken in this sense, the statement that "both the body and the spirit of their Messiah are from God" means a denial of humanity or of a human nature in Jesus, and the sect thus described here by Saadia is to be identified with the Monophysites or, as they are known to the Muslims, the Jacobites. The Jacobites are described by the Muslims as believing that "the Word was transformed into flesh and blood, so that God became the Messiah and was manifest in his body, or rather He was himself the Messiah." [3] This

[1] *Emunot ve-De'ot* II, 7, p. 90, l. 18.
[2] Shahrastānī, *Milal*, p. 172, ll. 6-7.
[3] *Ibid.*, p. 179, ll. 19-20; cf. Ibn Ḥazm, *Fiṣal*, I, p. 49, l. 9.

is exactly what Saadia meant to say about the first sect, for from his subsequent criticism of this sect it is clear that his statement that "both the body and the spirit... are from God" means that "some part of God became body and spirit." [1]

The second sect is described by him as that which believes that "his body was created but his spirit is from the Creator." [2] This reflects exactly the following Muslim conception of the Nestorians: "They maintain that Mary did not give birth to God; she gave birth only to the man; and that God did not beget the man; He begot only the God." [3] What Saadia therefore means to say of the second sect is that they believed that the humanity in Jesus was created, that is to say, was given birth by Mary, but that the divinity in him was "from the Creator," that is to say, was begotten by God.

The third sect is described by him as that which believes that "both his body and his spirit were created but that there was in him another spirit from the Creator." [4] This formula, I take it, is made up of two formulations of the Christology ascribed by Muslim writers to the Malkites, that is, to those who followed the Decree of Chalcedon (451). The first part of Saadia's formula, namely, "both his body and his spirit were created," reflects exactly that formulation of the Malkites' view which reads: "Mary bore the God and the man." [5] The second part of Saadia's formula, namely, "but there was in him another spirit from the Creator" reflects that formulation of the Malkites' view which, after stating that the Malkites believe that in Jesus there are two natures, a human and a divine, adds that they believe also "that the Messiah is a hypostasis (اقنوم) of the nature of God only, and it is an uncompounded nature, being [un]derived

1 *Emunot ve-De'ot* II, 7, p. 91, ll. 5-6.
2 *Ibid.*, p. 90, l. 19
3 Ibn Ḥazm, *Fiṣal,* I, p. 49, ll. 6-7.
4 *Emunot ve-De'ot* II, 7, p. 90, ll. 19-20.
5 Ibn Ḥazm, *Fiṣal,* I, p. 49, l. 4.

from the two aforementioned natures." [1] This last statement, evidently, was taken by Saadia to mean, and perhaps that is exactly what it meant, that Jesus was born with two natures, a human and divine, and then another divine nature was added to it. If this is what the last statement meant, it was based upon a misunderstanding of the Chalcedonian Decree stating that "one and the same Christ" is "in two natures" and that these two natures are "in one person and one hypostasis," namely, "God the Word." [2] What the Creed means is that of the two natures in Jesus, the divine and the human, the divine nature, that is, the Word, is both a person and a nature, whereas the human nature is only a nature, and therefore it is the divine nature that constitutes the one person. [3]

Thus the first three sects mentioned by Saadia are the Jacobites, the Nestorians, and the Malkites, those whom Muslim historiographers describe as "their fundamental sects (عمدتهم)" [4] or "their main sects." [5] These three sects, while differing in their Christological views, were all orthodox in their view on the Trinity, as is testified by Yaḥyā ibn ʿAdī, who says that, with regard to the orthodox conception of the Trinity, "the three sects" are fully in agreement. [6] Ordinarily, in Muslim works dealing with Christianity, the Malkites are mentioned first, then come the Nestorians and the Jacobites, [7] and the Malkites are described by Masʿūdī as "the

[1] *Al Ghazālī: Réfutation Excellente de la Divinité de Jésus Christ d'aprè les Évangiles*, Texte établi, traduit et commenté par Robert Chidiac (1939), p. 32, ll. 12-15 of the text, and cf. correction of reading on p. 87 of the introductory material.

[2] *See* Dnezinger et Bannwart, *Enchiridion Symbolorum* (1922), § 148.

[3] On the meaning of this, see the chapter on "The Mystery of the Incarnation", in my *Philosophy of the Church Fathers*, I, pp. 364-433.

[4] Ibn Ḥazm, *Fiṣal* I, p. 48, l. 22.

[5] Shahrastānī, *Milal*, p. 173, l. 11.

[6] *Petits* (above p. 1, n. 2), p. 55, l. 1 ff.

[7] *Cf.* Masʿūdī, *Murūj al-Dhahab* (ed. Barbier de Meynard et Pavet de Courteille 1861-77), I, p. 200; *Al-Tanbīh wa'l-Ishrāf* (ed. de

pillars (عمد) and the pivot (قطب) of the Christians."[1] and by Ibn Ḥazm as "the most improtant of the three sects (اعظمها)."[2] Saadia, however, as will have been noticed, reverses the order, putting the Jacobites first and then the Nestorians and Malkites. The explanation, it seems to me, is that Saadia has arranged these sects in the order of his direct acquaintance with them. Born in Egypt, where he lived up to the age of twenty-three or thirty-three, he first became acquainted with the Jacobite view, for in Egypt the Jacobites were the dominant Christian sect. Then when he settled down in Irak he became acquainted with the Nestorian Christology, for in Irak the Nestorians were the dominant Christian sect. The Malkites who flourished mainly in Christian countries and in Muslim Spain always remained to him a far-off sect. He therefore puts them last. So also, it may be added, the work on the refutation of the divinity of Jesus, attributed to Ghazālī,[3] which was written in Egypt,[4] in its dealing with the Christologies of these three sects, similarly puts the Jacobites first.

The fourth sect is described by Saadia as that which "assign to him the position of prophet only, interpreting the sonship of which they apply to him just as we interpret the biblical expression 'Israel is my first-born son' (Exod. 4: 22), which is merely an expression of esteem and high regard, or as others (Muslims) interpret the description of Abraham as the 'friend' of God (Surah 4: 124)."[5] On the face of it, this description reflects the various heretical Christologies which shared in common the denial of the divinity of Jesus, such as the Christology of the followers of Paul of Samosata, which was known to the Muslims as the view that "Jesus

Goeje, 1894), p. 142, l. 11; p. 154, l. 4; *Ibn* Ḥazm, *Fiṣal* I, pp. 48, 49; Shahrastānī, *Milal*, pp. 173, 175, 176.

1 Masʿūdī, *Murūj*, I, p. 200.

2 Ibn Ḥazm, *Fiṣal* I, p. 48, l. 23.

3 *Op. cit.*, above p. 18, n. 1.

4 *Ibid.*, pp. 25-35.

5 *Emunot ve-Deʿot* II, 7, p. 90, l. 21-p. 91, l. 2.

was the servant of God and His apostle like all the other prophets"[1] or that "he was an upright created servant";[2] and as the Christology of the Arians, which was known to the Muslims as the view that 'Jesus was a created servant";[3] and as the Christology of the Macedonians, which was known to the Muslims as the view that "Jesus was a created servant, a man, a prophet, an apostle of God like the rest of the prophets."[4] All these heretical Christologies may be described as reflecting the Ebionitic type of Christology, which was one of the three types of Christology that had existed in Christianity from the earliest time.[5] Ebionites as a sect or as a group of sects, it may be remarked, had disappeared before the rise of Islam and no longer existed at the time of Saadia. It is the common Christology of these three heretical sects that would thus seem to be reflected in Saadia's fourth sect. But there is the following question. Inasmuch as this type of Christology was known to the Muslims to have been shared by three sects and these sects were known to them to antedate the Nestorians and the Jacobites, why does Saadia designate those who followed this type of Christology as a single sect[6] and why does he describe them as a sect which appeared only recently?

The explanation which I should like to suggest is that, though the Christological view ascribed by Saadia to this fourth sect is exactly like that of the Samosatenians, Arians and Macedonians, it is not any of these sects that he has reference to here. His reference here is rather to an entirely new sect which we have reason to believe arose among Christians shortly before Saadia's birth in the same part of the Muslim world in which Saadia wrote his book. It happens

[1] Ibn Ḥazm, *Fiṣal* I, p. 48, ll. 13-14.
[2] Shahrastānī, *Milal*, p. 176, l. 12.
[3] Ibn Ḥazm, *Fiṣal* I, p. 48, l. 9.
[4] *Ibid.*, ll. 19-20.
[5] *Cf.* section on "Heresies with Regard to the Born Christ" in *The Philosophy of the Church Fathers*, I, pp. 587-606.
[6] *Emunot ve-De'ot*, II, 7, p. 91, l. 3.

that the Koran, while rejecting the orthodox Christian type of Christology, upholds the Ebionitic type of Christology in such verses as "And they say, God hath a son. No!" (2: 110); "The Messiah, Jesus, son of Mary, is only an apostle of God" (4: 169); "The Messiah, son of Mary, is only an apostle" (5: 79). We know that debates between Christians and Muslims on this Christological view had been going on ever since their first encounter. We know that Christians as a minority group in Muslim countries were not entirely impervious to Muslim influence We know also that the Christian Arabic literature, through its discussions of all sides of the Christological problems, had kept alive among Christians in Muslim countries a knowledge of the Ebionitic type of Christology of the heretical Samosatenians, Arians, and Macedonians and also a knowledge of all the arguments in favor of it. What with all this, is it not possible that a certain group of Christians in Muslim countries, shortly before the time of Saadia, succumbed to Muslim influence and adopted a type of Christology that was more agreeable to their Muslim masters? That the Christology of this fourth sect was advanced in an effort to accommodate itself to the Muslim environment is indicated by the fact that one of the ways, mentioned by Saadia, whereby this sect tried to explain why, with their denial of the divinity of Jesus, they still continued to call him son of God, was by referring to the Muslims' explanation of the expression "Abraham, the friend of God," [1] which had come into use on the basis of the Koranic verse, "And God took Abraham for His friend" (4: 124). Elsewhere, on the basis of a passage in Shahrastānī, I have shown how at about the end of the eighth century, that is, somewhat over three quarters of a century before the birth of Saadia, under the impact of Islam, a modified conception of the Trinity appeared among a certain group of Nestorian Christians in Adiabene on the Tigris,[2]

[1] *Ibid.*, p. 91, l. 2.

[2] *Cf.* my paper "An Unknown Splinter Group of Nestorians," *Revue des Études Augustiniennes*, 6 (1960), pp. 249-253.

which is in that part of the Muslim world where Saadia's work was written. Elsewhere, again, on the basis of another passage in Shahrastānī, I have shown that some of these Nestorians, following "Photinus and Paul of Samosata," held the following view: "The Messiah took his origin from Mary; he is a righteous servant and created, except that God has honored him and favored him because of his obedience and called him 'son' by adoption and not by begetting and union."[1] This is exactly the view ascribed here by Saadia to the fourth sect.

Saadia's criticism of all these four Christologies is based upon principles which, he says, he has already discussed, or is about to discuss, in other parts of his work, and so we shall forgo the discussion of it here.

[1] Cf. my paper "More about the Unknown Splinter Group of Nestorians," *ibid.*, 11 (1965), pp. 217–222.

I 2

JUDAH HALEVI ON CAUSALITY AND MIRACLES

Halevi's discussion of causality[1], which is included within his discussion of free will, is, like his discussion of free will, aimed directly at the orthodox Kalam, which denied both free will and causality, but indirectly it is also aimed at those philosophies which in their theories of causality went too far in restricting or eliminating the power of God.

The discussion of causality begins with a classification of events in the world[2] in their relation to God as the Prime Cause, giving first a general twofold classification and then a more detailed fourfold classification. Combining these two classifications, we get one classification consisting of two main divisions, under the first of which are two subdivisions and under the second are three subdivisions. The first main division consists of events which may be described by the term used in the second classification as "divine," [3] and this is subdivided into (a) those "traceable to the Prime Cause... according to primary intention," [4] and (b) those "obediently coming forth from the Prime

1. *Cuzari* V, 20, p. 336, 1. 28—p. 338, 1. 23; p. 337, 1. 26—p. 339, 1. 19 (ed. Hirschfeld).
2. Referred to as: (1) אלמעלומאת: הידיעות, "cognizable things" (or, according to another reading recorded in the Wilna edition העלולים [=אלמעלולאת]: "effects"; (2) אלתאתיראת: המעשים, "actions", "effects".
3. אלאהי״ה: אלהיים.
4. מיוחסות אל העלה הראשונה... על הכונה הראשונה

Cause and having no other cause whatsoever except God's will." [5] The second main division consists of events described as those "traceable to the Prime Cause.. by way of concatenation" [6] or "through intermediate causes" [7] and this is subdivided into (a) "natural," (b) "acidental," and (c) "optional."[8] Reversing the order of the two main divisions, I shall deal first with the second main division, and of this second main division I shall leave out "optional" events, for such events constitute a problem by itself, with which I shall deal elsewhere in connection with Halevi's discussion of free will. I shall start my discussion with events designated as "natural".

Natural events are described by Halevi as those which result "from intermediate causes which are prepared for them and bring them to the extreme end of their perfection, as long as no hindrance arises from one of the other three types of causes,"[9] and these are illustrated by the example of the burning of a piece of wood by fire. [10] The example is deliberately chosen. It is directly aimed at Ghazali, who, in his defense of the Kalam view of the denial of causality says that he will use "only one single example, namely, the burning of cotton through contact with fire," [11] concerning which he maintains that "the agent of the burning . . . is God, either through the intermediacy of angels or without any intermediary,"[12] thereby rejecting the view of some anonymous philosophers whom he quotes as saying that "the agent of the burning is fire only and that it is a natural agent." [13] Evidently having these two explanations of the act

5. מהסבה הראשונה יוצאים (נאפדה) [ו]על כל פנים (ולא בד) אין להם סבה זולת רצון האלהים יתברך.

6. מיוחסות אל העלה הראשונה . . . על דרך ההשתלשלות.

7. מסבות אמצעיות.

8. אכתיאריה: מבחריים; אתפאקיה: מקריים; טביעיה: טבעיים.

9. מסבות אמצעיות מוכנות להם ומגיעות אותם אל תכלית שלמותם בעוד שלא ימנע מונע מאחד מהשלשה חלקים.

10. שרפת האש על הדמיון לקירה (אלכ׳שב״ה) הזאת.

11. *Tahafut al-Tahafut* XVII, §2, p. 278, 1. 8 (ed. M. Bouyges).

12. *Ibid.* §4, p. 278, 1. 13 — p. 279, 1. 2.

13. *Ibid.* § 3, p. 278, 11. 10—11.

of burning in mind, Halevi offers a detailed description of the act of the burning of a piece of wood which is in opposition to both of them. Against Ghazali's own explanation he tries to show how the act of burning is brought about by intermediate natural causes; and against the anonymous explanation he tries to show how the intermediate natural causes terminate at God as their Prime Cause. His description of the causal process that brings about the act of burning is as follows.[14] First, there are the respective properties of the fire and the piece of wood, for by nature (מן שאן : מדרך = πέφυκε[15]), he says, fire which is "fine and hot and active" affects the piece of wood which is "porous and passive." Then, he says, "if thou seekest the causes of these processes, active as well as passive, thou wilt not fail to discover them. Thou mayest even discover the causes of their causes." Third, he goes on to say, "thou arrivest at the spheres, then at the causes of the spheres." Finally, he concludes, thou arrivest "at the Prime Cause." What "the causes of the spheres" may be will be discussed later.

Another argument, aimed, again, directly at Ghazali and exclusively at him, occurs later in the course of his discussion. It happens that Ghazali starts his defense of the denial of causality with the general statement that upon the rejection of causality "depends the possibility of affirming the existence of miracles which infringe upon the ordinary."[16] Halevi counters this by the following argument: "If all new things that arise were the immediate effects of the design of the Prime Cause, then they would, each in its turn, be created anew at every moment and we could then say that the Creator created the whole world anew at this very moment, with the result that there would be nothing

14. *Cuzari* V, 20, p. 338 11. 6—12; p. 339, 11. 3—9.

15. Thus the Arabic *min shān* is used as a translation of the Greek πέφυκε "by nature", in *Categ.* 10, 12a 28 (cf. Arabic version of the *Organon*, ed. A. Badawi).

16. *Tahafut al-Falasifah*, Phys. §6, p. 271, 11. 10—11.

in miracles for man to wonder at them, and still less to assent to beliefs on account of them."[17] In other words, if there is nothing that is ordinary and natural, there is nothing extraordinary and supernatural.

Against the assumption that certain causes are only material and natural is also argued by Halevi in two other places of his work. In one place, speaking of "the philosophers" in general, but meaning a special kind of philosophers, he attributes to them the view that prime matter is transformed into four elements only "by the movements of the spheres."[18] In opposition to them, he argues that it is "God who caused fire to become fire and earth to become earth for some reason which He deemed appropriate."[19] In another place he refers to "some philosophers" who were of the opinion that minerals, and inanimate objects in general, are the result of the various mixtures of the elements, which mixtures are determined solely by the motions of the spheres, without any forms of divine origin.[20] This view, too, is rejected by him, indirectly, in the course of his discussion, when he makes the general statement that what philosophers attribute to an act of nature should be attributed to what is ultimately an act of God.[21]

Accidental events are described by Halevi as those which result "likewise from intermediate causes, but accidentally, not by nature or according to a regular order or by design; nor are they prepared for a certain perfection, at which, once they arrive at it, they stop.

17. *Cuzari* V, 20, p. 340, 11. 12—14; p. 341, 11. 8—12.
18. *Ibid.* V, 2, p. 296, 1. 20; p. 297, 11. 21—22.
19. *Ibid.* V, 5, p. 300, 11. 1—2; p. 301, 11. 1—4:
ולמה לא נאמר . . . הוא אשר שם האש אש והארץ ארץ לחכמה אשר ראה אותה יתברך.
20. *Ibid.* V, 10, p. 306, 11. 5—6; p. 307, 11. 5—6.
21. *Ibid.* 306, 11. 17—19; p. 307, 11. 17—19:
ועל האמת שהבורא יתברך ינהיגם בתכונה מהתכונות, קרא אותה התכונה ההיא אם תחפוץ או נפש או כח.

The proviso with regard [to a hindrance arising from] the other three types of causes is to be made also in the case of these effects." [22]

No example is given here by Halevi as an illustration of accidental causes. But later, in the same chapter, he illustrates them by quoting David's words about Saul, "or he will go down into battle and perish" (1 Sam. 26:10), upon which he simply comments: "and this is accidental cause."[22a] In Aristotle they are illustrated by the example of a man who goes to a place for a certain purpose, and because he happens to be there he gets a sum of money.[23] Abraham Ibn Daud, who, like Halevi, enumerates four types of causes, divine, natural, accidental, and optional, similarly illustrates accidental causes by quoting the words "or he shall go down into battle and perish," upon which, however, he comments: "This is an illustration of the accidental kind of cause, against which man has the power to guard himself [by not volunteering to go down into battle, where he may accidentally perish] and also has the power [to volunteer to go down into battle] and expose himself to danger and thus [accidentally] be felled; and it is with reference to such a kind of cause that it is said: 'Blowing cold winds are in the way of the froward; he that keepeth his soul holdeth himself far from them' (Prov. 22:5)." [24] In quoting the verse from Proverbs as an illustration of accidental causes, Abraham Ibn Daud had in mind the rabbinic inference from it that "everything is in the power of Heaven, except illness from cold draughts."[25] The example of "illness from cold draughts" alluded to by Abraham Ibn Daud must have also been in the mind of Halevi when he indicated that ac-

22. *Ibid.* V, 20, p. 338, 11. 20—22; p. 339, 11. 16—18:
ואין להם הכנה לשלמות יגיעו עדין ויעמדו אצלו, ומתנים בהם בחלקים השלשה.

22a. *Ibid.*, p. 344, ll. 5—6; p. 345, l. 1.

23. *Phys.* II, 5, 196b, 33—197a, 5.
והמקריים מסבות אמצעיות גם כן, אך הם במקרה ולא בטבע ולא בסדר ולא בכונה,

24. *Emunah Ramah* II, vi, 2, p. 97.

25. Quoted *ibid.* p. 96; cf. *Ketubot* 30a.

cidental causes may be interrupted by a hindrance arising from the other three types of effects, one of which is optional effects, that is to say, acts performed by man's own free will.

We now come to those events of which he gives the two definitions quoted above, but to both of which he undoubtedly meant to apply the term "divine," which is used by him only in connection with the effects under his second definition. The "divine" events in his first classification, which are described as "traceable to the Prime Cause . . . according to primary intention," are illustrated by the example of "the arrangement and composition visible in animal and in plant and in the spheres, which no intelligent observer could possibly ascribe to mere accident; he could only sacribe it to the design of a wise agent, who puts everything in its proper place and give it its due portion."[26] I am going to show that the type of events under this description is only partly "divine"; partly it is "natural." For every one of the three examples by which this type of events is illustrated here can be shown to have been said by Halevi elsewhere in his work to contain certain things which are brought about by intermediate natural causes and certain things which are brought about by the direct action of God. Such a distinction may perhaps be discerned also here in the expression "the arrangement and composition visible in animal and in plant and in the spheres," which may mean that only "the arrangement and composition" in these three realms of nature are "according to primary intention," whereas other things in them are by "the concatenation [of causes]."

Let us then see what things in plants and animals and the celestial spheres are, according to Halevi, due to intermediate

26. *Cuzari* V, 20, p. 338, 11. 2—5; p. 337, 1. 27 — p. 339, 1. 2:
ודמיון הדרך הראשון הסדור וההרכבה הנראים בחי ובצמח ובגלגלים אשר לא יתכן למשכיל המשתכל שיחסהו אל המקרה אך אל כונת עושה חכם ישים כל דבר במקומו ויתן לו חלקו.

natural causes and what things in them are due to the direct action of God.

As for animals and plants, the distinction within them of natural effects and divine effects is brought out pointedly in several places. In one place, having in mind the process of growth and reproduction in general, he argues that, while "the elements and the moon and the sun and the stars perform actions by way of warming and cooling and moistening and drying and their consequences," still "the act of shaping and of determining the size and of bringing forth and of all acts in which there is evidence of planned sagacity can be ascribed to a wise agent who is powerful and capable of pre-ordaining the measurement of things."[27] Taking up then the procreation of human beings especially, he argues that, while the parents "aid matter in receiving human form from the wise Creator," one must deny them the faculty of "creating the child."[28] The direct action of God in case of plants and animals and human beings is further explained by him in the statements that "the form by which one plant is distinguished from another and one animal from another is not the work of the four natural elements but a divine effect issuing from God"[29] and that similarly "the calculation of the proportions which is required by the human form belongs exclusively to Him who created it."[30] In a passage

27. *Ibid.* I, 77, p. 30, I. 28 — p. 32, 1. 4; p. 32, 1. 4; p. 31, 1. 28 — p. 33, 1. 4:
יש ליסודות ולשמש ולירח ולכוכבים פעלים על דרך החמום והקירור וההרטבה והיובש והתלויים בהם... אבל הציור והשיעור וההזרעה וכל אשר יש בו חכמה לכונה לא יתיחס כי אם לחכם היכול המשער (=אלמקדד; בנדפס: אלקאהר = האדיר, המנצח).
See my comments on this passage in nn. 19—20 on pp. 142—143 of my paper "Halevi and Maimonides on Design, Chance, and Necessity," *Proceedings of the American Academy for Jewish Research*, 11 (1941). Above, pp. 38—39.

28. *Ibid.* p. 32, 11. 5—8; p. 33, 11. 5—7:
כאשר ירחיק מהאיש והאשה יצירת הולד בהתחברם, אך הם עוזרים לחומר המקבל צורת האדם מאת המצייר החכם.

29. *Ibid.* III, 23, p. 178, 11. 6—7; p. 179, 11. 7—8:
כי הצורה אשר בה יהיה עצם צמח מבלתי צמח וחי מבלתי חי איננה מן הטבעים אך מעשה אלהי מאת האלהים יתברך.

30. *Ibid.* p. 178, 11. 23—24; p. 179, 11. 22—23:
ושעור הערכים שראויה להם הצורה האנושית איננו כי אם ליוצרה יתברך.

dealing exclusively with the procreatim of man, he begins by saying that its intermediate natural causes are "the sperm and blood," "the organs of generation," and "the [vital] spirits and the faculties." He then adds that all these intermediate causes "are not active, but are causes in a material or in an instrumental sense, for the sperm and blood are the matter of the man [to be born] and the organs of generation connect them, and the [vital] spirits and the faculties are tools which employ them under the will of God, in order to carry to completion his configuration, delineation, growth, and nature."[31] A little later, in support of this view, that in the birth of man there is a divine cause above the material causes, he says: "Just as Galen, speaking of the formative faculty (*al-kuwwah al-mutasawwirah*: *koah ha-mesayyer*) places it above all other faculties and thinks that it does not arise out of the mixture [of the four natures] but by reason of something divine."[32] The references are to Galen's statements that each of the elementary parts of the body, that is, the tissues, are produced by the four natures, moisture and dryness and coldness and warmth, which are called the "alterative faculties' *(ἀλλοιωτικαὶ δυνάμεις)* whereas the bringing together of these so that they become organs is due to what he calls the "formative faculty" *(διαπλαότικὴ δύναμις)* which he describes as "doing everything for some purpose"[33] and as "creator" *(δημιουργός)*[34] and as "wise."[35]

It is, however, to be noted that, despite his quoting Galen in support of the view that the generation of man has a divine cause in addition to the material causes, there is a difference between his own conception of the divine cause and Galen's conception of

31. *Ibid.* V, 20, Prop. 2, p. 348, 11. 8—14; p. 349, ll. 4—10.
32. *Ibid.* V, 21, p. 354, 11. 4—6; p. 355, 11. 4—6:

כאשר אמר גאלינוס בכח המצייר (פי אלקוה אלמתנצורה) וישים לו יתרון על שאר הכחות ורואה שאיננו מחמת המזג אבל לענין האלהי.

33. *De Naturalibus Facultatibus* I, 6 (ed. Kühn, Vol. II, pp. 11—15).
34. *De Usu Partium Corpus Humani* VI, 13 (III, p. 476).
35. *Ibid.* X, 15 (III, p. 838); XI, 14 (III, pp. 910—11).

it. To Galen, God is only an ultimate and remote cause, whereas to Halevi. as we have seen from the passage quoted above, the formation and the shaping of man as an individual human being are direct actions of God. Such a distinction is to be made also, I believe, between him and those theistic philosophers upon whose statements, either openly or allusively, he draws in his arraignment of those materialistic philophers who denied any immaterial causes altogether.[36] Thus in his discussion of the augmentative and generative faculties of the soul, Halevi tries to show how some of their functions are performed by God through intermediate causes and how others are performed by Him directly. It is to be noted that, though Halevi's discussion of the generative faculty, like Ghazālī's discussion of it, [36a] is aimed at the philosophers, especially Avicenna, his view on the subject differs from that of Ghazālī's, for, according to Ghazālī, as I have shown elsewhere, the denial of intermediate causes applies to every function of the generative faculty.

As for the celestial spheres,[36b] the distinction within them of natural effects and divine effects is similarly brought out in several places.

In one of the passages he argues that it is God who by His will or command "caused the heavens to rotate continuously and the uppermost sphere to carry along [that is, to move] all the other spheres, without being in place and without having an inclination in its motion, and the earth to be fixed firmly, standing still at the center of the uppermost sphere, without being rolled, and without

36. Cf. Section on "The Wisdom of Nature", on pp. 139—158 of my paper referred to above in n. 27.

36a. *Tahafut al-Falasifah* XVIII, 5, p. 279, l. 7–p. 280, l. 1.

36b. Cf. section on "Celestial Spheres," pp. 119—129, in my paper referred to above in n. 27, where I deal with other problems arising from the same passages on the celestial spheres that are dealt with here. There I tried to show that none of the passages contained arguments merely from irregularity against necessity. Here I try to show that, arguing against the philosophers, Halevi maintains that in the processes of growth and procreation God acts in some parts directly and in other parts through intermediate causes.

anything to rest upon, and He causes the arrangement of the universe to be what it is with reference to quantity, quality, and shapes." [37]

The same view is stated by him even more clearly in a parallel passage: "The divine wise will ordained the rotation of the uppermost sphere, which completes one revolution in every twenty-four hours and causes other spheres to rotate along with it." [38]

In another passage, Halevi makes the King of the Khazars say: "And I should like to discuss with my opponent concerning the uppermost sphere itself. What is it that causes it to rotate? Is it the result of chance or not?" [39] The answer expected is, of course, that it is caused to rotate by God.

From all this we may gather that, while the rotation of the uppermost sphere is caused by God, directly by Him, the rotation of the inner spheres is caused by God through the intermediacy of the outermost sphere. Inasmuch, however, as this statement about the rotation of the inner spheres in both his passages reflects Aristotle's statement that "the sphere of the fixed stars is that which carries along all the other spheres" [40] and inasmuch as, according to Aristotle, each of the inner spheres is moved by the sphere of the fixed stars through the intermediacy of the sphere immediately enclosing it, we may assume that Halevi, too, held

37. *Cuzari* II, 6, p. 74, 11. 23—27; p. 75, 11. 23—27:
מה הדבר אשר שם אצלך השמים סובבים תמיד והגלגל העליון נושא הכל ואין מקום לו ואין נטייה בתנועתו וכדור הארץ מרכז עומד באמצעיתו מבלי נטייה ולא סבה, ושם סדר הכל על מה שהוא עליו מהכמות והאיכות והתמונות.
Cf. my comments on this passage in nn. 1—8 on pp. 119—20 of my paper referred to above in n. 27.

38. *Ibid.* V, 2, p. 296, 11. 17—19; p. 297, 11. 18—20:
ואחר כן חייב חפץ האלהים וחכמתו סביב הגלגל העליון אשר יסוב פעם בכל עשרים וארבע שעות ויסבב עמו כל הגלגלים.

39. *Ibid.* V, 7, p. 301, 11. 11—12:
ואני אדבר עמו על הגלגל העליון עצמו, מה הוא שיגלגלהו, ההיה הדבר ההוא במקרה אם לא.

40. *Metaph.* XII, 8, 1073b, 25—26.

that each of the inner spheres is moved by the uppermost sphere through the intermediacy of the sphere immediately enclosing it. Accordingly, when in his description of the intercatenation of causes of the act of burning quoted above he says, "thou arrivest at the spheres, then at the cause of the spheres, and then at the Prime Cause," he means by "the causes of the spheres" the "uppermost sphere" and the sphere immediately enclosing each sphere.[41]

Still further information about how the uppermost sphere is moved directly by God and the inner spheres are by way of the intercatenation of causes may be gathered from another set of passages.

In one passage, speaking of "the heaven," he says that it is "an instrument employed by the sole will of God, without the intervention of any intermediate causes."[42] In view of the fact that, as we have already seen, the inner spheres are, according to him, moved by intermediate causes, the denial of intermediate causes here of "the heaven" must refer to the uppermost sphere, which at the time of Halevi meant the ninth sphere, namely, the starless sphere. According to Aristotle, one of the meanings of the term "heaven" *οὐρανός* and the one which he mentions first, is "the extreme periphery of the whole,"[43] that is, the uppermost sphere, which at the time of Aristotle meant the eighth sphere, namely, the sphere of the fixed stars.

It will be noticed that the Arabic term used by Halevi here for heaven is in the singular (*al-samá*), whereas in another place,

41. The *Kol Yehudah, ad loc.*, says that the causes of the spheres here refers to angels. But see below at nn. 68—71.

42. *Cuzari* IV, 3, p. 234, 11. 8—9; p. 235, 11. 8—9:
כן רומזים אל השמים, מפני שהוא כלי משמש בחפצו גרידא, מבלתי סבות אחרות אמצעיות ביניהם.

43. *De Caelo* I, 9, 278b, 11—12.

where the term "heaven" is contrasted with "the uppermost sphere," the Arabic term used by him for it is the plural (*al-ṣamawât*).[44]

From two other passages we get still further information about spherical movement.

In one passage, referring to the commonly held view that "each movement [of the spheres] comes from a soul, and each soul has an Intelligence, and this Intelligence is an angel separated from mattter, so that they call these Intelligences god[s] and angels and secondary causes and other names like these," he dismisses it as "subtleties profitable only for speculation."[45] Similarly, in another place, speaking of the various grades of angels, he says that some angels "are lasting, and are perhaps those spiritual beings of which the philosophers speak, whose views, however, we have neither to refute or to adopt."[46] The manner in which the identification of Intelligences with angels is dismissed in both these passages, it may be remarked, is reminiscent of Ghazali's dismissal of the same theory by stating that, while on purely religious grounds this theory "cannot be refuted,"[47] no knowledge of it can be attained "by rational demoustration."[48]

From all this we may gather that, while Halevi admits that the inner spheres are moved by God through the intermediacy

44. *Cuzari* II, 6, p. 74, 1. 24; p. 75, 1. 24. However, elsewhere Halevi uses these two forms of the word indiscriminately. Cf. I, 8, p. 14, 1.3; p. 15, 1, 3; I, 25, p. 18, 1. 8; p. 19, 1, 8; IV, 1, p. 228, 1. 4; p. 229, 1, 2.

45. *Ibid.* V, 21, p. 354, 11. 15—27; p. 355, 11. 16—23. The Arabic term אללה in this passage is undoubtedly a corruption of אלהה. The statement here that the Intelligences are "gods" goes back to *Metaph.* XII, 8, 1074a, 38—1074b, 14, and there the Greek θεοί (1074b, 2) is translated by the Arabic *alihah* (*cf. Averroess Tafsir ma ba'd at-tabi'at*, ed. M. Bouyges, 1938—48, p. 1687, 1. 3).

46. *Ibid.* V, 3, p. 234, 11. 8—9; p. 235, 11. 8—9.

47. *Tahafut al-Tahafut* XIV, §2, p. 239, 1. 8.

48. *Ibid.*, §3, p. 240, 1. 3. Cf. my discussion of the entire problem in "The Problem of the Souls of the Spheres from the Byzantine Commentaries on Aristotle through the Arabs and St. Thomas to Kepler", in *Dumbarton Oaks Papers*, 16 (1963), 67—93. In *Studies*, I, 22—59.

of the uppermost sphere and the spheres immediately enclosing them, he denies the existence of Intelligence identified with angels as intermediate causes either of the uppermost sphere or of the inner spheres.

Here, again, it is to be noted that, though Halevi's discussion of the rotations of the celestial spheres, like Ghazali's discussion of them, is aimed at the philosophers, his own view on the subject differs from that of Ghazali's, for, according to Ghazali, as I shall show elsewhere, the denial of intermediate causes applies to the rotation of every sphere.

All these "divine" events in the first classification, though said by Halevi to be caused by God "according to primary intention," are not what he would call miracles. For, as may be gathered from his criticism of Ghazali quoted above, [49] events are regarded by Halevi as miracles only when they meet the following two conditions: (1) they must be caused directly by God; (2) they must be deviations from the manner in which the same events ordinarily occur. However, in the case of all the examples of events described by Halevi as being traceable to God "according to primary intention", such as the special form given to each plant and each animal and each human being and the variety of motions given to the different spheres and planets, all these events meet only one of the aformentioned conditions: they are caused directly by God, but they are not deviations from a manner in which they ordinarily occur. They cannot, therefore, be regarded as miracles.

Not so, however, are the "divine" effects which in his second classification, the fourfold classification, are described as "obediently coming forth from the Prime Cause and having no other cause whatsoever except God's will." Of such divine effects Halevi says that when they take place, they are hindrances to

49. Cf. above at n. 17.

effects which he describes as "natural." [50] Divine effects of this kind are thus outside the order of natural effects. This is what Halevi elsewhere calls "miracles" [51] and "signs," [52] for miracles are referred to by him as events which are "not natural events" [53] or as being "outside the order of the natural world" [54] or as "an infringement on ordinary events" [55] or as "outside the ordinary custom and nature." [56]

Miracles are divided by Halevi in one place into those which consist in "the creation of things" and those which consist in "the transformation of one thing into another." [57] In another place, corresponding to this twofold division, the two divisions of miracles are said by him to consist in the creation by God of something "out of what was nonexistent" and in the use made by Him of something "from among existent things." [58] As an example of the first type of miracle, he mentions the creation of the two tables of stone, which was an act of creation out of nothing. [59] To this he subsequently adds "the manna" and alludes to "other things." [60] As an example of the second type of miracle, he mentions the en-

50. *Cuzari* V, 20, p. 338, 1. 19; p. 339, 1. 18, quoted above at n. 9.
51. *Ibid.* I, 7, p. 12, 1. 22; p. 13, 1. 22: מעגזאת: מופתים; *ibid.* I, 67, p. 28, 1. 20; p. 29, 1. 19: מעגזאת: נפלאות.
52. *Ibid.* 1, 83, p. 36, 1. 4; p. 37, 1. 5: איאת: אתות.
53. *Ibid.* p. 36, 1. 12; p. 37, 1. 12: לא טבעיה: לא מצד הטבע.
54. *Ibid.* III, 17, p. 164, 11. 19—20; p. 165, 11. 18—19:
כארגה ען נטאם אלעאלם אלטביעי: יוצאות מסדר העולם הטבעי
55. *Ibid.* I, 67, p. 28, 1. 20; p. 29, 1. 20: כרק אלעאדאת: שנוי המנהגים. I, 83, p. 36, 1. 5; p. 37, 1. 5; V, 21, p. 354, 1. 6; p. 355, 1. 7:
כרק עאדאת: שנות מנהגים;
56. *Ibid.* II, 54, p. 114, 1. 5; p. 115, 1. 5: כאריג ען אלעאדה ואלטביעה: יוצא מן המנהג והטבע.
57. *Ibid.* I, 68, p. 28, 11. 20—21; p. 29, 1. 20:
אכתראע עאין או קלב עין אלי עין
אכרי: בריאת דברים או הפך דבר אל דבר אחר.
58. *Ibid.* I, 89, p. 40, 1. 28 — p. 42, 1. 1; p. 41, 11. 26—27: ולא מה שברא לו ית־
ברך ממה שלא היה נמצא (ממה לא יכין מוגודא) ולא ממה שהעביד לן מן הנמצאים
(סכר לה מן אלמוגודאת).
59. *Ibid.* p. 42, 11. 1—2; p. 41, 1. 28.
60. *Ibid.* I, 91, p. 42, 11. 17--18; p. 43, 11. 17—18.

gravement of the writing of the ten commandments upon them, the division of the Red Sea, and the shaping of the air into the form of sounds which convey the word of God to the prophet.[61] Both these types of miracle, he says, are caused directly by God, who employed no "tool" and no "intermediary causes,"[62] and the purpose of both these types of miracles is "to prove [the wisdom] of the Creator of the world and His power to do whatever He pleases whenever He pleases."[63] The characteristics of a miracle, then, according to Halevi, are that they are created directly by God on a special occasion for a certain definite purpose. And so in another place, grouping together these two types of miracle, such as "the manna," which he has already assigned to the first type, and "the division of the Red Sea," which he has already assigned to the second type, and adding to them "the plagues of Egypt" and "the pillar of a cloud," which he would undoubtedly assign to the second kind, and describing both of them as acts of creation, he says that "the Creator of the world created these things designedly and immediately."[64] How he would explain the Talmudic saying that some of the plagues of Egypt were performed either through Moses or through Aaron or through both[65] he does not say. Probably he would argue that Moses and Aaron were not really "intermediary causes" in the strict sense of the term; they were especially bidden by God on those occasions to perform certain acts outside the order of nature. This, according to him, may be regarded as one of the ways in which miracles are wrought. The conception of God acting through intermediate natural causes means, according to him, His delegation of power to some part of the world, such as Intelligences or spheres or elements, to act in a certain regular way all the time. It will be recalled how

61. *Ibid.* I, 89, p. 42, ll. 3—10; p. 43, ll. 2—10.
62. *Ibid.* p. 42, l. 7; p. 43, ll. 6—7.
63. *Ibid.* I, 67, p. 28, ll. 21—22; p. 29, ll. 20—21; cf. I, 91, p. 42, ll. 13—18; p. 43, ll. 13—18.
64. *Ibid.* II, 2, p. 72, ll. 26—28; p. 73, l. 7 — p. 75, l. 1.
65. *Tanhuma*: *Exodus, va-Era* 14; *Exodus Rabbah* 12, 4, and 15, 27.

in the passage quoted above Ghazali argues against intermediate natural causes by maintaining that "the agent of the burning . . . is God, either through the intermediacy of angels or without any intermediary." [66] Evidently angels, to Ghazali, are not intermediary natural causes. Evidently so are Moses and Aaron to Halevi. Thus "prophets and pious sages" are described by him not as causes but as "primary instruments of the divine will which . . . performs miracles through them."[66a]

If angels, to Halevi, are, like Moses and Aaron, not intermediate natural causes, then, in the pasages quoted in which he expresses doubt about the view that angels, identified with the Intelligences, are the movers of the spheres [67] and explicitly states that God employs the heaven as an instrument without the intervention of any intermediate causes, [68] his doubt may be taken to refer only to angels conceived as Intelligences and as intermediate natural causes. He would not thus deny that angels, conceived as direct messengers of God, could be the movers of the spheres at the direct bidding of God and in obedience to His will. Such a view is not unknown in the history of religious thought. Thus Theodore of Mopsuestia, in his commentaries on the Epistles of St. Paul, of which there was an Arabic translation, [69] commenting on Colossians 1: 16, where various orders of angels are enumerated, says that "some of them command the air, some the sun, some the moon, some the stars, some some others, in order that they move all things in accordance with the task imposed upon them God, to the end that all things may exist together."[70] Perhaps also, in one of the minor Midrashim, where angels are

66. Cf. above at n. 12.

66a. *Cuzari* IV, 3, p. 234, ll. 21—23; p. 235, ll. 21—24.

67. Cf. above at nn. 45, 46.

68. Cf. above at n. 42.

69. Cf. G. Graf, *Geschichte der christlichen arabischen Literatur*, I, (1944). p. 355.

70. *Theodori Mopsuesteni in Epistolas B. Pauli Commentarii*, ed. H. B. Swete, Vol. I (1880), pp. 270—271.

described as "superinending (*ha-memunim*) over the earth, the sun, the moon, the stars, and twenty-six spheres,"[71] the superintendence over all those celestial bodies ascribed to the angels may mean that they are the movers thereof.

According to Halevi's statements in the passages quoted, then, all the miracles, including the miracles of the two tables, the engraving upon them, and the manna, were especially created by God on certain special occasions either out of nothing or out of something, and all of them are described by him as being infringements upon nature or custom. In another passage, however, he gives us what would seem to be a different explanation of miracles. In that passage, Halevi quotes the rabbinic statement that ten things, which are treated in Scripture as miraculous, were created on the sixth day of creation in the twilight.[72] Among these ten things are "the manna," "the writing," and "the tables" upon which the writing was composed. Commenting on this statement Halevi says: "[The purpose of this statement] is to bring about a harmonization between the Torah and nature, for nature asserts [a fixedness of] the ordinary, whereas the Torah acknowledges [the possibility of] an infringement upon the ordinary. An harmonization between them may be brought about by [assuming that] the ordinary events which are infringed upon are only in accordance with nature, and this because [as the rabbis say] in the six days of creation this infringement upon ordinary events had been stipulated with those events and agreed upon with them by the eternal will."[73] The allusion is to the rabbinic statement that God made a stipulation with everything that was created in the six days of creation to deviate from its normal course of behavior on certain predetermined occasions.[74]

71. *Ke-Tapuah ba—'ase ha—ya'ar*, in Eisenstein's *Ozar Midrashim*, p. 262b.

72. *M. Abot* V, 6.

73. *Cuzari* III, 73, p. 222, ll. 23—28; p. 223, l. 26 — p. 225, l. 3.

74. *Genesis Rabbah* 5, 5.

Here there would seem to be a contradiction. In the former set of passages he speaks of "the tables," "the writing engraved upon them," and "the manna," as well as of all the other scriptural miracles, as having been new creations either out of nothing or out of something, infringing upon nature and the ordinary course of events, and enacted by God on special occasions, and here he says of "the tables," "the writing engraved upon them," and "the manna," as well as all other scriptural miracles, that they are in accordance with nature, on the ground that their occurrence was stipulated at the time of the creation of the world.

Perhaps, if confronted with this difficulty, Halevi would have answered as follows: The stipulation was not that the nature which God established in the world at the time of its creation should always follow a regular course of action except on certain prearranged occasions, when it should deviate from that course and produce certain prearranged miracles; the stipulation was that it should always follow a regular course of action except on certain occasions, when it would please God to create miracles. Miracles are thus indeed infringement upon the ordinary course of nature, and are indeed direct creations of God, but at the same time they are in accordance with nature, for this is how, from the very beginning of its creation, nature was to run its course, mostly, in a regular manner, but occasionally, at the behest of God, in a miraculous manner.

13

MAIMONIDES ON THE UNITY AND INCORPOREALITY OF GOD

THE OPENING CHAPTER on the *Mishneh Torah* is a sort of commentary on the following three commandments: (1) "I am the Lord thy God" (Exod. 20: 2); (2) "Thou shalt have no other gods before me" (Exod. 20: 3); (3) "Hear, O Israel: The Lord our God, the Lord is one" (Deut. 6: 4). In his comment on the first of these three commandments, which he takes to be basis of the doctrine of the existence of God, he sketches briefly his philosophic arguments for the existence of God, with implications also for his unity and incorporeality,[1] of which he later gave a more fully and more systematic presentation in his *Moreh Nebukim*.[2] In his comment on the second of these three commandments, he simply says that the denial of polytheism, which this commandment enjoins, together with the belief in the existence of God, enjoined by the preceding commandment, constitutes "the great fundamental principle upon which every other commandment depends."[3] As for his comment on the third of these three commandments, which contains the doctrine of the unity of God, I shall discuss it here more or less fully, pointing out the hidden logic of its structure and the cryptic philosophic allusions in its wording.

His comment on this commandment begins with the following statement: "This God is one: He is not two nor more than two but one in the sense of there not being anyone among existent individuals whose oneness is like His oneness."[4] By this he means to say that this commandment is

[1] *Yesode ha-Torah* I, 1-6.

[2] *Moreh Nebukim* II, 1-2.

[3] *Yesode* I, 6.

[4] *Ibid.* I, 7.

not a mere restatement in positive terms of what is negatively stated in the commandments "Thou shalt have no other gods before me;" it means something more than that. The term "one" in its application here to God is unlike the term "one" in its application to other beings, and similarly the terms "two and more than two," the negation of which is implied here in the term "one," are unlike the terms "two and more than two" the negation of which is implied in the term "one" applied to other beings, and therefore this positive commandment means more than the negative commandment.

He then goes on to explain how the use of the term one here in its application to God is unlike its use in its application to other beings. First, having in mind what Aristotle calls "one in species,"[5] by which is meant the application of the term one to many distinct individuals, say Socrates, Plato, and Aristotle, on the ground that they all share in the same species, namely, manhood, he says that "God is not one after the manner of the oneness in species, which comprises many individuals,"[6] that is to say, God is not described as one simply on the ground that He shares with other gods in the same species, namely, Godhood. Second, having in mind Aristotle's statement that, "when pieces of wood are made one by glue," they are to be described as one "in virtue of their being continuous,"[7] and may thus be described as "one piece of wood or one body,"[8] despite the fact that "a body" is that which is "divisible according to quantity in three directions (τριχῇ),[9] he says that "God is not one after the manner

[5] *Metaph.* V, 6, 1016b, 31-32.

[6] *Yesode* I, 7. Cf. Maimonides' own definition of species as that which "comprises a number of individuals" (*Millot ha-Higgayon* 10.

[7] *Metaph.* V, 6, 1015b, 36-1016a, 1.

[8] *Ibid.* 1016a, 7-9.

[9] *Ibid.* 1016b, 27-28. The expression "divisible according to quantity (κατὰ τὸ ποσὸν) is used here by Aristotle in contrast to what he would call "divisible according to form (κατ' εἶδος)." Cf. *ibid.* 1016b, 23. By the divisibility of a body "according to quantity" Aristotle means its actual breaking up into parts, whereas by the divisibility of a body "according to form" he means its being subject to such intellectual distinctions as matter and form, genus and specific difference.

of the oneness of a body, which is divisible into parts,"[10] the conclusion being that the scriptural doctrine of the unity of God excludes from God any divisibility into parts into which a body is quantitatively divisible.

Thus, this positive commandment differs from the negative commandment in two ways: First, the negative commandment could be taken to mean that, while other gods are prohibited, there do exist other gods who share with God in His divinity, differing from Him only as individuals of the same species differ from each other; this positive commandment, however, in which the expression "the Lord is one" is taken to mean that God is not one in species, is a denial of the very existence of other gods conceived as sharing with Him in His divinity. Second, in the negative commandment only other gods are prohibited; in this positive commandment, the "two and more than two," which are indirectly prohibited by the use of the term "one," refer not only to two and more than two other gods but also to two and more than two parts into which God, if conceived as a body, would be divisible. In other words, this positive command to believe in one God prohibits indirectly not only the belief in a plurality of gods but also the belief in a plurality of parts within the one God—parts analogous to the quantitative parts of a body.

These two meanings of the positive command to believe in the oneness of God, he goes on to show, are mutually implicative, its meaning that there are not many gods which share in a common species implies that God is not a body and its meaning that God is not a body implies that there are not many gods sharing in a common species. First, having in mind Aristotle's statement that "all that are many in number

[10] *Yesode* I, 7. In the Hebrew expression here the terms מחלקות and קצוות are used synonymously in the sense of "parts," as has been shown by D. Baneth in his paper לטרמינולוגיה הפילוסופית של הרמב"ם in *Tarbiz* 6 (1935), p. 30, n. 1—and this despite the fact that the Aristotle's statement, which I have shown to be reflected in Maimonides' statement here, contains a term which means "three directions."

have matter," [11] that is to say, only bodies can be numbered, and also having in mind the philosophic principle formulated by himself later in his *Moreh Nebukim*, namely, that bodiless beings can be numbered only when they are related to each other as causes and effects, [12] he argues that, "if there were many gods [among which was included our God], then they would [all] have to be bodies, for things which are subject to number and at the same time are equal with reference to [the origin of their] existence [that is, they are not related to each other as causes and effects] cannot be differentiated from each other [in order to be subject to number] except by accidents which accrue to bodies," [13] Second, having in mind the view subsequently advanced by him in *Moreh Nebukim* that Aristotle's proof of the incorporeality of the Prime Mover from the eternal continuous circular motion of the celestial spheres could similarly be used as a proof for the incorporeality of the one God when even the continuous circular motion of the celestial spheres is assumed to be created, [14] he argues: "If the Creator were a body... His power would be finite... but...the power of God is infinite and incessant, seeing that the celestial sphere is continuous in its motion, and so, since God is not a body, there cannot accrue to Him any of the accidents of bodies whereby He could be differentiated from any other god. Therefore, there cannot be but one God," and the oneness of this one God is, of course, as before, not a oneness according to species. It is unity in the sense of its inclusion of incorporeality, he triumphantly concludes, that is meant by the commandment, "Hear, O Israel: The Lord our God, the Lord is one." [15]

So far, however, his proof for the incorporeality of God is based only upon the implication of his initial assumption that the term "one" predicated of God in the commandment of

[11] *Moreh* II, Itrod., Prop. 16.
[12] *Yesode* I, 7.
[13] *Moreh* II, 2.
[14] *Yesode* I, 7.
[15] *Metaph.* XII, 8, 1074a, 33-34.

the unity of God is unlike the term one in its predication of other beings. But what scriptural evidence is there for this initial assumption? In answer to this question, Maimonides, of course, does not quote any scriptural verse explicitly stating that the term "one" predicated of God in the commandment is unlike the term one in its predication of other beings. But he quotes three scriptural verses in which the one God of the commandment is described in terms which imply incorporeality and consequently, by his preceding reasoning, the term "one" predicated of God in the commandment is unlike the term one in its predications of other beings. Having in mind Aristotle's definition of place as "the boundary of the containing body, at which it is in contact with the contained body," [16] which means that no body can be contained at the same time by more than one body and hence cannot be at the same time in more than one place, he quotes the verse, "The Lord thy God is in heaven above and upon the earth beneath" (Deut. 4: 39) and argues that, if God were a body, He could not be at the same time "in two places," [17] that is, both in heaven and upon the earth. Second, having in mind Aristotle's statement that "figure" (σχῆμα: شكل), such as straightness and curvedness, is a species of the category of the accident of quality, [18] which thus belongs to a body, he quotes the verse (Deut. 4: 15), "You saw no manner of figure (תמונה)," [19] from which he wants us to infer that God is not a body. Third, without the aid of any philosophy,

[16] *Phys.* IV, 2, 212a, 5-6.

[17] *Yesode* I, 8.

[18] *Categ.* 8, 10a, 11-16; cf. Arabic translation of the *Categores* in *Organon Aristotelis in Versione Arabica Antiqua*, ed. Badawi, p. 33.

[19] *Yesode* I, 8. I have translated the Hebrew *temunah* in Maimonides' quotation here of Deut. 4: 15 by "figure" rather than by "likeness" for the following reason. Maimonides himself in *Morah* I, 3, p. 18, 1. 6, explains the meaning of *temunah* in Deut. 4: 25 and 4: 15 by the Arabic *shakl*, which in the Arabic translation of the *Categories* is used as atranslation of the Greek σχῆμα, "figure," in the passage quoted in the preceding note. It is to be noted, however, that the term *temunah* in both Deut. 4: 25 and Deut. 4: 15 is translated in

he derives from the verse, "To whom will you liken Me, that I should be equal?" (Isa. 40: 25), that "if God were a body, He would be like other bodies." [20] Of these three arguments, only the third, it will have been noticed, is based exclusively on a scriptural verse. Thus his purely scriptural evidence that the oneness of God in the commandment includes incorporeality is based upon the scriptural teaching of the unlikeness of God to other beings.

Maimonides has thus arrived at the conclusion that the mandatory command to believe in the unity of God includes also a mandatory command to believe in His incorporeality. Then, having in mind the Talmudic saying that "anyone who worships an idol is a heretic," [21] and evidently taking this to include anyone who, while not actually worshipping an idol, "acknowledges (מודה)," as he says, "that idolatory is true" [22] and evidently, also, taking the acknowledgment of polytheism to be the same as the acknowledgment of idolatry, he includes among his five classes of heretics "anyone who says that there are... two or more [gods] and anyone who says that there is one God but that He is a body and possesses a figure (תמונה)." [23]

With this rigid conception of the incorporeality and unity of God, Maimonides takes up the question of the many corporeal terms and terms implying corporeality by which God is discribed in Scripture. Among the terms mentioned by him are included the terms "living" and "knowing" [24]—terms which are usually included in what was known in Mus-

the Septuagint by ὁμοίωμα, in Onkelos by *demut*, and in Saadia by *shibh*, all of which mean "likeness."

[20] *Yesode* I, 8.

[21] *ʿAbodah Zarah* 26b.

[22] *ʿAkum* II, 6.

[23] *Teshubah* II, 7.

[24] *Yesode* I, 11-12. Maimonides uses here the term חכמה as synonymous with the term דעת or דיעה used by him later in II, 10 and both these terms are used by him as the equivalents of the Arabic علم, "knowledge." Cf. Baneth, *art. cit.*, *s. v.*

lim and Jewish philosophy of that time as the problem of divine attributes.[25] With regard to all these terms, he first makes the general statement that they are not to be taken literally, quoting in support of this the Talmudic saying, "The Torah speaks according to the language of men."[26] But then he takes up especially the attributes "living" and "knowing," quite evidently using them as an example of all the attributes. With regard to knowledge and to attributes in general he makes the following statements:

First, having in mind Ghazālī's rejection of the philosophic view quoted by him in the name of Avicenna, that "God does not know other things by first intention, but He knows His essence as the principle of the universe and from this follows His knowledge of the universe by second intention, for . . . it is inconceivable that He should know His essence as principle of that which is other than Himself, without that other entering into His knowledge by way of implication and necessary consequence,"[27] he reaffirms the philosophic view by saying: "Because God knows Himself and discerns His greatness and glory and essence, He knows all and nought is hidden from Him[28]. . . . Hence God does not discern the creatures and know them by reason of themselves, as we know them; He knows them by reason of Himself. In fine, it is because He knows Himself that He knows all, for the All is dependent upon Him for its [coming into existence and its continuance of] existence."[29]

Second, having in mind the view of the Muslim Attributists that in God there exist eternal attributes which are other (*ghayr*) than God and different (*ḫilāf*) from God[30] and super-

[25] Cf. *Moreh* I, 53; Saadia, *Emunot ve-Deʿot* II, 4.

[26] *Berakot* 31b.

[27] *Tahāfut al-Falāsifah* VI, 24, p. 174, ll. 5-8 (ed. Bouyges).

[28] *Yesode* II, 9.

[29] *Ibid.* II, 10.

[30] Ibn Ḥazm, *Fiṣal* II, p. 126, ll. 22-24; IV, p. 207, ll. 7-10 (ed. Cairo, 1317-27).

added (*zā'idah*) to God [31] and also having in mind their defense of this view, through their spokesman Ghazālī, by contending that the unity of god does not mean absolute simplicity,[32] he says against it: "God discerns and knows His essence [and thereby He knows other things], and [whatever] He knows is not in virtue of a knowledge extraneous to Himself, as is the case in our knowing, for, in our case, we and our knowledge are not one and the same, whereas, in the case of God, He and His knowledge and His life are all one and the same in every respect and from every aspect." [33]

Third, having in mind that among the Attributists some expressed their belief in attribute by a formula of the type of "God is living in virtue of life and He is knowing in virtue of knowledge," [34] and having also in mind the stock Mu'tazilite argument against attributes, which, as stated by Wāṣil b. 'Aṭā', reads: "He who posits an eternal thing (*ma'na*) and attribute (*ṣifah*) posits two gods," [35] he says: "If God were living in virtue of life and knowing in virtue of knowledge, there would be many gods, He and His life and His knowledge." [36]

Fourth, having again in mind Ghazālī's rejection of the philosophic principle that "God is the knower and the knowledge and the known, and that all the three are one," [37] he says against it: "God is one in every respect and from every aspect and in every sense of unity, from which it follows that He is the knower and the known and the knowledge itself, all the three being one."[38]

Thus under the guise of his discussion of the terms "living"

[31] Shahrastānī, *Nihāyat*, p. 181, l. 3 (ed. Guillaume); Averroes, *Kashf*, p. 56, ll. 3 and 7 (ed. Müller).

[32] *Tahāfut al-Falāsifah* VII, p. 193, ll. 2-4.

[33] *Yesode* II, 10.

[34] Shahrastānī, *Nihāyat*, p. 181, ll. 1-2.

[35] *Idem, Milal*, p. 31, l. 19.

[36] *Yesode* II, 10.

[37] *Tahāfut al-Falāsifah* I, 15, p. 31, ll. 3-9; IV, 43, p. 182, l. 12 - p. 183, l. 4; XIII, 15-16, p. 232, l. l. 11 - p. 234, l. 4.

[38] *Yesode* II, 10.

and "knowing" Maimonides was dealing in his *Mishneh Torah* with what was technically known in Islam as the problem of attributes. The terms "life" and "knowledge," as I have shown elsewhere, [39] constituted one of the several pairs of attributes which formed the subject of discussion at the beginning of the problem of attributes. As in Judaism, and as also in Islam, there was no native reason for the rise of a doctrine like that of attributes and as the special external reason which had given rise to the problem of attributes in Islam, namely, the influence of Christianity, [40] did not exist in Judaism, Maimonides, like all the Jewish philosophers of the Arabic period before him, came out against attributes and thus, like all those Jewish philosophers of that period before him, he aligned himself with the Muslim Muʿtazilites.

But here three questions arise in our mind.

First, from Maimonides' inclusion among heretics "anyone who *says* that there is one God but that He is a body and possesses a figure" are we to infer that a heretic is only he who actually *says* that God is a body? Suppose, then, a person who does *not say* that God is a body but he happens to be one of those whom Maimonides describes as "the multitude" who cannot conceive in their mind of the existence of anything that is not a body [41] and hence cannot help but think of God as a body, would he be a heretic?

Second, again, from Maimonides' inclusion among heretics "any one who *says* that there are... two or more [gods]" are we to infer that a heretic is only he who actually *says* that there are two or more gods? Suppose, then, one who actually says that there is only one God but also says that the God, who is one, possesses attributes, would he be a heretic? Indeed Maimonides reproduces with approval the Muʿtazilite argument to the effect that a belief in attributes

[39] Cf. my paper "The Muslim Attributes and the Christian Trinity," *Harvard Theological Review*, 49 (1956), 1-18.

[40] Cf. *ibid.*

[41] *Moreh* I, 46, Arabic ed. Joel, p. 66, ll. 15-19; *Maʾmar Teḥiyyat ha-Metim*, *Ḳobeṣ* II, p. 8c; ed. Finkel, § 11.

implies a belief in many gods, [42] but still, while he does indeed repeat this statement of the Muʿtazilites, he does not use it in the same sense. As used by the Muʿtazilites, it means literally many gods, for as can be shown, [43] their criticism is based upon the view that eternity means deity, a view which they adopted from the Church Fathers, who adopted it from Philo. Maimonides, however, who rejects the view that eternity means deity, [44] uses the charge that attributes imply many gods only in a negative sense, namely, that they imply a denial of the unity of God, and this because they imply corporeality, which to Maimonides is tantamount to a denial of unity. But the implication of corporeality in attributes is, according to Maimonides, to be arrived at only by philosophic reasoning, which sees in the assumption of any intellectual distinction in God a divisibility implying corporeality; it is not directly contained in the scriptural denial of corporeality, which, according to Maimonides, as we have seen above, denies only the divisibility of God into quantitative parts like the quantitative divisibility of a body. The question therefore is whether one who professes the unity of God, but asserts that God has attributes, is a heretic or not.

Third, in view of the fact that Maimonides' inclusion of the belief of the incorporeality of God in the belief of His unity ultimately rests on the scriptural teaching of the unlikeness of God to other beings, suppose, then, a person who, mindful of the scriptural denial of likeness, resorted to the device of some Muslims, who, mindful of a similar denial of likeness in the koran (42: 9; 112: 4), said that God is a body unlike other bodies, [45] would he be a heretic?

[42] *Yesode* II, 10.

[43] To be discussed in my forthcoming work *The Philosophy of the Kalam*.

[44] To be inferred from his comment on Plato's theory of a pre-existent eternal matter in *Moreh* II, 13, as compared with Tertullian's argument against it in *Adversus Hermogenem* 4.

[45] *Moreh* I, 76 (2); cf. Ashaʿarī, *Maḳālāt*, p. 33, ll. 10-11; p. 208, l. 1 (ed. Ritter); Averroes, *Kashf*, p. 60, ll. 13-15.

An answer to the first question may be derived from Maimonides' own discussion of the mandatory command to believe in the unity of God and the prohibitive command not to believe in many gods.

The commandment enjoining the belief in the unity of God which reads, "Hear, O Israel: The Lord our God, the Lord is one" (Deut. 6: 4) is paraphrased by Maimonides in his *Sefer ha-Miṣvot,* written originally in Arabic, simply as "a command which imposes upon us the belief (אמונת: אעתקאד) in the unity [of God]." [46] but in his *Mishneh Torah,* written in Hebrew, it is paraphrased by him more precisely as a command ליחדו, [47] which literally means "to unify Him," but, by analogy of the term מיחדים in the statement "and we unify (מיחדים) His name twice daily, saying, 'Hear, O Israel: The Lord our God, the Lord is one'," [48] it really means to declare His unity by the recitation twice daily of the verse which begins with the words "Hear, O Israel." Thus the command to believe in the unity of God, legally, does not mean merely to believe in one's heart that God is one; it means to declare openly, by word of mouth, that God is one.

Similarly the commandment prohibiting polytheism, which reads, "Thou shalt have no other god before Me" (Exod. 20: 3), is paraphrased by Maimonides in Arabic simply as "a prohibition which prohibits us from believing (האמין: אעתקאד) in a deity besides god." [49] In Hebrew, however, it is paraphrased by him more precisely as a command that "one is not to cause to come up (יעלה) into his thought that there is another deity

[46] *Sefer ha-Miṣvot,* Positive 2. However, at the end of his discussion of this commandment, Maimonides explains that it means "the confession (ההודאה: אלאקראר) of unity and the belief therein." This shows that, though the Arabic term *tauḥīd* by itself may mean "profession of the unity of God," it is used here by Maimonides in the simple sense of "unity of God," just as in that simple sense does he quite evidently use its corresponding Hebrew term *yiḥud* in *Mishneh Torah, Yesode* I, 7, and in *Moreh Nebukim* I, 50.

[47] *Yesode,* Preface, Commandment 3.

[48] *Canticles Rabbah* 7, 11 (on 2: 6).

[49] *Sefer ha-Miṣvot,* Negative 1.

besides the Lord."[50] That the Hebrew word יעלה here is to be taken as the causative *hif'il* rather than the intransitive *ḳal* is quite evident from his subsequent statement that "whoever causes to come up (המעלה) into his mind that there is another besides this God, violates a prohibition, as it is said, 'Thou shalt have no other gods before Me'."[51] What the expression "causes to come up into his mind" means here may be gathered from what Maimonides says with regard to the acknowledgment of idolatry, with which, as we have seen, the acknowledgment of polytheism is identified by him.[52] Now with regard to the acknowledgment of idolatry he says that "he who acknowledges (מודה) that idol-worship is true, even if he does not worship an idol, is committing the sin of reviling and blaspheming the honored and the revered name of God," adding that "the same laws and regulations apply to both the idolater and the blasphemer."[53] But inasmuch as legally one is not a blasphemer unless he blasphemes the name of God by spoken word,[54] we may conclude that the prohibition of acknowledging idolatry as true means the acknowledgment of it as true by spoken word. Again, inasmuch as to Maimonides the acknowledgment of polytheism as true is the same as the acknowledgement of idolatory as true, we may conclude that the acknowledgment of the existence of "two or more [gods]," which he describes as heresy, must be an acknowledgment by spoken words. Finally, inasmuch as the heresy which attaches to the acknowledgment of the corporeality of God is derived by Maimonides, as we have seen, from a Talmudic statement which he understood to mean that he who only acknowledges idolatry, without actually worshipping an idol, is a heretic and, inasmuch as such an acknowledgment must be by spoken words, we may conclude that the heresy which he attaches to the acknowledgment of the corporeality of God must also be by spoken words.

[50] *Yesode*, Preface, Commandment 2.

[51] *Ibid.* I, 6.

[52] Cf. text between nn. 22 and 23 above.

[53] *'Akum* II, 6.

[54] *Ibid.* II, 7.

Thus, according to Maimonides, one is not included among his five classes of heretics, unless he actually *says* that he believes in many deities and also unless he actually *says* that God is a body.

As for the second and third questions, a partial answer to them may be derived from a responsum written by Maimonides to the prorelyte Obadiah, in which he says as follows: "The Muslims are not [what is legally called] idolaters [and polytheists]: idolatry has long been cut off from their mouth and from their heart. They attribute to God a unity in the true sense of the term, a unity to which there is no reproach.[55] By "Muslims," as may be gathered from the context, he means the generality of orthodox Muslims. Now the generality of orthodox Muslims believed that God possessed attributes. Moreover, while most of the orthodox Muslims believed that God is not a body and that similarly his attributes, though real things and other than God, are not bodies, there were some Muslims in good orthodox standing, such as those whom Averroes describes as "The Ḥanbalites and their many followers," who believed that "God is a body unlike other bodies"[56] and by the same token they believed that attributes are also bodies unlike other bodies. It is both these types of orthodox Muslims that are described by Maimonides as not being polytheists and as having a true conception of the unity of God. This quite clearly shows that from a strictly legally religious viewpoint non-Jews who professed that God is one but that he possesses attributes and similarly non-Jews who professed that God is one but that he is a body unlike other bodies are not polytheists. But the question still remains whether the same ruling would apply also to Jews who, while professing the unity of God, profess also that God has attributes or that God is a body unlike other bodies.

An answer to this question in both its phases is to be found in the *Moreh Nebukim*.

[55] *Teshubot ha-Rambam* 160 (Ḳobeṣ p. 34d), 369 (ed. Freimann, p. 335).

[56] Averroes, *Kashf*, p. 60, ll. 14-15.

I shall deal first with that phase of the question which relates to the assertion by a Jew that God, who is one, is a body unlike other bodies.

Likeness between God and other beings, according to Maimonides, is implied only when the same term, which is predicated of God and of other beings, is used either in a univocal (*mutawāṭi'*: *muskam*) sense or in an ambiguous (*mushakkik*: *mesuppak*) sense. There is no implication of likeness between God and other beings if the same term is predicated of them in an equivocal (*mushtarak*: *meshuttaf*) sense,[57] for any term predicated of God equivocally is, according to Maimonides, in meaning, the negation of the opposite of that term and, in form, the affirmation of the identity of that term with the essence of God and hence unlike the same term predicated of other beings. Thus, for instances, if the term "knowing" is used equivocally, then the proposition "God is knowing" is, in meaning, the negation of ignorance but, in form, it is the affirmation of knowledge that is identical with the essence of God and hence unlike the knowledge of any other being.[58] In the case of the term "body," however, Maimonides would not allow its predication of God even when used in an equivocal sense, and this, as he says, is for the following reason: "The prophetic books have never applied to God even metaphorically anything that is considered by ordinary people as an imperfection or that is conceived by one as being incompatible with God, though such a term is not different from those other terms which are used in those books as descriptions of God."[59] The term body, which includes the term matter, is taken to imply imperfection, according to Maimonides, not only by "the prophetic books" but also by the philosophers.[60]

57 *Moreh* I, 56.

58 Cf. my paper "Maimonides on Negative Attributes," *Louis Ginzberg Jubilee Volume*, 411-446. Above, pp. 195-230.

59 *Moreh* I, 47, p. 70, ll. 9-11, cf. pp. 439-440 in my paper referred to in the preceding note.

60 *Moreh* I, Introd., p. 8, l. 27 - p. 9, l. 3; I, 17; III, 8, p. 309, l. 24 - p. 310, l. 9.

Thus, according to Maimonides, on the basis of the mere scriptural teaching of the unlikeness of God, one should be allowed to predicate of God the term "body," with the qualification that he is unlike other bodies plus the understanding that the term body is used in an equivocal sense. He is against its predication of God only on the ground of the observed fact that Scripture avoids applying to God terms with any implication of imperfection, even with the understanding that those terms are to be taken in non-literal sense, and "body" to him is a term which implies imperfection.

The same inference may also be drawn from his criticism of some of the Muslim Mutakallimūn who tried to prove the incorporeality of God from His unlikeness to other beings, which is taught in the Koran in the verses "Nought is there like Him" (42: 9) and "There is none equal with Him" (112: 4).[61]

His chief arguments against this proof for incorporeality are two. His first argument is evidently from the viewpoint of the Mutakallimūn themselves, who believe that all terms are predicated of God in an ambiguous sense, that is, according to a difference of degree. Speaking, then, for these Mutakallimūn, Maimonides says that they could refute this proof by arguing that there is no likeness between God and created bodies, for created bodies "are not like God in every respect"[62] and so, conversely, God is not like them in every respect, that is to say, there is always some degree of difference in the likeness between them. In fact, it is to these Mutakallimūn that, as can be shown, he refers at the beginning of his work where he speaks of certain anonymous "people" who thought that God is a body, but is "the greatest and most splendid [of bodies],"[63] that is to say, the term body is applied to God in an ambiguous sense. The second argument is from his own viewpoint, according to which all terms are predicated of God in an equivocal sense, that is, in a sense according to which terms

[61] *Moreh* I, 76 (2)
[62] *Ibid.*, p. 160, ll. 18-19.
[63] *Ibid.* I, 1, p. 14, ll. 10-11.

predicated of both God and created beings are alike only in sound but not at all in meaning. Arguing then from his own viewpoint and describing that argument as "more telling," he contends that, even if it is admitted that there is no likeness between God and other beings, God can be described as a body, provided one uses the term body in an equivocal sense, so that there is absolutely no likeness between the term body predicate of God and the same term predicated of created beings.[64] His closing remark, "would that I knew how this vulnerable view [that is, that God is a body] can be refuted by these queer methods of theirs which I have made known to you,"[65] shows that he did mean his argument to be a mere argument *ad hominem* but that he really believed that the mere denial of likeness, such as found in Scripture, does not lead to a denial of God's being a body, if the term body is used in an equivocal sense and, especially, if its use in that sense is explicitly emphasized by the qualifying phrase "unlike other bodies."

Here, then, we have evidence that for a Jew the mandatory command to believe in the unity of God, which is taken by Maimonides to include a denial of the corporeality of God, may be satisfied by denying that God is a body like other bodies. Accordingly, when in his *Mishneh Torah* Maimonides condemns as heretic "anyone who says that there is one Lord but that He is a body and possesses a figure;" he means thereby only one who says that God is a body like other bodies which possess a figure; anyone who says that God, who is one, is a body unlike other bodies and use the term body in an equivocal sense is not, legally, a heretic.[65a]

I shall now take up that phase of the question which relates to the assertion by a Jew that God, who is one, possesses attributes.

That religiously the denial of corporeality and the denial of

[64] *Ibid.* I, 76 (2), p. 160, ll. 21 ff.

[65] *Ibid.*, p. 161, ll. 9-10.

[65a] The rejection of the use of the expression "God is a body unlike other bodies" in *Moreh* I, 1, refers to Muslims who use it not in an equivocal sense. Cf. my *The Philosophy of the Kalam*.

attributes are not of equal standing is brought out by Maimonides in a passage in which he shows how these two denials are to be taught differently to two different types of people.

"With regard to the remotion of corporeality as well as the removal of likeness and passivity from God," he says, "it is a matter which must be made clear and explained to everyone according to his capacity and its acceptance, on the authority of tradition, must be taught to children, women, illiterates, and those of subnormal intelligence, just as they are taught to accept on the authority of tradition that God is one, that he is eternal, and that none but he is to be worshipped." He then goes to say that, if, after having accepted this doctrine, they become perplexed as to the meaning of terms implying corporeality and passivity and likeness by which God is described in Scripture, they should be told that all such terms are used in a metaphorical sense, in a sense unlike the sense in which the same terms are used in describing other beings. Mentioning especially the terms "existence," "life," and "knowledge," terms which Muslim attributists usually include in their lists of attributes, he says that all these unsophisticated people are to be taught on the mere authority of scriptural tradition that these terms are predicated of God in an equivocal and not in an ambiguous sense, adding that the equivocal use of these terms has also been demonstrated by arguments derived from "the natural sciences."[66] He then goes on to say that, if these unsophisticated people claim that they cannot understand what all these metaphorical and equivocal interpretations of a scriptural text mean, they should be told: "The interpretation of this text is understood by scholars; as for you, all you have to know is that God is not a body and is free of bodily passion... that he is not to be likened to any other thing... that the words of the prophets are true and have an interpretation." The urgency of such instruction to unsophisticated people is finally explained by

[66] *Ibid.* I, 35, p. 54, l. 28-p. 55, l. 7; p. 54, ll. 2 20.

him on the ground that "it is not meet that [for the want of instruction] one should become set in the belief that God is corporeal or in the belief that He is anything pertaining to bodies any more than it is meet that [for the want of instruction] he should become set in the belief that there is no God or that in association with God there is another god or that a being other than He may be worshipped.[67]

His statement about the teaching of the denial of attributes reads briefly as follows: "As for the discussion of attributes, namely, how they are to be negated of God and what the meaning is of those terms which are attributed to Him. . . they are matters which are not to be discussed except in chapter-headings, as we have mentioned, and also only with an individual described [by us above as possessing certain qualifications, among which is included training in various plutsophic disciplines]."[68]

The contrast between the denial of corporeality and the denial of attributes is quite clear. That God is not a body and that terms implying corporeality by which God is described in Scripture should not be taken literally must be taught to everybody on the authority of mere scriptural tradition and must be accepted implicitly by those so taught. The denial of attributes, however, is to be taught, evidently by means of rational demonstration, to individual students who have already received preliminary training in certain prescribed philosophic desciplines. But, it will be noticed, no mention is made of the need of an implicit acceptance on the part of the student of his master's rational conclusion as to the denial of attributes. The denial of attributes is thus not regarded by Maimonides as being, legally, included in the mandatory command to believe in one God and consequently the assertion of a belief in attributes is not regarded by him as heresy.

An inference to the same effect is to be drawn also from

[67] *Ibid.*, p. 55, ll. 7-5.
[68] *Ibid.*, p. 54, ll. 20-28; cf. ibid. I, 34, Third Cause.

his chapters on attributes. In the first of these chapters, there occur the following five statements:

1. "Just as it is impossible that God should be a body, so it is impossible that He should possesse an essential attribute."[69]

2. "As for him who believes (חאמין: אעתקאד) that God is one but possesses many attributes, he says (אמר: קאל) by his spoken word that God is one but believes Him in his thought to be many." [70]

3. "This is like the saying of the Christians: God is one but also three and the three are one." [71]

4. "So also is the saying of him who, despite his remotion of corporeality [from God] and his belief in [His] absolute simplicity, says that God is one but possesses many attributes and that He and His attributes are one." [72]

5. "When thou...shalt become a possessor of understanding...thou shalt then be one of those who form a concept (יצייר: יתצוّר) of the unity of God and not one of those who say it with their mouth but form no concept of it in their mind and are thus of the kind of people of whom it is said: Thou art near their mouth, and far from their reins [Jer. 12: 2]." [73]

The first thing to find out about this passage is whether the Attributist who is the target of his criticism is Muslim or Jewish. For while the "thou" in statement 5 is quite evidently addressed by Maimonides to his prospective Jewish reader, it is not quite certain whether the "he who" in statements 2 and 3 and the "one of those" in the expression "not one of those" in statement 5 refer to a Jewish or to a Muslim Attributist, for references to various types of Muslim Attributists abound in these chapters on attributes. Let us then try to find out whom Maimonides had in mind by these anonymous references in this first chapter on attributes.

[69] *Ibid.* I, 50, p. 75, 11. 6-7.
[70] *Ibid.*, 11. 7-8.
[71] *Ibid.*, 11. 8-9.
[72] Ibid., 11. 9-11.
[73] *Ibid.*, 11. 16-20.

A cue to the identity of the Attributist criticized here by Maimonides is to be found in his description of that Attributist as one who, "despite his remotion of corporeality [from God] and his belief in [God's] absolute simplicity," maintains that "God is one but possesses many attributes." Now this description does not fit Muslim Attributists, for Muslim Attributists, through their spokeman Ghazālī, deny that the unity of God means absolute simplicty.[74] And this is the crux of the problem on which they differ from the Muctazilites. Indeed, they admit that God is incorporeal, or that his corporeality is unlike any other corporeality, but they deny that the denial of corporeality implies simplicity and hence a denial of attributes. Exactly whom Maimonides had in mind in his criticism here is not clear. In the literature on the subject, as far as I know, there is no mention of anyone who believed in the simplicity of God and, despite this belief, insisted upon the belief in attributes. Maimonides quite evidently is not arguing here against any particular proponent of attributism. He is discussing here the problem theoretically, trying to show to his Jewish readers that on the assumption of the belief that the unity of God means simplicity, there can be no belief attributes, and that consequently no Jew who believes in absolute simplicity of God can believe in attributes.

The "he who," then, in statements 2 and 3 and the "one" in "not one of these" in statement 5 is a Jew, and one and the same Jew. Now in statement 4, this Jewish Attributist is described as "he who *says* that God...possesses many attributes" and similarly in statement 5 he is told that with his growth in understanding, he will be "not one of those who *says*" that God has many attributes. Consequently statement 2, despite its reading, should be taken to mean: "As for him who *believes* [and hence also *says*] that God is one but possesses many attributes, he *says* by his spoken word that he is one but *believes in his thought* to be many," to whom later in

[74] Cf. above at n. 32.

statement 5 the verse, "Thou art near their mouth, and far from their reins" is applied. Now, since, according to Maimonides, as we have seen, one is not included among his five classes of heretics unless he actually *says* that God is many, the Attributist here who, by *saying* that God possesses many attributes, is described as being one who only "*believes in his thought*" that God is many, is not included by Maimonides in his five classes of heretics.

Finally, the same inference may be drawn from Maimonides' comparison of the Jewish would-be Attributist to Christian Trinitarians.

In Islam, the Christian doctrine of the Trinity was objected to on two grounds. On purely religious grounds, it was charged with being polytheistic. This charge was already raised against it in the Koran, in such verses as "Say not Three...God is only one God" (4: 169) and "They are infidels who say, God is the third of the three, for there is no God but one God" (5: 77). According to the testimony of John of Damscus, the Muslims called the Christians ἑταιριασταί, "associators," [75] a term reflecting the Koranic term *mushrikūn*, which is used for what we call polytheists. Following this common Muslim charge of polytheism against Christianity, Maimonides similarly characterizes the Christians as idolaters, that is, polytheists. [76] On philosophic grounds, the doctrine of the Trinity, with its assertion both that God is one and that God consisted of three persons each of whom is to be called God, was charged with being an infringement on the Law of Contradiction. [77] Now in his statement about the Trinity, it will be noticed, the objection implied is that it is an infringement on the Law of Contradiction and not that it is poly-

[75] John of Damascus, *De Haeresibus* 101 (PG 94, 768 B).

[76] *ʿAkum* IX, 4. Were it not for Muslim influence, there is reason to believe that Maimonides, like rabbis in Christian countries, would not have characterized Christians as idolaters and polytheists.

[77] This argument against the Trinity is reproduced by Yaḥyā b. ʿAdī in his apologetic treatises. Cf. A. Périer, *Petits Traités Apologétiques de Yaḥyā Ben ʿAdī*, p. 46, 1. 7 - p. 47, 1. 7; p. 64, 11. 6-7.

theistic. The question is, why did he not use against it the religious objection of its being polytheistic?

Then, there is also a question with regard to his statement about the Jewish would-be attributist, whom he describes here as believing that the unity of God means absolute simplicity. Now, according to Maimonides' own view, on the strict basis of scriptural teaching, the unity of God means simplicity only in the sense that it excludes any division into parts into which a body is quantitatively divisible.[78] Absolute simplicity, in the sense of exclusion of the logical destruction of genus and specific difference, is based purely on philosophic reasoning. Why then does he have to assume here that his Jewish Attributist believes that the unity of God means absolute simplicity?

The answer to these questions is, I imagine, as follows. Maimonides wanted to show that the Christian doctrine of the Trinity and the belief in attributes are open to the same objection. Now of the two objections to the doctrine of the Trinity, the religious one could not apply to the belief in attributes, for Maimonides, in his responsum to Obadiah the proselyte has already decided that legally the Muslims who believed in attributes were not polytheists[79] and he saw no reason why he should not extend the same legal decision to a Jew who believed in attributes. Similarly the philosophic objection to the doctrine of the Trinity could not apply to the belief in attributes, if the Jew who professed it did not believe that the unity of God meant his absolute simplicity, for Maimonides could not but agree with Ghazālī's contention[80] that the belief in attributes is not objectionable if the unity of God is not assumed to mean absolute simplicity. And so what did Maimonides do? He made the Jewish Attributist believe in the absolute simplicity of God, whereby, like the Christian Trinitarians, he laid himself open to the objection that he was infringing upon the Law of Contradiction.

[78] Cf. above at nn. 9 and 10.

[79] Cf. above at n. 55.

[80] Cf. above at n. 32.

Thus, again, according to Maimonides, a Jew who says that God is one but possesses attributes is not to be included among his five classes of heretics. Consequently, his opening statement (statement 1) that, "just as it is impossible that God should be a body, so it is impossible that He should possess an essential attribute," only means that it is logically impossible; it does not mean that the assertion of attributes, like the assertion of corporeality, is heresy.

The upshot of our discussion here is that within each of such beliefs as the incorporeality and the unity of God and the denial of attributes Maimonides draws a line of demarcation. To assert of God, who is one, that he is a body unlike other bodies, wherein the term body, predicated of God, is used in an equivocal sense, is, according to Maimonides, not heretical, but still he is opposed to the predication of the term body of God even with that qualification. Again, the true unity of God, according to Maimonides, means absolute simplicity, but still Muslims who deny that the unity of God means absolute simplicity are said by him to have an irreproachable belief in one God and similarly Jews who deny it are not heretics. Then, also, the assertion of attributes, according to Maimonides, is incompatible with the belief in the unity and incorporeality of God, and he even says that it is tantamount to the assertion of a belief in many gods, but still he says that Muslims who assert a belief in attributes have an irreproachable belief in the unity of God and are not to be regarded as polytheists and similarly Jews who assert a belief in attributes are not heretics.

For all these seemingly paradoxical views, we are going to show, there is a good reason. Underlying all these lines of demarcation drawn by Maimonides within all these beliefs is the fact that matters of belief, just as matters of action, are included under the traditional 613 commandments, [81] and consequently matters of belief are to be treated like matters of action. Now in matters of action a line of demarca-

[81] *Sefer ha-Miṣvot, Shoresh* 9.

tion, rigidly defined by law is, drawn between what one is required to do and what one is not allowed to do. So also in matters of belief, according to Maimonides, a line of demarcation, rigidly defined, must be drawn between what one is required to believe and what one is not allowed to believe. Again, in matters of action, a distinction is made between what is "along the line of legal requirement (שורת הדין) and what is "beyond the line of legal requirement" (לפנים משורת הדין).[82] So also, in matters of belief, according to Maimonides, a distinction is to be drawn between what may be called "along the line of required belief" (שורת האמונה) and what may be called "beyond the line of required belief" (לפנים משורת האמונה). Then, again, in matters of action, that which is "beyond the line of legal requirement" is called "a rule of piety" (מדת חסידות).[83] So also, in matters of belief, according to Maimonides, that which is "beyond the line of required belief" is to be called "a rule of piety," but, in the case of matters of belief, the "rule of piety," according to him, is to include what may be called "the rule of philosophic speculation" (מדת העיון הפילוסופי).[84]

In accordance with these conceptions of his with regard to the lines of demarcation that are to be drawn within anything pertaining to religious belief, Maimonides has arrived at the conclusion that, even though by the strict requirement of scriptural belief one is allowed to say that God, who is one, is a body unlike other bodies, provided the term body is used in an equivocal sense, still by the rule of piety one is not to apply the term body to God even with the addition of that qualifying phrase and with the use of the term body in that sense, inasmuch as Scripture never describes God by terms connoting imperfection, and body is one of such terms. Conversely, even though by the rule of philosophic speculation the belief in the unity of God is to mean absolute simplicity,

[82] *Mekilta, Amalek* 4 (ed. Lauterbach, II, p. 182).
[83] *Baba Meṣiʿa* 52b; Maimonides, *De ʿot* I, 5; *ʿAbadim* IX, 8.
[84] Cf. expression עיון פילוסופי in *Moreh* II, 1.

still those who deny this have an irreproachable conception of the belief in the unity of God, inasmuch as, on the basis of the strict requirement of scriptural belief, the unity of God excludes only that divisibility into parts which is analogous to the quantitative divisibility into parts to which a body is subject. Similarly, even though by the rule of philosophic speculation the belief in attributes is incompatible with the belief in the absolute unity of God, which philosophically implies corporeality, still those who assert that God, though one, possess attributes are not polytheists nor deniers of the unity of God, inasmuch as, on the basis of the strict requirement of scriptural belief, the belief in attributes is not incompatible with the belief in the unity of God.

14
STUDIES IN CRESCAS

It is not often given to a book to be taken up for detailed examination by two eminent scholars. Such good fortune has fallen to my *Crescas' Critique of Aristotle* in the reviews by Professor Julius Guttmann in *Zeitschrift der Deutschen Morgenländischen Gesellschaft*, N.F. 11 (1933), pp. 225–232, and by Professor Isaak Heinemann in *Monatsschrift für Geschichte und Wissenschaft des Judentums*, 76 (1932), pp. 487–489. That they should find themselves in disagreement with some of the statements in the book was naturally to be expected; that I should not agree with their disagreements is likewise quite natural. But the differences between us, which I am to discuss here, are more than the mere bandying of words between reviewers and author. They will prove, I hope, to be of general interest to students of Hebrew philosophic texts.

Guttmann

1. In a work like Crescas' *Or Adonai* which was completed only about one hundred and forty-five years before its appearance in print (1410–1555) and of which we have eleven manuscripts, one of which was apparently written by a student of the author and another was executed forty-seven years after the composition of the work, we should hardly expect to find any great number of corruptions which would not correct themselves in the various manuscripts. If despite all the manuscripts difficulties of reading do still appear in the text, we should naturally expect them to be due to inadequacies of style in the original composition rather than to corruptions at the hands of copyists—especially since we have reason to believe that no definitively revised text of the work ever emanated from the author (cf. pp. 703–704). Consequently, in attempting to remove these difficulties of reading, we should naturally be inclined to follow the method of

interpretation rather than that of emendation. This indeed is the principle which I have followed in the study of those portions of the *Or Adonai* which are included in the *Crescas' Critique of Aristotle*. Only in a limited number of instances, where the corruption of the text was quite obvious and no conceivable interpretation could remove it, have I allowed myself to emend the text or to suggest an emendation—and this on the assumption that such instances of corruption might have been careless slips in the original text. A list of such conjectural emendations is given in the "Index of Subjects and Names," p. 732, under "Text." But Professor Guttmann thinks that I should have been more lavish with my conjectural emendations, and as an illustration he suggests three such emendations. I shall discuss them here one by one.

(a) On p. 196, ll. 6–8, in the passage וזה שהמקום המיוחד לחלקים המתנועעים בעצם בתנועת הכל איננו מקיף שוה נבדל באופן שיהיה לו ערבות ודמיון לכל חלקי המקום כאשר חתר Guttmann suggests the change of המקום to המקומם. This change is unacceptable. Though Crescas uses the term המקומם a few lines later (p. 196, l. 16), in this particular passage its use is impossible, and for the following reason: Whenever the refluxion of the elements toward their natural localities is explained by desire, the explanation always means that the elements have a desire for their natural localities and not that the natural localities have a desire for their elements. Thus also Crescas throughout his discussion speaks of the object having האותות, ערבות, or דמיון for its place (cf. p. 196, ll. 15–20) and not of the place having האותות, ערבות, or דמיון for its object. Likewise in the passage quoted by me from Averroes' *Epitome of the Physics* (see p. 444, n. 62) the objects are said to have תשוקה, ערבות, and דמיון for their place, but not the other way around. To change in this passage המקום to המקומם, as suggested by Guttmann, would make Crescas say that it is the place which has ערבות ודמיון for the object, but this would not be in accordance with what we should expect him to say.

To strengthen his contention Guttmann further says: "Dass der vorliegende Text unmöglich ist, zeigt die Übersetzung W's die ganz wilkürlich an Stelle des Raumes das Raumobjekt zum Subjekt des Satzes macht." To this I say that there is nothing arbitrary in my translation. The pronoun לו does not refer, as is assumed by Guttmann, to שהמקום in the passage וזה שהמקום המיוחד לחלקים המתנועעים בעצם בתנועת הכל. That it cannot refer to שהמקום I have already shown in the preceding paragraph. Logically לו refers to לחלקים which is used here by Crescas in the distributive sense for the reason that in his mind the word לחלקים referred to כל אחד מחלקיו on p. 151, l. 19. Grammatically, however, it may be taken to agree with הכל. That this is so may be clearly seen from the passage which immediately follows. In my translation I have tried to bring out this construction of the text. Of course, had Crescas submitted his text to me for revision, I would have advised him to change here לו to להם, to make it agree grammatically with לחלקים to which he meant it to refer, and would have pointed out to him that לו might be mistaken to refer to שהמקום and might thus lead to impossible suggestion of emending המקום to read המקומם. But inasmuch as Crescas evidently had submitted his text to nobody for revision, nor had he revised it himself (cf. pp. 703–704), our duty is to find out what he meant to say, and in the light of this to explain what he actually does say.

(b) In the passage שסביב קטבי הכדור דבר נח (p. 198, l. 3) Guttmann makes two emendations. First, he changes שסביב to שיסובו. Second, he changes קטבי to קטרי. The passage thus emended reads: שיסובו קטרי הכדור דבר נח.

The first change evidently has suggested itself to Guttmann by his desire to rewrite the text of Crescas in order to make it read like the underlying sources reproduced in the notes. In these sources instead of the preposition סביב the finite verb יסבוב is used. But if Guttmann's שיסובו is to be taken, as it evidently must, in the sense of "moving circularly" and not simply in the sense of "surrounding"—for otherwise his suggested change would be quite purposeless—then it would be necessary for him further to emend the text by inserting the preposition על before דבר נח. In the underlying sources quoted by me the expressions read גשם גבנוני נח עליו יסבוב and גשם נח עליו יסבוב (p. 451, n. 70). But if we were to emend the *Or Adonai* on the basis of its underlying literary sources, then we should have to rewrite large portions of the work. The fact is, departure from his literary sources is one of the characteristic features of Crescas' method of literary composition. Such examples of departure occur even in places where there is no obvious reason for them and they occur often even at the expense of clearness. The explanation I have offered for this is that "the collection of material and especially the abstracts of literature used in the composition of the work were prepared by students" (cf. p. 23, and p. 30). In this particular instance there is no conceivable need for the emendation suggested by Guttmann.

Similarly unnecessary is the change of קטבי to קטרי. The Hebrew קטב is the Arabic قطب, the latter of which means both (a) axis and (b) either extremity of an axis. So also the equivalent Greek term πόλος means both axis and either extremity of an axis. In the sense of *axis* the term קטב is thus the equivalent of the term קטר which means *diameter*. While the prevalent meaning of קטב in Hebrew philosophic literature is that of the extremity of an axis, its use in the sense of axis is not unknown. Thus in *Emunot we-De'ot*, I, 3, Fifth Theory, in the statement והוא שלקחתי קטבי (اقطاب) דבריהם וסבבתי עליהם אופן (لولب) העיון (*Kitâb al-Amânât wa'l-I'tiqâdât*, ed. S. Landauer, p. 49) it is quite clear that the Hebrew קטבי as well as the Arabic اقطاب is used in the sense of "axis" about which the אופן, *wheel*, or the لولب, *tube*, turns. Incidentally, it may be remarked that the use of the term אופן in Judah Ibn Tibbon's translation would seem to indicate that he had before him the reading دولاب, *wheel*, instead of لولب, *tube*. The term קטרי, suggested by Guttmann, would mean here *diameters* which would be practically the same as the term קטבי in the sense of *axes*. The meaning of the passage as I have explained in my notes is the same whether we read קטבי or קטרי. It is as follows: Given a sphere which rotates on various axes (קטבי), in my reading, or diameters (קטרי), in Guttmann's reading, then at the crossing point of these axes, or rather at the centre of the sphere (l. 3: שסביב קטבי הכדור = l. 4: שהנקודה אשר במרכז או בקטבים), there would be something stationary. In my English translation, however, the term "pole" is inaccurately used. Without consulting dictionaries I substituted it for the term "axis" which I had originally used, assuming that like the Greek *πόλος* it is used both in the sense of axis and in the sense of either extremity of an axis, and somehow associated it with the word "pole" in the sense of "rod"—an erroneous association which, I have since discovered, is quite common. These two words in English, as I have now learned, have different etymologies, and the English "pole," which corresponds to the Greek *πόλος*, is never used in the sense of "axis" but always in the sense of the "extremity of an axis." Evidently, this English word has been derived not directly from the Greek but indirectly through the Latin *polus*, which is likewise used only in the sense of the "extremity of an axis." Consequently, in my translation, the term "axis" should be used for the term "pole." But there is no need for changing the reading קטבי to קטרי on the ground urged by Guttmann, though realizing how easy it was for the author or copyist to confuse קטבי and קטרי I could not oppose the reading קטרי by reason of my general opposition to unnecessary conjectural emendation. All I contend is that in this instance either word can be used with equal propriety. I have retained the extant reading because there was no compelling reason for changing it.

(c) In the passage הנה מלא כל הארץ כבודו שהוא יסוד העיבור (העבור) שביסודות כבודו Guttmann suggests to change יסוד העיבור to יסוד העובי. Now, if a term meaning "crass," "coarse," or "gross" would satisfy him in this context, why not change it to יסוד העיכור or היסוד העכור or still better to יסוד העפר? Any one of these readings would be better than his יסוד העובי, inasmuch as they would all retain the final ר. But the very fact that as soon as a conjectural emendation is suggested there appear at once three equally good terms to which the extant reading can be changed shows how hazardous and arbitrary such emendations are. But I have shown, and I believe quite convincingly (pp. 459–462, notes 92–93), that the entire passage with its use of the term כבוד reflects Cabalistic discussions of the Sefirot and this naturally leads one to expect that the term יסוד העיבור must likewise contain an allusion to Cabalistic terminology. To change it to any other term would destroy that allusion and would thus strip the term of the special significance which we feel it must have here in this particular Cabalistic context.

In a private communication, Dr. G. Scholem, of the Hebrew University, suggests that Crescas' explanation of מלא כל הארץ כבודו by יסוד העיבור reflects the Biblical expression בטן המלאה *the body of the pregnant* (Eccles. 11, 5). This is an excellent suggestion. But his contention that this dispenses with the assumption that the term יסוד הָעִיבור contains an allusion to the Sefirot does not follow. On the contrary, it may be taken as a corroboration of that assumption.

2. Crescas' statement ולזה גם כן לא יתחייב שגדר הבלתי בעל תכלית יצדק על חלקיו כמו שלא יתחייב זה בקו הלמודי ולא יתחייב הרכבה בו כלל אלא מחלקיו (p. 178, ll. 24–26) is the most difficult in the entire work. It is most difficult because it is most deceptive by its simplicity. Ostensibly it maintains that an infinite is not to be thought of as composed of infinites any more than a mathematical line is to be thought of as composed of points—which is an obvious truism. And this is the sense in which all students of Crescas who happened to comment upon this passage had taken it to mean. In my discussion of this passage (n. 1, pp. 391–396) I noticed the difficulty of this simple understanding of the passage and suggested an explanation which would remove that difficulty. The explanation consists in a distinction supposed to have been in the mind of Crescas between divisibility and compositeness. According to this distinction it would be possible to speak of an immaterial infinite, which is infinite by its essence, to be divisible into parts which are similarly infinite in their essence without necessarily having to assume that the definition of an infinite as that which is without limits would apply to those parts and thus also without having to assume that the whole would be composed of parts which are infinites in the sense of being actually without limits. The analogy of the mathematical, I have shown, was introduced by Crescas only for the purpose of illustrating the distinction between divisibility and compositeness. Now, one can argue back and forth against this distinction as one can argue back and forth against similar subtle distinctions made by all mediaeval philosophers and by Crescas himself elsewhere. In fact, the discovery, maintenance, and rejection of imperceptible distinctions of this kind are the constituent elements of the

greater part of the philosophic speculations found in mediaeval writings. The critical student of these writings, however, must constantly be on his guard against turning himself into a contemporary of the authors whom he studies and against engaging himself in a discussion of the intrinsic merits of the arguments which he is trying to interpret. All he is called upon to do is to establish the plausible reasonableness of those arguments. Still more must he guard himself against the temptation of removing difficulties of texts by making the authors of the texts say things which are contrary to what they actually do say. In the passage in question I have shown the plausible reasonableness of the argument which I assume to lie behind the very words used by Crescas, without attempting to change those words. Consequently my interpretation must stand until it is challenged by some other and more plausible interpretation, and one which could be equally construed with the text as it now reads.

But Guttmann offers an interpretation of the text which makes Crescas say what he does not say. He thinks that Crescas' argument could be strengthened by drawing an analogy not between an infinite and a "mathematical line" but between the infinite and a "mathematical circle," and consequently he makes Crescas use that analogy of a "mathematical circle." To quote: "Das will auch das Beispiel von der mathematischen Linie sagen. So wenig wie der Teil eines Kreises wieder ein Kreis ist, braucht der Teil eines Unendlichen ein Unendliches zu sein." But I should like to ask Professor Guttmann the following question. Crescas says definitely בקו הלמודי, which means "mathematical line" and not a "mathematical circle" for which the terms in Hebrew would be בעגול הלמודי. Does Guttmann mean to say that when Crescas explicitly wrote קו he meant עגול? Or, does he mean to emend the text here and change קו to עגול?

3. In my interpretation of Crescas' argument against Altabrizi I have shown that the argument is based upon a distinction between the infinite and what is known as the indefinite. This distinction is not only implied in this particular passage, offering a rational interpretation of the argument contained in it, but it is also implied in the passages quoted in the same note and

in subsequent notes. The distinction has not been read by me into this passage out of a desire to make Crescas anticipate Spinoza, for as far as this particular distinction is concerned, Spinoza had before him more immediate and much more explicit sources from which he could have derived it, as I have shown in my essay on Spinoza referred to in that note. (This essay has since been reprinted in my *The Philosophy of Spinoza*, Vol. I, Ch. VIII). The interpretation offered by Guttmann for the passage is only a paraphrase of the text, and if it is to be made to mean anything, it must be assumed to imply that distinction between the infinite and the indefinite which he rejects.

4. On p. 198, ll. 14–15 I take the passage וכבר היה ראוי להיות כן, כי המקום היה ראוי שיהיה שוה למקומם כלו וחלקיו which follows Crescas' own conclusion with regard to the definition of place, as an additional argument in support of his conclusion which in itself has been arrived at after a series of other arguments. The opening words וכבר היה ראוי להיות כן quite obviously indicate that supplementary nature of the argument. I have furthermore reproduced a passage from Albo's *'Iḳḳarim*, where it occurs among other arguments taken from Crescas, and have shown how Albo's more elaborate restatement of the argument throws light upon this brief and almost meaningless statement of Crescas (p. 199, n. 80). In another place I have shown that in this elaborate restatement of Crescas' brief argument we may see "a faint echo of the classroom discussion of Crescas' lectures on philosophy" (p. 30). Now, Guttmann does not raise any objection against the interpretation I have given of this argument in the light of its paraphrase by Albo. He only expresses his disagreement and says that this argument in question refers to the argument previously stated by Crescas more fully on p. 196, ll. 5–14.

Now, I am going to show that this argument cannot be a restatement of the argument on p. 196, ll. 5–14.

First, Crescas enumerates three main arguments against Aristotle's definition of place (pp. 194–196), and then as a result of these arguments he gives his own definition of place (p. 198, ll. 13–14). If the passage under consideration, which immediately follows this definition, is, as Guttmann says, a repetition of the second of the three arguments previously advanced by Crescas, the question may be raised, What need was there for Crescas to repeat himself? Why did he not repeat the other two arguments? There is nothing peculiar about the second argument that Crescas should want to repeat it more than the other two. Certainly what is required here is a new additional argument in corroboration of his conclusion—perhaps an argument which occurred to Crescas only after he had arrived at his conclusion.

Second, verbally this argument does not agree with the second of Crescas' three arguments to which Guttmann makes it refer. The second argument reasons from the use of three terms, namely, מקיף, שוה, and נבדל, which according to Aristotle are all essential to his definition of place (cf. p. 443, n. 60). In this passage Crescas reasons only from the use of the term שוה; the other two terms do not occur in it. The argument does, however, verbally agree with Albo's argument, for Albo's argument, too, reasons only from the term שוה. Furthermore, in Albo this argument is given in addition to another argument which, as I have shown in my notes, reflects Crescas' second argument (cf. pp. 448–449).

5. On p. 686, after discussing Crescas' classification of the nine accidents into two groups, one including quantity, figure and position, which he characterizes as inseparable, and the other including the remaining accidents, which he characterizes as separable, I say "a similar division of accidents is found" in Algazali. I quote and translate Algazali's passage in which the accidents are divided into two groups, one including quality and quantity, characterized by him as accidents "the conception of whose essence does not require the conception of something external," and the other including the remaining accidents, characterized by him as "those which require attention to something external." In the course of my discussion, in order to establish the similarity between these two twofold classifications of accidents, I explain in note 5, p. 687, that Crescas' "figure" and Algazali's "quantity" in the first group of accidents mean the same thing. Then in note 8, p. 689–690, I explain why "position" is placed by Crescas in the first group of accidents and by Algazali in the second group of accidents, my explanation

being that the term "position" is used by them in two different senses. Nowhere in my discussion do I say that Crescas and Algazali characterize their respective twofold classifications of accidents by the same terms. I purposely avoided making such a statement because I did not want to enter into a discussion of that question, which I had in mind to reserve for some other occasion. So guarded was I against committing myself to such a statement that toward the end of note 8, p. 690, in trying to explain why Algazali does not include "position" with "quality" and "quantity," i. e., Crescas' "inseparable" accidents, I was careful in saying that Algazali "includes 'position' among the accidents which *Crescas characterizes* as 'separable'."

Now Guttmann has nothing to say with regard to the similarity between the two classifications and with regard to my arguments proving that the two classifications are essentially the same despite their apparent differences, but he argues that Crescas describes his twofold classification as "inseparable" and "separable" whereas Algazali describes them by some other terms, which I have myself reproduced in my notes, and he somehow implies that all I was trying to do was to say that both Crescas and Algazali describe their respective twofold classifications by the same terms—something which I did not discuss at all. As for the question whether Crescas' and Algazali's two characterizations of their respective twofold classifications are the same or not I also differ from Guttmann. But I shall not discuss it here, as this is not a point at issue at the present.

6. Professor Guttmann agrees with my historical analysis of the concept of duration and with my tracing it to Plotinus. But he thinks that I have gone too far in my analogy between Crescas (and also Albo) and Plotinus. Despite his demur, I still maintain the correctness of my statement that if indefinite time or duration is assumed, as it is by Crescas and Albo, to be independent of motion and to exist in mind only, then if such indefinite time is said to have existed before the creation of the world it is to be assumed that it existed, like everything else prior to creation, in the thought of God, and in this sense only have I said in connection with Albo and later also in connection with Crescas that "prior to the existence of our thought, we may be justified

in assuming that Albo conceived it [duration] to be the activity of God's thinking just as Plotinus conceived it to be the activity of the universal soul" (p. 657). As against this Guttmann argues that such an analogy would imply that the thinking activity of God would be temporal as the thinking activity of Plotinus' universal soul. In this argument Guttmann is overlooking one important distinction. The thinking activity of Plotinus' universal soul which constitutes indefinite time or duration is itself not temporal. It becomes temporal only by the fact that it is measured by the motion of the spheres which co-exist with the universal soul. Consequently, if we assume that indefinite time or duration prior to the creation of the world is identical with the activity of God's thinking, this by itself logically would not imply temporality in God's thinking.

But Guttmann maintains that not only would it logically imply temporality in God but that it would also contradict the view explicitly expressed by Crescas, Albo, and all the mediaeval philosophers. "Sie müsste dazu führen, dass dem Denken Gottes, wie dem Leben der Weltseele bei Plotin, eine zeitartige Erstreckung zugeschrieben würde, während Crescas und Albo mit allen anderen mittelalterlichen Denkern die absolute Überzeitlichkeit Gottes behaupten." This statement is correct only in part—in that part of it which refers to Albo. The reference to mediaeval thinkers in general and to Crescas in particular is too sweeping and not quite correct. The facts in the case are briefly as follows: Those who define time after Aristotle as something connected with motion naturally deny any ascription of temporal relation to God, as, for instance, Maimonides in *Moreh Nebukim* I, 52. Those, however, who like Plotinus define time only as a definite portion of indefinite time or duration and make the latter independent of motion differ on the problem of the applicability of indefinite time or duration to God. The problem is openly discussed in scholastic philosophy (cf. Suarez, *Disputationes Metaphysicae*, Disp. L, Sec. III, II, Genevae, 1614, Tom. II, p. 458). In Jewish philosophy, while there is no open discussion of the problem, a difference of opinion may be discovered. Crescas, for instance, as a result of his rejection of the Aristotelian definition of time argues against Maimonides for the admission of attributes implying temporal relation, evidently meaning by that indefinite time or duration (cf. *Or Adonai*, I, iii, 3, ed. Vienna, p. 23b; cf. also my "Crescas on Problem of Divine Attributes," in *Jewish Quarterly Review*' n. s. VII (1916), pp. 181–182). Albo, on the other hand, excludes not only definite time but also indefinite time or duration, or, as he calls it, absolute time, as an attribute of God (*'Iḳḳarim*, II, 18). I have touched upon this aspect of the problem in my *The Philosophy of Spinoza*, Vol. I, pp. 363, 369.

7. In his criticism of my interpretation of the last passage in Crescas' criticism of Maimonides' Proposition VIII, Guttmann argues, in effect, that what we expect here is a total rejection of Maimonides' proposition on the part of Crescas in order to make it impossible for Maimonides to use it in his first proof of the existence of God, whereas according to my interpretation Crescas does not reject the proposition but only limits its application. All I can say to this is that my interpretation of the passage in question in Crescas' criticism of Proposition VIII was not worked out without regard to its bearing upon Crescas' criticism of Maimonides' proofs of the existence of God. In my study of Crescas' criticism of these proofs, which by a regrettable last-minute decision has been omitted from my *Crescas' Critique of Aristotle*, I show how the limited application of Proposition VIII was sufficient for Crescas to disqualify it as a supporting premise in Maimonides' first proof for the existence of God.

Heinemann

Throughout the work I have quoted extensively from the unpublished commentaries of Averroes. Many of these quotations are parallels of passages I have quoted from Maimonides or of Maimonides' propositions upon which my discussion was based. Still these innumerable passages did not impress me as indicating any knowledge on the part of Maimonides of the writings of his contemporary Averroes, and so on pp. 322–323, where I raise the question of Maimonides' knowledge of Averroes, I make the general statement that "a sort of argument from silence would seem to point to the conclusion that the *Moreh* was written in complete ignorance of the works of Averroes" and then proceed to discuss the question from the testimonies of Crescas, Shem-Ṭob, Joseph Kaspi, and Isaac Abravanel. To all this Heinemann makes the laconic comment: "Gegen W's Meinung dass Maimuni im More Ibn Roschd nicht benutzt habe, vgl. Munk, Guide III, 86.3." The reader will undoubtedly be led to believe that the passage in Munk referred to contains definite proof that Maimonides did make use of Averroes in the *Moreh*. But nothing of the kind is to be found there. All that Munk does is to quote Averroes' interpretation of *Physics*, II, 7, 198a, 24f., after he has shown that that passage in the *Physics* is the basis of a statement by Maimonides in *Moreh*, III, 13. Munk introduces his quotation from Averroes by the following words: "Ce passage, que Maimonide a eu sans doute en vue, est ainsi expliqué par Averroës." I do not know for what purpose Munk has quoted Averroes there. Maybe it was merely for illustrative purposes. Certainly it was not for the purpose of showing the dependence of Maimonides upon Averroes, for there is nothing in the content or the form of these two passages to show such a dependence. Both these passages are merely expanded paraphrases of Aristotle, the like of which is to be found in Themistius and probably also in the other commentaries on Aristotle accessible to both Averroes and Maimonides. The only distinctive expression which occurs in both these passages is *unum secundum subjectum* in Averroes (according to the Latin version quoted by Munk) and (אחד במין, ואחדא באלנוע) in Maimonides. But the fact that one uses *subjectum* and the other מין (*species*) shows that the two passages are independent of each other. Maimonides' use of אחד במין, furthermore, reflects the expressions τῷ εἴδει ταὐτὸ τούτοις used by Aristotle (198a, 26), ταὐτὸν ὢν αὐτῷ κατὰ τὸ εἶδος probably used by Themistius (ed. Schenkl, 57, 24n.), and τῷ εἴδει μόνον used by Simplicius (ed. Diels, 364, 10). Though Simplicius' commentary on the *Physics* is not known to have been translated into Arabic, still the passage from which the expression quoted is taken may have been copied by Simplicius from Alexander's lost commentary on the *Physics* of which there was an Arabic translation. Incidentally I may remark that Averroes' statement that the efficient, formal, and final causes "sunt unum secundum subjectum" is the opposite of Simplicius' statement *οὐ κατὰ τὸ ὑποκείμενον οὐδὲ τῷ ἀριθμῷ ταὐτόν ἐστιν* (364, 9–10).

2. "So lassen die sprachgeschichtlichen Ausführungen das Syrische ganz ausser Betracht." The desirability of consulting the Syriac translations of Aristotle for a reconstruction of the history of the transmission of Aristotelian terminology and philosophy has been a truism ever since Steinschneider called attention to it in his *Die arabischen Uebersetzungen aus dem Griechischen* (1897), p. 6. That I was not unconscious of this fact I have made quite clear when I referred to the uninterrupted continuity of Aristotelian scholarship "from the days of the Lyceum through the Syriac, Arabic and Hebrew schools of philosophy" (p. 7). The reviewer, however, does not seem to be aware of the fact that to a large extent this desired end will have to remain unfulfilled, owing to the unavailability, with the exception of some parts of the *Organon*, of the Syriac translations of Aristotle. But apart from this general observation, his stricture is entirely irrelevant. In the work reviewed by him, I had before me certain specific problems of terminology to deal with, well-nigh 500 in number. The only pertinent question is this: In how many instances have I failed to consult available Syriac texts which I should have consulted? Or, to how many instances can the reviewer point where the absence of the Syriac equivalents has led to an erroneous conclusion? I assume, of course, that the reviewer did not mean that even if there was no appropriate text to quote, I should have supplied the missing Syriac link by conjecture and with the help of lexicons, merely for the sake of adorning my pages with Syriac characters.

3. "Aber auch die Verwertung des griechischen Denkens bei W. (der die doxographische Überlieferung nach Plutarch statt nach Diels zitiert) ist unzureichend." I shall leave the reviewer's general comment out of consideration. In the court of learning no less than in the court of justice an indictment must rest upon evidence. But let us consider his definite charge that I quote Plutarch rather than Diels. In order to clarify the nature of the issue raised by Heinemann I may say that in my notes I have quoted certain views of Greek philosophy needed for my purpose

from the *De Placitis Philosophorum*, which is traditionally ascribed to Plutarch and is included in every edition of Plutarch's works. To this Heinemann objects and contends that I should have quoted these views from Diels' *Doxographi Graeci* where the *De Placitis* is reproduced in parallel columns with Stobaeus' *Eclogae*. Heinemann evidently has not examined the purpose of my quotations from Plutarch. Plutarch is quoted in my book six times. Once he is quoted for the purpose of getting the right shade of meaning of a Hebrew term translated from the Arabic (p. 588). Once again he is quoted for the purpose of accounting for the occurrence of a certain phrase in certain Arabic and Hebrew reproductions of Aristotle's definition of place which does not occur in Aristotle himself (p. 363). Once more he is quoted for the purpose of getting an exact formulation of Plato's definition of time (p. 639). Three times he is quoted for the purpose of getting a clear formulation of different views on gravity and levity (p. 411) and on vacuum (pp. 400, 417), which in the passages quoted by me from Aristotle were only vaguely described. In all these six instances it was not simply Greek sources that I needed, but a Greek source which was known at least to Arabic authors. Plutarch was such a source, for his *De Placitis Philosophorum* was translated into Arabic. As for Stobaeus, however, there is no record that he was known to Arabic philosophers. Under these circumstances, I submit that it would have been stupid for me to quote from Diels rather than from Plutarch.

4. In the sixth chapter of my Introduction I pointed out a general similarity between Crescas and the sixteenth century critics of Aristotle. All of them, I said, tried to free themselves from the thralldom of Aristotle by turning to the views of "the early Greek philosophers" (p. 114). The particular views which I discussed there in this connection are: (1) the existence of a vacuum, (2) the identification of space with the vacuum, (3) the infinity of that space, (4) the plurality of worlds, and (5) atomism. All these views are well known to have been held by pre-Aristotelian philosophers and are constantly referred to and argued against by Aristotle himself in passages which I have quoted in my Notes. Now let us see what my reviewer has to

say about all this: [1] "Natürlich sieht W., dass der Aristotelismus bereits im Altertum seine Gegner hatte und dass deren Einspruch im Mittelalter nachwirkt. [2] Aber der einzige ernsthafte Wettbewerber, den W. berücksichtigt (S. 120), ist der Atomismus." The first sentence, it will be noticed, is an inaccurate restatement of what I have said. I did not speak of the opposition to Aristotle found among his successors, but of the views of his predecessors, "the early Greek philosophers," rejected by Aristotle. This misunderstanding of my reference to "the early Greek philosophers" has led him to his second sentence which is wrong both as a statement of what is known about the views of these early Greek philosophers and as a restatement of my discussion of the subject, for certainly Heinemann cannot deny the accuracy of my attribution to the pre-Aristotelian philosophers the views which I have enumerated above in addition to atomism, namely, the existence of a vacuum, the identification of space with the vacuum, the infinity of that space, and the plurality of worlds.

5. The reviewer then proceeds to suggest: "In Wahrheit weisen manche der von W. hervorgehobenen Abweichungen mindestens ebenso sehr auf den Einfluss der Stoa (s. o. S. 480): so die Vereinheitlichung des Weltbildes (S. 118f.) und der Ersatz des nur denkenden Gottes durch den wollenden und schaffenden (S. 122f.; dazu Heinemann, Poseidonios' met. Schr. II, 34f.). With regard to the first statement, all I can say is that there is nothing in the Stoic teachings corresponding to particular phases of the continuity of nature which I happen to discuss on p. 118f. With regard to the second statement, I must say again that on p. 122f. I do not discuss the "Ersatz des nur denkenden Gottes durch den wollenden und schaffenden." What I do discuss there is the substitution of an immaterial God by a God who is predicated by the attribute of extension. Were I to discuss the "Ersatz des nur denkenden Gottes durch den wollenden und schaffenden" in Crescas or in Jewish philosophy in general, I would certainly not attribute it to the influence of the Stoics.

6. Once the reviewer has introduced the Stoics, he digresses from his review to suggest that the Stoics are responsible for Crescas' views on the soul and on determinism, neither of which problems is discussed by me in the work under consideration.

I have no means of knowing what the reviewer's conception of Crescas' views on the soul and determinism are. According to my conception of Crescas' position on these problems, the assumption of a Stoic influence is gratuitous and impossible. Equally gratuitous is the reviewer's suggestion that Crescas' view on the love of God was formed under the influence of Christian theology. Certainly the reviewer cannot be unacquainted with the history of that concept in Hebrew literature.

7. In the Preface of my work (p. IX) I make the statement that the Talmudic method applied by Crescas to the study of Aristotle will be applied by me to the study of Crescas. In the chapter on method (pp. 24–29) I give an analysis of what I consider the logic underlying the Talmudic method of text-study which I characterize as the "hypothetico-deductive method of text interpretation" (p. 25). In the course of my discussion I say: "Now, this method of text interpretation is sometimes derogatorily referred to as Talmudic quibbling or pilpul. In truth it is nothing but the application of the scientific method to the study of texts" (p. 27). In criticism of this the reviewer says: "Nach S. 24ff. soll er nach talmudischer Methode arbeiten; diese Behauptung kann aber nicht überzeugen, da W. die Unterschiede dieser Methode von derjenigen des Aristoteles und seiner Kommentare garnicht herausarbeitet." Evidently the reviewer wanted to object to something I have said, but could not make up his mind whether to object to my identification of the Talmudic with the scientific method or to accept my identification and then, on that score, to object to the description of my method as Talmudic, and so he combined the two objections and finds fault with my use of the expression "Talmudic method" on the ground that I failed to explain how it differs from the scientific method. Now, I do not feel that I have to apologize for my describing the subtleties of reasoning displayed by Crescas in handling philosophic texts as a manifestation in the field of philosophy of the traditional native Jewish method of studying texts which is generally associated with Talmudic literature. Nor do I feel the need of apologizing for the statement that in attempting to retrace the processes of Crescas' reasoning I have consciously followed this old method of Jewish learning, though

externally I have tried to conform to all the accepted canons of modern scholarship. But realizing the prevalent misconceptions about this native method of Jewish learning I felt it my duty to show by an analysis of it that it is essentially a scientific method of text-study. That I have succeeded in my attempt to rehabilitate this misunderstood Talmudic method is quite evident from the reviewer's complaint that he finds no difference between it and the method followed in the best type of scholarly research.

But while Heinemann seems to have become so much convinced of the scientific nature of the Talmudic method that he objects to my singling it out as something peculiar, my friend and colleague, Dr. George Sarton, in his review of *Crescas' Critique of Aristotle* in *Isis*, XIV (1930), pp. 240–244, contends that in my statement that "Pilpul is nothing but the application of the scientific method to the study of texts" I confuse "the truth in the worst manner." "For," he continues, "the essence of the scientific method is precisely not to stop at words but to investigate as directly as possible the realities which these words are meant to represent . . . From that point of view, pilpul is as antagonistic to scientific thinking as anything can be" (*ibid.*, pp. 242–243). In this criticism Dr. Sarton has committed a fallacy which in the language of the logic of pilpul may be described as the fallacy of "wheat "and "barley." What I have tried to establish in my description of pilpul on pp. 24–27 may be reduced to a formula which runs as follows:

> Pilpul to the *study of text* is as
> Scientific method to the *study of nature.*

What Dr. Sarton argues against is a formula which runs as follows:

> Pilpul to the *study of nature* is as
> Scientific method to the *study of nature.*

8. In the sixth chapter of my Introduction I say: "In the history of philosophy, the opposition to Aristotle had at various times assumed different forms. Aristotle was opposed, because some of his views were found to contradict certain Biblical

traditions; he was also opposed, because his reasoning on many important points was found to be logically unsustainable; and finally he was opposed, because the method of his approach to the study of nature was found to be empirically inadequate" (p. 124). With regard to Crescas, I say that his criticism of Aristotle belongs to the second of the three stages I have enumerated. As against this the reviewer says: "Das genügt nicht. C. bekämpft vielmehr als bewusster Jude und als religiös fühlender Mensch den Anspruch des 'Griechen' (W. 539!) auf Erkenntnis des letzten Lebensziels, da ein solcher Anspruch der Thora und ihrem unvergleichlichen Wert zu nahe trete; er empfindet überdies, ähnlich wie Gazzali, Jehuda Hallevi und später Cordovero, die Unmöglichkeit, auf die aristotelische Metaphysik Religion zu begründen." The reviewer, as will be noticed, is confusing here the motives which he thinks had prompted Crescas and the others in refusing to accept Aristotle's philosophy as the basis of their religion and the technique they employed in refuting the Aristotelian philosophy itself. Whatever their motives, and I have touched upon it in a general way on p. 13 in my Introduction, the technique used by Gazzali, Jehudah Hallevi, and Crescas belongs to what I describe as the second kind of criticism of Aristotle. They do not hurl Biblical verses against Aristotle, nor do they hurl weights down from the leaning tower of Pisa. They all try to show that Aristotle's reasoning is fallacious. Let anyone read a few consecutive pages in Gazzali's *Tahafut al-Falasifah*, or in the Fifth Part of Jehudah Hallevi's *Cuzari*, or in the text of Crescas reproduced in my book, and he will become convinced of the truth of my contention. Thus also, for instance, a theologian of today, who may refute the metaphysical assumptions of modern science by arguments drawn from experimental science, may still be actuated in his criticism by the same motives as Crescas, Jehudah Hallevi and Gazzali.

ADDITIONAL NOTES TO *CRESCAS' CRITIQUE OF ARISTOTLE*

1. P. 421, end of n. 35. In connection with my attempt to explain how the Arabic حركة in the Iḥwan al-Ṣafa's classification of discrete quantities came to stand for Aristotle's λόγος in his classification of discrete quantities in *Categories*, 6, 4b, 20–25, I may add that the connecting link may be the Greek προφορά which combines the ideas of both movement and utterance. Thus in *Enneads* II, ix, 1, Plotinus speaks of κίνησις καὶ προφορά (ed. Creuzer et Moser, Paris, 1855, p. 94, ll. 29–30). Furthermore, in *Enneads*, I, ii, 3, he describes λόγος ἐν προφορᾷ as something discrete-μεμερισμένος (*ibid.*, p. 10, ll. 22–23).

2. Pp. 594–598, n. 24. A parallel to Crescas' insistence upon the removal of the distinction between the matter of the sublunar elements and the matter of the translunar bodies (cf. pp. 103–104) may be found in Bruno's *De Immenso et Innumerabilibus*, Liber IV, Cap. 1–2. The following are the headings of these two chapters: "Caput I. Septem argumenta quibus Arist. et alii probant diversam esse substantiam corporum superiorum et inferiorum istorum. Caput II. Responsio ad argumenta haec et similia." Descartes takes a similar position on the same problem in *Principia Philosophiae*, II, 22: "Thus the matter of the heavens and of the earth is one and the same."

3. P. 626, n. 22. Additional parallels to the principle maintained here by Crescas are to be found in Descartes, *Principia Philosophiae*, II, 41, reproduced by Spinoza in *Principia Philosophiae Cartesianae*, II, Prop. 19.

4. P. 641, end of n. 11. The analogy between flowing water and time which is used by Abraham bar Ḥiyya and Hillel of Verona is reproduced by Abraham Herrara in the name of Torquato Tasso in *Sha'ar ha-Shamayim*, III, 4: "But as for time, which is an image and likeness of it [i. e., eternity], it is like a flowing stream, swift in its course, quick in its activity, the activity of motion, and in the course of its motion parts of it pass away and disappear and other parts come into being and take their place."

אמנם הזמן אשר נתהווה בדמותו וצלמו, הנו כנהר שוטף קל המרוץ מהיר

במלאכתו מלאכת התנועה, ועם מרוצתו ותנועתו יכלה ויפסיד חלקיו הראשונים ויחדש .וירויח במקומם אחרים.

The analogy is used by Plutarch after his restatement of the view, which he ascribes to the Stoics, that there is "a time future and past but no time present": "These men's conception, therefore, of time is not unlike the grasping of water, which, the harder it is held, the more it slides and runs away" (*De Communibus Notitiis Adversus Stoicos*, XLI–XLII).

15
ISAAC IBN SHEM-TOB'S UNKNOWN COMMENTARIES ON THE *PHYSICS* AND HIS OTHER UNKNOWN WORKS

Cod. Heb. 45 in Munich is an anonymous supercommentary on Averroës' Intermediate Commentary on Aristotle's *Physics*. Steinschneider, in his *Die hebräischen Übersetzungen des Mittelalters*, p. 116, ascribes it to Isaac Albalag. He repeats this ascription in his *Die hebräischen Handschriften der Kgl. Hof- und Staatsbibliothek in München*, p. 30. The grounds upon which this identification of authorship is based can be only surmised. In the text of the supercommentary the name Isaac occurs in the oft-repeated expression אמר יצחק. On the fly-leaf Albulak (אלבולק) is given as the name of the author. Now, Isaac Albulak is unknown in Hebrew literature whereas Isaac Albalag is well-known as the translator of two parts of Algazali's *Maḳaṣid al-Falasifah* and also as the author of a commentary on that work. In that commentary, furthermore, Isaac Albalag refers to himself as having been an assiduous student of the *Physics* for many years. (ואני זה כמה ימים לא זזתי מלעיין בס' השמע, Munich, Cod. Heb. 110, f. 207, quoted in the *Übersetzungen*, p. 116, n. 61.) It was therefore natural for Steinschneider to conclude that this supercommentary was the result of Albalag's many long years of study of the *Physics*.

Internal evidence, however, abounds which conclusively proves Steinschneider's ascription to be erroneous. First, the supercommentary quotes Levi ben Gershon whose literary activity probably did not begin until after the death of Albalag. Second, Moses Narboni (החכם הרב מאישרו וידאל ז"ל—Maestro Vidal Blasom) is mentioned in the supercommentary and is referred to as already dead, but Moses Narboni flourished somewhat later than Albalag. Finally, in no less than three places is Ḥasdai Crescas mentioned by name and the *Or Adonai* quoted. Inasmuch as Isaac Albalag flourished during the second half of the thirteenth century he could not very well be the author of a work which contains references to Crescas whose activity did not begin until the latter part of the fourteenth century. The name Albulak on the fly-leaf is of no consequence, for it is written in a different hand and is most probably the erroneous conjecture of some cataloguer.

Fortunately there exists another copy of the same supercommentary in Cambridge University Library (Mn. 6. 25), with which STEINSCHNEIDER evidently was unacquainted, and this leads us to the identification of its author. This Cambridge University volume resembles in shape and appearance another volume of manuscripts in the same library which contains commentaries on the *De Anima* and *De Generatione et Corruptione*. All the three commentaries are written in the same hand and bear unmistakable internal evidence of having been composed by the same author and of having been originally bound together. In the latter two commentaries, too, the expression אמר יצחק occurs frequently. Though the full name of the author is not anywhere mentioned in the manuscript, the colophon at the end of the second codex would seem to supply the deficiency. It reads as follows:

" The work is done and finished, praise to the Lord eternal. May no harm befall the scribe until an ass shall scale a ladder. The work was completed by me, Abraham Ibn Adret, here at Aguilar di Campaha, when I was a student of philosophy under that inexhaustible fountain, the consummate scholar, Rabbi Isaac Ibn Shem-Tob, on Sunday, the seventeenth day of the month of the second Adar, in the year two hundred and thirty-one of the sixth millennium of the era of creation (1471). And in order that a man of the street may not come and claim this book as his own, I have affixed hereto my seal and name."

תם ונשלם, תהלה לאל עולם, הכותב לא יוזק עד שיעלה חמור בסולם. והיתה השלמתו על ידי אברהם ן' אדרת בכאן באגולאר די קנפואה, בלמדי זאת החכמה מהמעיין המתגבר, החכם, השלם, הר' יצחק ן' שם טוב, ביום ראשון, שבעה עשר ימים לחודש אדר שני, שנת מאתים ואחד ושלשים לפרט היצירה. וכדי שלא יבא אחד מן השוק ויאמר שלי הוא, חתמתי שמי פה

אברהם מ'
יוסף ן' אדרת
ס"ט

A colophon found at the end of Isaac Ibn Shem-Tob's commentary on the Hebrew translation of the second part (Metaphysics) of Algazali's *Maḳaṣid al-Falasifah* and reproduced by STEINSCHNEIDER in his *Übersetzungen*, p. 320, n. 408 similarly mentions Aguilar di Campaha and gives the first of Adar, 1498, as the date of the completion of the work. It is interesting to note that both these manuscripts were completed in Adar, the end of the winter term in Jewish schools. Evidently the commentaries were the result of actual class-room lectures. There is all reason to believe, therefore, that Isaac the author of the super-commentaries is none other than Isaac Ibn Shem-Tob mentioned in the colophon. In SCHILLER-SZINESSY's unpublished catalogue of the Hebrew manuscripts in the Cambridge University Library these three works are ascribed, evidently as a guess, to Isaac Ibn Shem-Tob, and the same name is written in pencil on the manuscripts themselves. It may also be mentioned, that in the commentary on *De Generatione et Corruptione* Isaac Albalag's commentary on Algazali's *Maḳaṣid al-Falasifah* is cited and Isaac Albalag himself is referred to in terms that leave no room for doubt that he is not the Isaac who is named in the commentaries as their author.

In this commentary on the *Physics*, Isaac Ibn Shem-Tob mentions several times another commentary of his on the *Physics*, referring to it as "our first commentary" (ביאורנו הא'), or sometimes simply "our commentary on this book" (ביאורנו לזה הספר).[1] Similar references to "our first commentary on the *Physics*" (ביאורנו הא' לספר השמע) are also found in his *De Anima* and *De Generatione et Corruptione*. In the last-named work there is a reference near the end of the book to the "first and second commentaries on the *Physics*" (כבר ביארנוהו בשלמות בביאור הא' והב' מהשמע). It is clear that by the "second commentary" he refers to the work in the libraries of Munich and Cambridge University. But so far no trace has been found of the "first commentary." It happened that in examining the Hebrew manuscripts in the Library

[1] Cf. Tractate I, Summa iii, Chapter 1:
כונת אריסטו בזה הכלל כלו לבאר התחלות ההויה מה הם ובמה הם, ולפי שזה הדרוש הוא עמוק עד מאד ראינו לפרשו מלה במלה, ואעפ"י שכבר ביארנו זה הדרוש על אמתתו בביאורנו לזה הספר, עם כל זה ראינו לפרשו על אמתתו על דרך אחר מלה במלה ולעשות ספקות אחרות זולת מה שכתבנו שם, כי אין רצוננו לכפול הביאור.
Similarly in Tractate I, Summa ii, Section 2, Chapter 2.
The distinction between פירוש and ביאור which appears to be made in this quotation is not observed by the author. Elsewhere he calls also this second commentary ביאור.

of Trinity College, Cambridge, of which there is a published catalogue by SCHILLER-SZINESSY,[2] I have succeeded in identifying Cod. R. 8. 19. 3 as Isaac Ibn Shem-Tob's "first commentary." Furthermore, I believe that it can be conclusively shown that Cod. R. 8. 19. 2, which is another commentary on the *Physics*, is also the work of Isaac Ibn Shem-Tob and must have been written by him after his "second commentary" and may thus be designated as his "third commentary." These two commentaries are bound together in the same volume and are described by SCHILLER-SZINESSY as anonymous in which he is followed by STEINSCHNEIDER in his *Übersetzungen*, p. 121. Though in style and general method of exposition these two commentaries bear no resemblance to Isaac Ibn Shem-Tob's commentary already identified as the "second," and though the familiar expression אמר יצחק does nowhere occur in them, there is still the following irrefutable evidence to show that they are the "first" and a "third" commentary by the same author.

(1) In Tractate II, Summa i, Chapter 1 of the "second commentary" on the *Physics*, Isaac Ibn Shem-Tob raises an objection against the statement that nature is the principle and cause of rest as well as of motion (*Physics* II, 1, 192b, 21–22). He discusses two possible solutions of one of which he says that it is mentioned by him in his "first commentary" but he no longer finds it satisfactory. Both these solutions are found in Cod. R. 8. 19. 3. Cod. R. 8. 19. 2, however, contains only the solution approved of in the "second commentary."

1 Trinity College Library, R. 8. 19. 3	2 Munich, 45, and Cambridge University Library, Mm. 6. 25	3 Trinity College Library, R. 8. 19. 2
ויש לשאל, איך אמר	ועוד יש למספק שיספק ויאמר, איך	וא״ת, והלא התנועה
שהטבע הוא התחלה	אמר אריסטו שהטבע הוא סבת מנוחה,	קנין, והמנוחה העדר,
למנוחה, כי המנוחה	והמנוחה העדר, וא״א שיהיה דבר נמצא	והנה הקנין שהוא
העדר, והעדר אין לו	סבת ההעדר, אחר שההעדר איננו מפעולת	מציאות צריך סבה,
התחלה וסבה. ועוד	פועל. נוסף על זה שא״א שיהיה הדבר	אבל המנוחה שהוא
איך אמר שהטבע הוא	סבה למקבילו, כי יתחייב מזה שיהיה	העדר אין לה סבה, כי
סבת התנועה והמנוחה,	אוהב לו עם היותו אויב אחר שהם	ההעדר אינו מפעולת
והרי הם מקבילים, וא״כ	מקבילות, וא״א שנשיב על אלה הספקות	פועל. והתשובה בזה,
איך יהיה סבתם אחת.	מה שהשבנו אליהם בבאורנו הרא־	כי אמרנו בכאן מנוחה

[2] A Description Catalogue of the Arabic MSS. .... in the Library of Trinity College, Cambridge, by E. H. PALMER with an appendix .... by SCHILLER-SZINESSY, 1870.

אינו ר"ל העדר התנועה או השנוי, אבל ר"ל שלמות התנועה, כי צורת האבן עד"מ הוא התחלת תנועת האבן למטה, והיא התחלת המנוחה במטה שהיא שלמות התנועה. אבל אינה התחלת המנוחה למעלה שהוא העדר התנועה למעלה. ובזה ג"כ יותר הספק שאין הטבע התחלת דבר והפוכו — שאין הטבע התחלת מנוחת האבן למעלה, שהוא העדר התנועה למעלה, אבל הוא התחלה למנוחה אשר למטה, שהוא שלמות התנועה למטה.

מ"ב, כ"א, פ"א.

ש ו ן שהעדר סבת הקנין הוא סבת ההעדר, והוא כי יתחייב מזה שיפסד הטבע בעת היות הדבר נח, עם היות זה שקר מבואר, וזה שהטבע לעולם הוא קיים עם הנמצא הטבעי, מתנועע היה או נח.

. . . .

והספק הד', והס' הח' יותרו ג"כ במה שבאר אריסטו בה' מזה הספר. שהמנוחה נאמרת על המנוחה במה שממנו ועל המנוחה במה שאליו, ושהמנוחה במה שממנו הוא העדר התנועה, לא המנוחה במה שאליו. וזה כי הוא יותר ראויה שתקרא שלמות מאשר יהיה העדר. ואחר שזה כן, נאמר שהוא כוון הנה באמרו שהטבע הוא סבה למנוחה, שהוא מה שאליו התנועה, לא המנוחה שהוא העדר. וזהו אשר כוון באמרו והתנועה הנה והמנוחה וכו', ר"ל שהתנועה והמנוחה אשר לקח בזה הגדר שהוא המנוחה במה שאליו, שהוא רוצה בה המנוחה שהוא הפסק התנועה. ובזה שאמרנו שהמנוחה הנה רצה בו המנוחה במה שאליו התנועה, שהוא שלמות לתנועה לא העדרה, יסתלק הספק הקודם, לא במה שאמרנו בביאורנו הא', כמו שכבר אמרתי אליך.

מ"ב, כ"א, פ"א.

והתשובה לזה: כי מה שאומר בכאן מנוחה, אין הכונה בו המנוחה הקודמת שהוא העדר התנועה, אבל המנוחה שהוא הפסק התנועה, והיא שלמותה, וא"כ איננה העדר, וג"כ אינם ב' מקבילים. ומה שאמר שהתנועה הנה והמנוחה, שר"ל ההשתנות במוחלט והעדרו, ר"ל הפסקו, ונוכל לומר, שאמר זה, לפי שהתנועה במוחלט מקביל למנוחה במוחלט, וזאת המנוחה איננה העדר, לפי שהוא שלמות התנועה. או נאמר שהטבע סבת התנועה והמנוחה מב' צדדים: כמי שנאמר עד"מ שהטבע התחלת הצמיחה בזמן אחד ושלא יצמח בזמן אחר.

מ"ב, כ"א, פ"א.

(2) A similar case occurs in Tractate II, Summa iii, Chapter 2 in his discussion of an apparent contradiction between two statements, found in Averroës' commentary but not found in the corresponding passage of Aristotle, as to whether hexadactylism is the work of nature or of chance. In the "second commentary," after solving the difficulty he refers to an additional solution given in the "first commentary," which he, however, rejects as being no longer satisfactory to him. The solution of the "second commentary" as well as an additional solution is found in Cod. R. 8. 19. 3. Here, again, Cod. R. 8. 19. 2 contains only the approved solution of the "second commentary."

1

Trinity College Library, R. 8. 19. 3

יש לשאל, איך אמר בכאן שהאצבע הו׳ חודשה מההזדמן ובפ׳ ד׳ מזה המאמר אמר שחודשה מהטבע.

ונשיב לזה, שהכונה בזה לומר שלא נתחדשה מהטבע במוחלט ,אבל מהזדמן הטבע. או נאמר שלקח בכאן שם הטבע על מה שיורה על מנהג טבעי, וידוע כי האצבע הששית אינו מנהג טבעי.

מ״ב, כ״ג, פ״ב.

2

Munich, 45, and Cambridge University Library, Mm. 6. 25

ועוד יש למספק שיספק ויאמר כנגד הטענה הב׳ שההפך אמר למעלה בתחלת זה המאמר, וזה ששם אמר שהאצבע הו׳ נתחדש מהטבע. וא״א שנאמר שכונת אריסטו הנה באמרו שלא נתחדש מהטבע הוא על המנהג הטבעי, כמו שאמרנו בביאורנו הא׳, כי אם יהיה כן, כבר יהיה הטבע וההזדמן דבר אחד, הפך מה שרצה לבאר הנה.

. . . .

״והספק הג׳ יותר ג״כ בשנאמר שכוונת אריסטו באמרו שהאצבע נאמר שהוא נתחדש מההזדמן ולא נאמר שנתחדש מהטבע הוא שהאצבע הו׳ נאמר שהוא נתחדש מההזדמן שקרה לטבע, לא מהטבע סתם. ועם זאת התשובה שעשינו הנה בזה הספר לא יתחייב ס׳ כלל, וזה ששם לא אמר שהאצבע הו׳ נתחדש מהטבע סתם כי אם מההזדמן שקרה לטבע, והראיה עליו הוא שזה האצבע לא נתחדש על המנהג הטבעי, ולא מהפעולות המסדרות בטבע, והוא לא אמר בזה. וזאת התשובה שעשינו הנה לזה הספק הוא ע״ד האמת, לא על מה שאמרנו בביאורנו הא׳, מאשר הוא טעות שנפל בספרים, כי לא אמרתי שם מה שאמרתי כי אם ע״ד העברה.

מ״ב, כ״ג, פ״ב.

3

Trinity College Library, R. 8. 19. 2

וא״ת, והלא כבר התבאר שעל הו׳ אצבעות נאמר ג״כ שהם בטבע וא״כ נראה שהטבע וההזדמן שהם דבר אחד. והתשובה, כי ההזדמן כבר הוא בדברים הטבעיים כמו בדברים הבחיריים, ומה שנאמר באצבע הו׳ שהוא בטבע ר״ל שההזדמן הוא בדברים אשר בטבע.

מ״ב, כ״ג, פ״ב.

(3) In Tractate III, Summa ii, Chapter 4, at the end of an answer to the eighteenth objection to Aristotle's definition of motion there is in the " second commentary " the following statement: " This answer differs from the answer given by ourself to the same objection in our first commentary." In Cod. R. 8. 19. 3 the same objection occurs with a different answer.

2

Munich, 45, and Cambridge University Library, Mm. 6. 25

[י״ח] ועוד יש לאומר על מ״ש אחר זה והוא שהתנועה לדבר הוא לו מצד מה שבכח לא מצד מה שבפועל שזה בלתי צודק אבל בהפך, אחר שהמנוחה הוא העדר והתנועה הוא קנין והדבר שהוא בכח מצד מה שהוא בכח הוא נעדר והדבר שהוא בפעל הוא נמצא וסבת הקנין הוא קנין בהכרח וסבת ההעדר הוא העדר. ואחר שזה כלו כן, מבואר מאד שהוא מחוייב כפי זה שתבא התנועה מצד הפועל לא מצד הכח, הפך מ״ש אריסטו הנה.

. . . .

ונאמר ג״כ בהתרת הספק הי״ח במה שכבר התבאר בה׳ מזה חספר שהמנוחה תאמר על ב׳ ענינים, על המנוחה שהוא במה שממנו ועל המנוחה שהוא במה שאליו. ושם נתבאר שהמנוחה במה שממנו שהוא העדר התנועה, ושהמנוחה במה שאליו שהוא שלמות התנועה ותכליתה לא העדר. ואחר שזה כן, שהוא מחוייב בהכרח שתהיה התנועה באה מצד הכח, אחר שכל תנועה הויה, והכח הוא העדר בצד מה ואחר כל העדר יש הויה, כמו שנתבאר בא׳ מס׳ הויה והפסד. והמנוחה אשר דברינו עתה בה הוא העדר, והתנועה הוא הויה וקנין ודבר נמצא, וכל העדר מחויב בהכרח שתבא אחר המציאות, למה שאחר כל הויה העדר, כמו שהתבאר בהויה והפסד ג״כ. וזה הספק היה גדול ועצום אלו היה הכח סבת התנועה, כי יתחייב שתהיה ההעדר סבת הקנין, והתנועה סבת המנוחה, כי יתחייב מזה שתהיה הקנין סבת ההעדר, אבל כאשר לא היה זה אלא שאחר הכח תבא התנועה, כלומר אחר המנוחה, ושאחר המנוחה תבא התנועה, לא יתחייב ספק כלל.

וזאת התשובה מתחלפת לתשובה שעשינו בזה הס׳ בביאורנו הא׳, ובעבור זה עשינו זה הס׳ במקום הזה. מ״ג, כ״ב, פ״ד.

1

Trinity College Library, R. 8. 19. 3

ויש לעיין בזה הפרק שני דברים: האחד, שאנו אומרים שהדבר לא יתנועע מצד שהוא בכח, לפי שמזה הצד הוא נעדר . . .

ותשובת זו השאלה יתבאר בח׳ מזה הספר.

. . . .

ונאמר אחר זה שהמתנועע אעפ״י שלא יתנועע מצד מה שהוא בכח וג״כ לא יתנועע מצד שהוא בפועל שיתנועע מצד מה שהוא בכח ובפעל על זה הדרך: שחומר הביצה עד״מ הוא יתנועע בעצם מצד שבכח, אבל מצד שיהיה בכח לא יוכל להתנועע, הצורה ישימהו בפועל ויתן לו מציאות כדי שיוכל להתנועע. וכשהחומר מתנועע מצד שהצורה שמהו בפועל מתנועע הצורה ג״כ עמו, לפי שהוא עם החומר ומתנועע במקרה.

מ״ג, כ״ב, פ״ד.

(4) In Tractate IV, Summa i, Chapter 1 he discusses the question as to what would be the proper conversion of the proposition " that which is non-existent is not in place " (cf. *Physics* IV, 208 a, 30), at the end of which he says: " The interpretation given here of Aristotle's text would seem to be true according to Aristotle's view as stated in the *De Interpretatione*, whereas the interpretation given in our first commentary is more preferable in accordance with the view set down in the *Analytica Priora*. It is up to you to choose any one of the three explanations we have given of the Philosopher's words in this passage, namely, our two explanations in the first commentary and the one here." Now, Cod. R. 8. 19. 3 contains two explanations in the course of which references are made to the *Analytica Priora*. The discussion of the same question in Cod. R. 8. 19. 2 follows that of Cod. R. 8. 19. 3.

1
Trinity College Library, R. 8. 19. 3

וזה לסכלותם בהתהפך: ר"ל שהם הפכו הקדמת מה שאינו נמצא אינו במקום ואמרו מה שאינו במקום איננו נמצא ומזה נמשך להם שיהיה כל נמצא במקום.

ויש מפרשים שההפוך הנאות בזאת ההקדמה הוא אמרנו איננו במקום מה שאיננו נמצא, לא כמו שאמרו הם. וזה בלתי נאות, לפי שהגזרה המתהפכת הוא שנעשה מן הנשוא נושא ומן הנושא נשוא, ובזה [ה]הפוך אעפ"י שנשתנה הסדר עדיין נשאר כה הנשוא נשוא והנושא נושא. ויהיה זה במדרגת מי שאמר כל אדם ימצא צדיק, ימצא צדיק כל אדם, שמובן שתי ההקדמות דבר אחד. ולפי

2
Munich, 45, and Cambr. Univ. Library, Mm. 6. 25

וזה לסכלותם בהתהפך: אריסטו בא לבטל ראיתם מאשר ההפוך שהם עושים הוא טעות וסכלות גמור. וסבת זה איננו דבר אלא שכבר יתבאר בס' מליצה שיש הפוך בצד אחת והוא המרת המצבית בענין שיהיה נשאר הנושא נושא והנשוא נשוא, לא שנשים הנושא נשוא והנשוא נושא. והוא כמו שאומר אריסטו שם, ימצא האדם צדיק, ימצא צדיק האדם. וזה כי לעולם באלו הגזרות הנושא נשאר נושא והנשוא נשאר נשוא. וזה כי מלת האדם שהוא נושא לעולם

3
Trinity College Library, R. 8. 19. 2

וזה לסכלותם בהתהפך: ר"ל שההקדמה הוא כל מה שאיננו נמצא איננו במקום. וההפיכה הישר הוא איננו במקום כל מה שאיננו נמצא. והוא צודק. והם מהפכים ההקדמה בזה האופן, כל מה שאיננו במקום איננו נמצא, ומזה יחייבו שכל נמצא הוא במקום. וזה ההפוך הוא בלתו צודק, כי כבר התבאר בהקש כי בהפוך ההקדמות צריך שלא ישנה ההקדמה אשר ירצה להפכה ושלא יחסר ושלא יוסיף בה לא תיבה ולא אות ולא שנוי אחר כלל, אלא שיהיה מן הנושא

נשוא ומן הנשוא נושא. ובהפוך זאת ההקדמה שנו אותה שהמירו תיבת מה שהיה מונח עם מלת איננו נמצא והניחוה במלת איננו במקום.

וגם כן זאת ההקדמה היא מחייבת מיסרת ולא שוללת. וזה כי אמרנו כל מה שאיננו נמצא הוא כמו אמרנו כל בלתי נמצא, שר"ל כל נעדר, אינו במקום. וההקדמה המחייבת לא תתהפך כוללת כי אם חלקית. והתפיסה הישרה היא קצת מה שאיננו במקום אינו נמצא, שאם כל נעדר אינו במקום קצת מה שאינו במקום הוא נעדר, והוא צודק. ומה שמורה שהיא מחייבת הוא תיבת כל שהיא חומה מחייבת כוללת ולא חומה שוללת, כי החומה השוללת הוא אין אחד. וגם כן החומה השוללת לא יבא עמה אח"כ מלת איננו נמצא ואינו במקום. ואם הנחה שוללת כמו אין דבר אחד ממה שאינו נמצא שיהיה במקום יצדק הפיכה בהכרח והוא אין דבר אחד ממה שיהיה במקום שהוא אינו נמצא.

מ"ד, כ"א, פ"א.

נשאר נושא ומלת צדיק שהוא נשוא לעולם נשאר נשוא. ואין חלוף בין אלו הגזרות אלא בהמרת המצבית לבד. ואחר שזה כן, מבואר מאד סכלות אלו האנשים בזה ההפוך, וזה כי הם הפכוהו נושא לנשוא והנשוא לנושא. ולא היה ראוי לעשות זה כפי מה שאמרנו עתה, אלא שימיר המצבית לבד ושישאר הנושא נושא והנשוא נשוא. ואין העיון לזה כלל אלא בשנאמר איננו במקום מה שאיננו נמצא. וזה כי לעולם בזאת ההקדמה המהופכת נשאר הנושא נושא והנשוא נשוא. וזה כי מלת מה שאיננו נמצא הוא נושא בזאת ההקדמה, כמו שהיתה בראשונה, ומלת איננו במקום הוא נשוא בזאת ההקדמה, כמו שהיתה בתחלה. ואין סבת זה הדבר אלא שאנחנו לא אמרנו בזאת ההקדמה, לא שאנחנו מודיעים שאי"א שיהיה במקום אותו הדבר אשר הנחנו על שהוא מתואר בשיש לו מקום או שאין לו מקום.

וזה הפי' שעשינו הנה בדברי אריסטו זהו הנראה כפי אשר אמר אריסטו בס' מליצה, ומה שפירשנו

זה הסדר כל הקדמה מחייבת כוללת יתהפך כוללת, שהרי נוכל לומר כל אדם חי, חי כל אדם, וזה הפך מה שהונח בספר ההקש.

אבל הפירוש הנאות בזה הוא שסכלותם בהתהפך הוא לפי שזאת ההקדמה לא ימלט או שיהיה שוללת א מוסרת. ואם הוא שוללת, כמו שהוא האמת, א"כ יהיה מובן זאת ההקדמה כמו אמרנו אין אחד ממה שאיננו נמצא שהוא במקום, שזהו סדר ההקדמה השוללת הכוללת. והפוך זה יהיה אין אחד ממה שהוא במקום שאיננו נמצא, ולא יתחייב להם מזה מה שרצו לחייבו. ואם רצו להפכה כמו שיהיה ההפוך מה שבמקום איננו נעדר, לפי שאיננו נמצא כח הוראתו הוראת מלה נפרדת, והוא אמרנו נעדר, לא שיקחו מלת איננו עם מלת במקום, לשהוא חלק מן הנשוא, שהרי תיבת השלילה איננה חלק מן הנושא ולא מן הנשוא אבל הורה על היחס שיש ביניהם. ואם אמרו שהוא גזרה מוסרת, והביאו ראיה לזה לפי שהחומה בה היא בתאר גזרה מחייבת, לפי שבא בה מלה כוללת, ואם היתה שוללת היה מן הראוי [הוראת :read] אין אחד, כמו שהתבאר בספר מליצה, לזה נשיב שמה שלקחו מלת איננו עם מלת במקום שעשו כראוי, לפי שתיבת ההסרה הוא הלק מן הנשוא, אבל טעו בהפכם אותה כוללת, שהרי

התבאר בספר ההקש שהמחייבת הכוללת תתהפך חלקית. מ״ד, כ״א, פ״א.	בו בביאורנו הראשון הוא נראה יותר כפי מה שהתבאר בספר ההקש. ועליך לבחור איזה מהג׳ פרושים שעשינו בזה המקום בדברי הפלוסוף, שנים מה שעשינו שם וזה מה שעשינו הנה. ואין צריך לזכרם הנה מפני שלא יקרה מזה הכפל הבאור. מ״ד, כ״א, פ״א

All these considerations conclusively prove that these two anonymous commentaries belong to Isaac Ibn Shem-Tob and are his "first" and "third" supercommentaries on Averroës' Intermediate Commentary on the *Physics*. Furthermore, bound together with these two works are a few fragments of still another commentary on the *Physics* (Cod. R. 8. 19. 1) which resembles the former two in general style and form. It is not impossible that these fragments are the remains of a "fourth" commentary by Isaac Ibn Shem-Tob. He who has written three commentaries on the *Physics* and who, according to the testimony of his pupil, was "an inexhaustible fountain" might have written a fourth commentary. As a teacher actively engaged in expounding the text of the *Physics* to successive classes of students, he must have found it necessary to revise his notes from time to time and hence this series of four commentaries.

Isaac Ibn Shem-Tob has hitherto been known to bibliographers as the author of four works not all of which are extant: (1) A commentary on the *Moreh Nebukim* which is referred to by Moses Alashkar in his *Hassagot*. (2) A commentary on the second part (Metaphysics) of the Hebrew translation of Algazali's *Maḳaṣid al-Falasifah* (Paris, Cod. Heb. 906) in which he refers to (3) a treatise of his own on the problem of creation and (4) a treatise on metaphysical problems (See *Übersetzungen*, p. 320). With the establishment of his authorship of these commentaries we are enabled to add not only these works to his credit but also other works which he mentions in these commentaries as either having already written them or proposing to write them. Altogether Isaac Ibn Shem-Tob may be considered as the author of fourteen works, as follows:

I. Extant Works

1. First commentary on the *Physics* (Trinity College, Cambridge, Cod. R. 8. 19. 3).
2. Second commentary on the *Physics* (Munich, Cod. Heb. 45; Cambridge University, Mm. 6. 25).
3. Third commentary on the *Physics* (Trinity College, Cambridge, Cod. R. 8. 19. 2).
4. Fourth commentary on the *Physics* (probably his), (Ibid. Cod. R. 8. 19. 1).
5. Commentary on *De Anima* (Cambridge University, Mm. 6. 31. 1).

This commentary on *De Anima*, according to the author's own testimony, is based upon Aristotle's text with Averroës' Long Commentary: אמר יצחק, אחר אשר ביאר זה הכח הדברי על השלמות כפי יכלתנו, ראוי לומר הדרושים היוצאים ממנו ... אלו המה הדרושים היוצאים מזה הכח הדברי, וכבר פרשנו אותם על השלמות בפירושנו הנה דברי אריסטו עם ביאור בן רשד על המלה. ויהי׳ העוזר על הטוב אשר גמלנו ועזר אותנו לבאר זה הכח על השלמות כפי כונת אריסטו כפי מה שהבין ב״ר מדבריו. נשלם המאמר.

6. Commentary on *De Generatione et Corruptione* (Ibid. Mm. 6. 31. 2).
7. Commentary on the second part (Metaphysics) of Algazali's *Maḳaṣid al-Falasifah* (Paris, Cod. Heb. 906).
8. Commentary on the *Moreh Nebukim*, mentioned by Moses Alashkar in his *Hassagot*, in 2 and in 6, in the latter of which it is referred to as follows: אמר יצחק, אני מכחיש שהגרמים השמימיים אינם פועלי ההויה וההפסד באמצעות הכחות השופעות מהם כמו שאמר הרב האלהי במ׳ ראשון מס׳ המורה בפ׳ ע״ב מחלק הראשון כמו שבארנו שם על השלמות בבאורנו לאותו הספר. Ms. British Museum, Or. 1388, contains only Part I. Cf. Margoliouth, *A Catalogue of the Hebrew and Samaritan Manuscripts in the British Museum*, Part III, p. 218.

Of these works Nos. 1, 2, 5 and 6 were completed before 1471. See colophon at the end of No. 6 quoted above. No. 7 was completed in 1489. See colophon quoted in *Übersetzungen*, p. 320, n. 408.

II. Lost Works

9. עץ הדעת, mentioned in 2 and 5.
10. מאמר בחדוש העולם, mentioned in 2, 6: במאמרנו חדוש העולם, and 7: מאמר בחדוש העולם.
11. Commentary on Averroës' אגרת על אפשרות הדבקות, mentioned in 5. See quotation under 12.
12. Projected commentary on Abubekr Ibn Tofail's חי בן יקטן, mentioned in 5: אמר יצחק . . . ובן״ר חקר עליו ובאר אפשרותו באגרת הדבקות אשר לו, וגם אבובכר אל טפל חקר אליו בס׳ חי בן יקטן וביאר ג״כ אפשרותו ... אמר יצחק, זה הדרוש הנעלה והנשגב ב״ר עשה אגרת או על אפשרות הדבקות עם הנפרד מעטת הכמה וגדולה באיכות, וזה כי שם הביא מופתים רבים על אפשרות זה הדבקות, ואנחנו פרשנוה כפי דעתו, ובארנו שם שהמופתים שעשה שם הם כלם מופתים חזקים. ואם האל יאריך ימינו נבאר ג״כ ספר אחר גדול האיכות שעשה החכם השלם אבובכר בן אלטפל על דבקות השכל הנפרד עם השכל ההיולאני.
13. Commentary on the Hebrew translation of Algazali's *Makaṣid al-Falasifah*, mentioned in 2 and 5: ואנחנו כבר בטלנו זאת הדעת בפירושנו לספר דעות הפלוסופים. He refers to this book both by Isaac Albalag's title דעות הפלוסופים and by Judah Nathan's title כונות הפלוסופים. This commentary is probably not identical with the extant commentary on Part II of the *Makaṣid*, for the latter evidently was not completed before 1489, whereas this one is mentioned in a work which was already completed in 1471.
14. דרושים אלהיים, mentioned in 7.

It is interesting to compare the literary activity of Isaac Ibn Shem-Tob with that of his older brother Joseph Ibn Shem-Tob and of his nephew Shem-Tob ben Joseph Ibn Shem-Tob. They were all prolific writers of commentaries on standard philosophic texts. This must have become a sort of family specialization with them as translation had been with the Tibbonites. They also show a common interest in their choice of subject. All of them wrote commentaries on the *Moreh Nebukim* and on selected works of Averroës. They all were critical students of Ḥasdai Crescas, showing a rather hostile attitude toward him, as a result, perhaps, of their reaction against the opposition to philosophy on the part of their father, Shem-Tob Ibn Shem-Tob. The works of Isaac and his nephew Shem-Tob contain rather caustic remarks about the author of the *Or Adonai* and Joseph is not only the friendly translator of Crescas' work against Christianity (בּיטול עקרי הנוצרים) but also its severe critic.

16

THE PROBLEM OF THE ORIGIN OF MATTER IN MEDIAEVAL JEWISH PHILOSOPHY AND ITS ANALOGY TO THE MODERN PROBLEM OF THE ORIGIN OF LIFE

OF the many topics which are included under the general problem of creation the one upon which I should like to dwell in this brief survey is the specific problem of the origin of matter. Three views were held by mediaeval Jewish philosophers with regard to the origin of matter. First, matter was created by God *ex nihilo*. Second, matter existed from eternity alongside of God. Third, matter emanated from the essence of God. Of these three views, the first forestalled the problem, the second was merely an evasion of the problem, and the third, emanation, while meant to be a solution of the problem, really became a problem in itself.

The emanation theory as to the origin of matter presented to the mediaeval mind a problem analagous to, but the reverse of, the present-day problem as to the origin of life. Today, beginning with matter as the starting point of the process of evolution, we ask ourselves how did life originate. In the Middle Ages, beginning with God, or pure spirit, as the starting point in the process of emanation, they asked themselves how did matter originate. To appreciate the full significance of this problem to the mediaeval philosophers we must recall that emanation to them was a form of natural causality especially applicable to the action of spirit upon matter [1] and because of that the process of emanation had to conform to all the laws of natural causality. Now, one of the accepted principles of natural causality was that from a simple cause only one simple effect can be produced,[2] the necessary corollary of which was summed up in the dictum that matter cannot be produced from form nor form from matter — a dictum which may be traced back to the principle *ex nihilo nihil fit*. The mediaevals thus set out on their discussion of the origin of matter with a presumption in favor of a principle *omne materiale e materiali* just as today we set out on

[1] Cf. Maimonides, *Moreh Nebukim* II, 12.

[2] Cf. *Ibid*. II, 22.

the discussion of the origin of life with a presumption in favor of the principle *omne vivum e vivo.*

It is my purpose to show that in their attempts to solve the problem mediaeval Jewish philosophers resorted to hypotheses which logically stand in the same relation to the problem of the origin of matter as the various hypotheses offered today stand in relation to the problem of the origin of life.

The first hypothesis found in Jewish philosophic literature in explanation of the origin of matter may be called ahylogenesis, and we may consider it as the counterpart of the modern hypothesis of abiogenesis advanced in explanation of the origin of life. It is a bold statement to the effect that a certain portion of the divine spiritual essence was converted directly into matter out of which the world was formed. This view is reproduced by Saadia [3] as one of the thirteen theories of creation which he had gathered from various sources, non-Jewish as well as Jewish. What was the particular source of this view cannot be definitely determined. While on the whole it resembles the general theory of emanation insofar as it traces matter to the divine essence, denying on the one hand creation *ex nihilo* and on the other the independent existence of an eternal matter, it differs from emanation on two important points. In the first place, in emanation matter is an overflow of the totality of the divine essence, whereas in this view it is the transformation of only part of the essence.[4] In the second place, in emanation the procession of matter from God is indirect and remote, whereas according to this view it is direct and immediate. It is not impossible, however, that in the many theories of emanation, which are much older than Plotinus and which are to be found in sources outside the *Enneads*, there must have been one version which made matter arise directly from a part of the divine essence. The existence of such a view is reflected in the arguments of Christian theologians, such as Tertullian [5] and Augustine,[6] who argue explicitly against a view that the world like the Logos was created directly out of a part of the divine essence.

A second hypothesis advanced in Jewish philosophic literature is Avicenna's version of Plotinus' theory of emanation.[7] In this version a

[3] Cf. *Emunot ve-Deot* I, 2, Third View.

[4] Cf. J. Guttmann, *Die Religionsphilosophie des Saadia,* p. 49 f.

[5] *Adversus Hermogenem,* ch. 2.

[6] *De Natura Boni contra Manichoes*, ch. 27.

[7] See, e.g., Abraham ibn Daud, *Emunah Ramah* II, iv, 3, and Maimonides, *Moreh Nebukim* II, 22.

new attempt is made to solve the problem discussed by Plotinus as to the origin of matter by maintaining that in the process of emanation a new cause appears which is directly responsible for the rise of matter. This new cause does not proceed from God nor does it come from without, but is the concomitant of a new relation which, not present in God, appears in the first Intelligence by the very nature of its being an emanation. Formally, this new version of the theory of emanation is stated as follows: There is God who is necessary existence by his own nature and whose object of thought is his own self. The product of his thought is an Intelligence. This Intelligence, having a cause for its existence, is only possible by its own nature, but inasmuch as it is the necessary product of God's thinking, it is necessary by virtue of its cause. Thus a duality appears in the nature of the First Intelligence owing to its relation to God as effect to cause. And a similar duality appears also in its object of thought. Its thinking of God, who is necessary existence, produces another Intelligence; its thinking of itself, which is possible existence, produces matter, or more correctly, a sphere. In analogy to the modern explanation of the origin of life by what is known as emergent evolution we may call this explanation of the origin of matter emergent emanation. It says in effect that matter is not the resultant of spiritual causes, but rather an emergent, arising as something unpredictable out of a new relation which makes its appearance in the first emanated Intelligence.

A third hypothesis for the rise of matter from God is quoted by Maimonides in the name of some anonymous philosophers to whom he refers as "some of the latter-day philosophers."[8] They are presented by him as those who, while believing in the eternity of the world, still describe God as "the Maker of the World, who freely chose that it should exist, who designed it, and who particularized it so that it should be as it actually is."[9] This description is taken by Maimonides to mean the same as the view held by the Neoplatonized Aristotelians of his time, namely, that the world emanated eternally from God, except that they take this eternal emanation to be not an act of necessity but rather an act of free will and design, for, he says, according to them, "in assuming that God acts from eternity, there is no difference whether we describe God as one who acts, as one who wills, as one who designs, or as one who par-

[8] *Moreh Nebukim* II, 21 (Arabic text, ed. Munk, p. 46b, 1. 7). The reference would seem to be to "the philosophers" whose view on the divine attribute of will is reproduced by Ghazali in his *Maḳāsid* al-*Falāsifah*, p. 162, 1. 17 ff. Behind this passage of Ghazali there would seem to be Alfarabi's passage in his *Kitāb al-Jam' bayn Ra' y al-Ḥakīmayn Aflāṭūn al-Ilāhī wa-Aristūtālīs,* p. 23, 11. 13–19 (ed. Dietereci in his *Alfārābī's philosophische Abhandlungen,* 1890).

[9] *Ibid.* (11. 8–9).

ticularizes,"[10] for all these descriptions are assumed to be eternal. This description of the eternal process of emanation by the terms will and design does for emanation what the various types of vitalism do for evolution. It renders emanation teleological instead of its being purely mechanical, intelligently creative instead of blindly causative; it transforms a necessary process into a free activity. As an explanation of the rise of matter, volitional emanation is not a device invented *ad hoc* but rather the application of a generally established principle. According to the accepted theories of causality there is a well-recognized distinction between an agent acting by necessity and one acting by design. In the case of the former a simple cause can only produce a simple effect. In the case of the latter, "a single agent that acts with design and will, and not merely by the force of the laws of nature, can produce different effects."[11]

These three hypotheses which I have enumerated with regard to the origin of matter are subjected to a searching criticism by Maimonides. Against the view which we have chosen to call ahylogenesis he invokes the generally accepted proposition that there must be some relation between cause and effect, that quality cannot be the origin of quantity, nor quantity of quality, that a form cannot emanate from matter, nor matter from form.[12] Against emergent emanation he argues that, while it is sufficient to explain the origin of a simple matter, it fails to account for the origin of the variety and multiplicity of material substances. For emergent emanation, argues Maimonides, is still a necessary process. What it does is simply to introduce a new additional cause which, again, acts by necessity. While this new cause could indeed produce one simple matter, the question still remains how could it produce the sphere, and fixed stars within the sphere, the luminous and non-luminous stars and also the other bodies, each of which has its own matter and its own form.[13] Equally unacceptable to Maimonides is volitional emanation. "These philosophers," he says, "have changed the term necessity, but have retained its meaning."[14] Neither design nor will can be eternal, for, according to Aristotle's own reasoning, "if things had come into existence by the design of one possessing design, they would not have existed before they were designed," and so also "the meaning of the true essence of will is to will (at one time) and not to will (at another time)."[15]

In opposition to Maimonides, though not directly answering him, is

[10] *Ibid.* (11. 20–21).
[11] *Ibid.* II, 22, Prop. 3.
[12] *Ibid.* Prop. 2.
[13] *Ibid.* Passage immediately following Prop. 4.
[14] *Ibid.* II, 21 (p. 47a, 11. 2–3).
[15] *Ibid.* II, 19 (p. 40a, 11. 2–3).

the view of Crescas. In the first place, he argues that the essence of will is not temporal action but rather purposive action. Given therefore an agent whose purpose is contained within himself and whose means of attaining that purpose are not determined by external circumstance, and you can have eternal action which is also volitional.[16] In the second place, Crescas boldly denies the distinction between creation *ex nihilo* and emanation from the divine essence — a distinction which has been tacitly assumed in Jewish philosophy and openly maintained in Christian theology ever since the Arian controversies. Creation *ex nihilo*, he argues, is a negative term, meaning simply a denial of creation from an eternal matter; on its positive side, it means nothing but emanation from the divine essence.[17]

The inherent difficulties of emanation brought about a revival in Jewish philosophy of the view that matter has an independent origin, having existed from eternity alongside of, and apart from, God. Compared again to the modern theories as to the origin of life this view may be considered analogous to the theory advanced by Lord Kelvin and Helmholtz that life has an independent origin having come down to our earth from other cosmic bodies, where, presumably, it must have existed from eternity. The chief exponent of this view in Jewish philosophy is Gersonides, in the fourteenth century, but it had many followers before him. It is generally assumed that this view was introduced into Judaism from Greek philosophy, under the influence of Plato, and the attempt to reconcile it with the Biblical account of creation is a species of theological rationalization. I think, however, that it can be shown that the belief in the eternity of a formless matter, or chaos, is the survival of an early native Jewish tradition and that it reflects more truly the original meaning of the first verses of Genesis than the belief in creation *ex nihilo*, which is undoubtedly a later development. The stock argument against the assumption of an eternal matter, in both Jewish and Christian theology,[18] is that it would be a second God, equalling God in his chief attribute of eternity. Gersonides, in answering this difficulty, argues that even by denying eternity as the unique attribute of God, God could still maintain his character as a deity by virtue of his power over the eternal formless matter.[19] But to this Crescas rejoins, as follows: To assume first an eternal matter independent of God and then to make it subservient to God's action is purely arbitrary.[20]

This, in brief, is a summary of solutions offered in mediaeval Jewish

[16] *Or Adonai* III, i, 5, Vienna edition f. 69a.

[17] *Ibid.*

[18] Cf. Tertullian, *Adversus Hermogenem,* ch. 4.

[19] *Milhamot Adonai* VI, i, 18, Third Doubt.

[20] *Or Adonai* III, i, 4, f. 68a.

philosophy for the problem of the origin of matter. Its analogy to the modern problem of the origin of life, I believe, has been fully established. As against abiogenesis we have ahylogenesis. As against emergent evolution we have emergent emanation. Corresponding to vitalism we have volitional emanation, and corresponding to the theory of the extraneous origin of life we have the theory of the extraneous origin of matter. The chief difficulty of emanation, as we have seen, arose from the assumption of a contrast between God and the world as between pure spirit and matter and of the existence of a causal relation between them. To minds more daring two new alternative solutions would probably have suggested themselves, namely, the obliteration of that contrast between God and the world, either by denying the materiality of the world or by denying the immateriality of God. While the former solution does nowhere occur in Jewish philosophy, the latter was one of the youthful heresies of Spinoza which in time became the keynote of his system. The starting point of Spinoza's philosophy is the rejection of creation in any sense whatsoever. The opening chapters of his *Short Treatise* and the first six propositions of his *Ethics* is a revision of the mediaeval discussion of theory of emanation and a criticism of the futile attempts to explain the derivation of a material world from a God who is pure thought.[21] By force of the internal difficulties of emanation, of which the mediaevals themselves were not unaware, Spinoza was led to the conclusion that God is not thought of which matter, or extension, is an emanation but rather a substance of which both extension and thought are attributes.

[21] Cf. my paper "Spinoza on the Unity of Substance" in *Chronicon Spinozanum* II.

17

ST. THOMAS ON DIVINE ATTRIBUTES

When St. Thomas posed the question how, on the basis of what in his view cannot be predicated of God, are we to explain the terms which are predicated of God in Scripture, he examined the various explanations which had been advanced in the course of the history of the problem. Five such explanations are discussed by him : negation, causality or relation, eminence, equivocation and with it also univocation, and analogy. Of these, he rejects equivocation as well as univocation, but accepts the others. The philosophical and theological aspects of St. Thomas' explanations of divine attributes have been discussed by many, and by none with greater distinction than by Professor Gilson. In this paper, presented as a token of high regard and admiration for my good friend Professor Gilson, I shall confine myself to comments on the philological aspect and historical background of these explanations.

1. *Via Negationis*

"Negation" and "remotion" are used by St. Thomas indiscriminately in the technical sense of logical propositions which are negative in quality.[1] "Negation", which is a translation of the Greek ἀπόφασις, is an Aristotelian term. "Remotion" reflects the Greek ἀφαίρεσις and, when used in its logical sense of "negation", is not Aristotelian. It is first used in that sense by Albinus and, following him, by Plotinus[2] and, following both of them, by the Greek Church Fathers,[3] among them

(1) *Cont. Gent.* I, 14.

(2) Cf. my paper "Albinus and Plotinus on Divine Attributes", *Harvard Theological Review*, 45 (1952), pp. 115-130. In *Studies*, I, 115-130.

(3) Cf. my paper "Negative Attributes in the Church Fathers and the Gnostic Basilides", *Harvard Theological Review*, 50 (1957), pp. 145-156. In *Studies*, I, 131-142.

pseudo-Dionysius Areopagita and John Damascene, both of whom are quoted by St. Thomas in his discussion of divine attributes. It happens, however, that in the Latin versions of Dionysius[4] and John Damascene[5] available to St. Thomas, the Greek term αφαίρεσις is rendered *ablatio*. Quite evidently St. Thomas, for some reason, substituted *remotio* for *ablatio*.

A similar substitution by St. Thomas of an expression suggesting the term *remotio* for the term *ablatio* is to be found in a comment of his on a passage in Aristotle's *Metaphysics*.

The passage in Aristotle, in the Latin translation used by St. Thomas, reads: *illius enim absentia* (ἀπουσία) *negatio est.*[6] In the Latin translation of Averroes' Long Commentary on the *Metaphysics*, also used by St. Thomas, this passage reads: *quia negatio est ablatio unius,*[7] where *ablatio* translates the Arabic *nafy.*[8] Averroes' own comment on it, in its Latin translation, reads: *negatio nam est ablatio (nafy) alicuius negati simpliciter.*[9] St. Thomas' parallel comment on the same passage reads: *quia negatio dicit tantum absentiam alicuius, scilicet quod removet, sine hoc quod determinet subiectum.*[10] It is quite evident that St. Thomas' explanation of Aristotle's statement as meaning *quod removet, sine hoc quod determinet subiectum* is based upon Averroes' explanation of it as meaning *ablatio alicuius negati simpliciter*, and thus the term *remotio*, which is implied in the expression *quod removet*, is indirectly substituted by St. Thomas for the term *ablatio*.

In the case before us, however, in connection with the problem of attributes, St. Thomas' substitution of the term *remotio* for *ablatio* as the equivalent of *negatio* may perhaps be due to the influence of two sources. One of them is the Latin translation of Maimonides' *Moreh Nebukim*, which was made from al-Ḥarizi's Hebrew version. In that Latin translation, the term *remotio* is used as a translation of two Hebrew terms, *harḥakah*[11] and *biṭṭul*[12], both of which are translations of the Arabic *nafy*, which in turn reflects the Greek ἀφαίρεσις. Now it happens that as a translation of the second of these two Hebrew terms,

(4) St. Thomas, *Expositio in Librum b. Dionysii de Divinis Nominibus*, Caput. VII, Lectio IV, corresponding to *De Div. Nom.* VII, 3 (*P. G.* 3, 872 A).

(5) *De Fide Orthodoxa. Versions of* Burgundio *and* Cerbanus, edited by E. M. Buytaert, (1955), 4, 4, p. 41, l. 35; Greek text, I, 4 (*P. G.* 94, 800 B).

(6) *Metaph.* IV, 2, 1004 a, 14-15

(7) Averroes, *In IV Metaph.*, *Text.* 4, fol. 68 E (*Aristotelis Opera*, Venice, 1574).

(8) Averroes: *Tafsir ma ba'd at-tabi'at*, p. 317, l. 3 (ed. Bouyges, Vol. I, 1938).

(9) Comm. 4, fol. 69 B; Arabic, p. 320, ll. 16-17.

(10) St. Thomas, *In IV Metaph.*, Lectio III, No. 565 (ed. M.-R. Cathala, Turin, 1915).

(11) *Dux seu Director dubitantium aut perplexorum* I, 1, fol. 5 a, l. 39 (ed. Paris, 1520).

(12) *Ibid.* I, 50, fol. 18 b, l. 3.

the term *remotio* occurs in connection with the problem of attributes. Moreover, in that Latin translation, such expressions as *nominationes attributivae removentur ab eo*[13] and *nomina remota*[14] are used in the discussion of attributes even when the original Arabic underlying the Hebrew is not any form of the verb *nafa* or of the adjective *nafiyy*. The other possible source is the Latin translation of Algazali's *Maḳāṣid al-Falāsifah*. In that Latin translation, in the chapter dealing with divine attributes, the terms *remocio* and *removeri* occur as translations of the Arabic *nafy*[15] and from the context one may judge that these two Latin terms are used in the same sense as *negacio* and *negari*.

In Aristotle, the term "negation" is distinguished from the term "privation" (στέρησις), and so was also later the term "remotion" distinguished from the term "privation". The distinction between these two terms is illustrated by the contrast between the propositions "A is not seeing" and "A is blind", the difference between these two contrasting propositions being that in the case of the former the subject A may by its very nature not be seeing, as, for instance, an inanimate object, whereas in the case of the latter the subject A must be one who by nature should be seeing. This distinction between "negation" and "privation" is dwelt upon by St. Thomas in his commentaries on the works of Aristotle and is illustrated by him by the propositions *A non est videns* and *A est caecus*.[16] Now propositions which are affirmative in quality but in which the predicate is with a negative prefix or suffix, such as "A is unseeing" or "A is sightless", are treated by Albinus and Plotinus[17] and Gregory of Nyssa and Dionysius and John Damascene[18] as negative propositions. St. Thomas, however, in his comment upon a passage in which Aristotle happens to treat of propositions with a negative prefix or suffix under "privation"[19], says that such proposition are used both as "negations" and "privations"[20]—a view which I have shown to be justifiable on the basis of certain statements in Aristotle.[21] Accordingly in his *Summa Theologiae*, describing a proposition with a negative prefix as "privation", with the assumption that it is used in the sense of "negation", he says that "although in God there is no privation, still...

(13) *Ibid.* I, 58, fol. 22 b, ll. 26-27.

(14) *Ibid.* I, 59 (misprinted 58), fol. 23 b, l. 31.

(15) *Algazel's Metaphysics*, p. 88, ll. 29 and 32 (ed. J. T. MUCKLE, 1933); Arabic: *Maḳāṣid al-Falāsifah*, p. 181, ll. 2-3 (ed. Cairo, n. d.).

(16) *In IV Metaph.*, Lectio III, No. 565; cf. *Peri Hermeneias* I. Lectio IV, No. 1 (Leonine ed., Rome, 1882).

(17) Cf. *op. cit.* (above n. 2), p. 125.

(18) Cf. *op. cit.* (above n. 3), pp. 148-150.

(19) *Metaph.* V, 22, 1022 b, 32-33.

(20) *In V Metaph.* Lectio XX, No. 1074.

(21) Cf. *op. cit.* (above n. 3), pp. 154-155.

He is known to us by way only of *privation* and *remotion*, and thus there is no reason why certain *privative* terms should not be predicated of God; for instance, that He is incorporeal and infinite."[22] Elsewhere the examples which he uses to illustrate the way of remotion are such negative propositions as "God is not an accident" and "God is not a body."[23]

St. Thomas himself refers to Dionysius as his authority for negative attributes.[24] But the theory of negative attributes is already found, among the Church Fathers, in Clement of Alexandria and Gregory of Nyssa[25] and, at about the time of Clement of Alexandria, also in Plotinus, and before all of them also in Albinus,[26] who was the first, as far as we know, to formulate this negative interpretation of attributes. But the use of negative attributes throughout its history before St. Thomas follows a certain pattern. Let us see whether St. Thomas follows that pattern.

One characteristic feature with regard to negation as conceived by both Albinus and Plotinus is that it is not necessary for one to describe God by predicates which are negative in form, such, for instance, as the proposition "God is not corporeal" or "God is incorporeal"; one may predicate of God terms which are affirmative in form provided he uses them in a meaning which is negative.[27] This conception of negative attributes is also to be found among Church Fathers, such as Gregory of Nyssa and Dionysius,[28] and also among Muslim[29] and Jewish[30] philosophers.

St. Thomas does not fully agree with this twofold use of negation as a solution of the problem of attributes. While he is willing to allow the use of negative predicates when they are negative in form, as in the propositions "God is not a body" or "God is incorporeal", because, as he says, "names which are said of God negatively... do not signify His substance,"[31] he is opposed to giving a negative meaning to such affirmation predicates as "good, wise, and the like". Referring to "some" who have given negative meaning to "all such names", he concludes: "Hence they assert that when we say that God is living

(22) *Sum. Theol.* I, 11, 3, ad 2.
(23) *Cont. Gent.* I, 14.
(24) *In 1 Sent.* 35, 1, 1 c; *De Potentia* 9, 7, Obj. 2.
(25) Cf. *op. cit.* (above n. 3).
(26) Cf. *op. cit.* (above n. 2).
(27) Cf. *op. cit.* (above n. 2), p. 125.
(28) Cf. *op. cit.* (above n. 3), pp. 148, 152.
(29) Cf. my paper "Avicenna, Algazali, and Averroes on Divine Attributes", *Homenaje a Millás Vallicrosa*, Vol. II, 1956, pp. 545-571. In *Studies*, I, 143-169.
(30) Cf. my paper "Maimonides on Negative Attributes", *Louis Ginzberg Jubilee Volume*, 1945, pp. 411-446. Above, pp. 195-230.
(31) *Sum. Theol.* I, 13, 2 c.

we mean that God is not like a lifeless thing, and the same in like manner applies to other names." He then adds: "This was thought by Rabbi Moses."[32] He makes, however, two exceptions. One exception is made by him explicity, and that is with regard to the term "one", which, though affirmative in form, is predicated of God in a negative sense.[33] The reason for this exception is undoubtedly Aristotle's statement that "one" means "indivisible",[34] which is reflected in St. Thomas' own statement that one "imports privation"[35] and that it is so called "from the privation of division."[36] The other exception is with regard to the term "eternal", the negative interpretation of which is implied in his statement that "eternal" means "immovable" and refers to that which "has no beginning and no end".[37]

Now the special reference to Maimonides is quite understandable, for Maimonides explicitly stresses the negative interpretation of terms which are affirmative in form. Even the use of "good", "wise" and "living" as examples of such affirmative terms which are to be negatively interpreted can be traced to Maimonides, for among the affirmative terms which are to be negatively interpreted Maimonides explicitly mentions the terms "wise" and "living"[38] and, though the term "good" is not explicitly mentioned by him, he happens to say in another part of his work that "good" means "life"[39] and so, by implication, the term "good" as a divine attribute, like the term "living", is to be interpreted negatively. But who are the others whom St. Thomas had in mind when he describes this view as having been held by "some"? He certainly could have meant the "philosophers" whose views are expounded by Algazali in his *Makāṣid al-Falāsifah.* But in that work only the terms "one" and "eternal" are mentioned as being interpreted negatively,[40] and both "one" and "eternal" are interpreted by St. Thomas himself negatively. The "philosophers" whose views are expounded by Algazali are Alfarabi and Avicenna, and in the works of these philosophers some other affirmative terms are interpreted negatively. Thus, it can be shown the Alfarabi interpreted the term "wise" negatively, and Avicenna says explicitly that the terms "good", "willing" and "generous"

(32) *Ibid.*
(33) *Ibid.* I, 11, 3, ad 2.
(34) *Metaph.* III, 3, 999 a, 2 ; V, 6, 1016 b, 23-24; VII, 17, 1041 a, 18-19.
(35) *Sum. Theol.* I, 11, 3, Obj. 2.
(36) *Ibid.* I, 11, 4, Obj. 1.
(37) *Ibid.* I, 10, 1 c ; *Cont. Gent.* I, 15 ; *Compend. Theol.* I, 5.
(38) *Moreh Nebukim* I, 58 ; Latin I, 57.
(39) *Ibid.* I, 42. Latin I, 41, fol. 15 b, ll. 3-4 : *expositio boni vita est.*
(40) Latin, p. 63, ll.-15-18 ; Arabic, p. 151, l. 4. A larger list of terms to be interpreted negatively is to be found in his *Tahāfut al-Falāsifah* V (cf. *op. cit.* [above n. 29], p. 554), a work unknown to St. Thomas, but even that list does not contain "good" and "wise".

may be interpreted negatively.[41] Perhaps St. Thomas somehow got wind of their view. But did St. Thomas know that Gregory of Nyssa said that the term "good" (ἀγαθός) when predicated of God means the same as the expression "unsuceptible of evil (ἀνεπίδεκτος πονηρίας)," and that the term "ever-living (ἀεὶ ζῶν) means "immortal" (ἀθάνατος)?[42] And did he know that Albinus applied the negative interpretation to the term "self-complete" (αὐτοτελής) and that Plotinus applied it to the term "self-sufficient" (αὐτάρκης), but that both of them interpreted the term "good" not as a negation but rather as a causal relation?[43]

If St. Thomas were to use an argument from silence in order to get support for his view, he could have referred to St. Augustine, who as illustrations of the statement that "God is ineffable", which was introduced by Philo,[44] and of the inference which he himself draws from that statement namely, that "we more easily say what He is not than what He is", uses such negative propositions as "the earth is not God", "the sea is not God", and the like.[45] Similarly as an illustration of his statement, "Thou canst not reach to what He is; reach to what He is not", he uses the negative proposition," god is not body, not the earth, not the heaven, not the moon, not the sun, not these bodily things."[46] And so also, in an attempt to show that terms predicated of God are not to be taken as accidents adjoined to the essence of God but are to be understood "according to substance or essence", he uses as illustrations such negative terms as "immortal", "incorruptible", and "unchangeable" and such affirmative terms as "eternal", "living", "wise", "powerful", "beautiful", "righteous", "good", "blessed", and "spirit", but of these affirmative terms only the term "eternal" is interpreted by him negatively. The term "eternal", as we have seen, together with the term "one", is treated also by St. Thomas as an exception and is interpreted negatively. With reference to some of these affirmative terms, namely, "living", "wise", "powerful", and "beautiful", St. Augustine says that they are to be taken in a sense unlike that in which they are applied to creatures, that is, in what St. Thomas would call the eminent sense, but he does not interpret them negatively.[47] In Philo, too, on the basis of the principle of the ineffability of God, such negative terms as "unborn", "unbribable", "invisible", and the like are predicated of God, but no attempt is made by him to interpret affirmative terms negatively.[48]

(41) Cf. *op. cit.* (above n. 29), pp. 553-554.
(42) *Contra Eunomium XII* (*P. G.* 45, 953 D).
(43) Cf. *op. cit.* (above n. 2), p. 125.
(44) Cf. my discussion in *Philo*, II, pp. 110.
(45) *Ennaratio in Psalm.* 85, 12 (*P. L.* 37, 1090).
(46) *In Joann.* 23, 9 (*P. L.* 35, 1588)
(47) *De Trinit.* XV, V, 7-8.
(48) Cf. *op. cit.*, II, pp. 126 ff.

2. *Via Causalitatis*

The attributes which St. Thomas describes as "by way of causality" *(per viam causalitatis)* or "by cause" *(per causam)* or "causally" *(causaliter)*[49] are also described by him as "names... which signify God's relation to creatures" or which "express... His relation to something else, or rather, the relation of creatures to Him."[50] The description of this type of attribute as causative and as relative reflects that type of relation which Aristotle describes as the relation of "the active to the passive"[51] or the relation of "agent and patient."[52] Historically this kind of divine attributes was introduced by Philo, who describes them as signifying the property of God to act and expressing a sort of relation.[53] There is also an implication of this kind of causal attributes in both Albinus and Plotinus.[54] Dionysius, in a passage quoted by St. Thomas as his authority for his causal interpretation of divine attributes,[55] describes them as signifying a knowledge of God attained through the conception of "the cause of all things"[56] and, in another passage, describes them as predicates drawn "from all manner of causes (αἰτίας) and powers (δυνάμεις)."[57] John Damascene, also in a passage quoted by St. Thomas,[58] describes any predicate of this kind as expressing "some relation (σχέσιν τινὰ) or an operation (ἐνέργειαν)."[59] And so also Augustine allows the predication of God of terms which signify "making" *(faciendum)*[60] or which are predicated of God "relatively *(relative)* in respect to the creature."[61] Causal relation as an interpretation of divine attributes is also common in Muslim[62] and Jewish[63] philosophy.

Here, again, St. Thomas, as we have already seen from the passage

(49) *1 Sent.* 22, 1, 2, Obj. 2; 8, 4, 3 c.
(50) *Sum. Theol.* I, 13, 2 c.
(51) *Metaph.* V, 15, 1020 b, 30.
(52) *Phys.* III, 1, 200 b, 30.
(53) Cf. *op. cit.*, II, pp. 137-138.
(54) Cf. *op. cit.* (above n. 2), pp. 121-125.
(55) *1 Sent.* 35, 1, 1 c; *De Potentia* 9, 7, Obj. 2.
(56) *De Divin. Nomin.* VII, 3 (*P. G.* 3, 872 A). Cf. St. Thomas' Commentary on it, Cap. VII, Lectio IV.
(57) *Ibid.* I, 8 (597 A). Cf. St. Thomas' Commentary on it, Cap. I, Lectio III.
(58) *Sum. Theol.* I, 13, 2, Obj. 1.
(59) *De Fid. Orth.* I, 9 (*P. G.* 94, 836 A).
(60) *De Trinit.* V, viii, 9.
(61) *Ibid.* V, xvi, 17.
(62) Cf. *op. cit.* (above n. 2), pp. 552-553.
(63) Cf. my paper "The Aristotelian Predicables and Maimonides' Division of Attributes", *Essays and Studies in Memory of Linda R. Miller*, 1938, pp. 201-234, especially pp. 225-227. Above, pp. 161-194.

quoted, is willing to allow causal predicates which express "God's relation to something else, or rather, the relation of creatures to Him." By this, I take it, he means that the predicates must be terms which externally, in form, express causative actions, such, for instance, as "creator", "ruler", "legislator", and the like, all of which express, as he says, "God's relation to something else". His additional revisionary statement, "or rather, the relation of creatures to Him", means to emphasize that the relation is a non-reciprocal relation, and hence not what Aristotle requires of a true relation;[64] it is only some sort of relation, inasmuch as the creature, or creature, depends upon God, God, as creator, does not depend upon creature. This is the reason why Philo calls such predications of action not simply relative but rather "relative, as it were" (ὡσανεὶ πρός τι)[65] and also why John Damascene calls it "some relation" (σχέσιν τινά).[66]

But, as previously in the case of negations, St. Thomas is opposed to the relative or causal interpretation of terms which externally, in form, do not express causative action, mentioning "good, wise, and the like" and going on to explain as follows: "Others say that these names applied to God signify His relationship towards creatures: thus in the words 'God is good' we mean God is the cause of goodness in things; and the same interpretation applies to other names."[67] In this case no mention is made of Maimonides.

Who are those "others" who interpreted "good, wise, and the like" as causal or relative terms?

Alanus ab Insulis has been mentioned as the one referred to by "others".[68] But Alanus is not the only one who applied the causal or relative interpretation to terms which in form do not express causal or relative actions. Besides, Alanus does not mention "good" and "wise"; he mentions only "just *(justus)*, kind *(pius)*, strong *(fortis)*". For the record, let us enumerate representative types of philosophers, even those unknown to St. Thomas, who applied the causal or relative interpretation to "good, wise, and the like". To begin with, Albinus interprets "good", when applied to God, to mean "He does good to everything according to its [receptive] ability and is the cause of every good" and he interprets "truth", when, too, applied to God, as meaning that "He is the principle of every truth", and similarly Plotinus interprets

(64) *Metaph.* V, 15, 1021 a, 26-28 ; *Categ.* 7, 6 b, 28-30.

(65) *De Mut. Nomin.* 4, 28.

(66) *De Fid. Orth.* I, 9 (*P. G.* 94, 336 A).

(67) *Sum. Theol.* I, 13, 2 c.

(68) Cf. note *ad loc.* in the Ottawa edition of the *Summa Theologiae*, referring to *Theol. Reg.*, reg. 21 (*P. L.* 210, 631).

"good" to mean that "He is good for other things, if they are able to receive some part of it," and "living" he interprets to mean "He gives life".[69] Then, among the Church Fathers, Dionysius in his *De Mystica Theologia*,[70] referring to his interpretation of divine attributes in his *De Divinis Nominibus*, evidently to his causal or relative interpretation, mentions "existence" and "life" and "wisdom" and "power" as attributes to which that interpretation of his applies. Among Muslim and Jewish philosophers, Avicenna and Algazali describe "good" *(ḫair)* as either relative or negative,[71] Saadia describes "wise" as an explanation of the term "creator",[72] and Maimonides describes "wise" and also "living", which, as we have seen, means "good", as belonging to those attributes of God which "describe actions"[73] and which are applicable to God only "when we regard them in relation to His creatures."[74]

But here a question may be raised. In view of the fact that Maimonides describes the attribute "wise" and the like as signifying God's "actions" and as being used "in relation to His creatures," why does not St. Thomas specifically mention "Rabbi Moses" here, as he did in the case of negative interpretation? Is there any significance in the omission of the name of Maimonides here?

The answer is "yes".

The fact is, Maimonides does not admit "relations", even causal relations, as divine attributes. In the very same chapter from which we have quoted his statement that the attribute "wise" and the like are "in relation to His creatures," when he happens to repeat that statement, he adds, "according to the manner of our explanation of the true meaning of relation, to wit, that it is only in the imagination and not in reality."[75] The reference is to his discussion in an earlier chapter (I, 52; Latin I, 51) of "relations" and to his rejection of them, even if they are causal relations, on the ground that a true relation, as defined by Aristotle, must be reciprocal and the relation between God and creatures cannot be reciprocal—a difficulty which Philo and John Damascene, as we have seen, tried to dodge by the use of the expressions "a relation, as it were" or "some relation."[76] But he does allow terms which express action

(69) Cf. *op. cit.* (above n. 2), pp. 125-126.

(70) *De Mystica Theologia* 3 (*P. G.* 3, 1033 A).

(71) Cf. *op. cit.* (above n. 29), p. 554.

(72) *Emunot ve-De'ot* II, 4.

(73) *Moreh Nebukim* I, 53. Latin, I, 52, fol. 19 b, ll. 40-41 : *ideoque omnes nominationes quae inveniuntur in libris attributae creatori, nominabunt opera.*

(74) *Ibid.* Latin, fol. 20 a, ll. 11-12: *sic ergo probatur tibi quod istae dispositiones non conveniunt ei cum intendimus in substantia eius, sed cum intendimus creata ipsius.*

(75) *Moreh Nebukim* I, 53 end. Latin I, 52, fol. 20 a, ll. 20-21 : *Per viam autem quam exposuimus de veritate comparationis, quia est cogitatio non vera.*

(76) Cf. above at nn. 66, 67.

as predicates of God and he also interprets such adjectival predicates as "living", "powerful", "wise", as actions (*op. cit.* I, 53 [52]). The difference between "action" and "causal relation" as conceived by Maimonides, is this. "Action" means a proposition consisting of two terms, a subject and a finite verb, illustrated by Maimonides by the propositions, "A made this door", "A built this house", "A wove this garment." "Causal relation" means a proposition consisting of three terms, subject, copula, and predicate, illustrated by Maimonides by the proposition, "A is the father of B." The distinction between these two types of propositions corresponds to the distinction known as propositions of the second adjacent and propositions of the third adjacent.[77]

Now according to Maimonides the proposition "God is good" may be used in the sense of "God does good" but may not be used in the sense of "God is the cause of goodness in things", for the former is to him an "action", the latter a "causal relation". This distinction, as I have shown elsewhere, is traceable to a passage in Aristotle.[78] St. Thomas evidently, penetrated into the meaning of Maimonides' attributes of "action" and consequently, when he was arguing against those who interpreted "God is good" to mean "God is the cause of goodness in things",[79] that is to say, as a causal relation, he did not mention Maimonides.

And so, according to St. Thomas, while certain terms which are predicated of God may be interpreted as negations or as causal relations, no such interpretations can be given to terms described by him as being predicated of God "absolutely and affirmatively",[80] that is to say, terms which are adjectival and affirmative in form.

Still terms, such as "good, wise, and the like" are found to be predicated of God in Scripture "absolutely and affirmatively"' What, then, do these terms mean, seeing that they can be neither relative nor negative? The answer given by St. Thomas is that they are to be interpreted in two senses: first, in an eminent sense; second, in an analogical sense.

3. *Via Eminentiae*

The eminential interpretation *(per viam eminentiae)*[81] is described by St. Thomas also as the excellential interpretation *(per modum*

(77) Cf. *op. cit.* (above n. 64), pp. 225-232.
(78) Cf. *op. cit.* (above n. 30), p. 412.
(79) *Sum. Theol.* I, 13, 2 c.
(80) *Ibid.*
(81) *1 Sent.* 22, 1, 2, Obj. 2 ; cf. 35, 1, 1 c : *per eminentiam.*

excellentiae).[82] Both these expressions are based upon the term ὑπεροχῇ, which is used by Dionysius[83] and the term ὑπεροχική, which is used by John Damascene,[84] the former of whom is quoted by St. Thomas as the authority for his use of the eminent sense.[85] However, the terms *eminentia* and *eminens* are not used as translations of ὑπεροχῇ and ὑπεροχική in the Latin translations of the works of Dionysius and John Damascene which were used by St. Thomas. In the translation of Dionysius the term used is *excessu*;[86] in that of John Damascene the term used is *superbundativa*.[87] In Dionysius these eminential attributes of God are expressed by the use of the prefix "super" *(hyper)* before the attribute in question, such as "super-good" (ὑπεράγαθος), "super-God" (ὑπέρθεος), "super-substantial" (ὑπερούσιος), "super-living" (ὑπέρζωος), and "super-wise" (ὑπέρσοφος).[88] which, incidentally, reflects Plotinus' use of "super-beautiful" (ὑπέρκαλος)[89] and "super-intellection" (ὑπερνόησις)[90] as attributes of the Divinity and Proclus' use of "super-substantial" (ὑπερούσιος), "super-living" (ὑπέρζωος) and "super-intellect" (ὑπέρνους) as predicates of, as he says, "every god."[91] Moreover, according to Dionysius the prefix "super" *(hyper)* need not be actually expressed; one may use any laudatory predicate of God with the understanding that it means in an eminent sense, for in a passage, in which he refers to the passage containing the list of predicates with the prefix "super" *(hyper)*, he says that in that latter passage has been explained in what sense the terms "good", "being", "life", "wisdom", and "power" are predicated of God.[92]

This is exactly what St. Thomas means by the way of "excellence" or "eminence". Every adjectival term, which is affirmative in form and cannot be explained as a causal relation, is to be predicated of God as if it had the particle "super" prefixed to it, denoting thereby that the term is predicated of God in an "excellent" or "eminent" sense. What that excellent or eminent sense means is explained by him in a passage, where, dealing with the predicate "knowing", he says: "We find that the more some things approach the First the more nobly they share in knowledge, as men more than brute beasts and angels more than men, whence

(82) *Sum. Theol.* I, 13, 1 c.
(83) *De Div. Nom.* 7, 3 (*P. G.* 3, 872 A)..
(84) *De Fid. Orth.* I, 4 (*P. G.* 94, 800 C).
(85) 1 *Sent.* 35, 1, 1 c ; *De Potentia* 9, 7, Obj. 2.
(86) *Expos. in Divin. Nomin.*, VII, Lectio IV.
(87) *Op. cit.* (above n. 5), 4, 5, p. 21, l. 46 ; Greek text, I, 4 (*P. G.* 94, 800 C).
(88) *De Divin. Nomin.* I, 5 (*P. G.* 3, 593 CD) ; I, 7 (596 C) ; *De Myst. Theol.* i, 2 (1000 B).
(89) *Enn.* I, viii, 2.
(90) *Ibid.* VI, viii, 16.
(91) *Institutio Theologica* 115.
(92) *De Myst. Theol.* 3 (*P. G.* 3, 1033 A).

it necessarily follows that in God there should be found to exist the most noble knowledge".[93] Now this superlative degree of knowledge, or of any other predicate, which St. Thomas allows of God could not mean something which, however superlative, had some numerical relation to something similar predicated of creatures, for with regard to knowledge he explicitly says that "the knowledge of God extends to infinite things"[94] and that "the knowledge of the infinite is infinite."[95] Accordingly God's knowledge is infinite and, being infinite, it can have no numerical relation to the finite knowledge of any creature. Similarly, with regard to God's power, he argues that it must be infinite and that «the infinite exceeds the finite beyond all proportion».[96] By the same token, he would argue that all other predicates of God must be infinite and hence must have no numerical relation to similar predicates applied to creatures. Thus predicates which St. Thomas interprets in the excellent or eminent sense mean predicates which are applied to God in an infinite sense and have no numerical relation to similar predicates applied to creatures.

But here a question may be raised. Are not predicates which are applied to God in an infinite sense and have no relation to similar predicates applied to creatures really negations, the negation of finitude and of numerical relationship? Dionysius seems to have thought so, for after his enumeration of the eminent predicates "super-good", "super-God", "super-substantial", "super-living", and "super-wise", he says that all these eminent predicates and others like them belong to what he describes as "eminent remotion" (ὑπεροχικὴ ἀφαίρεσις),[97] that is to say, they are remotions expressed in the form of eminence. Similarly when John Damascene interprets "darkness" to mean "super-light" (ὑπὲρ τὸ φῶς), he refers to this interpretation of "darkness" as "eminent remotion" (ὑπεροχικὴ ἀφαίρεσις),[98] that is to say, it is eminence expressed in the form of remotion. Maimonides, while not dealing with what St. Thomas calls "eminence", deals with what is implied in eminence, namely, the absence of numerical relation Thus, starting with the premise that there can be no numerical relation between any predicate of God and any similar predicate of creatures, he concludes that all attributes predicated of God in affirmative propositions must be taken as equivocal terms, by which he means that they are negative in meaning.[99] Since eminence implies negation, how, then, could

(93) *1 Sent.* 35, 1, 1 c.
(94) *Sum. Theol.* I, 14, 12 c.
(95) *Ibid.* III, 10, 3, Obj. 2.
(96) *Ibid.* I, 105, 8, Obj. 2.
(97) *De divin. Nomin.* 2, 3 (*P. G.* 3, 640 B).
(98) *De Fid. Orth.* I, 12 (*P. G.* 94, 848 B); cf. I, 4 (800 C).
(99) *Moreh Nebukim* I, 56; Latin, I, 55; cf. *op. cit.* (above n. 30) p. 413.

St. Thomas justify the indiscriminate application of the eminential interpretation to all attributes, after he had explicitly rejected the interpretation of "good, wise, and the like" as negations?

In answer to this question, I imagine, St. Thomas would try to show that there is a difference between interpreting "good, wise, and the like" negatively and interpreting them eminentially, even though the latter also implies negation. For, he would argue, in the problem of divine attributes the basic assumption is that one must not only have a right conception of God but one must also express that right conception of God in appropriate terms, and appropriate terms are those which would not lead the unwary into any kind of misapprehension. In his opinion, he would conclude, the kind of misapprehension which he had found to be feared of in the use of the negative interpretation is not to be feared of in the use of the eminential interpretation.

4. *Neque Univoce Neque Aequivoce*

Two modes of interpreting divine attributes, described as « univocal » *(univocus)* and "aequivocal" *(aequivocus)*, are both rejected by St. Thomas.[100]

The term *univocus* is the conventional Latin translation of the Greek συνώνυμος, which Greek term, in its logical use as distinguished from its rhetorical use,[101] is explained by Aristotle as referring to a term which applies to things in the same sense, without any difference at all, as for instance, the term "animal" in its application to "man" and "ox".[102] No reference is made by St. Thomas to anyone who interpreted divine attributes univocally; probably he knew of nobody who did so; the subject is discussed by him as a mere hypothetical suggestion. Indeed, Maimonides intimates that the Muslim Mutakallimun were of this opinion. But in the Latin translation of the work of Maimonides used by St. Thomas this intimation of Maimonides, which even in the original is not quite clear, was still further made vague. The statement of Maimonides in the Arabic original, as well as in its two Hebrew versions, reads as follows :

> "Nor should you think that these terms are predicated [of God] in an ambiguous sense, for terms which are predicated in an ambiguous sense are those which are predicated of two things between which there is a similitude in respect to something, which something is an accident in both of them, without constituting the essence of either of them;

(100) *Sum. Theol.* I, 13, 5 ; *Cont. Gent.* I, 32-34; *De Verit.* 2, 11 c ; *De Pot.* 7, 7 c ; *Compend. Theol.* I, 27.

(101) *Rhet.* III, 2, 1405 a, 1-2.

(102) *Categ.* 1, 1 a, 6-12.

but none of the things attributed to God are accidents, according to the view of anyone who has speculated on the subject, whereas the attributes predicated of us are all accidents, according to the opinion of the Mutakallimūn. Would that I knew, therefore, wherefrom came the similitude [between God's attributes and ours], so that they could be included under one definition and be predicated in a univocal sense (Arabic: *bi-tawāṭu'*, Hebrew: *be-haskamah*), as they assert."[103]

The same statement in the Latin translation reads as follows:

> Nec putes quod illa nomina sint ambigua vel per transumptionem dicta, quia nomina quae sic dicuntur conveniunt in duobus inter quae est similitudo aliquo modo, et illud in quo conveniunt est accidens et non intrat in substantiam alicuius istorum. Ista vero quae attribuuntur Creatori non sunt accidentia, secundum quemlibet magistrum speculationis. Dispositiones autem illae quae nobis conveniunt omnes sunt accidentia, secundum sensum Loquentium. Velle scire, nolle, unde provenit similitudo per quam contingat ea terminus idem et dicantur convenire, sicut putant.[104]

The use of the term *convenire*, in the third word before the last in the Latin quotation, instead of the term *univoce* or *secundum univocationem*, which is required by the underlying Arabic and Hebrew terms, has failed to bring out the fact that the Mutakallimūn, according to Maimonides, interpreted divine attributes univocally.

The term *aequivocus* is the conventional Latin translation of the Greek ὁμώνυμος, as used by Aristotle. In what sense Aristotle uses this term may be gathered from three passages, one in the *Categories*, another in *De Partibus Animalium*, and a third in the *Physics*. In the *Categories* the term equivocal has only one sense, which is illustrated by the term "animal" in its application to a "man" and to the "picture of a man".[105] In *De Partibus Animalium* he similarly uses the term "equivocally" (ὁμώνυμος) with reference to "man" in its application to a living body and a dead body of a man and the term "hand" to a real hand and to a hand of bronze or wood.[106] In the *Physics*, however, Aristotle enumerates three senses of the term equivocal.

The first of these three senses is described by him as the application of a term to things which are "very much distant [from one another]".[107] In his comment on this statement Simplicius explains this first sense of "equivocal" as applying to a term whose different senses are "those

(103) *Moreh Nebukim* I, 56.
(104) *Op. cit.*, I, 55, fol. 21 b, ll. 13-19.
(105) *Categ.* 1, 1 a, 2-3.
(106) *De Part. Animal.* I, 1, 640 b, 33-641 a, 1.
(107) *Phys.* VII, 4, 249 a, 23-24.

which originate casually (ἀπὸ τύχης)."[108] This explanation reflects Aristotle's statement in his *Nicomachean Ethics* that the term "good" cannot be applied to various things which are only "casually equivocal" (ἀπὸ τύχης ὁμωνύμοις).[109] Porphyry, in an enumeration of the various senses of the term equivocal, which is based upon this one of Aristotle, similarly describes the first type as that whose various senses originated "casually" and illustrates it by the example of the name "Alexander" which refers both to the son of Priam and to the son of Philip of Macedonia.[110]

The second sense of the term equivocal is described by him as the application of a term to things which "possess a certain similitude (ὁμοιότητα)."[111] In Simplicius this is explained "as images to their prototypes"[112], which quite evidently refers to Aristotle's use of the term equivocal in the *Categories*, where it is illustrated by the example of "man" and "the picture of a man."[113] The same illustration of this second sense of equivocal terms is also used in Porphyry.[114]

The third sense of the term equivocal is described as a term applied to various things which "are near either in genus or in analogy, on which account they seem not to be equivocal though they really are."[115] What is meant by being near "in genus" is of no concern to us here; but, as to what is meant here by being near in "analogy" is illustrated by Simplicius by the Greek term ἀρχή, "beginning", "principle", "source", in its application to "a spring", "the heart", "the unit", "the point", and "the ruler", for all of them bear a relationship to something as that of a "beginning" or "principle" or "source," a relationship which may be expressed in the following proportion—spring: river : : heart: animal : : unit: number : : point: line : : ruler: city.[116] All this reflects Aristotle's own definition and illustrations of "analogy", which we shall discuss in the next section of this paper.

It is the first sense of the term equivocal mentioned by Aristotle in the *Physics*, the one identified by his commentators with the "casually equivocal", that St. Thomas rejects as an interpretation of divine attributes. Thus in his *Compendium Theologiae*, the statement that terms are not predicated of "God and other things... in an altogether equivocal sense *(omnino aequivoce)* is explained as "those which are

(108) *Simplicius in Physica*, ed. Diels, p. 1096, l. 29
(109) *Eth. Nic.* I, 6, 1096 b, 26-27.
(110) *Porphyrius in Categorias*, ed. Busse, p. 65, ll. 22-24.
(111) *Op. cit.* 249 a, 24.
(112) *Op. cit.*, p. 1096, l. 30.
(113) *Categ.* 1, 1 a, 2-3.
(114) Porphyry, *op. cit.*, p. 65, ll. 25-30.
(115) *Op. cit.*, 24-25.
(116) *Op. cit.*, p. 1097, ll. 2-4.

casually *(casu)* equivocal".[117] The expression "in an altogether equivocal sense" used here is the same as the expression "in a purely equivocal sense *(pure aequivoce)*" used in the *Summa Theologiae* in his rejection of this kind of interpretation of divine attributes.[118] Moreover, in his *Summa Theologiae* he explicitly says that the expression "in a purely equivocal sense" does not apply to the term "equivocal" used as a description of the term "animal" in its application to "a real animal and a pictured animal",[119] by which he means that it does not apply to the second sense of the term equivocal mentioned in the *Physics*,[120] the implication being that it applies only to the first sense, which St. Thomas in his commentary on the *Physics* illustrates by the term "dog" in its application to "the celestial star and the barking animal",[121] an illustration which is like that of "Alexander" in its application to the Son of Priam and the son of Philip used, as we have seen above, by Porphyry as an illustration of the "casually equivocal." The illustration of the term "dog", it may be remarked in passing, is an old one. It occurs in Philo[122] and in John Damascene.[123]

In his discussion of the equivocal interpretation of divine attributes in *Summa Theologiae* I, 13, 5c, St. Thomas refers to "some" *(aliqui)* who have approved of it, without specifying who they are. In *De Potentia* 7, 7c, however, after stating that certain persons were of this opinion *(quidam... dixerunt)*, he adds that "Rabbi Moses is of this opinion, as is clear from his words." Who, then, are those others besides Maimonides who interpreted divine predicates equivocally? Let us trot out all the possible candidates, including those who were unknown to St. Thomas.

First, there are the Gnostics Basilides and his son Isidore. Hippolytus, speaking of their interpretation of divine attributes, says: "Aristotle, born many generations before Basilides, was the first to discourse, in the *Categories*, upon the subject of equivocal terms (ὁμώνυμα), which these men expound as their own and as a novelty."[124] Here it would seem that both Basilides and Isidore interpreted divine attributes equivocally. But it is doubtful whether the term "equivocal" is used here in that strictly technical sense which is meant by St. Thomas'expression *pure aequivoce*. In the passage quoted, it will be noted, Hippolytus refers

(117) *Compend., Theol.* I, 27.
(118) *Sum. Theol.* I, 13, 5 c,
(119) *Ibid.* I, 13, 10, ad 4.
(120) Cf. above at nn. 110-113.
(121) St. Thomas, *In VII, Phys.*, Lectio VIII, No. 8 (Leonine ed., Rome, 1884) cf. *In Metaph.*, Lectio I, No. 535.
(122) *De Plant. Noe* 37, 151
(123) *Dialectica* 31 (*P. G.* 94, 596 B).
(124) *Refutatio Omnium Haeresium* VII, 20, 5 (ed. Wendland).

to Aristotle's use of the term "aequivocal" in his *Categories*, that is, *Categories* 1, 1a, 1-6. But the term "equivocal" in the *Categories*, as we have seen, was not taken by Greek commentators of Aristotle to have been used in the sense of what St. Thomas calls *pure aequivoce.*

Second, there is Alfarabi. In a passage dealing with divine attributes, he refers to them as "equivocal terms" *(al-asmā' al-mushtarakah).*[125] But his immediate explanation that these attributes are predicated of God and creatures according to prior and posterior shows that he did not use the term "equivocal" in the strictly technical sense of "purely equivocal" but rather in the sense of "ambiguous" in which, as we shall soon see, the term "equivocal" was sometimes used in Arabic philosophy.

Third, there is Averroes' Long Commentary on the *Metaphysics*, which was known to St. Thomas, and reference to which is given in the Ottawa edition of the *Summa Theologiae* in a note on I, 13, 5c. In that Long Commentary, Averroes says: "And therefore this term knowledge is predicated in an equivocal sense *(aequivoce; arabic: bi-ishtirāk)* of God's knowledge and ours."[126] A similar statement occurs in his *Tahāfut al-Tahāfut.*[127] But here, again, it is doubtful whether Averroes really uses the term "equivocal" in its strictly technical sense of pure equivocation, and this for several reasons. First, we know that Averroes was acquainted with the difference between the use of "equivocal" in its loose sense and its use in its strictly technical sense of pure equivocations, for, commenting upon a passage where Aristotle says that the terms "much" and "equal" and "one" and "two" are equivocal,[128] he says: "But it is to be noted that these terms are not pure aequivocals *(aequivoca pura)* but are of that mode of equivocals which are called ambiguous."[129] Second, in his refutation of Algazali, Averroes argues that such terms as "existent" *(al-maujūd)*, "thing" *(al-shai)*, "being" *(al-huwiyyah)*, and "substance" *(dhāt)*[130] and also the term "intellect"[131] are predicated of God neither as univocal terms *(asmā' mutawāṭi'ah)* nor as equivocal but as what he calls ambiguous terms *(asmā' mushakkikah).* Third, the reason given by him in his Long Commentary on the *Metaphysics* for describing "knowing" as an equivocal divine predicate, namely, that "God's knowledge is the cause of that which exists, whereas that which

(125) *Kitāb al-Siyasāt al-Madaniyyah*, p. 20, l. 14 (ed. HYDERABAD, 1346 A. H.); cf. *op. cit.* (above n. 29), p. 555.

(126) AVERROES, *In XII Metaph.*, Comm. 51, fol. 337 B; Arabic: *Tafsir ma ba'd attabi'at*, p. 1708, l. 3 (ed. M. BOUYGES, Vol. III, 1948).

(127) *Averroes: Tahafot at-tahafot* XII, § 7, p. 462, ll. 4-5 (ed. M. BOUYGES, 1939).

(128) *Phys.* VII, 4, 248 b, 15-21

(129) AVERROES, *In VII Phys.*, Comm. 26, fol. 328 I.

(130) *Tahafut al-Tahafut* VII, § 4, p. 369, ll. 3-13.

(131) *Ibid.* VII, § 37, p. 387, ll. 11 ff.

exists is the cause of our knowledge"[132] reflects, as we shall see, the general description of ambiguous terms. On the whole, the term "equivocal", in Arabic philosophy, unless modified by the term "pure" or "absolute" or contrasted with the term "ambiguous", does not necessarily mean equivocal in the strict sense of the term. Thus, while St. Thomas may have had Averroes in mind when he spoke of more than one who interpreted divine attributes as equivocal terms, it is not quite certain that Averroes really interpreted them as such.

Maimonides, I make bold to say, was the first, and the only one, who knowingly set out to interpret divine attributes in what he himself describes as "in a purely equivocal sense" (Arabic: *bil-ishtirāk al-maḥḍ;* Hebrew of al-Ḥarizi: *be-shittuf amitti*, and of Ibn Tibbon: *be-shittuf gamur*).[133] This expression is translated in the Latin translation of al-Ḥarizi's Hebrew version, used by St. Thomas, by the words *aequivoce pure*,[134] the very same words used by him in his *Summa Theologiae.* In his treatise on Logic, it may be remarked in passing, Maimonides illustrates that which he calls "equivocal in a purely equivocal sense"[135] by two examples, on of which is the term "dog" in its application both "to the celestial constellation Canis and to the animal which barks".[136]

5. *Secundum Analogiam*

As the opposite of terms used either univocally or equivocally, which he rejects as divine attributes, St. Thomas mentions terms used "according to analogy" *(secundum analogiam)* or "analogically" *(analogice)*, which he accepts as divine attributes.[137] By the time of St. Thomas the Greek term *analogia* had already long been domesticated in the Latin language, so that in the Latin translations of Aristotle, used by St. Thomas, the Greek ἀναλογία is sometimes merely transliterated into the Latin *analogia*,[138] though sometimes it is translated by *similitudo*[139] or *proportionalitas.*[140] Most often, however, it is translated by *pro-*

(132) *Loc. cit.* (above n. 126).

(133) *Moreh Nebukim* I, 56, Latin, I, 55.

(134) Which is much closer to the original Arabic than to the Hebrew, from which it was directly translated. Is it possible that the Latin translator made use also of the Arabic original?

(135) The Arabic original here, we assume, was *bil-ishtirāk al-maḥḍ*, as in *Moreh Nebukim* I, 56.

(136) *Millot ha-Higgayon* 13

(137) *Sum. Theol.* I, 13, 5 c.

(138) *Metaph.* V, 6, 1016 b, 32; See κατ ἀναλογία in *Metaph.* XII, 4, 1070a, 31; XII, 4, 1070 b, 26; *Eth. Nic.* (*Antiqua*) I, 4, 1096 b, 28.

(139) *Phys.* VII, 4, 249 a, 25.

(140) *Eth. Nic. (Antiqua)* V, 6, 1131 a, 31.

portio.[141] As to its meaning, Aristotle, in the *Nicomachean Ethics*, says that "analogy (ἀναλογία) is equality of ratios (λόγων)",[142] and he illustrates it in one place of that work, by the proportion A: B: : C: D,[143] and, in another place of the same work, by the term "good" in its application to "intellect" and "sight", on the ground that "intellect is to the soul as sight to the body."[144] This use of the term "analogy" is, of course, reproduced by St. Thomas in his Commentary on the *Nicomachean Ethics*.[145]

But then St. Thomas uses the term analogy in senses which do not occur in Aristotle.

First, in his *Summa Theologiae* he says that the term "animal" is predicated of "a real animal and a pictured animal" not "in a purely equivocal sense" but rather "in an analogical sense."[146] An example like this, as we have seen, is used by Aristotle in the *Categories* as an illustration of "equivocal", and it is this example which both Simplicius and Porphyry, as have seen, use as an illustration of the second sense of the term equivocal in the *Physics*, described by Aristotle as applying to things which "possess a certain similitude."

Second, in his Commentary on the *Metaphysics*,[147] St. Thomas applies the term analogical to that which Aristotle describes as a term "used in many senses (λέγεται πολλαχῶς), but with reference to one, and to one certain nature and not in an equivocal sense."[148] This is subdivided by Aristotle into two sub-senses.

The first sub-sense of this multivocal, but non-equivocal, term is illustrated by Aristotle, as explained by St. Thomas in his Commentary,[149] by the application of the term "health" to "a diet," "to medicine", to "urine", and to "an animal", and of the term "medical" to a physician, to a student of medicine, to a drug, and to a scalpel.[150] These terms "health" and "medical" are said to be used "multivocally" and not "univocally" because they are applied to different things for different reasons, for a diet is called healthy because it preserves health, medicine because its produces health, urine because it is a symptom of health, and an animal because it is receptive and susceptive of health, and

(141) *Phys.* IV, 8, 215 b, 29 ; VIII, 10, 266 b, 19 ; *Metaph.* V, 6, 1016 b, 34 ; 1017 a, 2 ; VII, 4, 249 a, 25

(142) *Eth. Nic.* V, 6, 1131 a, 31 ; cf. *Metaph.* V, 6, 1016 b, 34-35.

(143) *Ibid.*, 1131 b, 5-6

(144) *Ibid.* I, 4, 1096 b, 28-29.

(145) St. Thomas, *In I Eth. ad Nic.* Lectio VII ; *In. V*, Lectio V.

(146) *Sum. Theol.* I, 13, 10 ad 4.

(147) St. Thomas, *In IV Metaph.*, Lectio I, No. 535.

(148) *Metaph.* IV, 2, 1003 a, 33-34.

(149) *Op. cit.*, Nos. 537-538.

(150) Cf. *Top.* II, 3, 110 b, 16-19 ; *Metaph.* XI, 3, 1060 b, 36-1061 a, 7.

similarly a physician is called medical because he has mastered the art of medicine, a student because he is capable of learning the art of medicine, and a drug and scalpel because they are necessary for the art of medicine. Still these two terms in their multivocal usages are not equivocal terms, for in all their variety of application they are related to one thing, the former to "health", the latter to the "art of medicine".

The second sub-sense of this multivocal, but non-equivocal, term is illustrated by the term "being" (τὸ ὄν, *ens*) in its application to "substance" (ουσία) and to the "affections (πάθη) of substance",[151] that is to say, the qualitative accidents of substance,[152] and by the same token to all the other accidents of substance, for all these accidents, again, are "related to one principle" (πρὸς μίαν ἀρχήν)[153] that is to say, to substance, in which all accidents exist as in a subject and apart from which they cannot exist. And because accidents exist only in substance and through substance, Aristotle says that the term "being" applies "first" (πρώτως) to substance and "next" (ἑπομένως) to accidents,[154] that is to say, it applies to substance and accidents according to the distinction of "prior and posterior", where the terms "prior" and "posterior" are to be understood to mean "cause" and "effect".[155]

How, then, did St. Thomas come to apply the term analogical to these two cases, namely, (1) to Aristotle's second sense of the term equivocal in the *Physics;* (2) to Aristotle's two sub-senses of multivocal non-equivocal terms in the *Metaphysics.*

I venture to offer two explanations.

The first explanation, which applies only to the first of the two cases mentioned, is to be found in St. Thomas' understanding of the use of the term "similitude", in the Latin translation of Aristotle, in the sense of "analogy".

In several places of his writings, St. Thomas uses the expression *similitudo analogiae*,[156] sometimes adding after *analogiae* the words *vel proportionis*.[157] This Latin expression may be traced to the expression ἡ ἀνάλογον ὁμοιότης in Aristotle.[158] Now the second sense of the term equivocal in *Physics* VII, 4, 249a, 24, is described by Aristotle as terms which possess τινα ὁμοιότητα, which in the Latin translation used by St. Thomas reads: *quandam similitudinem.* In view of the fact that to St. Thomas, as well as to Aristotle, there was a certain kind of "simi-

(151) *Ibid.*, 5-7.
(152) Cf. *Scholia in Aristotelem*, ed. C. A. Brandis (1836), 638 b, 31 sqq.
(153) *Loc. cit.*, 6.
(154) *Metaph.* VII, 4, 1030 a, 21-22 ; cf. VII, 1, 1028 a, 10-20.
(155) *Categ.* 12, 14 a, 10-13.
(156) *2 Sent.* 16, 1, 2, ad 5 ; *De Potentia* 3, 4, ad 9.
(157) *1 Sent.* 31, 2, 1, ad 2.
(158) *De Part. Animal.* I, 4, 644 b, 11

litude" which he described as that "of analogy", we may assume that he took the expression *quandam similitudinem* here in the sense of analogy, and this perhaps on the additional ground that in the third kind of equivocal terms in *Physics* VII, 4, 249a, 24-25, the Greek ἢ ἀναλογίᾳ is translated in the Latin version used by St. Thomas by *aut similitudine,* where from Simplicius' Commentary on this passage,[159] which was available to him in Latin translation, he could have learned that *aut similitudine* here is used in the sense of *aut analogia.*

The second explanation, which applies to both cases, is to be found in St. Thomas' recognition of the fact that the Aristotelian term "analogical" is the same as the post-Aristotelian term "amphibolous" or "ambiguous".

In his discussion of analogy St. Thomas says that though the idea in analogies is not "totally diverse as in equivocals," still an analogical term is "a term which, after a certain manner, is used in many senses" *(nomen quod sic multipliciter dicitur).*[160] Now the expression *multipliciter dicitur* used here by St. Thomas reflects Aristotle's expression λέγεται πολλαχῶς, in connection with which Aristotle says that of terms which are λέγεται πολλαχῶς there are those which are used "not equivocally... but in some other way".[161] In Alexander's commentary on Aristotle's *Topics* these terms, "used in many senses... not equivocally... but in some other way", are described an "amphibolous" or "ambiguous" terms (ἀμφίβολα).[162] From a combination of these two statements it may be gathered that what Alexander calls "ambiguous" St. Thomas calls "analogical". Now it happens that the Arabic philosophers adopted from Alexander the term "ambiguous" (Arabic: *mushakkikah*)[163] and used it as a description of any kind of multivocal term which while, not equivocal in the strict sense of "casually equivocal", is also not univocal, and hence is the equivalent of "analogical", for, according to Aristotle, the analogical differs, on the one hand, from the "casually equivocal"[164] and, on the other, from "one in genus",[165] that is to say, from the univocal.[166] Now it happens that the second sense of the term univocal in the *Physics*, which in the original Greek is described as possessing "a certain similitude", is in the Latin translation from the Arabic translation from the Greek, which was available to St. Thomas,

(159) Cf. above at nn. 115-116.
(160) *Sum Theol.* I, 13, 5 c.
(161) *Top.* II, 3, 110 b, 16-17 ; *Metaph.* IV, 2, 1003 a, 33-34.
(162) *Alexander in Topica*, ed. M. Wallies (1891), p. 97, ll. 22-23 ; p. 152, ll. 7-8.
(163) Cf. my paper "Amphibolous Terms in Aristotle, Arabic Philosophy, and Maimonides", *Harvard Theological Review*, 31 (1938), pp. 151-171. In *Studies* I, 455-477.
(164) *Eth. Nic.* I, 4, 1096 b, 26-28.
(165) *Metaph.* V, 6, 1016 b, 32.
(166) *Categ.* 1, 1 a, 6-12.

described as "possessing a certain ambiguity".[167] We may, therefore, assume that it is because of this description of the second sense of the term equivocal in the *Physics* as "possessing a certain ambiguity" that St. Thomas applies to it the term "analogical". For a similar reason St. Thomas also applies the term analogical to the two sub-senses of multivocal non-equivocal terms in the *Metaphysics*, for these terms are described by Aristotle as "terms used in many senses," and the expression "terms used in many senses", which Alexander and the Arabs have taken to mean "ambiguous", St. Thomas, as we have seen, has taken to mean "analogical".

There are thus, according to St. Thomas, altogether four senses of the term "analogical", corresponding to Aristotle's second and third senses of the term "equivocal" in the *Physics*, the third sense of which being the same as the "analogical" in the *Nicomachean Ethics*, and his two sub-senses of multivocal non-equivocal terms in the *Metaphysics*. They are as follows: *first*, a term applied to two things because one is the image of the other, as "man" is applied to a real man and to his picture; *second*, a term applied to two things because the relation of one of these things to a third thing is like the relation of the second of these two things to a fourth thing, as "good" is applied to intellect and to sight because intellect is to mind as sight to eye; *third*, a term applied to several things because they are all related in various ways to one thing, as the term "healthy" is applied to diet, medicine, urine and animal, or the term "medical" is applied to physician, student, drug, and scalpel, because they are all related to one thing, to "health" or to the "art of medicine"; *fourth*, a term applied to two things because one of the things is the subject in which and through which the other exists, as the term "being" is applied to "substance" and "accident". This last kind of analogy is described as that which is "according to prior and posterior" *(secundum prius et posterius)*, where the term prior is used in the sense in which it is applied, according to Aristotle, to a thing which in some respect is the cause of the existence of another thing.[168]

In the light of these four senses in which St. Thomas uses the term analogical, the question is, which of these senses is accepted by him as the interpretation of divine attributes? To answer this question, let us examine in chronological order representative passages in which he deals with analogy.

The earliest discussion of the analogical interpretation of divine attributes occurs in his *De Veritate*,[169] which was composed during the years 1256-1259. In that work, St. Thomas begins with a distinction

(167) Averroes, *In VII Phys.*, Text. 31, fol. 331 E; Comm. 31, fol. 331 I.
(168) *Categ.* 12, 14 b, 11-13.
(169) *De verit.* 2, 11 c.

between two senses of the term analogy. One of these senses he calls "proportion" *(proportio)* and is explained by him as that in which one of two things has a relation to the other, such as, for instance, 2 is the double of 1. The second sense of analogy he calls "proportionality" *(proportionalitas)* and is explained by him as that in which two proportions are similar to one another, such as, for instance, 6: 3 : : 4:2. This distinction between *proportinalitas* and *proportio* is based upon the terminology used in the Old Latin translation of the *Nicomachean Ethics*, in which Aristotle's statement ἡ γὰρ ἀναλογία ἰσότης ἐστὶ λόγων[170] is rendered *proportionalitas enim aequalitas est proportionis.*[171] Strictly speaking, then, only *proportionalitas* represents what Aristotle in this passage calls *analogia; proportio* does not represent here *analogia*; it represents only what Aristotle calls here λόγος, *ratio*, "ratio". St. Thomas, however, not knowing what the underlying Greek terms here were, took the term *analogia* to include also *proportio*. The reason why he thought that *analogia* includes here *proportio* is that the term *proportio*, as we have seen,[172] is the most common translation of the Greek *analogia* in the Latin translations of the works of Aristotle used by St. Thomas, and moreover, there is one short passage in the Latin translation of *Metaphysics* V, 6 (1016b, 32 and 34, and 1017a, 2) where the terms *analogia* and *proportio* are used interchangeably. In fact, St. Thomas explicitly says *secundum analogiam, idest proportionem*,[173] thus identifying "analogy" with "proportion".

With this distinction between the two senses of analogy, St. Thomas proceeds to illustrate them by examples.

His first sense of analogy, that which he calls "proportion" but is really "ratio", corresponds to two senses of analogy in our classification, the *fourth* and the *third* respectively. As corresponding to the *fourth* sense in our classification, it is illustrated by the same example as that which we have reproduced from Aristotle in our classification, namely, the term "being" in its application to substance and accidents. As corresponding to the *third* sense in our classification, it is similarly illustrated by the same example as that which we have reproduced from Aristotle in our classification, namely, the term "healthy" in its application to urine and animal.

His second sense of analogy, that which he calls "proportionality", corresponds to the *second* sense in our classification and is illustrated by an example which is only a slightly modified form of the example which we have reproduced from Aristotle in our classification. It is the term

(170) *Eth. Nic.* V, 6, 1131 a 31 ; cf. above at n. 142
(171) St. Thomas, *In V Eth. ad Nic.*, Lectio V.
(172) Cf. above at nn. 138-141.
(173) *Sum. Theol.* I, 13, 5 c.

"sight" as applied to bodily sight and to the intellect, "because", he says, "intellect is in the mind as sight is in the body".

Of these two senses of analogy, St. Thomas rejects the first, which is the *fourth* and *third* in our classification, as an interpretation of divine attributes, and accepts only the second, which is also the *second* in our classification. In his subsequent writings, however, we shall now try to show, he reversed himself and accepted that sense of analogy which corresponds to the *fourth* sense in our classification.

In his *Contra Gentiles*,[174] which was composed at about 1260, St. Thomas, again, distinguishes between two senses of analogy. One sense, which corresponds to the *third* in our classification, is illustrated by the same example as that which we have reproduced from Aristotle in our classification, namely, the term "healthy" in its application to animal, medicine, food, and urine. The other sense, which corresponds to the *fourth* in our classification, is similarly illustrated by the same example as that which we have reproduced from Aristotle in our classification, namely, the term "being" in its application to substance and accident.

Of these two senses of analogy St. Thomas selects the second, corresponding to the *fourth* in our classification, as an interpretation of divine attributes.

A distinction between two senses of the term analogy is also to be found in *De Potentia*,[175] which was composed during the years 1265-1268. One sense, corresponding to the *third* sense in our classification, is described as that in which "something is predicated of two things on account of their relation to some third thing" and is illustrated by a term borrowed from the illustration which we have reproduced from Aristotle in the *fourth* sense of our classification, but it is used in such a way as to form an illustration like that which we have reproduced from Aristotle in the *third* sense of our classification. It is the term "being" as applied to "quality and quantity on account of their relation to substance". What he means to say is that "being" is applied to "quality and quantity", because "quality" and "quantity" are both related to one thing, a third thing, namely "substance", for they both exist in substance, and "substance" is that which is primarily called "being." The other sense, corresponding to the *fourth* sense in our classification, is described as that in which "something is predicated of two things on account of the relation of one of them to the other" and is illustrated by the same example as that which we have reproduced from Aristotle in the *fourth* sense of our classification, namely, the term "being" in its application

(174) *Cont. Gent.* I, 34.
(175) *De Potentia* 7, 7 c.

to "substance" and "quality", that is to say, to "substance" and "accident".

Of these two senses of analogy St. Thomas, as in *Contra Gentiles*, approves of the second, which is the *fourth* in our classification.

A similar distinction between two senses of the term analogy is given by St. Thomas in his *Summa Theologiae*,[176] which was composed during the years 1265-1272. Here, too, he distinguishes between two senses of analogy. The first sense, corresponding to the *third* in our classification, is described as that in which "many things are proportional to one", and is illustrated by the same example as that which we have reproduced from Aristotle in our classification, namely, the term "healthy" in its application to medicine and urine, for medicine and urine are both related to one thing, that is health, since medicine is the "cause" of it and urine a "symptom" of it. The second sense, corresponding to the *fourth* in our classification, is described as that in which "one thing is proportional to another" and is illustrated by a term borrowed, again, from the illustration we have reproduced from Aristotle in the *third* sense of our classification, but it is used in such a way as to form an illustration like that which we have reproduced from Aristotle in the *fourth* sense of our classification. It is the term "healthy" in its application to "medicine and an animal", for of these two things, one, namely medicine, bears a causal relation to the other, namely, animal, "since medicine", he says, "is the cause of the health of an animal".

Of these two senses of analogy he, again, approves of the second, which corresponds to the *fourth* in our classification.

Finally, in his *Compendium Theologiae*, composed in 1273, he says that terms are predicated of God and other things "according to analogy, that is, according to a proportion to one *(secundum proportionem ad unum)*."[177] Here the expression *secundum proportionem ad unum* is rather vague, for it may be an abridged form of *secundum quod multa habent respectum ad aliquod unum* (*Cont. Gent.* I, 34) and hence the *third* sense in our classification, or it may be an abridged form of *secundum quod duorum attenditur ordo vel respectus... ad unum ipsorum (ibid.)* and hence the *fourth* sense in our classification. However, the description of analogy here as being *secundum proportionem ad unum* and the subsequent distinction between terms "predicated priorily of creatures" and terms "predicated priorily of God" correspond exactly to an article in the *Summa Theologiae* where analogy is similarly described simply as being *per respectum ad unum* and where a distinction is similarly made between terms which are "predicated priorily of creatures" and terms

(176) *Sum. Theol.* I, 13, 5 c.
(177) *Compend. Theol.* I, 27.

"predicated priorily of God."[178] And inasmuch as we have already seen that the analogical interpretation of divine attributes adopted by St. Thomas in the *Summa* is of the *fourth* sense of analogy in our classification, the same sense of analogy must have undoubtedly been meant by him in his *Compendium*.

The analogical interpretation of divine attributes insisted upon by St. Thomas, as against Maimonides' equivocal interpretation, is not without precedent. All the Arabic philosophers interpret divine attributes as ambiguous terms,[179] which, as we have seen, is the same as analogical terms. Even Alfarabi and Averroes who happen to use the term equivocal as a description of divine attributes mean by equivocal, as we have seen, ambiguous.[180] The kind of ambiguity in accordance with which they interpret divine attributes is the same as the *fourth* kind of analogy in our classification, usually described as being "according to prior and posterior", that is, as a relation of cause and effect, and is illustrated by the term "being" as applied to substance and accident, for substance is the subject and hence also the cause in which and through which accidents exist. Before the Arabic philosophers, the analogical interpretation of divine attributes is to be found in Albinus and Plotinus. Though their conception of analogy is derived from Platonic sources, and not, as in St. Thomas and the Arabic philosophers, from Aristolelian sources, still they mean by it terms predicated of God and other beings because of the causal relationship that exists between God and other beings.[181] The only one in the history of philosophy who openly rejected "analogy", under the guise of "ambiguity", as an interpretation of divine attributes is Maimonides.[182]

But here a question may be raised. The analogical interpretation of divine attributes ultimately means their interpretation as causal relations. This, as we have see, is what Alexander and the Arabs meant by "ambiguity" and this is also what St. Thomas means by "analogy", for, at the conclusion of his explanation of the analogical interpretation of divine attributes, he says: "Hence, whatever is said of God and creatures is said according as there is some relation of the creature to God as to its principle and cause, wherein all the perfections pre-exist excellently."[183] Since analogy implies causal relation, how then, could St. Thomas justify his indiscriminate application of the analogical interpretation to all attributes, after he had explicitly rejected

(178) *Sum. Theol.* I, 13, 6 c.
(179) Cf. *op. cit.* (above n. 29).
(180) Cf. above at nn. 123-130.
(181) Cf. *op. cit.* (above n. 2), pp. 121-123.
(182) Cf. my paper "Maimonides and Gersonides on Divine Attributes as Ambiguous Terms", *Mordecai M. Kaplan Jubilee Volume*, 1953, pp. 515-530. Above, pp. 231-246.
(183) *Sum. Theol.* I, 13, 5 c.

the interpretation of "good, wise, and the like" as causal relations?[184]

In answer to this question, too, I imagine, St. Thomas would try to show that there is a difference between interpreting "good, wise, and the like" as causal relations and interpreting them analogically, even though the latter also implies causal relation. For, again, he would argue, the problem of divine attributes assumes not only that one must have a right conception of God but also that one must express that right conception of God in terms so appropriate as not to lead the unwary into any kind of misapprehension. In his opinion, he would then conclude, the kind of misapprehension which he had found to be feared of in the interpretation of "good, wise, and the like" as causal relations is not to be feared of in their interpretation as analogies.

Let us now sum up the result of our discussion.

In our discussion of *via negationis*, we have tried to show how St. Thomas came to use the term remotion as the equivalent of negation and how in a limited sense he also uses the term privation as the equivalent of negation. We have also tried to show how the negative interpretation of attributes did not start with Dionysius, who is often spoken of as the father of the so-called negative theology. Finally, we have tried to identify those referred to by St. Thomas as "some", from whom he differed as to the indiscriminate application of the negative interpretation to all terms which are affirmative in form, suggesting that St. Thomas could have found support for his view in St. Augustine.

In our discussion of *via causalitatis*, we have traced the history of this mode of interpretation. We have, again, tried to identify those referred to by St. Thomas as "others", from whom he differed as to the indiscriminate application of the causal or relative interpretation to all terms which are not causal or relative in form. Finally, we have tried to explain that there may be a good reason why his discussion here of causal relation, unlike his discussion of negation, contains no reference to Maimonides as one of those from whom he differed.

In our discussion of *via eminentiae*, we have, again, traced the history of the eminential interpretation of divine attributes. We have also tried to show how the eminential interpretation ultimately amounts to the same as the nagative interpretation, and hence we tried to explain how St. Thomas, who rejected the negative interpretation of certain attributes, still interpreted them eminentially.

In our discussion of *neque univoce neque aequivoce*, we have tried to explain why St. Thomas makes no reference to anyone who interpreted attributes univocally. We have also tried to determine which of the

(184) *Ibid.* I, 13, 2 c; cf. above at n. 47.

three senses of the term equivocal found in Aristotle is referred to by St. Thomas as the "purely" equivocal, which is rejected by him as an interpretation of divine attributes. Finally we have tried to show that there is no evidence that anyone besides Maimonides ever explicitly interpreted divine attributes as equivocal terms.

In our discussion of *secundum analogiam*, we have tried to show how in Aristotle analogy is used only in one sense and how in St. Thomas it is used in four senses, and hence we have tried to explain how St. Thomas came to add these three senses of analogy. We have also tried to show how of the four senses of analogy only one sense is accepted by St. Thomas as an interpretation of divine attributes and how there is a difference between his *De Veritate* and his later writings as to which one of the four senses of analogy is to be used as an interpretation of divine attributes. Finally we have tried to show how analogy implies causal relation, and hence we have tried to explain how St. Thomas, who rejected the interpretation of certain attributes as causal relations, still interpreted them an analogies.

Appendix

I tried to answer, in the foregoing, the question raised by me why in dealing with the negative interpretation of attributes St. Thomas ascribes it to Maimonides, whereas in dealing with the causative interpretation of attributes he does not similarly ascribe it to Maimonides. A more likely answer to the question is the following.

In his Commentary on the Sentences (*I Sent.* 2, 1, 3, ad tertium), written between 1254-1256, St. Thomas mentions both Avicenna and Maimonides as using the negative and the causative interpretations of attributes, and under each of these interpretations he gives two forms of interpretation, which we shall designate as Form I and Form II, and this Form II can be shown to reflect more closely the interpretations used by Maimonides. In *De Potentia* (Quaest. VII, Art. V), written between 1265-1267, he mentions only Maimonides as using these two methods of interpretations and under each of these two interpretations he gives only what corresponds to Form II in his Commentary on the Sentences, thus indicating that when he mentions only Maimonides as the user of these two methods of interpretation he ascribes to him only Form II. Now in *Summa Theologica* I, 13c, which part was written between 1266-1268, practically during the same time as *De Potentia*, for the negative interpretation he gives Form II, which in *De Potentia* he ascribes to Maimonides, whereas for the causative interpretation he gives Form I, which in *De Potentia* he does not ascribe to Maimonides. This, then, is the reason why here in the *Summa*, the negative interpretation is ascribed to Maimonides, whereas the causative interpretation is not ascribed by him to Maimonides.

18

ANSWERS TO CRITICISMS OF MY DISCUSSION OF PATRISTIC PHILOSOPHY

Three eminent scholars, Professors Robert M. Grant,[1] T. A. Burkill,[2] and Cyril C. Richardson,[3] in their reviews of my Religious Philosophy, have raised certain problems touching on topics in Patristic philosophy. The problems are of such importance as to call for further consideration.

I

In my attempt to show how, beginning with the Apologists, the Logos in John was interpreted in terms of the Philonic Logos, I remarked that, "from internal evidence of their writings, we may gather that they used the works of Philo as a sort of commentary upon Scripture" (p. 39). Upon this Professor Grant comments: "It may be so, . . . But I miss the presence of such evidence as one certainly finds in regard to the early Alexandrians."

If by evidence is meant what a pavement-beating policeman investigating a crime would mean by it, namely, eyewitnesses, then Professor Grant is right, for none of the Apologists, unlike the Alexandrians, refers to Philo by name. But prosecuting attorneys, as well as attorneys for the defense, look not only for eyewitnesses but also for circumstantial evidence, and scholarship is the proper use of circumstantial evidence. The circumstantial evidence in establishing the use of Philo by the Apologists is to be found in a comparison of their interpretation of certain scriptural verses with Philo's interpretation of the same verses. This is the method which has always been followed by students of Philo as well as by those of the Church Fathers. It is by this method that Carl Siegfried, for instance, in his Philo von Alexandria (1875), has shown the influence of Philo upon the scriptural interpretation of the Church Fathers, and he deals there not only with the

[1] Speculum 38 (1963), 164–65.
[2] The Philosophical Review 72 (1963), 257–60.
[3] Union Seminary Quarterly Review 18 (1963), 179–80.

Alexandrians and the later Fathers but also with the apocryphal Epistle of Barnabas, the anonymous Epistle to Diognetus, and such Apologists as Justin Martyr, pseudo-Justin, Tatian, Athenagoras, and Theophilus. The same method was followed by other students, among them Paul Heinisch in Der Einfluss Philos auf die älteste christliche Exegese (1908), in which, again, he begins with Barnabas and continues with the Apologists and others. By this time the influence of Philo upon the scriptural interpretation of the Apologists is to be considered a scholarly, established commonplace, concerning which, of course, Professor Grant is entitled to have his own private opinion.

II

Quoting me as saying that "Apollinarianism . . . was never called a Judaistic heresy," Professor Grant comments: "It is not quite correct. The eschatology of Apollinarius, at least, is called 'Judaism' by Basil (P. G., XXXII, 989 C) and Gregory of Nazianzus (P. G., XXXVI, 197 C and 1297)."

First, let me correct two misprints in the reference to P. G.— 989 C should read 980 C and XXXVI should read XXXVII.

Second, the "eschatology of Apollinarius" belongs to what is specifically known as "Millenarianism," and Millenarianism is something distinct and different from Apollinarianism. The latter is a Christological theory and, as the name implies, it is identified with Apollinaris, who was its founder. The former, an eschatological theory generally branded as Judaistic, was held by many Church Fathers, and Apollinaris only happens to share in it. But, though Apollinaris happens to be a Millenarian, the term Apollinarianism does not by any stretch of language include Millenarianism. I am quite certain that, if Professor Grant asked any one of his students what Apollinarianism was and the student answered that it was the belief that Christ, after his second coming, would rule on earth for one thousand years, he would not give that student credit even for half an answer. What, therefore, Basil and Gregory of Nazianzus branded as "Judaism" in Apollinaris was his Millenarianism; what in Apollinaris I dealt with was his Apollinarianism, and the twain are not to be confused.

Third, I did not say, as quoted by Professor Grant, that "Apollinarianism . . . was never called . . . a Judaistic heresy." From long experience I have learned to be careful about making universal negative assertions. What I did say was that "Apollinarianism, as far as I know, was never called . . . a Judaistic heresy" (p. 157). I am glad to see that, also as far as Professor Grant knows, Apollinarianism was never called a Judaistic heresy.

III

Commenting upon my distinction between the mythological conception of God as "begetter" and the scriptural conception of God as "artisan" (p. 145), Professor Grant asks "why the analogical description of God as a begetter is any more 'mythological' than that of God as an artisan."

If one uses the term "mythological" as the equivalent of the term "mythical" and in the sense of "having no foundation in fact" and "fictitious," and if, added to this, one thinks that any conception of God is fictitious and has no foundation in fact, then Professor Grant is right in his contention that both God as begetter and God as artisan are equally to be described as mythological. But if one uses the term "mythological" as a description of that which is to be found in what is technically known as Greek mythology, then only God as begetter is "mythological," for the gods in Greek mythology, in contradistinction to the God of Hebrew Scripture, happen to be begetters. It is in this sense that the term "mythological" was explicitly used by me.

IV

Professor Grant wonders whether I was right in my explanation that Augustine was led to his particular conception of concupiscence by the Latin version of Wisdom 8:21. He explains it on the ground of Augustine's struggle with sexual problems. So also did I wonder, and in the concluding sentence of my discussion I stated the problem in the following words: "As for his concupiscence, it is not clear whether it is based upon his own personal experience before his conversion or whether it is based upon a misunderstanding of the Latin translation of a Greek verse in the Book of the Wisdom of Solomon" (p. 176; cf. p. 167). I am glad to see that Professor Grant has cast his vote in favor of the first alternative suggested.

V

In the Sermonette at the conclusion of the book I said with reference to the Greek philosophic conceptions of God that some of them were regarded by the Fathers of the Church as "the paltry result of the blind groping of human reason for a truth which can be known only by faith and revelation" and that most of them were regarded as "only polite and empty phrases for the honest atheism of the fool in Scripture" (p. 271). Against this Professor Grant refers to "the favor which Xenophanes found in the eyes of Irenaeus and Clement of Alexandria" and to "the universal, though partial, revelation of the Logos in Justin and Clement."

In The Philosophy of the Church Fathers, in the light of which this statement in the Sermonette is to be read, I have discussed in great detail the attitude of the Fathers of the Church toward the religious beliefs of the Greek philosophers. The Fathers had all started with the assumption that the philosophers, by their God-given reason, discovered certain views about God which approximated the views about God as taught in the revealed Scriptures. But at the same time they all denied that the philosophers had ever reached the true scriptural view of God. Greek philosophers, I have shown, are divided by the Fathers into theists and atheists, but even the theists are regarded by them as having wrong conceptions about God, and often, because of these wrong conceptions about God, even the theists are called by them atheists, their theism thus being virtually dismissed as mere verbalism. Accordingly, while in their polemics against polytheism and idolatry or in their apologies for Christianity the Fathers are in the habit of invoking the names of philosophers who happen to speak of one unanthropomorphic deity or of trying to show how some philosophers anticipated the Christian doctrine of the Logos, they never really thought that these philosophers had a knowledge of the whole truth about God or of the whole truth about the Christian Logos. And so, even though some of the Fathers, in their propaganda against polytheism and idolatry, praised Xenophanes for his speaking of a God who is one and unlike mortal beings, they would never admit that his God was exactly the same God in whom they themselves believed. They knew, as we may gather from Hippolytus (Refutatio Omnium Haeresium, I, 14), that the God of Xenophanes did not create the world and they also knew, as they could have gathered from Aristotle (Metaph., I, 5, 986b, 21–27), that the God of Xenophanes was identical with the world. To the Fathers, therefore, Xenophanes' views on God, like those of any other Greek philosopher, were either "the paltry result of the blind groping of human reason for a truth which can be known only by faith and revelation" or "only polite and empty phrases for the honest atheism of the fool in Scripture."

VI

While Professor Grant tried to pin-prick certain particular statements in my collection of essays, Professor Burkill tried to brush away some of its main theses and conclusions.

Referring to my general thesis that the synthesis effected by Philo between Scripture and philosophy became the common view of the Church Fathers and to my attempt to interpret the Prologue in John in terms of Philo's Logos, he says: "Philo undoubtedly effected a synthesis of Hebraic and Greek thought, but syncretism had long been the order of the day in the Hellenistic world, and in all probability Christian theology would have taken on its synthetic character independently of Philonic influence. We cannot be sure that the author of the fourth gospel knew Philo's works; Gnosticism may have been operative in this connection, but Gnosticism is not discussed."

The facts in the case are as follows:

(1) In the very first chapter of my Philo I called attention to certain attempts made before the time of Philo to harmonize pagan popular religions with Greek philosophy, but pointed out certain fundamental differences between the two kinds of harmonization. At the conclusion of each chapter in Philo and in

many places in The Philosophy of the Church Fathers, I tried to show how the harmonizations of Scripture and philosophy by the Church Fathers were directly under the influence of Philo. Whether even without Philo the Fathers of the Church would have attempted to harmonize Scripture and philosophy is a plausible assumption. Whether the result of their harmonization would have been the same as it is now is a matter of conjecture. But it happens that Philo came before them and it also happens that all kinds of evidence show the influence of Philo upon them.

(2) To doubt John's knowledge of Philo is not a scholarly dogma which must not be violated. It only means that John in his Prologue does not mention Philo by name. But so does he not mention there any other name. And yet modern scholars have tried to identify the sources of his Prologue, and some of them even mention Philo. In The Philosophy of the Church Fathers I have shown by arguments evidential, terminological, and contextual how, beginning with the Apologists, the Fathers interpreted the Prologue of John in terms of the Philonic Logos. In my preliminary chapters on the New Testament, which were primarily meant to provide a background for the variety of Patristic views, I presented a detailed interpretation of the Logos in terms of a Philonic background, such as we have reason to believe was assumed by the Fathers, and pointed out certain vaguenesses which were responsible for the different interpretations that arose later among the Fathers. If everything I have said on the subject is to be shown to be wrong, it will have to be done by something more than the mere statement that "we cannot be sure that the author of the fourth gospel knew Philo's works."

(3) It is simply not true that Gnosticism is not discussed by me. I have a whole chapter on Gnosticism in The Philosophy of the Church Fathers (pp. 495–574). In that chapter I tried to show (a) that Gnosticism as we know it never existed before the rise of Christianity; (b) that the various syncretisms which are embodied in what is known to us as Gnosticism were never known by the name of Gnosticism before they became syncretized with Christianity; (c) that the Gospel of John and the Gnosticism of Cerinthus were two different attempts to interpret the Pauline teaching of a preëxistent Christ, the one in terms of the Philonic

philosophy and the other in terms of a certain system of syncretic paganism; and (d) that the common view that Gnosticism was the first to try to harmonize Christianity with philosophy, summed up by Harnack in his statement that Gnosticism is "the acute secularizing and Hellenizing of Christianity," is not substantiated by evidence, summing up my own conclusion in the statement that Gnosticism is "a verbal Christianization of paganism." Gnosticism, accordingly, had nothing to do with the Prologue to John.

VII

Referring to my attempt to present Philo and the Church Fathers as consistent thinkers and especially to my statement that Origen's description of the soul as being essentially immortal and indestructible does not mean an agreement with Plato that the soul could not be destroyed, if God ever willed to destroy it, he says: "Insufficient allowance seems to be made . . . for the possibility that Philo and the patristic thinkers may not have been wholly consistent in their philosophizing. For instance, Origen could have held, after Plato, that the soul is essentially immortal *and*, after biblical teaching, that the sovereign Creator could destroy the soul."

The facts in the case are as follows:

(1) In both my works, Philo and The Philosophy of the Church Fathers, I enumerated certain "scriptural presuppositions," based solely on faith, to which, according to both Philo and the Fathers, philosophy had to be made to harmonize and, if it could not be made to harmonize, had to be rejected. In this, despite one's natural human desire to allow for the possibility of their being inconsistent, they all, Philo and the Fathers, just happen to be consistent, though there are differences between Philo and the Fathers, and also among the Fathers themselves, as to the exact meaning of some of the scriptural presuppositions. Sometimes, however, they express themselves in a way which seems to be inconsistent with what they have been found to consider as their unshakable scriptural presuppositions. In all such instances, I always try to make a careful study of the terms and

phrases used by them in order to find out whether the inconsistencies are real or only verbal. During a half century and over of busying myself in such matters I have discovered that it is wisest always to act on the assumption that the great religious thinkers of the past are less likely to have been inconsistent in their fundamental beliefs than in the language used by them in expressing those fundamental beliefs, and I have thus learned to curb my natural lazy inclination to cry inconsistency whenever any one of them is found to use different terms in expressing some fundamental belief of his.

(2) With regard to Origen, my brief statement, as indicated in n. 13 on p. 71, is based upon a fuller discussion of the subject in the as yet unpublished second volume of The Philosophy of the Church Fathers. Here is a digest of some of the conclusions of that discussion.

Though Origen makes no direct reference to Plato, some of his characteristic views on the origin and immortality of the soul, by which he is known to differ from other Church Fathers, reflect Platonic views, which he changed in some fundamental aspects in order to harmonize them with certain scripturally based views as he understood them. His own view on immortality, as expressed in his assertion that the soul is essentially immortal and indestructible, was meant by him to be opposed to the view of two of his predecessors among the Greek Fathers, namely, Justin Martyr and Irenaeus, as well as to the view of Plato.

Justin Martyr, wishing to express his view on immortality in opposition to Plato's view, argues that the soul "lives not by being itself life, but as partaking of life," and this because "God wills it to live," and consequently "it will no longer partake of life when God does not will it to live, for life is not a property of the soul as it is of God" (Dial. 6). As to the question whether God will ever will to destroy the soul, Justin makes two seemingly inconsistent statements, which scholars have tried to harmonize. In the same work in which he argues that immortality is by the will of God because the soul only partakes of life, he also argues: "I do not say, indeed, that all souls die," but "some which have appeared worthy of God never die, whereas others are punished as long as God wills them to exist and to be punished" (ibid. 5), the implication thus being that after their punishment they may be destroyed. In another work, however, speaking of the wicked, he says that they are to undergo "eternal punishment" (I Apol. 8). Similarly Irenaeus, on the basis of scriptural verses, argues that "the soul itself is not life, but partakes of the life bestowed upon it by God" (Adv. Haer. II, 34, 4) and that consequently he who is righteous will receive life "for ever and ever," but he who is wicked "deprives himself of continuance for ever and ever" (ibid. II, 34, 3), the implication being, again, that the soul of the wicked may be destroyed. But in another place he speaks of the punishment of "those who do not believe the Word of God" as being "eternal" (ibid. IV, 28, 2).

Origen, however, has already arrived at his doctrine of the apocatastasis, according to which by the will of God there is to be not only no destruction of the soul but also no eternal punishment. So, having in mind those passages in which Justin and Irenaeus argue that, because the soul only partakes of life, immortality was bestowed upon it only by the will of God, and that, because immortality was bestowed upon the soul by God's will, God may will to destroy it, Origen begins his discussion of the immortality of the soul (De Princip. IV, 9 [36]–10 [37]), or rather "the immortality of rational natures," which includes the immortality of the human soul, by stating, like both Justin and Irenaeus, that the soul is immortal only because it "partakes" of something else. But to him that something else of which the soul partakes differs from the something else of which, according to Justin and Irenaeus, the soul partakes. According to the latter two, that something else is life, and hence they conclude that the soul itself is not life. Origen, however, on the basis of the scriptural statement, "And God said: Let us make man after our image and likeness" (Gen. 1:26), in which the term "man" is taken by him, after Philo (Opif. 69; Fug. 69), to mean the rational human soul, argues that the something else of which the human soul partakes is "the divine nature," and hence he concludes that the human soul was created by God to be like His own nature essentially both immortal and indestructible, and this conclusion of his he supports by other scriptural verses. By this Origen has placed the indestructibility of the human soul among the many impossibilities which, according to himself, God by His will and wisdom created in the world, and consequently, just as all the other impossibilities could, again, according to himself, be changed by God if He ever willed to change them, so also the human soul could be destroyed by God if He ever willed to destroy it. Origen thus did not combine two inconsistent views. What he did was to extend, on the basis of scriptural verses, the will or grace by which, according to Justin and Irenaeus, God bestowed upon the soul immortality to include also the bestowal of indestructibility, admitting, however, that just as according to Justin and Irenaeus God has the power to withdraw the immortality, so also according to himself God has the power to withdraw the indestructibility.

VIII

Referring to my comment on Cullmann's view that Jesus awaited death "with strong crying and tears" because he had no conception of the immortality of the soul, Professor Burkill says: "Occasionally a complicated matter is made to seem remarkably simple, as when Cullmann's thesis that for Jesus death meant the annihilation of the soul is 'refuted' by the bare citation of talmudic tradition regarding the belief of Rabban Johannan ben Zakkai. Actually, the gospel traditions are such as to make it extremely difficult to determine what precisely the sentiments of Jesus were in specific situations."

The facts in the case are as follows:

(1) While I do not agree with Cullmann's thesis, I do not discuss it in the essay under review, though I do discuss it in the as yet unpublished second volume of The Philosophy of the Church Fathers. This essay, entitled "Immortality and Resurrection in the Philosophy of the Church Fathers," was to start with a statement to the effect that to the Fathers of the Church the beliefs in the resurrection of the body and the immortality of the soul were inseparably connected with each other. But as the essay was originally delivered as an Ingersoll Lecture on the Immortality of Man at the Harvard Divinity School one year after Cullmann had delivered his Ingersoll Lecture, it occurred to me to preface my statement about the Church Fathers with a brief comment on

the striking thesis in Cullmann's Ingersoll Lecture the year before. Paraphrasing his description of two scenes, the one of how Socrates faced death cheerfully and without complaint and the other of how Jesus faced death "with strong crying and tears," I restated his inference from the latter scene that Jesus did not believe in the immortality of the soul. Commenting on this inference from the latter scene, I said: "Let us depict for you another scene, one laid not in far-off Athens about 492 years before the crucifixion but in a village about thirty miles from the place of the crucifixion and only about half a century after its occurrence." Then, after retelling the story of how Johannan ben Zakkai wept before he died not because of his disbelief in the immortality of the soul but because of his belief in the judgment that awaited every human being after death, I said: "This, ladies and gentlemen, is exactly the reason why Jesus awaited death . . . with strong crying and tears," cautiously remarking, however, that, though we are told that in Jesus there was no sin, "certainly there was not in him the sin of being righteous in his own eyes." At the conclusion of this exordium, I said: "But whatever one may be pleased to prove with regard to what Jesus thought of immortality and resurrection, to the Fathers of the Church these two beliefs were inseparably connected with each other." If this last statement failed to make it clear that my refutation here was only of the inference drawn by Cullmann from the manner in which Jesus faced death and not of his thesis as such, then either I must train myself to write more clearly or the reviewer must learn to read more carefully.

(2) As for his admonition against the oversimplification of the difficulties of the complicated gospel traditions about the teachings of Jesus, the reviewer is applying what is no doubt a generally useful piece of advice to a concrete case which he evidently has had no occasion to examine closely. No complicated difficulties in the gospel reports of the sayings of Jesus on resurrection gave rise to Cullmann's thesis. The only argument advanced by Cullmann himself in support of his thesis, besides his inference from his comparison of Socrates and Jesus in the manner in which they faced death, is his own peculiar notion that the Jews at the time of Jesus had no conception of an immortal soul.

IX

Commenting on my Sermonette entitled "The Professed Atheist and the Verbal Theist," he argues that on the basis of the view expressed in it, "presumably, the philosophy of the Vedanta, for example, is godless and therefore not properly religious," and he deplores the fact that "even in university circles accession to the pulpit is still taken to be an opportunity for the public expression of narrow dogmatism."

I thoroughly agree with Professor Burkill that the term religion does not imply the belief in any particular conception of God. In fact, I even admit that there would be no misuse of the term religion if one should refer to some special hobby of his as his religion on the ground that it is his "ultimate reality" or "ultimate concern." But in that Sermonette I dealt with two special types of religion, the religion of the Greek philosophers and the religion of Hebrew Scripture. Both these religions were based upon the belief in what they each called God, of whom they each had a special conception, and these religious Greek philosophers described as Godless or atheists all those who did not believe in what they conceived of as God, and similarly Hebrew Scripture speaks of a fool who said there is no God. Now it happens that, when followers of the scriptural type of religion compared their own conception of God with that of the theistic Greek philosophers, they unanimously denied that those theistic Greek philosophers had a true conception of God, with the implication that they were theists only verbally. When, therefore, we find nowadays some theistic philosophers whose conception of God is like that of the theistic Greek philosophers, then, historically, from the viewpoint of the exponents of the scriptural type of religion, their theism is only a verbal theism. That is all that the Sermonette was trying to convey. There is no suggestion in it that such verbal theists are not religious or that they can have no religion. There is no suggestion in it even of denying them the right to expropriate the religious vocabulary and rituals and institutions that grew out of the belief in the scriptural conception of God. It merely suggests that such an expropriation would mark a radical, revolutionary break in what throughout its history was held to be essential to the scriptural type of religion, without, however, attempting to express an opinion as to the relative merits of the old-fashioned theology and the new-fashioned theology or to discuss the relative narrowness of their respective dogmatisms.

X

While Professors Grant and Burkill approached my collection of essays critically, the approach of Professor Richardson may be described as appreciative. But toward the end of his review he throws out two suggestions of criticism. First, he raises the question "whether modern developments in logic do not make a good deal" of my manner of argument "old-fashioned." I, too, would like to question whether any modern logician, expressing himself in symbols, would claim for his art some magical power enabling him to reduce to ashes studies in the history of religious philosophy based upon the use of old-fashioned logical reasoning, even when such studies do occasionally venture to show the continuity between some past historical religious problems and the same religious problems that are still being discussed today. Second, referring to my discussion of what Philo and the Church Fathers and later religious philosophers meant by the infinity of God in the sense of His unknowability and His infinite power and His infinite goodness, he remarks, less questioningly now, that "one can hardly deal with infinity . . . in categories which antedate [the mathematical infinite of] Georg Cantor." One would like to refer this remark to Mr. Ko-ko, the celebrated Lord High Executioner of Titipu, famous for his ditty,

> The flowers that bloom in the spring,
> Tra la,
> Have nothing to do with the case.

19

ANSWERS TO CRITICISMS OF MY DISCUSSIONS OF THE INEFFABILITY OF GOD

I

In my paper "The Knowability and Describability of God in Plato and Aristotle,"[1] I tried to show that (1) Plato described God in affirmative terms, but that despite this (2) he argued against the knowability and describability of God which means that God could be described in affirmative terms, and that (3) Aristotle similarly described God in affirmative terms, which terms he considered as definitions consisting of genera and species. In that paper I also quoted passages to the effect that (4) in comments on Plato's statement that "it would be impossible to declare Him [that is, God] to all men" (*Timaeus* 28C) Clement of Alexandria and Celsus took it to mean that God is ineffable, whereas Origen took it to mean that God is effable.[2] In my *Philo*, I further tried to show how by reasoning based upon both Scripture and philosophy Philo arrived at the conclusion that (5) God is unknowable and ineffable and unnameable in the sense that He cannot be defined in terms of genus and species[3] and (6) how, under the influence of Philo, this conception of the unknowability, ineffability, and unnameability of God was accepted by the Church Fathers and subsequently by the philosophers of the three religions, Christianity, Islam, and Judaism.[4] In that work, I also tried to show that, insofar as a negative generalization can be established, it can be established that (7) in the extant Greek philosophic literature no philosopher prior to Philo described God as unknowable and ineffable and unnameable in the Philonic sense of these terms.[5]

Let us now see how these discussions of mine of the ineffability of God were criticized, confining myself only to such criticisms that try to refute any of my views by the quotation of passages and not by the mere expression of dissenting opinions.

First, J. Moreau[6] and John Whittaker[7] refer to Plato as having de-

[1] Cf. *Harvard Studies in Classical Philology*, 56–57 (1947) 233–249, reprinted in *Studies in the History of Philosophy and Religion*, v. I, 98–114.

[2] *Studies*, I, pp. 103–104.

[3] *Philo*, II, pp. 94–126.

[4] *Ibid.*, pp. 149–160.

[5] *Ibid.*, pp. 111–118.

[6] *Revue des Etudes Anciennes* 60 (1958) 446–448, quoted with evident approval by Louis H. Feldman in his "Scholarship on Philo and Josephus," *Studies in Judaism (1937–1962)*, Yeshiva University.

[7] "Basilides on the Ineffability of God," *Harvard Theological Review* 62 (1969) 368, n. 4.

scribed God by the term ineffable in *Epistola* VII, 341C. This is not so. Plato does not deal there with God; he deals there with a certain branch of philosophy, concerning which, after saying "I certainly composed no work in regard to it," he says "nor shall I ever do so in the future, for it is nowise as effable as other disciplines," that is to say, as translated by Jowett, "there is no way of putting it in words like other subjects."

Second, Wilfred L. Knox [8] refers to a passage in Cicero's *Tusc. Disput.* I, 10, 22 which, according to him, refutes my claim that "the conception of the ineffability or unnameability of God is not found in any other Greek philosopher," for, he says, it is found in Cicero, and Cicero may be assumed to follow "a Greek model." This is, again, not so. Cicero does not speak there of God; he speaks there of the fifth element, aether, concerning which he says that Aristotle "employs a fifth class without a name" (*quintum genus adhibet vacans nomine*), thus referring to Aristotle's statement that aether has no proper name (*De Caelo* I, 3, 270b, 20–24).[9]

Third, Henry Chadwick [10] refers to a passage in Cicero's *De Nat. Deor.* I, 12, 30 (Diels, *Dox.* Gr. 537) and, quite evidently having in mind Plato's statement in *Timaeus* 28C that "it would be impossible to declare Him [i.e. God] to all men," states that "Plato says in the *Timaeus* that the father of this world cannot be named." [11] The meaning of this statement is vague. First, inasmuch as among the many gods known to the Greek and Latin speaking peoples of the time some gods were known by proper names and some were known as nameless, Cicero's statement here may only mean that the proper name of the father of the world is unknown, thus referring to the fact that Plato in his *Timaeus* ascribes to his Demiurge, that is the Craftsman, no proper name.[12] Second, if Cicero's statement is taken here to mean, as in Philo, that God is unnameable because His essence is unknowable, then we can only say that

[8] *Journal of Theological Studies* 49 (1948) 211.

[9] Cf. my discussion in *The Philosophy of the Church Fathers*, I, pp. 85–86, and nn. 89–94, of attempts to identify Aristotle's God with his fifth element in passages quoted in the names of Athenagores, Clement of Alexandria, the *Recognitiones* of Clement of Rome, and Lactantius.

[10] *Classical Review* 63 (1949) 24–25.

[11] In the same passage, Cicero refers to Plato's "books of the Laws" where Plato is quoted by him as saying "that no inquiry at all ought to be made into what God is." The reference is to the opening words of a discussion in *Laws* VII, 821A, where, however, in the course of the discussion it is made clear that the nature of God is a fit and possible subject of inquiry. Cf. also *Laws XII*, 966C and Cicero's own subsequent comments in the same passage in *De Natura Deorum* III on Plato's treatment of God in his *Timaeus* and *Laws*.

[12] This explanation may apply also to Seneca's description of God as having no name referred to in my *Philo*, II, p. 113 at n. 25. Cf. also my discussion in *Philo*, II, pp. 115–116, of the expression "the unknown God" in Acts 17:23.

Cicero anticipated Clement of Alexandria and Celsus who, as I have shown, so interpreted Plato's statement in *Timaeus* 28C.[13]

Fourth, John Whittaker [14] refers to the occurrence of the description of God by the term ineffable "in the Hermetic Poimandres, perhaps not later in date than the career of Basilides . . . " (*Corpus Hermeticum* [ed. A. D. Nock, I, 31, II, 2, 19, 2]). Thus, according to Whittaker himself this description of God by the term ineffable occurred in a work which was composed about a century after Philo. Besides, the *Corpus Hermeticum* is generally acknowledged to show both Philonic and Christian influence.

Fifth, John Whittaker [15] again refers to the occurrence of the description of God by the term ineffable in "a work ascribed to the early Pythagorean Lysis, which can hardly be later in date than Basilides, . . . cf. Athenagoras, *Suppl.* 6 (PG 6, 901A)." Thus here, again, according to Whittaker himself the description of God by the term ineffable occurred in a work which was composed after Philo.

It will be noticed that all these five criticisms deal only with the seventh of these seven topics which I have dealt with in my discussions of the subject of the ineffability of God and that of these five criticisms of this single one of the seven topics the first two are definitely wrong and of the remaining three the first is doubtful and the second and third are post-Philonic.

II

In my paper "The Twice-revealed Averroes," [16] I showed that propositions with an inseparable negative particle prefixed to the predicate (in Greek with alpha privative), such as "incorporeal," "unequal," are treated by Aristotle either as "negatives" or as "privatives." [17] In my paper "Negative Attributes in the Church Fathers and the Gnostic Basilides," [18] I tried to show that the reason why all the Church Fathers describe God as "ineffable," whereas Basilides rejects the description of God by the term "ineffable," is that the former take the term "ineffable" to have a "negative" meaning, whereas the latter takes it to have a "privative" meaning; both these meanings, as I have shown, are in good use according to Aristotle.

[13] Cf. above at n. 2. Chadwick quotes also a passage from Philo's *De Gigantibus* 8 against my view that Philo denied the existence of souls in the spheres (*op. cit.*, p. 25, Col. 1). I myself have quoted that passage from *De Gigantibus* and explained it (cf. *Philo* I, p. 364). Evidently Chadwick does not agree with my explanation.

[14] *Op.* and *loc. cit.* above n. 7.

[15] *Ibid.*

[16] Cf. *Studies*, I, pp. 371–401.

[17] *Ibid.*, pp. 387–389 and 140–141.

[18] *Ibid.*, pp. 131–142.

In his refutation [19] of my explanation that Basilides' rejection of the application of the term "ineffable" to God is due to his taking the term "ineffable" to have a "privative" meaning, Whittaker tries to show that the term "incorporeal" is rejected in application to God by many who quite evidently believe that God is "incorporeal" in its "negative" meaning. To prove this he quotes the Apocryphon of John which declares that the first principle is "neither corporeal *nor incorporeal*" (*Gnosticism: An Anthology*, ed. R. M. Grant, London, 1961, p. 71) and adds that "a similar claim is made by Philo . . . Clement of Alexandria, Origen" and others.[20]

Now, if Whittaker had continued his researches in the texts quoted by him, he would have discovered that the Apocryphon of John, not far from its statement that God is "neither corporeal nor incorporeal," says that God is "the indestructible . . . and imperishable" and he would then undoubtedly have asked himself why the Apocryphon does not allow one to say that God is "incorporeal" but does allow one to say that God is "indestructible" and "imperishable." He would have similarly discovered that Philo, Clement of Alexandria, and Origen, for instance, to whom he had referred as having applied to God the description "neither corporeal nor incorporeal" applied to Him also the simple description "incorporeal" [21] and he would then undoubtedly have asked himself why the same term "incorporeal" is sometimes rejected and sometimes used by them as a description of God. The only answer that could be given to that question is that, like Aristotle, these quoted sources used terms with inseparable prefixed negative particles both as "privatives" and as "negatives," so that, as descriptions of God, in the expression "neither corporeal nor incorporeal" the term 'incorporeal" in its contrast to the term "corporeal" is used by them in a "privative" sense, but when the terms "indestructible" and "imperishable" are used singly or when the same term "incorporeal," is used singly, then, like the single term "ineffable," these terms are used by them in a "negative" sense. When, therefore, we find that Basilides, unlike all others, does not allow the use of the single term "ineffable" as a description of God, we are justified in concluding that the reason for this is that he is using the term "ineffable" in its "privative" sense.

[19] *Op. cit.* (above n. 6), p. 370, at n. 9.

[20] *Ibid.*, at nn. 10–15.

[21] Cf. Indexes of their respective works.

20

INFINITE AND PRIVATIVE JUDGMENTS IN ARISTOTLE, AVERROES, AND KANT

In Aristotle judgments are divided with respect to quality into two types, the affirmative and the negative, of which the propositions "A is B" and "A is not B" are the respective examples.[1] But under affirmative judgments Aristotle mentions two other types of judgments, which though affirmative in quality are negative in meaning. First, a proposition in which the predicate is what he calls a privation (στέρησις),[2] such as the terms "blind" (τυφλός) and "toothless" (νωδός).[3] Second, a proposition in which the predicate is what Aristotle calls an indefinite term (ὄνομα ἀόριστον),[4] but which through Boethius has been known in the history of philosophy as an infinite term (*nomen infinitum*),[5] as, for instance, the term "not-just" in the proposition "the man is not-just."

In Aristotle no special terms are used to distinguish these three types of propositions, namely (1) affirmative and negative propositions, (2) propositions with privative predicates,[6] and (3) propositions with infinite predicates. Through his commentators, however, these three types of propositions came to be designated respectively as (1) simple propositions, (2) privative propositions, and (3) infinite propositions.[7]

Now, with regard to negative and privative propositions, Aristotle draws a sharp distinction between them. In negative propositions, he says, the predicate may be negated of a subject even if that subject can never naturally possess that predicate, as, for instance, the term "one" which can be negated of a subject even if the subject cannot naturally be one,[8] but a

---

1 *De Interp.*, c. 6, 17a, 25–26.

2 *Categ.*, c. 10, 10a, 26–12b, 5; *Metaph.*, IV, 2, 1004a, 10–16.

3 *Categ.*, 12a, 34.

4 *De Interpr.*, c. 2, 16a, 32.

5 Boethius' commentary on *De Interpr.*, Prima Editio, I, c. 2 (ed. C. Meiser, Vol. I, p. 51, 1, 23).

6 The expression πρότασις στερητική is used by Aristotle in the sense of negative proposition. Cf. Bonitz, *Index Aristotelicus*, s.v.; Prantl, *Geschichte der Logik*, I, p. 195, n. 330.

7 Cf. *Ammonius De Interpretatione*, ed. A. Busse, p. 161, 11, 7–9, and p. 163, 1. 14: πρότασις ἁπλῆ, στερητική, ἀόριστος; Boethius, *op. cit.*, Secunda Editio, IIII, c. 10 (Vol. II, pp. 277–278); *propositiones simplicae, propositiones privatoriae, propositiones infinitae.*

8 *Metaph.*, IV, 2, 1004a, 10–16; cf. Schwegler's commentary *ad loc.* (Vol. III, p. 156, §14).

privation cannot be affirmed of a subject unless its opposite habit could be naturally possessed by it, thus the term "blind" or "toothless" cannot be affirmed of a subject unless the subject could naturally possess "sight" or "teeth."[9] Alexander illustrates this distinction by the example of the term "wall," "for," he says, "the expression 'is not seeing' may indeed be appropriately said both of a blind man and a wall, the latter of which is absolutely incapable of having sight . . . not so, however, is the case of blindness."[10] In other words, you can say "the wall is not seeing" but you cannot say "the wall is blind." But no such statement is made by Aristotle with regard to predicates which are infinite terms, such as, e.g., not-seeing. The question may therefore be raised whether according to Aristotle the term "not-seeing" could be predicated of a wall. Indeed the proposition "it is not-day (*οὐχὶ ἡμέρα ἐστί*)", which Aristotle would call an "infinite judgment" is described by the Stoics as a "negative judgment" (*ἀποφατικὸν ἀξίωμα*),[11] but Stoic usages are not decisive in the interpretation of Aristotle.

Though in the passage quoted above with regard to privative propositions Aristotle makes no distinction between propositions in which the predicate is only privative in meaning but not in form, as, e.g., the term "blind," and predicates which would seem to be privative both in meaning and in form, as, e.g., the term "toothless," in another passage he seems to put terms which have as their prefix the Greek *alpha privative* into a special class by itself. In that passage, discussing the meaning of "privation," he makes the general statement that "there are as many kinds of privations as there are words which derive their negations from the *alpha privative*," and as illustrations of such privations he mentions the terms "unequal" (*ἄνισον*), "invisible" (*ἀόρατον*) and "footless" (*ἄπουν*).[12] Furthermore, in contradistinction to the privatives "blind" and "toothless," concerning which he says that "it is a universal rule that each pair of opposites of this type has reference to that to which the particular 'habit' is natural,"[13] he would seem to say concerning privatives formed with the *alpha privative* that they can be affirmed of subjects which do not naturally possess the opposite habit. For in this passage under consideration, privative propositions are divided by him into three types. First, propositions of the type "the plant is eyeless." Second, propositions of the type "the mole is

---

[9] *Categ.*, c. 10, 12a, 27–34.

[10] Alexander in *Metaphysics*, ed. M. Hayduck, p. 327, 11, 18–20: *τὸ γὰρ οὐχ ὁρᾷ καὶ ἐπὶ τοῦ τυφλοῦ ἀληθὲς καὶ ἐπὶ τοῦ τοίχου, ὅς οὐδὲ ὅλως ὄψεως δεκτικός . . . οὐχ οὕτω καὶ ἡ τυφλότης.*

[11] Diogenes, VII, 69.

[12] *Metaph.*, V, 22, 1022b, 32–36.

[13] *Categ.*, c. 10, 12a, 27–29.

sightless" or "the blind man is sightless." Third, propositions of the type "the man is blind."[14] Now of these three types of privative propositions, only the third conforms to the universal rule laid down by Aristotle himself with regard to privative propositions. In the case of the first of these three types of propositions the privation "eyelessness" is affirmed of a plant, even though plant belongs to a genus which naturally does not possess the habit of being endowed with eyes. In the case of the second type of these three judgments, the privation "sightlessness" is in the first instance affirmed of a mole, even though a mole belongs to a species which naturally does not possess the habit of "sight" and in the second instance it is affirmed of a blind man, who, as a particular individual, i.e., a blind man, does not naturally possess the habit "sight."[15] Inevitably, therefore, the universal rule laid down by Aristotle was not meant by him to apply to propositions in which the predicate is a term prefixed by an *alpha privative*. Corroborative evidence for this conclusion may be found in Aristotle's oft-repeated statement that we can say of a "voice" that it is "invisible" (ἀόρατος),[16] even though a voice cannot naturally possess the habit of being "visible." Probably the distinction which Aristotle meant to draw was one between terms which are privative only in meaning and not in form, such as "blind," and terms which are privative both in meaning and in form, such as "unseeing," and if he puts the term "toothless" (νωδός) in the same class with the term "blind" it is because the negative prefix νη- was of rare and only of poetic use and therefore terms having it as their prefix were not considered by him as being in the same class as terms having the *alpha privative* as their prefix.

This distinction in Aristotle's conception of privative propositions has, as far as I know, not been noticed.[17] In Boethius, the typical example of a privative proposition is the proposition "*est iniustus homo*,"[18] though the term *iniustus* represents the Greek ἄδικος. The Stoics, too, use the proposition "the man is inhumane (ἀφιλάνθρωπος)" as an illustration of what they call a "privative proposition" (στερητικὸν ἀξίωμα),[19] but here, again, Stoic usages are not to be taken as decisive in the interpretation of Aristotle.

[14] *Metaph.*, V, 22, 1022b, 22–29.

[15] This is what I understand to be the meaning of the three types of privation in this chapter. Other interpretations are given in the Oxford translation of the *Metaphysics* by Ross and in the Loeb translation by Tredennick. Cf. below the discussion of Averroes and Avicenna.

[16] *Phys.*, III, 5, 204a, 13–14; V, 2, 206b, 10–11; *Metaph.*, XI, 10, 1066a, 36.

[17] Cf. the discussion of the passages in question in Zeller, *Die Philosophie der Griechen*, II, 2⁴, p. 216, n. 7 (*Aristotle*, I, p. 226, n. 6).

[18] Boethius, *op cit.*, Prima Editio, II, c. 10 (Vol. I, p. 133); Secunda Editio, IIII, c. 10 (Vol. II, p. 277).

[19] Diogenes, VII, 70.

In our analysis of Aristotle's statements with regard to infinite and privative judgments we have thus come upon two generally unnoticed points. First, there is the question whether an infinite term, such as "not-seeing," can according to Aristotle be predicated of a subject which naturally cannot see. Second, there seems to be in Aristotle a distinction between a privation which is only privative in meaning, such as "blind," and a privation which is privative also in form, such as "unseeing." Both these points, we shall now try to show, are subjects of discussion in the interpretation of Aristotle in Arabic philosophy.

But before we begin to deal with the relevant texts in question, let us make two comments on the Arabic translation of two Greek terms.

First, the Arabic translation of what Aristotle calls ὄνομα ἀόριστον, and Boethius translates by *nomen infinitum*, is *ism ghair muḥaṣṣal*.[20] But for what Ammonius and Boethius call "infinite judgment" the Arabic uses the expression *qaḍiyyah ma'dūlah*. As for the meaning of that Arabic expression there is some uncertainty. Johannes Hispalensis in his translation of Ghazali's *Maqāṣid al-Falāsifah* renders this expression by *propositio privativa*;[21] Horten renders the term *ma'dūlah* by *infinita*[22] and Goichon renders it by *équivalente*.[23] None of these, as can be readily seen, are exact translations of the Arabic term. Now the Arabic term *ma'dūlah*, among its many meanings, has also the meaning of "deviated," and it is in this sense that it was taken by mediaeval Hebrew translators of Ghazali's *Maqāṣid al-Falāsifah* who render it by either *musar* or *noṭeh*.[24] Taken in this sense the expression *qaḍiyyah ma'dūlah* literally means "a deviated proposition" and may therefore be taken as a translation of the Greek πρότασις ἐκ μεταθέσεως or κατά μετὰθάεσιν, i.e., "proposition by transposition," which was used by Theophrastus as a description of what Boethius calls "infinite proposition."[25] The Arabic expression may therefore be translated by "transposed proposition."

Second, in the passage ir the *Categories*, Chap. 10, quoted above, the

---

[20] See "Glossar," s.v., p. 39, col. 1, in I. Pollak's edition of Isḥāq ibn Ḥonain's Arabic translation of the *De Interpretatione* (*Die Hermeneutik des Aristotles*, Leipzig, 1913).

[21] Quoted in Prantl, *Geschichte der Logik*, II², 1885, p. 373, n. 260. In the Latin translation of Averroes' *Epitome of the Organon*, made from the Hebrew, the corresponding Hebrew term *musarim* is translated by *remotiva*; cf. quotation below, n. 38.

[22] M. Horten, *Die spekulative und positive Theologie des Islam*, 1912, p. 203.

[23] A.-M. Goichon, *Lexique de la Langue philosophique d'Ibn Sina*, 1938, §411.

[24] The former in Judah ben Nathan's translation, MS. Jewish Theological Seminary, Adler 1015, p. 23a; the latter in Isaac Albalag's translation, MS., *ibid.*, Adler 131, p. 9b.

[25] *Ammonius de Interpretatione*, ed. A. Busse, p. 161, 11. 10 and 28; *Alexander in Priora Analytica*, ed. M. Wallies, p. 397, 1. 2; cf. Prantl, *op. cit.*, I, pp. 357–358, nn. 30–33; Zeller, *op. cit.*, II, 2⁴, p. 221, n. 4 (I, p. 232, n. 2).

term "toothless" (*νωδός*) is translated by the term *adrad*,[26] which like the term "blind" is privative only in meaning and not in form. Consequently, the universal rule laid down by Aristotle in that passage with regard to propositions with privative predicates could be taken by readers of his works in Arabic translation to apply exclusively to predicates which are privative only in meaning and in no way privative in form. They did not have to make an exception, as suggested by us above, of predicates which in Greek have the poetic negative prefix *νη-*.

The source which contains the clearest statement of what may be considered as constituting the Arabic traditional interpretation of Aristotle with reference to the two points mentioned by us is to be found in the commentaries of Averroes.

First, with regard to privative propositions of the type "A is unseeing," we shall reproduce his comment on Aristotle's discussion of the various meanings of "privation."[27] In that comment, Averroes enumerates seven types of privation. The first three are illustrated by propositions in which the predicates are terms which are privative in meaning but positive in form, such as, for instance, the term "bald," "blind," "naked," "poor," "squint-eyed," and "cripple-bodied."[28] The common characteristic feature of these types of proposition is that the subject in question, while having certain "privations" predicated of it, could naturally also possess the opposite habits and thus be described as "hairy," "seeing," "clothed," "rich," "straight-eyed," and "straight-bodied," corresponding to what Aristotle says of the opposites of "privation and habit" that "it is a universal rule that each of a pair of opposites of this type has reference to that to which the particular 'habit' is natural."[29] The last four types of privations are illustrated by the following propositions: "God is immortal (*lā mā'it*) and incorruptible (*lā fāsid*)," "the donkey is irrational (*lā nāṭiq*)," "the woman is unmanly (*lā dhakar*)"; and "the boy is ignorant (*lā 'āqil*)."[30] The com-

---

[26] Cf. *Averroès: Talkhīç Kitāb al-Maqōulāt*, ed. M. Bouyges, Beyrouth, 1932, p. 97.

[27] *Metaph.* V, 22, 1022b, 22ff.; *Epitome of the Metaphysics* (ed. C. Quirós), I, 47, pp. 26–27.

[28] Cf. *Epitome of the Metaphysics*, *loc. cit.* The use of the terms "blind," "naked," and "poor" as illustrations of privation is to be found in *Aristotelis Fragmenta*, ed. v. Rose, §119, 1498a, 36–38: "Blindness is of those privations which are according to nature; nakedness is of those which are according to custom; privation of money is of those which exist in use" (*τυφλότης μὲν τῶν ἐν φύσει, γυμνότης δὲ τῶν ἐν ἔθει, ἀργυρίου δε στέρησις τῶν ἐν χρήσει παραγινομένων.*)

[29] *Categ.*, c. 10, 12a, 27–29.

[30] *Epitome of the Metaphysics*, I, §47, p. 27. The Latin translation (*Aristotelis opera*, Venice, 1574, Vol. VIII, p. 361 H-I) translates the last three propositions by (1) "asinus non est rationalis," (2) "cum dicimus foeminam non esse marem," and (3) "cum dicimus puerum non esse doctum," in all of which the translator has missed the main point of the illustrations, for all his propositions are negative and not privative.

mon characteristic feature of all these propositions is that the subjects in question have certain 'privations' predicated of them even though they cannot possess the opposite 'habits' and cannot therefore be described, in the case of God, as being 'mortal' and 'corruptible', in the case of the donkey, as being 'rational', in the case of the woman, as being 'manly', and, in the case of the boy, as being 'learned', reflecting thus the implications of Aristotle's statements quoted above with regard to propositions in which the predicate is a term privative in form.[31]

But here a question comes up. In Arabic, which has no privative prefixes or affixes, no distinction can be made between an infinite term, such as "not-seeing," and a term which is privative in form, such as "unseeing." Both of them are expressed by a separable negative particle followed by the participle in question. Consequently when Averroes says here that you can say of God that He is *lā mā'it* and *lā fāsid*, and of a woman that she is *la dhakar*, and of a donkey that it is *lā nāṭiq* and of a boy that he is *lā 'āqil*, the question is whether these terms were meant by him to be taken as privations in form, namely, "immortal," "incorruptible," "unmanly," "irrational," and "ignorant," or whether they were meant by him to be taken as infinite terms, namely, "not-mortal," "not-corruptible," "not-manly," "not-rational," and "not-learned." The same question may also be raised with regard to Aristotle's statement quoted above that we can say of a voice that it is "invisible," whether the Greek word for "invisible," which in Arabic must be translated by the use of a separable negative particle, was taken by Averroes to mean "invisible" or "not-visible." In other words whether Averroes was conscious of the fact that the Arabic separable negative particle followed by a participle or adjective translates two different forms of predicates in Greek, and also whether he made any distinction between these two forms of predicates with regard to their application to subjects which cannot naturally possess the opposite habits.

In answer to this we shall try to show that Averroes definitely disapproves of the use of an infinite predicate, such as "not-seeing," of a subject which cannot naturally possess the habit "seeing," and therefore when he

Similarly Horten (*Die Metaphysik des Averroes*, 1912, pp. 27–28) translates them by (1) "Der Esel ist nicht vernünftig," (2) "Das Weib besitzt nicht die männliche Natur," and (3) "So sagen wir von dem Knaben, dass er nicht den vollen Gebrauch der Vernunft habe." So also S. van den Bergh (*Die Epitome der Metaphysik des Averroes*, 1924, p. 20) translates them by (1) "Wie wenn wir sagen vom Esel, dass er nicht vernünftig ist," (2) "so wenn wir sagen von der Frau, dass sie nicht männlich ist," and (3) "wie wenn wir sagen vom Knaben, er sei nicht gelehrt." Similarly Quirós in his Spanish translation (Averroes: *Compendio de Metafisica*, 1919, p. 44) translates these three examples as negative propositions instead of privative propositions.

[31] Cf. above, nn. 12–16.

does allow, in the passage quoted, the use, for instance, of such terms as *lā mā'it* and *lā fāsid* of God, these terms were inevitably meant by him to be taken in the sense of "immortal" and "incorruptible" rather than in the sense of "not-mortal" and "not-corruptible."

The passage in which Averroes expresses himself clearly on this point is his comment upon Aristotle's discussion in *De Interpretatione*, Ch. 10, of the distinction between the negative proposition "man is not just" and the infinite proposition "man is not-just." His comment reads as follows: "When we say 'man is not just', the statement may apply both to a man who is wicked and to a man who is neither wicked nor just, that is, an uncivilized man or a boy. But when we say 'man is not-just', the statement applies only to a man who is wicked, for our predicate 'not-just' signifies a privation, and privation is the remotion of a habit from a subject in which it would naturally exist at a time when it would naturally exist in it."[32] The meaning of this passage is quite clear. An infinite term like "not-just" is the same as a privative term "wicked" and consequently an infinite judgment is like a privative judgment and not like a negative judgment. The term "not-just" therefore cannot be predicated of a subject which cannot naturally possess the habit of "justice."

In another passage he not only repeats his view that infinite propositions are of the same status as privative propositions but he also indicates that propositions with a predicate which is privative in form is the equivalent of negative propositions. He says: "Some propositions are transposed,[33] and these are those propositions in which the predicate is an infinite noun or verb,[34] as when we say, for instance, 'Socrates is not-healthy'. This occurs in propositions which are not used in the Arabic language. Some are privative propositions, and they are those propositions in which the predicate is a privative noun or verb. It is a universal rule that privation is [predicated of a subject as] the absence of a habit which would naturally exist in the subject at a time it would naturally exist in it,[35] as when we say, for instance, 'Socrates is blind' or 'Plato is sick'. The force of infinite terms in those languages in which they are used is like the force of privative terms, for our saying 'not-seeing' is of the same order as our saying 'blind' and our saying 'not-healthy' is of the same order as our saying 'sick'. In-

[32] Middle Commentary on *De Interpretatione*, *Aristotelis opera*, Venice, 1574, Vol. I, 1, p. 86A: "Nam cum dicitur, homo non est iustus, verificatur de homine iniusto et de homine qui non est iniustus neque iustus, qui sive est incivilis vel puer. Sed cum dicitur, homo est non iustus, significat privationem. Privatio autem est ablatio rei ab aliquo, cui nata est inesse, tempore quo nata est inesse ei."

[33] Latin: "remotivae," see above n. 21.

[34] With reference to an "infinite verb" (*ἀόριστον ῥῆμα*), see *De Interpr.*, c. 3, 16b, 12–14.

[35] Cf. *Categ.*, c. 10, 12a, 27–29; cf. above, n. 14.

asmuch as infinite terms are not used in the Arabic language, the negative particle is regarded by Arabic logicians as one of the ambiguous particles, for sometimes they use it generally and mean thereby merely privation,[36] and sometimes they mean thereby absolute negation.[37] It is this consideration that has compelled men of the art of logic to treat of transposed terms, for if we are not careful about these terms and pay no heed to their being technically equivalent to privations, we might be led into error and take that which is infinite to mean negation, and vice versa."[38]

The implication of this passage is quite clear. Such an expression as *lā baṣīr* in a nominal proposition wherein the copula is omitted is in ordinary Arabic not used in the sense of what logicians call the infinite "is not-seeing." It is ordinarily used in the sense of "is not seeing" or "is unseeing,"[39] the latter of which is to be taken as being in its logical sense a negative like the former "is not seeing." Evidently there must have been a traditional interpretation of Aristotle among the Arabic philosophers to the effect that a term privative in form like "unseeing" was to be distinguished from a term privative only in meaning like "blind."

In the light of these explicit statements of Averroes we may explain certain statements in Avicenna with regard to infinite and privative judgments which are not so explicit.

Avicenna, in his discussion of infinite and privative judgments makes the following statements.

First, propositions are to be divided into three types, described as simple (*basīṭah*), transposed (*ma'dūlah*)[40] and privative (*'adamiyyah*).[41] The

[36] As, e.g., in the use of *lā baṣīr* in the sense of "is not-seeing."

[37] As, e.g., in the use of *lā baṣīr* in the sense of "is not seeing" or "is unseeing."

[38] Averroes' *Epitome of De Interpretatione*, Ch. IV, in *Aristotelis opera*, Venice, 1574, Vol. I, 2, p. 41 I: "Et earum sunt remotivae, et sunt illae, quarum praedicatum est nomen vel verbum imperfectum: sicut si dixerimus Socrates est non sanus: et hoc est in orationibus, quae non usitantur in lingua Arabum. Et quaedam sunt privativae, et sunt quarum praedicatum est nomen privativum, vel verbum privativum. Privatio autem universaliter est, quod deficiat habitus, cuius consuetudo est, quod sit in eo subiecto in hora, qua solet esse in eo: sicut si dixerimus Socrates est caecus, et Plato aegrotat. Vis autem nominum inperfectorum in idiomatibus, quae utuntur eis, est vis nominum privativorum, quia dictum nostrum non videns est in gradu dicti nostri caecus: et dictum nostrum non sanum est in gradu dicti nostri aegrum. Quoniam autem non fuerunt ista nomina in lingua Arabum, fuit dictio negationis apud eos ex dictionibus ambiguis, quia ipsi aliquando proferunt ipsam simpliciter, et volunt per eam rem privationis, et aliquando volunt per eam negationem absolutam. Et hoc est, quod cogit homines huius artis loqui per nomina remotiva, quia nos dum non cavemus ea, et imponemus eis istam impositionem, possibile est quod erremus, et accipiamus quod est imperfectum loco negationis, et contra."

[39] Caspari-Wright, *A Grammar of the Arabic Language*, II, §82, d, *Rem*. b, p. 227.

[40] *Najāt* I, Cairo, 1331 A.H., p. 22, ll. 4–7.

[41] *Ibid*., p. 24, ll. 7–11.

terms by which these three types of propositions are designated, as we have seen, do not occur in Aristotle; they are the same as those used by his Greek and Latin commentators.

Second, infinite propositions, illustrated by the proposition "Zaid is not-seeing," are expressed in Arabic in two ways: (a) a nominal proposition which contains a copula, namely, *Zaid huwa ghair basīr;*[42] (b) a nominal proposition in which the copula is omitted, namely, *Zaid lā baṣīr.*[43]

Third, the following distinction is to be drawn between a simple negative proposition and an infinite proposition. A simple negative proposition may be true even of a non-existent subject, whereas an infinite proposition can be true only of subject which has existence. Thus, taking the sphinx as an example of that which does not exist, he says it may be true to say "the sphinx is not seeing," but it cannot be true to say "the sphinx is not-seeing."[44]

Fourth, the terms *ghair baṣīr* can be predicated of any subject that happens to be without sight, irrespective of the fact whether (1) it naturally possesses sight, or whether (2) it naturally does not itself possess sight but its genus or species possesses sight, or whether (3) neither itself nor that which is predicated of it (i.e., its genus or species) possesses sight.[45] As against this, he says, in a privative proposition, such as "Zaid is severe (*jā'ir*)" or "the air is murky (*muẓlim*)," the terms "severe" and " murky " can be predicated only of a subject which either itself or its species or genus can naturally possess the opposite habit of being "lenient" and "bright."[46]

Fifth, with reference to the proposition *Zaid lā baṣīr*, he says that its meaning depends upon the intention of him who uses it. If he means by it *inna Zaid laisa huwa bi-baṣīr*, i.e., Zaid is not seeing, it is a negative proposition; but if he means by it *inna Zaid huwa lā baṣīr*, i.e., Zaid is not-seeing, it is a transposed proposition.[47]

Now his fifth statement is exactly the same as the statement we quoted above from Averroes with regard to nominal propositions in which the copula is omitted and the predicate is preceded by the negative particle *lā*. But his fourth statement, wherein he seems to say that the infinite term "not-seeing" (*ghair baṣīr*) can be predicated even of a subject which naturally has no sight would seem to be contradictory to Averroes' explicit statement that such an infinite term is like the privation "blind" which can

---

[42] *Ibid.*, p. 22, l. 9.

[43] *Ibid.*, p. 23, ll. 13–14.

[44] *Ibid.*, p. 23, ll. 2–6.

[45] *Ibid.*, p. 23, ll. 6–10; *'Ishārāt*, ed. J. Forget, 1892, p. 28, ll. 10–13.

[46] *Najāt*, p. 24, ll. 9–11.

[47] *Ibid.*, p. 23, ll. 12–13; *'Ishārāt*, p. 27, l. 15—p. 28, l. 10; cf. a similar statement reproduced from the *Shifā* in I. Madkour, *L'Organon d'Aristotle dans le monde arabe*, pp. 169–170.

be applied only to a subject which naturally possesses sight. Now there is nothing impossible in the assumption that there is a difference of opinion between Avicenna and Averroes on this point, for they differ on many points in the interpretation of Aristotle. But, if there is such a differences of opinion between them on this point, it is strange that Averroes should make no allusion to it, for Averroes usually calls attention to his differences with Avicenna.

We shall therefore try to show that there is no difference of opinion between Avicenna and Averroes on this point.

In Arabic, as we have already pointed out, owing to the lack of inseparable negative prefixes, both the privative "unseeing" and the infinite "not-seeing" were expressed in the same way, either by *ghair baṣīr* or by *lā baṣīr*. Let us assume then that this kind of privative term became somehow confused with the infinite term, so that both these kinds of terms came to be known as "infinite terms" and propositions formed with both these kinds of terms as predicates also came to be known as "transposed propositions." But let us also assume that despite this confusion there still survived a tradition that one kind of such propositions has the force of a privative proposition and the other kind has the force of a negative proposition. It is for this reason, therefore, that both Averroes and Avicenna, as we have seen, try to explain the twofold meaning of the proposition *Zaid lā baṣīr*. Similarly we may now assume that the two statements, namely, the third and fourth, made by Avicenna with regard to the expression *ghair baṣīr* have reference to the two distinct meanings of that expression. When in his third statement he says that the predicate *ghair baṣīr* can be affirmed only of an existent subject, the predicate in question is the infinite "not-seeing"; but when in his fourth statement he says that this predicate *ghair baṣīr* can be affirmed even of a subject which does not naturally possess sight, the predicate in question is the negative "unseeing."

That these two statements of Avicenna refer to two different kinds of predicates can be established by a study of the literary sources of these statements. Both of them are based upon statements in Aristotle.

Avicenna's third statement that a transposed proposition can be true only of an existent subject, whereas a negative proposition can be true even of a non-existent subject is based upon the following statement in Aristotle. "In the case of 'privation' and 'habit', if the subject is non-existent at all, neither proposition is true. . . . But in the case of 'affirmation' and 'negation', whether the subject exists or not, one is always false and the other true."[48] Now in this passage Aristotle definitely deals with the privation 'blind' as the opposite of the habit 'seeing.' Avicenna, as

[48] *Categ.*, c. 10, 13b, 20–29.

will be noticed, applies what Aristotle says with regard to the privation 'blind' to the infinite *ghair baṣīr*. It is therefore reasonable to assume that by *ghair baṣīr* Avicenna means the infinite "not-seeing," thus agreeing with Averroes' explicit statement that the infinite "not-seeing" is logically the equivalent of the privation "blind."

Avicenna's fourth statement to the effect that the predicate *ghair baṣīr* may be predicated of any subject deprived of sight irrespective of the fact whether (1) it naturally possesses sight, or whether (2) it naturally does not itself possess sight but its genus or species possesses sight, or whether (3) neither itself nor its genus or species naturally possesses sight, reflects the following statement of Aristotle, in which the three possibilities mentioned by Avicenna are given in reverse order. "We speak of 'privation' (1) if something has not one of the attributes which a thing might naturally have, even if this thing itself would not naturally have it . . . (2) if, though either the thing itself or its genus would naturally have an attribute, it has it not . . . (3) if, though it would naturally have the attribute, and when it would naturally have it, it has it not."[49] Now in our analysis above of this passage, as well as of Averroes' commentary thereon, we have shown that the predicates in the case of all these three types of propositions are terms which are privative in form. It is therefore reasonable to assume that Avicenna's *ghair baṣīr* is his parallel statement here was meant by him to be taken in the sense of "unseeing."

Part of Avicenna's discussion of infinite judgments is restated also by Ghazali. Taking the proposition "Zaid is not-seeing (*ghair baṣīr*)" as the subject of his discussion, he describes it as a "transposed proposition" (*qaḍiyyah ma'dūlah*), explaining that the infinite "not-seeing" has the same meaning as the privation "blind" (*a'ma*), and, like Avicenna, he adds that while in negative propositions the subject may be something non-existent in infinite propositions the subject must be something existent.[50] From his statement that the infinite term "not-seeing" means the same as the term "blind" it is quite evident that the term "not-seeing" can be predicated only of a subject which naturally does possess the habit of "sight."

Indirect light on these various types of proposition is thrown also by Maimonides. With regard to negations, he follows Aristotle when in his discussion of the negative attributes of God, as, e.g., in such a proposition as "God is not mortal," he says that this negation does not imply that it negates of God that which He could naturally possess.[51] Then with regard

---

[49] *Metaph.*, V, 22, 1022b, 22–28.

[50] *Maqāṣid al-Falāsifah* I, p. 22, l. 14—p. 23, l. 4. Like Avicenna in *'Ishārāt*, p. 28, l. 1, Ghazali (p. 22, l. 13) refers to Persian as a language in which the copula is not omitted in nominal propositions.

[51] *Moreh Nebukim* I, 58.

to privation, he also follows Aristotle when he says: "Nothing can have a term of 'privation' as its predicate except that in which the 'habit' opposite to that 'privation' can naturally exist, for we do not say of a wall that it is foolish or blind or dumb."[52] Incidentally, the example of a wall is taken from Alexander's commentary on the *Metaphysics*.[53] But then in another place he says that "we do say concerning a wall that it is not seeing."[54] Now the Arabic for that which I have provisionally translated by "is not seeing" is *lā baṣīr*, the very same expression which according to both Avicenna and Averroes may mean either the infinite "not-seeing" or the privative "unseeing." But since Maimonides says that *lā baṣīr* can be predicated even of a wall, which means that the proposition in question is of the same status as a negative proposition, we may assume that it is to be understood here, as in the similar statements of Avicenna and Averroes, in the sense of "unseeing." Though Maimonides makes no direct statement as to the status of infinite propositions, we may also assume that like Avicenna and Averroes he takes them to be of the same status as propositions in which the predicate is a privative term of the type of the term "blind" and not of the type of the term "unseeing."[55]

As a result of our discussion then we know that according to a traditional interpretation of Aristotle in Arabic philosophy a distinction is to be made between a proposition of the type "A is not-seeing" and a proposition of the type "A is unseeing." The former, the infinite proposition, is to be regarded as the equivalent of the privative proposition of the type "A is blind," so that the term "not-seeing" could not be affirmed of a subject which naturally cannot possess sight. The latter, the privative proposition of the type "A is unseeing," is to be regarded as the equivalent of the negative proposition "A is not seeing," so that the term "unseeing" can be predicated even of a subject which cannot naturally possess sight.

We have already pointed out that in Latin philosophy no distinction was made between a privative predicate of the type of "unseeing" and a privative predicate of the type of "blind." Nor, as far as I know, did Latin interpreters of Aristotle try to throw light on the question whether infinite propositions like "A is not-seeing" is the equivalent of privative propositions of the type of "A is blind," or of negative propositions like "A is not seeing." Hobbes indeed takes the proposition "*homo est non lapis*" as an example of a negative proposition,[56] but it is not clear whether

[52] *Millot ha-Higgayon*, Ch. 11.

[53] Cf. above n. 10.

[54] *Moreh Nebukim* I, 58.

[55] Cf. my paper "Maimonides on Negative Attributes" in the Ginzberg Volume, pp. 411–446. Above, pp. 195–230.

[56] *Opera Latina*, 1839, I, p. 31.

this was meant by him to be in opposition to Aristotle's conception of an infinite judgment, or whether it was meant by him to be an interpretation of it, or whether unknowingly he confused an infinite proposition with a negative proposition. Similarly when Wolff describes an infinite proposition as a proposition which in reality is affirmative and not negative, but it has the appearance of a negative proposition,[57] it is also doubtful whether by the last statement he meant that in an infinite proposition like "A is not-seeing" the subject "A" could be something which naturally had no sight. A similar uncertainty is also to be found in Baumgarten's statement that "an affirmative proposition, in which there is a negation, is called infinite."[58]

Through Wolff, it is generally assumed, Kant learned of the old conception of an infinite judgment. The only innovation introduced by him, it is again generally assumed, was in making it into a third kind of judgment under quality and placing it by the side of the affirmative and the negative judgments,[59] and the question was therefore raised whether the introduction of that innovation was at all necessary.[60] But in the light of our discussion of what, according to the Arabic tradition, was the meaning of infinite and privative judgments in Aristotle, the departure of Kant from Aristotle, perhaps unknown to himself, was more fundamental. If the soul is assumed not to be mortal by its very nature, then according to Aristotle, in contradistinction to Kant, it could be said of it that "it is not mortal" but it could not be said of it that "it is not-mortal." Moreover, among the expositors of Kant it is said that his model proposition of an infinite judgment, namely, "the soul is not-mortal" is the same as the proposition "the soul is immortal."[61] According to the traditional interpretation in Arabic philosophy, however, Aristotle would maintain that inasmuch as it is assumed that the soul cannot naturally be mortal, it could be affirmed of it that it is "immortal" but it could not be affirmed of it that it is "not-mortal."

Let us summarize the result of our discussion.

---

[57] Ch. Wolf, *Philosophia Rationalis sive Logica*, §§208–209: "Si negandi particula non refertur ad copulam, sed ad praedicatum, vel subjectum; propositio negativa non est, sed aliquam ejus saltem speciem habet . . . propositio, quae speciem negativam habet, sed revera affirmativa est, infinita dicitur."

[58] A. G. Baumgarten, *Acroasis Logica*, §217: "Propositio affirmans, cui inest negatio, dicitur infinita."

[59] Kant, *Logik*, §22, *Anm.* 3; *Kr. d. rein. Vern.*[1], p. 70.

[60] Cf. W. Hamilton, *Lectures on Logic*, 1866, I, pp. 253–255; Th. Ziehen, *Lehrbuch der Logik*, 1920, pp. 638–640.

[61] Cf. W. T. Krieg, *Logik*, 1833, §55, *Anm.* 3: "*animus est non-mortalis = immortalis*"; C. F. Bachmann, *System der Logik*, 1928, §84, *Anm.* 2: "Die Seele is *nicht-sterblich* (*unsterblich*)."

An analysis of the various texts of Aristotle brings out the fact that he distinguishes four types of proposition.

First, a negative proposition of the type "A is not seeing."

Second, a privative proposition of the type "A is unseeing," in which the predicate is privative in form.

Third, a privative proposition of the type "A is blind," in which the predicate is only privative in meaning.

Fourth, an infinite proposition of the type "A is not-seeing."

With regard to the first type of proposition, Aristotle explicitly says that the subject "A" can be something which naturally never possesses sight, as, e.g., a wall. The same may also be inferred with regard to the second type of proposition.

With regard to the third type of proposition, he explicitly says that the subject "A" must be something which naturally would possess sight, as, e.g., a man.

But with regard to the fourth type of proposition, he does not say whether it is like the first and second types of proposition or like the third type. Nor is any light shed on the subject by Greek and Latin commentators and in general by the western tradition of Aristotle.

From Arabic commentators, however, it may be gathered that the fourth type of proposition in Aristotle is like the third type.

As a result of this analysis and interpretation of Aristotle, the differences between him and Kant are two.

First, with regard to negative propositions of the type "A is not seeing," in which, according to Aristotle "A" can be a "wall," whereas according to Kant it cannot.

Second, with regard to infinite propositions of the type "A is not-seeing," in which according to Aristotle "A" cannot be a "wall," whereas according to Kant it can.

21

GOICHON'S THREE BOOKS ON AVICENNA'S PHILOSOPHY*

Despite its title, the first of the three books of Dr. Goichon does not deal with what is technically known in the history of mediaeval philosophy as the problem of essence and existence. In its strictly technical sense, the problem of essence and existence is a logical problem of predication which may be formulated as a question whether the term existence when predicated of a subject affirms something which is added to the essence of the subject or whether it affirms something which is identical with the essence of the subject. Directly through the works of Avicenna and more so indirectly through Averroes' discussions of the problem, in which Avicenna is held up as the exponent of the view that existence is an accident superadded to the essence of the subject, Avicenna has become associated in western philosophy with that particular view, though historically he is not the originator of it. In the work before us, though this problem in its technical sense is not overlooked, it is used in the title in a much broader sense. It serves as a sort of framework for the entire metaphysics of Avicenna.

The use of this specific problem as a general framework for the entire metaphysics of Avicenna is quite a legitimate device and one may cite as a precedent for it the work of Rivaud in which the philosophy of Spinoza is presented under the general title of "Les notions d'essence et d'existence dans la philosophie de Spinoza" (1906). Still I do not believe that the rearrangement of the topic of Avicenna's metaphysics under these two contrasting terms is any im-

* A.-M. Goichon. *La Distinction de l'Essence et de l'Existence d'après Ibn Sīnā (Avicenne)*. Paris. Desclée de Brouwer. 1937. pp. xvi+546.

Idem, *Lexique de la Langue Philosophique d'Ibn Sīnā (Avicenne)*. Paris. Desclée de Brouwer. 1938. pp. xiv+496.

Idem, *Vocabulaires Comparés d'Aristote et d'Ibn Sīnā*. Paris. Desclée de Brouwer. 1939. pp. xvi+48.

provement upon the order which he himself has followed in his own systematic writings. From the point of view of historical investigation, quite the contrary, any deviation from the original order in which a system of philosophy is presented is in some respects a vitiation of one of the essential characteristics of the system itself. The order chosen by a philosopher for the presentation of his problems is in itself a part of his philosophy. The disposition of the topics of metaphysics in Avicenna's philosophy follows a certain predesigned and well-devised plan, which has deep historical roots and which has also had a far-reaching historical influence. This plan is in itself an integral part of his philosophy.

Still, under the contrast of the concepts of essence and existence, Dr. Goichon manages to deal in logical sequence with every problem dealt with by Avicenna in his formal treatises on metaphysics. Beginning with a discussion of the concept of being or existence, she deals with such topics as the definition of metaphysics in terms of being, the meaning of being and thing, being and unity, being as substance and as accident, and being as truth (pp. 1-28). Proceeding from this to a discussion of the concept of essence, she deals with the problem of universals and predicables (pp. 29-129). A discussion of the relation between essence and existence, including a restatement of Avicenna's view that in God they are identical, whereas in the world they are distinct, naturally follows as the next topic (pp. 130-155).

Inasmuch as the contrast between the identity of essence and existence in God and their distinction in the world implies also contrasts between God as necessary and the world as possible, God as actual and the world as potential and finally God as cause and the world as effect, the author enters into a detailed discussion of these three contrasting concepts (pp. 156-334). Under the last of these three contrasting concepts, she deals with all the variety of problems which are involved in the dependence of the world upon God as its cause (pp. 203-334), such as the nature of creation and emanation, the order of the process of emanation,

God's knowledge and will in the act of creation, the eternity of the process of creation and the intermediaries between God and the world, such as the Intelligences or angels, from among which the Active Intellect and the part it plays in prophecy is singled out for special discussion.

God and the world, each considered in itself, are, as is to be expected, the last two topics discussed by the author (pp. 335-493). Under God, she discusses Avicenna's proof for the existence of God from possibility and necessity (pp. 335-338) and a variety of topics which are generally included under the heading of the nature of God or divine attributes, such as the self-sufficiency of God and the identity of His essence with truth, goodness, love and life (pp. 355-374). Under the world, she discusses such topics as matter, form, body, the principle of individuation and the world of immaterial beings (pp. 377-493).

This wide range of topics, in their new arrangement devised by the author, covers the entire field of metaphysics as treated by Avicenna in the fourth Book of his *Shifa'* and the third Book of his *Najāt*. Now every student of philosophy knows that none of these topics was invented by Avicenna. They all go back to some source and they are all, in the form in which they are stated by Avicenna, the result of a long process of historical development. Dr. Goichon, however, does not go in for genetically historical studies. When she discusses Avicenna's concept of being, for instance, she does not try to find out how the various topics under this problem have developed from Aristotle's definition of metaphysics as being *qua* being (*Metaphysics* VI, 1, 1026a, 31-32) and from his fourfold division of being into being by accident, being in the sense of truth, being as potential and as actual, and being according to the ten varieties of the categories (*ibid.* V, 7, 1017a, 7 ff.). Again, when she discusses Avicenna's concept of essence, she does not try to find out how the topics dealt with in this discussion have developed from Aristotle's treatment of the predicables in the various parts of his *Organon* and from his scattered statements about the nature of universals in various places in his works. Similarly when she discusses Avicenna's conception of God as the Necessary Being, she does not try to find out how this conception has developed from Aristotle's brief statement that God is the Absolutely Necessary (*Metaphysics* XII, 7, 1072b, 10-13). When she discusses Avicenna's conception of the order of the process of emanation, she does not try to find out how this has developed from the order of the process of emanation as conceived by Plotinus. And so also with every other topic dealt with in the book. Every one of these topics has a long and complicated history—a history which is to be followed up not as a mere aesthetic satisfaction to a prying intellectual curiosity but rather as a primary and essential requirement for an exact and thorough understanding of the full significance of Avicenna's own position. But not having gone into this kind of inquiry, as the author herself admits (*Vocabulaires,* p. xi), she did well, I believe, in refraining from scattering some casual references to ancient sources, such as Aristotle and Plotinus. To do so would have been easy, but it would hardly have met the situation. In most cases there is a wide gap between any single ancient source and the corresponding statement by Avicenna—a gap which can be filled only by a complete and painstaking study of the problem in each particular case. Any historical study of this kind if it is done at all, should be done properly or else it should be omitted altogether. To have omitted historical investigations in a work like this on Avicenna is no defect; it is only a self-limitation on the part of the author of the scope of her undertaking. To have attempted to do it haphazardly would have been indeed a serious defect.

Limited though the book is with respect to external historical sources, it abounds in passages quoted from the writing of Avicenna with certain selections of parallel passages from the writings of Farabi and Ghazali. According to the author's own statement, no less than 2,500 passages are quoted in carefully prepared translations (*Lexique,* p. x). Owing to the inaccessibility of the works of Avicenna to the general student of philosophy, the work of Dr. Goichon, besides its being a study of Avicenna, has the additional merit of a source book.

Another valuable feature of the book is its many studies of terminology. Especially notable is its discussion of the Arabic terms for essence (pp. 30-45) and of the terms expressing the concept of creation (pp. 244-258). To these studies of terminology, which are scattered throughout the first of the three books (*Distinction*), the author has added a second book (*Lexique*) in which 792 Arabic terms are minutely defined in their various shades of meaning and copiously illustrated by appropriate quotations both in the original Arabic and in translation. A third book (*Vocabulaires*), described as a supplement to the second book, provides 450 Greek equivalents to as many Arabic terms.

In the *Lexique*, where the chief purpose of the author was to determine the fine shades of the meaning of terms out of the internal evidence of Arabic texts, she has purposely omitted Greek equivalents, for the reason, as she declares, that there are not always Greek equivalents for certain shades of meaning which Arabic philosophic terms have acquired in the course of their history (*Vocabulaires,* p. viii), and consequently in her *Vocabulaires* she has confined herself to terms for which exact Greek equivalents could be found. While the statement is on the whole true, it exaggerates, in my opinion, the impossibility of finding Greek equivalents for the special meanings which philosophic terms have acquired in Arabic literature. Intensive studies of the history of the problems as well as of the texts in which such terms are used in their special meaning will often bring to light, I believe, their exact Greek equivalents. I shall try to illustrate this point by the example of a few terms which the present reviewer once had occasion to investigate.

The term *wahm* in its technical sense of what the Scholastics call *aestimatio* is declared by the author to have no Greek equivalent (*Vocabulaires,* p. 40). But I have shown, by a study of the history of the problem, that this term reflects the Greek terms σύνεσις, φρόνησις and πρόνοια as used by Aristotle in connection with animals (*cf.* my "The Internal Senses in Latin, Arabic and Hebrew Philosophic Texts," *Harvard Theological Review,* 28 (1935), pp. 89-90). Incidentally, under *ẓann* (*Lexique,* § 405), the author should have recorded Avicenna's use of the term as an equivalent of *wahm* (*cf.* "The Internal Senses," *ibid.,* p. 100, n. 43, and also p. 93, n. 22, and p. 106, n. 64). It may also be remarked that the references to Aristotle's *De Anima* III, 9, 432a, 16; III, 2, 426b, 10; and *Analytica Posteriora* II, 19, 99b, 35 which the author suggests as possible sources for *wahm* (*Vocabulaires,* p. 40) have nothing to do with *wahm.* The τὸ κριτικόν implied in all these three passages refers only to the element of discrimination which according to Aristotle is to be found in the external senses (*cf.* commentaries of Rodier and Hicks on *De Anima,* 432a, 16).

For *fikr* in its various forms the term διάνοια is given by the author as the Greek equivalent (*Vocabulaires,* p. 25). This is true for the original meaning of the term *fikr.* But the term is also used by Avicenna in its newly acquired meaning as a designation of one of the internal senses, and the author herself reports this special use of the term under *mufakkirah* (*Lexique,* § 524). Now the Greek equivalent of this special use of *fikr* is not διάνοια but rather φαντασία λογιστική or βουλευτική (*cf.* "The Internal Senses," *op. cit.,* pp. 91-92).

In trying to assign Greek equivalents to Arabic philosophic terms one must never lose sight of the distinction between terms which are equivalents both etymologically and in meaning, and terms which are equivalents only in meaning but differ in etymology. This distinction is quite often overlooked by Dr. Goichon in her *Vocabulaires.* In many instances, when Greek etymological equivalents could be found for their corresponding Arabic terms, she gives terms which are equivalents in meaning only. I shall illustrate this by several examples.

For *ḥāfiẓah* the author gives the Greek μνήμη (*Vocabulaires,* p. 8). Etymologically the Arabic for this Greek term is *dhākirah*. *Ḥāfiẓah* is its equivalent only in meaning. I have shown that the use of *ḥāfiẓah* in the sense of memory reflects the Greek σωτηρία used by Plato in *Philebus* 34A and John of Damascus in *De Fide Orthodoxa* II, 20, also the Greek συντήρησις used by Galen in connection with memory in *Definitiones Medicae* 124 (*Opera Omnia,* ed. Kühn, XIX, 381) and perhaps also the term ἕξις in the expression φαντάσματος ἕξις used by Aristotle in connection with memory in *De Memoria et Reminiscentia,* 1, 451a, 15-16 (*cf.* "The Internal Senses," *op. cit.*, p. 102, n. 49).

For *riyāḍīyah* the author gives the Greek μαθηματική (*Vocabulaires,* p. 8, under *Ḥikmah*). Etymologically the Arabic for this Greek term is *ta'līmīyah,* for which, by the way, the author does not give its use in the sense of mathematics (*Lexique,* § 457). The Arabic *riyāḍīyah,* I have shown, reflects the Greek προπαιδεία (or rather παιδεία) which Plato uses as a description of mathematics in *Republic* VII, 536 D. (*cf.* my "Classification of the Sciences in Mediaeval Jewish Philosophy," *Hebrew Union College Jubilee Volume,* 1925, p. 268, n. 22). It is interesting to note that one of the Hebrew translations of the Arabic term *riyāḍah* is the Biblical word *musar* which in the Septuagint is often translated by παιδεία (*cf.* my "Additional Notes to . . . the Classification of the Sciences," *Hebrew Union College Annual,* 3 (1926), p. 372).

For *ḥalla* the author gives the passive Greek δέχεσθαι (*Vocabulaires,* p. 8). Etymologically there is no connection between these two terms. I have once suggested that the Arabic *ḥalla* reflects the Greek ἔπειμι which is used exactly in the same sense by Plotinus when he speaks of form as coming upon, or entering into (ἔπεισι), matter (*Enneads,* II, 4, 8, ed. Didot, p. 75, 1. 44. *cf.* my *Crescas' Critique of Aristotle,* 1929 p. 544, n. 11).

For the term *maḥall* the author gives the Greek δεκτικόν, *réceptacle* (*Vocabulaires,* p. 8). However, there is no etymological connection between these terms. Furthermore, there is a good Arabic etymological equivalent of this

Greek term in the term *qābil* (*cf.* Ghazali, *Maqāṣid al-Falāsifah* II: Metaphysics I, Cairo, without date, p. 90, ll. 8-14). The author refers to *Categories,* 5, 4a, 11, as evidence for her explanation of the term *maḥall.* But in that passage the Greek δεκτικόν is translated by the Arabic *qābil* (cf. Bouyges, *Averroès: Talkhiç Kitab al-Maqoulat,* 1932, p. 33, l. 141 of text at bottom of page). I therefore suggest, though I have no textual evidence at hand to support this suggestion, that *maḥall* reflects the Greek χώρα and ἕδρα (*Timaeus* 52 A and *cf. Physics* IV, 2, 209b, 11-12) which Plato identifies with matter on account of the fact that matter like these two terms is also a "receptacle": ὑποδοχή (*Timaeus* 51 A) or a "participant": μεταληπτικόν (*Physics* IV, 2, 209b, 12-13 reflecting μεταλαμβάνον in *Timaeus* 51A). The latter of these terms, however, was taken in the Arabic version of the *Physics* to mean "recipient of change"; for, according to the Latin translation of that Arabic version, it was rendered into Arabic by "*illud . . . quod recipit mutationem*" (*Aristotelis Opera, Venetiis, apud Iuntas* 1574, Vol. IV, p. 126 L) which is interpreted by Averroes as "*illud quod recipit mutationem et successionem formarum*" (*ibid.,* com. 15, p. 127 C). The Greek χώρα and ἕδρα and the Arabic *maḥall* all have the same essential meaning—*place, position, abode.*

An understandable slip is the author's use of the Greek συνώνυμον as used in *Categories,* 1, la, 6, as the equivalent of the Arabic *ism murādif* (*Vocabulaires,* p. 13 under *Smw*). This is not quite correct. In Aristotle, as Liddell and Scott will tell us, the term συνώνυμον has two meanings. In logic, it means a term which is applied to two things which are the same in genus but differ in species and it is usually translated by the Latin *univocus.* In rhetoric, it refers to words which have a different form but the same meaning. Now in Arabic, the Greek term in its logical sense is translated by *ism mutawāṭi',* whereas the same term in its rhetorical sense has the same meaning as the term "synonym" in English and is translated by *ism murādif* (see, *e. g.*, Bouyges, *Averroès: Talkhiç Kitab al-Makoulat,* p. 6, 1. 5 of text at bottom of page; Ghazali, *Maqāṣid al-Falāsifah* I: Logic, p. 11; *cf.* D. Z. Baneth, "La-Terminologiyyah ha-Philosopfit shel ha-Rambam," *Tarbiz,* 6 (1935), p. 35). Consequently the Arabic for συνώνυμον in *Categories,* 1, 1a, 6, is not *ism murādif* but rather *ism mutawāṭi'*.

For *taṣdīq* the author gives πίστις as the Greek equivalent (*Vocabulaires,* p. 15). Etymologically, however, the Arabic for this Greek term is *īmān* or *i'tiqād*. But still in Arabic translations from the Greek, the Greek πιστεύειν is sometimes translated by the Arabic *taṣdīq*, as, for instance, in the Arabic translation of *Metaphysics* III, 2, 997b, 18 (cf. Bouyges, *Averroès: Tafsir Ma Ba'd at-Tabi'at,* 1938, p. 208, 1. 5). Undoubtedly, the Arabic term *taṣdīq,* like so many other Arabic terms, has acquired a new meaning, and this new meaning, again as in the case of so many other Arabic terms, must have been acquired by it as a result of its close association with that term whose meaning it has acquired. In this particular case, I believe, the explanation is to be found in the old definition of belief (*īmān, i'tiqād*) in terms of truth (*taṣdīq*) which was current in Arabic philosophy (*cf.* Shahrastani, *Kitāb al-Milal wal-Niḥal,* ed. Cureton, p. 62, 1. 20, and p. 73, 11. 2-3; Maimonides, *Moreh Nebukim* I, 50 beginning; *cf.* also D. Kaufmann, *Geschichte der Attributenlehre in der jüdischen Religionsphilosophie des Mittelalters,* p. 369, n. 9).

A similar consideration may also explain the use of the term *taṣdīq* in the statement that all knowledge is either *taṣawwur* or *taṣdīq,* which occurs so often in Arabic books on logic and which the author herself quotes from Avicenna's *Najāt* (*Lexique,* § 347). On the whole, this distinction reflects Aristotle's distinction between φάσις and κατάφασις (*De Interpretatione,* 4, 16b, 27-28) of which the corresponding Arabic terms are *lafẓah and ījāb* (*cf.* I. Pollak, *Die Hermeneutik des Aristoteles in der arabischen Übersetzung des Isḥāk Ibn Ḥonain,* 1913, p. 6). Now as for the change of φάσις to *taṣawwur* it has been explained as being due to the Stoic restatement of Aristotle's distinction as a distinction between φαντασία and συγκατάθεσις (*cf*. Paul Kraus, "Abstracta Islamica," p. 220, in *Revue des Études Islamiques*, 9, 1935). The use of the term *taṣdīq*, however, is not explainable by its corresponding Stoic term, for they are not etymological equivalents. Here, again, the explanation is to be found in the fact that Aristotle defines ἀποφαντικός in its affirmative sense (κατάφασις) in contradistinction to its negative sense (ἀπόφασις) as that which contains truth: τὸ ἀληθεύειν (*cf*. *De Interpretatione*, 4, 17a, 2-3, and 6, 17a, 25-26), and so also the term συγκατάθεσις is used by the Stoics as a criterion of truth.

Etymologically, then, the Greek equivalent of *taṣdīq* is ἀληθεύειν.

In the light of the preceding discussion, furthermore, Avicenna does not always use *taṣawwur* as the equivalent of the Greek νόημα (*Vocabulaires*, p. 15). In other Arabic texts the term *taṣawwur* is definitely used in the sense of imagination as one of the internal senses (*cf*. "The Internal Senses," *op. cit.*, p. 105, n. 61; *cf*. also p. 100, n. 42; 104, n. 58; p. 108, n. 73). On the whole, it would seem that the Arabic *taṣawwur* has the general meaning of being represented by a form, and it is always to be determined from the context whether it is an intellectual form or an imaginative form. This may be inferred from the fact that in *De Anima* III, 3, 427b, 27, τὸ νοεῖν is translated not by *al-taṣawwur* but rather by *al-taṣawwur bi-al-'aql* (*cf*. Averroes' Middle Commentary on *De Anima ad loc.*, MS. Paris, Bibliothèque Nationale, Cod. Heb. 1009) and it is said to consist partly of imagination φαντασία, *takhayyul*) and partly of judgment (ὑπόληψις, *ra'y*) (*cf*. *De Anima*, *loc. cit.* 28).

We do not hesitate to assert that these works of Dr. Goichon on Avicenna contain notable contributions to our knowledge of Arabic philosophic terminology as well as valuable material for further study and research.

22

SYNEDRION IN GREEK JEWISH LITERATURE AND PHILO

Professor Zeitlin, with his usual thoroughness and attention to original sources, has raised and discussed the question as to the use of the term synedrion in the sense of a court of justice prior to the Jabneh period (*JQR*, 36, 1945, pp. 109-140). But, as it sometimes happens in investigations of this kind, however far one may probe, some considerations are overlooked. I wish to call attention to a few of such considerations.

It is true that the term *synedrion* in Greek is used in the sense of council as the opposite of the term *dikasterion* which is used in the sense of a court of justice. Schürer (*Geschichte*, II[4], p. 243, n. 14), who happens to remark that in later Greek it is used in the sense of court, refers only to Hesychius in support of his remark. But Hesychius is late, in the 5th century C. E., and he quotes no passages from earlier literature as illustrative of this new use of the term *synedrion*. The only purpose of Schürer's reference to Hesychius in this connection was evidently to show that a pagan author, who presumably was not influenced by the Palestinian Jewish usage of the term, gives *dikasterion* as the only meaning of *synedrion*. The article on "Synhedrion" in Pauly-Wissowa contains only one reference to a special use of the term synhedrion (col. 1346, ll. 20 22) which may have some bearing upon the Hebrew use of the term sanhedrin as a body concerned with religious laws and rites, and that is its use in the sense of a body of counsellors which had supervision over the improvement and the interpretation of the laws relating to the rites of the mysteries, without, however, having the power of changing those laws. (Cf. also col. 1352, ll. 44 ff.)

Still, even if the term *synedrion* was never used among non-Jews in the sense of a court of justice, one can see how that term, once introduced into Judaism, would acquire that new meaning. For in the form of government which they enjoyed, the Jews, unlike the Greeks, had no such an institution as a purely deliberative council existing apart from judiciary bodies. In the Bible indeed "elders" are spoken of as counsellors (I Kings 12.6-8; Ezek. 7.26; Ezra 10.8), but they are also described as exercising the function of judges (Deut. 22.15-19; 25.7-9; Job 32.9), thus showing that they were at once counsellors and judges, and they continued to exercise these two functions also after the biblical period. When therefore the organized body of elders, which flourished continuously during the period of the second commonwealth under a succession of different names, began to be called synedrion — a term which in the Greek meant council — quite naturally that term acquired also the meaning of a court of justice.

This new meaning of the term synedrion among the Jews appears already in the pre-tannaitic Jewish literature written in Greek. A close examination of the context of some of those very same passages quoted by Professor Zeitlin to show the exclusive use of the term synedrion in the sense of council will show quite the opposite, that it is used in the sense of a court of justice.

Let us examine the passages quoted by Professor Zeitlin.

Of the eight verses quoted from the Book of Proverbs (p. 111) in at least one verse, 22.10, the term synedrion is quite unmistakably used in the sense of a court of justice, for it is given there as a rendering of the Hebrew word דין. This has already been pointed out by Schürer (*loc. cit.*). But the evidence of this verse is even stronger than was supposed by Schürer, for undoubtedly, instead of the masoretic וישבת דין, the Septuagint had here the reading וישב בית דין (comp. C. H. Toy's Commentary *ad loc.*), which makes the term *synedrion* here used as a translation of the Hebrew *bet din.*

Of the three verses quoted from Ben Sirah (p. 112) one definitely points to the use of the term synedrion in the sense of a court of justice. For when the Greek version of Ben Sirah says "sit (*synedreue*) not in judgment with sinners" (11.9), the word judgment (*κρίσις*, ריב) here, which both in Greek and in Hebrew has the technical meaning of a law-suit, quite conclusively shows that the noun synedrion implied in the verb *synedreue* is a court of justice. Similarly in the quotation from the Psalms of Solomon (p. 112), when in the Greek version of that book the profane man who is said to sit in the "synedrion" of the pious (4.1) is subsequently said to be "severe of speech in condemning sinners in judgment (*κρίσει*) and his hand is first upon the sinner as though acting in zeal" (4.2–3), it is quite evident that the "synedrion" spoken of is a court of justice, for the last statement quite evidently refers to Deut. 17.7 and 13.10 which deal with the execution of the judgment of a court of justice. So also in the passages quoted from Josephus (p. 113), when Josephus says that Herod "assembled a synedrion of his friends and relations and accused (*κατηγόρει*) this wretched woman of numerous misdeeds," (*Bell. Jud.* I, 29, 2, 571) the term "accused," for which the Greek used here has the technical meaning of bringing legal charges, clearly shows that the synedrion called together by Herod had a quasi-judicial character.

With reference to the passages in Philo (p. 112), it can be shown, I believe, that in three or four places the term synedrion is used in the sense of a court of justice.

First, in *Quod Omnis Probus Liber Sit* 2, § 11, speaking of men who are not guided by reason, Philo says of them figuratively that "their unstable synedrion is always open to bribes from those who are brought to trial (*κρινομένων*)." The context quite clearly indicates that the allusion here is to a synedrion in the sense of a court of justice.

Second, in *Legatio ad Gaium* 44, §§ 349–350, Philo complains that Caligula acted not as a judge (*δικαστής*) sitting with his "synedroi" but as an accuser (*κατήγορος*). The terms "judge" and "accuser" quite clearly show that the term "synedroi" in this passage is used in the sense of members of a court of justice.

Finally, there are two parallel passages which, when taken together, show conclusively that at least in one of them Philo uses the term synedrion in the sense of a court of justice. In one passage (*De Praemiis et Poenis* 2, § 28), there occurs the expression *συνέδριον καὶ δικαστήριον*; in another passage (*De Vita Contemplativa* 3, § 27), there occurs the expression *συνέδριον καὶ βουλευτήριον*. Now, if the conjunction *καὶ* is used in both passages to join two contrasting terms, then in the first passage the term *synedrion*, being used in contrast to the term *dikasterion*, is definitely a council, but in the second passage, being used in contrast to the term *bouleuterion*, the term *synedrion* is definitely a court of justce. And if the conjunction *καὶ* is used on both passages to join two terms of the same meaning, then in the first passage the term *synedrion* is definitely a court of justice, whereas in the second passage it is definitely a council.

Professor Zeitlin is undoubtedly right in his view that prior to the destruction of the second Temple there were in Jerusalem two Sanhedrins. This view, elaborately developed by Büchler, may be supported on many grounds. But Professor Zeitlin's present attempt to show that the term synedrion was never used before the rise of the school of Jabneh in the sense of a court of justice (*bet din*), while plausible, cannot be sustained on the basis of the evidence marshalled by him. Especially vulnerable is his statement (pp. 126–127) that "the term Sanhedrin never occurs prior to the destruction of the Temple in tannaitic literature." Of course, it does not occur in tannaitic literature prior to the destruction of the Temple, because the entire tannaitic literature as we have it comes from a period after the destruction of the Temple. But certainly Professor Zeitlin does not mean thereby to say, as in fact some scholars do actually say, that every statement found in the tannaitic literature with reference to conditions in Judaism before the destruction of the Temple, or before the rise of Christianity, is to be taken as a later fictitious invention of the rabbis. I imagine what Professor Zeitlin means to say is that the tannaitic literature is to be assumed to contain two types of material, one reflecting earlier usages and teachings and the other reflecting later innovations, and that the use of the term *sanhedrin* as synonymous with *bet din* in every tannaitic passage is a later innovation. Now the main proposition is true enough. But when he wants us to believe that the use of the term *sanhedrin* for *bet din* which occurs in the tannaitic literature is a later innovation, he is assuming something which, I must admit, sounds plausible, but for which he has no evidence. One cannot arbitrarily select from the tannaitic literature that which suits one's purpose and declare it to belong to a time before the destruction of the Temple, or before the rise of Christianity, and with equal arbitrariness reject anything that does not suit one's purpose and declare it as a later innovation. There is no internal evidence of a positive and objective nature by which one could be justified in saying definitely that the use of the term sanhedrin as synonymous with *bet din* in such tannaitic sources as M. Sanhedrin I, 6, or in Sifra, va-Yiḳra (ed. Weiss, 19a) is a later invention of the Jabneh period. And as for external evidence, we have seen how Greek Jewish writers before the Jabneh period used the term *synedrion* in the sense of *bet din*.

23

TWO COMMENTS REGARDING THE PLURALITY OF WORLDS IN JEWISH SOURCES

ON P. 213, N. 23, OF HIS PAPER in *JQR* for January, 1965, Dr. Lamm refers to *Berakot* 32b as containing a statement about the existence of a plurality of worlds. This is incorrect. The statement does not deal with the existence of a plurality of worlds. It deals with the existence of a plurality of stars in the signs of the zodiac which are in the heaven called *raḳiʿa,* that is, the second of the seven heavens (cf. *Ḥagigah* 12b), in this world of ours.

On p. 215, a statement in Saadia's *Commentary on Sefer Yeṣirah* is reproduced by him to read as follows: "Those who do accept the idea of many worlds believe that the talmudic statement refers to successive worlds, the present one being the 18,000th." On the basis of this reading of the statement, he concludes that none of those who accepted the idea of many worlds interpreted the talmudic passage as referring to simultaneous 18,000 worlds and, in conformity with this conclusion of his, he analyzes the entire passage in Saadia.

All this is incorrect.

The statement does not say that "those" who accept the idea of many worlds take the talmudic 18,000 worlds to mean successive worlds; what it says is that "some of those" who agree with the talmudic saying take its 18,000 worlds to mean successive worlds (cf. Arabic text, p. 6, 11. 3-4, and French translation, p. 20, 11. 2-5, in Lambert's edition of the work). The statement thus quite evidently implies that others who agreed with the same talmudic saying took its 18,000 worlds to mean not successive worlds but rather simultaneous worlds.

A correct analysis of the entire passage, of which the foregoing statement is the conclusion, is as follows:

1. Restatement of the view of a third groups of Platonized Atomists who believed in the simultaneous existence of innumerable worlds, all of them having been created out of preëxistent eternal atoms (p. 5, ll. 8-9). For the identification of these three groups with a view combining Atomism with Plato, see discussion in my paper "The Kalam Problem of Nonexistence and Saadia's Second Theory of Creation" in this *Quartely*, N. S., 36 (1946), pp. 385-387.

2. Remark about someone who might think that the talmudic saying about the existence of 18,000 worlds is similar to the saying of the third group of Platonized Atomists about the simultaneous

existence of innumerable worlds followed by Saadia's comment that the talmudic saying differs from the saying of that group of the Platonized Atomists in that "he who gave utternace to this saying about the 18,000 worlds maintained that every one of these worlds was created by God out of nothing" (p. 5, ll. 10-14).

3. Reference to some unnamed philosophers who believed in the simultaneous existence of a plurality of worlds equal in number to the number of stars in this world (p. 5, ll. 14-19).

4. Repetition of the talmudic saying about 18,000 worlds with the addition of a scriptural proof-text, upon which Saadia comments as follows: "Our people are not of one mind with regard to this saying [of the Talmud] and so, having reported [and explained] that saying, we let it go and passed on to our next statement. But some of those who agree with this saying [of the Talmud] believe that it refers to one world after another, this world in which we are being the 18,000th" (p. 5, l. 19-p. 6, l. 4).

In this last quotation, the statement "our people are not of one mind with regard to this saying" refers to oral discussions among contemporaries of Saadia about the 18,000 worlds of the talmudic saying. References to oral discussions among his contemporaries about various topics are similarly to be found in his *Emunot ve-De'ot*. Among those contemporaries of his who discissed that talmudic saying about the 18,000 worlds, some did not agree with it, believing as they did, like Saadia himself, in one world; others, however, agreed with it, but of these, some interpreted its 18,000 worlds, like Saadia, as referring to simultaneous worlds, each of them created out of nothing, whereas others interpreted them as referring to successive worlds, each of them, again, created out of nothing. All this is in line with what I tried to show in *Philo* that, while Philo himself has laid down the belief in the unity of the world as a fundamental scriptural doctrine, none of the subsequent religious philosophers, whether Jewish or Christian and, I may add, also Muslim, followed him on this point. As a rule, like Philo, they followed the Platonico-Aristotelian conception of one world; still they did not make it a mandatory religious belief, but allowed one to believe in many worlds, whether simultaneous or successive, provided only that each of the worlds was believed to have been created by God according to what was considered as the right conception of creation. This is exactly the position of Saadia.

Evidence that among Arabic-speaking Jews close to the time of Saadia (d. 942) there were those who took the talmudic statement to mean 18, 000 simultaneous worlds is to be found in the use made of it, quite evidently under Jewish influence, by some Muslim commentators on the Koran. As reported by Baghdādī (d. 1037) in his *Uṣūl al-Dīn* (ed. Istambul, 1346/1928), p. 34, ll. 4-5, some commentators, on the basis of the plural *al-ʿālamīna* used in the Koran (1 : 1 and *passim*), say that "God has 18,000 worlds, every one of them being like the perceptible world."

24

COLCODEA, קולקודיא

Professor Efros in *JQR*, XXXVI (1945), p. 79, was right in suspecting that the term קולקודיא was Arabic and in trying to find some appropriate Arabic term of which the term in question could be a corruption. He hit upon the right term in Goldziher's note on the discussion of the Active Intellect in pseudo-Baḥya's *Ma'ānī al-Nafs*, p. 42*, though he did not hit upon the right explanation.

The question of how the term *colcodea* in Latin characters and קולקודיא in Hebrew characters came to be used in the sense of "giver of forms," which is one of the appellations of the Active Intellect, is dealt with by M. Steinschneider in his *Die hebraeischen Uebersetzungen*, p. 563, n. 183, and *Die arabische Literatur der Juden*, pp. 28–29, and also by C. A. Nallino in "La 'Colcodea' d'Avicenna et T. Campanella", *Giornale Critico della Filosofia Italiana*, VI (1925), pp. 84–91. I shall present here briefly what may be gathered from their discussion, with the interspersion and addition of a few comments of my own.

Nallino shows that the first mention of the term *colcodea* as being the original Arabic for the expression "giver of forms" occurs in a commentary by Niphus (1473–1546) on the Latin translation of Averroes' *Tahāfut al-Tahāfut* published in 1497. Commenting upon a passage in which Averroes ascribes the term *dans formam* (read: *formas*) to "Avicenna and others," he says: "arabice tamen colcodea." In two other places in the same commentary he makes the same remark with regard to the expression *dator formarum*. Similar remarks occur also in his *De intellectu libri sex*, written in the year 1492, and *Metaphysicarum disputationum dilucidarium*, written in the years 1507–1510. In all these places, it is quite evident, that Niphus, not knowing that the Latin *dans formas* or *dator formarum* was a literal translation of the Arabic *wāhib al-ṣuwar*, assumed that the underlying Arabic term was *colcodea*.

The next to use the term *colcodea* in the same sense is *Zimara* (1460–1532). In his *Solutiones contradictionum in dictis Averrois*, published in the year 1508, in a passagae corresponding to *Metaphysics* XII, comm. 38, he connects *dator formarum* with *colcodea* by the disjunctive conjunction *seu* (comp. *Aristotelis opera*, Venice, 1574, Vol. VIII, fol.

421 v 2). The same connection of these two terms by *seu* occurs also in an anonymous marginal note on Averroes' Long Commentary on *Metaphysics* XII, comm. 18 (comp. *op. cit.*, fol. 304 A–B).

From these two authors the term *colcodea* passed over into the writings of Campanella (1568–1639).

As for the use of that term by Jehiel of Pisa (d. c. 1567–72 in *Minḥat Ḳena'at,* Nallino seems to have known about it, as well as about Kaufmann's query, only from Steinschneider's reference to it in his *Die arabische Literatur der Juden*, p. 29, for he repeats a typographical error of the latter, giving p. 36 instead of 30. He describes its occurrence on p. 30 as "the only appearance" of that term in the book, even though Steinschneider refers also to its occurrence on p. 67. He refers also to Kaufmann as having found "no parallel in other Hebrew books," even though Kaufmann quotes the corresponding passage in Joseph Solomon Delmedigo's *Nobelot Ḥokmah,* p. 17b, in his note on *Minḥat Ḳena'ot,* p. 67, and even though Steinschneider himself refers also to "Josef del Medigo." The use of the term in the *Minḥat Ḳena'ot,* says Nallino, "is undoubtedly due to Niphus and to Zimara." To this conjectural comment it may be added that Niphus is mentioned in the *Minḥat Kena'ot* on p. 33.

To the same Latin sources is quite evidently also due the use of that term by Joseph Solomon Delmedigo (1591–1655) in his *Nobelot Ḥokmah,* p. 17b. The spelling קולכודיאה instead of קולקודיאה as in the *Minḥat Ḳena'ot,* p. 67, is undoubtedly due to the fact that the author has used Niphus' commentary on Averroes' *Tahāfut al-Tahāfut* in its edition of 1517, where the spelling of *colcodea* is *colchodea* (comp. quotation in M. Bouyges' edition *Averroes*: *Tahafot at-Tahafot,* 1930, p. 407). The influence of Niphus is quite evident also on Delmedigo's discussion of the subject matter.

But the question may now be raised as to how Niphus came to assume that the Arabic term underlying the Latin *dans formas* or *dator formarum* was *colcodea.* From the data gathered by Steinschneider and the discussion of Nallino the answer may be presented as follows.

In Arabic, ther term *kadkhudā,* which is of Persian origin (كد خدا, *kad khuda*), means literally "master of a house." It is in this literal sense, quite evidently, that the term is used in the passage quoted by Goldziher in his note on pseudo-Baḥya's *Ma'ānī al-Nafs,* p. 42*, in which the Active Intellect is described as being "by the order of God the housemaster of the elementary things"; and it is to be noted that the term *kadkhudā* is not used there by itself as one of the several appellations of the Active Intellect. This term, however, is used also technically in the astrological sense of the "Master of a House," corresponding to the same astrological meaning of the similar Greek term *οἰκοδεσπότης*. As a result of this astrological use, the term has also acquired the special meaning of "lifetime" or the "duration of life," inasmuch as the duration of one's life was supposed to have been determined by the particular Master of the House who happened to have presided at the time of birth (comp. G. Flügel, *Al-Kindī*, p. 24, No. 70). It is in this sense that the term is used in the title of the astrological work *al-Hīlāj wal-Kadkhuda* by Sahl ibn Bishr (c. 820). Now in the Latin astrological literature, the term *al-kadkhudā*, which it has taken over from the Arabic, appears under various forms, among them *alcochoden* and *acolhodebia*, and is translated in various ways, among them also *dans vitam*. By confusing *dans vitam* with *dans formam*, it is assumed, Niphus came to say that the underlying Arabic term for *dans formam* or *dans formas* or *dator formarum* was what he reproduces as *colcodea*.

In this explanation, it will be noticed, there is one gap. It fails to account for the verbal transition from *dans vitam* to *dans formam* or *formas*, though there is a logical transition between them. I believe the explanation can be improved a little.

The expression *dans vitam* as a translation of the term *alcochoden* is, according to Steinschneider, to be found in Alchabitius. Nallino must have relied upon this reference in Steinschneider when he explains *alcochoden* as meaning *daotre della vita*, for he gives no reference in support of this meaning. However, in the printed text of Alchabitius' *Liber isagogicus*, Venice, 1482, which I have examined, I did not find the expression *dans vitam* as a translation of the term *alcochoden*. The passage found there reads as follows: "*De alcochoden. Et hoc alcochoden q. e. significator vite idest dominus annorum: vel dans annos*" (unnumbered fol. 23 r). Let us assume now that in the text used by Niphus, perhaps a manuscript, the words *dominus annorum vel dans annos* were abbreviated in such a way as to lead Niphus to read them *dominus animarum vel dans animas*. Such an assumption is justifiable, for on the reverse side of the same folio, last line, in the same printed text, "alcochoden" is said to mean *dn̄s ãni.*, which, but for the stroke over the letter *a*, would stand for *dans animas*. Now it happens that in that passage in Averroes' *Tahāfut al-Tahāfut* in which the expression *dans formas* occurs, and to which Niphus has added his remark *arabice tamen colcodea*, the terms *forma* (*ṣūrah*) and *anima* (*nafs*) are repeatedly used as alternatives (Comp. Arabic ed. Bouyges, p. 407, ll. 2–15; Latin with Niphus' commentary, Lugduni, [1529], fol. 219b–220a; *Aristotelis opera*, Venice, 1574, Vol. IX, fol. 101 L–102 A). Moreover in Algazali's *Maqāṣid al-Falāsifah*, with the Latin translation of which Niphus was undoubtedly acquainted, the expression *dator animarum* (*wāhib al-nufūs*) does actually occur (comp. Latin ed. J. T. Muckle, p. 182, l. 20; Arabic, p. 301, l. 3). One can readily see how Niphus, with his belief that the Arabic *alcochoden* means *dans animas*, could have assumed that the Arabic term underlying the "giver of forms," which to him meant the same as the "giver of souls," should be the term *alcochoden*, which term he reproduces from memory, on the basis of its various forms, as *colcodea*.

25
SOME GUIDING PRINCIPLES IN DETERMINING SPINOZA'S MEDIAEVAL SOURCES

THE hunt for mediaeval Hebrew and Latin sources of Spinoza is an old and venerable game. I myself have done some hunting in this field, and the chase for me has by no means come to an end with the publication of my book on *The Philosophy of Spinoza*, for by its mere publication a book does not become to its maker a closed masoretic text in which the right of emendation is to be exercised only by higher and lower criticism. Since the appearance of that book I have gathered some three hundred additional passages of miscellaneous origin. Some of these call for revision of certain statements in the book or for the improvement of certain infelicities of expression or for the expansion of certain views too briefly expressed. For the greater part, however, they are merely duplicates of passages I have used and serve only to confirm my statement that the passages quoted or referred to in the book are not "irreplaceable by similar passages from other works, though I have always tried to select passages which are most suitable for our purpose" and furthermore that "it would be quite possible to rewrite considerable portions of this work by substituting other quotations for those used by me, without necessarily changing my present analysis and interpretation of the *Ethics*, for the passages quoted are only representative of common views which are current in the philosophic literature of the past" (Vol. I, p. 18).

But for any game not to degenerate into a mere scramble it must be played according to certain fixed rules. Such rules I have worked out for myself in the pursuit of my own studies of Spinoza and have described them in a general way in the opening chapter of the book. In order to show how these rules have been applied in actual practice I shall analyze here a few concrete cases in greater detail than I have done in the book and with the use of new additional material. These cases will illustrate certain characteristic phases of the problem which one is confronted with in trying to determine the fitness and relevancy of passages that are to be brought into play in the interpretation of Spinoza.

The most elementary and the most obvious method of determining a relationship between two texts is similarity of expression. But as every student of such matters knows, external similarities, like appearances in general, are very deceitful. Quite often where our indiscriminating eye may at first see only similarities, closer observation subsequently discovers far-reaching differences. A case in point is Spinoza's reproduction, in the name of philosophers, of two arguments against the conception of God as a corporeal substance, which I discuss briefly in Vol. I, pp. 260–261. As the source of his second argument can be determined with absolute definiteness, I shall take up this argument first. In his own language the passage reads as follows: "A second argument is assumed from the absolute perfection of God. For God, they say, since He is a being absolutely perfect, cannot be passive (*pati*); but corporeal substance, since it is divisible, can be passive." The immediate source of this argument, I have shown, is Descartes in his *Principia*, I, 23. And so, as far as Spinoza is concerned, it is quite futile to look for any other source. But in my discussion of the subject I added for mere historical background that this argument "is implied in Maimonides' fourth proof for the existence, unity and incorporeality of God from the concept of actuality and potentiality" (Vol. I, p. 261). My reference here to this particular proof of Maimonides and my use of the word "implied" were deliberately and cautiously chosen, for Maimonides has three arguments against the corporeality of God, in addition to those he reproduces in the name of the Kalam in *Moreh*, I, 76. First, an argument from the fact that every corporeal object is composed and hence must be the effect of a cause. Second, an argument from the fact that every corporeal object is divisible and has dimensions and hence must be subject to accidents. These two arguments are formally and fully stated in *Moreh*, II, 1, end; they are also referred to in *Moreh*, I, 35, quoted by me in Vol. I, p. 260. The argument from composition is also used by him in his third proof for the existence, unity and incorporeality of God in *Moreh*, II, 1, and is referred to by him in his preliminary remarks to the arguments of the Kalam in *Moreh*, I, 76. But in addition to the argument from *composition* and *causedness* and the argument from *divisibility* and *accidents*, Maimonides has an argument from the fact that corporeal substance is *potential* and hence *passive* and hence *imperfect*. The primary place of this argument is in his fourth formal proof for the existence, unity and incorporeality of God in *Moreh*, II, 1. There, however, only the term *potential* (בכח) is used but not the terms *passive* and *imperfect*. But in *Moreh*, I, 35, Maimonides refers to this argument and adds the other two terms. He says: "There is a perfect being, not a body nor a potency (כח) in a body, namely, God, who is not subject to any kind of imperfection and hence is also in no way subject to passivity (התפעלות)."

Now unguardedly and without careful consideration of all the facts in the case one could erroneously conclude, on the mere ground that Descartes derives his passivity of corporeal substance from its divisibility, that the Cartesian argument from *passivity* and *imperfection* is the same as Maimonides' argument from *divisibility* and *accidents*; or, by transforming the term *causedness* into the term *imperfection*, one could conclude, still more erroneously, that it is the same as Maimonides' argument from *composition* and *causedness*. We need, however, only study the wording and phrasing and structure of all these passages to come to the conclusion that if any analogy to the Cartesian argument reproduced by Spinoza is to be found in Maimonides, it is not in his argument from *divisibility* and *accidents* nor in his argument from *composition* and *causedness* but in his argument from *potentiality*, which he himself explains elsewhere as an argument from *passivity* and *imperfection*. Incidentally it may be added that Thomas Aquinas has an argument from *potentiality* (*Cent. Gent.*, III; 20), which may be considered as one of the sources of Descartes' argument from *passivity* and *imperfection*.

The source of Spinoza's first argument, however, is more difficult to determine. In his own language it reads as follows: "First, that corporeal substance, in so far as it is substance, consists, as they suppose of parts, and therefore deny that it can be infinite, and consequently that it can pertain to God." Now superficially this argument would seem to be the same as the common mediaeval argument from composition which we find, as I have mentioned, in Maimonides and which we also find in Thomas Aquinas (loc. cit.). But upon closer observation it will be noticed that they are not the same, for the common argument from composition arrives at its conclusion from the *causedness* of composite objects, whereas this argument of Spinoza arrives at its conclusion from the *finitude* of composite objects. It happens, however, that the finitude of bodies has been used by mediaeval philosophers as an additional and distinct argument against the corporeality of God. It is reproduced as such by Maimonides in the name of the Kalam (*Moreh*, I, 76, 3rd Argument) and it is also treated as an independent argument by Thomas Aquinas (loc. cit.). Spinoza himself reproduces it with approval in the name of philosophers as an argument against the conception of God as a "body" (*corpus*), as distinguished from the two arguments, of which he disapproves, against the conception of God as a corporeal substance (*substantia corporea*) (see Vol. I, p. 259). The conclusion one is forced to arrive at is that the first argument reproduced by Spinoza is synthetic in its structure, made up of two distinct arguments; and once one arrives at this conclusion one can find an allusion to it, as I have pointed out, in the words with which Spinoza introduces this argument (Vol. I, p. 260).

Furthermore, the expression "consists . . . of parts" (*constat . . . partibus*) used by Spinoza in this first argument can be shown to have been used by him not in the strict sense of the argument from *composition* or of the argument from *divisibility* or of the argument from *imperfection* but in the general sense of the *simplicity* of God which combines under it all these three arguments. Thus in *Short Treatise*, I, 2, §18, 11.12–15, he says: "Since extension is *divisible*, the *perfect* being would have *to consist of parts* (*van deelen bestaan*) and this is altogether inapplicable to God, because he is a *simple* being."[1] Consequently, if this expression "consists . . . of parts" is taken to refer in general to the *simplicity* of God, its conflation with the argument from finitude has its precedent in Heereboord's argument for the

[1] The cross-reference "Cf. below, p. 269," in n. 3, p. 260 of Vol. I, of my book, should be omitted, as the reference to "11.13–15" before the quotation from *Short Treatise*, I, 2, §18, in n. 1, on p. 269, is a misprint for "11.15–18."

simplicity of God which, he says, is to be deduced "from His infinity" and which reads as follows: "Nothing infinite is composed of other things . . . But God is an infinite Being" (*Meletemata*, ed. 1665, p. 79, Col. 2, §III). Incidentally it may be remarked that arguments against the corporeality of God are sometimes included under the general topic of the simplicity of God, as, for instance, in Thomas Aquinas' *Summa Theologica*, I, 3, 1.

As a result of this discussion we find that Spinoza has three arguments in connection with the general problem of the corporeality of God, one, of which he approves, against the crude conception that God is a "body," and two, of which he disapproves, against the philosophic conception that God is "corporeal substance." Of these three arguments, only one, the argument from *passivity* and *imperfection*, has been traced to a direct immediate source. In the case of the others, only analogies and a general historical background have been provided.

When, unlike the preceding case, the question is not one of the establishment of general analogies or of a direct source of a simple statement in Spinoza, but one of the establishment of a direct source of a complicated discussion, still greater care must be taken in the selection of material. I discuss such cases in the opening chapter of the book. "In determining these direct sources," I say, "it is not the similarity of single terms or even of single phrases that guide us, for in the history of philosophy terms and phrases, no less than the ideas which they express, have a certain persistency about them and they survive intact throughout their winding transmigrations. It is always a term or a phrase as imbedded in a certain context, and that context by its internal structure and by a combination of enveloping circumstances, that help us to determine direct literary relationships" (Vol. I, p. 15).

A good example of this is to be found in the three "distinctions" which Spinoza makes in connection with the problem of the infinity of corporeal substance in one of his letters to Meyer. Of these three distinctions the first two are self-explanatory. They deal respectively with the distinction between an essential infinite and what may be called an accidental infinite and with the distinction between the infinite and the indefinite. In my discussion of the subject I have shown how each of these two distinctions reflect old discussions both in Hebrew and in non-Hebrew sources (Vol. I, pp. 271–286 and pp. 288–291). His third distinction, however, is not clear in its original statement. All that Spinoza says on this point is that those who deny the infinity of corporeal substance "did not distinguish between that which we can only understand by reason but cannot imagine, and that which we can also imagine." He does not, however, explicitly state here how this distinction would apply as an answer to the various difficulties which have been raised against the existence of an infinite corporeal substance. From his subsequent use of the distinction between imagination and understanding in the same letter to Meyer it is evident that he has meant to use it as an auxiliary and subordinate part of his first distinction, and that both of them taken together were meant to obviate the difficulty arising from the fact that corporeal substance was supposed to be divisible into parts and to be composed of parts. But if this were the only meaning of that third distinction, the question naturally arises, why did Spinoza count it as a third distinction? and why also did he place this distinction between imagination and intellect after the distinction between the infinite and the indefinite and not after the distinction between the essential and the accidental infinite to which, according to his subsequent use of it, it belongs?

An answer to this can be found if we consider the three "distinctions" given by Spinoza in his letter to Meyer in their relation to the three "examples" which he reproduces in *Ethics*, I, Prop. 15, Schol., as the arguments of those who deny the infinity of corporeal substance, and if we further consider both these "examples" and "distinctions" in their relation to three arguments reproduced by Crescas against the existence of an infinite magnitude and his respective three refutations of these three arguments. Now the three "examples" of Spinoza correspond respectively to the three arguments of Crescas. Furthermore, the first two distinctions of Spinoza correspond also respectively to the first two refutations of Crescas. Spinoza's third "distinction," however, does not correspond to Crescas' third refutation in its entirety. But toward the end of his third refutation Crescas adds the following statement: "This, to be sure, is remote from the imagination, but reason compels us to understand it so," which in its turn reflects a similar distinction by Maimonides in connection with his general argument against the Kalam proposition that "everything that can be imagined is to be also admitted by reason" (*Moreh*, I, 73, Prop. 10).[2] Consequently when Spinoza in his third "dis-

[2] It must not be assumed, however, that whenever the qualifying phrase "in imagination" occurs in the *Moreh* or in any other philosophic work it is to be understood to imply a contrast with the term "reason" and hence it is to be taken as the source of Spinoza's third distinction. Sometimes the phrase "in imagination" may have the general meaning of "in thought" as contrasted with the phrase "in fact" or "in actuality" (cf. the contrast between במחשבה, באלוהם and בפועל, באלפעל in *Hobot ha-Lebabot*, I, 8, Arabic: pp. 60, l. 23 — 61, l. 1). Thus, for instance, when Abraham ibn Daud says in his description of a continuous quantity (כמה מתדבק), such as body, surface, line and time, that "in a body it is possible to assume a surface which would divide it by an *imaginary division* (חלוקה מדומה)" and that similarly "a surface may be *imagined* (ידומה) to be divided by a line and a line by a point, and time may be *imagined* (ידומה) to be divided by an instant" (*Emunah Ramah*, I, 1, pp. 5–6), the meaning of his statement is that the division of these continuous quantities is only "in imagination" but not "in actuality."

tinction" states rather vaguely and without specific application to any particular kind of difficulty raised against the infinite that "they did not distinguish between that which we can only understand by reason but cannot imagine, and that which we can also imagine," we have reason to believe that it is a reminiscence of the concluding statement of Crescas' third refutation of that third argument of his which corresponds to the third example of Spinoza (Vol. I, p. 294). Referring therefore to my treatment of this subject as one of the outstanding examples of the method by which a direct source of Spinoza is to be determined, I say: "When, again, we are in a position to affirm with reasonable certainty that it is Crescas from whom Spinoza has taken over in Scholium to Proposition XV of *Ethics* I the three 'examples' by which his 'opponents' prove the impossibility of an infinite extension and in refutation of them the three 'distinctions' which he mentions in Epistola XII to Meyer, it is not because these 'examples' and 'distinctions' are to be found in Crescas, for as individual 'examples' and 'distinctions' they are to be found also in other authors; it is only because these three 'distinctions' are used by Crescas as refutations of three arguments which correspond respectively to the three 'examples' of Spinoza" (ibid., p. 16).

A combination of context, historical background and the careful wording of Spinoza's own statements will sometimes

Averroes, in his description of continuous quantity, supplies the right contrast of the phrase "in imagination" when he says: "Discrete quantity is that which has parts *in actuality* (*in actu*, בפועל) . . . Continuous quantity is that which has not parts *in actuality* (*quae non habet partes in actu*, אשר [אין] לו חלקים בפועל), such as one line and one surface" (*Epitome of the Organon*: *Categories*, Latin: *Aristotelis Opera*, Venice, 1574, Vol. I, Part III, p. 39 f.; Hebrew: Riva di Trento, 1559, p. 6b). In this sense also is to be understood Maimonides' statement in *Moreh*, I, 76, 1st Argument, that "he is one continuous body (גשם אחד מדובק) not susceptible of division except *in imagination* (והמא, במחשבה)." Spinoza's distinction, as I have shown, is not one between continuous and discrete.

guide us in the right direction toward a successful identification of the sources of some of his references or allusions. A case in point is my discussion of Spinoza's reference to the term "glory" (Vol. II, pp. 311–316). This reference to "glory" occurs in connection with his discussion of the state of immortality which to him as to many others before him consists in the union of the human mind with God through love. He describes the state of immortality by four terms, namely: "salvation" (*salus*), "blessedness" (*beatitudo*), "liberty" (*libertas*) and "regeneration" (*Wedergeboorte*). These four terms, as I have shown, are all taken from the Christian theology, and are to be found in the New Testament. But then, after mentioning three of these four terms, Spinoza adds that "this love or blessedness is called glory in the Sacred Writings." From the context of the passage it is quite clear that what Spinoza means to say is that the state of immortality which is love and is called "salvation," "blessedness," "liberty" and "regeneration" is also called "glory," and it is called "glory" in the "Sacred Writings."

Now the use of the term "glory" as a designation of the state of immortality is characteristically Christian, though occasionally it occurs also in Jewish sources. In Christian theology, the term "glory" is in common use as a designation of the heavenly splendor and the ultimate blessedness of the righteous. A collection of Latin passages illustrating the Christian use of the term *gloria* is to be found in *Thesaurus Linguae Latinae*, p. 2077, ll. 22 sqq. and p. 2083, ll. 51 sqq. So common is this use of the term "glory" in mediaeval Christian literature that it has been retained as one of its common meanings in modern languages, including English. In Jewish theology, however, the term "glory" as a designation for the state of immortality is not common. With the exception of the interpretation of the term *kabod* in certain passages of the Bible by certain Bible commentators and with the exception also of the term *ziw* in the well-known talmudic description of the world to come as a place where "the righteous sit with their crowns on their heads and enjoy the glory of the Shekinah" (Berakot 17a), one cannot think offhand of the use of the term *kabod*, or of similar other terms which can be translated by "glory," as a designation of the state of immortality. It is certainly not used in ordinary writing. The question, therefore, that I have raised in my book was as to where in the "Sacred Writings" is the term "glory" used, or was understood to be used, in connection with immortality, and for this I suggested Psalm 16.8–11 and Psalm 73.24, with Ibn Ezra's commentaries thereon.

Since the publication of the book I have collected new material from Christian commentaries on the Bible, both Old and New Testaments, with reference to their interpretation of the term "gloria" in various places. Three of these I shall mention here. First, not only Ibn Ezra, whom I have quoted in my book, interprets the term "glory" in Psalm 73.24, as referring "to the union of the soul of the righteous with the supernal incorporeal and immortal beings" (Vol. II, p. 316) but also Albertus Magnus in his commentary on Psalms interprets the term as referring to the union with the person of Christ. "*Cum gloria suscepisti me*, in gloriosa scilicet unione cum persona Filii" (*Opera Omnia*, ed. Vivès, Vol. 16, p. 256). Second, in his *Enarratio in Psalmum XXXVI, 8*, drawing upon the statement "non sunt condignae passiones hujus temporis ad futaram gloriam quae revelabitur in nobis" in Romans 8.18, St. Augustine asks and answers: "What will be our future glory, if not to be equal to angels and to see God?" (Migne, *Pat. Lat.*, Vol. 36, Col. 368). Third, and this settles the matter definitely, Spinoza's statement under consideration, namely, "hic Amor, seu beatitudo in Sacris codicibus Gloria appellatur" is directly based upon Thomas Aquinas' statement "illa beatitudo in Sacra Scriptura frequentissime gloria moninatur" (*Cont. Gent.*, III, 63). However, of the many frequent occurrences of this use of the term "glory" in the Sacred Writings to which Thomas Aquinas refers, he mentions only one scriptural verse, namely, "Let the saints exult in glory" (Psalm 149.5). It is interesting to note that also Ibn Ezra interprets the verse as referring to immortality and the hereafter. He says: "[*Let the saints exult in glory*, that is], let them exult in the glory that they shall exist eternally, [the term 'glory'] thus referring to their soul or to the hereafter."[3]

But not only must one be on guard to observe differences between apparently similar phrases and passages and arguments but one must also study the various shades of differences in the use of single terms. The history of philosophic terminology is full of all kinds of tricks, and no sooner do we find a term meticulously and scrupulously defined than we discover somewhere either explicitly or by some subtle implication that it also has some other meaning. In my study of Spinoza I constantly had to search for these uncommon distinctions in the use of terms, and I was always careful to substantiate my findings by appropriate quotations from the various philosophic literatures. Thus when I happened to say that Spinoza's substance or God was both immanent and transcendent, I disarmed criticism of my use of these terms on the part of those who are accustomed to think of them as antithetical terms by giving a history of their meanings and also by showing how "genus" is both immanent and transcendent (Vol. I, pp. 319–323). When Spinoza himself described this immanent-transcendent substance or God by the term "whole" and tried to explain the particular

[3] יעלזו בכבוד הזה שיעמדו לנצח והטעם על נשמותם או לעתיד לבוא.

sense in which he used that term, I similarly justified his special use of the term by appropriate texts (Vol. I, pp. 323–328). When I myself rendered Spinoza's immanent-transcendent whole by the term "universal," I was quite mindful of the fact that universals to Spinoza were only names and I justified the use of the term "universal" by the statement: "Or, to make use of a modern distinction, God or substance or the whole is according to Spinoza a concrete or real universal, whereas attributes are according to him only abstract universals" (Vol. I, p. 328). But it was inevitable that occasionally, either through neglectfulness or through reliance upon the resourcefulness of the reader, I should forget to mention the special sense in which I used certain terms in explaining some statement by Spinoza. Thus, for instance, when, in my attempt to explain why Spinoza's immanent-transcendent whole or substance or concrete universal is "conceived through itself," I said "inasmuch as it is a *summum genus*" (Vol. I, p. 76), I should have added that I used the term *summum genus* in a sense analogous to that in which Philo refers to God as "the supremely generic" (τὸ γενικώτατον), i. e., the highest genus, in his *Legum Allegoriarum Liber*, II, 21, §86. Perhaps, also, I should have pointed out that *summum genus* is a term which is of common use in philosophy as a description of "substance" as well as of all the other categories, though with regard to "being" it is generally maintained that it is not the *summum genus* of the categories into which it is divided.

But phrases and terms, even when properly treated in all their similarities as well as differences, are important for the study of Spinoza only in so far as they help to throw light upon the meaning of his statements as well as upon the genesis of his views and the processes of his reasoning. In the study of Spinoza it is quite useless to follow his own advice with regard to the study of Bible, that is, to try to extract the meaning of his doctrine out of the contents of his own writings. For to try to explain some of Spinoza's vague and enigmatic utterances on one topic by his similarly vague and enigmatic utterances on another topic is like trying to find the value of an unknown X by equating it to an unknown Y. The known quantities by which the values of the unknown quantities of Spinoza are to be determined are those clear philosophical texts and problems of the past, out of which Spinoza's own statements and problems have been hewn. If, for instance, his definition of attribute is vague and lends itself to different interpretations each of which is subject to certain inherent difficulties, the problem cannot be solved by the aid of statements of Spinoza on other topics, which are equally as vague, equally liable to being misunderstood and equally in need of interpretation. If an analysis of the mediaeval problem of divine attributes is suggested as a key to the interpretation of Spinoza's definition of attribute, it is not merely to furnish certain analogies of expression for the curious, but to draw attention to the fact that every conceivable difficulty that has been raised against either of the two alternative interpretations of Spinoza's attributes have also been raised against either of the two analogous alternative mediaeval theories of divine attributes, and that all these difficulties in the case of the mediaeval problem have been answered by their respective proponents to their own satisfaction. Methodologically, then, the task of the student of Spinoza is first to discover out of Spinoza's own utterances with which side of the problem he has consciously aligned himself and then to try to find, on the basis of analytical analogies in the mediaeval problem of divine attributes, how Spinoza would answer to his own satisfaction, even if not to the satisfaction of others, the inevitable difficulties that could be raised against whatever position he has decided to take. For ultimately there is an element of arbitrariness in the position taken by any philosopher on any speculative problem; beyond that arbitrary limit discussion is likely to become purely verbal.

Of the new passages referred to at the beginning of the paper the greater part are from scholastic writings. In some future new edition of the book, it is hoped, these passages will be distributed throughout the text so that every Hebrew reference on any essential point will be matched by a parallel non-Hebrew reference. At present the number of Hebrew references in the book is about two-thirds of all the references — somewhat less than 600 out of a total of over 900. The preponderance of Hebrew references occurs especially in Chapters IV, V, VII, XI, XII, XIII and XX, in connection with the discussion of the unity and simplicity of God, of divine attributes, of creation, of freedom of the will, of divine knowledge and of immortality — topics which by mere coincidence happen to correspond to those problems in which Maimonides' influence upon scholastic writings is most in evidence. As against this, however, the discussion of the cognitive faculties, of imagination and memory, of truth, of the stages of knowledge, of will, of emotions and of virtues, in Chapters XIV, XV, XVII, XVIII and XIX, contains comparatively few Hebrew references. While in a number of instances these new Latin passages are more appropriate to certain texts of Spinoza or more closely connected with them than the Hebrew passages used, and will therefore have to be substituted for the latter, for the most part they have proved to be only parallels of the Hebrew, and their contemplated addition to the text is to be only for the purpose of showing that the sources used in the analysis and interpretation of Spinoza's *Ethics* are well-known and reputable mediaeval staples and not some outlandish rabbinic concoctions. On the whole the rule still holds that in seeking to determine the sources of Spinoza "we [must] go first to Hebrew philosophic literature for our documents" but "in order not to create the erroneous impression that the material drawn upon is unique in Hebrew philosophic literature, we [must] quote, or refer to, similar passages in the works of Arabic and scholastic authors" and that "when the occasion demands, scholastic sources are [to be] resorted to in preference to the Hebrew" (Vol. I, p. 14).

26

SPINOZA'S MECHANISM, ATTRIBUTES, AND PANPSYCHISM

PHILOSOPHERS have so long been in the habit of seeing in the detailed researches of science and scholarship a heedless neglect of wholes that it was quite natural for Professor Grace A. De Laguna, on finding herself in disagreement with some of the conclusions of my rather detailed study *The Philosophy of Spinoza,* to declare that while the book is "valuable" and "indispensable" as a detailed investigation, it did not do right by "Spinoza's system as a whole" (*Philosophical Review,* May, 1935). Of her disagreements three are specified, and Mrs. De Laguna has been thoughtful enough to state her case against me fully and clearly, by showing wherein my interpretation appears to her to present certain difficulties. I am grateful to her for raising these difficulties, for it affords me an opportunity to clarify my position.

1. Extension and Thought, Descartes, and Mechanism.—My discussion of the attributes of extension and thought falls into two parts. First, I try to unfold the reasoning which has led Spinoza, in opposition to all philosophers, including Descartes, to deny that matter and form are substances and to reduce them to attributes. Second, I try to explain why Spinoza has changed the terms matter and form to extension and thought. I show how throughout the history of philosophy matter was associated with extension, and among my instances I also mention the fact that Descartes defined matter as extension (I 235). In another place, speaking of the duality of matter and form, I add, "or, as it was better known in the fashionable philosophy of Spinoza's own time, of extension and thought" (I 79). Descartes, then, was not altogether overlooked by me; he was merely treated as part of a larger tradition.

In criticism of this, Professor De Laguna maintains that "it misses the essential aspect of Spinoza's thought that he derives from Descartes" and then proceeds to present her own version of the Cartesian background from which alone, according to her, Spinoza could have derived his doctrine of extension and thought.

Now it is the contention throughout my study of Spinoza that while we may ascribe to Spinoza a knowledge of any conceivable text in Descartes that may help us to explain his cryptic utterances, we must not ascribe to him a foreknowledge of modern textbooks on Descartes. Spinoza was too close to the original sources of philosophy to allow himself to fall into the error of considering every statement he found in Descartes as something peculiarly Cartesian. When Spinoza read in Descartes that "the nature of matter or body . . . consists in its being extended in length, breadth, and depth" (*Princ. Phil.* II 4), he saw in it a philosophic commonplace which occurs in Aristotle (*Physics* IV 1, 209a4-5; *De Caelo* I 1, 268a23-24) and is variously interpreted by mediaeval philosophers, one of its interpretations being, as I have shown, that extension is the essence of matter. When he further read in Descartes that he does not "accept or desire any other principle in physics than in geometry" (*Princ. Phil.* II 64), he saw in it merely a reiteration of a philosophic commonplace as to the existence of necessary logical laws in nature. Spinoza himself, as I have pointed out (I 53), uses his geometrical analogies in this sense. When he discovered that Descartes himself did not adhere to his geometrical conception of nature and admitted the existence of free will in God and man, trying to explain human freedom, as Mrs. De Laguna so aptly puts it, by "man's will mysteriously acting through the pineal gland", he saw in it only one other attempt at a mysterious explanation of the action of a free will within a world governed by necessary laws. In Spinoza's own discussion of free will and final causes we find, on the basis of textual evidence, that his arguments are directed as much against mediaeval authors as against Descartes (*cf.* Chs. xii and xvii). In fact, his arguments against final causes are aimed primarily at the mediaevals and Heereboord. It is noteworthy that, throughout his allusions to Descartes which I have identified in the *Ethics* and throughout his discussions of Descartes' views on matters purely metaphysical in his correspondence, Spinoza treats Descartes as an exponent of traditional philosophy.

But Professor De Laguna thinks that I have failed to interpret Spinoza's doctrine as a whole because I have not said that in all his arguments against final causes, which are mainly directed against authors other than Descartes, Spinoza was merely trying to extend a Cartesian positive doctrine beyond the limits set for its operation by Descartes himself; for "Spinoza could not simply deny final causality. . . . He must replace it with some *positive* doctrine, and this doctrine is the mechanism he inherits from Descartes and makes universal" (my italics).

I take exception to this statement on two grounds:—

In the first place, Spinoza's argument, as he himself develops it in the *Ethics,* begins with the conception of God as acting without will and design; and from this premise he arrives at his denial of final causes in nature and free will in man (*cf.* I 424). This is evident from the very structure of the *Ethics.* He does not argue reversely, as Professor De Laguna suggests, from Descartes' mechanism of nature to a denial of freedom in man and design in God. Even in his correspondence, where he argues directly against Descartes' assertion of the freedom of the will, Spinoza does not confront him with the logical consequence of the latter's mechanism of nature, but argues from his own conception of God as acting without will and design (*cf.* for instance, *Letters* 21, 43, 58).

In the second place, the term mechanism cannot be spoken of as a "positive doctrine", for it is only a description of the denial of final causes but not an explanation. Teleology, to be sure, can be loosely spoken of as a positive doctrine, because it implies some positive principle, such as God or some of its more polite equivalents in current philosophy. But mechanism, if it is thoroughgoing, does not imply any positive principle, whether it is the thoroughgoing mechanism of the ancient Atomists, according to the mediaeval as well as Spinoza's conception of it, or the equally thoroughgoing mechanism of Spinoza. In the former it means the denial of God; in the latter it means the denial of will and design in God. If the term mechanism is applied to Descartes and to others like him despite their belief in a God endowed with will and acting by design, it is only by the courtesy of modern historians of philosophy. But, for that matter, the same courtesy might with equal propriety be extended to all the mediaeval philosophers who believed in necessary laws of nature preordained by an unknown will of God. Though these mediaeval philosophers continued to speak of final causes, the term really was nothing with them but a verbal designation for what they believed to be the revelation in the world of some divine purpose unknown to men—exactly the position taken by Descartes with all his verbal denial of final causes. To say, therefore, as Professor De Laguna does, that Spinoza replaced the mere denial of final causality by the "positive doctrine" of mechanism is to reduce Spinoza to the intellectual level of the village freethinker who tantalized his bucolic listeners by declaring that he did not have to explain the origin and order of the universe by the existence of a God, as he could explain everything by the existence of atheism.

2. *The "Nonsense" of Subjective Attributes.*—In his *Way of All Flesh,* Samuel Butler describes the shock which young Mr. Pontifex received when he read in Dean Alford's notes that despite the contradictions in the various accounts of the Resurrection in the Gospels the whole story should be taken on trust. Such an implicit faith in the integrity of any kind of scripture against the striking evidence of facts has, alas, disappeared from almost every field of learning. It is refreshing to see that it is still alive among students of the scripture of Spinoza, as when, for instance, Professor De Laguna maintains that even if the "historical evidence" is in favor of the subjective interpretation of Spinoza's attributes, such an interpretation must be discredited because "it makes nonsense of a great thinker". But the "nonsense" of the subjective interpretation is really nothing more than the fact that it presents certain difficulties according to the contention of Mrs. De Laguna. These difficulties, however, I shall try to show, are due to a

misreading of the meaning of the term "invented", which I have used in connection with the subjective interpretation. Professor De Laguna takes the term to mean the invention by the mind of something of which substance is devoid, whereas what it really means is the invention by the mind of certain universal terms, referred to as attributes, to describe the actions or power of substance.

Since my subjective interpretation of attributes has proved to be the most disturbing part of my study on Spinoza, I shall try to restate it in its salient features.

That attributes are only perceived by the mind is a common expression throughout mediaeval philosophy and down to the time of Spinoza. When we examine, however, the meaning of this expression in its various contexts, we find that it sometimes means that attributes have a certain kind of real existence in the essence of God but an existence which can be *discovered* only by the mind, and sometimes it means that they have no objective existence at all but are only *invented* by the mind. Now according to both these views the attributes of God are admitted to be perceived by the human mind only through the various manifestations of God's actions, which actions receive the name attributes when they are transformed into adjectives and thus become universalized by the mind. But here the problem of universals comes into play. Those who held a nominalistic conception of universals, *i.e.*, universals are only *invented* by the mind, had no difficulty at all in asserting that all the various actions of God are attributes, inasmuch as the plurality of such nominalistic attributes does not imply a plurality in the essence of God. All propositions about God, therefore, assume with them a subject-predicate relation. Those, however, who considered universals as having some kind of real existence, *i.e.*, the mind only *discovers* them, could not consider the various actions of God as attributes without implying the existence of a plurality in the divine essence. They therefore had to resort to the following alternative: (a) either to maintain that such a plurality in the divine essence was not inconsistent with its simplicity, (b) or to maintain that propositions about God do not express a subject-predicate relation. In the latter case, it was usually said that in all propositions about God the predicate always expresses a dynamic relation, that is to say, it always expresses a pure action, the assumption being that a variety of actions can proceed from a simple essence without implying a plurality of elements in it.

Now Spinoza starts like all mediaevals with the conception of God as pure activity, or, as he himself says, "the power of God is His essence itself", meaning by power that which "He and all things are and act" (*Ethics* I 34). But unlike those mediaevals against whom he especially argues, namely, the emanationists, he considers the activity of

God to be not only understanding but also motion. These two activities are what Spinoza calls the two immediate infinite modes. From these two immediate infinite modes follow the two finite modes, mind from the former and body from the latter. Then mind, according to Spinoza, universalizes the various manifestations of these two activities of God and transforms them respectively into the attributes of thought and extension. Following tradition, Spinoza defines attribute as that "which the intellect perceives of substance, as if constituting its essence". But he does not tell us whether he meant by it that the intellect *discovers* the attributes or whether he meant by it only that the intellect *invents* them—the problem upon which, as we have seen, the mediaevals were divided. The question can be answered only indirectly by the following considerations: (1) The terms Spinoza uses in connection with attributes are like those used by mediaevals who denied the real existence of attributes in substance. (2) His statements about universals point to a nominalistic conception. (3) The emphasis with which he insists upon the simplicity of substance as something which logically follows from his definition of attribute points to a subjective theory of attributes. This last type of evidence, however, I consider only as corroborative of the first two, for Spinoza, like some of the mediaevals whom I have referred to, could have found a way of showing that the simplicity of substance is not inconsistent with its containing a plurality of real attributes, even though he does not explicitly argue that point. When, however, a question on this point was raised by de Vries, Spinoza's answer was that the attributes are merely "names", *i.e.*, invented by the mind (*cf. Letter* 9).

When Professor De Laguna therefore asks how, if the attributes of thought and extension are invented by the mind, there could be a mind to invent them, or where did material things come from, the answer is, in the words of Spinoza himself, that the mind follows from the immediate infinite mode of the absolute intellect and that material things follow from the immediate infinite mode of motion, both of these immediate infinite modes being actions of the infinite power of substance, the power which is the essence itself of substance; and it is through these actions that substance appears to the mind as having the attributes of thought and extension.

3. Unity of Nature and Omnia Animata.—If the unity of nature were a principle which Spinoza advanced as a religious dogma, and we were fundamentalists who accepted his dogma literally, then of course we would also have to accept Spinoza's *omnia animata* in its literal sense as implying the existence of consciousness of some degree in all things; for otherwise, as Professor De Laguna rightly argues, "the unity of nature breaks down". But the unity of nature with Spinoza is merely the carrying out of the principle of necessary causality to its logical conclusion, and it can mean no more than what is warranted by that principle. The principle itself is that there can be nothing in the effect which is not in the cause, which reflects the old philosophic axiom *ex nihilo nihil fit*. It is as a result of this principle that Spinoza argues, as I have shown, that inasmuch as there is extension in the universe there must be extension in God (I Ch. iv). It is by the same reasoning, too, that Spinoza had to assume consciousness in God: since there is consciousness in some finite modes (I 329; II 337) and since also he pleased to think of God as the cause of modes (II 342). But the converse of this principle, namely, that everything in the cause must be in the effect, is not true, especially when the effect is removed from the cause by the interposition of intermediate causes. Moreover, in the case of Spinoza, by the very same eternal necessity by which modes are according to him unlike substance in their being finite and temporal and imperfect (I 397-398), they are also different from one another; and some of them are still further unlike substance in their being devoid of consciousness. We must not lose sight of the fact that while Spinoza has rejected the traditional belief in creation he has not anticipated the modern theory of evolution. To him the universe in its complexity was not the result of an evolutionary process; it was a static universe fixed in its present form from eternity. Living things and non-living things, beings endowed with consciousness and beings devoid of it, thinking beings and non-thinking beings—all these existed side by side in their present form from all eternity. There is no break therefore in the unity of nature, as understood by Spinoza, when we say that he did not assume that all finite modes are like God and man in the possession of consciousness. If man is still "a kingdom within a kingdom", his kingdom is no longer of Heaven. The "kingdom" which Spinoza denies man is not that of his occupying a special realm in nature, delimited by certain special properties he possesses in the universal order of things, but rather, as Spinoza explicitly states, that of his having "an absolute power over his own actions" and of his being "altogether self-determined" (*Ethics* III, Preface). His *omnia animata* need not therefore on that account be taken literally; it means, as I have tried to show, that all things may be said to have an *anima* in the same sense as in the older philosophy all things were said to have a *forma*.

But Professor De Laguna seems to think that, because Spinoza qualifies his statement that all things are besouled by the phrase "in different degrees" (*diversis gradibus*), the differences must be only quantitative or qualitative and not specific, and that consequently the souls of all things must differ only in the *degree* of the consciousness which they all possess and not in the fact of their having consciousness or of their not having it. This reasoning from the use of the term "degree" is not conclusive. In philosophic Latin, the expression *diversi gradus* or *diversitas gradus* means also a difference in natural perfection which implies a specific difference. The following quotation from Thomas Aquinas will show that the expression *diversis gradibus* here in Spinoza is to be understood in the sense in which I have taken it: "In material substances different degrees (*diversi gradus*) in the perfection of nature constitute a difference in species. . . . For it is manifest that mixed bodies surpass the elements in the order of perfection, plants surpass mineral bodies, and animals surpass plants, and in every genus one finds a diversity of species (*diversitas specierum*) according to the degree of natural perfection" (*Quaestiones Disputatae: De Anima,* Art. 7, Resp.). Now the term "species" (εἴδη) by which Thomas describes the elements, mixed bodies, plants, and animals, is what is also known as "forms"—the Aristotelian term to which, as I have shown (II 46-48, 59), Spinoza's "souls" corresponds. These Aristotelian "forms" are described by Thomas as *diversi gradus* just as Spinoza describes his "souls" by *diversis gradibus*. The differences of degree which Thomas finds between the forms of elements, mixed bodies, plants, and animals, consist in the fact, as we know, that elements and mixed bodies have no power of nutrition, growth, and reproduction, which plants have, and that plants have no power of sensation, which animals have. The differences of degree which Spinoza finds between the various souls are of a similar nature, and they include among them, as may be inferred from his own statements, also the following difference, namely, that man has consciousness which other things have not (II, 59-61).

Ultimately there is an arbitrary element in the philosophy of Spinoza as there is an ultimate element of arbitrariness in every system of philosophy. When Spinoza has rejected by logical reasoning the hypothesis of an immaterial God and of creation and of emanation, he could have assumed the universe to be only an aggregate of modes, or what he calls *facies totius universi,* existing by its own necessity in its present form from eternity. Epicurean atomism of antiquity thus saw no need for the assumption of a cause to explain the origin of the world; and while Spinoza disapproves of this view, applying to it the mediaeval opprobrium of "chance" (I, 318, 422), he does not undertake to disprove it. The substance or God which he supplies serves no other purpose except, to quote my own words, that of "an infinite logical crust which holds together the crumbs of the infinite number of finite modes" (I 398; II 343). For the existence of that substance or God he offers no proof except the three forms of his ontological argument, which is nothing but the assertion that we have a clear and distinct idea of its existence (I, Ch. vi). But, having assumed its existence and having conceived its relation to the universe of modes as that of cause to effect, he had to play the game of causality according to its accepted rules. He was thus quite logical in reasoning from the nature of the effects of substance to its own nature and in assuming that it cannot be devoid of anything which is found in its effects; and so he arrived at the conclusion that it must have extension and thought, and also consciousness as a condition of thought. But there was no logical compulsion, and no rule of the game requiring him, to reverse the reasoning and to endow all effects, contrary to observation, with thought and consciousness. And it is in accordance with these considered views of Spinoza that his casual and qualified *omnia animata* is to be understood.

27

TOWARDS AN ACCURATE UNDERSTANDING OF SPINOZA

IT IS not strange that my interpretation of twelve out of the first thirteen propositions of *Ethics* I, which appeared in *Chronicon Spinozanum,* I, II, and III, should have been found by the reviewer, Mr. Joseph Ratner, in the issue of March 4 of this JOURNAL, to be inconsistent with his understanding of certain other passages in the *Ethics.* All of his objections, leaving out of consideration his general expressions of disapproval, are of the nature of contradictions which he believes to have been found in passages of the *Ethics* not as yet explained by me according to the method I am trying to apply to Spinoza as a whole. I believe I have sufficiently shown, by evidence which according to all established standards of literary criticism is accounted as valid, that Spinoza's terms and expressions have a history of their own and are often used by him in a sense to which the ordinary student of modern philosophy has no immediate access. While I can not undertake here to explain fully the passages cited against me by the reviewer, I wish to indicate briefly my own method of approach.

Against my statement that "Spinoza's substance is a whole transcending the universe which is the sum of the modes (not necessarily excluding its being also immanent in the universe)" he quotes Proposition 18 of *Ethics,* I, that "God is the immanent and *not* the transitive cause of all things" (p. 125). The reviewer seems to be quite certain that the term "transitive" here, or rather the Latin *transiens,* means the same as "transcendent," inasmuch as both are used as opposites of the term "immanent." When in the course of time I come to discuss Proposition 18, I hope to show that there are many shades of meaning to the term "immanent," that there are many shades of opposition to it, and that Spinoza's *transiens* and my use of the term "transcending" do not exactly express the same shade of opposition to the term "immanent."

My argument that Spinoza could not have considered Substance as "a physical quantitative whole" in the sense of "the aggregate sum of the modes" (*Chronicon Spinozanum,* I, p. 109 f.) is countered by the reviewer by the statement that according to Spinoza "God is among an infinite number of other things, an infinite corporeal Being" (p. 125), meaning thereby, evidently, that according to Spinoza God is what I tried to prove He is not, namely "the aggregate sum of the modes." If the reader cares to look into *Ethics,* I,

Prop. XV, Schol., to which the reviewer refers as the source of his statement, he will find that what Spinoza is trying to prove there is "that extended substance is one of the infinite attributes of God," which is quite another matter. What I consider to be Spinoza's conception as to the relation of the essence of Substance to the attributes and the modes, on which point the reviewer's own understanding of the matter is used by him as an argument against me (p. 126), the reader can partly gather from the chapters already published, and as for the rest I must beg his indulgence until the publication of the chapter on the attributes of extension and thought.

Against my statement that Spinoza's Substance is unknowable in its essence the reviewer exclaims: "Truly a remarkable pronouncement, when we consider that Spinoza defines substance" (p. 125). But may it not be said that Spencer defined God as the unknowable? And did the reviewer stop to think for a moment how many kinds of definition were abroad at the time of Spinoza, and of what nature are the Definitions of Spinoza, and what was their purpose?

He also cites against this unknowability of Substance Proposition 47 of *Ethics,* II, that "the human mind possesses an adequate knowledge of the eternal and infinite essence of God" (p. 125). Now, there are several kinds of knowledge, according to Spinoza, and we therefore find him speaking of God as being knowable in one sense, but as being unknowable in another. It is with reference to the unknowability of God in one of the senses of knowledge that Spinoza says in Epistola L: "Of His essence we can form no general idea." I have discussed this question in the opening paragraph of Section IV of the third chapter (*Chronicon Spinozanum,* III, p. 165), which the reviewer has completely overlooked. I am taking the liberty of quoting from myself a few sentences: "The God or Substance of Spinoza, like the God of medieval rationalists, is unknowable in his essence. He may indeed, in Spinoza's view, be immediately perceived by intuition as a clear and distinct idea, but He is not subject to knowledge that defines its object in terms broader and more general. When Spinoza argues against the mediæval conception of an unknowable God, he simply argues for the view that God can be known, after a manner, even though He can not be defined in terms of genus and species."

The reviewer further quotes against the unknowability of Spinoza's God Proposition 28 of *Ethics,* IV, that "the highest good of the mind is the knowledge of God and the highest virtue of the mind is to know God" (p. 125), and he also argues that an intellectual love of an unknowable God would be "pure charlatanism" (*Ibid.*). The reviewer apparently misunderstands the unknowability of God to mean a sort of agnosticism with respect to God's existence or even a denial of God's existence. A similar misunderstanding of the meaning of negative terms occurs elsewhere in the review, as I shall point out later. The fact is, the idea of an unknowable God is as old as theology. Whatever the implications of this expression, it does not connote doubt as to the existence of God. Theologians have, therefore, never found any difficulty in making an unknowable God an object of love as well as a source of law and in continuing to use the language of piety by extolling the knowledge of God as the greatest of all virtues.

In my discussion of Spinoza's Definition of God (*Chronicon Spinozanum,* III, pp. 146–147) I tried to show that it was meant to be a reproduction of a medieval definition, and on the basis of what I proved to be its literary source I said with regard to Spinoza's definition that "by eternal he means *here* infinite time" (*Ibid.,* p. 147). The reviewer, failing to notice, apparently, that the adverb "here" is the equivalent of the more colloquial "in this here place," quotes against me Spinoza's well-known Definition of "eternity" (p. 127).

In the chapter, "Spinoza on the Simplicity of Substance," I attempted to show that in Propositions VIII, IX, and X of *Ethics,* I, Spinoza endeavors to prove of Substance what he has affirmed of God in Definition VI. This parallelism or analogy between substance and God is briefly outlined by me on page 147 in *Chronicon Spinozanum,* III. In the subsequent pages it is fully worked out, and on page 164, in taking up Proposition IX, I say: "The next step in the parallelism between substance and God is to show that by infinity in both cases is meant the possession of infinite attributes." This is the simple meaning of the "parallelism between substance and God" which the reviewer finds "difficult to understand" and "very curious" (p. 127).

It is interesting to watch with what facility the reviewer plays words against words and equates terms without apparently being aware of what they actually stand for in Spinoza. He thus finds a contradiction between my statement that there is not any relation between the essence of God and that of other beings and Spinoza's statement in Epistola IV that God has something actually in common with created beings (p. 127). What Spinoza means by the latter statement is simply to affirm that God has the attribute of extension (see "Spinoza on the Unity of Substance" in *Chronicon Spinozanum,* II, pp. 97–98). This, however, does not establish a relation between the essence of God and the essence of other beings any more than the existence of something in common between God and the human mind, in the medieval theory of emanation, established a relation between the essence of God and the essence of the human mind. The only relation that this "something in common" establishes is that of cause and effect, as I have pointed out in my second chapter (*Ibid.*, p. 100 f.).

He further finds fault with the statement that God is "infinite" also in the sense of being "indeterminate." He argues that inasmuch as "indeterminate" is the equivalent of "indefinite" it can not be the equivalent of "infinite," for Spinoza expressly distinguishes between the "infinite" and the "indefinite" (p. 128). It happens that Spinoza distinguishes "indefinite" from "infinite" by restricting it to the sense of "immeasurable," as will be gathered from my next chapter in the forthcoming fourth volume of the *Chronicon Spinozanum.* As for the term "indeterminate," I have used it in its legitimate sense of "indefinable" as the privative of *determinatio* used by Spinoza in his dictum: *Determinatio negatio est* (Epistola L).

The reviewer also seems to show a lack of appreciation of the method of critical textual study even in its simplest form. In trying to explain the meaning of Proposition IX, I pointed out that it must be taken as the major premise of a syllogism in which the minor premise and the conclusion are to be supplied. This I thought was necessary in order to complete what I consider to be the main argument contained in Propositions VII to X. To prove my contention I referred to a parallel passage in Epistola IX (*olim* XXVII) where the very same Proposition is quoted as the major premise of the very syllogism that is wanted according to my interpretation in the *Ethics.* This I think should be conclusive to any one who has ever worked independently on source material and tried to extricate a connected thought from several mutually supplementary texts. I don't see with what relevancy the reviewer brings in what he happens to think of Pollock's interpretation of Proposition VII of the Second Part (p. 127).

It is sometimes disheartening to notice the break in the continuity of philosophic modes of expression when students of modern philosophy, however well informed otherwise, find themselves quite at a loss and uncomfortable in the presence of terms which were common stock-in-trade from the time of Aristotle throughout the Middle Ages and were still a common commodity in the times of Descartes, Spinoza, and Locke. The reviewer thus can not grasp the technicality of the expression "prior in nature" in the sense of the priority of the more universal to the less universal or of animality (which to the reviewer is the same as "animals") to rationality (p. 126).

Similarly he seems to be puzzled by the negative interpretation of such expressions as "to be conceived through itself" or "to be in itself" and to him it can not mean anything but that the thing so conceived or so said to be does not exist (p. 126).

But still, while not being at home in common medieval forms of expression the reviewer feels quite confident that he knows *a priori* the difference between medieval and modern philosophy, and assures us that "Spinoza in every particular is a full-blooded modern," and that his God is not the God of Maimonides (p. 124). I must confess that I am not always sure as to what is medieval and what is modern in philosophy. But this much I can say with certainty, that I find nothing medieval in Maimonides' approach to the problem of religion except his modernist lack of logical consistency in raising the superstructure of a traditional religious system upon a purely scientific conception of God. The advance made by Spinoza is not in modifying Maimonides' conception of God, but rather in escaping that logical inconsistency. Starting out with the identical premises, he consistently carries on his reasoning to its logical conclusion. He thus ceases to be a medieval and becomes a modern. But it is as a critic of the medievals that he appears to us in his writings, it is from their premises that his own discussion arises, and for this reason I believe in emphasizing Spinoza's rôle as the last of the medievals no less than his rôle as the first of the moderns.

28

SOLOMON PAPPENHEIM ON TIME AND SPACE AND HIS RELATION TO LOCKE AND KANT

Towards the end of the eighteenth century, among the first Jews who gained their way into general literature there was a predominance of those who worked in the field of philosophy. Some of them, like Solomon Maimon and Moses Mendelssohn, achieved fame and distinction either through the profundity of their thought or through the elegance of their table talk. Others, less famous, like Marcus Herz and Lazarus Bendavid, succeeded only in enshrining themselves in an occasional foot-note in the history of German philosophy or in being included among those who also lived and philosophized, but still they will always be remembered as the pages, if not the armor-bearers, of Kant. That philosophy should have been the vehicle through which the first linguistically emancipated Jews should break into the world's literature was only natural, for outside the Bible philosophy was the only field of knowledge which the Jews shared in common with the rest of Europe. It is characteristic of all these early Jewish pioneers in European letters that even in their new state they continued to draw upon their early knowledge and training and to show the unmistakable influence of their early traditions and interests. Mendelssohn wrote a commentary in Hebrew on Maimonides' logic and composed books on psychology and theology which abound in old-time allusions. Solomon Maimon not only borrowed his surname from Maimonides but published a commentary in Hebrew on the latter's *Moreh Nebukim* and also discussed Maimonides' philosophy in his German autobiography. Among the kind of Jews to whom these men belonged they marked the transition from mediaeval to modern philosophy just as in an earlier generation Spinoza performed a similar function among Jews of another kind and Descartes among Christians. By the vicissitudes of life and education they formed a link, as it were, between the Jewish philosophic tradition and the European. To this goodly list of names I now wish to add that of SOLOMON PAPPENHEIM.

SOLOMON PAPPENHEIM (1740–1814) is not altogether a stranger to philosophy. Two of his works on the proofs of the existence of God, one entitled *Beiträge zur Berichtigung der Beweise vom Dasein Gottes aus der Reinen Vernunft* and the other *Abermaliger Versuch über den ontologischen Beweis vom Dasein Gottes*, were published in Breslau in 1794 and 1800 respectively. Both of these books, as may be judged from their titles, follow in the trail of KANT's *Critique of Pure Reason.* But it will be of interest to know that in an earlier Hebrew work of his, which is nothing more than a study of Hebrew synonyms, there is a discussion of the conceptions of time and space which, it is our purpose to show, is a characteristic blending of Jewish and European philosophy, especially LOCKE and KANT.

The book entitled *Yeri'ot Shelomoh* (Part i) was published at Dyhernfurth in 1784, about three years after the appearance of the *Critique of Pure Reason* (1781), long enough for the author to have become acquainted with KANT's discussion of time and space. The passages under consideration are introduced by the author as a sort of philosophic excursus at the beginning of his discussion of the Hebrew word for "time."[1] There is no mention of any names of authors or sources in those passages except for a vague reference to "some of the philosophers."[2] The argument of PAPPENHEIM is rather difficult to follow, as his style is purely literary and entirely unlike the accepted style of Hebrew philosophic writings with its precise and technical terminology. Still from behind the veil of his eloquence we can detect the main drift of his thought and identify the sources he followed as well as the views he meant to criticize.

In order fully to appreciate the fine points of PAPPENHEIM's discussion we must first attempt to reconstruct the background of his knowledge, or his mass of apperception, as it were, with regard to the general problems of time and space. This can be easily done,

[1] *Yeri'ot Shelomoh* f. 6, r. a: טרם התחלנו לדבר על שמות המורות על הזמן עצמו ועל כל המתיחם אליו ראינו מן הצורך להעיר תחלה על הזמן עצמו מה הוא.

[2] מקצת המחקרים (*loc. cit.*) קצת מן החוקרים (f. 8, v. b).

assuming, as we have reason to do, that he was well versed in the standard philosophic texts of his time, Jewish as well as non-Jewish. From Maimonides' *Moreh Nebukim*[3] and its commentaries as well as from other standard Hebrew works on philosophy he must have become acquainted with Aristotle's definition of time with all its implications. According to this definition time is an accident of motion, inseparable from motion and hence from space and body, and since it could not exist without motion and body there could be no time prior to the creation of the world, if the world is assumed to be created. He must have also been acquainted with the question whether time is ideal or real, or, as the mediaevals put it, whether time is in the mind or outside the mind, and also with Aristotle's position on this question that time, being the number of motion, is partly real and partly ideal.[4]

From JOSEPH ALBO's *Ikkarim* II, 18, he could have learned of another kind of time, which is pure duration, succession and continuity, independent of motion and space and magnitude. For says ALBO: There are two kinds of time. One, " unmeasured duration conceived only in thought, having existence prior to the creation of the world as well as after its passing away." This is " absolute time " in which there is no distinction of equality and non-equality. The other kind of time is that which is " counted and numbered by the motion of the sphere, and to this applies the distinction of prior and posterior, of equal and unequal."[5] The first kind of ALBO's time can be traced to an old un-Aristotelian definition, which I have already discussed elsewhere;[6] the second is time in the Aristotelian sense. The first kind of time, or rather duration, furthermore, is purely ideal, that is, it arises in the mind and exists only in the mind, and requires no body and motion or space. It has not even that partial objectivity or reality that Aristotle ascribes to time as he defines it.

These Jewish sources must have been supplemented by his reading of LOCKE and LEIBNITZ, for there is evidence, as we shall see anon,

[3] *Moreh Nebukim* II, Introduction, Proposition XV.

[4] *Physics* IV, 14, 223 a, 21 ff.

[5] וזה אף אם יהיה הזמן המשך הבלתי משוער המדומה במחשבה, שהוא נמצא תמיד קודם בריאת העולם ואחר העדרו . . . . שההמשך הוא הזמן בשליה . . . . ויהיה הזמן לפי זה שני מינים, ממנו נספר ומשוער בתנועת הגלגל, ויפול בו הקודם והמתאחר והשוה והבלתי שוה, וממנו בלתי נספר ומשוער, והוא המשך שיהיה קודם מציאות הגלגל, שלא יפול בו השוה והבלתי שוה.

[6] " Note on Crescas's Definition of Time," *Jewish Quarterly Review*, n. s. X, 1–17.

that he was acquainted with the writings of both these authors. In LOCKE's discussion of time he must have found an expression of views the like of which he had already met in Jewish sources, especially ALBO. Time, according to LOCKE, is not the measure or number of motion (*Essay Concerning Human Understanding* II, xiv, § 6). Its essence is duration and succession, which is a product of the mind. What is generally called time is duration set out by measure (*ibid.*, § 17). And because it is independent of motion and magnitude it could exist prior to the creation of the world (*ibid.*, § 24–25). If PAPPENHEIM had read Spinoza he must have found in him also a similar distinction between duration and time (Epistola XII *olim* XXIX).

Similarly with regard to space he must have gathered from Jewish sources, especially CRESCAS and ALBO, of the existence of two views. On the one hand, there was the view of Aristotle that space is the external, enclosing boundary of a body with its corollary that there could be no space without a body. On the other hand, there was another view, mentioned by Aristotle but explicitely rejected by him,[7] according to which space is identified with the distance or interval or vacuum, which has only the capacity of being filled by a body but which in itself is independent of body. This definition of space is favored by CRESCAS (*Or Adonai* I, ii, 1, Vienna edition, p. 15 b) and by ALBO (*Ikkarim* II, 17). A definition similar to this he must have also found in LOCKE, for according to him space is distance (*Essay* II, xviii, § 3). In a certain sense, these two contrasting definitions of space may be said to correspond to the two definitions of time, both revolving upon the question whether time and space are dependent upon body or not.

To a mind nurtured upon these traditional speculations about the nature of time and space the views of KANT would naturally appeal only as another one of those theories that came out to deny their reality. Its original marks of distinction would be overlooked by him. What would stand out in his eye as of the greatest significance in KANT's discussion of the problem is its insistence upon the denial of the reality of time and space as something independent of the mind and more especially the repeated statements that they were not accidents or qualities subsisting in a subject. The latter point would

[7] *Physics* IV, 4, 211 b, 6 ff.

at once suggest to his mind the old un-Aristotelian definition of time which likewise denied that it is an accident. He would thus throw it in together with those definitions of the middle ages or with that of Locke which defined time as duration or which found duration as something different from time, maintaining that it exists only in the mind of him who comprehends it.

This is how all the historical threads are brought to a focus in Pappenheim. Following his philosophical precedents he tries to answer the question whether time is real or not, and if the former, what is its nature. From this he tries to draw the logical conclusion as to whether time could have existed prior to the creation of the world. Pappenheim's discussion throughout is devoid of any direct reference to opposite views; no names of authorities or opponents are mentioned; there is only a vague allusion to the prevalent ignorance of the true nature of time among "some of the philosophers," and to "the view held by some philosophers on this subject."[8] He is especially painstaking in calling attention to the importance and originality of his own view on the subject. But whatever we shall finally find his own view to amount to, we shall first try to follow him step by step in the deployment of his argument and to show his complete dependence upon Locke's chapters on space and time in his *Essay Concerning Human Understanding.* He follows Locke closely in the main outline, diverting from him occasionally only to digress into some of the by-ways of the problem or to elaborate his point by additional explanations and illustrations. But these digressions, too, are often suggested by other parts of the *Essay*, and as for the elaborations one is sometimes led to suspect that they are taken from some contemporary German philosophic writings. Leibnitz' *New Essays Concerning Human Understanding* shows its influence as does also, in one important point, as I hope to show, Kant's *Critique.*

Pappenheim sets out by defining time as *duration* and space as *distance.* For *duration* he uses the term המשך, which is also used by Albo, translating it himself by the German *Die Dauer.* For *distance* he uses the term מרחק, to be found also in Albo (רחק) and elsewhere, translating it again by the German *Die Weite.* It is, however, neither Albo nor any other Jewish source but rather Locke whom Pappenheim

[8] *Yeri'ot Shelomoh* f. 6, r, a: שהעלמתי גדולה היא אצל מקצת המחקרים; f. 8, v. b: להנחת קצת מן החוקרים בענין הזה.

is following here, for he proceeds to draw a further distinction between the two senses in which the term *space* (מקום עצמו, מקום, *Der Raum*) may be used, one in the sense of *distance* (רחוק, *Die Weite*), which applies only to the length between two bodies, and the other in the sense of *void* (החלל הרקני) or *capacity* (הכנה לקבל הגשמים), which applies to the entire *interval* (רווח מקום). This distinction is given by LOCKE in his *Essay* II, xiii, § 3. It would furthermore seem that his immediate literary source must have been the corresponding passage in LEIBNITZ' *New Essays*, for PAPPENHEIM's description of *distance* bears a closer resemblance verbally to the latter than to the former, and then also the term *interval* as another word for *capacity* occurs only in LEIBNITZ.[9]

After thus defining the terms time and space PAPPENHEIM proceeds to explain their nature. They are conceptual quantities (כמויות עיוניות) and hence apply to both material and spiritual beings. They are furthermore numerical quantities (כמות מספרי). Accordingly they are capable of infinite increase as well as of infinite divisibility. This characterization is also based upon LOCKE, who similarly speaks of time and space, or rather duration and expansion, as "abstract conceptions," which do not intimate the idea of body, and also as being capable of greater or less quantities to infinity (*Essay* II, xv, § 1 f. Cf. xiii, § 4; xv, § 9). It is LOCKE, too, who speaks of number as furnishing us with the idea of infinity in connection with space and duration (*ibid.* II, xvii, § 9 ff.).

But while at first PAPPENHEIM makes rather a sweeping statement that both time and space apply alike to spiritual and material beings, he then veers about and hastens to make a qualification, stating that spiritual beings are to be excluded from any spatial relation.

9

LOCKE

This space, considered barely in length between any two beings, without considering anything else between them, is called distance; if considered in length, breadth, and thickness, I think it may be called capacity.

(*Essay* II, xiii, § 3.)

PAPPENHEIM

...והמקום מתעצם על צד הרחוק שאם נשער שיהיה כאן גשם משהו מונח בין מזרח למערב בדרך משל מיד נדע בבירור שיש כאן הפסק בין רוח מזרח לרוח מערב ושאינן נוגעות זו בזו, כי אותו משהו גשם מפסיק ביניהם ועל כן הם מרוחקות ונפרדות זו מזו. ואותו הרחוק הכמות המפסיק נקרא מקום (דיא וייטע). ובשתוף השם יקרא גם כן החלל הרקני מקום, והוא מצד שיש בו הכנה לקבל הגשמים אבל באמת לא יקרא זה כי אם רווח מקום לא מקום עצמו (דער רוים).

(*Yeri'ot Shelomoh* f. 6, r.)

LEIBNITZ

PH. L'espace considéré par rapport à la longueur, qui sépare deux corps, s'appelle distance; par rapport à la longueur, à la largeur, et à la profondeur on peut l'appeller capacité.

TH.... On peut dire que la capacité ou plutôt l'intervalle...

(*Nouveaux Essais* II, xiii, § 3.)

He begins his qualification with the following expression: " But there is a difference between the spiritual and the material beings." He then explains the difference by saying that material beings have two kinds of extension, by way of duration and by way of distance, whereas spiritual beings have only one kind of extension, that by way of duration. He closes his remarks on this point by saying: " But this is outside the scope of our discussion." [10] We have good reason to ask ourselves here. Why this sudden change of view? Why drag in this problem which according to the author's own statement is " outside the scope of our discussion "? All this, to our mind, can be explained only by again referring to LOCKE.

Toward the end of a long comparison between duration and space (or expansion), LOCKE says: " But there is this manifest difference between them, that the ideas of length which we have of expansion are turned every way ... but duration is but as it were the length of one straight line " (*Essay* II, xvi, § 11). The similarity in the turn of speech between this passage and PAPPENHEIM's digression is quite apparent. But more than this. LOCKE then proceeds to raise the question whether spiritual beings are in time and space. He declares that as for time it applies to all beings, whether spiritual or material. But " whether angels and spirits have any analogy to this, in respect to expansion, is beyond my comprehension " (*ibid.*). What PAPPENHEIM does in his digression is simply to reproduce LOCKE's question, which is left open, and answer it negatively.

The question raised by LOCKE as to the spatial and temporal relation of spiritual beings is a mediaeval inheritance. In Jewish philosophy time and, for that matter, space are said to be inapplicable to spiritual beings, under the Aristotelian definitions of these terms.[11] But if, in opposition to Aristotle, time is defined as duration and space as distance there is a certain sense in which they may be said to apply even to God. CRESCAS maintains that under the un-Aristotelian definition of time attributes expressing temporal relations may be applied to God (*Or Adonai* I, iii, 3, p. 23 b). In his identification of space with the unfilled vacuum or distance, he also finds justification

[10] *Yeri'ot Shelomoh* f. 6, r. b: אלא שיש הפרש בין הנבראים הרוחנים לגשמים, כי הגשמים יש להם ב' מיני התפשטות על צד ההמשך ועל צד הרחוק.... אבל הרוחני אינו נופל זולת תחת מין אחד מן ההתפשטות, והוא ההתפשטות ההמשכותי.... ואין זה מכלל דברינו. ונשוב אל הענין ונאמר.

[11] *Moreh Nebukim* II, Introduction, Proposition XV; *Or Adonai* I, 1, 15.

for the old rabbinic dictum that God is the place of the world (*ibid.* I, ii, 1, p. 15 b).[12] ALBO, on the other hand, denies the applicability to God of either of these two terms even under their un-Aristotelian definitions (*Ikkarim* II, 17–18). It is interesting to note that LEIBNITZ in his criticism of LOCKE with regard to the inapplicability of space to spiritual beings refers to the same dictum as CRESCAS by saying that "some have believed that God is the place of things" (*New Essays* II, xiii, § 17). Of course, this dictum, in so far as it occurs in non-Jewish sources, may be traced back to Philo[13] and one need not ascribe it to a rabbinic origin. LEIBNITZ himself mentions Lessius and Guericke as having been of this opinion. Still leaving out God, who is called the place of the world, it may be definitely stated that in mediaeval Jewish philosophy, under the un-Aristotelian definitions of time and space, spiritual beings are said to be in time but not in space.[14] Thus while the question was introduced by PAPPENHEIM under the influence of LOCKE, his solution of it is based upon Jewish sources.

In the course of his discussion as to the nature of space LOCKE says that its definition does not really explain its nature. "If any one asks me what this space I speak of is, I will tell him when he tells me what his extension is" (*Essay* II, xiii, § 15). But one knows as little of the nature of extension as of the nature of space. According to its definition, as ordinarily given, "extension is to have parts that are extended." But to say this is tantamount to saying that "extension consists of extended parts," which hardly explains its nature. LOCKE compares it to the question as to what a fibre was, which could hardly be answered by the statement that "it was a thing made up of several fibres." The same question is also raised by PAPPENHEIM with reference to both time and space, introducing it, like LOCKE, by the phrase: "Any one may now ask us." Like LOCKE he finds that his definitions of time and space, the former as duration and the latter as distance, do not really explain their nature. They are only tantamount to saying that time and space consist respectively of small parts of duration and of small parts of distance. Again

[12] *Genesis Rabbah* 68, 9.

[13] *De eo quod a Deo mittantur somnia* I, 11.

[14] That incorporeal beings have no spatial relations, see *Or Adonai* I, 1, 3: בדברים אשר להם סדר במצב..... בדברים אשר להם סדר בטבע.

ABRAHAMS.

like Locke he compares it to the question as to what wood was. "If a man asked us what the nature of wood was," we would fail to answer the question satisfactorily by saying "that the wood concerning which he asks is a thing made up of smaller pieces of wood."[15] Unlike Locke, however, Pappenheim is not satisfied by merely stating the problem and leaving it unsolved. He proceeds to solve it by laying down first two preliminary propositions. These propositions, too, as we shall see, can be traced back to Locke, but their discussion by Pappenheim shows the unmistakable influence of some other literary sources. In one instance, I hope to show, it was that of Kant's *Critique*.

First, Pappenheim distinguishes between two processes of generation or coming-to-be (הויה). One he calls "saltatory generation" (הויה דולגת), the other "aggregative generation" (הויה מתלקטת). The terms may perhaps sound less awful if we attempt to translate them into Latin: *Generatio per saltum, generatio per aggregationem.* Whether these terms are of his own coinage or have been copied by him from somebody else is hard to determine. The distinction between these two terms, however, judged by his explanation, is like that between "timeless or instantaneous change" (שנוי בזולת זמן) and "temporal or gradual change" (שנוי בזמן) found in Jewish philosophy.[16] It may also correspond to Locke's distinction between simple and complex substances (*Essay* II, xxiii, § 1) or between single and collective substances (*ibid.* II, xii, § 6. Cf. II, xxiv). His own illustration of "saltatory generation" is that of a geometrical line each part of which is a line, and of "aggregative generation" is that of the circumference of a geometrical circle (העגול ההנדסי), the parts of which are not circles but arcs (קשתות).[17] Like coming-to-be, passing-away or corruption (העדר הנמצאים) is also either "saltatory" or "aggregative," i.e., instantaneous or gradual. Furthermore, corresponding to these two kinds of generation and corruption there are two processes of the formation of ideas (הוית הציורים), "saltatory

[15] *Yeri'ot Shelomoh* f. 6, r. b—v. a: ואם כן איפו אי אפשר שיהיה ההמשך הזמני שהוא אמנם סך מקובץ מהמשכות קטנות הבאות זו אחר זו שיהיה הוא הזמן עצמו, והמרחק המקומי אי אפשר שיהיה הוא המקום עצמו, כאשר הוא אמנם סך משופע מרחקים קטנים. ואלו שאלנו אדם על עצם העץ מה הוא.... ואף גם אלו היינו משיבים לו יותר מדוקדק שהעץ שהוא שואל עליו הוא דבר מורכב מעצים קטנים, גם בזה לא היינו מספיקים תשובת שאלתו.

[16] *Or Adonai* I, 1, 4. Altabrizi's commentary on Maimonides' twenty-five propositions (prop. IV) uses the expression השנוי פתאום אי לא פתאום. Cf. Mendelssohn's *Sefer ha-Nefesh* I, § 16—17: העדר פתאומי, הויה פתאומית (בלי זמן) שיעדר בזמן, שיתהוה בזמן.

[17] *Yeri'ot Shelomoh* f. 6, v. cf. also f. 8, r. a.

ideas" and "aggregative ideas." From his further description of these two kinds of ideas it is evident that he means thereby the old distinction, formally stated by LOCKE, between intuitive and demonstrative knowledge (*Essay* IV, ii, § 1–2). "Saltatory ideas"[18] are ideas which leap in to one's mind and are perceived immediately; "aggregative ideas" are ideas which are gathered up gradually by means of reasoning and through intermediary stages.

Then, in his second proposition, PAPPENHEIM draws a distinction between three senses in which the term "existence" or "being" (מציאות) may be used: "Substantial being" (מציאות עצמיי), "accidental being" (מציאות מקריי), and מציאות על צד ההתגלות, which we shall translate here by "phenomenal being." The last term התגלות, however, is used by the author in several other senses. Taking the word in its literal meaning of "appearance" he combines it with other words to mean appearing, to the eye, in the imagination, *to* the mind and *in* the mind, and he seems to use these expressions in the technical senses of "phenomenon," "image," "idea" and "intuition" respectively.[19] Or, we may put it in another way. On etymological grounds, in its literal meaning of "appearance," he uses it in the sense of (1) *phenomenon*[20] and (2) *phantasm*, the latter in the sense of an image or picture of both the imagination and the mind. On historical and lexicographical grounds, in its derivative meaning of *divine revelation* and *prophetic inspiration*, he uses it also in the sense of *intuition*. Thus מציאות על צד ההתגלות, which we have translated by phenomenal being, may also be translated by fictitious, conceptual and intuitive being.

Of these three kinds of being only the first two are considered by him as having real existence; the third is not to be classed at all among real beings.[21] The first two he defines very clearly and leaves no doubt as to what he means by them. "Substantial being" is that which subsists by itself and is dependent only upon the

[18] Compare the expression *saltus in demonstrando*.

[19] The following passages illustrate the use made by the author of the term:

על צד המציאות בציור ובמחשבה (f. 7, r. b)
שהם מתגלים כך לעינינו (*ibid.*)
ואלה המצואים הצוריים (*ibid.*)
המתגלה... במוחש.... והמתגלה גם כן כך במושכל. (f. 7, v. b)

[20] MENDELSSOHN translates "Phenomenon" by האיון (*Sefer ha-Nefesh* II).

[21] *Ibid.*, f. 7, r. b: ועוד מין אחר נמצא יש לנו, אבל הוא בלתי ראוי להכנס בסוג המציאות כלל, והוא המציאות על צד ההתגלות, והיא דבר הבלתי נמצא בישות בפני עצמו, גם לא בישות על צד הרכיבה, כי אם על צד המציאות בציור ובמחשבה.

creative power of God, in conformity with the traditional definition of substance. "Accidental being" is that which does not subsist by itself but is dependent upon some other created being for its support—the traditional definition of accident. As illustrations of accidental being he mentions quantity (כמות, *Die Menge*), sound, color, odor, and refers to other terms of the same kind. His definition and illustration of the third class of being are not so clear. The term "phenomenal" by which it is designated and the example of "priority in place"[22] by which he illustrates it would seem to indicate that he means thereby any external relation. But, then, the term which we have translated by "phenomenal" is also used by him, as we have already mentioned, in the sense of "intuitive," "fictitious" or "ideal." While there is a common underlying meaning to all these terms, namely, the negation of reality, in consequence of which we may be justified in designating this third class of being as "unreal being," the question still remains how did Pappenheim get to this involved terminology.

The answer to this question, it seems to me, may be found in the complexity of the sources which we have reason to believe were used by Pappenheim in his discussion of the threefold classification of being. His basic source was undoubtedly Locke's threefold classification of complex ideas into substances, modes and relations (*Essay* II, xii, § 3). Mode is only another word which Locke, like Spinoza, substituted for the old traditional term accident, the latter term, according to Locke's contention, being "of little use in philosophy" (*Essay* II, xiii, § 19–20). Leibnitz, however, in his criticism, tried to reinstate the term accident (*New Essays* II, xiii, § 19). By relation Locke means a great variety of relations, among which he also mentions the "relation of place" (*Essay* II, xxvi, § 5). Here, again, Leibnitz adds that the ideas of relations are "the poorest in reality" and have "something of the essence of reason" (*New Essays* II, xxv, § 1).

Locke's classification, therefore, with Leibnitz' modifications and explanations, accounts for Pappenheim's threefold classification of being, for his designating the first two by terms "substantial" and "accidental," for his illustrating the third one by the example of "priority in place," for his characterizing it as unreal, and for his

[22] *Ibid.*, ומעין זה המין הוא מה שנקרא קדימה במקום.

describing it by a term which, as we have seen, is used by him, in the sense of any subjective form of reason or imagination. But why did he not use, like LOCKE, the term relation for his third class of being, and what made him lend the additional meanings of "phenomenal" and "intuitive" to the term by which he describes it? This, I believe, can be accounted for by the influence of KANT's *Critique*.

KANT introduces the problem of time and space by asking, as does here PAPPENHEIM, which of the three possible kinds of being they are, and his enumeration of his three possible kinds of being, again as in PAPPENHEIM, is reminiscent of LOCKE's classification of complex ideas. KANT asks himself: "Are they real beings [i.e., substances]? Or, if not that, are they determinations or relations of things, but such as would belong to them even if they were not perceived [i.e., modes or accidents]? Or, lastly, are they determinations and relations which are inherent in the form of intuition only, and therefore in the subjective nature of our mind [i.e., relations]?"[23] Under the guise of the Kantian vocabulary we can discover here the terms substance, mode or accident, and relation, the last one in the sense of being "in the subjective nature of our mind," as LOCKE's relations are described by LEIBNITZ. He also calls this last kind of being "the form of intuition," by means of which we combine all our internal and external sensations into phenomena. Phenomena only, therefore, or things so far as they are perceived by us and appear to us, are in time and space, which to him are the forms of intuition. Thus the term *intuition* with its inseparable companion term *phenomenon* is introduced by KANT in the description of the third class of being known as *relations*, and from KANT, we may safely conclude, it was taken over by PAPPENHEIM.

Like KANT, and undoubtedly following him, PAPPENHEIM tries to answer the question as to the nature of time by first determining what kind of being it is. Exactly like KANT he asks himself: Are they substances? Are they accidents? Or, are they relations existing only in the mind? KANT answers that they are neither the first nor the second but the third, existing only in us as something wholly subjective, or, as he describes them, they are "pure forms of sensuous intuition." PAPPENHEIM, however, in opposition to KANT, but following

[23] MÜLLER's translation (1881), p. 20.

the Aristotelian and mediaeval tradition as well as LOCKE, answers that they are of the second class of being, namely, accidents or modes.[24] Time and space are to him accidents belonging to the category of quantity, but each representing a different kind of quantity, the one being *duration* and the other *distance*.[25] As accidents they have no independent existence but require some external subject for their support. The subject of space must be a body; the subject of time need not be a body, it may also be a spiritual being, but it must be created.[26] In both cases the subject of time and of space must have external reality. There is no space unless a body occupies it; there is no time unless something, not necessarily a body, endures in it.

Time and space are further continuous quantities and belong to what PAPPENHEIM chose to call "saltatory generation." And here PAPPENHEIM enters upon a lengthy explanation of the nature of continuous quantities and their infinite divisibility.[27] There is nothing new in that explanation which sounds to us merely as an echo of what has been said on the subject ever since Aristotle, though its immediate literary source must have been, again, LOCKE's discussion of the same subject, which culminates in the statement that "every part of duration is duration too, and every part of extension is extension, both of them capable of addition or division in infinitum" (*Essay* II, xv, § 9). PAPPENHEIM, however, elaborates the discussion by introducing many new illustrations the origin of which may undoubtedly be traced to contemporary German philosophic literature. He also refers to additional arguments on the question of infinite divisibility both which he himself has devised and which may be found in the works of others.[28]

[24] *Yeri'ot Shelomoh* f. 7, v. b: אחרי אשר הראנו שאין הזמן והמקום לפי הנהתנו אך סגולות מקריות נשואות על נושא חוץ להם.

[25] *Ibid.*, וכאשר קימנו לנו שהזמן והמקום אמנם הם סגולת הדברים כפי התגלתם ולא נחייב להם שום עצם בפועל כי אם עצם הכמות שהוא סגולת המספר המרובה לא נשאר לנו כי אם לידע ולהודיע אותן הסגולות מה הם בעצם, והתרנו לנו שהם עצמים מתעצמים אם על צד ההמשך ואם על צד הרחוק.

[26] *Ibid.*, f. 7, v. a b: הנה בזה קימנו לנו שהזמן והמקום הם ממין הנמצאים המקריים שאין להם מציאות מופשטות, כי אם מציאות מה שהם נשואים אל נושא חוץ מהם....ובעצמות המקום מעיד לנו החוש על זה....ואותו לא נמצא עומד נפרד בפני עצמו משום אופן, כי אם על אופן שימצא שם כבר גשם הנושא אותו.... ומעצמות המקום....נוכל להקיש על עצמות הזמן....ולא ימצא גם כן במציאות פרדי בשום אופן כי אם כשימצא שם נברא שיש לו מציאות בפועל. Cf. above his discussion as to the relation of time to spiritual beings.

[27] *Ibid.*, f. 8.

[28] *Ibid.*, f. 8, v. a: ובגוף הדבר עצמו שיהיה כל כמות מוכן להלוקה בב"ת מבלי שנגיע אל חלק ממנו הבלתי מקבל עוד החלוקה יש לנו ראיות מספיקות מה שיארך כאן זכרם מלבד אותן הנמצאות כבר בדברי זולתינו.

Compared with the two definitions which mark the age-old controversy as to the nature of time and space, the controversy which has its exponents in Aristotle, on the one hand, and in CRESCAS, ALBO and LOCKE, to name but a few, on the other, PAPPENHEIM's position amounts to a compromise. From Aristotle he has accepted the view that time and space exist only when body exists and thus have an existence which is only accidental. But unlike Aristotle he denies that time is the number or measure of motion and that space is the external boundary of body. On this point he agrees with Aristotle's opponents, CRESCAS, ALBO and LOCKE, for instance, and defines time as duration and space as distance. But unlike CRESCAS, ALBO and LOCKE he would not say that space and time could exist without a subject. He insists that time is a duration in which there must be something to endure and that space is a distance in which there must be a body to occupy it.

By adopting this definition of time and space PAPPENHEIM is enabled to come out in opposition to KANT and LOCKE on two important issues. Defining time and space as accidents he establishes thereby their reality—a reality which is only partial and conditional, to be sure, the reality of accidents which depend on something else for their existence. He is thus opposed to KANT who again and again denies that time and space are accidents or qualities, maintaining that they are subjective forms of our intuition. By further insisting upon the inseparability of time and space from some created object, PAPPENHEIM also comes out in opposition to LOCKE, whose definition he otherwise follows, on the question of the existence of time prior to the creation of the world and of the separability of space from body. According to both CRESCAS and LOCKE the necessary corollary of their identification of time with duration and space with distance is that time existed prior to the creation of the world and that the idea of space was independent of the idea of body (*Essay* II, xiii, § 24; xiv, § 24 ff.; xv, § 2–3, § 7. Cf. CRESCAS, *Or Adonai* I, ii, 1, p. 15 b, and I, ii, 11, p. 19 b). To PAPPENHEIM, however, there was no time prior to creation and there can be no space without body. It is with reference to this issue that PAPPENHEIM begins the last paragraph of his discussion—a paragraph which seems to be aimed directly at LOCKE[29]—by addressing his reader: "From all that has

[29] See LOCKE's arguments for the existence of duration prior to the creation of the world in *Essay* II, XIV, 28—30.

been said you can know and understand clearly the wide difference between our conception of time and space and the view held by some philosophers on the same subject."[30] This is what he himself has evidently considered as his own original contribution to the subject.

The concluding statement of Pappenheim is likewise addressed to his readers. "Try to understand this solution of the problem and keep it well in your mind, for it will prove of the utmost importance. Its value will dawn upon you when you come to pry into the subtleties of the higher speculations, for thereby you will rid yourself of the many doubts which confuse man's views in matters metaphysical."[31] There is in this passage an insinuation of the lively discussions on time and space that were aroused in philosophic circles, and in Jewish no less than in others, on the appearance of Kant's *Critique.* We know from Solomon Maimon's autobiography how he happened to come across a chance copy of Wolff's *Metaphysics* in a butter-shop, how stirred he was on reading it, how he compared it with the views of Maimonides, dashed off a criticism of it in Hebrew and rushed it off to Mendelssohn. Pappenheim may have gotten his copy of Kant's *Critique* in a less casual way, but so impressed must he have been by its opening pages that he immediately dashed off his own views, such as they were, in the language in which Jews still philosophized, and rushed them off to his printer to be inserted as an introductory essay to his discussion of the Hebrew word for "time" in his *Yeri'ot Shelomoh.*

[30] *Yeri'ot Shelomoh* f. 8, v. b: ותדע ותשכיל ממוצא הדברים המפרש הרב שבין הנחתנו בעצם הזמן ומקום להנחת קצת מן החוקרים בענין הזה.

[31] *Ibid.*, f. 9, r. a: והבן זה הענין ודעהו מאד כי רב הוא. ותועלתו ימצא לך בקרבתך אל העיון בענינים הדקים כי יסלק מעליך ספיקות רבות המשבשות את הדעות בענינים האלהיים.

APPENDIX

אצילות ויש מאין אצל קרשקש

אצילות ובריאת יש מאין הן שתי דעות על דבר מוצאו של העולם העומדות זו כנגד זו. האחת, בתפיסתה הפילוסופית, היא מיסודו של פליטינוס, אם כי החוקרים הערביים שלפני אבן רשד, והרמב"ם עמהם [1], יחסו אותה גם כן אל אריסטוטוליס. השנית יסודה בספר מקבים ב', פרק ז', פסוק כ"ח, אם כי הרמב"ם [2], וכן גם רובם של החוקרים בימי הבינים, יחסו אותה אל תורת הבריאה שבספר בראשית. יש צד שוה בין שתי הדעות האלו, והוא ששתיהן מניחות, שהתהוותו של העולם תלויה בסבה ראשונה שהיא האלהים. אבל נבדלות הן זו מזו באופן הסברתן את התהוותו של העולם בסבתיותו של האלהים. תורת האצילות מניחה שהעולם יצא מתוך עצמותו של האלהים, בעוד שתורת יש מאין מניחה, שהעולם נברא על ידי האלהים מאין ומאפס גמור. ועוד שני הבדלים יש ביניהן לפי מובניהן המקובלים. לפי תורת האצילות, התהוותו של העולם מעצמותו של האלהים היא התהוות חיובית ונצחית; לפי תורת יש מאין, בריאתו של העולם על ידי האלהים היא פעולה רצונית ובעלת התחלה זמנית.

שתי הדעות האלו הן נושא דבריו של קרשקש באחת מטענותיו על תורת החידוש של הרלב"ג [3]. במרוצת הטענה ההיא, הוא מתאמץ להוכיח שהמושג יש מאין אין מובנו „שהאין יהיה הנושא כאמרנו הזנג'אר [4] מהנחשת" אלא מובנו הוא „שנתהווה אחר ההעדר"; וכן גם מושג האצילות אין מובנו אלא „שהחומר והצורה יחד שניהם נאצלו אחר ההעדר". ומכיון ששני המושגים האלה מובנם אחד, הוא הולך ומסיק, ששני המושגים בעצמם הם אחד, אם כי מובעים הם במלות שונות. בדרך אגב הוא מציע גם־כן שהאצילות אפשר לה להיות „אם על דרך החיוב ואם על דרך הרצון" ומזכיר הוא גם כן את ההבדל שביניהן בנוגע לשאלה של רצוניות והתחלותיות זמנית.

קרשקש כדרכו תמיד יותר משהוא מביע את רעיונותיו הוא מרמז אליהם. דבריו במקום הזה, כמו בכל מקום, יש בהם משום גילוי טפח וכיסוי טפחיים, וכדי שיובנו כל צרכם, לכל האצור והכמוס בהם, טעונים הם ביאור שלם כמעט לכל מלה. אבל בהערתנו

1 מורה נבוכים, ח"ב, פכ"ב.

2 שם, ח"ב, פי"ג, הדעת הראשון.

3 אור ה', מ"ג, כ"א, פ"ה.

4 שם, דף ס"ט, עמ' א, שורה י"ג (דפוס וינה). כך היא הגירסא בכל כתבי־היד. במלה ערבית זו, זנג'אר, שפירושה הוא חומצת הנחושת, כמו המלה היוונית קלקנתוס שבלשון חז"ל, השתמש קרשקש גם כן במקום אחר באמרו: „כאלו תאמר, שחומר הנחושת אפשר שיהיה זנג'אר" (שם, מ"א, כ"א, פכ"ד). בנדפס הגירסא פה במקום הזה „הנגזר מהנחושת". לפי גירסא זו, פירושו של „הנגזר" פה הוא „הפסל", והוא כמו „האנדרטא" במשלו של אריסטוטוליס המובא למטה.

הקצרה הזאת נייחד דבורנו רק על מקורותיהם ומקבילותיהם של שלשה ענינים שהוא דן בהם בטענה זו, והם: (א) שהבטוי יש מאין פירושו יש אחר אין; (ב) שאצילות אפשר לה להיות גם כן רצונית; (ג) שאצילות כוונתה אחת עם יש מאין.

צור מחצבתה של התאמצותו של קרשקש להראות שמלת „מאין" פירושה „אחר אין" הוא פרק אחד באריסטוטליס, שבו הוא דורש בפירושו של המלה „מן"[5]. המלה „מן", הוא אומר, היא בעלת הרבה משמעיות, וביניהן הוא מזכיר את שתי המשמעיות, שהבאנו אותן מקרשקש. יש שהמלה „מן" מורה על החומר, שממנו נעשה איזה דבר, ובתור משל הוא מביא את המאמר „האנדרטא הוא מהנחושת". אבל יש שההוראה של המלה „מן" היא „אחר", כלומר אחר בזמן, כמו למשל באמרנו: „מיום יבוא לילה ומשקט יבוא סער", שפירושו של המאמר הזה הוא, שאחר יום יבוא לילה ואחר שקט יבוא סער.

השתמשות כזו בדבריו של אריסטוטליס כדי ליתן פירוש חדש לבטוי יש מאין אנו מוצאים גם אצל תומס מאקווינו. מתקשה הוא תומס במאמר המסורתי, שבריאת העולם היא מאין ושואל: „המלה מ ן מורה על יחס אל איזה סיבה, וביחוד אל סיבה חמרית, כאמרנו, שהאנדרטא היא מהנחושת. אבל האין אי־אפשר לו להיות חומר של הנמצא או גם סיבה אחרת כל שהיא של הנמצא. ובכן מלת ב ר א (שבבראשית) אין כוונתה עשיית יש מאין"[6]. תשובתו על פירכא זו מיוסדת על דבריו של אריסטוטליס בפירושו למלת מן, „באמרנו שיש נתהווה מאין", אומר תומס, „המלה מן, או יותר נכון האות מ"ם, שבמאין אינה מורה על סיבה חמרית אלא על סדר, כאמרנו מבוקר יבוא צהרים, שפירושו הוא אחר בוקר יבוא צהרים". אבל אחר שהשיב את התשובה הזאת, הוא הולך ומוסיף ביאור עליה, ומתוך ביאורו תצא עוד תשובה לפירכא שלו. לפי תשובתו זו השניה, מובנו האמיתי של „נתהווה מאין" fit ex nihilo, הוא „לא נתהווה מדבר", non fit ex aliquo. ובין שני המשפטים האלה יש, לפי דעתו, הבדל הגיוני. המשפט הראשון, „נתהווה מאין", הוא משפט חיובי, ולכן יש לטעות בו, שכוונתו היא, שהאין הוא הנושא החמרי, שממנו נתהווה העולם. אבל המשפט השני, „לא נתהווה מדבר", הוא משפט שלילי ואי־אפשר לטעות בו ולפרשו, שה„דבר" הוא הנושא החמרי שממנו נתהווה העולם[7].

יש לשער, שתומס לא חידש את התשובות האלו מעצמו לגמרי. מושפע היה בזה במקצת מהרמב"ם. אמנם הרמב"ם אינו דן בגלוי על מובנו של הבטוי יש מאין, ואין הוא מציע בהדיא, שמובנו האמיתי של הבטוי יש מאין הוא או (א) נתהווה אחר ההעדר או (ב) לא נתהווה מדבר. אבל בניסוחו של האמונה המסורתית בחידוש העולם הוא מדקדק בלשונו ואומר כי דעת כל מאמין בתורת משה היא (א) שהבורא המציא את העולם „אחרי אפיסה אמיתית מוחלטת" („אחר ההעדר הגמור" בהעתקת אבן תיבון) post privationem veram et absolutam, או (ב) שהבורא המציא את כל הנמצאים „לא

5 עיין: *Metaphysica*, V. 24

6 עיין: Thomas de Aquino, *Summa Theologica* I, 45, 1, obj. 3

7 עיין: Ibid., ad 3

מדבר (לא מן שי)", non de aliquo [8] כבר הצעתי במקום אחר [9], שהרמב"ם בהשתמשו פה בבטוי "לא מדבר" כוונתו היתה בזה לפסול את הבטוי "מלא דבר", שתרגומו הלטיני הוא de nihilo או ex nihilo, מפני שהבטוי "מלא דבר" יש בו מקום לטעות, שמובנו הוא ש"לא דבר" הוא הנושא החמרי של היש הנברא ממנו. הרי יודעים אנו, שמפני טעם זה גם סעדיה בפירושו לספר יצירה מניח את הכלל: "אנחנו אומרים הוא ברא דבר לא מדבר (לא מן שי) ואין אנחנו אומרים הוא ברא דבר מלא דבר (מן לא שי)" [10]. בודאי ראה תומס את הדיוק בדבריו של הרמב"ם ונזכר דיונו של אריסטוטוליס על מובניו השונים של מלת מן וגם הדיונים שלו על ההבדלים השונים שבין משפט חיובי ובין משפט שלילי והלך והכין מסממניהם מרקחת של פירכא ותשובה על מובנו של הבטוי "יש מאין".

מלבד הרמז שאנו מוצאים ברמב"ם אל הצעתו של קרשקש, שמלת "מאין" פירושה "אחר העדר", הנה מוצאים אנו בו גם כן עוד עיון אחר משלשת העיונים של קרשקש, שהזכרנו למעלה, והוא שהאצילות יכולה להיות רצונית. הוא אומר: "דע כי מן האחרונים מן הפילוסופים האומרים בקדמות העולם מי שאומר שהשם יתעלה פועל העולם ובוחר מציאותו ומכוונו ומיחדו על מה שהוא עליו, אלא מן השקר, שיהיה זה בעת בלתי עת, אבל כן היה ויהיה תמיד" [11]. כוונתו של מאמר זה הוא, שאיזה מן הפילוסופים האחרונים, שהלכו אחר אריסטוטוליס בקדמות העולם, שהיא לפי פירושו של הרמב"ם אצילותו התמידית של העולם מעצמותו של האלהים, פרשו ממנו בזה, שהאמינו שהאצילות התמידית הלזו היא בבחירה ובכוונה ובהתיחדות, כלומר, ברצון.

מי הם אלה האחרונים מן הפילוסופים אין הרמב"ם מגלה לנו. אבל יש רגלים לדבר, שאלפראבי היה מבעלי דעה זו. גם הוא, אחרי שהוא מבאר שתורת קדמות העולם לאריסטוטוליס היא באמת תורה של אצילות תמידית של העולם מעצמותו של האלהים, מוסיף ואומר: "ומי שעיין בדבריו על האלהות בספרו הידוע בשם תיאולוגיה לא יהיה הענין מסופק בעיניו, שאריסטוטליס קיים מציאות הורא ומחדש לזה העולם. והענין בדבריו ברור הוא כל כך עד שאי־אפשר לו להיות נעלם מעיני כל איש. ושם בספר ההוא התבאר, שהחומר חדשהו הבורא יתעלה שמו לא מדבר ושעל ידי הבורא יתברך התגשם ושעל ידי רצונו אז התכונן" [12]. ובכן לפי דבריו אלה של אלפראבי, אריסטוטוליס, הסובר שחדושו והתגשמותו והתכוננותו, או התדרגותו, של חומר העולם

8 עיין מורה נבוכים, ח"ב, פי"ד (פי"ג), הדעת הראשון, לפי העתקת אלחריזי שעליה מיוסדת ההעתקה הלטינית, שהשתמש בה תומס. עיין גם: *Rabi Mosei Aegyptij Dux sen Director dubitantium aut perplexorum,* Lib. II, cap. XIV, fol. XLVI b, lb. 12 et 15 .Paris, 1520

9 עיין בסוף מאמרי המוזכר למטה בהערה 14.

10 עיין תפסיר כתאב אלמבאדי, פצל ד', הלכה ה', עמ' 84, שור' 4—3, בספר: *Commentaire sur le Séfer Yesira . . .* par Mayer Lambert, Paris, 1891.

11 מורה נבוכים, ח"ב, פכ"א.

12 עיין "כתאב אלג'מע בין ראיי אלחכימין אפלאטון אלאלאהי ואריסטוטוליס", בספר: *Alfarabi's Philosophische Abhandlungen,* ed. F. Dieteaici, 1890, S. 23.

היא על ידי אצילות תמידית. סובר גם כן, שהאצילות התמידית הלזו היא על ידי האלהים ורצונו.

נוסף על זה, מכלל דבריו של אלפראבי יש להסיק, שלפי דעתו תורת האצילות של אריסטוטוליס היא גם כן תורת יש מאין. בדבריו שהבאנו למעלה הוא אומר שבספר התיאולוגיה של אריסטוטוליס „התבאר שהחומר חדשהו הבורא יתעלה לא מדבר". והנה בכל ספר התיאולוגיה שלפנינו אין כל זכר לחידוש החומר מלא דבר. להפך, החומר לפי דעת הספר הזה התאצל מעצמותו של האלהים [13]. ואם בכל זאת מיחס אלפראבי אל הספר הזה תורת יש מאין, אין זה אלא משום שלפי דעתו תורת האצילות ותורת יש מאין אחת הן.

עקבותיה של השקפה זו על דבר הזדהותה של תורת האצילות עם תורת יש מאין ניכרים גם כן בדעותיהם של ההוקרים האלוהיים המוסלמיים שלפני אלפראבי. מפי אלה שמסרו לנו את דעותיהם על המדברים המוסלמיים למדים אנו על מחלוקת אחת, שהיתה ביניהם בנוגע למובנו של המושג נעדר (מעדום). כת אחת מהם סברה שהנעדר הוא לא דבר (לא שי); אבל כת אחרת טענה ואמרה שהנעדר הוא דבר מה (שי מא). מחלוקת זו, כפי מה שבארתי אותה במקום אחר [14], טומנת בקרבה שתי השקפות שונות על דבר חידושו של העולם, ויסודותיהן של שתי ההשקפות האלו הם שני פירושים שונים על הנוסחה המקורית שבה היתה מובעת האמונה המקובלת על דבר חידוש העולם.

ואלה הם ראשי הפרקים של תולדות שני הפירושים האלה וחילוקי הדעות בחידוש העולם, שהסתעפו מהם.

ראשית, במקומו של הבטוי „יש מאין" שרגילים אנו להשתמש בו עכשיו, היו בראשונה משתמשים בבטוי „יש מלא נמצא". כך היא הנוסחה לפי ספר מקבים ב', פרק כ"ח, וכך היא הנוסחה גם אצל רוב אבות הכנסיה הנוצרית שכתבו יוונית. המדברים המוסלמיים קבלו את ראשית ידיעתם בחקירות על תורת החידוש מאבות הכנסיה הנוצרית האלו. ולזאת בודאי קבלו מהם גם כן את הבטוי „יש מלא נמצא", שבשפתם הערבית נהפכה ל„יש מנעדר", מפני שהבטוי היווני „לא נמצא" מתורגם היה בערבית במלה „נעדר" (מעדום).

שנית, הבטוי היווני „לא נמצא" (μὴ ὄν), שתרגומו בערבית הוא „נעדר". כבר היו לה בספרות הפילוסופית שני מובנים. אריסטוטוליס בעצמו אומר שהבטוי הזה, לפי דעתו הוא, כוונתו „אין" [15], אבל האפלטונים משתמשים בו במובנו של „חומר" [16]. ובכן המדברים המוסלמיים בקבלם מאבות הכנסיה הנוצרית את האמרה, שחידוש העולם היה מנעדר, פירשו אותה בשני אופנים, לפי שני המובנים של מלת נעדר, שכבר היו ידועים להם מהספרות הפילוסופית. לפי דעת הכת האחת כוונתה של האמרה הזאת היתה שהעולם נברא מאין או מלא דבר, בעוד שלפי דעת הכת האחרת כוונתה היתה

13 עיין דוד נימרק, תולדות הפילוסופיה בישראל, ח"א, עמ' 162.

14 עיין מאמרי: "The Kalam Problem of Nonexistence and Saadia's Second Theory of Creation", *Jewish Quarterly Review*, N. S., 36 (1946), 371—391. Above, p. 338.

15 עיין: *De Generatione et Corruptione*, I, 3, 318a, 15

16 עיין: *Physica*, I, 9, 192a, 6—7

שהעולם נברא מחומר, כלומר, מחומר קדום, שממנו נברא העולם לפי דעתו של אפלטון.

שלישית, אלה מן המדברים שבארו את האמונה המסורתית של חידוש נמצא מנעדר במובנה האפלטוני של הידוש העולם מחומר קדום לא הסתפקו במה שכינו את הנעדר בשם חומר. הם כינו אותו, כמו שראינו, גם כן בשם „דבר מה". יתר על כן, עוד הוסיפו לכנות אותו בשם עצם (ג'והר) ולתאר אותו בתור דבר שהוא ידוע ושיוגד עליו (מא יעלם ויכבד ענה). והנה השם „דבר מה" והשם „עצם" אינם נמצאים באפלטון בתור כינויים להחומר, וכן גם אין אנו מוצאים, שהוא מתאר את החומר בתור דבר שהוא ידוע ושיוגד עליו. אבל מוצאים אנו שפלוטינוס קורא להחומר בשם „דבר מה", ואת ה„חומר המושכל" שלו, כלומר, האידיאה של החומר, הוא מכנה בשם „עצם" [18]. וכן אנו מוצאים שאפלטון בעצמו מתאר את האידיאות שלו בתור דברים שאפשר להם להיות נושאי ידיעתנו [19] ודבורנו [20].

רביעית, החומר המושכל של פלוטינוס, כלומר, החומר אשר בעולם המושכל שלו, או האידיאה של החומר, הוא לפי שיטתו אצילות מעצמותו של אלהים, ועולמנו המוחש גם כן התאצל על ידי אמצעיים מעצמותו של האלהים.

מצרופי הידיעות האלו עולה לנו שאלה המדברים, שהכניסו באמונת-החידוש המסורתית את דעתו של אפלטון התחילו בבטוי המסורתי „יש מנעדר", שכוונתו המקורית היתה „יש מאין". אחר שבארו את הבטוי הזה במובנו הפלטוני של יש מחומר קדום, תפסו את החומר הקדום הזה במובנו של החומר המושכל או האידיאה של החומר, שבשיטתו של פלוטינוס, ולכן מתארים הם אותו בשם „דבר מה" ו„עצם" ובתור „דבר שהוא ידוע ושיוגד עליו". אבל, לפי שיטתו של פלוטינוס, התאצל גם העולם על ידי אמצעיים מעצמותו של האלהים. ובכן הבטוי המקורי של האמונה בבריאת יש מאין קיבל אצלם מובן של אמונה באצילות מעצמותו של האלהים. בקצרה, שתי תורות אלו נעשו אצלם לאחת.

הבעיה על דבר היחס שבין אצילות ויש מאין דנו עליה גם-כן אבות הכנסיה הנוצרית והבאים אחריהם, האסכוליסטיקים [21].

היו ביניהם אלה שקיבלו את תורת האצילות של פלוטינוס והרכיבו אותה על האמונה המסורתית של בריאת יש מאין. ביחוד אנו מוצאים הרכבה כזו אצל יוהניס סקוטוס אריגינא. ה„אין" שבבטוי „יש מאין", הוא אומר, פירושו הוא דבר, שאין לו כל תוארים, כלומר, דבר שאי-אפשר לתארו בשום שם ומלה מפאת היותו בלתי מושג בחוש או בשכל. וכיון שהאלהים הוא הוא הנמצא היחידי, שאי-אפשר לנו לתארו בדברים

17 עיין: *Enneades*, II, 4, 16

18 עיין: Ibid., II, 4, 5

19 עיין: *Cratylus*, 440 B

20 עיין: *Parmenides*, 135 C

21 עיין מאמרי: "The Meaning of ex *nihilo* in The Church Fathers, Arabic and Hebrew Philosophy, and St. Thomas", *Mediaeval Studies in Honor of Jeremiah Dennis Mathias Ford*, Harvard University Press, 1948, pp. 353—370; *Studies*, I, 207.

ועוד אני מוסיף לדון בענין זה בספרי על „הפילוסופיה של אבות הכנסיה הנוצרית", העומד להיגמר בקרוב.

ולהשיגו אף בשכל, אי לזאת הבטוי „יש מאין" פירושו התאצלותו של העולם מעצמותו של האלהים, שהוא „אין" בבחינה זו [22].

מטעם זה ממש הגיעו גם בעלי חכמת הקבלה שלנו לידי הזדהות של אמונת האצילות שלהם עם האמונה המסורתית של יש מאין [23]. ברם, ה„אין" שבשיטתם אינו האלהים; ה„אין" שבשיטתם הוא האצול הראשון מהאלהים, הנקרא „כתר עליון" או „ספירת הכתר", אבל הוא נקרא „אין" אצלם, מאותו הטעם עצמו, שהאלהים נקרא „אין" אצל אריגינא — „בשביל שהוא נעלם מלהשיגו" [24] או בשביל שהוא „דבר שאינו נתפס כל עיקר" [25] או מפני „היותה נסתרת מכל הנבראים ואין מי שיוכל להתבונן בה זולתי לשמע אוזן" [26].

אבל אצל הנוצרים הזדהותן של שתי התורות האלו, אצילות ויש מאין, היתה רק דעתם של יחידים. רוב חוקריהם האלוהיים, כפי שאפשר להיווכח מחקירותיהם על חידוש העולם ועל תורת השילוש שלהם, מבדילים ביניהן. בחקירותיהם על חידוש העולם הם מדיינים תמיד עם כת היודעים ועם פלוטינוס ומתאמצים להוכיח, שהעולם נברא מאין ולא התאצל מעצמותו של האלהים. וכן גם בחקירותיהם בתורת השילוש הם מתווכחים תמיד עם אריוס וסיעתו וטוענים, שהבן נולד, כלומר נאצל, מעצמותו של האלהים, ולא היה נברא מאין. רעיון זה, שיש הבדל בין אצילות ויש מאין, מובע באופן ברור ונמרץ על ידי אבגוסטינוס. באחד מספריו, לאחר שהרבה לספר בשבח העולם ולקלס את פלאי הטבע, הוא פונה כלפי האלהים ואומר: „מאין על ידך, ולא מעצמותך, הם נבראו" [27]. ובמקום אחר באותו הספר, שוב הוא נושא את עיניו אל האלהים ואומר: „אתה בראת את השמים ואת הארץ לא מעצמותך כי אילו נבראו מעצמותך, אז היו שווים אל בנך יחידך ומתוך כך גם אליך בעצמך" [28]. וכן גם תומס מאקווינו אומר: „הבן נולד לא מאין אלא מעצמותו של האב", אבל העולם, לאידך גיסא, נברא היה „מהנעדר, כלומר מאין" [29].

היוצא לנו מדברינו, שדעתו של קרשקש בזיהויין של אצילות ויש מאין כבר היתה לה מהלכים בפילוסופיה של הנוצרים והמוסלמים וגם בחכמת הקבלה שלנו. אבל בכל זאת יש הבדל בין דעתו של קרשקש ובין דעתם של כל אלה שקדמו לו. כל אלה שקדמו לו הניחו בראשונה את תורת האצילות בתור האמונה העיקרית שלהם בחידוש ורק אחר־כך, בתור ויתור קצת להמאמינים בתורת החידוש המסורתית, קיבלו מהם את הבטוי „יש מאין" ודרשוהו כמין חומר בהסכם לתורת האצילות. לא כן קרשקש. אמונתו העיקרית

22 עיין: Johannes Scotus Erigena, *De Divisione Naturae*, I, 15 (PL 122, 463 B); III, 5 (634 CD); III, 22 (686 A—688 A).

23 עיין: Gershon G. Scholem, *Major Trends in Jewish Mysticism*, pp. 25, 217—218, 401, nn. 40—41.

24 עיין הקדמה לפירוש הראב"ד לספר יצירה (ווארשא, תרמ"ד), דף ג', ע"א.

25 עיין ס' הפליאה (פשמישל תרמ"ד), דף י"ד, ע"ג.

26 עיין ס' שערי אורה (אורבך, תע"ה), דף ק"ח, ע"ב.

27 עיין: Augustinus, *Confessiones*, XIII, 33, 48

28 עיין: Ibid., XII, 7, 7

29 עיין: *Sum. Theol.* I, 41, 3 C

בחידוש היא האמונה המסורתית ביש מאין, שמובנה האמיתי, כמו שכבר הניח הרמב״ם ואחריו גם תומס מאקווינו[30] הוא, גם לפי דעתו, בריאת יש אחר העדר. ורק אז, לאחר שקיבל את האמונה ביש מאין במשמעותה האמיתית המסורתית, הוא מתאמץ להוכיח, שתורת האצילות, בניתוחה ההגיוני, מובנה האמיתי הוא גם כן בריאת יש אחר העדר ובכן גם־כן יש מאין.

השפעתו של קרשקש בזיהוייו של תורת האצילות ותורת יש מאין ניכרת בשפינוזה. יש שורה של הקדמות בספר המדות שלו וגם פרק אחד במאמר הקצר שלו, שאינם אלא התווכחות עם בעלי האצילות[31]. מטרתו של שפינוזה בהקדמות האלו ובפרק ההוא היא לבטל את דעתם של בעלי האצילות — שהיא באמת גם דעתם המקובלת של רוב החוקרים האלוהיים שבימי הביניים — שהאלהים הוא בלתי בעל חומר, ולהקים במקומה את דעתו שלו, שהאלהים הוא בעל חומר, או, לפי הניסוח החדש שלו, שהאלהים הוא בעל התפשטות. וכדי להגיע אל מטרה זו הוא טוען כנגד בעלי האצילות ואומר: אם תתעקשו לומר שהאלהים הוא בלתי בעל התפשטות ושהעולם, שהוא בעל התפשטות, התאצל מעצמותו של האלהים, נמצא, שאתם מאמינים באפשרותה של בריאת התפשטות מלא־התפשטות, ובכן בעל־כרחכם, למרות כל הכחשותיכם וכפירותיכם, אתם מאמינים באפשרותה של בריאת יש מאין — ואז הוא הולך וחוזר על כל הערעורים הישנים, שעירערו מעולם על יש מאין. טענה פשוטה זו יוצאת אמנם מהרצאתו המלאכותית של שפינוזה — אותו החיקוי ההשתעשעותי של הסדר ההנדסי — כשהיא מרוסקת ומסובכת ומעומעמת. אבל עם כל התרסקותה והסתבכותה ועימעומה בוקע ועולה ממנה קולו הברור של קרקשקש הקורא ואומר, שאין בין אצילות ויש מאין ולא כלום ושכל המודה באצילות כאילו מודה ביש מאין.

30 עיין: ibid. I, 45, 3 c ש׳ שתומס משתמש במלת emanatio, אצילות, במובן של creatio, בריאה (למשל: Ibid., 45, 3 c). אבל זהו רק ענין של פירוש מלה בעלמא, ואינו מורה על זיהוי של אצילות ויש מאין.

31 עיין פירושי על הקדמות ב׳—ו׳ מח״א של „ספר המידות" ועל פרק ב׳ מח״א של ה„מאמר הקצר" בספרי: *The Philosophy of Spinoza*, I, pp. 79—111.

עדותו של קלמנס מאלכסנדריה

על מנהג בלתי ידוע בעבודת יום הכפורים בבית המקדש

בקטע כ״ז מכתביו של תיאודוטוס, שהגיעו אלינו על ידי אחד מאבות הכנסיה הנוצרית, קלמנס מאלכסנדריה 1), שהיה בן דורו של ר׳ יהודה הנשיא, נמצא כתוב: „הכהן בהכנסו לפנים מן הפרוכת השנית היה מסיר את הציץ אצל מזבח הקטורת״. מתוך דבריו אלה משמע, שכהן גדול בעבודתו ביום הכפורים, לפני הכנסו אל קודש הקדשים, גם אחרי שכבר החליף את בגדי הזהב בבגדי הבד שלו בלשכת בית הפרוה, עוד היה נושא את ציץ הזהב על מצחו, והיה הולך ונושא אותו עד שהגיע אל מזבח הזהב, שהיה עומד בהיכל סמוך אל קודש הקדשים, ושם הסירו. וכנראה הניח את הציץ שם במקום גלוי אצל מזבח הזהב.

למנהג כזה אין כל זכר במקורות העברים, ועל פי השקפה ראשונה נראים דבריו של תיאודוטוס כאלו הם טעותו של גוי מן המין הרגיל והמצוי, שאין לשום לב עליהם. אבל מכל מקום, הואיל ואין במקורות העברים סתירה מפורשת לדבריו, הרי על פי הכלל הידוע, שאין מפריכין מן השתיקה צריכים אנו לפחות לעיין, אם אין בעדותו של גוי זה, המסיח לפי תומו. איזה קורטוב של אמת היסטורית. הן יוכל היות שבדבריו אלו נשתמרה איזה מסורה על מנהג קדום, ששרר בבית המקדש בזמן מן הזמנים ורק על פי מקרה נשכח ולא נכתב בספר.

אבל כדי להוציא את הקורטוב של אמת מתוך העדות הזאת, עלינו להעמיד בראשונה את דבריו של תיאודוטוס על כוונתם הנכונה. כידוע היה כהן גדול ביום הכפורים פושט את בגדי הזהב ולובש את בגדי הבד שלו פעמים. בבגדי הבד שלבש בפעם הראשונה היה נכנס אל קודש הקדשים פעמים אחדות, זו אחר זו, וכניסתו הראשונה היתה כדי להקטיר שם את הקטרת של יום הכפורים. בבגדי הבד שלבש בפעם השנית היה נכנס אל קודש הקדשים רק פעם אחת, הכניסה האחרונה לכניסותיו, כדי להוציא משם את הכף והמחתה. ומכיון שבין הלבישה הראשונה של בגדי הבד

1) עיין בספר The Excerpta ex Theodoto of Clement of Alexandria של Robert Pierce Casey (1934), צד 60, ובהערה שלי על צד 122, ובספר Patrologia Graeca של Migne, כרך IX עמוד 671.

וכניסתו הראשונה אל קודש הקדשים על הכהן הגדול היה למלאות עבודות אחדות המיוחדות ליום הכפורים, כגון הוידויים, ההגרלה וזריקת הדם, וכל אלו העבודות היו נעשות רק בבגדי הבד, הרי מן הנמנע היה, שבכל שעת עסוקו בהן היה נושא את ציץ הזהב על מצחו. וכן אין מתקבל על הלב, שאחרי שגמר את העבודות המיוחדות האלו ובעודנו לבוש בגדי הבד יחזור אל לשכת בית הפרוה, או אל מקום אחר שבמקדש, ששם השאיר את בגדי הזהב שלו, ונתן שנית את ציץ הזהב על מצחו — וכל זה רק כדי להסירו מיד אצל מזבח הזהב. ברור הוא איפוא, שמנהג כזה, אם התקיים כלל, יכול היה להתקיים רק לפני הכניסה האחרונה אל קודש הקדשים, ששום עבודה אחרת לא הפסיקה בינה ובין לבישת בגדי הבד. לפיכך כשתיאודוטוס אומר, ולו גם מכללא, שכהן גדול נכנס לקודש הקדשים מיד אחרי שהסיר את ציץ הזהב והניחו על יד מזבח הקטורת, כוונתו היא לכניסה האחרונה, או, מה שמתקבל יותר על הדעת, הוא ערבב את המעשים, המתלוים לכניסה האחרונה עם אלה שבכניסה הראשונה.

ומכיון, שברור הוא שדבריו של תיאודוטוס, אם נקבל שאינם קלוטים לגמרי מן האויר ושיש בהם איזה יסוד היסטורי, יכולים להיות מוסבים רק על מנהג, שהיה נהוג לפני הכניסה האחרונה אל קודש הקדשים, הרי עדותו לא רק שאינה מופרכת מן הקבלה הישראלית, אלא יש גם בידינו להראות על סמך של מקורות עברים, שמחלוקת אחת בין חכמי ישראל על דבר סדר עבודת יום הכפורים בבית המקדש יכולה היתה, בתנאים ארעיים מיוחדים, לגרום למנהג כזה, שיצמח ויתקיים לפי שעה, ואחר כן, עם סור התנאים הארעיים, שהולידוהו, שיחלוף ויעבור.

כידוע ישנה מחלוקת בספרות ישראל על דבר זמנה של הקרבת התמיד של בין הערבים ביום הכפורים. ממקומות אחדים נשמע שהתמיד והקטורת של בין הערבים היו חלים שניהם אחר יציאתו האחרונה של כהן גדול מקודש הקדשים (ספרא, אחרי פ״י; יומא ל״ב ע״א). ממקומות אחרים מוכח שהתמיד של בין הערבים חל לפני הכניסה האחרונה אל קודש הקדשים, ואולם הקטרת הקטורת של בין הערבים היתה אחר יציאתו של כהן גדול משם (משנה יומא פ״ז מ״ד; ירושלמי יומא, מ״ד ע״ב; השוה לחם משנה יד החזקה, עבודת יום הכפורים, פ״ב ה״ב). ואף על פי שהמחלוקת הזאת שנויה בספרות התנאים שלאחר החרבן, הרי אפשר הוא ששתי הדעות המתנגדות האלו מראות על חלוקי השקפות ביחס אל סדר העבודות האלו, שהתקיימו בין הבתים של הפרושים עצמם לפני חרבן בית המקדש. אם כך הדבר, הרי יש לשער עוד, שכל אחד מהבתים האלה התאמץ בזמנים שונים להכניס את דרכו הוא בעבודת בית המקדש, כמו שקרה במחלוקותיהם של הצדוקים והפרושים על אודות עבודת בית המקדש, שכל אחת מהכתות בקשה להשליט את דרך העבודה המיוחדה משלה (עיין יומא י״ט ע״ב; סוכה מ״ח ע״ב). במצב שכזה, הרי אינו יוצא מגדר האפשרות, שכאשר היתה יד בני הדעה הזאת על העליונה בעבודת בית המקדש, שלפיה קרבן התמיד של בין הערבים קרב לפני הכניסה האחרונה, היו כופין את הכהן הגדול להניח את ציץ הזהב במקום

גלוי על יד מזבח הקטורת בתור הוראה לרבים שהקטרת הקטורת של בין הערבים באה מיד אחר יציאתו מקודש הקדשים ואין התמיד מפסיק ביניהן.

דוגמא לקביעת מנהג חדש בעבודת בית המקדש לשם פרסום ניגוד לדעה אחרת יש למצא במנהג החדש שקבעו הפרושים, הדורש מאת כהן גדול להגביה את ידו בנסוך המים בעבודת השחרית של חג הסכות. תקנה זו נקבעה על ידיהם אחרי שאלכסנדר ינאי, שנמשך אחרי הצדוקים, שהיו בועטים בנסוך המים, שפך את המים על רגליו (עיין סוכה מ״ח ע״ב). וכן גם ההשבעה שהיו רגילים להשביע את הכהן הגדול בערב יום הכפורים היתה מפני המחלוקת שבין הפרושים והצדוקים בנוגע למקומה של הקטרת הקטורת של יום הכפורים (עיין משנה יומא פ״א מ״ה ובגמרא י״ט ע״ב). ובכן אפשר הוא גם כן, שאותו המנהג להניח את ציץ הזהב על יד מזבח הקטרת, שאליו רמוזים דבריו של תיאודוטוס, נבע מן מחלוקת, שבין הפרושים עצמם, על דבר זמנו של הקרבת התמיד של בין הערבים, אם לפני כניסתו האחרונה של כהן גדול אל קודש הקדשים או אחר צאתו משם.

ובכן בין העדיות שלנו יכולים אנו עכשיו להוסיף משנה חדשה כזו: העיד קלמנס איש אלכסנדריה על עבודת יום הכפורים בבית המקדש. שמעתי בשם תיאודוטוס ששמע מפי זקנים וזקנים מזקנים, בו ביום שגברו האומרים תמיד, כף ומחתה, וקטורת, התקינו שיהא כהן גדול מניח את ציץ הזהב על יד מזבח הקטורת לפני כניסתו האחרונה אל קודש הקדשים כדי להוציא מלבם של האומרים כף ומחתה, תמיד, וקטורת.

General Index

Abelard, Peter, 326
Abiogenesis, 492
Abrabanel, Isaac, 294–296, 329
Abraham bar Hiyya, 118, 477
Abucara, 396
Abu Hashim, 200–201, 228, 341
Active Intellect, 31, 34, 63–67, 96, 108
Aegidius, 312
Ahylogenesis, 492, 494
Alanus ab Insulis, 504
Albalag, Isaac, 303, 306, 312, 479, 481
Albertus Magnus, 587
Albinus, 497, 499, 500, 502–504, 522
Albo, Joseph, 330–332, 465–468, 608, 613
Alchabitius, 575
Alchemists, 41, 45–47
Alexander of Aphrodisias, 209–211, 244, 470, 517, 543
Alexander Jannaeus, 632
'Allāf, 202
Alpha Privative, 543–544
Ambiguous Terms, 231–235, 280–281
Ammonius, 188–189, 218, 545
Analogy, 514–523
Angels, 90–91, 113, 426
Antiattributists, 399, 401
Apocatastasis, 533
Apocryphon of John, 541
Apollinarianism, 526
Apollinaris, 408
Apologists, 525
Arians, 396, 398, 412–413, 628
Aristotle, 124, 424–425, 434–435, 437, 498, 503, 515, 624–626; Ambiguous terms, 244; Atoms, 364–365, 373–374; Celestial Spheres, 5, 25, 424–425; Chance, 2–3, 18, 29, 30–31; Definition, 166–168; God, 226; Nature, 35–55; Negation, 209–211, 214, 215; One and Many, 198; Opposites, 207, 337–340; Place, 437; Predicables, 168–171, 175–176, 188, 251–252; Prime Mover, 253–254; Propositions, 163–164, 238, 249, 267, 542; Relations, 183–184, 294–295; Time, 296–298, 468
'Arsh, 93
Ash'arites, 200, 224–225, 228, 403, 405
Atheism, 536
Atomists, 2, 5
Atoms, 350–354, 359–376
Attributes, 164–337, 398–400, 439, 450–457, 596–597
Augustine, 100, 492, 502–503, 527, 587, 628
Averroes, 78, 181, 198, 215, 218, 242–243, 365–366, 445, 469–470; Celestial Intelligences, 336; Essence and Existence, 306–308, 310; Privative Propositions, 546–549, 551; Refutation of al-Ghazali, 275–276; Unity, 308–309; Universals, 277–288
Avicebron, *see* Ibn Gabirol, Solomon
Avicenna, 172–174, 181, 198, 215, 217, 242; Definition, 166–167; Emanation, 333; Essence and Existence, 249, 253–254, 271–276, 303–305, 311–312; God's Knowledge, 437; Goichon's books, 556–565; Negation, 492, 500, 505; Nominalism, 257; Privative Judgments, 549–552; Rejection of Conceptualism, 258–259; Simplicity, 254–256; Universals, 277, 315; Unity, 309

Baghdadi, 341, 350, 572
Bahya ibn Pakuda, 6–7, 187, 197, 324
Balaam, 210
Basil, 526
Basilides, 512, 540–541
Batinites, 76, 118
Baumgarten, A. G., 554
Belief, 163–164
Bendavid, Lazarus, 606
Boethius, 542, 544–545
Bruno, Giordano, 477
Buechler, A., 568
Burkill, T. A., 525, 529

Cajetan, 307
Campanella, T., 574
Categories, 176–177, 251, 302–303
Causality, 361, 415–432, 503
Celestial Spheres, 15–26, 423–426
Celsus, 538
Cerinthus, 530
Chadwick, Henry, 539
Chalcedonian Decree, 409–411
Chance, 1–2, 29–34
Christology, 70–73, 407
Cicero, 539
Clement of Alexandria, 100, 500, 528, 538, 541, 630–632
Conceptualism, 258
Conjectural emendation, 459
Corporal Form, 378
Correlations, 295
Crescas, Asher, 295
Crescas, Hasdai, 458–469, 479, 490, 584; Critics, 326–329; Emanation, 495, 623–629; Essence and Existence, 309–313; Influence, 329–332; Negative Attributes, 298–301, 323–324; Positive Attributes, 291–292, 316–322, 333; Relative

Attributes, 293–296; Time, 297–298; Unity, 313–314
Cullmann, O., 534

Definition, 166–174, 242–243
De Laguna, G. A., 593–598
Delmedigo, Joseph Solomon, 574
Democritus, 2, 342, 362, 365, 371, 373–374
Descartes, René, 477, 578, 593–594
Description, 242
Desire, 459
Determination, 23–25
Dualists, 395
Duran, Profiat, 295
Duration, 467

Ebionites, 412–413
Ecphantus, 374
Efros, I., 573
Elements, 32–34
Emanation, 8–15, 332–336, 492–496, 623–629
Eminence, 506
Empedocles, 386
Enoch, 46
Epicurus, 2–3, 6, 29, 370–372, 595
Equivocity, 198–199, 231, 233, 509–510
Essence, 198, 302–308, 404, 556
Existence, 249, 271–275, 283, 317–318, 323, 331

al-Farabi, 75; Alchemy, 46; Ambiguous terms, 231, 234, 242, 513, 522; Attributes, 233, 493, 501; Chance, 2; Emanation, 333, 625–626; Essence and Existence, 198; Identity, 266
Father, 398, 401
Friedlaender, M., 295

Gabriel, 64
Galen, 30–31, 40, 48, 386, 422
al-Gazali, 218, 476, 499, 505, 522; Ambiguous terms, 233–235, 242; Attributes, 174–175, 441; Causality, 416–417, 423, 427; Emanation, 3, 11–15; Existence, 271–275, 310, 313; God's Freewill, 22, 58–60; God's Knowledge, 439; Influence, 151
Gersonides, 479; Attributes, 224, 235, 282–286; Essence and existence, 310; Eternity of Matter, 150, 495; Reputation, 331; Unity, 313
Giver of Forms, 573
Gnostics, 530, 628
Goichon, A–M., 545, 556–565
Goldziher, I., 75, 76, 118, 573
Goodness, 321
Grant, R., 525–527
Greeks, 120–127
Gregory of Nazianzus, 526
Gregory of Nyssa, 499–500, 502
Guttmann, Jacob, 338
Guttmann, Julius, 227–228, 458–469

Halevi, *see* Judah Halevi
Hanbalites, 445
Harizi, 498
Harnack, A., 531
Heaven, 425
Heereboord, 581–594
Heinemann, I., 469–476
Heinrich, Paul, 526
Helmholtz, 495
Heresy, 441
Herrara, Abraham, 477
Herz, Marcus, 606
Hesychius, 566
Hexadactylism, 483–484
High Priest, 630–632
Hillel of Verona, 479
Hippolytus, 512, 529
Hobbes, Thomas, 553
Holy Spirit, 64, 87–89, 113, 398, 401
Horten, M., 75, 545

Ibn Adi, Yahya, 393–394, 410
Ibn Aknin, Joseph, 312, 335
Ibn Daud, Abraham, 174–175, 334, 381–382, 419, 584
Ibn Ezra, Abraham, 587
Ibn Gabirol, Solomon, 89, 324, 363, 365
Ibn Hazm, 403, 405, 410
Ibn Kullab, 403
Ibn Shem Tob, Isaac, 327, 481–490
Ibn Shem Tob, Joseph, 138, 157, 490
Ibn Shem Tob, Shem Tob, 295, 490
Ibn Tibbon, Judah, 46, 383–384
Ibn Tibbon, Samuel, 384–385
Ibn Zaddik, Joseph, 187, 239
Ideas, 347
Iḫwān al-Ṣafā, 73, 75–76, 102–103, 118, 477
Indefinite Term, 216, 355–356
Infinity, 320
Intelligence, 279, 322, 325–326
Irenaeus, 528, 532–533
Isaac Israeli, 360–363
Isaac the Sabian, 79
Isidore, 512

Jehiel of Paris, 574
Jesus, 71, 534
Jews, 102–103, 120–127

Johannan ben Zakkai, 534
Johannes Hispalensis, 545
John Askunages, 394
John of Damascus, 453, 498–499, 503–505, 507, 508, 512
John Scotus Erigena, 627
John Philoponus, 243, 394, 530
Joseph Caspi, 186–187
Josephus, 567
al-Jubbā'i, 200, 341, 350
Judah Halevi, 324, 476; Amr Ilahiyy, 68–85, 95–96; Attributes, 187; Celestial Spheres, 5–25; Contrast with Maimonides, 1–8, 58–59, 60–62; Emanation, 9–13; Ethical Doctrine, 153–159; Hebraism, 139–160; Miracles, 57–58; Prophecy, 86–107; Sublunar Phenomena, 26–36; Wisdom of Nature, 35–47
Justin Martyr, 99, 528, 532

Kabbalah, 628
Ka'bī, 341
Kalam, 6–7, 23–25, 127–128, 415, 581
Kallen, H. M., 122
Kant, Immanuel, 222, 267, 554, 606, 617
Kelvin, Lord, 495
Khaiyāt, 341, 350
Knox, W. L., 539

Lamm, N., 570
Law of Contradiction, 453, 454
Leucippus, 342
Life, 404
Likeners, 399, 401
Locke, J., 608–619
Logos, 69–77, 525
Lysias, 540

Macedonians, 412–413
Maimon, Solomon, 295, 406
Maimonides, 78, 340–341; Attributes, 161–194, 196–230, 250–271, 291–302, 322, 501, 504–506; Celestial Spheres, 25–26; Contrast with Halevi, 1–8, 58–59, 60–62, 116–118; Creation, 357, 624–625; Emanation, 13–15, 493–494; Hellenism, 129–138, 159–160; Miracles, 57; Prophecy, 107–116; Sublunar Phenomena, 32–34; Time, 297–298, 608; Wisdom of Nature, 58–57
Malkites, 409–411
Mas'ūdī, 410
Matter, 348–349, 377–392, 491, 626–627
Mendelssohn, M., 606
Millenarianism, 526
Miracles, 55–58, 417, 427–432
Monophysites, 408, 410
Monopsychism, 314
Moore, G. F., 326
Moreau, J., 538
Moscato, Judah, 18
Moses ben Joseph of Lucena, 385, 388, 390
Moses Halavi, 274, 286–290, 332, 335–336
al-Mukammas, David, 202, 401
Munk, S., 295, 470
Mu'tazilites, 361, 441

Nahmanides, 326
Nallino, C., 573
Narboni, Moses, 187, 210, 309, 479
Naturalists, 47
Nature, 35–55, 139–159
al-Naẓẓām, 199–203, 361
Negation, 209–222, 497–499
Nestorians, 71–72, 409–412
Neumark, D., 338
Niphus, 573
Nominalism, 257, 279
Nonexistent, 339–350

Opposites, 207, 339
Origen, 531–533, 538, 541

Pappenheim, Solomon, 607–620
Paul of Samosata, 411, 413–414
Philo, 93, 99, 104–106, 346, 502–504, 512, 525, 538, 541, 568, 571
Photinus, 414
Photius, 394
Place, 465
Plato, 367, 627; God, 40, 124, 279, 538; Ideas, 258, 343–344, 347–349; Immortality, 532
Plotinus, 181, 344, 477; Attributes, 503–505, 507, 522; Duration, 467–468; Emanation, 492–493; Matter, 89, 348–349, 627; Negation, 497, 499–500, 502
Plurality, 254–255
Plutarch, 40, 368, 371, 471–472, 477
Polytheism, 453
Porphyry, 40, 177–178, 229, 252, 511, 515
Possibility, 274–276
Prayer, 149–150
Predicables, 168, 176–177, 229, 251–252
Privation, 207–224, 499, 542
Proclus, 507
Procreation, 421–422
Property, 201
Prophecy, 62–68, 95–118
Propositions, 163–166, 188–192, 542
Pseudo-Dionysius the Areopagite, 498–499, 503, 505, 507–508

Pythagorus, 373–374

Ratner, J., 601
al-Rāzi, Fakhr al-Din, 76, 118
al-Rāzī, Muhammad ibn Zakkariyya, 360
Relation, 180–185, 259–260
Remotion, 497–499
Rest, 482–483
Richardson, C. C., 525, 537
Rivaud, 556

Saadia, 93, 203, 331, 505, 571; Atomism, 359–360, 366–376; Creation, 6–7, 492, 625; Matter, 382–386, 390–392; Trinity, 77, 390–414
Sabellians, 396, 398–399, 404
Sabians, 46, 78–79
Sahl ibn Bishr, 575
al-Salihi, 341
Samosatenians, 412–413
Sarton, G., 475
Schiller-Szinessy, 481
Scholem, G., 463
Schuerer, E., 566
Sects, 396–397
Sefer Yezira, 93, 325
Sefirot, 325, 462
Seth, 46
Shahrastani, 40, 45–47, 72–73, 75, 333–334, 341, 362–363
Shalom, Abraham, 246, 294, 296, 300, 314, 328
Siegfried, Carl, 525
Simplicius, 470–471, 510–511, 515
ben Sirah, 567
Socrates, 123
Son, 398, 401
Space, 609, 611
Spencer, H., 602
Spinoza, 124, 277, 465, 477, 496, 577–605, 609, 629
Spiritualists, 46
Spontaneous Generation, 42
Steinschneider, M., 479, 573
Stobaeus, 472
Stoics, 35, 39–40, 47–48, 51, 215, 242, 343, 473–474, 477, 543–544
Suarez, 468
Substance, 516
Synedrion, 566–569

al-Tabrizi, 464
Talmudic Method, 474–475
Tasso, Torquato, 477
Tautology, 204
Teicher, J., 228
Teleology, 595
Terminology, 560
Tertullian, 492
Themistius, 42–44, 470
Theodore of Mopsuestia, 71–72, 430
Theodotus, 630–632
Theophrastus, 40, 218, 595
Thomas of Aquinas, 588, 599; Attributes, 235, 238, 240, 487–524; Creation, 357, 624–625, 628
Time, 296–298, 467–469, 477, 608, 610
Trinity, 73–75, 326–327, 393–407, 453, 628
Tritheites, 394

Unity, 308, 317–318, 323, 397
Universals, 247–249, 252, 257–259, 277–290, 302, 314–316, 596
Univocals, 509–510

Vaiśeṣika, 342
Vedanta, 536
Vegetative Soul, 39, 51
Vitalism, 492

Wasil ibn ʻAtā, 440
Whittaker, J., 538, 540, 541
Wolff, J. C., 554

Xenocrates, 365
Xenophanes, 528–529

Yom Hakippurim, 630–632

Zeitlin, S., 566
Zeno, 40
Zimara, 573

Index of Terms

Arabic

'Adam, 342
Amr ilāhiyy, 52–53, 68–85, 95–96, 107–108, 118–119
'Araḍ, 1
Aṣl basīṭ, 385, 387

Dhāt, 170

Faḍīlah, 66
Fayḍ, 10, 108
Fikr, 561
Fi'l, 191

Ghayriyyah, 404–405
Ghayr muḥaṣṣal, 216, 355, 545

Ḥāfiẓah, 561
Ḥakīm, 51
Ḥalla, 562
Ḥāmil al-jamī', 15
Ḥarakah, 477
Hayūlā, 360, 377–385
Ḥifẓ, 52
Ḥirāsah, 52

Ilhām, 64, 67
Ishtirāk, 185
Ism, 170
Ism murādif, 563
Istiqisāt, 390
Ittifāq, 1

Jawhar, 389

Kadkhuda, 574
Kā'in, 301
Kalimah, 77
Khamīrah, 377
Khaṭṭ, 367
Khuluq, 36

Lāhūtiyyah, 70–73
Lubāb, 101
Luzūm, 2

Māddah, 377–385
Ma'dūm, 340–341
Maḥall, 562, 563
Māhiyyah, 170, 304
Ma'nā, 400–404, 440
Mawjūd, 302–304, 340
Mayl, 16
Muḍādah, 339
Muḥīṭ, 9
Mushakkikah, 231, 446, 513
Mushrikūn, 453
Mushtarakah, 231, 446, 513
Mutaqābilāt, 339
Mutawāṭi'ah, 231, 446, 513

Nabiyy, 100
Nasab, 42

Qaḍiyyah ma'dūlah, 217–218, 545
Qawl, 170–171
Quṭb, 461–462

Rasm, 242
Riyāḍiyyah, 562
al-Rūḥ al-'amīn, 64
Rūḥ al-qudus, 64
Rūḥāniyy, 351

Sanad, 16
Sharḥ, 70–71
Ṣifah, 400–403, 440
Ṣūrah jismiyyah, 378

Ṭabī'iyyūn, 47
Tabrīz, 39
Tadbīr, 51
Ta'khīr, 234–235
Talaṭṭuf, 51
Taqdīr, 38
Taqdīm, 234–235
Taṣwīr, 38
Ṭīnah, 353, 377, 381–382

'Umm, 353, 385
'Unṣur, 385–389

Wahm, 560–561
Waḥy, 64, 67
Waliyy, 100

Greek

Amphibola, 231
Antikeimena, 339
Aphairesis, 497
Apophasis, 209, 497
Aretê, 66

Charakteristika, 400
Choristé hylê, 360
Chymos, 386

Diaplasis, 38

Ekmageion, 353, 377, 381–383
Enantia, 339
Enklisis, 16
Eupaideutos, 51

Hetairistai, 453
Homônyma, 231, 233, 510–512
Horos, 169
Hylê, 377–381
Hyper-, 507

Logos, 163, 170–171
Logos apophantikos, 163

Noêtikos, 312

Onoma aopiston, 216, 542
Ouranos, 19
Ousia, 304

Phronimos, 51
Physis, 37
Pneumatikos, 351
Pragmata, 400–401, 403
Pronoêtikê, 40
Prophora, 477

Rêma, 191
Rizôma, 386

Sterêsis, 209
Stoicheion, 381, 390
Symbebêkos, 1
Synechein, 52
Synônyma, 271, 509

Ti, 343
Tyche, 1

HEBREW

Beriah, 37
Bilti magiah, 217
Bilti nishlam, 217

Elohim, 141–142
Even kedumah, 389
Eẓem, 171

Galgal ha-mazzalōt, 20
Gezarah nōtah, 217

Ḥakham, 51, 55
Hanhagah, 51
Ḥasid, 100–101
Havayah Doleget, 614
Havayah mitlakketet, 614
Ḥefeẓ, 326
Hemshekh, 610
Ḥiyyūv, 2
Hizdamen, 1
Ḥōmer, 353, 377–385

Inyan elōhī, 68–85

Kav, 367
Kevōd Adonai, 86, 90, 92–94
Kotev, 461–462

Le'ut, 299
Limmūd, 64, 101

Ma'alah, 66
Ma'amar, 170–171
Mahūt, 170–304
Makkīf, 9
Malkhut Adonai, 86, 90
Mammash, 391–392
Merḥak, 610
Meshekh, 384
Meshuttaf, 231, 280, 446
Mesuppak, 231, 280, 446
Meẓiūt, 304, 615
Mikreh, 1
Mishpat musar, 217
Muskam, 231, 280, 446

Neṭiyyah, 16
Nevūah, 64, 101
Nōse' ha-kol, 15

Perush, 170–171
Pe'ūlah, 191

Raẓōn, 326
Ruah ha-kodesh, 86–89

Shamayim, 20
Shefa', 108
Shekhīnah, 86, 90
Shelīlah, 268
Shem, 170
Shemīrah, 52
Shinnuy, 405

Shi'ūr, 38
Sibbah, 16
Sikhlut, 299
Sōter, 299

Tafel, 212
Te'alah, 387–388
Tō'ar, 324

Yahas, 40
Yesh me-'ayin, 623–629
Yesōd ha-'ibbur, 462–463
Yeẓīrah, 37
YHWH, 141

Ẓiyyūr, 38
Zulatiyyut, 404–405
Ẓurōt, 10

LATIN

Ablatio, 498
Aequivocus, 510–514
Aestimatio, 566
Analogia, 514–523

Calcodea, 573–576

Diversi gradus, 599

Esse, 304–305
Essentia, 304–305
Ex nihilo, 357

Influentia, 108
Intellectus, 326

Largitas, 108

Materia propinqua, 378

Nomen infinitivum, 542, 545

Proportio, 42
Propositio privativa, 42

Quidditas, 304–305

Remotio, 498–499

Transiens, 601

Univocus, 509

Via causalitatis, 503–506
Via eminentiae, 506–509
Via negationis, 497–502